THE CRAFT OF
QUALITATIVE
LONGITUDINAL
RESEARCH

An engaging, timely and tremendously generous guide to qualitative longitudinal research. This book will be of great value to both readers already using this method and those new to the field. **Julia Cook, University of Newcastle**

Bren is *the* authoritative voice of qualitative longitudinal enquiry and methods. Her accessible and engaging style is both informative and captivating and makes this text a must read. **Anna Tarrant, University of Lincoln**

Written by a world-renowned scholar, this is a seminal text for qualitative longitudinal research. Bren Neale's wealth of experience, thought-provoking reflections and synthesis of other key studies, provides an accessible, comprehensive and timely guide for researchers, students and teachers. **Susie Weller, University of Southampton**

Exploring social life over time opens up exciting research possibilities, Bren Neale provides a lucid and insightful guide to all aspects of qualitative longitudinal research. This engaging, informative and readable book is gold standard. Highly recommended. **Jane Millar, University of Bath**

A sensitive and thorough examination of qualitative longitudinal research, Neale's volume presents the rewards, challenges and ethical demands of researching lives and communities through time. She sets out the history and value of QL, offers a clear discussion of the necessary craft and commitment to collaboration and shared authority, and provides examples of cases that illustrate themes and strategies. A superb and authoritative history and guide. **Anya Peterson Royce, Indiana University**

THE CRAFT OF QUALITATIVE LONGITUDINAL RESEARCH

Bren Neale

Los Angeles | London | New Delhi
Singapore | Washington DC | Melbourne

Los Angeles | London | New Delhi
Singapore | Washington DC | Melbourne

SAGE Publications Ltd
1 Oliver's Yard
55 City Road
London EC1Y 1SP

SAGE Publications Inc.
2455 Teller Road
Thousand Oaks, California 91320

SAGE Publications India Pvt Ltd
B 1/I 1 Mohan Cooperative Industrial Area
Mathura Road
New Delhi 110 044

SAGE Publications Asia-Pacific Pte Ltd
3 Church Street
#10-04 Samsung Hub
Singapore 049483

Editor: Jai Seaman
Assistant editor: Lauren Jacobs
Production editor: Victoria Nicholas
Marketing manager: Fred Preston
Cover design: Shaun Mercier
Typeset by: C&M Digitals (P) Ltd, Chennai, India

Library of Congress Control Number: 2020944545

British Library Cataloguing in Publication data

A catalogue record for this book is available from
the British Library

ISBN 978-1-4739-9543-7
ISBN 978-1-4739-9544-4 (pbk)

For Alan
and our next generation:
Jess, Danny, Rachel and Sarah

There do not exist *things* made, but only in the making, not *states* that remain fixed, but only states in process of change ... in the process of becoming. [We] arrive at fluid concepts, capable of following reality in all its windings. (Henri Bergson, 'Introduction to Metaphysics' in *The Creative Mind* 1946 [1903]: 188, 190)

[Class] is not a thing, it is a happening ... Not this or that part of the machine, but the way the machine works once it is set in motion ... the friction of interests – the movement itself, the heat, the thundering noise. ... [T]he definition can only be made in the medium of time, that is, action and reaction, change and conflict. (E.P. Thompson, *The Poverty of Theory* 1978: 85)

For groups, as well as for individuals, life itself means to separate and to be re-united, to change form and condition, to die and to be reborn. It is to act and to cease, to wait and rest, and then to begin acting again, but in a different way. And there are always new thresholds to cross. (Arnold van Gennep, *The Rites of Passage* 1960 [1909]: 189)

TABLE OF CONTENTS

ABOUT THE AUTHOR

Bren Neale is Emeritus Professor of Life Course and Family Research at the University of Leeds, UK, and a Fellow of the Academy of Social Sciences. She was the director of the ESRC-funded Timescapes study from 2007 to 2012. She has contributed to advances in qualitative longitudinal methods across academia, government and the voluntary sector, both in the UK and internationally, and continues to provide training and support in this methodology for new and established researchers.

ACKNOWLEDGEMENTS

This book is built on the accumulated wisdom of generations of researchers who have pioneered qualitative longitudinal research. It has been a privilege and pleasure to meet and work alongside a good number of these researchers in recent years. This was made possible through a series of research grants from the Economic and Social Research Council, including a methodological fellowship, national and international seminar series, and funding for a five-year programme of QL research and archiving (the Timescapes study). I owe a particular debt of gratitude to my Timescapes colleagues, and to the affiliated researchers, archivists, legacy data researchers and time theorists who enriched the programme. This was a cutting-edge environment in which to develop the ideas for this book. It has also been a pleasure to be part of an international network of QL researchers, which has grown rapidly over the past two decades, and to have the opportunity to deliver courses and training programmes to international researchers from many fields of scholarship. Through these events, I have met many enthusiastic proponents of QL methodology, and each time I have learnt something new about its power and creativity, and its capacity to grip and inspire people.

At the core of QL enquiry, shaping our research methods and ethics, can be found the research participants, whose contributions make our research possible. Over a long research career, I have 'walked alongside' many people, of all ages and living in many different circumstances. They have generously shared the stories of their lives with me, and enriched my own life in the process. This book is in no small measure a tribute to them.

More specifically, many colleagues offered ideas and advice, or donated materials as this book was taking shape. I'd particularly like to thank Libby Bishop, Ann Del Bianco, Maureen Haaker, Kahryn Hughes, Sarah Irwin, Hannah Kinsey, Linzi Ladlow, Jane Millar, Hanna Pettersson, Fiona Shirani, Anna Tarrant, and Rachel Proudfoot and the Timescapes Archive team. At Sage, I am grateful to Jai Seaman for the invitation to write this book and for her support throughout; and to Lauren Jacobs and the Sage production team for gently steering the project through to completion. Finally, special thanks (and apologies) to my family members, not least to Jess for her technical wizardry, and to Alan for being there every step of the way.

INTRODUCTION

At a time when social forces are making instability a way of life, researchers are developing new modes of enquiry that take account of the dynamic nature of people's lives. Approaches to 'thinking dynamically' have triggered the beginning of an intellectual revolution, one that blends insights from across the social sciences, merges quantitative and qualitative methodologies, combines macro and micro views of society and exploits the power of international comparison. (Leisering and Walker 1998: xiv)

Qualitative longitudinal research (hereafter QL research) is an evolving methodology for exploring the dynamic nature of people's lives. While QL studies are rich and varied, they share a common purpose: to follow the fortunes of individuals and groups in real-time to discern how their lives unfold. Time, process, continuity and change are the driving forces for QL enquiry. As the quotation above suggests, this mode of research is part of a broad **temporal turn** in social enquiry that has gradually emerged since the latter decades of the 20th century.

QL research has developed in piecemeal fashion across different research traditions and substantive fields, a process reflected in the varied labels and acronyms used to describe it (QL, QLR, QLS, LQ, LQS, QPS, Longitudinal Ethnography, Qualitative Panel Studies, Real-Time Research, Longitudinal Process Research, and related labels that appear throughout this book). It typically takes the form of small-scale, in-depth studies of individuals or groups, which unfold slowly over time to generate rich, situated data about dynamic processes. With its dual identity (both longitudinal and qualitative), QL research spans two established methodological traditions. As a small but vital component of the longitudinal canon, it seeks to follow the same individuals or collectives (households or varied forms of organisation) prospectively, walking alongside them to capture 'change in the making' (Bergson 1946 [1903]; Wright Mills 1959). With its roots in the interpretivist philosophical tradition, and framed by a processual logic of enquiry (detailed in Chapter 2), QL research explores dynamic processes through an in-depth, qualitative lens. It accords priority to the way humans narrate, understand and shape their unfolding lives and the evolving world of which they are a part, using ethnographic, case study and narrative methods to flesh out a detailed, processual picture. The key features of QL research are set out in Box 0.1.

Box 0.1   What is Qualitative Longitudinal Research?

- QL research is a distinctive form of temporal enquiry that follows people's lives as they unfold. It aims to shed light on how processes of change and continuity are created, navigated, lived and experienced for both individuals and groups; and how temporal processes emerge, develop, grow or dissipate through time (Abbott 1995b). Time, process, continuity and change are at the forefront of enquiry, along with a drive to discern the nature, causes and consequences of change. The focus may be on individual life course transitions, or studies of dynamic processes in organisations, or other forms of collective life.

- QL research follows the same individuals or groups (a panel of participants) in 'real' time, to discern changes and continuities as they occur. Through the longitudinal frame of a study, 'snapshot' visions of the social world are turned into qualitative 'movies' that look both forward and backward in time. QL studies are creatively fashioned, with flexible time frames, tempos and sample sizes. Designs can mirror the tempo of real lives and enable a processual understanding of the changing fortunes of participants (detailed in Chapters 2 and 11).

- As a form of qualitative enquiry, this methodology utilises ethnographic, case study and participatory methods, alongside narrative interviewing, to gain an in-depth picture of continuities and changes. Studies are typically small-scale. This produces an intimate form of movie that gives weight to people's individual and collective accounts, and their subjective understandings. It takes agency, subjectivity and reflexivity seriously. 'Walking alongside' participants creates a new terrain for the ethical conduct of a study.

- The lived experiences of individuals and groups can be placed in a broader (meso, macro) context of socio-historical processes operating across the social fabric. These broader processes are anchored in and understood through the changing lives of the research participants. It is here that biography and history intersect.

- The combination of its key features gives this methodology considerable immediacy and explanatory power. It has the capacity to explore how and why life course processes unfold, in distinctive ways, for varied individuals and groups, in particular contexts of change. Generalisations in QL research are qualitative in nature, that is, they explore and integrate a mosaic of diverse phenomena and evidence, rather than extrapolating from what is assumed to be an archetypal or typical case. Exploring dynamic processes through a qualitative lens, and following lives where they lead, requires flexibility, openness and an exploratory approach. This is a creative mode of enquiry, an intellectual craft, based on imaginative thinking and expression (Wright Mills 1959).

Through the rich combination of its features, QL research offers unique insights into a world that is fluid, complex and unpredictable. This suggests that it is part of a developing theoretical orientation, an emerging tradition for social research that offers new and exciting ways to know and understand the social world.

Thinking through Time

While QL research is conducted *through* time, it also engages with the temporal dimensions of experience, opening up the potential to 'think dynamically' in creative, flexible and innovative ways. The importance of time has long been recognised in social-scientific research, but, as our introductory quotation shows, it has taken on new significance with the recognition of rapid social change in the contemporary world. Time is the lynchpin for understanding the nature of lived experiences, and the essentially dynamic relationship between personal lives and wider historical processes (Wright Mills 1959). It is *through time* that we can begin to grasp the nature of social change and continuity, how these fluid processes unfold, and the ways in which structural forces shape the lives of individuals and groups, and, in turn, are shaped by them. Indeed, given their dynamic relationship, it is *only* through time that we can gain a better appreciation of how agency and structure, the personal and social, the micro and macro dimensions of experience are interconnected and how they come to be transformed (Neale and Flowerdew 2003). Moreover, **fluid enquiry** invites us to broaden our vision, to bring rich flows of time more centrally into the picture (detailed in Chapters 2 and 3). This requires a shift in focus from static structures to dynamic processes, and the nurturing of a broader imaginary about the complexities of a fluid world.

In all forms of temporal research, time is the driving force for research design and practice. For QL researchers, time is a powerful design strategy, the medium through which studies are conducted and data analysed. But, as indicated above, it is also a rich theoretical construct and theme of enquiry that shapes how data are generated and interpreted. One of the distinctive features of QL research is its capacity for a rich and flexible engagement with time. Yet this gives rise to a number of questions. How exactly do QL researchers engage with time? How does time, as a social construct, feed into research design, practice, ethics and analysis? Underpinning these questions is another: how is time itself conceptualised and understood? More broadly, what is the place of QL research within the established canon of socio-historical studies, and how does time transform qualitative research design and practice? These basic questions about temporal theory, design, practice and development are explored and addressed in this book.

An Evolving Methodology

QL enquiry is hardly new. It is rooted in a long-established tradition of socio-historical studies that have evolved in piecemeal fashion over the past century. What is relatively new, however, is the growing reflexivity of QL researchers, who are increasingly crafting and documenting this approach and exploring its theoretical underpinnings. A critical mass of methodological scholarship has developed over the past two decades, reflecting a growing sophistication in the way QL research is being conceived and designed. This, in turn, has fuelled a widespread interest in and rapid uptake of QL studies across the academy. If QL research was a fledgling methodology around the turn of the millennium, this is no longer the case. Researchers from a wide range of disciplines in the arts, humanities, social and applied sciences are routinely seeking to incorporate QL methods into their research designs. Studies range from the lived experiences of health, welfare and migration, to the dynamics of family life, employment, education, criminal careers, transport, energy use, bio-diversity, environmental management, legal systems, organisational change, and evolving cultures of language, leisure and the arts. New studies appear almost daily; for every study cited here, there will be numerous others in this rapidly expanding field.

In addition, QL research is now increasingly used as an exploratory, evaluation or navigational tool in health, education, welfare and other policy-related settings. Understanding processes of change and continuity is vital in policy domains where people are required or encouraged to change their practices, or need to adapt to changing circumstances or environments (Molloy et al. 2002; Farrell et al. 2006; Corden and Millar 2007; Millar 2007; Calman et al. 2013; Patrick 2017; Stich and Cippolone 2017) (for examples of longitudinal impact studies, see Box 12.2).

Time, as both the framework for a study and a rich theme of enquiry, can be incorporated into any form of qualitative enquiry across any substantive field, creating a rich and diverse body of scholarship. Longitudinal ethnography is a well-established field. But other formulations of real-time longitudinal enquiry in the interpretivist tradition (longitudinal biography, longitudinal narrative research, longitudinal re-studies, longitudinal case study research, and longitudinal processual research) are all beginning to flourish, each with their own subtle methodological inflections (detailed in Part 1 of this book). This creates a rich and heterogeneous field of enquiry.

To give one example, over the past decade qualitative psychologists using interpretative phenomenological analysis (IPA) have begun to develop a longitudinal approach to their small-scale, intensive case studies. Known as longitudinal IPA (LIPA), much of this research is concerned with charting lived experiences as people adapt to intricate changes in their physical and emotional health and well-being, following illness, trauma, or transitions into new networks of care and support (see Snelgrove 2014; Shaw et al. 2016; Spiers et al. 2016; Thomson, Ross et al. 2017; Nizza et al. 2018 (featured in Box 10.5); and, for a review of key literature, see Farr and Nizza 2019; see also Box 4.6 and Box 10.5, where LIPA studies are showcased).

These broad developments in QL research have global reach and influence. Beyond the four nations of the UK, studies are flourishing across Europe, Australia, Canada and the USA, and beginning to appear in parts of the Middle East, Asia and the global South, including sub-Saharan Africa. Funding has been provided by the UK central and devolved governments, British and international funding councils, independent research organisations such as the Joseph Rowntree and Nuffield Foundations, national and European funding agencies, and global agencies such as the World Health Organisation. In a parallel development, long-running TV documentaries that trace unfolding biographies, for example the *Seven Up* series and *Child of Our Time*, have popularised this approach and demonstrated its enduring appeal for global audiences (Apted 1999).

Amid this rapid expansion, there have been calls for more guidance on the conduct of QL studies, and for some standardisation of methodological techniques (Calman et al. 2013; McCoy 2017). Clearly, the exploratory, flexible and porous nature of this methodology warns against a prescriptive approach (Dawson 2003; Thomson and McLeod 2015). The rigour of QL research depends on flexible designs that can be fine-tuned to mirror a diverse, dynamic and complex world. Moreover, its application across widely disparate fields of enquiry confounds any idea of standardisation or strict labelling. As the chapters in this book illustrate, researching qualitatively through time is a craft that requires creative skills, innovation, flexibility, sensibility, an open knowledge base, and fine judgement on the part of the researcher (Dawson 2003; Thomson and McLeod 2015).

Nevertheless, crafting a QL study requires an adequate grounding in temporal theory, methods and ethics, and the skills to balance flexibility and continuity, and creativity and precision in the way studies are fashioned (Barley 1995). Expanding on and updating an earlier, introductory volume (Neale 2019), this book aims to bring the growing interdisciplinary literature on QL research into a coherent framework; to provide a more comprehensive understanding of the key conceptual, methodological and practical issues involved in carrying out a QL study; and to explore its potential for creative applications across a range of substantive fields.

Each chapter in this book is designed to take the reader on a short research journey. In the introductory section, the first chapter (Qualitative Longitudinal Research: Mapping the Field) explores the contours of QL methodology, traces its historical roots and locates it within the broad canons of longitudinal and socio-historical studies. The second chapter (Time and the Processual Turn: Fluid Enquiry) explores the foundations of QL research in the interpretivist tradition of social research, and traces the development of fluid notions of time, process, causality and complexity in social enquiry. Chapter 3 (Time and the Life Course) builds on insights from

Chapter 2 to consider the life course as a key organising framework for QL research, and explores how varied flows of time can feed into and enrich life course and longitudinal studies. The Timescapes framework developed here forms a conceptual tool kit that researchers can use as a bridge between temporal theory and research practice.

The second section of this book explores the crafting of QL enquiry. Chapter 4 (Design and Sampling in Qualitative Longitudinal Research) considers the many ways in which QL studies are fashioned and the journeys that QL researchers undergo as their studies progress. It explores how different flows of time may be used empirically to build the longitudinal frame for a study and to determine a sampling strategy. Chapter 5 (Longitudinal Ethics: Walking Alongside) considers the journeys that researchers take with their participants: how they are recruited into a study and their involvement sustained, and the ethical terrain within which these processes occur. Chapter 6 (Generating Qualitative Longitudinal Data) details the range of tools and techniques, including multi-media participatory tools, that may be used in the field to explore fluid processes.

The third section of this book focuses on the journeys that researchers take with their data (and, more generally, with legacy data). Chapter 7 (Managing Qualitative Longitudinal Data: Ethics and Practicalities) explores how researchers manage the 'oceans' of data that they generate, in the context of a growing drive to ensure that data are preserved and sustained for future use. Chapter 8 (Working with Legacy Data) explores how QL researchers, as both producers and users of legacy data, can draw upon pre-existing datasets to broaden their socio-historical and comparative insights, as part of an emerging culture of open data access and collaborative sharing and re-use.

Chapters 9, 10 and 11 focus on analytical strategies and practice, dimensions of the research process that are complex and currently poorly documented. Chapter 9 (Qualitative Longitudinal Analysis: Basic Strategies) sets out the analytical strategies that shape and provide an anchor for a QL study from start to finish. Abductive logic is explored here as the conceptual underpinning for QLA. Chapters 10 and 11 (Cases and Themes in Qualitative Longitudinal Analysis; Process and Synthesis in Qualitative Longitudinal Analysis) focus on the conduct and practicalities of QLA. The case-led, thematic and processual facets of analysis are explored in these chapters, along with the varied ways in which these can be integrated to create a balance between depth, breadth and temporal reach. A prototype for a QLA tool kit is set out in these chapters, which researchers can draw upon to suit their own needs. The discussion concludes with a consideration of the culminating act of analysis: how temporal processes can be narrated and visually conjured and conveyed to a wider audience.

The concluding chapter (Looking Back, Looking Forward) draws together key themes in this volume to consider the many strengths and challenges of QL methodology, and the status of its evidence base. In a field where findings have no temporal fixity, where veracity has to be built on shifting grounds, the quality and value of QL knowledge and evidence are crucial considerations. The value of a modest, open and ethically responsible approach to QL enquiry is reflected on here, while the potential for longitudinal impact studies is also illustrated. Finally, a number of areas for future development are considered. Throughout the text, readers are directed to key empirical and theoretical sources, along with illustrative materials to flesh out the picture.

Further Reading

Relatively few dedicated texts exist for QL methodology. For classic texts, Saldaña (2003) continues to stand out as a key resource, while Dawson (2003) is a useful resource from the perspective of organisational research. Short overviews are provided in Molloy et al. (2002) and Holland et al. (2006). A concise, interdisciplinary introduction to the field is provided in Neale (2019), while Derrington (2019) offers a practical entry-level text, focused primarily on educational research. Key literature is grouped together in a range of edited collections that have a disciplinary focus: Anthropology (Foster et al. 1979; Kemper and Royce 2002; Howell and Talle 2012); Sociology (Thomson et al. 2003; McLeod and Thomson 2009; Neale et al. 2012; Thomson and McLeod 2015); Social Policy (Corden and Millar 2007; Patrick et al. in press); Organisation Studies (Huber and Van de Ven 1995; Hassett and Paavilainen-Mäntymäki 2013; Langley and Tsoukas 2017); and International Development (Camfield 2014). Finally, integrative reviews of QL studies in particular disciplines are beginning to appear, for example in the fields of medical research (Calman et al. 2013), nursing (SmithBattle et al. 2018), longitudinal IPA (Farr and Nizza 2019) and education (Neale 2020a).

Calman, L., Brunton, L. and Molassiotis, A. (2013) 'Developing longitudinal qualitative designs: Lessons learned and recommendations for health services research', *BMC Medical Research Methodology*, 13 (14): 1–10.

Camfield, L. (ed.) (2014) *Methodological Challenges and New Approaches to Research in International Development*. London: Palgrave Macmillan.

Corden, A. and Millar, J. (2007) 'Qualitative longitudinal research for social policy', *Social Policy and Society*, 6 (4). Themed Section.

Dawson, P. (2003) *Reshaping Change: A Processual Perspective*. London: Routledge.

Derrington, M. (2019) *Qualitative Longitudinal Methods: Researching Implementation and Change*. Washington, DC: Sage.

Farr, J. and Nizza, I. (2019) 'Longitudinal interpretative phenomenological analysis (LIPA): A review of studies and methodological considerations', *Qualitative Research in Psychology*, 16 (2): 199–217.

Foster, G., Scudder, T., Colson, E. and Kemper, R. (eds) (1979) *Long-term Field Research in Social Anthropology*. New York: Academic Press.

Hassett, M. E. and Paavilainen-Mäntymäki, E. (eds) (2013) *Handbook of Longitudinal Research Methods in Organisation and Business Studies*. Cheltenham, UK: Edward Elgar.

Holland, J., Thomson, R. and Henderson, S. (2006) *Qualitative Longitudinal Research: A Discussion Paper*. Working Paper No. 21, South Bank University: Families and Social Capital Research Group.

Howell, S. and Talle, A. (eds) (2012) *Returns to the Field: Multi-temporal Research and Contemporary Anthropology*. Bloomington, IN: Indiana University Press.

Huber, G. and Van de Ven, A. (eds) (1995) *Longitudinal Field Research Methods: Studying Processes of Organisational Change*. London: Sage.

Kemper, R. and Royce, A. (eds) (2002) *Chronicling Cultures: Long Term Field Research in Anthropology*. Walnut Creek, CA: AltaMira Press.

Langley, A. and Tsoukas, H. (eds) (2017) *The Sage Handbook of Process Organizational Studies*. London: Sage.

McLeod, J. and Thomson, R. (2009) *Researching Social Change*. London: Sage.

Molloy, D. and Woodfield, K. with Bacon, J. (2002) *Longitudinal Qualitative Research Approaches in Evaluation Studies*. Department for Work and Pensions Working Paper No. 7. London: HMSO.

Neale, B. (2019) *What is Qualitative Longitudinal Research?* London: Bloomsbury Academic.

Neale, B. (2020) 'Researching educational processes through time: The value of qualitative longitudinal methods', in M. Ward and S. Delamont (eds) *Handbook of Qualitative Research in Education*, 2nd edition. Cheltenham: Edward Elgar, pp. 101–13.

Neale, B., Henwood, K. and Holland, J. (eds) (2012) 'Researching lives through time: The "timescapes" approach', *Qualitative Research*, 12 (1). Special issue.

Patrick, R., Treanor, M. and Wenham, A. (eds) (2021 in press) 'Qualitative longitudinal research for social policy: Where are we now?', *Social Policy and Society*. Themed Section.

Saldaña, J. (2003) *Longitudinal Qualitative Research: Analyzing Change through Time*. Walnut Creek, CA: AltaMira Press.

SmithBattle, L., Lorenz, R., Reangsing, C., Palmer, J. and Pitroff, G. (2018) 'A methodological review of qualitative longitudinal research in nursing', *Nursing Inquiry*, 25 (4): e12248.

Thomson, R. and McLeod, J. (2015) 'Editorial Introduction: New frontiers in qualitative longitudinal research', *International Journal of Social Research Methodology*, 18 (3): 243–250.

Thomson, R., Plumridge, L. and Holland, J. (eds) (2003) 'Longitudinal qualitative research', *International Journal of Social Research Methodology*, 6 (3). Special issue.

PART 1

INTRODUCING QUALITATIVE LONGITUDINAL RESEARCH

The opening chapters in this book explore the methodological foundations for QL research, focusing in particular on its history and development, its conceptual underpinnings, and the ways in which QL theory and method are intertwined. Overall, the chapters trace the development of key interpretive, temporal and processual ideas, from the early 20th century through to the present day, thereby locating QL methodology within established bodies of theoretical knowledge.

Chapter 1 (Qualitative Longitudinal Research: Mapping the Field) establishes the distinctive features of this mode of research, and traces its historical development as a form of real-time (longitudinal) and real-world (qualitative) enquiry. Its place within the broad canons of longitudinal enquiry and socio-historical research is mapped out here. In the process, the distinctive ways in which QL research engages with temporal processes, its capacity to 'walk alongside' people, to mirror the flux of the world and 'follow reality in all its windings' (Bergson 1946 [1903]) comes into sharper focus.

Chapter 2 (Time and the Processual Turn: Fluid Enquiry) establishes the place of QL research in the interpretivist tradition of social research. Human agency, subjectivity and lived experiences are central sources of explanation, enabling an understanding of real world processes 'from the inside'. QL research is also part of a broad processual 'turn' in social enquiry, which has brought a shift in focus from the form that social pheonomena take, their structural components, to their relational and dynamic elements. As key thinkers such as Bergson and E. P. Thompson saw, it is the dynamic relationship between things that matters, not the things in themselves. More specifically, the chapter explores the temporal underpinnings for QL research, highlighting time not simply as a 'fixed' linear entity, but as a fluid, non-linear and experiential phenomenon. Re-thinking time in this way transforms our understanding of change, continuity and causality. Causality emerges here as a complex phenomenon, with multiple, fluid and relational dimensions. Throughout, the value of QL research as a mode of fluid enquiry, with the capacity to discern how complex causal processes unfold, is clarified.

In Chapter 3 (Time and the Life Course) the rich ideas on fluid time and complex causality developed in Chapter 2 are applied to the empirical study of life course processes. This field of enquiry is particularly well suited to the application of longitudinal methodologies. How biographies and collective biographies are shaped are important questions for QL researchers. The discussion introduces three temporal horizons, turning points, transitions and trajectories, which are commonly used to trace how lives unfold. The intersecting nature of these temporal constructs is explored. The chapter concludes with a broader consideration of how time, as a theoretical construct, can be woven into empirical enquiry. Five intersecting flows of time, or timescapes, are outlined here as a conceptual tool kit that researchers can draw upon to craft their own studies. Establishing the methodological credentials of QL research in these chapters creates a bridge between temporal theory and method. The overall aim is to provide a solid conceptual foundation upon which QL research design and practice can be built.

1

QUALITATIVE LONGITUDINAL RESEARCH: MAPPING THE FIELD

Key Points

- **Defining qualitative longitudinal research**: QL research follows the same individuals or groups in real-time as their lives unfold, turning a diachronic 'snapshot' of social life into a longitudinal 'movie'. The methodology is grounded in an interpretive, processual logic of enquiry: longitudinal methods that follow participants through time are combined with in-depth, narrative, ethnographic and/or case study methods that give insights into lived experiences. This creates an intimate, up-close-and-personal movie.
- **The development of QL research**: QL research is part of the longitudinal canon, but has evolved over the decades from three main fields of socio-historical research: longitudinal ethnographies carried out by anthropologists; community re-studies carried out by sociologists; and biographical studies (life history, oral history and narrative studies) that merge sociological, historical and humanistic insights. The methodology is commonly employed in studies of people who are the focus of health, social care or welfare concern; in studies of life course transitions; and in studies of change management processes in organisations and groups.
- **QL studies may be conceived and developed in varied ways**. They may take the form of prospective QL studies, designed from the outset as processual, through-time studies. Alternatively, they may opportunistically follow up earlier 'snapshot' studies to create QL **re-studies**; or they may take the form of nested QL studies, which are embedded within a large-scale, longitudinal survey. Designs vary in their scale, intensity and longitudinal reach.

(Continued)

- **QL research is both prospective (forward looking) and retrospective (backward looking)**. Both prospective and retrospective lenses are needed in the generation and analysis of QL data. Cases may also be followed intensively through regular or frequent visits to the field, or extensively through 'punctuated' revisits. These two tempos may be combined as a study unfolds. QL research is rooted in a micro-understanding of the unfolding lives of individuals. The wider socio-historical contexts in which these processes occur are an important part of the picture.

Introduction

In the first decade of the 21st century … what was an area of work scarcely acknowledged beyond groups of committed oral historians, occasional sociologists, auto/biographers and ethnographers has become a vast and constantly changing and expanding ferment of creative work … [that] thrive[s] on invention. (Bornat 2008: 344)

In our opening quotation, a leading oral historian reflects on the rapid and creative development of biographical forms of socio-historical research since the turn of the millennium. Much the same could be said for the way QL enquiry has evolved and flourished over the past two decades. The aim of this introductory chapter is to map out and delineate the contemporary field of QL research, and to trace its development through varied strands of socio-historical scholarship over the past century. In the process, its distinctive features are highlighted.

The discussion begins with longitudinal and life course research, and goes on to consider a range of studies that make up the broad field of qualitative socio-historical studies: longitudinal ethnographies, socio-historical re-studies, and biographical enquiry (life history, oral history and narrative research). The differences between these fields are more a matter of disciplinary tradition than strong methodological divisions. Since they are not static or set in stone, there is scope for a creative blending of approaches over time.

Engaging with Time: Key Dimensions

All temporal research constructs a moving picture of social processes, turning a frozen moment in time, a 'snapshot' of social life, into a '**movie**' (Leisering and Walker 1998: 265; see also Giele and Elder 1998; Berthoud 2000; Weis 2004). While a snapshot is created **synchronically**, in the moment, a qualitative movie develops **diachronically**, telling an unfolding story through time. However, temporal movies can be created in a rich variety of ways. How they are produced and what they tell us about social processes vary across different disciplinary traditions. Their similarities and differences stem from their engagement with three planes of time that are set out in Box 1.1.

Box 1.1 Foundational Planes of Time

Prospective–Retrospective (Past, Present, Future)

This plane of time is concerned with how people orient themselves to the past, present and future: either prospectively (looking forward), retrospectively (looking back), or both. In its purest form, longitudinal research is *prospective*: it follows the same people in real-time, capturing changes and continuities as they occur and anticipating them in the future. A *retrospective* approach, on the other hand, explores dynamic processes through hindsight, a gaze backwards in time from the vantage point of the present day. In QL research, the temporal gaze is directed back and forward in time, oscillating between the two. Both of these temporal lenses are essential in the generation and analysis of QL data.

Intensive–Extensive (Time Frames and Tempos)

This plane of time is concerned with the time frames or duration of temporal processes, alongside the tempo of events, their spacing and regularity, and whether they occur intensively over the short term, or extensively over longer-term horizons. For our purposes in this volume, the *time frame* of a QL study reflects the overall time span through which it is conducted, while its *tempo* reflects the number, spacing, frequency and duration of visits to the field. Taken together, time frames and tempos constitute the longitudinal frame for a QL study. A spectrum of approaches may be discerned: cases may be traced *intensively* via frequent or continuous visits to the field; or they may be traced *extensively* through regular, occasional or 'punctuated' revisits over many years or decades (Burawoy 2003). In QL research, these two tempos may be combined as a study evolves.

Micro–Macro (Scales of Time)

Events and experiences unfold at different scales of the social fabric (personal, interpersonal, institutional, biographical, generational, historical). Any rounded analysis of unfolding processes will need to explore how different facets of the social fabric, operating within different domains of experience, intersect; how, for example, lived experiences mesh with, and unfold against, a backdrop of shifting policy processes. This requires creative approaches to research design and sampling. Understanding the micro–macro plane through a temporal lens is vital.

(Continued)

The relationship between agency and structure, biography and history is essentially dynamic: it is only through time that we can understand how these different scales of the social fabric are interconnected, and how they come to be transformed. In QL enquiry, wider socio-historical processes are anchored in and understood through the unfolding lives of individuals and groups.

The planes of time outlined in Box 1.1 form core elements in a framework for mapping and visualising time that is set out in Chapter 3. They can be designed into QL research in flexible and creative ways, as Chapter 4 will show. QL researchers are likely to gaze both forward and backward in time, enabling a more nuanced understanding of dynamic processes, and they may combine intensive and extensive tempos in their research designs. In mapping the field of QL research, this chapter illustrates how temporal researchers use these flows of time in their study designs. The exercise begins with a consideration of longitudinal and life course research, before going on to consider the broad canon of qualitative socio-historical studies.

Longitudinal and Life Course Studies

Longitudinal research, whether quantitative or qualitative, has a prospective design: it produces 'movies' that unfold in real-time, charting dynamic processes as they occur. Prospective tracking is commonly combined with a retrospective gathering of data on past times (Scott and Alwin 1998). While the focus of enquiry may straddle individuals, collectives or wider socio-historical processes, the purest form of these studies is the **panel design**, which follows the same individuals, households or other collectives (a longitudinal 'panel' of participants) as their lives unfold (Ruspini 2002: 4). A panel study is synonymous with, and a good short hand for, a prospective longitudinal study.

The alternative is a **recurrent cross-sectional design** that recruits different cohorts at each wave and interviews them just once. To give one example, a mixed methods longitudinal study of 20 social housing estates in the UK, conducted over 25 years, involved four waves of visits and interviews that were carried out in 1982, 1988, 1994 and 2005 (Tunstall and Coulter 2006). Data were gathered via observations, in-depth interviews with local housing managers and senior local authority officials, joint discussions with resident groups, and brief street interviews with random local residents. Supplementary legacy data (census returns, local housing policy documents, and so on) also informed the study and were analysed after each wave. The result was a series of snapshots that revealed changes in the nature of the housing associations at each point in time. Standard community-based re-studies commonly utilise this design (see below).

Such studies generate **time series data**, often gathered over relatively extensive periods of time, that can discern broad patterns of change at an aggregate or population level, but not at the micro-level of individual biographies (Ruspini 2002: 4; Grossoehme and Lipstein 2016; discussed further in Box 10.6). A useful distinction between this approach and panel designs is provided by Abbott (1995b), who uses the metaphor of a school of fish swimming in a lake (the 'variable' space). The recurrent cross-sectional approach explores changes in the composition and shape of the whole school of fish at each point in time. The panel approach, in contrast, looks at the paths of the individual fish over several time periods (Abbott 1995b: 206). While both forms of longitudinal design yield insights into dynamic processes (and may be effectively combined; see Box 4.9), the biographical continuity offered by panel designs gives unique insights into processes of change and continuity within the life course, between generations and through history (Elliott 2005; Neale et al. 2012). They also allow wider processes of social change to be anchored in and understood through the changing lives of individuals and small groups. These panel designs are the main focus of this book.

The life course is a central organising framework for the conduct of longitudinal panel studies. This is explored in more detail in Chapter 3, but some salient points are drawn out here. As the name implies, the focus is on how the course of a life unfolds through time. This can be understood *biologically* (an age-related process from birth to death) and *biographically* (how a life is individually crafted and socially constructed from cradle to grave). It can also be understood *collectively* (how lives are shaped, socially and institutionally, within and across the generations), *historically* (the chronological times into which people are born and live out their lives) and *geographically* (the places and local cultures that give shape and form to unfolding lives). In other words, while individual biography is integral to life course research, so too is a concern with how lives unfold collectively, and how individual and collective lives shape and, in turn, are shaped by wider socio-historical processes (Elder 1994; Elder and Giele 2009).

The life course is a vital lynchpin for discerning the links between biography and history. The impetus for exploring these dual processes and their complex intersections was provided by Wright Mills (1959), who saw this as the central challenge of the sociological imagination. His concern was to translate the personal troubles of biography into public issues of history and society:

> Neither the life of an individual, nor the history of a society can be understood without understanding both. ... We cannot hope to understand society unless we have a prior understanding of the relationship between biography and history ... [the task is to] continually work out and revise your views on the problems of history, the problems of biography and the problems of social structure in which biography and history intersect. (Wright Mills 1959: 3, 225)

It is generally accepted among life course researchers that the complex intersection of these factors is best understood through a longitudinal lens. Yet, teasing out the varied factors that shape unfolding lives across the micro–macro plane is also a perennial challenge (see Chapter 3). How life course research is approached depends on how these micro–macro domains are understood, and the relative priority accorded to them, creating a diverse and amorphous field of study (Neale 2015).

Quantitative Longitudinal Research

Thus far, our discussion has focused on features that are common to longitudinal enquiry, whether quantitative or qualitative. While both are prospective in their orientation to time, they operate at different scales, tempos and time frames of enquiry. This produces different kinds of movie. **Quantitative longitudinal** survey, cohort and panel studies began to develop in the United States in the late 1920s, primarily in the fields of medicine and child development, although on a relatively small scale (for overviews of developments, see Phelps et al. 2002, Ruspini 2002 and Pearson 2016). Regardless of their precise scale, quantitative longitudinal studies chart changes in broad patterns of social behaviour through the generation of big 'thin' data that can be analysed statistically, using event history modelling and other techniques (Elliott et al. 2008).

The scale of such studies varies: a community-based study will recruit many hundreds of participants (e.g. the *Longitudinal Harlem Adolescent Health* study, Brunswick 2002), while a nationally representative study (e.g. the 1958 cohort of the *National Child Development* study) will recruit many thousands. Either way, these studies illuminate large-scale patterns of change based on the production of numerically 'representative' data. Panel members are likely to be asked a series of semi-structured questions at regular intervals (typically every year for a longitudinal panel study, and every five years for a birth cohort study; Ruspini 2002: 4). In general, then, tempos tend to be well-regulated and extensive, with time frames stretching over several decades of change.

Given the scale and duration of these studies, the focus tends to be on the measurement of change: what changes, for whom, the direction and extent of change, and where, when and how often change occurs. Data on the spells of time that people spend in particular states, for example in a state of poverty or cohabitation, produce a broad, chronological picture of change across a study population (Leisering and Walker 1998). Time is operationalised here in a particular way: the focus tends to be on the duration, sequencing and phasing (bracketing) of life course transitions and states, and the basic unit of analysis is the spell of time that people spend in a particular state (Leisering and Walker 1998). Here, time has a certain geometric quality to it:

Longitudinal research of this sort … certainly gives us a dynamic picture, a movie rather than a snapshot. But the movie takes a particular form. The focus on spells of time, which follow (or deviate from) a presumed linear sequence in the life course, turns the movie into a series of disjointed pictures or movie 'stills'. (Neale and Flowerdew 2003: 191–2)

Given their scale, these longitudinal studies create a bird's eye view of the social world, a 'long shot', that is panoramic in scope. The result is an **epic movie**, a highly valuable 'surface' picture of social dynamics. However, it is a movie in which the intricacies of the plot and the fluid twists and turns in the story line are hidden from view (Neale and Flowerdew 2003).

Qualitative Longitudinal Research

In contrast to its large-scale cousin, QL research is located within the interpretivist tradition of qualitative research (detailed in Chapter 2), where it has an equally venerable history. As will be shown below, it is rooted in a patchwork of qualitative socio-historical studies that has developed over many decades. QL research combines the dynamic power of longitudinal designs, with in-depth narrative, ethnographic and/or case study methods, which give insights into lived experiences of continuity and change. One of the earliest QL studies to be conducted in the UK is featured in Box 1.2.

> **Box 1.2** A Classic QL Study – *Round about a Pound a Week* (Pember Reeves)
>
> This study, commissioned by the Fabian Society and set in Lambeth Walk in London, was conducted as part of a social policy intervention (The Mothers Allowance Scheme), designed to support low-income families with a newborn child (Pember Reeves 2008 [1913]). Of the 42 'respectable' working families initially recruited into the study, 34 were followed on a weekly basis over the space of a year. The researchers documented in vivid detail the lives of the mothers and their families: their living conditions in small, overcrowded housing; the tenor of their daily lives, including arrangements for sleeping, shopping and cooking, and their daily battles against dirt and vermin; their weekly budgets, diets and health; and their lived experience of parenthood, marriage, work and neighbourhood. In a study full of perceptive humanity, the researchers reveal the fast-changing fortunes and precarious life chances of these families.
>
> *(Continued)*

In fashioning this study, Pember Reeves drew upon earlier surveys on poverty carried out by Booth (1902–3) and Rowntree (1901), but added the human detail and a micro-dynamic understanding of poverty that the surveys lacked. The study shows that there is no discrete category of the poor, no fixed underclass and no unitary or static experience of poverty; it highlights instead the complex mixture of shifting events and precarious circumstances that shape the volatile fortunes of low-income families.

In the mould of Pember Reeve's pioneering study, QL research typically takes the form of small-scale, in-depth studies of individuals or groups, who are followed intensively over relatively modest time frames to generate rich, situated data about their lives. The tempo for a QL study tends to be more intensive and flexible than its larger-scale cousin. Here, creativity and flexibility are just as important as precision and continuity. Patterns of revisits vary, with each wave of data generation used to inform the next (Smith 2003). A micro-dynamic focus is more deeply embedded in this form of longitudinal enquiry.

Placing the individual or small collective at the centre of investigation, the concern is not simply with how concrete events, changes and continuities can be measured, but with how processes of change unfold: the trigger points, turning points and pivotal moments that initiate change or lead to equilibrium, along with the micro–macro elements in the social fabric that provide the driving force for change. The more intensive and continuous the time spent in the field, the greater the likelihood that fluid, processual insights will be generated (see Chapters 2 and 11 for processual thinking and analysis).

In these designs, time is harnessed to the immediacy and vitality of human experience. QL research engages with human hearts and minds: it provides access to the 'inner logic' of lives (Laub and Sampson 1998), discerning how change is created, negotiated, lived and experienced. At the heart of this approach lies a concern with the dynamics of human **agency** – the capacity to act, to interact, to make choices, to influence the shape of one's life and the lives of others. Agency is a dynamic concept, embodying notions of action, process, change, continuity, endurance, and bringing notions of causality to the fore (Hitlin and Elder 2007; Hammersley 2008).

Of equal importance is human **subjectivity** and **reflexivity**: the shifting meanings that events, circumstances and social processes hold for those who experience them. Midgley (2014) reminds us that these subjective facets of human experience are just as important for our verifications of the social world as any objectively defined fact or process. Subjective accounts are not fixed, and the past and future are 'reworked' as people overwrite their biographies and strive for coherence in the evolving narratives of their lives (Kohli 1981; Halbwachs 1992; Neale and Flowerdew 2003; Cohler and Hostetler 2004; Holland and Thomson 2009). There is also a need to acknowledge and engage with the reflexivity of researchers in their evolving interpretations (Pollard with Filer 1996; Thomson et al. 2002; McLeod and Thomson 2009).

By their very nature, then, agency and subjectivity are dynamic concepts, affording opportunities to discern changing perceptions, values, aspirations and strategies over time, alongside concrete changes in events or circumstances. With its responsive tempo and sensibilities, QL research has been likened to the process of 'walking alongside' people to discern change as it occurs (Neale and Flowerdew 2003; see Chapters 5 and 6). One of the strengths of researching intensively, in real-time, is this capacity to glean something of the life as lived and experienced, alongside the life as told (Bruner 1984: 7).

Returning once more to the movie metaphor introduced earlier, QL research offers us an up-close-and-personal or **intimate movie**, providing insights into *how and why* the social world unfolds in varied ways, for specific individuals and groups, in particular settings of change (Neale and Flowerdew 2003; Neale 2015). Being 'up close and personal' does entail some limitations. The depth of QL enquiry, the relatively small sample sizes and the relatively modest time frames are likely to constrain the breadth of evidence and findings (although it is possible to build a broader, comparative picture; see Chapter 8). Moreover, the longitudinal frame of a study may not match or capture the momentum of unfolding lives. Caveats may therefore be needed about the limited longitudinal reach and tempo of a study, and about how much it can reveal, particularly about longer-term trajectories and broader processes of social change.

In the post-war years, the idea of using ethnographic methods over extended periods of time to discern processes of social change was being promoted in the US among Chicago School scholars (see, for example, Becker and Geer 1957; and for a short account of the Chicago School and its mosaic of empirically based community studies and life histories, see Becker 1966). From the 1970s, QL studies began to appear more regularly in Britain and the USA, although, as will be noted below, the sense of a distinctive methodology with its own credentials and identity was to come later. Studies at this time included vivid case-history analyses of varied life course transitions (e.g. adjusting to divorce and separation, Hart 1976; and becoming a mother, Oakley 1979). Three examples of late 20th century longitudinal real-time studies are set out in Box 1.3. They reflect three areas of social enquiry where QL methodology is commonly applied: studies of people who are the focus of health, social care or welfare concern; studies of life course transitions; and studies of change management processes in organisations or community groups. Two of these examples illustrate different ways in which change is not simply managed but is actively crafted in human affairs.

Box 1.3 Late 20th Century Longitudinal Ethnographies and Case Studies

Cycles of deprivation? An ethnographic case study: In designing this anthro-pological study, Coffield et al. (1980) took their cue from Radin (1987 [1933]), an early proponent of longitudinal ethnography. From 1975 to 1978, the researchers followed the fortunes of four low-income, three-generational families (parents, part-ners and children) who were living on varied social housing estates in an industrial town in the English Midlands. The families were recruited through social workers and were experiencing multiple deprivations in their lives. The researchers aimed to enter the social worlds of the families. Fieldwork extended over three years (detailed in Box 4.6). **Participant observation** and life history interviews were combined with an intensive ethnographic design of continuous and flexible engagement with the families, yielding detailed biographies from the past to the present day. The case studies enabled the team to compare the diverging trajectories of the families. They were able to uncover the complex web of factors that could lead families into or out of poverty, and to investigate how and to what extent adverse experiences and cir-cumstances could become entrenched and be perpetuated down the generations.

Getting married – life course transitions: This ethnographic study (Neale 1985) of a major life course transition was inspired by anthropological studies on *rites of passage* (Richards 1956; van Gennep 1960 [1909]). It was set in a time when marriage was regarded as a key social institution, a marker of respectable family life in the UK. Twelve couples from the Old Bankside, a working-class slum-clearance neighbourhood of Leeds, were followed over the months leading up to their weddings (in church, chapel or register office). The aim was to discern the varied meanings and impact of this transition on the participants and their families, and the intricate means by which this change in status is crafted and accomplished. Fieldwork was carried out over an 18-month period during 1976–7, and involved participant obser-vation (frequent visits to the neighbourhood, attendance at community events, hen nights, filming at weddings) and many hours of in-depth, conversational interviews with the couples and their parents, both before and after the weddings. Tracing and revisiting these participants, to discern changes in their family lives and values over the past 45 years, would make for a fascinating study.

Processual longitudinal research – case studies of organisational change: In a landmark organisational study, Pettigrew (1979, 1985) explored how large cor-porations respond to external pressures to change and how they institute change management processes. He traced the histories, unfolding fortunes and fates of five teams of organisational developers, who were employed across the divisions of a major chemical company (ICI). The study drew on the tradition of anthropological case study enquiry, and was conducted over eight years (1975–83) through five waves of fieldwork. By the close of the study, only two of the five development teams were still in existence and these had undergone major transformations. Pettigrew interviewed a total of 134 people, including the developers, their clients and key managerial and trade union representatives, drawing out their backgrounds, aspirations, values, roles, rationales, resources and the structures of power in which they operated.

Over 40 of these participants were followed up for repeat interviews. Through his role as an ICI trainer and consultant, Pettigrew was also able to conduct this study 'from the inside', drawing on rich archival data dating back to the 'birth' of the teams in the 1960s, and incorporating elements of ethnographic engagement. He placed his case studies in the context of changing economic and industrial conditions in the UK. In this way, Pettigrew pieced together an evolving story, using prospective and retrospective data and a comparative, processual framework across the micro–macro plane.

The larger-scale and comparative nature of this study created some limitations. Pettigrew was unable to give a full account of the lived experiences and viewpoints of different employee groups, or a detailed consideration of their competing stories and claims. He presents a managerial perspective and tends to gloss over the political tensions of change management that are a feature of large-scale organisations (Dawson 2003). Nevertheless, he powerfully demonstrates how continuous, incremental (evolutionary) processes of change are interspersed with radical (revolutionary) change processes, thereby challenging the idea that change is a single event, or a discrete series of episodes.

The research featured in Box 1.3 illustrates the variations that may occur in the scale, intensity and longitudinal reach of a QL study. It is worth noting that, in each case, these studies were conceived and designed as prospective real-time QL studies that took their inspiration from the work of longitudinal ethnographers.

There are two other ways in which QL studies may be conceived and developed. They may take the form of **nested QL studies** that are part of mixed longitudinal designs (see Box 1.5 for an example). Or they may be conceived as QL re-studies, drawing for their inspiration on the community re-studies carried out by historical sociologists (see Boxes 1.7 and 1.8 below). Such 'follow up' studies develop opportunistically; they turn an earlier 'snapshot' study into a longitudinal design through a revisit to the field, usually with a gap of some years between the two waves. The impetus to return to the field is often driven by a deep curiosity on the part of the researcher to find out what has happened to 'their' participants (Weis 2004; see, for example, Henderson et al. 2007; Hermanowicz 2009, 2013).

In the latter decades of the 20th century, it was comparatively rare for prospective real-time QL studies, of the sort showcased in Box 1.3, to be conceived, let alone funded, although they have come into their own since. During this formative period, the developing patchwork of QL studies, with their varied designs and disciplinary affiliations, had no common or overarching label to unite them. It was not until the 1990s that references to qualitative longitudinal research, along with its varied acronyms, began to appear (Hallebone 1992; Saldaña 1995; Yates and McLeod 1996; Agren 1998; Wenger 1999). Bringing the twin dimensions of QL research – the longitudinal and the qualitative – together in this way has helped to create an 'umbrella' identity for an array of creative studies that share a common purpose and a core methodological approach.

Complementary Longitudinal Studies

The different kinds of longitudinal 'movie' outlined above have complementary strengths and weaknesses. Quantitative longitudinal research powerfully reveals the wholesale movement of study populations from one circumstance to another (e.g. into or out of the states of poverty, migration, marriage or ill health). QL research, in turn, has the potential to reveal why and how such journeys are undertaken, the factors that shape the journey, and how they are managed and experienced. In other words, this finely grained methodology offers a *processual approach* to social enquiry (see Chapters 2 and 11) that can address and explore the nuances of unfolding processes.

For example, are continued states bound up with stability, contentment, inertia, stagnation or 'lock-in'? How do transitions and trajectories unfold (linear or fluid, upward or downward, smooth or volatile, running in parallel or interconnecting)? How and why do these pathways converge or diverge across the cases in a sample? Is a journey planned or sudden, prescribed or imposed, joyous or traumatic? Is a transition straightforward and positive, or are there detours, setbacks or recursive loops along the way? QL research has the capacity to capture emotional as well as chronological journeys, and to discern the constellation of driving forces and pivotal moments through which lives unfold. Much like Homer's *Odyssey*, the nature and meaning of the journey assume just as much importance as the destination reached (Neale 2015).

Some of the most perceptive insights on the value of QL research come from life course researchers whose work straddles both traditions. These are illustrated in Box 1.4.

Box 1.4 The Value of Qualitative Insights in Longitudinal Enquiry

While demographic surveys show the magnitude and distribution of migration in entire populations ... only individual or family histories can reveal why one individual moves and another stays put. (Giele 2009: 236)

[A]lthough quantitative longitudinal research has the potential to provide very detailed information about individuals, what is lost in this approach ...

are the narratives that individuals tell about their own lives. ... The narrative approach allows for a more active, processual view of identity that shifts over time and is more context dependent. ... Quantitative research can never provide access to the *reflexive* individual. ... Without this element there is a danger that people are merely seen as making decisions and acting within a predefined and structurally determined field of social relations, rather than contributing to both the maintenance and metamorphosis of the culture and community in which they live. (Elliott 2005: 131)

Perhaps the most compelling evidence in support of these statements comes from individuals who have participated in both forms of enquiry. The following reflections are from two panel members in the large-scale *National Child Development* study (NCDS 1958 cohort) who, at the age of 50, took part in an innovative, qualitative wave of the study (Elliott 2010a):

The researcher comes, and they take the information from you. Sometimes it's just a question of a 'yes' or 'no' ... and I might want to put a 'maybe' there ... or something. And there's sort of areas where you think, 'oh, but they don't ask me that.' And, I think, 'they should know that' ... so this [life interview] for me is good 'cause I've been able to sort of say to you things that have gone on in my life that perhaps the NCDS haven't known about.

I have been quite open and [said] things ... to you that I probably haven't told a lot of other people. But you've probably got a picture now of what ... sort of person I'm like from that, and if you got somebody coming to your home every few years and ... asking some questions and going again, they're not getting to know the real person.

Bridging the Gap: Advancing Longitudinal Enquiry

Quantitative longitudinal studies have traditionally been seen as the 'gold standard' of life course research. In 2003, Heinz noted that such studies had made impressive progress in exploring the shape of life trajectories, through the use of event history and sequence-pattern analysis. However,

Qualitative life history or biography research seems to have made comparatively less visible progress. Through it has been recognised as an important complement to life event and trajectory studies ... it has yet to become a steady companion and resides at the margins of mainstream life course research. (Heinz 2003: 75)

This casting of QL research as a peripheral approach, of use only to augment the large-scale panel studies, is notably persistent:

> The field of life course studies has matured. There appears to be more consensus on methods of data collection and on analytical strategies ... Longitudinal survey research and panel studies are the principal way to chart changes in the life course over time, with other methods, such as ... ethnographic observation ... as important supplements. (Elder and Giele 2009: vii–viii)

Among longitudinal and life course researchers, particularly in the USA, knowledge of the growing corpus of QL studies and their theoretical underpinnings remains limited. QL researchers themselves are not always aware of developments in their field and may inadvertently lay claim to novelty for their own approach (see Hermanowicz 2016 and McCoy 2017: 442, who suggest that QL methodology lacks clear definition, 'experimental trustworthiness' or any grounding in established methodological traditions). But such views look increasingly at odds with the rapid, interdisciplinary advances in QL enquiry, and the increasingly sophisticated body of methodological literature that has accompanied this growth.

More generally, across the corpus of longitudinal research, qualitative and quantitative designs are increasingly seen as complementary and of equal worth. Many of the design issues faced by longitudinal researchers, such as attention to sample maintenance, and the need to respond flexibly to changes in the social fabric (see Chapter 4), are common to those working in both traditions (Phelps et al. 2002; Elliott et al. 2008). The many commonalities between these two traditions create a forum for a productive cross-fertilisation of ideas and insights.

Alongside such developments, there is a growing interest in ways to bridge the gap between these different scales of enquiry, to combine breadth and depth, or epic and intimate movies to good effect. In the quantitative tradition, scaled-down community-level surveys are developing that are no longer driven by the search for elusive, nationally representative samples (Rothman et al. 2013; see, for example, *Born in Bradford* at borninbradford.nhs.uk). The promotion of narrative and biographical approaches in large-scale longitudinal and life course enquiry is a significant advance (Cohler and Hostetler 2004; Elliott 2005; Sharland et al. 2017 and personal communication; Carpentieri, personal communication), while, in a variety of creative ways, QL methods are increasingly nested within, or linked to, complementary longitudinal surveys (Laub and Sampson 1998, 2003; Entwisle et al. 2002; Heinz 2003; Farrell et al. 2006; Burton et al. 2009; Elliott et al. 2010; Morrow and Crivello 2015; Gray et al. 2016; for examples see Boxes 1.5; 3.2; 4.7; 8.4; and, 11.2). In these studies, insights elicited through the quantitative, 'variables' approach used in large-scale surveys are usefully read against insights generated through qualitative, person-centred, processual, case study approach (Laub and Sampson 1998: 221; Van de Ven 2007).

The *Baltimore Beginning School Study (1982–2005)*, for example, tracked nearly 800 young people over two decades to shed light on their educational trajectories and life chances. In the late 1990s, the researchers began to conduct unstructured qualitative interviews with participants who had, for a variety of reasons, dropped out of school. This yielded some valuable insights and led the researchers to build this mixed design more centrally into their study. Their only regret was that they had not taken this step earlier (Entwisle et al. 2002: 176; Alexander et al. 2014).

There is potential for QL researchers to build collaborative ventures with existing large-scale longitudinal panel studies, through the development of linked or nested studies. A linked QL study runs alongside a larger study (see Box 4.7 for an example). A nested study can be created through a limited sharing of participants from a large-scale panel, and the addition of a new suite of qualitatively-driven questions that a larger study can address over a limited period of time. This creates comparable data across the two scales of enquiry (see Box 1.5). But, rather than piggy backing onto an existing study, a nested QL study can also be designed from scratch. A model example, which integrates a QL design into a larger-scale and more extensive longitudinal study, is given in Box 1.5.

At this point, it is also worth teasing out more clearly exactly what is being 'mixed' in a 'mixed' longitudinal study. There are obvious limitations in 'integrating' forms of data and evidence when they are drawn from such different research traditions, and where data are generated and analysed according to very different logics of enquiry. This can often mean that one form of enquiry is subsumed within the other, most commonly where either quantitative or qualitative insights are used as supplementary or illustrative material. The methodological complexities of working across these different scales are evident and need to be addressed. Further developmental work is needed on this issue, but it may be useful to think in terms of productively linking (rather than mixing) research questions, and forms of data and evidence that can tell very different but complementary stories about dynamic processes (Neale 2008; see also Blaikie and Priest 2017: 20–1 for a critique of the idea of 'mixed methods' as a research 'paradigm' in its own right; see also Chapter 8 for a discussion of integrative reviews that may aggregate such data and evidence).

Box 1.5 Nested QL Studies – The Bangor Longitudinal Study of Ageing

This study of the vulnerabilities and support needs of older people in rural Wales (Wenger 1999) clearly demonstrates the value of nested longitudinal studies that link qualitative and quantitative methods. For the survey element, over 500 people were interviewed in 1979, and survivors were traced and re-interviewed

(Continued)

at four-yearly intervals between 1983 and 1995. Open-ended questions and the recording of verbatim quotations were incorporated to provide a qualitative component to the survey data and a source of comparison across the two scales of enquiry.

Between 1983 and 1987, the researchers also conducted an intensive QL study of a random sub-sample of 30 people, aged 79 or above, who were drawn from the first wave of the survey. Over a five-year period, they were visited twice a year, often for half a day or longer, using a combination of life history and narrative-based interviews and participant observation. This yielded rich descriptions of their daily lives and lived experiences.

The qualitative data revealed insights into the lives of the participants that had either not been anticipated or had not been seen as relevant at the outset of the study. The overriding picture was of able and competent older people, who were leading independent lives and engaging in reciprocal forms of support with strong networks of family members, friends and neighbours: 'the assumption of dependency, which was to be measured, applied only to a minority' (Wenger 1999: 373). The researchers were able to trace the shifting composition, evolution and sustainability of these social networks over time. In a productive iteration between the two scales of the research, anomalies and puzzles from the larger survey were fed into the QL study and teased out through an in-depth lens, while insights from the QL study were fed back into the next waves of the larger survey, where they could be explored across a larger sample. This iterative approach between different scales of related data greatly enhanced the findings: 'What is certain is that the final conclusions and outcomes of the longitudinal study would have been quite different without the qualitative study and the collection of qualitative data at all phases of the project' (Wenger 1999: 376).

These attempts to accommodate different scales of longitudinal enquiry in the quantitative tradition have been matched by similar initiatives within the qualitative tradition. While QL research is traditionally equated with small-scale, situated enquiry, recent initiatives have seen a 'scaling up' of QL research in ways that can enhance the evidence base and combine depth with breadth of data and analysis. One line of development involves revisiting and aggregating legacy data drawn from varied QL and/or mixed longitudinal/recurrent cross-sectional datasets, including those held in the Timescapes Archive (Irwin et al. 2012; Irwin and Winterton 2014; Lindsey et al. 2015; see Chapter 8 for legacy data research, and Box 8.4 for some examples).

The development of **qualitative panel studies** (QPS) represents another way to 'scale up' a QL study (Burton et al. 2009; Morrow and Crivello 2015; Dwyer and Patrick 2020). As will be shown in Chapter 4 (Box 4.7), these studies are by no means small scale in terms of sample size, geographical coverage, team composition and/or temporal reach. In effect, they represent a third kind of movie, **intimate epics**, which are grounded in big 'rich' data and evidence, yet, crucially, retain their depth and explanatory power (Neale 2015). These varied attempts to bridge the gap between these two longitudinal traditions, to bring intimate and epic movies together, are relatively new developments, but they suggest the rise of a new and enriched methodological infrastructure within which longitudinal and life course research can advance and flourish.

Qualitative Socio-historical Studies

Sociology without history resembles a Hollywood set: great scenes, sometimes brilliantly painted, with nothing and nobody behind them. (Tilly 2008: 120)

Beyond the longitudinal and life course fields outlined above, QL research forms part of a vibrant canon of interpretive studies that has a broader temporal or socio-historical focus. The value of combining sociological with historical insights is beautifully captured in the quotation from Tilly, above. Such studies include the broader reaches of social history and historical sociology (e.g. Elias 1997 [1977]; Kynaston 2005; Tilly 2008), both of which rely on documentary legacy data (detailed in Chapter 8). We focus here on three fields of empirical socio-historical enquiry that, in varied ways, have underpinned the development of QL studies: **longitudinal ethnographies**, **socio-historical re-studies** and biographical research (life history, oral history and narrative studies). These fields of scholarship have fed into and helped to shape the development of QL enquiry. The aim here is to tease out the ways that these established fields of scholarship engage with time, and to discern the place of QL enquiry within them. The common threads within these disciplines tend to outweigh their differences; there are many parallel developments across these fields of enquiry, and a significant cross-fertilisation of methodological aims and approaches.

Longitudinal Ethnography

Social anthropologists have been conducting ethnographic research in small-scale, agrarian communities since the early 20th century. Many such studies are conducted longitudinally (Foster et al. 1979; Royce and Kemper 2002). The approach typically involves continuous, intensive ethnographic immersion (a mixture of participant observation and interviews over many months). This is followed by a more extensive engagement, sometimes over decades of revisits, by the same researcher (and, often, thereafter, by new generations of researchers who 'inherit' a particular field site). This produces a distinctive longitudinal frame. Howell (2012: 156) likens the process to dipping 'different nets in a teeming ocean, each time producing a different catch'.

She stresses, too, that the constituent elements of the ocean are transformed over time, and that informed ethnographers throw their metaphorical nets purposively rather than randomly, based on informed understandings of shifting local terrains (2012: 157).

Longitudinal ethnographies are essentially prospective in nature, with revisits anticipated and planned for. But they also entail a constant retrospective gaze, made possible through the extensive temporal reach of the studies over many years. The extensive longitudinal designs are the most distinctive and impressive feature of these studies, when compared to the more modest time frames that usually charac-terise QL studies (see Box 1.3). Longitudinal ethnographers are able to explore how lives are being *lived* as well as narrated, and how both lived and narrated lives change through time. Socio-historical re-studies in these evolving communities, conducted by the same or a different researcher after a lapse of many years, are also common (reviewed in Burawoy 2003).

Whether anthropological field research is 'truly' longitudinal (i.e. involving a continuous or regular field engagement with a prospective purpose) or a re-study (after a gap of many years), the focus tends to be on the changing community itself, rather than the individuals or small collectives who inhabit it. Nevertheless, the small scale of the community settings, and the intensive engagement through time, mean that anthropologists are able to develop a micro-dynamic knowledge of the lives of community members, particularly of their key informants, with whom they often forge close and enduring ties. Anya Peterson Royce (2002), for example, has been engaged in many decades of research in a Mexican Zapotec community, start-ing in the late 1960s. Over time, she became the official chronicler and photographer of life in the community, and acquired a much valued Zapotec family. She talks movingly of the ethics of becoming a Zapotec through time, and of the transforma-tions that have occurred in her own identity and sense of belonging through a lifetime of committed scholarship and enduring friendships.

Research carried out by Foster (1979, 2002) in the Mexican village of Tzintzuntzan provides a further example. The baseline phase of fieldwork, conducted in 1945–6, comprised six months of continuous ethnography, followed by monthly visits, each lasting a week. Twelve years later, in 1957, Foster revisited the community once again, and thereafter became committed to a lifetime of regular revisits (once or twice a year) that spanned half a century of change (Foster 1979, 2002). As Foster notes, his study bridges the gap between a continuous longitudinal field engage-ment and a more punctuated re-study, and he was able to look forward and backward in time to discern the impact of historical developments on the lives of the villagers. Like many long-term anthropologists, Foster developed an enduring commitment to the community he revisited, and, upon his retirement, 'passed the mantle' to a new generation of researchers (Foster 1979, 2002; Royce and Kemper 2002). (For an exploration of the ethics of this study, see Box 5.7; and for insights on how anthro-pologists share their legacy data with their successors, see Box 8.1).

The power to discern dynamic processes through longitudinal ethnography was initially slow to develop. While early empiricists visited the field on numerous occasions, each time developing a deeper knowledge of the communities, they produced a series of snapshots that had no temporal connection (Foster et al. 1979; Burawoy 2003; Howell and Talle 2012). The concern was to document bounded, 'traditional' societies, through an extended 'ethnographic present'. This was so much taken for granted that the historical moment when data were gathered was deemed irrelevant and the dates rarely recorded (Foster et al. 1979: 4; Fabian 1983; Royce and Kemper 2002). There were exceptions to this picture. Paul Radin (1987 [1933]), an historical ethnographer, who used life history methodology, argued that a proper understanding of cultures could only be achieved through '"intensive and continuous" long-term studies that recognised the particularities of individual lives' (1987 [1933]: 184–5).

It was not until the post-war years that anthropologists began to catch up with Radin's argument. There was a growing awareness that 'models of society that leave out time are inadequate ... our concern is not *whether* to study change, but *how* to study it' (Wilson 1977: 21). The recognition that social systems are dynamic and open-ended led to the development of methodologies that could capture these processes (Firth 1959; Foster et al. 1979). With each return visit to the field, the complexities of dynamic processes were becoming more evident. Continuity was no longer perceived as the norm, while processes of change were increasingly recognised as being integral to social life (Howell and Talle 2012: 16–17). This also led to greater reflexivity among anthropologists about their own personal and professional involvement in the communities under study. An example of how historical change may drive the evolution of a longitudinal ethnography is given in Box 1.6.

Box 1.6 A Classic Longitudinal Ethnography (Scudder and Colson)

In their longitudinal ethnography of the Gwembe Tonga in Zambia, Colson and Scudder (Scudder and Colson 1979, 2002; Colson 1984) made repeated visits to the community over five decades, from the 1950s to the 1990s. A conventional focus on the internal workings of kinship and ritual quickly gave way to a concern with the resettlement of the community after the building of the Kariba Dam, the absorption of the Tonga into a larger political economy in newly independent Zambia, and what this meant for their collective identity and citizenship. More recently, the researchers explored the lived experiences of the Tonga in facing the AIDS epidemic (Burawoy 2003; Howell and Talle 2012).

Over time, the researchers witnessed fundamental transformations in Tonga society that could not have been predicted: a transformation from isolated village subsistence farmers, to a culture with an emerging middle class who were actively

(Continued)

embracing new Zambian political and economic structures. The researchers also documented their own shifting relationships with community members as their concern for their fate grew, and as they and their key informants aged:

> What we can learn is related to our age. As we return again and again, we are perceived as ageing and different questions and behaviours become appropriate to us. ... in Gwembe I have found myself shifted from the role of young to middle-aged to old woman. Even my Tonga name has changed with that progression. And I myself am interested in different things. ... [I] pick up nuances which once passed me by when I did not have a three-generational knowledge of family linkages shared with other elders in the community. ... How the anthropologist records a funeral or a marriage or a cockfight, depends very much on where he or she sits and stands and with whom identification is made. (Colson 1984: 3–4)

Throughout their fieldwork, the researchers maintained their core anthropological focus on the twin processes of continuity and change in Tonga life. Like many of their colleagues, they were able to discern enduring values, practices and collective identities that remained intact through 50 years of community upheaval (Howell and Talle 2012). But they also documented profound changes in values and practices over the decades, in sexual mores and marriage practices for example, and in the rise of a cash economy that eclipsed the practice of reciprocal working parties, which had been fuelled by communal feasting and drinking. The researchers reflect, too, on the recursive nature of their study, as people look back and reinterpret the past from a new perspective:

> We have found people revising their memories as they tailor their ideas about the appropriate ordering of society to their experiences of the compromises involved in daily living. Moreover, their expectations of other people and of themselves, has changed drastically. ... They see themselves now as members of a world community within which they desire respect. ... They are much more likely to tell us what they want to hear about themselves, as they attempt to sustain a decent reputation before the world. ... We are not the same when we return, nor can we return to people who are the same. It was Heraclitus who said that we cannot step twice into the same river. I suspect that, until recently, few of us have been able to see how fast the river really flows. (Colson 1984: 3, 6, 8)

Since the late 1970s, longitudinal ethnography has advanced through a series of edited collections that have documented this approach and its power to discern the flow of lives 'through the stream of time' (Foster et al. 1979; Kemper and Royce, 2002: xv; Howell and Talle 2012). Earlier attempts to map out and describe social change have developed into theoretically rich approaches that more readily recognise and engage with the complexities of time (Howell and Talle 2012; Grandia 2015). In a recent stream of anthropological enquiry, time as the medium for conducting a study has given way to a focus on time as a theoretical construct and theme of enquiry. This is temporal research of a different order (Fabian 1983; Knight and Stewart 2016). But, overall, there is an enduring appeal in the use of longitudinal ethnography, or what Grandia (2015) calls 'slow' ethnography, for, in combining qualitative depth with extensive temporal reach, it represents one of the most powerful forms of QL enquiry. Perhaps more than in any other body of research, it is here, in the pioneering work of longitudinal ethnographers, that QL research was founded and began to gain its credentials as a distinctive methodology.

Socio-historical Re-studies

The ethnographic tradition described above fed directly into the development of socio-historical re-studies in Western societies. These began to appear in varied community settings in the first decades of the 20th century. As the name implies, a re-study involves revisiting and updating an earlier study to discover new insights about the past in relation to the present day. Newly generated data are brought into dialogue with the findings and data from an earlier study, creating the means for a direct comparison between the two (for comprehensive reviews, see Bell and Newby 1971; Crow 2002; Charles and Crow 2012; Crow 2012). Duncan (2012: 313) describes these studies as a 'sort of comparative research, but using comparisons over time, instead of over space'. These studies, with their community focus, commonly take the form of recurrent cross-sectional studies, as the discussion below will show.

It is possible to trace a long line of re-study scholarship, from the serial studies of 'Middletown' (the American city of Muncie; Lynd and Lynd 1929, 1937; Lassiter 2012), to contemporary re-studies in the town of Swansea, and the Isle of Sheppey (Rosser and Harris 1965; Charles et al. 2008; Crow 2012; Lyon and Crow 2012; Lyon 2017). In what was seen as a productive fusion of interpretive anthropological and sociological methods, the earlier studies often included researchers from both traditions, used a mixture of ethnographic and interview-based methods, and focused on communities as the unit of study. At the same time, they were pioneering a particular form of historical sociology that was being promoted more broadly within the social sciences (Wright Mills 1959; Gergen 1973; Abrams 1982; Elias 1997 [1977]; Tilly 2008). From the outset, there was an overriding concern with the intersecting processes of social change and continuity (the latter often framed at that time in terms of 'tradition'). This concern was not confined to the re-studies themselves but was also a preoccupation of the original researchers (see, for example, Stacey 1960).

The particular way in which early re-studies engaged with time has given this field a distinctive character. First, re-studies rarely seek to build understandings prospectively, tracing dynamic processes as they occur. In contrast to longitudinal ethnographies, which combine a prospective and retrospective gaze, here the gaze is retrospective, looking back to compare two snapshots in time, the past and the present day. Second, while longitudinal ethnographies tend to combine intensive and extensive tempos, re-studies are purely extensive. The original study and the re-study are typically separated by many years (at least a decade), creating significant historical reach. Researchers may attempt to trace a few of the original participants where these are known (see, for example, Stacey et al. 1975 and further studies reviewed in Crow 2012). But the backward gaze, the extensive reach over time and the community focus of these studies mean that the same individuals are rarely followed. These, then, are recurrent cross-sectional designs that limit the scope to discern how lives are unfolding biographically, or how biographical and historical processes intersect.

Overall, these studies have been marked by a pronounced break in continuity between the original research and the re-study. This tends to be reinforced where anthropological or socio-historical re-studies are carried out by second-generation researchers, who enter the field armed with a fresh, untrammelled vision (although, where possible, there will be some collaboration or at least consultation with the original researchers; see, for example, Lewis 1951 and Charles et al. 2008).

This break in continuity opens up new ways to think about the purpose of such research and the insights that might be generated. Indeed, some striking findings emerged in the post-war years that gave some urgency to these issues (Crow 2012). An illustration is given in Box 1.7.

Box 1.7 A Classic Re-study – Life in a Mexican Village (Lewis)

Oscar Lewis (1951) revisited the Mexican village of Tepoztlán in the 1940s, some 20 years after an earlier study had been conducted by Robert Redfield (1930). While paying homage to his predecessor, Lewis gained notoriety for comprehensively refuting the findings of his predecessor (on the ethics of managing this, see Chapter 8). Where Redfield had found homogeneity, integration and harmony in Tepoztlán society, Lewis uncovered heterogeneity, individualism and conflict. He accused Redfield of adopting 'the old Rousseauian notion of primitive peoples as noble savages and the corollary that, with civilisation, comes the fall of man' (Lewis 1951: 435). Redfield's work has since been described as the first of many anthropological ostriches that 'weathered the Mexican revolution in Tepoztlán without writing a word about it, lest it disrupt his description of a placid, harmonious peasant village' (Scheper-Hughes 2000, cited in Crow 2012: 411).

The stark difference between the findings of these two studies requires some explanation (Bell and Newby 1971; Crow 2012). Whether such discrepancies are the result of historical change, or changing researcher perceptions and preoccupations, or a mixture of these is not always clear. But, in this case, the differences largely reflected the changing methodological and theoretical orientations of the two researchers, rather than any wholesale change in Tepoztlán society

(Bell and Newby 1971; Crow 2012). Where Redfield was operating as a sole doctoral researcher, with relatively limited time in the field, and dependent on the accounts of only half a dozen key informants, Lewis was much better resourced. In the post-war years, he drew on more advanced and systematic fieldwork techniques, mobilised a large, multidisciplinary team of researchers, spent twice as long in the field, and interviewed over 100 individuals.

But perhaps the key difference across these two studies was the shifting theoretical orientation of the two researchers (Bell and Newby 1971: 77). Redfield was working in an anthropological tradition that, at that time, focused on the formal and ritualised aspects of the social world (those that tend to express collective values), while Lewis, working in an emerging sociological tradition, was concerned with the everyday worlds of the people and their economic and political livelihoods, tensions and struggles. As Bell and Newby (1971) note, since the questions that drove Lewis's research were quite different from those asked by Redfield, it is hardly surprising that the two studies produced different results. With hindsight, it is possible that the researchers were tapping into different facets of the dialectical forces of continuity and change, collective and individual action, harmony and conflict, which co-exist in creative tension with each other in any society, at any given time (cf. Gusfield 1967).

The example given in Box 1.7 suggests that there is some wisdom in the old anthropological adage that what we see depends mainly on what we look for (Lubbock 1892: 10). The preoccupations of researchers may lead them to miss compelling evidence about social processes. This suggests the value of working abductively, moving iteratively between the particular and the general, and between empirical observations and wider evidence (see Chapter 9 for an outline of abductive logic). By its very nature, temporal research confronts researchers with a basic insight: they are not neutral observers of change. They are part of the worlds they study, and deeply implicated in the very processes that they seek to describe and explain (Firth 1959; Burawoy 2003; Savage 2010: 163).

Lewis's research was one of the first of many re-studies to uncover limitations in an earlier study that require some re-working and refining (reviewed in Crow 2012 and Burawoy 2003). A recent re-study of the classic 'Middletown' community studies (Lassiter 2012) is also worth highlighting here. The early researchers (Lynd and Lynd 1929, 1937) painted a picture of a 'typical' American community undergoing social and economic change through the Great Depression. Their research, particularly their own re-study, conducted a decade on from the first, was innovative in focusing on the dynamics of class relations. However, a more recent re-study (Lassiter 2012) uncovered a major gap in the original research: a failure to explore the ethnic composition of the city and to document the lives of its African American inhabitants. Lassiter and his colleagues gave voice to a marginalised minority and, in effect, rewrote the history of Muncie from a more enlightened and ethically acceptable standpoint (for the ethics of revisiting earlier studies, including the re-studies conducted by Lewis and Lassiter, see Chapter 8).

These re-studies had far-reaching implications of a conceptual nature. First of all, the profound break in the tempo of re-studies throws into question the idea that researchers can simply replicate an earlier study, visit an identical setting (if not the same people), driven by the same theoretical premises, and use the same or similar methods to generate comparable data over time (Charles 2012). Indeed, the original study could no longer be regarded as a fixed, stable or definitive 'baseline' upon which a comparative re-study could be built. A re-study is better characterised in terms of building on and developing an earlier study, rather than baldy replicating it. After all, asking new questions and developing fresh interpretations is intrinsic to qualitative enquiry (Bornat 2013: 312). It is worth invoking Heraclitus once again here, who reminds us that it is not possible to step into the same river twice.

Related to this, it was becoming less clear that it was possible, or indeed desirable, to simplistically compare the past and the present. This was no longer seen as a sufficiently robust form of enquiry or source of explanation. The retrospective gaze needed to be refocused to allow for new questions to be asked about the past, and for existing evidence to be re-worked, re-interpreted and thereby enhanced. In short, there was a shift in focus towards a more reflexive, historical reconstruction of the past, seen through the lens of present-day scholarship.

Looking back in this more nuanced and reflexive way, with hindsight and from a new critical perspective, quickly became commonplace, and not only among second-generation researchers. The idea of recursively re-working the past applies to all researchers who invoke a retrospective gaze. Indeed, temporal researchers commonly go through a process of cumulatively building interpretations and re-interpretations of their data, interrogating them afresh from changing historical and conceptual vantage points, and responding to new themes, insights, theoretical questions and methodological refinements as they emerge (see Chapters 8 and 10 for further discussion on this theme).

Other transformations in the re-studies field were also occurring in the wake of Lewis's research. Communities were now increasingly seen as 'too large, too macro' (Frankenberg 1990: 188; Crow 2012); they could no longer be regarded as bounded units or microcosms of a wider society that could be studied in their entirety. While it was perfectly possible to carry out research *in* communities, studies *of* communities, as holistic entities, became increasingly contentious (Crow 2012). As a result, the temporal lens gradually shifted to studies and re-studies of discrete collectives within communities (e.g. employment, residential, religious or medical organisations), or the familial, gendered or generational dimensions of community life (Charles et al. 2008; Johnson et al. 2010; Lyon and Crow 2012). These changing orientations led to a revitalisation of re-studies in the latter decades of the 20th century. Indeed, there is an enduring appeal in revisiting a growing pool of classic 'legacy' studies, available through research archives, whose historical significance increases with each passing year (detailed in Chapter 8).

Overall, the particular strength of re-studies lies in their extensive tempo, bringing macro-historical processes into sharp relief, and enabling these processes to be re-visioned through a reflexive, retrospective gaze. However, re-studies carried out in this way cannot create the processual understanding that a prospective longitudinal frame would allow. Linked to this, there is less scope to follow the same individuals and thereby build a biographical understanding of change into the picture. In these dimensions of temporal design, classic re-studies and QL studies have notably different strengths and weaknesses.

However, the way re-studies engage with time is not set in stone. As shown earlier, the opportunity to follow up an existing 'snapshot' enquiry and turn it into a longitudinal one has become an attractive and cost-effective route for creating a QL study (see, for example, Hermanowicz 1998, 2009; Weis 2004; Henderson et al. 2007; Heath 2012). The fusion of re-study and QL methodology is nicely illustrated in the socio-historical comparative research of O'Connor and Goodwin (2010, 2012; Goodwin and O'Connor 2015). This is featured in Box 1.8. An equally compelling example can be found in the criminology research of Laub and Sampson (1998, 2003; see Box 3.2), who, after re-discovering and re-purposing a three-wave dataset dating from the 1940s, were able to trace the lives and criminal careers of a sample of delinquent 'boys', from their teenage years through to their 70s.

| Box 1.8 | A QL Re-study – Leicester Young Workers Study (O'Connor and Goodwin) |

Since 2001, O'Connor and Goodwin have been re-studying the *Leicester Young Workers* study, an investigation into the transition from school to work, which had been carried out by Norbert Elias and his colleagues in the early 1960s. A rich dataset had been generated, based on an interview-based survey with nearly 900 young adults. The data included contact details of the participants. Unfortunately, the research was never completed. For some 40 years, this treasure trove of data languished in a large number of box files in an attic storeroom in the Department of Sociology at the University of Leicester, before it was re-discovered, reconstituted and re-purposed.

O'Connor and Goodwin were able to 'read' the data from the earlier study in new ways, and shed fresh light on the precarious employment experiences of young people in the 1960s, thereby filling a major gap in our knowledge of youth employment and unemployment in post-war Britain (Goodwin and O'Connor 2015). They also used the original study as a baseline for a new study of youth transitions and

(Continued)

employment in Leicester, generating fresh insights on changing practices and circumstances over historical time.

Of particular significance for our discussion here, the researchers were able to trace, re-interview and reconstruct the biographies of around 100 participants from the original sample, retrospectively building a more processual understanding of their employment trajectories over four decades. This micro-dynamic data not only afforded some continuity from past to present, but enabled historical processes to be anchored in and understood through the changing personal lives of the participants (Goodwin and O'Connor 2015). In this way, a synchronic dataset, generated at a particular historical moment, was turned into an extensive, qualitative longitudinal dataset spanning a period of 40 years (O'Connor and Goodwin 2010, 2012: 486). (The process of retracing the sample in this study is documented in Box 5.4; and the use of participatory **visual methods** is explored in Box 6.10)

As O'Connor and Goodwin note, the potential to build QL re-studies in the future is ripe for development. This would require a greater focus on a processual understanding of lives, and, more pragmatically, the ability to identify and trace the original participants in a study. In turn, this relies on a commitment to preserve and archive the original unabridged dataset, complete with participant contact details, for the use of future generations of researchers (this core theme is developed in Chapter 7).

Biographical, Life History, Oral History and Narrative Research

Our mapping exercise concludes by considering a group of cognate disciplines (life history, oral history and narrative research) that are centrally concerned with the unfolding biographies of individuals. These fields share a common endeavour with the individual dimensions of life course research, albeit their methods for engaging with time tend to differ. Bornat (2004: 34) usefully observes that:

> The turn to biography in social science … coupled with a … grudging acceptance of the contribution of memory in historical research, has resulted in a proliferation of terms, schools, and groupings, often used interchangeably, some with a disciplinary base, others attempting to carve out new territory between disciplines. Labels such as oral history, biography, life story, life history, narrative analysis, reminiscence and life review jostle and compete for attention. What is common to all is a focus on recording and interpreting … the life experiences of individuals. (Bornat 2004: 34)

These **biographical studies** represent a powerful blend of insights from the socio-logical, historical and humanistic traditions. This field evolved within the sociology of Western societies (notably the life history research conducted within the Chicago School in the 1920s and 1930s: Thomas and Znaniecki (1958) [1918–21]; Becker 1966 [1930]; Shaw 1966 [1930]). Thereafter, the approach fell quickly into decline, but was subsequently revived in the post-war years. Since that time, it has gradually coalesced into a recognised field of socio-historical research, with global reach and influence (Merrill and West 2009; Goodwin 2012).

The development of this field in the post-war years of the 20th century was driven by a desire to counter the growing dominance of positivist social survey research (see Chapter 2). In its concern with broad patterns of human behaviour, such research tended to erase individuals from the historical record (Bertaux 1981). Thomas and Znaniecki (1958 [1918–21]) were, perhaps, the first to establish the value of subjective accounts as a source of meaning and insight, but the message has since been reinforced by each new generation of researchers (see, for example, Portelli 2016 [1979].

While precise methods vary, a biographical approach involves the narrative con-struction and analysis of individual lives (or significant dimensions of these lives), which, taking a lead from Wright Mills (1959), are then placed within their socio-historical contexts (Hatch and Wisniewski 1995; Miller 2000). As Miller (2000: 22) notes, life stories cannot be told without a constant reference to historical change. Working across the micro–macro plane requires a move from the particular to the general, maintaining the integrity of the former while elaborating on the latter (Bertaux 1981; Denzin 1989; Miller 2000; Andrews 2007). This creates a rich fusion of sociology and history, but this is history 'from below' (Perks and Thomson 2016).

The aim is to encourage the creative, interpretive story-telling of lives in ways that remain close to the experiences of those under study, and that views socio-historical processes from their perspective (Roberts 2002; Andrews 2008; Goodwin 2012). The agenda, then, has been to create a people's history through oral testimony (Thompson 1981); to bring subjective life histories to bear on an understanding of socio-historical processes (Bertaux 1981; Hareven 2000); and to establish and vali-date a humanistic, processual approach to social enquiry (Plummer 2001).

The rich methods used across this broad corpus of biographical studies to generate insights into unfolding lives, have fed directly into the field techniques used by QL researchers. The production of **narratives** (spoken or written accounts of connected events), that are generated as a joint venture between participant and researcher, is a core element of this methodology. Narratives are ancient forms of knowledge and expression, the means by which we story our lives, and make sense of our lived expe-riences (Flyvbjerg 2007; Plummer 2019). They are 'styles of telling' but also 'stories of experience' and 'ways of knowing' that create meaning for both participant and researcher (Hatch and Wisniewski 1995; McAdams 2008; Riessman 2008). Narratives lay claim to process, contingency and change as their distinguishing features

(Andrews et al. 2008; Riessman 2008); indeed, as will be shown in later chapters, they are the prime means of exploring and conveying how complex, temporal processes unfold. Time is said to lie at the heart of narrative thinking: 'we can neither think ourselves without thinking time, nor think time without thinking ourselves' (Brockmeier 2001, cited in Andrews 2008: 94).

Time in Biographical Research

The varied fields of biographical research alluded to above tend to engage with time in similar ways. Life stories are generally constructed through a retrospective gaze rather than prospectively, in real-time. The focus has tended to be on the life as told, rather than the life as lived, reinforcing the need for specialist skills in drawing out people's stories. Moreover, biographical researchers tend to generate these retrospective accounts at one moment in time, through a single visit to the field (Miller 2000: 40). Where a series of interviews is conducted, the aim is to excavate further: to seek clarification and to gain greater depth of insight, rather than explore continuities and changes through time. These synchronic/retrospective designs are easier and cheaper to manage than prospective QL studies, but they do not allow for a processual understanding of lives in the making.

However, as we have seen for re-studies, these differences are not set in stone. As our opening quotation from Joanna Bornat shows, like all socio-historical researchers, social biographers and oral historians are creative and adaptable. This has resulted in some exciting fusions of biographical, oral historical and QL designs, and the development of what has recently been called *longitudinal biography* (King and Roberts 2015). For example, the oral historians involved in the Timescapes study developed a panel design for *The Oldest Generation* study (Bornat and Bytheway 2008, 2010; Bytheway 2011). Through two waves of in-depth, life journey interviews, the researchers were able to explore biographies prospectively, looking forward as well as backward in time, and they rose to the challenge of discerning how those living in deep old age both perceive and 'live out' the future for themselves and their families.

Closing Reflections

In this introductory chapter, the place of QL enquiry has been explored in relation to the established canons of longitudinal and life course research, and the broad field of socio-historical studies. In the process, some of its distinctive features have been highlighted, not least its capacity to discern how lives unfold in real-time, through a rich, processual, qualitative lens.

Since the 1990s, QL research has found a broadly based rationale and a unifying identity, which has given it an established place within the canons of longitudinal and socio-historical studies. But it remains an open, creative and evolving form of research. Thompson (1981: 290) observes that social biographers and oral historians are 'jackdaws' rather than methodological purists, **bricoleurs**, who are adept at teasing out a variety of evidence to piece together a richer, composite picture of lives and times. The same can be said for QL researchers. They draw liberally on longitudinal and re-study designs to fashion the time frames and tempos for their studies, and adopt a mixture of ethnographic, case study, biographical and narrative methods to create the necessary depth and richness of temporal insight. Indeed, QL enquiry represents a rich amalgam of methods drawn from these varied bodies of scholarship.

Mapping the fields of longitudinal and socio-historical research in this chapter has illustrated some of the subtle differences, commonalities and synergies that exist between these varied modes of enquiry. As we have seen, among longitudinal researchers there is an emerging interest in working across and bridging the divide between large- and smaller-scale studies. At the same time, researchers engaged in varied forms of socio-historical research are exploring the interface between their own traditions and QL enquiry, and, in some cases, consciously adopting the QL label to frame their studies (see, for example, O'Connor and Goodwin 2010, 2012; O'Reilly 2012; Stanley 2013, 2015; King and Roberts 2015). These are porous fields of enquiry, with a great deal of cross-fertilisation between them, and scope for much more. The discussion suggests the value of working across the spectrum, blending different methodological traditions in a creative approach to research design.

The many ways of designing and conducting a QL study are explored in Parts 2 and 3 of this volume. Before this, however, our discussion turns to the rich bodies of theoretical knowledge on time, process, causality and complexity, which provide the conceptual foundations for QL enquiry.

Further Reading

For classic QL ethnographic studies, Coffield et al. (1980) is highly recommended, while, for QL re-studies, the work of Lewis (1951) and O'Connor and Goodwin (2010, 2012) stands out. For nested QL studies, Wenger (1999) provides a clear and concise introduction, while Laub and Sampson (2003) and Gray et al. (2016) provide excellent examples of research based on mixed longitudinal designs. On longitudinal enquiry more generally, Elliott (2005) and Leisering and Walker (1998) offer landmark discussions of theoretical and methodological developments, while Phelps et al. (2002) and Pearson (2016) provide fascinating insights into the design and development of large-scale longitudinal studies. Across the broad canon of socio-historical studies, the following works are particularly recommended: on longitudinal ethnography, Kemper and Royce (2002) and Howell and Talle (2012); and on re-studies, the collection of articles in the special issue of *The Sociological Review* (Charles and Crow 2012). For biographical, life history and narrative forms of research, Plummer's (2001) rich and engaging text is essential reading for the QL researcher; while Hatch and Wisniewski (1995), Andrews et al. (2008) and Merrill and West (2009) are also highly recommended.

Andrews, M., Squire, C. and Tamboukou, M. (eds) (2008) *Doing Narrative Research*. London: Sage.

Charles, N. and Crow, G. (2012) 'Community re-studies and social change', *The Sociological Review*, 60. Special issue.

Coffield, F., Robinson, P. and Sarsby, J. (1980) *A Cycle of Deprivation? A Case Study of Four Families*. London: Heinemann.

Elliott, J. (2005) *Using Narrative in Social Research: Qualitative and Quantitative Approaches*. London: Sage.

Gray, J., Geraghty, R. and Ralph, D. (2016) *Family Rhythms: The Changing Textures of Family Life in Ireland*. Manchester: MUP.

Hatch, J. and Wisniewski, R. (eds) (1995) *Life History and Narrative*. London: Falmer.

Howell, S. and Talle, A. (eds) (2012) *Returns to the Field: Multi-temporal Research and Contemporary Anthropology*. Bloomington, IN: Indiana University Press.

Kemper, R. and Royce, A. (eds) (2002) *Chronicling Cultures: Long Term Field Research in Anthropology*. Walnut Creek, CA: AltaMira Press.

Laub, J. and Sampson, R. (2003) *Shared Beginnings, Divergent Lives: Delinquent Boys to Age 70*. Cambridge, MA: Harvard University Press.

Leisering, L. and Walker, R. (eds) (1998) *The Dynamics of Modern Society*. Bristol: Policy Press.

Lewis, O. (1951) *Life in a Mexican Village: Tepoztlan Restudied*. Urbana, IL: University of Illinois Press.

Merrill, B. and West, L. (2009) *Using Biographical Methods in Social Research*. London: Sage.

O'Connor, H. and Goodwin, J. (2010) 'Utilising data from a lost sociological project: Experiences, insights, promises', *Qualitative Research*, 10 (3): 283–98.

O'Connor, H. and Goodwin, J. (2012) 'Revisiting Norbert Elias's sociology of community: Learning from the Leicester re-studies', *The Sociological Review*, 60: 476–97.

Pearson, H. (2016) *The Life Project*. London: Allen Lane.

Phelps, E., Furstenberg, F. and Colby, A. (eds) (2002) *Looking at Lives: American Longitudinal Studies of the Twentieth Century*. New York: Russell Sage Foundation.

Plummer, K. (2001) *Documents of Life 2: An Invitation to a Critical Humanism*. London: Sage.

Wenger, C. (1999) 'Advantages gained by combining qualitative and quantitative data in a longitudinal study', *Journal of Aging Studies*, 13 (4): 369–76.

2

TIME AND THE PROCESSUAL TURN: FLUID ENQUIRY

Key Points

- **The interpretivist tradition**: In its qualitative dimensions, QL research has its roots in the interpretivist tradition of social enquiry. This holds that the social world is experienced, interpreted, constructed, reconstructed and transformed by its members through their everyday actions and interactions with others. QL enquiry accords priority to human agency, subjectivity and lived experience as the means to reach a deep understanding of the social fabric and its dynamic nature. Since this research is situated in time and space, findings are provisional, requiring modesty on the part of the researcher.
- **Temporal theory**: In its longitudinal dimensions, QL research has its roots in a rich body of temporal theory, ranging from the works of Bergson to Adam. Time can be understood in both 'fixed' and 'fluid' ways, i.e. in terms of the measurements of the clock and calendar, and in terms of the flux and flow of human events and experiences. Both fixed and fluid notions of time are important for QL enquiry. Time is an important theme of investigation, as well as the framework through which a study unfolds. Change, continuity and causality are transformed when seen through a fluid lens.
- **The processual turn**: The importance of time in social enquiry has led to a widespread processual 'turn' that straddles the social and natural sciences. This recognises the social world as a complex, dynamic, fluid web of events, actions and experiences that are perpetually oscillating, interacting and unfolding through time. The aim of social enquiry is to capture this reality in

(Continued)

flight, to trace processes backwards and forwards in time, using the non-linear logic of **abduction** (detailed in Chapters 9 and Chapter 11).

- **Complexity theory**: A processual world view underpins the rise of complexity theory, which brings interpretive, fluid understandings more centrally into the social and natural sciences. Embracing complexity is a foundational principle of interpretivist enquiry. But its importation into the natural sciences is challenging the deterministic, predictive and linear thinking of classical positivism. This has created an enhanced status for interpretive forms of enquiry across the social and natural sciences.

- **Fluid enquiry**: If the social world is fluid and processual, then we need fluid modes of enquiry to investigate and understand it. There is a growing appreciation that interpretive forms of research, particularly those that utilise a mixture of longitudinal, ethnographic, case study and narrative methods, have unique value in this enterprise. This has profound implications for the future development of QL research.

Introduction

There do not exist *things* made, but only in the making, not *states* that remain fixed, but only states in process of change ... in process of becoming. ... Rest is ... apparent, or rather, relative. ... [We] arrive at fluid concepts, capable of following reality in all its windings. (Bergson 1946 [1903]: 188, 190)

Events and processes are ... complex because they necessarily exceed our capacity to know them. ... [We need] the capacity to think six impossible things before breakfast. ... [to create] metaphors and images for what is ... almost unthinkable. Slippery, indistinct, elusive, complex, diffuse, messy, textured, vague, unspecific, confused, disordered ... intuitive, sliding, unpredictable ... Each [metaphor] is a way to open space for ... an unformed, but generative flux of forces and relations that work to produce particular realities. ... In this way of thinking, the world is not a structure, something we can map with our social science charts. We might think of it instead as a maelstrom or a tide-rip ... filled with currents, eddies, flows, vortices, unpredictable changes, storms, and with moments of lull and calm. ... We begin to imagine what research methods might be if they were adapted to a world that included and knew itself as tide, flux and general unpredictability. (Law 2004: 6–7)

These observations from a metaphysical philosopher, writing around the turn of the 20th century, and a contemporary sociologist and organisational researcher, reflect much of what is compelling about the dynamic study of lives. They alert us to a basic insight: if the social world is fluid, then we need fluid modes of enquiry to investigate and understand it.

Bergson was a pioneering temporal thinker, who developed a new metaphysics based on fluid time, duration, the continuous process of becoming, and the embedded, emergent, unpredictable nature of change. For Bergson, these temporalities can be grasped through creative intuition, interpretation and lived experience, aspects of reality that provide a bridge between metaphysical and scientific understandings. Bergson's insights and their widespread influence across the social and natural sciences are threaded through this chapter.

A century later, Law argues for an approach to social enquiry that moves beyond conventional structural thinking to explore the complexity, fluidity and unpredictability of social processes. Like many 'processual' methodologists, Law does not engage explicitly with time, temporality or longitudinal methodology (a point elaborated on below). But he is clear that social realities are brought into being in a continual process of production and reproduction. These opening quotations encompass continuity as well as change, times of waiting, resting, lull and calm that are embedded within the rhythms of daily life. With a social constructionist understanding that our modes of enquiry do not simply describe social realities but help to create them, Law makes a plea for research methods that are in tune with and able to capture the enduring flux of the world. His reflections suggest that our capacity to follow Bergson, to 'arrive at fluid concepts, to follow reality in all its windings' has yet to be fully grasped, and remains an ongoing challenge for social research. But at least the task is now more widely recognised.

In their varied ways, these quotations provide a fitting starting point for this chapter. We begin by exploring two broad areas of theoretical development, which reflect the dual nature of QL methodology. The first concerns the philosophical roots of QL research in the interpretivist tradition of qualitative enquiry. The second concerns is the grounding of QL enquiry in a rich body of temporal theory. Starting with the pioneering work of Bergson, we trace the development of ideas about time in social theory that span a century of scholarship. The discussion then moves on to discuss a third major theme: a widespread **processual turn** in the social sciences. This has been articulated, in particular, among critical realists, who focus on causal processes, and, more recently, by social complexity theorists, who have brought fluid forms of enquiry into mainstream social science.

The chapter concludes by considering the relationship between the longitudinal and qualitative dimensions of QL research, between a fluid, processual understanding of the world, and interpretivist understandings. It suggests that these do not simply sit alongside each other for, as Bergson recognised, they are conceptually bound together. Just as qualitative enquiry is transformed when time is brought centrally into the picture, so time is transformed when seen through a qualitative lens. Law's insight that a fluid world needs to be mirrored in our research methods heralds a shift in the relative status of interpretivist and positivist social science, and suggests the need to rethink the rationale for social enquiry, to reconsider afresh what insights it can convey.

Two broad ways of conceptualising time are outlined in this chapter: fixed (linear, absolute) time, the structural realm of the clock and calendar, and fluid (non-linear, multi-dimensional) time, the social and experiential realm of lived experience (Neale 2015, 2019). This notion of the duality of time is a common theme in the work of time theorists, where it appears in many guises. It appears, for example, in Aristotle's distinction between *chronos* (chronological, sequential time) and *kairos* (qualitative, spontaneous time) (Chaplin 2002; Dawson 2013); in Bergson's (1910 [1889]) distinction between measurable quantitative time *(Temps)* and qualitative or lived time *(Durée)*; and in Adam's (1990) distinction between *Events in Time,* and *Time in Events.* It also maps neatly onto the methodological distinction drawn in Chapter 1 between the 'epic' and intimate 'movies' of longitudinal research.

This distinction between fixed and fluid time is nicely reflected in the everyday metaphors that we use to grasp the intangible nature of time. On the one hand, spatial metaphors (life journeys, passages, transitions, pathways, sequences, thresholds, horizons, forward/backward, before/after, and so on) are commonly used to capture a sense of lives unfolding through a chain of events. They imply a sense of purpose, and a linear, orderly direction of travel, although temporal journeys are by no means necessarily linear, sequential or orderly. These metaphors reflect what Bergson (1910 [1889]: 122) calls 'the deeply ingrained habit of setting out time in space'.

On the other hand, the imagery of waves, tides, rapids, turbulence, flows, storms and flash floods usefully captures the powerful fluidity and perpetual momentum of time. In its vastness and ever present motion, time has been likened to an ocean (Saldaña 2003: 5). Interspersed with these images are those that reflect calmer waters: drops, ripples, eddies, backwaters, streams, ponds and babbling brooks, which capture the delicate, enduring and almost imperceptible ebbs and flows of time. As our opening quotations make clear, while the tempo of our existence encompasses continuity as well as change, our lives are never static. It is worth reflecting in this regard that all of these metaphors, whether spatial or fluid, powerful or gentle, are dynamic: they conjure a sense of the ceaseless motion of the world, and its fragile, contingent, intangible nature.

Taking both fixed and fluid understandings of time into account is a necessary foundation for QL research design and practice. Time becomes more than a design strategy, the framework through which QL research is conducted (however important that is). In its fluid, qualitative dimensions, time can also be understood as a rich analytical concept and theme of enquiry that drives the generation and analysis of data. It is this latter conception of time, *time as theme,* as opposed to *time as framework,* which is the focus here. The discussion also draws out the different ways in which time is understood across three main traditions of social research: positivist, interpretivist and critical realist (Blaikie and Priest 2017; for a proliferation of different branches of realist thinking, each with their own labels, see Maxwell 2012).

The exploration of key temporal dynamics and processual concepts in this chapter paves the way for Chapter 3, which explores how fluid notions of time and causality can be built into qualitative longitudinal and life course research. These themes are then drawn together in Chapter 11, as the basis for processual analysis.

The Logic of Qualitative Enquiry: Understanding and Interpreting the Social World

The logic of qualitative enquiry, and its engagement with temporal processes, encompasses a range of intellectual positions and strands of scholarship that have developed over many decades, stretching back to the 19th century. Ideas about the nature of the social world (its ontology), and the best means to know and understand this world (its epistemology), are enduring themes that are refuted, re-enforced and refined by successive generations of social theorists and philosophers. These ideas, and the language used to describe them, are continually evolving of course, not least in the work of individual scholars. Interpretations of classical scholarship, the nature of particular theories, their provenance and originality are also continually contested and revised. It seems that the 'intellectual firmament' of social science enquiry is no less subject to flux and change than the social world that it seeks to study (Abbott 2016).

This is the case for varied research **paradigms**, including the interpretivist, positivist and realist traditions that are discussed below. Paradigms are integrated sets of conceptual ideas that achieve a dominant position in social research and provide a methodological blueprint for researchers to follow. As conceptual tools that offer alternative ways to know and understand the social world, paradigms are overarching, abstract concepts that feed into different research methodologies and practices. It is worth noting that paradigms have porous boundaries: they are continually shifting as new ideas come to prominence (the temporal 'turn' noted in the introduction to this book) and as others fade into obscurity. This is why they are described here, in more fluid terms, as research traditions. Moreover, 'there is no one-to-one correspondence between paradigms and research methods … most methods can serve more than one master' (Blaikie and Priest 2017: 21). Indeed, in a context where there is value in crafting a bespoke set of ideas to address particular research questions, loyalty to one paradigm becomes both unnecessary and undesirable (Blaikie and Priest 2017: 9, 238).

In this shifting picture, there is no unified approach to qualitative enquiry or to temporal theorising, making it notoriously difficult to generalise about these fields, or to succinctly trace their development. With these caveats in mind, the discussion here pieces together a number of key themes and concepts drawn from varied traditions of enquiry (interpretivist, positivist and realist) that have utility for QL enquiry. A variety of sources are used, including Adam (1990), Blaikie (2007), Maxwell (2012), and Blaikie and Priest (2017).

The Interpretivist Tradition

As a mode of qualitative enquiry, QL research operates within a broadly interpretivist intellectual tradition. This has its roots in two parallel streams of classical thought: **hermeneutics** (an interpretive framework) and **phenomenology** (a descriptive framework). During the 20th century, interpretive understandings fed into a mosaic of research methods that, in whole or in part, embrace a qualitative logic. Beyond the temporal fields outlined in Chapter 1, these include **ethnomethodology**, phenomenology, **symbolic interactionism**, and constructionist forms of **grounded theory**. These approaches reflect varied ontological positions and/or epistemological preferences, for example a commitment to detailed empirical description found among phenomenologists and ethno-methodologists. But these are not mutually exclusive fields and useful convergences are evident, for example the incorporation of social constructionist insights into grounded theory (Bryant and Charmaz 2007; Maxwell 2012). There is, too, a growing appreciation of abductive/retroductive logic. This is an interpretive form of reasoning and discovery that uses iteration to generate new insights from empirical evidence (Paavola 2006, 2014; Blaikie 2007; see Chapter 9). Taking a broad overview, it is possible to discern an interpretivist vision of the social world, which is outlined in Box 2.1.

Box 2.1 An Interpretivist Vision

Interpretivists hold that the social fabric of the world is constituted through individuals and groups and their interpersonal and collective beliefs, experiences, events, actions and interactions. Since this world is experienced, interpreted, constructed and reconstructed by its members through their everyday interactions and evolving social activities, these are the aspects of social reality that need to be investigated and understood. Priority is accorded to human agency, subjectivity and reflexivity: the web of meanings, values, passions, feelings, motivations and intentions that shape people's everyday lives and which underpin their actions.

It was in classical hermeneutics (Dilthey 2002 [1910]) that an interpretive approach first found its value, and the idea of **lived experience** was developed. This was understood as a complex mix of experiences, values and practices, a series of social actions and reflexive understandings, in which imaginative and accomplished humans interact with others in their environment to create and recreate their social world (Dilthey 2002 [1910]).

Bergson (1946 [1903]: 159–60), one of the earliest interpretive thinkers, makes a distinction between two ways of knowing something: 'the first implies going all around it, the second, entering into it ... [grasping it] from within, in what it is in itself'. An interpretive framework enables the social world to be investigated and understood 'from the inside'. This encompasses the interpretations of people themselves (their world views), to which, in abductive fashion, a further layer of meaning, the broader interpretations of researchers, may be added. In more recent theorising, these two systems of interpretation (lay/expert, participant/researcher) are understood to interact and influence each other, a process known as the **double hermeneutic** (Giddens 1984: 284).

This intricate world of agency and subjectivity, of practices, meanings and values, can be accessed through ethnography, rich narrative interviews and/or participatory methods; in short, through **thick description** (Geertz 1973). The focus is on meanings rather than measurements, narratives rather than numbers. Indeed, phenomenologists and ethno-methodologists are committed to an **idiographic** approach that focuses on the uniqueness of individuals and the particularities of their lives. Where generalisations are made, these are **qualitative generalisations** that are discerned not through statistical prevalence, or by extrapolating from a presumed archetypal or typical case, but abductively through a mosaic of empirically observed social practices, lived experiences, and structures of meaning and knowledge (van Gennep 1960 [1909]; Becker 1966; Hallebone 1992; Gobo 2004; Halford and Savage 2017; see Chapters 8 and 9).

Across the foundational methodologies listed above, it is possible to discern an interpretive vision of a real, but nevertheless socially constructed, social world, that is fluid and diverse, marked by multiple, intersecting social realities, and operating at different scales of complexity across the social fabric. An interpretive vision has implications for the nature of social knowledge and insight. Since this is situated enquiry, tied to particular social, temporal and spatial contexts, it is not possible to produce definitive findings or generalisations. Interpretations are, by their very nature, partial, plural, provisional and subject to re-interpretation (Holstein and Gubrium 2008; Maxwell 2012). This creates an enterprise for social enquiry that is exploratory, reflexive, creative and open to refinement.

Interpretive thinking underpins all forms of qualitative enquiry, including QL research. These ideas first emerged as a foil to the dominance of **positivism** in social enquiry. Classical positivism holds that the social world is made up of behavioural regularities that can be described as social 'laws', and that the social and natural worlds should be studied in the same scientific way: through a focus on universal knowledge, experimental control, determinism and simplistic, linear models of cause and effect. Hypotheses about these regular, linear patterns can be deductively tested, explained and verified 'from the outside', using systematic empirical observation (survey data across large, statistically representative samples), experimentation, statistical measurement and the analysis of variables (categories that vary across a sample, such as age, class and income). In classical positivist thinking, time becomes a theoretically interesting variable that is added to the others to produce an understanding of strictly linear, sequential causal processes (see Kelly and McGrath 1988 for a detailed exposition). However, the variables approach 'assumes that the past has no depth' (Abbott 1995b: 204). It locates events as a series of snapshots in time, but does not discern the intricate non-linear processes by which changes may have occurred.

The classical positivist view that universal and definitive findings can be produced has been modified over the decades, with a growing recognition that all scientific knowledge is provisional rather than law-based, and that explanations may be fallible. Nevertheless, the **neo-positivist** idea of an objective, scientific method based on statistical measurement and linear causality reached a position of dominance in the middle decades of the 20th century, and has proved remarkably resilient since. As suggested in Chapter 1 in relation to longitudinal enquiry, neo-positivist and interpretivist frames of reference are best seen as complementary. Yet it remains the case that, for many positivists, human concerns, intentions, experiences, meanings and actions, and their situated contexts, are characterised as too impressionistic, anecdotal, unsystematic and biased to be of value. For interpretivists, however, these dimensions of experience are the bedrock of social understanding, sources of deep insight that take us well beyond the formal, reductionist, surface understandings that can be gained by measurement alone.

Time in Interpretivist Thought

The incorporation of temporal insights into interpretivist thought has particular resonance for QL researchers. Ideas about the fluid nature of existence have a long pedigree, stretching back to the days of Heraclitus (530–470 BC). The fragments of his surviving writings include the insight that an individual cannot step into the same river twice, for both the individual and the river are perpetually changing. For Heraclitus, everything changes and nothing abides: the river is not an object but an ever-changing flow; the sun is not a thing but a flaming fire. Everything in nature is a matter of process, of activity, of change (Rescher, cited in Langley et al. 2013: 5). This view has been echoed down the ages, for example in the work of Michael Servetus, a 16th century humanist philosopher, who observed that at no time can you say, 'the world is this', for before you have finished saying it, the world has changed.

From the early days of the interpretivist tradition, time was woven into the theoretical picture. But how is time itself understood? Studying lives through time seems, at first glance, to be self-evident and straightforward, a matter of creating a moving, chronological picture that charts observable changes and discerns what happens next. This approach rests on orthodox positivist understandings of time as an empirical, linear construct, tied to the clock and calendar. Yet lives do not necessarily unfold in chronological order, through discrete stages, in one linear direction, or at a uniform pace. Nor do people experience time in these orderly ways (Kelly and

McGrath 1988: 55; Strauss 1997 [1959]: 93). Time can also be perceived as a fluid social construct that shapes and, in turn, is shaped through lived experience. These interpretive understandings of time are hardly new. They have evolved gradually over the decades through a wealth of socio-historical and temporal theorising (Adam 1990: 13). Key developments in this evolving picture that have relevance for QL enquiry are outlined below.

Our starting point is the work of French philosopher and Nobel Laureate Henri Bergson (1908 [1896]; 1910 [1889]; 1944 [1911]; 1946 [1903–22]). Bergson sought to overturn the classical positivist idea that time is sequential, uniform and linear, and entails an infinite series of 'now' points. He developed his ideas on 'lived' qualitative time, becoming and emergence through a series of writings spanning many decades. Key features of his temporal vision are set out in Box 2.2.

Box 2.2 Bergson's Vision of Time and Becoming

In *Time and Free Will* (1910 [1889]), Bergson held that the social world exists in a perpetual state of *becoming* rather than *being*. He distinguished between quantitative time (*temps*), the mechanistic nature of time embodied in the scientific world of the clock, and qualitative time (*durée*), the enduring dimensions of time that are lived and experienced: 'Usually, when we speak of time, we think of the measurement of duration, and not of duration itself. But this duration, which science eliminates, and which is so difficult to conceive and express, is what one feels and lives' (1946 [1922]: 13). Bergson saw that clock time does not endure. It is merely a succession of separate, discrete, sequential and spatialised constructs that give a snapshot view of a transition, much like a succession of fixed frames in a cinematographic reel, or a string of beads on a necklace (1946 [1903]: 185). These are engaging metaphors that have seeped into the writings of many contemporary researchers (see, for example, Glick et al. 1995; Abbott 2001; Neale and Flowerdew 2003; Gerrits 2008).

For Bergson, it is the relationship *between* things that matters, not the things themselves: 'what is real is the continual change of form: form is only a snapshot view of a transition' (1944 [1911]: 301/197). Lived time, for Bergson, encompasses a multiplicity of times which inhere simultaneously in the present day through the power of intuition, memory and imagination. The legacy of the past is always shaping both the present and the future, and adding something new to them (Bergson 1946 [1903]: 164): 'pure duration ... forms both the past and present states into one organic whole, as happens when we recall the notes of a tune, melting, so to speak, into one another' (1910 [1889]: 100). In other words, past, present and future are not separate, bounded realms, but relational realms that derive their meaning from each other. The meaning of the present moment depends on its

(Continued)

place in a larger whole, the multiplicity of time horizons that merge in the present moment. Times of settled states, of continuity in events and practices, are embedded within the ceaseless motion of becoming; ultimately, our social existence is dynamic and cannot stand still.

In Bergson's view, it is lived time (durée) that is the privileged dimension of time, while quantitative time (temps) is a mathematical abstraction that lacks the inner consciousness and experience of lived time. Bergson's view of the temporal world has further implications. For, if the world is in a perpetual state of becoming, then, in the tradition of Heraclitus, this also means that no two successive moments (routines, traditions, recurring events) are the same; in the ebb and flow of existence, things can never return to exactly where they were. Since the future can never be a mere re-arrangement of what has been, time is irreversible (Bergson 1910 [1889]).

Bergson's theories on the ceaseless fluidity of the world, and the multiplicities of lived time, were highly influential in the first decades of the 20th century, and enjoyed a resurgence from the 1960s, most notably in the philosophy of Deleuze (1988 [1966]), and in Prigogine's notion of thermodynamics as a science of becoming (Prigogine 1980).[1] His theories helped to shape the literary philosophy of writers such as Sartre and Proust, the pioneering life course theories of van Gennep (see Chapter 3), and they were elaborated, debated and refined by numerous social philosophers, theorists and social scientists, from James, Dewey, Whitehead, Mead and Sorokin in the USA, to McTaggart, Husserl, Heidegger, Mannheim and Luhmann in Europe (detailed in Adam 1990).

Among these developments, it is worth highlighting the incorporation of Bergson's philosophical ideas into the realm of socio-historical research and social theory. Dilthey (2002 [1910]), a sociologist and hermeneutic philosopher, established that phenomena are always situated within a larger socio-historical context, and that a full understanding of the social world requires an investigation of both dimensions: how the parts of this system are related to the whole. This was described by Dilthey and his followers as the **hermeneutic circle**, an iterative process by which researchers oscillate between the particular and the general, the individual and the social, interpreting the fragmented parts of the system from multiple vantage points, to produce new understandings.

---

[1] Varied reasons have been suggested for the gradual eclipse of Bergson's ideas during the 1930s, not least his ill health, which curtailed his career from the late 1920s, and his bold (some would say rash) critique of Einstein's theories. There is also the view that Heidegger appropriated some of Bergson's ideas and, without warrant, discredited others (Massey 2015). The rise of fascism in Heidegger's Germany may also have played a part. In 1940, months before his death, Bergson was required, under the anti-semitic laws of the Vichy Government in France, to either give up his identity as a Jew, or to renounce all the posts and honours that had been awarded to him. He chose the latter course.

In this context, Dilthey came to understand lived experience as an essentially temporal process, part of a dynamic, interconnected system, in which meaning is derived from understandings of the past, while purpose is projective, striving into the future. Experience is necessarily lived *through* time, for it can only be understood through the horizons and contexts of history, culture and geography (Dilthey 2002 [1910]; Makkreel 2003/4; Nelson 2004; and for a contemporary discussion of lived experience, see McIntosh and Wright 2019).

Similar ideas emerged as part of Mead's (1959 [1934]) symbolic interactionism, the notion that mind and self are continually emerging through relational social processes. Mead held that social processes are not invisible forces, but can be observed through symbolically mediated interactions between people (Becker 1966 [1930]). He also provides a useful elaboration of Bergson's view of the past. He acknowledges the irreversibility of time, but observes that when it comes to the meaning and interpretation of past events and experiences, how we make sense of them when we look back, some elements of the past are preserved, evoked and selected, while others are discarded. The continual process by which we recreate and reformulate our past experiences from the standpoint of the present makes the past as hypothetical as the future. It is here that the seeds of recursive understanding begin to emerge (detailed further below, and in Chapter 3 and Chapter 6). With his focus on the social dimensions of time, Mead also gives an enhanced status to Bergson's lived time. This, for Mead, is the essential element of temporality, the only real version of time. In Mead's account, fixed, quantitative time becomes a residual, abstract or virtual category with no perceptible value for social enquiry.

Bergson's ground-breaking ideas on the multiplicities of time were elaborated and refined in the work of a number of researchers. Husserl (1964 [1901–10]), for example, contributed the powerful insight that both past and future may be understood as horizons of time that are constituted through and integrated into the present moment. This idea was further developed by Husserl's pupil, Heidegger (1980 [1927]). Like Dilthey and Bergson before him, Heidegger reinforced the general idea that time has an emergent quality. But, taking as his starting point a broader view of temporality, beyond human consciousness and intuition, Heidegger held that there is no understanding outside of the broader reaches of history. Humans cannot step outside of their social world or the historical context in which they live. Alongside this focus on the more extensive, historical horizons of time, Heidegger also highlights the future as an important source of understanding and motivation (Bauman, cited in Blaikie 1993: 35). He held that our finitude, the arc of our individual existence from birth to death, is a constant feature of our daily lives, perpetually shaping awareness of our past and future time horizons (Adam 1990: 30). Ideas about the recursive nature of time were strengthened through such writings.

Over the course of the 20th century, classical ideas on the salience of time in social enquiry began to find proponents across the main disciplines of the social sciences, notably in anthropology, sociology, linguistics and psychology (Mannheim

(1952 [1924]; Wright Mills 1959; Gergen 1973; Abrams 1982; Fabian 1983; Ricoeur 1984–5; Radin 1987 [1933]; Strauss 1997 [1959]; Elias 2007 [1984]). These ideas began to gain wider currency when they appeared in the work of Giddens (1979, 1981, 1984). Like many of his contemporaries, Giddens was critical of the compartmentalisation of sociology, history and geography into separate disciplines and stressed that time–space relations cannot be pulled out of social analysis without undermining the whole enterprise (1984: 286).

These ideas were incorporated into Giddens's structuration theory. Drawing on Bergson's insights on the multiplicities of time, and the ideas of Husserl (see above), Giddens distinguishes between three horizons of time: (1) the here and now; (2) the duration of everyday lives; and (3) extended durations across the generations, across institutions and across history (Giddens 1981: 19–20). He holds that these time horizons are mutually dependent, intersecting and simultaneously co-existing, suggesting that a social-scientific focus on any one must always imply the others (see Chapter 3, where these ideas are applied to the temporal horizons of the life course).

It must be said that Giddens's (1979, 1984) temporal theorising has some notable limitations and inconsistencies (Archer 1982; Adam 1990; Blaikie 1993, 2007). In his concern to give agency and structure equal weight, Giddens presented these as symbiotic systems that operate simultaneously, in the moment, to reinforce and reproduce themselves. Related to this, his tendency to focus on the repetitions, endless replications and routinisation of the clock led him to present time as a reversible force: the past and future are perceived as identical realms, with no external means of distinguishing between them. Giddens's ideas on time, then, leave little room for temporality: no duration, momentum, tempo, pace or flow of time through which, individually or collectively, people might create, negotiate or transform their lives. This means that Bergson's rich ideas on becoming, emergence and transformation (see Box 2.2) are crowded out of his analysis (Adam 1990: 27).

Nevertheless, it was through the work of Giddens that the value of bringing time and space into social enquiry gained wider recognition. The implications of doing so were also sharpened: if the social world is endlessly varied across space, and individuals, groups and institutions are perpetually evolving through time, this makes it impossible to search for, let alone uncover, universal or definitive laws of social existence. This provided a major challenge to the dominance of classical positivist thinking in the latter decades of the 20th century.

Contemporary Understandings of Time

The many complex strands of temporal theorising touched on above were eventually brought together in a masterly synthesis by Barbara Adam (1990). Out of an extensive array of literature, which she characterises as 'a maze of conceptual chaos' (1990: 14–15), she produced a coherent vision of the nature of time and its significance for social theory. She subsequently elaborated on these ideas and applied them in the context of varied social and environmental fields of study (Adam 1995, 1998; Adam and Groves 2007).

Like Bergson and other theorists before her, Adam (1990) draws a distinction between quantitative and qualitative understandings of time, which she characterises as **events in time** and **time in events**. She explains that most of our social-scientific and common-sense assumptions about time are reflected in the 'fixed' time of the clock and calendar. Here, time is perceived as an invariant, chronological, linear feature of life, a quantity that is objective and measurable, with a relentless, regular and recurrent motion that is expressed numerically. Time becomes a line, a dimension along which change takes place (Adam 1990: 101). Past and future are seen as separate and identical realms, held apart by the relentless progression of the clock.

Time in this formulation provides an external structure within which our lives are measured, planned, organised and regulated. The assumption is that people experience time in a uniform way. In the process, time becomes a resource, a commodity, a site of power and control (Thompson 1967; Giddens 1981). And, for social enquiry, time becomes a variable to be measured alongside others. Under 'clock' time, then, lives progress and events occur *in time*, for time is external to them. Time becomes a shared background, an over-arching framework, a taken-for-granted presence, the constant and unvarying medium through which lives are lived and events unfold.

This view of time is a recent social construction within Western industrial societies, yet it is pervasive and of global significance, making it difficult to think beyond or outside it. Time is so extensively embodied in the mechanics of the clock that the clock *becomes* time. However, this model of time has its source in outmoded forms of scientific explanation and logic (the abstract positivism of Newtonian physics). As Adam (1998: 43) notes, 'in Newtonian science there is no room for uniqueness and creativity, contingency and contextuality, surprises and discontinuities, chaos and catastrophes'. In short, there is no room for social complexity or fluidity. Drawing on more recent and evolving scientific advances (from relativity theory to complexity theory), Adam offers a powerful way to rethink and transcend clock time. She turns our common-sense notions of time on their head to consider not *events in time*, but rather *time in events*. Her insights are set out in Box 2.3.

Box 2.3 Time in Events (Fluid Time)

For Adam (1990, 1998), temporality has a kaleidoscopic quality. It has no fixed path, but is perpetually emerging in multi-dimensional ways in varied local contexts. Objective, constant, one-dimensional clock time gives way to a plurality of times, held in a simultaneous relationship with each other, flowing and intersecting in

(Continued)

complex and unpredictable ways. These multiple flows of time, or timescapes, are embedded in our day-to-day lives, giving shape to our lived experiences. They are subjective, relational, embodied and context dependent, inhering in and emerging from our social events, practices and processes. As Bergson saw, in all their complexity and flux, events and processes do not occur *in time*; they *constitute* time. Time, as an integral part of the social fabric, becomes our creation.

Seeing time in this way transforms our understandings of change and continuity. In clock time, our focus is on what happens from one point in time to the next. Change is seen as an instrumental, concrete, linear process, a discrete turn in the path, while continuity is the process of sustaining (or reverting back to) a particular path. Studying these processes is an empirical matter of charting and documenting what happens next, in a sequential chain or chronology. However, change can also be understood, in Bergsonian terms, as pervasive and indivisible, a constant, unfolding presence that inheres in the myriad events, practices, processes and interactions that make up the social fabric. Change is perpetually occurring in a multitude of ways through the shifting world of experience: it is not something that happens to things; it is an inherent part of the nature of things. A fluid temporal frame invites reflection on the subtle, perpetual, circuitous and unpredictable nature of change: how it is managed, created and experienced; its scale and cumulative nature; and the extent to which it is planned, anticipated, expected, desired, re-worked or imposed on people (Flowerdew and Neale 2003).

This fluidity raises questions, too, about how change intersects with periods of lull or calm, the stability or inertia of continuing states, and the intricate oscillations that occur between the two. Pettigrew (1987: 649) notes that 'empirically and theoretically, change and continuity need one another'. These oscillating processes emerge and derive their meaning from each other, as well as from the social practices and unfolding contexts in which they are embedded (Saldaña 2003). As will be shown below, a similar transformation occurs in our understanding of causality, when seen from a fluid, qualitative perspective.

In teasing out the distinctions between *events in time*, and *time in events*, Adam makes clear that these are not either/or formulations. Both are empirical realities that influence everyday existence and both, therefore, need to be taken into account in social enquiry. Adam makes two further observations, which have important implications for how we understand social time in relation to the cycles of time found in the natural world. First, she observes that, through our clocks and calendars, we do indeed live *in time*, for we live with the rhythms of the natural world and the passing of the seasons. The diurnal cycle of day following night, the rising of the sun, the turning of the earth, and our seasonal events and activities (harvest, religious festivals, and so on) are cyclical forms of time that mirror and elaborate the natural rhythms of the universe. Fixed temporal processes, those of the clock and calendar, therefore have more than the abstract or residual quality recognised by Bergson and Mead. The paradox of time as an inexorably advancing and irreversible force (the arrow of time, the river that flows to the sea), and a cycle (the perpetual wheel of time) is resolved. These representations of time are not incompatible when we think of the dual movement of the wheel, which not only spins on its axis, but simultaneously moves forward along a path (Zerubavel 2003). **Cyclical time**, and its elaborations in human activities, creates a bridge between fixed and fluid time.

Second, drawing on neo-positivist scientific discoveries of the 20th century (relativity theory, thermodynamics, quantum mechanics, ecological biology, chaos and complexity theory), Adam shows that unpredictable, intersecting flows of time are not confined to the social world; they also permeate the natural and cosmic worlds. This is where our temporal awareness arises, for fluid time is an aspect of nature, of which our social world is a part (Adam 1990: 155–6). In these ways, Adam transcends the dualities not only of fixed and fluid time, but also of social and natural time, demonstrating their intrinsic and powerful connections.

In the broader, more fluid formulations offered by Adam, narrowly conceived clock time loses its dominance. It becomes one among many flows of time that make up our temporal world. For Adam, then, the key task becomes a holistic one: to transcend the dualities that stultify conventional investigations of time, and to discern and investigate the flows and rhythms of time, social and natural, linear and cyclical, quantitative and qualitative, fixed and fluid. This in turn requires an exploration of the intricate webs of their connections, how they are implicated in each other. Adam's contribution to social theory is far reaching. She creates an alternative vision of the nature of temporal reality, an alternative ontology of time.

The Processual Turn

We have seen that time, as a fluid, processual entity, has been recognised through a century of temporal scholarship, running from Bergson (1910 [1889]) to Adam (1990). As shown in Chapter 1, a dynamic, processual logic underpins all forms of temporal research, and has since provided the conceptual foundations for a range of QL studies, where processual and longitudinal enquiry are intrinsically bound together (see, for example, Pettigrew 1997; Dawson 2003; Bidart et al. 2013; Langley et al. 2013; Bidart 2019).

An engagement with fluid processes has been consistently articulated and developed by organisational QL researchers, who describe their field as longitudinal process research. The overriding focus is on 'how and why things emerge, develop, grow or terminate over time' (Abbott 1995b; Langley et al. 2013: 1). As we have seen, this requires a shift in focus from change as something that happens to things, to changing as an inherent part of the nature of things. From this perspective, structural entities such as organisations are seen as no more than temporary instantiations of ongoing processes (Langley et al. 2013: 5). For these researchers, processual thinking goes hand in hand with longitudinal enquiry, ensuring a deep and prolonged engagement that can bring processes to light (Pettigrew 1987, 1997; Huber and Van de Ven 1995; Tsoukas and Chia 2002; Dawson 2003, 2013; Langley et al. 2013; Mari and Meglio 2013; Langley and Tsoukas 2017). Bergson's legacy is clearly evident in these writings (and acknowledged, in particular, by Tsoukas and Chia 2002; Dawson 2013; and in Langley and Tsoukas 2017).

Beyond these avowedly temporal fields, processual ideas have seeped into the very foundations of interpretive enquiry. Overall, it is possible to discern a widespread processual 'turn' across the social and natural sciences, a paradigmatic shift in focus from static structures to dynamic processes, which creates a bridge between interpretive, neo-positive and critical realist thinking. Through a long line of theoretical and philosophical development, processual ideas have gradually coalesced into the varied sub-fields of *process philosophy* (Whitehead 1978 [1929]); *process sociology* (Elias 1997 [1977]; Sztompka 1991; Abbott 2001, 2016; Tilly 2008), *process organisation studies* (Dawson 2003; Hassett and Paavilainen-Mäntymäki 2013; Langley and Tsoukas 2017), and similar designations across other major disciplines (psychology, economics, political science, archaeology and theology).

In the USA, interpretive processual research can be traced back to Mead's symbolic interactionism (1959 [1934]), helped by his pragmatist philosophy (**pragmatism** holds that theories should be useful and derived from experience and practice). Processual thinking was central to the work of the Chicago School in the 1920s and 1930s, where it fed into the work of successive generations of US scholars, and formed core elements in the development of social constructionist studies, and constructionist grounded theory (Becker and Geer 1957; Mead 1959 [1934]; Strauss et al. 1963; Becker 1966 [1930]; Berger and Luckmann (1971 [1966]: 40–2); Glaser and Strauss 1971; Dey 1999; Strauss (1997 [1959]); Charmaz 2014). In a parallel development, in post-war Europe these same ideas played a pivotal role in advancing realist causality research, and, more recently, the development of complexity theory (both of which are discussed further below) (Cilliers 1998; Sayer 2000; Urry 2005; Blaikie 2007; Maxwell 2012).

The key elements of an interpretivist processual vision are set out in Box 2.4 (and detailed further in Chapters 6 and 11, where strategies for generating and analysing processual insights are explored).

Box 2.4 An Interpretivist Processual Vision

- **The nature of processes**: The social world is a web of intersecting events and practices that are perpetually flowing, oscillating and interacting as lives unfold. A processual vision requires a shift in focus from the form that social events take, their structural components, to their relational and dynamic elements. The driving assumption is that the world is not a steady state, a static structure, a mere *being*, but a dynamic entity, a *becoming*. The aim of social enquiry is to capture this reality in flight (Pettigrew 1997), through the generation and analysis of processual data that can be traced through time.

- **Time and processes**: By their very nature, processes are temporal: time inheres within them. They can be thought of as unfolding pathways, but where the course of the path, its nature, momentum and meaning, are just as important as the start or end point. Processes are sculpted in a multitude of ways. At one end of the spectrum, a conversation can be seen as a process that unfolds intensively over a few minutes, inviting analysis of its linguistic and dialogic elements, and the iterative nature of the exchange through which meanings emerge (Doehler et al. 2018). At the other end of the spectrum, processes may evolve extensively and organically over many decades, inviting understandings of broad, intertwined patterns of biographical, social, environmental and historical change (Elias 1997 [1977]; Tilly 2008). Beginnings and endings are 'ephemeral way stations' (Langley et al. 2013: 10). In other words, outcomes may be arbitrary rather than clear cut. How events unfold is not necessarily chaotic or random, but future effects are inherently unpredictable, particularly where they evolve slowly, imperceptibly and without visibility (for example, the slow burn, hidden effects of climate and environmental change; Adam 1998).

- **Causal flows**: Processes may or may not unfold as clear pathways marked by an orderly sequence of events and with a clear purpose (sense making, decision making, performing, producing, identifying, managing/creating change, and so on; Langley et al. 2013). There may be no fixed or unitary driving force or trigger point for change. With their open, intersecting and porous boundaries, processual pathways are intertwined with others, like skeins of thread, or a confluence of streams flowing within a river basin or spreading across a flood plain (Pettigrew 1997). This gives each process a unique, kaleidoscopic swirl of movement (Dawson 2003: 86). Discerning how a process unfolds in practice and what it means for those involved, requires insight into how these pathways intersect and influence each other.

- **How questions**: A processual focus affords insights into *how* the social world flows, *how* individual and collective practices, values and decisions interact, and *how* these elements of the social fabric are sustained or transformed through time (Van de Ven and Huber 1995; Pawson and Tilley 1997; Van de Ven 2007). 'How' questions are inherently processual. Arguably, they precede and encapsulate 'why' questions, which require singular, relatively clear-cut responses (Lofland et al. 2006: 158; Bidart et al. 2013). Or to put this another way, 'positivists tend to want to produce answers to *why* questions that can ultimately be counted: phenomenologists seek to understand *how* a person lives' (Plummer 2001: 140–1). Processes, in themselves, become important sources of meaning, for both time and causality are embedded within them.

Pettigrew (1987: 650) advises processual researchers to 'beware the singular theory of process', to look for 'patterns and idiosyncrasies, the actions of individuals and groups, ... the role of exceptional people and extreme circumstances, the enabling and constraining forces of the environment' and to 'give history and social processes the chance to reveal their untidiness'. For Pettigrew (1997), exploring the complexities of processes requires a holistic, case study approach to enquiry.

In line with the quotations from Bergson and Law at the start of this chapter, processual thinking requires some imagination, aided, as Pettigrew (1997) notes, by a new dynamic vocabulary: the language of becoming, emerging, recurring, ebbs and flows, fits and starts, forming, transforming, cumulating, dissipating, decaying, revitalising, and so on. The growing tendency to use narratives and metaphors to convey fluid processes, and to turn nouns into verbs, for example to think in terms of changing rather than change, or organising rather than organisation (Pettigrew 1987), are important means of creating a linguistic and narrative tool kit to encapsulate the flux of the world.

Causality and Complexity in Social Processes

As noted above, processual ideas are not confined to the interpretive tradition but have informed the development of neo-positivist and critical realist ideas across the social and natural sciences. From among the many strands of scholarship alluded to above, two developments are particularly worth highlighting. The first is a processual approach to causal explanations, developed by critical realists and QL organisational researchers. The second is the rise of complexity theories that are founded on a processual ontology (Richardson and Cilliers 2001). These developments are outlined below.

Complex causality

The search for causal explanations, an understanding of cause and effect, is deeply rooted in social enquiry, and in the flux of everyday life (Maxwell 2012). Causality is our way of making sense of the world. In the Aristotelian tradition, 'causes' are simply explanations, forms of reasoning that give meaning to our existence. In general, we want to know how things happen and why events and actions turn out in a particular way. Indeed, our credentials as researchers often depend on our capacity to explain these deeply embedded processes, although we may not use the language of causality (Lofland et al. 2006: 159; Hammersley 2008). As Maxwell notes, 'any argument that something "influences", "impacts", "shapes" or "transforms" something else is a causal claim' (Maxwell 2012: 42). Indeed, 'causal statements are pretty much inevitable in any discussion of human social and cultural life ... research reports ... will always contain ... implied causal mechanisms' (Seale 2018: 573). As shown in Chapter 1, QL research, with its capacity to follow people in real time and generate dynamic insights, is designed precisely to uncover an unfolding tale, to explore the causes and consequences of change and continuity in human affairs (Becker and Geer 1957; Maxwell 2004, 2012; Elliott 2005).

Added to this, an understanding of causal processes is vital in policy domains where people are required or encouraged to change their practices or adapt to changing circumstances, or where the effects of health, welfare, social care, educational or employment interventions need to be monitored and evaluated (Corden and Millar 2007). As various researchers point out, 'unless qualitative researchers are able to talk in cause/effect terms they will not have much to say to a policy community focused on the question, "what works?"' (Anderson and Scott 2012: 680; Donmoyer 2012).

Despite this, causality has long been a contested issue in social enquiry. The search for such explanations was seen by classical scholars, such as Dilthey, as a defining feature of predictive, measurement-oriented positivism, and not, therefore, a valid enterprise for interpretive enquiry. Qualitative understandings of causal processes were set back for decades through fears that the findings would be tainted by their positivist associations (Maxwell 2004; Hammersley 2008). Lincoln and Guba are particularly scathing: 'the concept of causality is so beleaguered and in such serious disarray that it strains credulity to continue to entertain it in any form approximating to its present (poorly defined) one' (1985: 141).

Part of the problem is that the language of causality and of causal mechanisms conjures up images of conveyor belt precision and narrow, instrumental, mechanistic processes that may bear little relationship to complex social realities. The *variance/inference* causal logic used by positivists relies on a combination of two temporal flows. The first is chronology (A is followed by B). The second is causality (A causes B). It is assumed that if A is typically followed by B, then A must cause B, particularly where this pattern occurs regularly and repeatedly across large samples (Abbott 2001; see Lofland et al. 2006 for a more detailed discussion).

In a context where we cannot observe causes, but can only observe sequences of events, the logic holds that we can infer causes from the sequences of events. Causality, then, is inferred from two or more snapshot visions of events (temporal variables) that are held together (correlated) by their consistently observed sequence in a linear chain. Causality is implied in the linear, orderly progression from past to present to future; cause and effect are intimately tied to this sense of chronology. Causality, as a predictive and instrumental relationship between cause and effect, is reduced here to regularity, repetition and sequence (Maxwell 2012: 37).

Some blistering attacks have been levelled at this inferential logic. Sayer (a critical realist) astutely observes that what causes something to happen may have very little to do with the number of times we observe it happening (Sayer 2000: 13). The link between causality and repetition and regularity becomes far too tenuous and simplistic. Moreover, on its own, the bald fact that A is followed by B may also tell us very little. As Abbott observes, events or occurrences have duration and may overlap, raising questions about the conceptual order or sequencing of things (Abbott 2001: 192). Related to this, there is what Abbott (2001: 193) calls the 'time horizon' problem: how do we account for processes that involve multiple, contingent sequences of events that are moving at different speeds, across different scales of the social fabric? In short, how far is it possible to tease out the different interlocking threads of a process that occur at different and overlapping tempos? And how do we account for the recursive feedback loops and effects that are integral to causal understandings? While we can discern a great deal from the intricate patterning of events and activities, with their different temporal rhythms, the sequence itself is likely to be just one element in a much more complex and fluid picture.

To give a relatively simple example, the logic used by positivists is akin to suggesting that a light is turned on or off because someone switches a light switch. Yet there is a great deal more to this act than meets the eye (Fleetwood 2014). It is located within a complex system of interacting elements, including the provision of a light bulb and its elements; localised factors tied up with wiring, fuses and electricity connections; and more distant factors related to energy supplies and economic and contractual relationships with suppliers. The suppliers, in turn, operate in a diverse, historically unfolding, technologically advancing global energy market.

In such a system, a multitude of interacting causal processes are at work at any one time, operating at varied scales and unfolding through varied tempos and horizons of time. Every event has multiple antecedents, spiralling backwards through time, and multiple consequences, spiralling forwards into the future, creating vast and ever expanding constellations of causal flows (Abbott 2001: 144, 192). As shown below (Box 2.5), how the distributed elements of this system operate and interact may not be known to the person who operates the light switch. In the maelstrom of complex social processes, there is no simple relationship between a cause and an effect. Indeed, there are no discrete causes that lead to discrete effects over discrete sequences of time. The attempt to trace effects back to a single cause, or through a clear-cut, linear sequence of events becomes far too simplistic.

There may, of course, be considerable value in discerning widespread correlations between discrete events and practices. For example, a broadly observed pattern that links smoking with ill health can trigger more detailed and situated investigations into how such correlations arise (Elliott 2005). Linking questions and data across different scales of longitudinal enquiry can have significant value here. Yet there is always the danger that inferential logic will produce flawed causal models that are too superficial, tenuous, narrow or spurious to be of value (Maxwell 2004; Anderson and Scott 2012; Westhorp 2018). Part of the problem is that variance/inference models of causality are spatially and temporally adrift, abstracted from real-world processes, events and practices, and the meanings and motives of those involved.

However, in recent decades, a more complex, processual approach to causality has emerged as an alternative to the simple variance/inference logic outlined above

(Byrne et al. 2009). This recognises the 'openness, contingency and contextually variable character of social change' (Sayer 1992: 107; Maxwell 2012). This new thinking has wrested causality from its positivist stronghold and made it a legitimate concern for qualitative enquiry (Maxwell 2012). It has gradually spread across a range of disciplines; indeed, it goes hand in hand with the processual 'turn'. This broad development has spawned a variety of approaches to understanding and investigating causal processes. The key differences are bound up with how time is understood, and the extent to which fluid (qualitative, non-linear) understandings of time and causality are recognised.

These variations can be illustrated by drawing out some parallels and differences between realist and interpretivist understandings of causality. Since the 1970s, **critical realist** research has developed a specialist focus on understanding observed regularities and patterns in events and processes, and the underlying causal mechanisms that drive them. The critical realist paradigm is described in detail elsewhere (Maxwell 2012; Blaikie and Priest 2017), but some of its key features are teased out here. As an established philosophical tradition, realism is based on the drive to understand a real world, comprising real relationships and processes, a world that is seen to exist independently of how we perceive or construct it. This creates a distinction between two aspects of reality: the world as it exists, elements of which may or may not be observable, and the world as it is constructed and interpreted. Exactly how these two aspects of reality are related to each other is the subject of extensive and ongoing debate, creating many diverging branches of realist thinking.

In some of these branches, there is a marked penchant for working with and developing theoretical models, on the grounds that if causal mechanisms cannot be observed, then they can at least be conceptually modelled and theorised (Blaikie and Priest 2017: 177). A standard formula is commonly applied, which seeks to model inputs, mechanisms and outcomes as they occur in particular contexts of change. In some quarters, such modelling runs the risk of becoming reductionist and hypothetical, of ironing out the complexities of real-world processes in ways that are far too abstract and simplistic (see critiques in Hedström and Swedberg 1998; Hedström and Ylikoski 2010).

However, in other branches of realist thinking, notably critical realism, realist ontology is productively combined with an interpretive epistemology (Maxwell 2012). Critical realists start from the observation that there can be no objective or certain knowledge of the world. Regardless of its independent existence, the social world can only be known through the interpretations of its members. This means that alternative interpretations have to be accommodated: 'our knowledge of the real world is inevitably interpretive and provisional' (Frazer and Lacy, in Maxwell 2012: 5). The notion that it is agents, individuals and collectives (not social structures) that have causal force and can bring about change is another important strand of realist thinking that chimes with interpretivist thinking (Harré, in Blaikie and Priest 2017). As Sayer observes, 'explanation requires mainly interpretive and qualitative research to discover actors' reasoning and circumstances in specific contexts – not in abstraction from them' (Sayer 2000: 23). For Maxwell (2004, 2012), what is needed is a commitment to detailed, contextually drawn case studies that will give direct insights into causal relationships. Where a case study approach is combined with intensive, longitudinal field engagement, and narrative approaches to analysis, these methods can yield rich data and insights based on participant meanings. In Maxwell's writings, realist and QL approaches are productively merged.

However, realist and QL interpretive approaches part company when it comes to how they engage (or fail to engage) with time. Realist causal models or explanation are often developed with no more than a passing reference to time, or, rather, with an implicit understanding of time as a fixed, linear entity (Westhorp 2018: 45). For QL researchers, in contrast, causal processes have to be understood within a temporal framework, and in fluid ways: 'Causality is neither singular nor linear. ... Changes have multiple causes, and are to be explained more by loops than lines' (Pettigrew 1995: 96). In what follows, an attempt is made to tease out the relational, multiple and fluid dimensions of complex causality (a theme developed further in Neale 2021 in press).

Causal processes are relational

Causal processes are inherently relational (Dall and Danneris 2019). Human agency and subjectivity, the shifting meanings that events and processes hold for those who experience and craft them, are central to causal understandings (Hammersley 2008; Maxwell 2012). The very notion of agency is founded on an understanding of the causal power of individuals and groups (Hammersley 2008). In policy-related research, understanding 'what works' relies on a prior understanding of 'how things work' (an essentially processual question; see Box 2.4), along with an understanding of 'what helps' and 'what matters' to people in particular circumstances and settings of change. This generates 'know-how' knowledge (Langley et al. 2013: 4). These more relational, collaborative, consultative and tailored forms of enquiry avoid a narrowly prescriptive and instrumental focus on 'what works'. They also suggest the value of longitudinal case studies in generating causal knowledge.

Causal processes are multiple

Causal processes need to be understood holistically. They unfold through a multitude of interacting threads, operating in different spatial settings and at different scales of the social fabric (Pawson and Tilley 1997; Sayer 2000; Anderson and Scott 2012; Maxwell 2012; see Box 2.4 for the tenets of processual thinking). Causality is recast here, for there is no simple or unitary relationship between a cause and an effect. Tracing effects back to a single cause is too simplistic when they are rooted in entangled webs of causality (Nowotny 2005). Fleetwood (2014) refers to this as 'thick' causality, which relies on thick descriptions of interacting events, processes, motives and meanings. In policy contexts, a failure to generate holistic, empirically driven understandings risks producing policy recommendations that treat the symptoms rather than addressing the root causes (Anderson and Scott 2012: 679). These varied insights suggest the need for pluralism and empirically grounded sensitivity in the way that causal investigations and explanations are framed (Maxwell 2004; Cartwright 2007).

Causal processes are fluid, contingent and unfinished

A temporal perspective on causality is currently under developed. But it is a vital dimension of causal understanding. Time does not stand still while causal processes unfold; the latter are not located in static environments. If causal processes are plural, operating through different settings and scales of the social fabric, they are also temporal, operating through varied horizons and tempos of time. If tracing back to a single cause is too simplistic, so too is tracing back through a clear-cut, linear sequence of events. Fluid causality invites an understanding of the complex flows and tempos of time through which events unfold.

Bringing time into the picture invites a more nuanced and fluid understanding of how causal processes operate, one that moves beyond the notion that there are discrete mechanisms, contexts, inputs and outcomes that can be separated out for analysis. The temporal location of these causal threads is continually shifting, such that an effect (or outcome) that is observable at one moment in time, may become a cause, a contextual factor or a mechanism at another (Westhorp 2018). The very idea of discrete causes, mechanisms or outcomes becomes problematic in this shifting, fluid landscape: 'whether something "wears the label" of context, mechanism or outcome at a particular moment in any analysis does not depend on its intrinsic nature' (Westhorp 2018: 55). It depends instead on its relational force and its temporal location in a uniquely unfolding process. Causal processes, then, operate on shifting ground. They have no temporal fixity, no discrete end point, other than an artificial one that is created as an artefact of the research process and its window of observation. As Abbott (2001: 145) notes, when we think through time, the idea of beginnings, middles and ends quickly gives way to a sense of endless middles.

Seeing causality in these complex, qualitatively driven ways has two major implications for future research. The first is that methods of enquiry need to be attuned to the flux of unfolding lives and events, including a sustained, longitudinal engagement in the field, and the generation and analysis of rich case narratives that can capture and convey how processes unfold. This is precisely what QL researchers seek to do, of course. But it is notable that this view is gaining ground more generally, in ways that may support the further expansion of QL methodology (Maxwell 2012).

Second, the basic characteristics of complex causality outlined above confront us with the enormously complex task of identifying the many threads that may play a part in a causal process, how they fit together and unfold, and their relative salience in shaping events and lives (a theme we return to in Chapter 11). Causal processes themselves are contingent and inherently unfinished, requiring us to capture them 'in flight', through small windows in time, and in situated corners of the social fabric.

This, in turn, necessitates greater modesty in our claims to causal understanding, and a need to reframe this enterprise in a more open, reflexive and diffuse way. One way to do this is to harness causal explanations more closely to the empirical realities of the lives and events that are under study. However far we tread beyond the views of our participants, we need to ensure that we step back into their shoes, to understand what matters to them, and to discern their own meanings, motivations and agency in the maelstrom of life events. This may be a better means of discerning the open-ended, fluid nature of social actions, reactions, effects and counter-effects in complex systems of change.

Complexity Theory

The rise of **complexity theory** in recent decades represents a further critical development for temporal research, offering further insights into our understanding of processes. Complexity theories are founded on a combination of systems theory and processual thinking (Richardson and Cilliers 2001; Urry 2005; Byrne and Callaghan 2014: 201). A major impetus came from the field of thermodynamics, where Prigogine's *From Being to Becoming* (1980) was inspired directly by Bergsonian philosophy. The basic tenets of complexity theory, which has developed its own technical language, are set out in Box 2.5. The discussion here draws principally on the social complexity theories of Cilliers (1998, 2005), Gerrits (2008) and Boulton et al. (2015).

Box 2.5 Social Complexity Theory

- **Social systems are fluid and dynamic**: Complexity theory holds that social systems are dynamic, non-linear and unpredictable. These systems (organised or connected groups of individuals), operating at different scales (local to global, biographical to historical) and within different social and natural settings, are in a constant state of flux (Boulton et al. 2015).

They can be thought of as relational **assemblages**, dynamic structures with open and fluid boundaries. Directly, or indirectly, the varied entities within a social or environmental system interact with and influence each other, and they do so reflexively, through recursive feedback or feed-forward loops that may re-shuffle (reaffirm, grow, adapt, condense) or transform the system.

- **The flow of interactions (causal flows)**: The influences that produce change, or lead to recurring states, are multiple and flow in all directions (Cilliers 1998, 2001). It is the rich flow and patterning of interactions between system entities which is important (rather than the entities themselves): how the interactions occur, the direction of influence, the paths or trajectories that are being followed, and their effects. These processes may be marked by **punctuated equilibrium** (erratic changes following periods of relative stability, identified in retrospect). But they may also be shaped through **path dependency**, inertial effects, whereby changes are incremental and cumulative, building through their own momentum; or **lock-in**, inflexibility or stagnation where the momentum for change dissipates or is actively suppressed (Gerrits 2008).
- **Myriad fluid patterns** may be identified that are not linear, consistent or predictable. Small fluctuations can produce disproportionate, discontinuous and unpredictable effects elsewhere in the system or beyond it (the 'butterfly' effect, where a small movement in one part of a system may be amplified to create a tidal wave elsewhere). It is important, also, to discern the momentum of interactions, for example how momentum may build to create a **tipping point** (Gladwell 2000), a point of no return that may flow into other systems and lead to a radically altered state. These push-and-pull factors can occur simultaneously and at random. At critical moments of instability, new constellations of entities may be spontaneously created. Their history shapes how they are constituted in the present and in the unfolding future. Traces of past and future remain in the system, giving systems their emergent nature: the future is always uncertain and characterised by multiple possibilities. These intricate patterns and flows can only be discerned through a retrospective lens (Gerrits 2008).
- **Social systems are complex, distributed and contingent**: Complex systems have a distributed nature, with change operating at multiple scales of influence. While strong pockets of power, influence and inequality may be discernible, there are no fixed, overriding, hierarchical or dominant 'levels' of influence that operate as fixed control points or external designers. The many structural configurations of a system (horizontal, vertical, fractal, fragmented, integrated) are continually open to adaptation or transformation

(Continued)

57

(Cilliers 1998: 2–3; 2001). With their intertwining structures and processes (Gerrits 2008: 20), systems are marked by a constant oscillation between continuity and change.

Because these influences are distributed, this also means that social systems are contingent: local actors will not be fully aware of the range or impact of their interactions across or beyond a system. And neither will researchers. This reinforces the constraints on generalising about causal processes, or creating predictive models, and highlights the imperative to understand the situated nature of complex systems and their unique temporal and spatial configurations (Cilliers 2001; Gerrits 2008).

The tenets of complexity theory set out in Box 2.5 represent an engaging amalgam of ideas drawn from systems and network theory, chaos theory and post-structuralism, driven by a fluid, processual ontology. The ideas in themselves are not new (Adam 1998; Blaikie 2007; Gerrits 2008), and they are likely to be familiar to, or at least resonate with, QL and other temporal researchers who work with the same fluid logic. Of course, embracing complexity has long been a core facet of interpretive enquiry, even if it is new to the natural sciences: 'it is interesting to see that notions such as "holistic", "historical" and "qualitative", which have traditionally been the hallmark of interpretive social sciences, are now appearing in the language of physicists' (Tsoukas and Hatch 2001: 996).

To date, complexity theories have developed primarily through scientific, neo-positivist applications based on mathematical modelling. This has created a hard, reductionist form of theorising, driven by a search for 'thin' causality, which, for Gomm and Hammersley (2001), is incompatible with the thick description of qualitative enquiry. But 'softer', more socially oriented or 'connectionist' forms of complexity theory are also emerging that embrace qualitative, narrative and longitudinal forms of exposition (Cilliers 1998, 2005; Richardson and Cilliers 2001; Tsoukas and Hatch 2001; Gerrits 2008; Bevan 2014; Boulton et al. 2015). The introduction of human agents into complex systems unsettles scientific or social-scientific theories that assume a drive towards predictable patterns, stability and equilibrium. As Gerrits (2008) explains, such ideas have no basis in social reality when the social fabric is just as likely to be marked by ongoing instability: 'The stability of a system is a matter of perception and this points at the existence of subjective, multiple, temporally different equilibria at any given time. ... Stability and change ... can occur simultaneously' (Gerrits 2008: 30–1).

In bringing together and integrating a range of pre-existing concepts, complexity theory offers a powerful and coherent framework for understanding the flux of the world (Gerrits 2008). Simple, linear, cause-and-effect models of change give way to a more fluid and unpredictable vision of social processes, a radical development that challenges the deterministic and predictive thinking of classical positivism, and the linear, atemporal theorising of critical realism. Indeed, it has been hailed as a new paradigm for social and scientific enquiry (Urry 2005; Blaikie 2007). Its strength lies in the broader, more inclusive framework that it provides for thinking about how processes unfold, one that straddles micro and macro understandings and engages with both fixed and fluid temporalities. For Urry (2005), this suggests that a new ontological understanding has been reached that collapses or dissolves the differences between the natural and social sciences. It would seem that, in complexity theory, the momentum of fluid, processual thinking has grown to reach a tipping point, creating a seismic and irreversible shift in our view of the world.

Time and the Processual Turn

In the discussion above, we have explored two parallel strands of dynamic scholarship. The first is the development of temporal theory, culminating in a synthesis of fixed and fluid time in the work of Adam. As noted in Chapter 1, this has spawned a broad **temporal turn** in social science enquiry in recent decades. The second is a parallel processual turn, rooted in Bergsonian philosophy, evident in the work of Mead and the Chicago School, and developed, in particular, by critical realists and by QL researchers engaged in longitudinal processual research. This has culminated in new understandings of causal processes, and the development of complexity theory in the work of Cilliers and others. Both of these 'turns' – the temporal and the processual – take as their starting point the temporal philosophy of Bergson; both are rooted in a complex, fluid ontology; and both straddle the social and natural sciences. But how far have these parallel bodies of knowledge influenced and enriched each other? How does the theoretically driven temporal turn relate to the more empirically driven processual turn? Where, exactly, does time fit into the processual turn? More precisely, where or how does *fluid* time fit into the processual turn?

In QL research, and in the broader socio-historical fields of research outlined in Chapter 1, fluid time and processual understandings are inherently intertwined (Adam 1998). A temporal understanding of the world is also central to the softer, social form of complexity theory propounded by Cilliers (1998, 2005), Gerrits (2008) and Boulton et al. (2015): 'any analysis of a complex system that ignores the dimension of time is incomplete, or at most, a synchronic snapshot of a diachronic process' (Cilliers 1998: 4).

But, across the fields of social enquiry more generally, the connections between time and process are much more tentative. As shown above in the context of critical realism, in many processual accounts time is marginalised (Adam 1990; Tsoukas and Hatch 2001; Bidart et al. 2013; Langley et al. 2013; Westhorp 2018). It appears as an implicit, linear category or is 'tacked on' to discussions as another variable, or an overarching plane of existence, in ways that take little account of its embedded nature or its analytical power.

Where time does appear, it is more likely to do so in the guise of fixed, linear time than in its fluid (non-linear, qualitative, experiential) dimensions. Indeed, this is so across all fields of social enquiry. Processes are most commonly equated with chronology, creating an overriding preoccupation with linear sequences and the discrete events, steps or stages through which an end point is reached (commonly known as **sequence analysis**). This, in turn, tends to produce a focus on change at the expense of continuity, leaving little room to consider the oscillations between the two. This is perhaps most evident in formal processual sociology (Abbott 2016), where sophisticated, measurement-based theories of linear stage and time-sequence analysis have been developed (reviewed in Abbott 1995a and 1995b; see also Archer 1982; Van de Ven and Poole 1995; Van de Ven 2007; Byrne and Callaghan 2014). Even in grounded theory, where processes are recognised to have a degree of indeterminacy, they are defined in linear fashion: 'A process consists of unfolding temporal sequences that may have identifiable markers with clear beginnings and endings and benchmarks in between. The temporal sequences are linked in a process and lead to change' (Charmaz 2014: 17).

This widespread recourse to sequence analysis is perfectly understandable. It is perhaps the most obvious starting point for processual enquiry, and may have particular salience where change is being actively crafted and managed (for example, in organisational and public policy fields, or in *Rites of Passage* (van Gennep 1960 [1909]), where the temporal ordering of a carefully crafted symbolic process becomes an important source of meaning; see Chapter 3). Yet, in light of the recent advances in temporal and complexity theory outlined above, a focus on sequences alone, and the recourse to fixed understandings of their significance, begins to feel too narrow and somewhat dated.

In much formal sequential analysis, there is too little room to explore the discontinuities, irregularities, sudden accelerations, trigger points and pivotal moments of change, or to aim for a more rounded and complex picture. As Stich and Cippolone (2017) observe in their QL study of urban school reforms in the USA, 'it is not just the passage of time that is important ... but also the accumulations, recursions, connections, relations, stabilizations and destabilizations that develop ... as time passes' (Stich and Cippolone 2017: 5). Similarly, Tsoukas and Chia point out the 'difficulties we face when we try to understand change by breaking it down to stages. By doing so, change is reduced to a series of static positions – its distinguishing features are lost from view' (Tsoukas and Chia 2002: 571). Moreover, 'putting categories into an order does not provide any process logic or explanation for a process, but only an artificial queue of (stages)' (Paavilainen-Mäntymäki and Welch 2013: 242). This was precisely the point that Bergson strove to make in his early writings (see Box 2.2).

There are many ways in which a fluid logic becomes submerged or simply disappears in processual enquiry, particularly in positivist, variance-based studies. This results in 'thin' explanations (Dawson 2013; Halinen and Mainela 2013; for the drawbacks this may create for QL analysis, see Chapters 9 and 10, and Box 10.5). As Halinen and Mainela (2013: 194) suggest, sequence mapping (an intermittent engagement with events) needs to be placed alongside flow mapping, which requires a deeper, more continuous engagement with unfolding lives (detailed in Chapter 11). Pettigrew neatly sums up the argument: 'Some processes may be linear, directional, cumulative and perhaps irreversible, while others may be non-linear, radical and transformational. Openness to these possibilities is a key intellectual requirement for the process scholar' (Pettigrew 1997: 339).

Currently, however, there seems to be a lag between theory and method, a lack of insight into how this new fluid ontology may be operationalised. In many quarters, researchers lack the theoretical language and appropriate tools of enquiry to work with fluid time:

> Inadvertently, social theorists employ the theories of machines for the elucidation of social processes. ... It is clear that all theories of interactive processes have to utilise time as an integral property of the system. Not the abstract non-temporal time of the measure, but the temporal *time in processes* has to become central to the analysis. (Adam 1990: 63) (emphasis added)

This observation was made some 30 years ago, but relatively little seems to have changed in the interim. There would seem to be an ongoing reluctance to engage with fluid time, or to invoke the in-depth, qualitative methodologies through which it may be discerned. This is illustrated, for example, in the complexity theorising of Byrne and Callaghan (2014), who engage with the idea of narrative, but then stretch the concept to include equation-based modelling, and, in a highly selective reading of Adam's theory, omit any reference to the fluidity of time, to *time in events* (see also Van de Ven (2007), who retreats into variance logic and the quantification of temporal processes). As Cilliers observes, 'there seems to be a growing resistance against theoretical positions which emphasise the *interpretive* nature of knowledge' (2005: 255).

Fluid Enquiry and Interpretivist Insights

These observations take us back to the pleas from Law (that open this chapter), and from Pettigrew (1995), Dawson (2003, 2013), Bidart et al. (2013) and other QL researchers, for the use of multiple field methods (longitudinal, ethnographic, narrative, case study) that, in combination, can capture the flux of the world. Social complexity theorists are making some headway here. Boulton et al. (2015) hold that seeing the world in terms of complex fluidity is closer to lived experience than the Newtonian idea of the world as a machine. They usefully ask: how can we research the complex world, in all its grittiness and granularity, 'not through mathematical models and theories but "in the flesh" through "being in it"'? (Boulton et al. 2015: 107).

They advocate **process tracing** as a means to identify chronologies and 'the causal links and pathways which lead actions through to impact' (Boulton et al. 2015: 190). In doing so, they make a clear commitment to working across fixed and fluid, sequential and non-sequential time. They also promote qualitative, narrative, case history, action research and real-time methodologies as the prime means to achieve these goals. Their general advice is to *be processual*: to follow processes and anticipate tipping points, to trace and represent the development of situations over time; to be open to multiple perspectives through a critical subjectivity; to allow for detours along the way, and to work both retrospectively and prospectively, to look both backward and forward in time (Boulton et al. 2015: 112–14).

The utilisation of QL case study methodologies as the foundation for complexity research is a further significant development, providing a solid base for their expansion in future (Pettigrew 1995; Dawson 2003; Gerrits 2008; Bevan 2014; see Chapters 6 and Chapter 10 for the development of case methodologies). In his QL case study of the co-evolution of human and environmental systems, Gerrits (2008: 24) stresses the value of continuous, detailed modes of observation that enable the intricacies of change to be pieced together in retrospect:

> Co-evolution is essentially a process and can only be understood longitudinally. … snapshots are not the right mode for longitudinal research. … The risk of taking snapshots at (fixed) intervals is that the oscillating nature of complex change will go unnoticed. … The nature of complexity makes it inevitable that it is reconstructed afterwards, and, in order to find these roots, a high resolution of past developments should be obtained. (Gerrits 2008: 24)

Intuition, Creativity and Narrative Power

Using an interpretive framework for exploring processes has profound implications for social enquiry. Returning once more to John Law's introductory quotation, researching a complex, fluid world necessitates going beyond what we can easily comprehend. This suggests the need to acknowledge intuition, imagination and creativity as both inevitable and valuable elements of social enquiry; to make allowances for the unexpected; and to speculate and draw on disparate forms of evidence. This takes us beyond objectivity and the formal, linear logics of deduction or induction to embrace fluid, abductive, interpretive forms of insight (Blaikie 2007: 57; see also Law 2004; Nowotny 2005; Boulton et al. 2015: 110–11; and Chapter 9). It is worth invoking Bergson on this point: 'The realm of experience ... with incomplete solutions and provisional conclusions ... is unfinished, but it pushes strong roots down into the real. ... A science founded on experience ... can attain the essence of the real' (Bergson 1946 [1922]: 46, 43).

Creative modes of enquiry that encompass experience, intuition, practical wisdom and the particularities of context (Flyvbjerg, in Nowotny 2005), acquire greater
meaning and worth when the production of definitive, universal evidence is no
longer a feasible goal. For Cilliers (1998, 2005), this creates the need for modesty in
our claims for social enquiry:

> The view from complexity argues the necessity of modest positions ... [the]
> need to resist the arrogance of certainty and self-sufficient knowledge. ...
> There will always be some form of creativity involved when dealing with
> complexity ... not in terms of flights of fancy or wild (postmodern) abandon,
> but ... in terms of a careful and responsible development of the imagination.
> (Cilliers 2005: 264–5)

Linked to these new, more open and exploratory aims for fluid enquiry, a narrative
framework for the production and presentation of evidence has undoubted value.
For Dawson (2013), processual enquiry requires researchers to be chroniclers and
story-tellers. Unfolding narratives with their rich metaphors are ideal means –
perhaps the only effective means – of conveying the complexities, nuances and
paradoxes of fluid processes, and the intricate intersections of past and future, of
hindsight and foresight (Van de Ven and Huber 1995; Tsoukas and Hatch 2001;
Langley et al. 2013; Plummer 2019). Narratives reveal ambiguities rather than tidying them away, enabling us to tell an evolving story that, by its very nature, is in a
state of becoming. By reflecting the contingent and emergent nature of the social
world, a narrative framework does not close off further interpretations, transformations or discoveries. Instead, it actively invites them (Boulton et al. 2015: 115–16;
see also Chapters 6 and Chapter 11).

We will return to these foundational themes in later chapters of this book, particularly in Chapter 11, where the rich processual ideas presented here are distilled
to create a framework for analysis. For now, our conclusion brings us back to the
starting point for this chapter: to the value of an interpretive framework for understanding fluid processes. Such an approach should no longer be seen as an optional
extra, a supplementary orientation: in a complex, fluid world, it is an essential foundation for responsible social enquiry.

Closing Reflections

In exploring the conceptual foundations for QL research in this chapter, we have
traced the development of two traditions of social enquiry. The first is an interpretive vision that sees the social world 'from the inside', through the subjectivity,
agency and lived experiences of those who inhabit it. The second is the development
of temporal theory, including the complex intertwining of 'fixed' clock time and

'fluid' experiential time, and the need to work across these dualities to achieve a more holistic understanding of social processes. The discussion reveals how these two dimensions of QL enquiry – the qualitative (interpretivist, real-world) and the longitudinal (temporal, real-time) – do not simply sit alongside each other. As Bergson recognised, the fluid components of the social world, the notions of becoming and emergence are integral to lived experience. Fluid time and subjective understandings are conceptually bound together in ways that enhance and transform them both.

This chapter has also traced the development of a processual turn in social enquiry. This has impacted on the way that causality is understood, and has culminated in the rise of a new theoretical orientation for discerning a complex world. The recent rise of complexity theory has shifted our attention away from formal, static structures towards a fluid ontology. But, more generally, exploring how far the processual turn has been informed by advances in temporal theory has revealed a lag between the two. It is interesting to compare the scripts in Boxes 2.2 to 2.5 above, and to discern the common threads that link Bergson's becoming and emergence with Adam's temporality, and, in turn, with the development of processual thinking and the more recent rise of complexity theory. A greater integration of these ideas would enrich and advance processual enquiry.

In particular, the need that has been highlighted in this chapter for fluid methods of enquiry, that can trace complex temporal processes 'in flight', has obvious implications for the expansion of QL research. Discerning change, continuity, causality and complexity through a fluid lens creates a seismic shift in thinking. Social complexity research is a fledgling field of enquiry, currently a theory in search of a methodological tool kit, offering huge potential to mobilise QL methods as part of this enterprise. Finally, the complexity and fluidity of the social fabric suggests the need to move away from the certainties of scientific facts, to value meanings as well as measurements, narratives as well as numbers, and to acknowledge that, just like the world that we study, our research evidence is always in the making. This requires a more modest understanding of what our research can tell us, alongside the cultivation of a more creative, intuitive, exploratory and open approach to social enquiry; in short, it requires an enhanced status for an interpretive vision of the social world.

Further Reading

Adam's *Time and Social Theory* (1990) is essential reading for this chapter. Valuable introductions to processual research and the merits of longitudinal case study methodology can be found in Pettigrew (1979, 1997), Bidart et al. (2013) and Hassett and Paavilainen-Mäntymäki (2013), while Tsoukas and Chia (2002) and Law (2004) stretch the imagination in exhilarating ways. Valuable discussions of causal processes can be found in Elliott (2005) and, from a realist perspective, in Maxwell (2004, 2012), and in Westhorp (2018), who provides a much needed critique of the temporal limitations of realist research. In complexity theory, Cilliers's (1998, 2005) clear and beautifully crafted expositions are a must-read, while Boulton et al. (2015) is down to earth, accessible and draws foundational ideas into social research practice. Gerrits's (2008) longitudinal case study of the fluid co-evolution of human and environmental systems represents a landmark development in QL complexity research.

For those wishing to explore the different theoretical approaches to social enquiry touched on here, Blaikie (2007) and Blaikie and Priest (2017) provide solid introductions. Finally, the philosophical works of Bergson are elegant and engaging. A useful entry point is his 'Introduction to Metaphysics' and other essays in *The Creative Mind* (1946 [1903]). Among a growing number of commentaries on Bergson's philosophy, Ansell-Pearson (2018) and Massey (2015) provide interesting overviews.

Adam, B. (1990) *Time and Social Theory*. Cambridge: Polity Press.

Ansell-Pearson, K. (2018) *Bergson: Thinking Beyond the Human Condition*. London: Bloomsbury Academic.

Bergson, H. (1946 [1903]) 'Introduction to metaphysics', in H. Bergson, *The Creative Mind*. New York: Citadel Press, pp. 159–200.

Bidart, C., Longo, M. and Mendez, A. (2013) 'Time and process: An operational framework for processual analysis', *European Sociological Review*, 29 (4): 743–51.

Blaikie, N. (2007) *Approaches to Social Enquiry*, 2nd edition. Cambridge: Polity Press.

Blaikie, N. and Priest, J. (2017) *Social Research: Paradigms in Action*. Cambridge: Polity Press.

Boulton, J., Allen, P. and Bowman, C. (2015) *Embracing Complexity*. Oxford: OUP.

Cilliers, P. (1998) *Complexity and Postmodernism: Understanding Complex Systems*. London: Routledge.

Cilliers. P. (2005) 'Complexity, deconstruction and relativism', *Theory, Culture and Society*, 22: 255–67.

Elliott, J. (2005) *Using Narrative in Social Research: Qualitative and Quantitative Approaches*. London: Sage.

Gerrits, L. (2008) *The Gentle Art of Co-Evolution*. Rotterdam: Erasmus University, www.Researchgate.net/publication/254805429

Hassett, M. E. and Paavilainen-Mäntymäki, E. (eds) (2013) *Handbook of Longitudinal Research Methods in Organisation and Business Studies*. Cheltenham, UK: Edward Elgar.

Law, J. (2004) *After Method: Mess in Social Research*. London: Routledge.

Massey, H. (2015) *The Origin of Time: Heidegger and Bergson*. Albany, NY: State University of New York Press.

Maxwell, J. (2004) 'Using qualitative methods for causal explanations', *Field Methods*, 16 (3): 243–64.

Maxwell, J. (2012) *A Realist Approach for Qualitative Research*. London: Sage.

Pettigrew, A. (1979) 'On studying organisational cultures', *Administrative Science Quarterly*, 24 (4): 570–81.

Pettigrew, A. (1997) 'What is a processual analysis?', *Scandinavian Journal of Management*, 13 (4): 337–48.

Tsoukas, H. and Chia, R. (2002) 'On organisational becoming: Rethinking organisational change', *Organisation Science*, 13 (5): 567–82.

Westhorp, G. (2018) 'Understanding mechanisms in realist evaluation and research', in N. Emmel, J. Greenhaugh, A. Manzano, et al. (eds) *Doing Realist Research*. London: Sage, pp. 41–57.

3

TIME AND THE LIFE COURSE

┌─ Key Points ─

- **Re-thinking the life course**: In this chapter, the notion of fluid enquiry, which was developed in Chapter 2, is applied to the study of the life course. The life course is a central organising framework for QL research (and for longitudinal enquiry more generally) and, like any dynamic social construction, it can be understood in both 'fixed' and 'fluid' ways. How biographies and collective biographies are shaped, and how causal processes are implicated in unfolding lives, are important questions for QL researchers.
- **Turning points, transitions and trajectories**: Turning points (trigger points), transitions and trajectories are presented here as nested horizons of time through which the life course unfolds. Their causal power resides in their subtle interactions and multiple, cumulative effects. A trigger point brings a change in perception or aspiration. This may or may not translate into a concrete or enduring change but it is likely to be the necessary precursor to such a change. Like all complex causal processes, turning points defy prediction; a retrospective lens is needed to understand their efficacy.
- **Timescapes**: Human lives are shaped through varied intersecting flows or planes of time. Within these planes, there are a multitude of time horizons, which move as the observer moves. Five planes of time are set out here, through which unfolding events and experiences can be explored: **prospective–retrospective** (past, present, future); **intensive–extensive** (time frames and tempos); **micro–macro** (scales of time); time–space (spatiality of time/temporality of space); and continuity–discontinuity (synchronicities of time). This framework is designed to provide a bridge between QL theory and method, and to explore how time, as a powerful theoretical construct, can feed

(Continued)

into and enrich empirical enquiry. It provides a conceptual tool kit that researchers can draw upon selectively to craft their own studies.

- **The importance of fluid time**: A focus on time in longitudinal and life course research is vital. But how time is understood, its nature and parameters, is no less so. Our vision will be impoverished if it is fixed solely on the clock and the calendar. Seeing things *qualitatively* through the lens of time produces a richness of understanding that can transform our vision of the social world.

Introduction

> For groups, as well as for individuals, life itself means to separate and to be re-united, to change form and condition, to die and to be reborn. It is to act and to cease, to wait and rest, and then to begin acting again, but in a different way. And there are always new thresholds to cross: the thresholds of summer and winter, of the seasons of the year, of a month or a night; the thresholds of birth, adolescence, maturity and old age; the threshold of death and ... for those who believe it ... that of the afterlife. (van Gennep 1960 [1909]: 189–90)

This quotation from an early 'armchair' anthropologist and pioneering processual thinker reflects much of what is compelling about the study of the life course. Van Gennep was one of the earliest scholars to use the organising principle of the life course to make sense of social practices, and the complex interweaving of continuity and change in unfolding lives. Through a careful analysis of a mosaic of legacy data on the rituals surrounding birth, initiation, marriage and death, he developed insights into life course processes that were in tune with local mechanisms and meanings of change. By grounding his enquiries in processual thinking and abductive logic, he brought Bergson's ideas about *becoming* centrally into empirical research.

Theoretically and methodologically, van Gennep was very much ahead of his time. He developed his *Rites of Passage* as a corrective to Durkheim's school of positivism, which, in the early years of the 20th century, wielded such power and influence in the French academy that the development of fluid enquiry was set back for decades.[1] Given the centrality of the life course to QL enquiry, van Gennep's processual insights provide a fitting starting point for our discussion.

---

[1] It seems that Durkheim and his colleagues blocked van Gennep from securing an academic post in France. They were also avid opponents of Bergson and his interpretivist vision (Clark 1973). Van Gennep's marginalisation continued throughout his life, and has since been described as an academic disgrace. While his *Rites of Passage* received a wider audience after his death, when it was translated into English, his translators placed their own interpretations on his work. In the process, they skewed his meaning and diluted the force of his arguments about the power of these rites as mechanisms of change (Neale 1985). The second edition of the English translation (introduced by David Kertzer) acknowledges this problem, but no up-to-date translation has been produced to rectify this disservice. Despite this, a growing body of writings on van Gennep are helping to secure his legacy (see, for example, Hochner 2018).

The broad aim of this chapter is to apply the temporal ideas and insights developed in Chapter 2 to understandings of the life course. The life course is broadly understood here as the flow of lives through time. It is a central organising framework for QL research (and for longitudinal enquiry more generally) and, like any dynamic social construction, it can be understood in both 'fixed' and 'fluid' ways. How biographies are shaped, and how causal processes are implicated in unfolding lives, are important questions for QL researchers and for life course researchers more generally. How wider processes of social change are anchored in and reflected through the changing lives of individuals and groups is also a central focus of enquiry.

Drawing on insights from Chapter 2, the chapter goes on to explore turning points, transitions and trajectories as nested horizons of time. These temporal constructions are far from simple empirical categories; their meaning and utility have been the subject of extensive debate. Here, we explore their fluid, processual and interlocking nature, and suggest that their causal power resides in their multiple temporal connections and configurations.

Drawing together key themes across Chapters 2 and 3, and building on an existing conceptual framework (Neale 2015, 2019), the final section of this chapter explores how time, as a rich theme of QL enquiry, can be used to enrich empirical investigation. Since the publication of Adam's (1990) treatise on time three decades ago (see Chapter 2), some progress has been made to import fluid temporal understandings into social research. On the whole, however, clock time continues to dominate longitudinal and life course research, particularly in the quantitative tradition. In many life course studies, an engagement with time is limited to working with calendar time as a design framework. But taking time seriously involves more than this. In exploring time conceptually, as a rich theme of enquiry, five intersecting planes or flows of time are outlined here, and their utility for QL research is considered. The overall aim of this chapter is to provide a bridge between theory and method, and to explore how fluid time, as a powerful theoretical construct, can feed into and enrich longitudinal and life course research.

Re-thinking the Life Course

As shown in Chapter 1, **life course research** is centrally concerned with the flow of human lives, the positions that people inhabit in the life span, their life chances and experiences relative to others, and the dynamics of these processes through the intertwining of biographical and historical time. Life course research explores how the biographical crafting of lives (from cradle to grave) is inscribed upon the universal, biological processes of ageing (from birth to death), and how these processes intersect with broader shifts and transformations in the social fabric.

The study of individual biographies or life journeys is a central component of life course research (Chamberlayne et al. 2000). The focus may be on the dynamics of specific 'phases' of the life course (e.g. youth, older life), or on transitions between these phases as people grow up and grow older. Transition from one status or circumstance to another (e.g. into and out of schooling, parenthood, employment, poverty, ill health or crime) is another key area for enquiry. The factors that shape life course transitions are important themes, along with the causal threads or mechanisms that mark or trigger change.

Longer-term trajectories are no less important: for example, the 'age' trajectory through childhood and adulthood into later life; the intergenerational 'family' trajectory through partnering and parenting into grandparenting; and the 'work' trajectory through education and un/employment into retirement. The intertwining of these varied trajectories and how they influence each other is another key site for investigation. It is through the long sweep of a life over decades that historical processes come more clearly into focus, and the cumulative influence of earlier life patterns on later life chances and experiences can be more fully investigated and understood (Elder 1974; Giele and Elder 1998).

While individual biography is integral to life course research, so too is a concern with how lives unfold collectively (interactively, relationally), and how individual and collective lives shape, and in turn are shaped through, broader processes of historical change. How life course research is approached depends on how these varied domains and scales of experience are understood, and the relative priority accorded to them. The flow of lives, then, can be conceptualised and investigated in a wide variety of ways, creating a diverse and amorphous field of study.

Understanding the life course in terms of the flow of human lives brings to the fore another of its key features: it is essentially a dynamic process, bound up with flows of time. While time is deeply implicated in the way that the life course is understood and researched, relatively little attention has been given to its temporal dimensions. Indeed, much longitudinal and life course research is empirically driven and under-theorised (Reiter et al. 2011). Yet, like all dynamic processes, the life course can be understood in both 'fixed' and 'fluid' ways. In other words, how the life course is perceived depends in large measure on how time itself is perceived:

> To study the experience of duration, the estimation of an interval ... or the timing, sequence and co-ordination of behaviour is to define time as duration, interval, passage, horizon, sequencing and timing. The conceptualisation is in turn imposed on the studies. ... Time does not 'emerge' from these studies but is predefined in the very aspects that are being studied. (Adam 1990: 94)

> Western notions of the ageing process are based on fundamental assumptions about chronology. We organise our temporal perceptions by connecting the past to the present, and this to the future, in linear terms. ... We divide

and mark our days with units of time, seemingly orienting our every action to clock and calendar. Life change and a linear chronology implicate one another. Our understanding of ageing and life change is circumscribed and propelled by our view of time passing – irresistibly, irreversibly, irretrievably, inevitably. The linear, progressive life course is an artefact of this chronology. (Holstein and Gubrium 2000: 35–6)

Methods for studying the life course reflect, map onto and reinforce the different ways in which time is understood. Heinz (2009a: 422) suggests two contrasting methodologies: a 'top down' positivist approach that works with fixed views of time, and a 'bottom up' interpretive approach that works with fluid time. From the perspective of 'fixed' time, the course of a life is conceptualised as a socially defined and institutionally regulated sequence of transitions that are reinforced by normative expectations (Heinz 2009b: 474, 479). Life is seen to unfold as a predictable passage through a number of pre-defined, developmental stages relating to the institutions of family, schooling, employment, health, and so on:

> There is a central life cycle theme … that underlies much of this research. …
> [using] panel data to show directly how people move from stage to stage. …
> The standard life course progressions are the regular and expected events
> of anyone's life. … We expect to marry and have children at a certain
> age, to retire from our jobs at another. … It is possible to show whether
> members of the sample move along the expected trajectory from year to
> year. … Particular expected events, and unexpected ones (e.g. divorce,
> unemployment), their incidence at particular ages, their prevalence across
> the population … constitute the individual life chances of a given state of
> society. (Berthoud and Gershuny 2000: 230)

Berthoud (2000) suggests eight life stages, ranging from dependent child to old/ infirm. This is one among many models of life course development, or of particular 'stages' within it (e.g. the models of childhood development suggested by Piaget, Erikson and others; Denzin 1977: 8). Researchers vary in the degree to which they present these stages as prescriptive models, and Berthoud is careful to avoid being overly deterministic. Nevertheless, models such as these are assumed to represent widespread patterns of behaviour and, in the process, they acquire the status of normative benchmarks against which to measure the actuality of people's lives.

To take one example, the idea of path dependency (introduced in Box 2.5) usefully conveys the idea that the momentum for change builds incrementally through cumulative events and interactions. The past is as much a creative as a constraining force, which may lead people to choose new and exploratory directions. However, the concept of path dependency is also commonly understood as a linear, predictive pattern, in which past events and experiences determine the present, which, in turn, determine the future. This has been couched as a relentless, inexorable process from which individuals cannot escape (Gershuny 1998; for a critique, see Neale and Flowerdew 2003). In such accounts, the life course is assumed to have a universal linearity and a seeming objectivity that place it outside and 'above' those whose lives are under study. It has been likened to an escalator that carries us along in a uniform direction (Glaser and Strauss 1971; Riley 1998). The result is that 'much … life course research does not analyse lives but presents the statistical history of cohorts' (Neugarten, cited in Heinz 2009b: 476).

An alternative, fluid way of understanding the life course is set out in Box 3.1.

Box 3.1   Fluid Understandings of the Life Course

From a fluid perspective, the life course is understood to be socially constructed through lived experiences, subjectivities, and the agency and social interactions of individuals and groups (Harris 1987; Holstein and Gubrium 2000). While recognising the structural opportunities and constraints within which all lives unfold, this approach foregrounds the variability of life journeys, and the many different ways in which these journeys are crafted, negotiated and experienced in different settings and contexts of change. **Social constructionists**, from van Gennep (1960 [1909]) onwards, have reflected this fluidity in their research (Neale 2015). Harris (1987: 27–8), for example, sees the life course as 'the negotiation of a passage through an unpredictably changing environment', while, for Holstein and Gubrium (2000), individuals are the everyday authors (or co-authors) of their lives:

> [T]he meaning of our experiences is artfully constructed, constantly emerging, yet circumstantially shaped. … The life course does not simply unfold before and around us; rather we actively organise the flow, pattern and direction of experience … as we navigate the social terrain of our everyday lives. … The construction of the life course is always ineluctably local. … Individuals never yield authorship of realities to deterministic structural imperatives. (Holstein and Gubrium 2000: 182–4, 210, 232)

In this more malleable, processual understanding of the life course, the flow of lives can be viewed as a rich tapestry of intersecting threads that are perpetually forming, transforming and unfolding in distinctive and unpredictable ways through the stream of time (see Boxes 2.4 and 2.5).

An interpretive (fluid, constructionist) understanding of the life course has further implications: the life course itself is far from a fixed entity. Historical and cross-cultural evidence challenges the idea of a standardised model of human development. Researchers have discovered, for example, that childhood and old age are relatively recent historical categories, emerging in response to wider demographic and structural changes in Western societies (Ariès 1962; Blaikie 1999). In contemporary life, too, there is a blurring of the boundaries around youth and adulthood, and between mid-life and older life. Age and generational categories (from infancy to deep old age) are fluid and shifting as people cross generational boundaries, and as life course categories expand or contract. As Hockey and James observe, 'we have to account for changes in the shape of the life course itself: it is not only individuals who change but the categories that they inhabit' (2003: 57).

That there is nothing fixed about the way the life span is conceptualised is reinforced in cross-cultural perspective. While something akin to the life course is recognised in all societies, age and generational categories are culturally defined and constructed (Holstein and Gubrium 2000). Social ageing, for example, may be calculated as an 'upward' journey to venerable old age in some societies, and a 'downward' journey to senility in others (Hockey and James 2003). Even the universal process of biological ageing varies cross-culturally in relation to environmental and genetic factors. The St Lawrence Eskimos, for example, recognise two simple life course categories (young and old), while other cultures use complex age-grading systems that provide the foundation for elaborate systems of social stratification and inequality (Holstein and Gubrium 2000).

As Holstein and Gubrium observe, 'the linear life course is merely one variant. ... [A]cross cultures we find depictions of ageing and life change aligning with local notions of time' (2000: 36). Seen historically, and in cross-cultural perspective, the rhythms of our lives are elaborated in a multitude of ways, producing distinctive understandings of ageing and the life course. This fluidity provides a challenge to the idea of clearly separated and universally recognised life phases or stages, which are linked through a linear and orderly set of steps that occur at prescribed times (Bynner 2007; Grenier 2012; Woodman and Wyn 2013).

Turning Points, Transitions and Trajectories

Exactly how biographies are shaped and what kind of causal processes are involved, are crucial questions for QL researchers, and for life course researchers more generally. **Turning points**, **transitions** and **trajectorie**s, temporal constructs that convey the dynamics of the life course, are vital tools in addressing these questions. A burgeoning literature has debated the meaning and definition of these concepts (Hackstaff et al. 2012), although, interestingly, relatively few accounts link these constructs or seek to discern their temporal connections.

Taking a lead from Bergson, Husserl and Giddens (see Chapter 2), these constructs are framed here as intersecting horizons of time. For Husserl, past and future are time horizons that are constituted through and integrated into the present moment. For Giddens (1981), horizons of time operate across different time frames or durations, from the intensity of here and now, to the durations of everyday life, to extended durations across the generations, across institutions and across the broader reaches of history. Giddens holds that these different time horizons are mutually dependent, intersecting and simultaneously co-existing, suggesting that a social-scientific focus on any one must always imply the others. As the discussion below will show, this provides a useful way to think about the relationship between turning points, transitions and trajectories.

Turning points/trigger points

The notion of a turning point is used here as a loose umbrella term to capture the plethora of critical events, pivotal moments, epiphanies and tipping points that may act as the triggers or drivers of change (Kupferberg 2012: 227). In processual analysis, they are the connecting forces that link events, actions and interactions together to create the momentum for change (detailed in Chapter 11). The rich metaphors used to describe these phenomena reflect subtle differences in their nature, suggesting that these concepts should be used with care (Clausen 1995, 1998; Carlsson 2012). A finely grained, qualitative lens is needed to discern these phenomena, which perhaps explains why they are often omitted in accounts that are concerned with wider structural processes of change (Wingens and Reiter 2011).

As the name implies, turning points are often viewed in instrumental and linear terms to mean a concrete change from one state to another. They are said to 'redirect paths' (Elder 1985: 35; Abbott 2001: 258). They have been described as fateful or critical moments – points in the life course that are 'highly consequential for a person's destiny' (Giddens 1991: 112; Thomson et al. 2002; Holland and Thomson 2009). Certainly, these phenomena may be bound up with critical life events or experiences, turning points in the literal sense – for example, at the moment of a birth or death, or when a tipping point is reached, a point of no return, following a growing momentum for change (Gladwell 2000; see also Chapters 2 and 11).

Conversely, turning points may be artfully constructed, socially prescribed and carefully planned, for example the ritualised entry into marriage, or the marking of a significant change, such as a topping out ceremony, or the awarding of a degree. Such pivotal moments have causal power: they are instrumental through their expressiveness, combining core 'speech acts' with powerful symbolic representations that place people at the fulcrum of change (Neale 1985).

The idea that turning points have causal efficacy, involving a concrete change in the direction of individual or collective lives, is widespread. It is for this reason, perhaps, that they are often subsumed within the broader category of transitions. However, this overly instrumental way of viewing these phenomena tends to obscure their meaning, and the subtle ways in which they may influence the course of a life. An alternative reading of these phenomena stresses their subjective, fluid nature and their subtle influence through the flows of time.

First, and perhaps most evidently, turning points are triggered in discrete and often striking moments in time. They have a fleeting quality, reflected in Denzin's (1989) description of epiphanies as transformational experiences. These take people to a different level, direction or quality of change, akin to the sudden, unexpected force of a flash flood or rainstorm (Saldaña 2003). Their power lies in their propensity to create or instil changes in an inner biographical disposition, a process in which individuals or collectives take stock of their circumstances, assess this reality, understand it anew and conjure a new imaginary future (Strauss 1997 [1959]; Hareven and Masaoka 1988; Denzin 1989; Clausen 1998).

While such arresting moments in time do not necessarily constitute life change in themselves, they are the potential agents or triggers of change. For this reason, it seems fitting to describe these experiential phenomena more specifically, as **trigger points** (cf. Laub and Sampson's concept of triggering events, 2003: 40). They are also simultaneously forward and backward facing, the lynchpins for bridging continuities and discontinuities, and marking and creating boundaries between past and future (Clausen 1995; Abbott 2001; Carlsson 2012; Kupferberg 2012).

By their very nature, trigger points occur in the moment, crystallising elements of past and present circumstances, changing perceptions, identities and understandings, and opening up the possibility of an alternative pathway for the future. For example, in her research with the Chewong, an Indonesian community, Howell (2012) documents how the tribe's religious elders arrived at a rapid re-think in their core beliefs about the status of Rattan, a sacred (and therefore untouchable) forest plant. As a result of this sudden and arresting change in their belief system, the tribe was able to take advantage of new and lucrative opportunities to harvest this plant and use it for trade. A turning point in the traditional practices of the tribe was wrought through a trigger point that transformed their core values.

This brings us to a second feature of turning points. Since they occur in the moment, their longer-term causal efficacy can only be determined through a backward gaze (Hareven and Masaoka 1988; Abbott 2001). While these phenomena may have significant power at the moment in which they occur, their effects may be short lived. The subjective significance and meaning attached to a particular trigger point may shift over time, with some assuming enduring causal power, while others fade into insignificance (Plumridge and Thomson 2003; Holland and Thomson 2009; Jost 2012). Of course, it may also be a challenge to identify a clear trigger point; events may evolve slowly, imperceptibly or through inertia, with no clear markers along the way. Turning points are best perceived, then, as subjectively defined phenomena, inhering in particular narratives of change, constructed with hindsight and, therefore, identifiable only in retrospect (Strauss 1997 [1959]; Denzin 1989; Clausen 1998; Abbott, 2001; George 2009). An illustration of this is provided in Box 3.2.

> **Box 3.2** Retrospective Understandings of Turning Points (Laub and Sampson)
>
> In the late 1980s, Laub and Sampson (1993, 1998, 2003) uncovered 60 boxes of case files in the basement of the Harvard Law School Library. These constituted the legacy data from a classic longitudinal study of 500 delinquent boys, based in Boston, which had been conducted by Sheldon and Eleanor Glueck in the early 1940s. The researchers traced a sub-sample of these 'boys', who were by then in their 70s, and conducted life history interviews with them as part of a mixed methods QL re-study. The new data revealed the zigzag fortunes of these men over the decades, and the many intersecting turning points (relating to marriage, home, employment, economic security, peer group and substance abuse) that had led some to resist offending, while others had persisted. The researchers reveal that it would not have been possible to predict the varied life paths and outcomes for these men at the outset of the research; it was only by looking back and reconstructing their lives in retrospect that the turning points, causal connections and pivotal moments could be clearly discerned. Whatever the power of prospective longitudinal enquiry, a complementary retrospective lens is vitally important in piecing together an unfolding picture (Laub and Sampson 2003; Gerrits 2008).

This way of understanding turning points represents a challenge to the idea that one single, discrete event, experience or epiphany has sufficient causal power to bring about another event, or to effect a concrete change in the direction of a life or, indeed, that individual agency alone can bring about such changes (Carlsson 2012: 4). In other words, if trigger points have any causal power, what is likely to make a difference is their cumulative impact, that is, how they are situated relative to each other through an unfolding process (Laub and Sampson 1993).

This was a key theme in van Gennep's (1960 [1909]) study of the rites of passage. He saw that an enduring change in the life course of an individual or group can be carefully crafted through the cumulative power of these rites (birth, marriage and death rituals are prime examples). These experientially evocative symbolic acts take a multiplicity of forms, but they have a common purpose and structure: they mark, mirror and inscribe a change in a person's status and identity. The rites symbolise a separation from a past life, a liminal state (a marginal, indeterminate or undefined state, a time out of time, 'betwixt and between'), and the start of a new journey on a different path. Van Gennep saw that these ritual acts lose their meaning if they are dislocated from the social and temporal contexts in which they occur. It is the constellation of the rites, their growing momentum through a cumulative sequence of actions and interactions, combined with their rich imagery, which gives them their meaning and causal significance.

Unlike fixed, instrumental entities, turning points may accumulate in varied ways: as carefully crafted mechanisms of change, as shown above; as incremental nudges, or 'rehearsals' along a pathway (Thomson et al. 2002, Holland and Thomson 2009; Negroni 2012); or as 'eddies' or 'drifts' or zigzag pathways in varied, sometimes random, and sometimes conflicting directions (the forces of push and pull, to and fro, as people try out new paths, revert back to old ones, forge ahead, or remain behind) (Howell 2012). They are, indeed, subject to a host of intervening social, structural and historical circumstances that may have an impact on a future path (Carlsson 2012). At pivotal moments, they operate at the crucial nexus between social structures and personal and collective agency (Kupferberg 2012: 227). They are not free-floating and do not operate in isolation; they are part of the interplay between individuals and the social and temporal worlds that they inhabit (Carlsson 2012).

Transitions and trajectories

Transitions are dynamic periods of the life course that constitute a concrete change from one status or circumstance to another (Millar 2007; Shanahan and Macmillan 2008). They may unfold over varied periods of time, at different paces and intensities, sometimes occurring suddenly through a rupture in life experience (a bereavement, an illness, a relocation, a job loss), or occurring almost imperceptibly through a mixture of biological, biographical, collective and historical change. They also vary in the extent to which they are planned, prescribed, managed or desired by those involved.

They may take the form of a series of mini transitions, managed and marked through key milestones and prompted by a series of trigger points that lead to a pivotal moment of change. For example, the processes leading to and following a birth, death or illness, or the preparations leading to a marriage or a retirement, are all transitional processes. They are marked by an accumulation of trigger points that, taken together, provide the momentum for change. As shown above, the extent to which transitions have clear temporal boundaries is unclear; without appropriate trigger points that can create a temporal marker, or drive a process forward, transitional states may become semi-permanent ways of life in themselves, without closure.

Transitions, in turn, are embedded within longer-term trajectories, the unfolding contours of lives stretching across the life span. These longer spans of time are marked by periods of continuity and steady states, as well as change. They are what Abbott (2001) calls 'master narratives', and they are influenced by a host of intervening factors across the micro–macro plane (Clausen 1998). The temporal dynamic of these master narratives is an extensive one, occurring over the longer term. As Heidegger (1980 [1927]) understood, the arc of our individual existence, from birth to death, is a constant feature of our biographies, perpetually shaping our awareness of the rhythm of our lives, the timing of events, and what we can or should be striving to achieve at different points in our biographies.

Over time, it is possible to discern how varied trajectories (family, work, home, and so on) intersect to create a unique biography; to explore how they are shaped through particular circumstances (e.g. 'upward' or 'downward' paths through privilege or poverty); or how they may unfold differentially (converging or diverging) for those with shared beginnings (Laub and Sampson 2003; see Box 3.2). Among many fruitful lines of enquiry are those that explore how, or whether, a particular transition (e.g. an early entry into parenthood) impacts on an overall trajectory (e.g. the broader socio-economic fortunes and life chances of young parents; Neale and Davies 2016; detailed in Boxes 10.2 and 10.3).

Over the longer term, too, the impact of external forces and the twin processes of continuity and change, stability and volatility on emerging trajectories are more clearly discernible, giving a particular pattern and shape to an unfolding life (Clausen 1998). Abbott (2001) reminds us that trajectories have an inertial quality; they are marked as much by stasis as change: enduring states, recurring patterns and structural equilibrium that may well overwrite, absorb or iron out the ripples of transitions and turning points (see, for example, Neale and Davies 2016; Millar and Ridge 2017; and Millar 2021 in press, who discern this pattern in their studies of the changing fortunes of disadvantaged parents).

In sum, trigger points, transitions and trajectories are inextricably linked. They represent interlocking and interdependent horizons of temporal experience that are nested inside one another, rather like Russian dolls. They operate through varied durations of time, from fleeting moments, to transitional pathways, to longer lines of development across the life span. The meaning and causal efficacy of a particular trigger point will depend on its temporal location within a transition, which in turn will be shaped by its place within the overall span of an unfolding life. It will be influenced, for example, by perceptions of the timing of events in a biography; the appropriate pace of change; how past and future expectations shape current experiences; the perceived investment that has been made in a particular transition or life path; and what is deemed feasible, appropriate or possible for those of a particular age or generation. These temporal connections and configurations in themselves have causal effects; it is their dynamic interdependence that is the source of their meaning (Shanahan and Macmillan 2008). This suggests that research designs should take all three temporal flows into account and investigate their simultaneous connections.

Timescapes: Flows of Time

We conclude this chapter by bringing together some of the rich ideas about time that have been considered above and in Chapter 2. A framework for engaging with time as a rich theme of QL enquiry is suggested here. It can be seen as a conceptual tool kit that researchers can draw upon when considering how to build temporal insights into their studies. This framework is one among many ways of thinking about time as an empirical category (Crow and Heath 2002). If time inheres in social events, interactions, practices, structures and processes, it can be discerned within and made the focus of any topic of social-scientific enquiry (Adam 1995). Myriad temporal dynamics may be pulled out for focused analysis, ranging from theoretically oriented studies of duration, frequency, sequence and timing (Flaherty 2011), to more empirically grounded studies of temporal horizons and oscillations, found, for example, in public and private time, work and free time, women's and men's time, and individual and global time (Nowotny 1994).

For our purposes here, time is mapped along five intersecting planes or flows of time (see Box 3.3). Drawing on Adam (1998), these planes can be thought of as **timescapes** that capture a range of temporal dynamics in unfolding processes (Neale 2007). A scape (a landscape, seascape, and so on) is a vista, a view of the world that changes in kaleidoscopic ways, depending on the position and disposition of the observer. Timescapes operate in a similar fashion, but in a temporal rather than spatial plane. Within these broad planes of time, a multitude of intersecting **temporal horizons** may be discerned. Time horizons are relative to their owners and to the contexts in which they appear, and, unlike boundaries, they are never reachable but occur along the line of our vision, moving as we move (Adam 1990: 31–2; Hitlin and Elder 2007).

The five timescapes identified in Box 3.3 are porous and flow into each other. They have theoretical and substantive value, as rich themes and topics of enquiry and analysis that researchers may selectively draw upon to enrich their studies. They are separated out here to illuminate the interface between temporal theory and research practice, and to provide a foundation for empirical investigation.

Box 3.3 Timescapes (Flows of Time)

- Prospective–retrospective (past, present, future)
- Intensive–extensive (time frames and tempos)
- Micro–macro (scales of time)
- Time–space (spatiality of time/temporality of space)
- Continuity–discontinuity (synchronicities of time)

Prospective–retrospective (past, present, future)

This plane of time is foundational in discerning the dynamic unfolding of lives and the way we orient ourselves to time. Looking to the future, prospectively, or to the past, retrospectively, are basic orientations that may be combined in the design of a

QL study (see Chapters 1 and 4). In turn, these same temporal orientations are part of the analytical strategies used by QL researchers. As shown in Chapter 2, past, present and future are enduring topics of theoretical enquiry, inviting understanding of the immediacy, immanence or distance of events from the present day. The broad idea is to think 'in time streams', looking at an issue in the present day, with a sense of how past and future are embedded in the present and implicated in how events unfold (Tsoukas and Hatch 2001: 1006). Abductive logic can be used to trace lives backward and forward in time and to oscillate between the two (see Chapter 9). This is the basic strategy used in tracing and mapping processes (see Chapter 11).

Past and future are foundational horizons of time, the yardsticks by which we orient ourselves to the passage of time. Like all unfolding processes, past, present and future can be understood in both fixed and fluid ways. **Fixed time** focuses our attention on chronology, a linear construct that proceeds in one direction and unfolds cumulatively and in sequence. It invites consideration of people's life journeys: the markers and vantage points that locate them on their way, where they have come from, where they are heading, the direction of travel, the sequence and intervals of events, and what propels them onwards or holds them back. This is the basic framework used in life journey interviewing (see Chapter 6).

In the fluid realm of temporality, or **fluid time**, however, the relationship between past, present and future is more complex. These are no longer separate states that progress chronologically; they are processes that flow into one another, suggesting that our understanding of the past is no more fixed than the future. The notion that the past is an interpretive realm can be traced back to the work of Mead (1959 [1934]), and to the philosophy of Kierkegaard, who observes that while lives are lived forwards in time, they must be understood backwards (Kierkegaard 1843, cited in Brockmeier 2000: 51–2). The temporal gaze is continually shifting as people look back and forth in the ever-moving present, constructing and reconstructing their past and future, overwriting their biography, re-interpreting opportunities and constraints, and confounding any sense of chronology and the orderly sequence of events. Citing Jean-Luc Godard, Saldaña notes that 'a story should have a beginning, middle and an ending, but not necessarily in that order' (Saldaña 2003: 7). These ideas remind us, once again, of the need to combine prospective with retrospective understandings.

Moreover, as Husserl understood (see Chapter 2), the horizons of past, present and future are simultaneously present and interacting at any one moment in time, and are continually under construction and reconstruction as the temporal gaze shifts. The momentum of our lives builds through a continual construction and reconstruction of past and future. These interlocking flows of time are in constant conversation with one another (Hardgrove et al. 2015). In other words, past, present and future are relational states that derive their meaning from each other. Understanding how individuals shape their biographies through the fluid stream of time becomes just as important as understanding transitions through fixed chronologies:

Invariably the stories we tell about ourselves, as well as those to which we attend as audience, are always ... anchored on shifting ground. ... We are forever re-scripting our pasts, making sense of the things that happened. This is true not only as narrators of our own lives, but also as narrators of the lives of others. This process of re-interpretation of events is one that is ongoing throughout our lives, as different parts of our past reveal themselves to hold increased importance, or to be void of meaning, depending not only on who we are, but critically, on whom we wish to become. (Andrews 2008: 94)

Every narrative about [the] past is always also a story told in and about the present, as well as a story about the future. This ... is much like the temporal structure of human life itself. ... Understanding a life is understanding the continuous oscillating of ... past, present and future. ... [T]he story of one's life almost always leaves the paths of chronology ...the autobiographical process does not follow chronological time but creates its own time, narrative time. (Brockmeier 2000, 52, 56, 59)

For QL researchers, revisiting past and future at each research encounter is a powerful way to understand these shifting processes. This is **recursive interviewing** (detailed in Chapter 6), a process which invites consideration of narrative change, a change in perception and meaning, as well as chronological change (Lewis 2007). How people may come to understand their past lives in a new light, and the scope that this provides for the researcher to revisit and re-interpret past accounts from a new perspective, is illustrated in Box 3.4.

Box 3.4 Looking Forward, Looking Back – Re-interpreting the Past

The first extract below is drawn from a study of post-divorce childhoods. The researchers revisited Helen, a 12-year-old, after a gap of three years. Her account differed markedly from the one she gave as a 9-year-old. In this second interview, she reflects on how she had reached a fresh understanding of her family relationships, as a result of which she had recently made the difficult decision to stop visiting her father. When we revisited her earlier interview, the seeds of her growing disquiet about her father were implicit in her reflections on what she would like for the future of her family:

Bren: Is there any thing you'd like for the future of your family? ...

Helen: (whispering) They don't like me to tell anyone this, but I like my mum more than my dad. ... I get poorly in my tummy when I go to my dad's. ... I wish he would get nicer. (Wave 1: aged 9)

(Continued)

Jennifer: Have your feelings about the divorce changed over the years?

Helen: Yeah, definitely, because I realised, I found out, you know, about my dad because I didn't really – well, I *did* know [about his temper] but not like, *know*, as in completely understand. ... 'cos dad was not treating [my brother] very well. That was when I started to see him less. And when I realised that I actually had the choice ... I didn't have to go. (Wave 2: aged 12)

Source: *Enduring Families Project*, Neale and Flowerdew 2007

The second extract is from a life history study of socialist activists. Elizabeth, a woman in her 70s, reflects back on her life and her long-standing commitment to left-wing politics:

When you look back, you see the path or paths that you've taken. The path would obviously not be so clear when you're groping up and finding it, would it? I mean it's rather like going up a mountain, you're sort of looking that way and that track and it looks too steep and you're going round ... Whereas when you're high up you can look back and see, and it sort of stands out much more clearly, things you didn't realize at the time. (Andrews 2008: 87)

As Andrews observes, through the metaphors of walking and climbing, 'the protagonist is forever coming to new vantage points from which to view what she/he has passed through' (Andrews 2008: 87).

The past, seen as hindsight, memory, heritage, legacies, reputations, and so on, becomes a powerful, subjective resource that plays an important role in life planning, the ongoing construction of social identities and the shaping of moral lives (Freeman 2010).

The future, meanwhile, is a neglected site of research, yet it inheres in and shapes everyday realities, and has the potential to reveal the nature of aspirations and the seeds of change (Adam and Groves 2007). For example, the extent to which people engage in life planning (the idea of 'choice' biographies) or live in an extended present which curtails their capacity to think about the long term, much less plan for it, are important topics of enquiry (Nowotny 1994). Brannen and Nilsen (2002) suggest that young people orient themselves to the future in three different ways: deferment, which keeps the future at bay; adaptability, which forges a future by responding to contingencies; and predictability, which strives for certainty and security over time. Concepts such as these have provided the foundation for a range of studies of youth transitions (see, for example, Henderson et al. 2007; Bidart 2019).

Imaginary futures are important topics of biographical enquiry (detailed in Boxes 6.4 and 6.5). Krings et al. (2013), for example, found that how their participants viewed the future in 2010 was substantially different from how they saw it in 2008, at the start of their study. Future accounts are usually seen as reflections of where people are on their life journeys at the moment in which the accounts are elicited. In other words, they are understood to have little or no predictive or causal power (Sanders and Munford 2008; Elliott 2010b; Hardgrove et al. 2015). However, they may have motivational power, the propensity to bring into focus possible future selves, the notion of 'becoming', and thereby to shape, nurture and strengthen inner biographical dispositions (Strauss 1997 [1959]; Worth 2009; Hardgrove et al. 2015). Arguably, how people orient themselves to the future may influence the paths they take, for people cannot work towards future aspirations unless they have the capacity to imagine them (Worth 2009; Hardgrove et al. 2015). In this way, the conjuring of an imaginary future can become a trigger point for change:

> There is, for the adolescent, the demand, or at least the opportunity to direct his thoughts both behind and ahead of the present moment; swinging rapidly from one perspective to another, comparing, predicting, regretting and resolving afresh; planning for the future but preserving continuity with the present; making the best of what has been, ensuring the best of what could come. (Veness 1962: 2)

Intensive–extensive (time frames and tempos)

As shown in Chapter 1, this plane of time is central to QL methodology: it shapes the time frame (the overall duration) for a study, and its tempo (the number, length and frequency) of visits to the field. In terms of its theoretical potential, this plane of time affords rich possibilities that take us beyond a fixed understanding of durations and linear sequences. It invites an exploration of the experiential intensity of life course processes: the tenor, pace, velocity and rhythms of time, the acuteness or chronicity of change, and whether time is perceived intensively, in the moment or the short term, or extensively, stretching over longer-term horizons.

Life states, for example, may be perceived as fleeting or enduring, temporary or permanent, while individuals may oscillate between change and continuity, action and inaction as their lives unfold. The work of enduring hardship or sustaining relationships, how people bide their time, is another important dimension of this plane of time. Alheit (1994) identifies two contrasting time horizons in the life course: everyday time, which is cyclical and involves spontaneity as well as routine, and lifetime, longer-term horizons that are retrospectively constructed in linear and sequential terms. How individuals reconcile these different horizons of time in making sense of their lives is a fruitful line of enquiry.

Closely allied to the tempo of time is its pace: our experiences of the rhythms, repetitions and velocity of time, the speed at which time is perceived to pass, and whether it is slowing down or accelerating. The pace of time emerges in varied ways, for example across the generations, where the pace of young childhood or deep old age is noticeably slower than the pace of youth or adulthood. Similarly, the speed and suddenness of change, and whether multiple changes occur in quick succession, are important dimensions of lived experience, inviting consideration of how change processes are managed (Flowerdew and Neale 2003). As a final example, time use and work–life balance studies, both qualitative and quantitative, have flourished over the past few decades. These are driven by a concern that life is speeding up and becoming more routinised, regulated and frenetic in industrial society (Gershuny 2000; Crow and Heath 2002; Rosa 2013; Wajcman 2015; see also related studies from The ESRC Centre for Time Use Research (UCL, University of London).

Studies that engage with this temporal plane commonly focus on the distinctions between industrial time (the rigid, impersonal tempo of the clock: Aristotle's *chronos*) and family, personal or holiday time (which is fluid, flexible, enduring and value laden: Aristotle's *kairos*) (Hareven 1982). Chaplin (2002) and Harden et al. (2012), for example, have explored how families oscillate between and manage these two contrasting tempos in their daily lives. Finally, Lemke (2000) suggests that we simultaneously inhabit a whole spectrum of time horizons, from the microscopic (where time is incomprehensible because it is fleeting and moves at lightning speed) to the cosmic (where time is incomprehensible because it is infinite and appears to stand still). The nested horizons of turning points, transitions and trajectories (explored above), with their different temporal intensities, are embedded within this grand, cosmic scheme.

Micro–macro (scales of time)

The centrality of this plane of time was established in Chapter 1. The interlocking scales at which events and experiences occur (from the personal to the social to the historical), are ever present in how lives unfold. As Riley notes, 'Changing lives … are in continual interplay with changes in society and its structures. Neither can be understood conceptually without the other' (1998: 29). Moreover, the intersection between these domains of experience is essentially dynamic: it is only through time that we can discern how these elements of the social fabric are connected and how they come to be transformed. We have seen above that the temporal gaze may be directed forwards to the future, or backwards towards the past, or it may oscillate between the two. Similarly, in the micro–macro plane, the focus of the temporal lens may be adjusted to produce a close-up vision of individual or interpersonal biographies, or a wide-angled view of social or historical processes.

As shown in Chapter 1, it was Wright Mills (1959) who first provided the impetus for temporal researchers to explore the interface between biography and history. However, he had little to say about how such a task might be accomplished, leaving successive generations of researchers to grapple with this problem (Giele and Elder 1998: 7; Shanahan and Macmillan 2008: xii). The development of a processual vision of unfolding lives, and the more recent rise of social complexity theory (outlined in Boxes 2.4 and 2.5), represent significant advances here, for they offer new ways to think about and investigate the interlocking flows of the social fabric.

A useful starting point in exploring the relationship between biography and history is the recognition that these are not discrete domains that can be viewed dualistically. They are part of a continuum of temporal dynamics, operating at different scales of the social fabric, within which lies the meso domain of collective lives (families, organisations, communities, generations, institutions, and so on). This domain of shifting social relationships and structures plays a crucial role in mediating between micro and macro, between biography and history (Riley 1998: 45). Nor is the meso domain simply located between micro and macro, for it constitutes an intersecting and interdependent scale of social experience and practice (Riley 1998: 45). Nielsen (2003) describes this as a subtle and ongoing interaction that produces societal change through a process akin to osmosis.

In like vein, Bronfenbrenner's (1993) ecological model of human development comprises five interlocking domains of influence that span the micro–macro plane. These are micro systems; meso systems; exo systems (in which at least one linkage in the chain has an indirect influence on the original person, for example the impact of employment on parents, and hence on their children); macro systems; and chrono systems. The last is an 'umbrella' temporal domain that pervades and envelops the others. In Bronfenbrenner's view, these varied domains are nested inside one another, like Russian dolls, and he proposes that research designs should investigate their simultaneous connections.

Bronfenbrenner's framework has been utilised in a variety of policy contexts where there is a need to understand how individual, interpersonal and institutional spheres of life influence each other over time, and to what extent lived experiences mesh with policy processes (Molloy et al. 2002; Lewis 2007; Neale 2016; Bidart 2019; see Chapter 4, Table 4.1 for a conceptual road map that spans this plane). Temporal researchers who work across this plane frame their enquiries in a variety of ways, exploring, for example, the intersection of individual, family and industrial time (Hareven 1982), or biographical, generational and historical time (Neale et al. 2012). Broadly similar schemas underpin large-scale longitudinal studies, this time couched in the quantitative language of age effects (biographical processes), cohort effects (collective processes across a cohort) and period effects (broad historical processes). Elder's comprehensive life course paradigm (1994; Elder and Giele 2009) follows a similar pattern, spanning the agency of individuals, linked lives or social ties to others, and historical and geographical location.

Re-focusing the temporal lens still further permits a close-up view of these micro–macro planes, and reveals further flows of time embedded within them. In the micro domain, for example, it is possible to discern both 'inner' and 'outer' constructions of biography, the former permitting insights into the psycho-social dynamics of identity and the place of emotions in the construction of psycho-biographies (Nielsen 2003; Thomson 2010a, 2012; Du Plessis 2017). Drawing on the work of Chodorow, Nielsen (2003) suggests that an individual's psychological make-up, the formation of subjectivities and motivations, can be seen as historical phenomena, inviting exploration of the interdependent dynamics between emotional realities, cultural constructions and historical context; in short, between self and society.

Similarly, the meso domain encompasses collectives of different scales, from small-scale family, friendship or interest groups, to larger institutional structures, to the complex machineries of government. It is in this domain that social structural configurations play a part in shaping and re-shaping human relations of care, support, dependency, solidarity, division, power and inequality. Finally, in the macro-historical domain, transformations in the social fabric are evident both locally and globally. The pace and tempo of such changes may range from tipping points – revolutionary 'flashpoint' or 'watershed' moments, such as the fall of the Berlin wall or a pandemic lockdown – to incremental, evolutionary and barely perceptible processes such as the changing place of women in the labour market, or the gradual shift from religious to secular society (Miller 2000).

While the value of working across the micro–macro plane is beyond doubt, it can create challenges for researchers. Methodologically, building macro-historical time into QL studies that have a limited longitudinal reach requires creative approaches to design, sampling and data generation, as the chapters in Part 2 of this book will illustrate. A more pressing and seemingly intractable issue concerns the theoretical challenge of teasing out micro-meso-macro influences and discerning their relative influence in how lives unfold. This raises doubts about the feasibility of identifying and disentangling, let alone explaining the multiple causal threads that operate across different scales of the social fabric and through different horizons of time and space (Giele and Elder 1998; Elliott 2005: 110–11; Brannen 2006: 150; Anderson and Scott 2012; and see Chapter 11 for a more detailed treatment of this theme).

Working round this problem requires a shift in focus. Rather than seeking unitary and definitive causal explanations, researchers need to aim for case-rich, authentic and plausible accounts of the constellation of fluid elements through which life course changes occur. Such accounts are rooted in the particularities of time, space and social context and their meaning is inherently provisional (Elliott 2005). As shown in Chapter 2, those who research complex temporal processes advocate modesty in presenting their explanations and insights. History teaches us that such modesty is a necessity of responsible scholarship (Cilliers 2005: 264–5).

Time–space (spatiality of time/temporality of space)

This plane reflects the when and where of time: the intrinsic connections between time and space as a means to locate and grasp the meaning and significance of events and experiences. *When and where* can be added to the interpretive questions of *how and why* to further enrich the meaning of social processes. While clock time is spatially adrift, abstract and 'empty', fluid time is grounded in real-world events and practices. It emerges within and is made tangible through varied spatial settings and local cultures, people's ways of life which may be distinctive in terms of geography, topography, language, material culture, everyday practices, and so on. May and Thrift (2001: 3) observe that multiple, dynamic time, 'is irrevocably bound up with the spatial constitution of society (and vice versa)'. Indeed, space and place are central to our understanding of the unfolding life course. The cultural environments into which we are born and grow up (from ghettos to leafy suburbs) exert a powerful influence on our sense of self, and how we position ourselves in relation to others (Compton-Lilly 2017). At the same time, a simple change of locality may enable people to establish new patterns of living, forge new identities or escape old ones (Elder 1994; Laub and Sampson 1998).

Working across this plane has produced some pioneering lines of enquiry in recent years, described variously as geo-dynamic or geo-biographical research, or latitudinal or transnational ethnography (Barnard 2012; Falola 2015; Lee 2015). A temporal orientation can be enhanced through a comparative, spatial lens. Taking a 'latitudinal' approach, for example, Barnard (2012) broadened his longitudinal ethnography of the Naro peoples of Botswana to include related hunter-gatherer groups living in multiple sites across the southern states of Africa. The spatial comparisons enabled him to discern more clearly the historical forces involved in changing hunter-gatherer culture (see also Howell 2012).

As a further example, Shaw (2001) used accounts from the Mass Observation archive and other documentary sources to investigate how the intensity and pace of social time vary across cultures, and across different spaces within cultures (urban/ rural, industrial city/small town life). She found significant variations in the amount of time allotted for work, rest, meals and other tasks of daily living. Time keeping also varies, in some cultures (such as Germany) driven by a rigid adherence to clock and calendar, and in others (Finland, Brazil and large parts of the global South) exhibiting a more unhurried approach, where people gather over hours or even days. Time in these slower places is more elastic and forgiving; 'finding time' to oneself, or simply 'being' as opposed to always 'doing', is more highly valued.

Alternatively, a spatial orientation can be enriched when seen through a temporal lens. Lee (2015), for example, traced the journeys of young Korean immigrants from New Zealand, where they had spent most of their childhoods, back to their homeland. She then followed up those who subsequently returned to their host country. By using a mixture of prospective tracking, ethnographic techniques and life history interviewing, she was able to shed light on the unfolding experiences of those whose lives straddle two cultures, and to discern how transnational identities and a sense of spatial belonging are forged through time.

Such studies show that spatial variations may create different experiences of time, while temporal variations may create different experiences of space (May and Thrift 2001: 3; Chaplin 2002). While time–space is pervasive in life experiences and processes, it offers particular scope for comparative investigations of geo-biographies, temporal geographies, migrations and resettlement, and for the study of 'liminal' (betwixt and between) spaces that create a different quality of time (Zerubavel 1981; Hockey and James 2003).

Continuity–discontinuity (synchronicities of time)

Our final plane of time was first identified by Aristotle as a central component of his distinction between *chronos* (fixed) and *kairos* (fluid) time (Bastian 2014). Synchronicities cut across all the flows of time outlined above, raising questions about how individuals oscillate between past, present and future, between personal and social time, biographical, generational and historical time, short- and longer-term time horizons, a fast and a slow pace of existence, and between biographical continuities and change. In short, we can consider here how people balance, reconcile or synchronise these different temporalities. There are many ways of exploring these temporal oscillations. An example, drawn from a large-scale longitudinal study with considerable historical reach, is provided in Box 3.5.

Box 3.5 Synchronising Biographical and Historical Time (Elder)

In his large-scale longitudinal research, Elder (1974; Elder and Pellerin 1998) drew on legacy data from the long-running *Berkeley Guidance* study and the *Oakland Growth* study to explore the impact of an adverse historical event (the Great Depression in the 1930s) on the life chances of two age cohorts of young people. The *Oakland* children experienced the Depression during their teenage years. They were more resilient and were able to contribute to their family income. The *Berkeley* children were eight years younger, and small dependants at the time of the Depression. They placed extra strain on their family resources, resulting in adverse effects for them and their families. A variety of other factors might also have contributed to the radically different fortunes of these two age cohorts, including their gender, the nature of family relationships, material resources and sources of income, their local environments and labour markets, and a host of intervening interpersonal and institutional factors. However, for Elder, their experiences could be explained, at least in part, by the differential timing of a cataclysmic historical event in their unfolding lives. Elder's findings sparked a widespread interest in how broader historical events are synchronised with individual life course processes.

On a smaller canvas, researchers have explored the timing of life course events within individual biographies. The timing of a transition into parenthood, for example, may be a challenge for those who do not conform to dominant perceptions of an appropriate age to have a child (Shirani and Henwood 2011; Neale 2016). Similarly, the discontinuities that may arise between individual lives and 'mainstream' practices and experiences (crime, drug addiction, homelessness, and so on) have yielded an enduring interest in how people manage, re-align or reconcile values and practices that are at variance with orthodox pathways and practices. There is huge scope to explore how people oscillate between sub-cultural and mainstream values and practices, and what may lead them from one to the other (see, for example, the case study of a prostitute in Plumridge and Thomson 2003; Lopez-Aguado's 2012 study of a street-gang intervention programme; and a study of the transitions of homeless people in Hodgetts et al. 2011, detailed in Box 6.11).

Discontinuities between personal lives and the mainstream can occur in a rich variety of ways, for example through changes in a working environment, migration, or a transition into parenthood, retirement or unemployment. A change in tempo can lead to a sense of dislocation, as people find themselves marching at an unfamiliar, hurried pace, or languishing in a world that feels too unstructured for comfort (May and Thrift 2001; Shaw 2001). Living 'out of time' may be a temporary state, and as 'time out' from a pressured or challenging life it may be highly valued (see Baraitser's (2013) exploration of family 'mush' time). But where it is associated with unplanned or unwanted transitions that become entrenched, living out of time can have a significant impact on life trajectories and on future health and well-being.

For those undergoing challenging biographical disruptions (bereavement, prolonged or chronic illness, job loss, forced migration, pandemic lockdowns, and so on), time may seem to shrink, creating a sense of disorientation or dislocation from the mainstream, such that the seamless flow of life from past to future is disrupted (Bury 1982; Lovgren et al. 2010). People commonly talk of 'taking each day as it comes' or 'living in the moment'. Living out of time means shortened time horizons, and a sense of the fleeting or ephemeral nature of time, which can make future planning impossible and lead to risky practices.

In their QL study of the financial implications of poverty, for example, Dearden et al. (2010) found that people acted rashly in running up huge debts. The overriding preoccupation with survival in the here-and-now led to a loss of care and concern for the past (burning bridges) and for the future (risky behaviour, a lack of aspiration, the loss of hope). This is the sense of **liminality** (time-out-of-time, betwixt and between) first identified by van Gennep (see above). The concept of liminality has been utilised in a range of studies to make sense of prolonged and challenging life states, such as chronic or terminal illness, entrenched poverty, 'doing time' in prison, forced relocation, long-term unemployment and homelessness (for a range of interesting examples, see Jahoda et al. 1972 [1932]; Kelly 2008; Blows et al. 2012; Neumann 2012; Szakolczai 2014; Bryant 2016).

Intersecting Timescapes

The five planes of time outlined above form a provisional basis for discerning a range of temporal dynamics in unfolding processes, which may feed into empirical investigation. These planes are clearly not discrete or stand-alone, for they intersect and flow into one another. Past, present and future, for example, can be understood at different scales of time (biographically or historically), in different spatial contexts, and through differential experiences of the tempo, pace and synchronicities of time. Endless possibilities exist to refine these planes, and to discern myriad connections across and beyond them.

Adam (1990) reminds us that, in focusing on one flow of time, we should not lose sight of the others. As parts of a larger whole, they are all implicated in how lives unfold. Nevertheless, our purpose here is not to promote an over-ambitious and unrealistic project for empirical enquiry. These flows of time are offered here as a starting point for considering how time, as a theoretical construct, can be imported into research design and practice. They are part of a conceptual tool kit for QL enquiry that researchers can draw upon selectively to inform and inspire their own projects.

Closing Reflections

Drawing on the notion of fluid time developed in Chapter 2, this chapter has explored ways to rethink the life course, and the nested horizons of turning points, transitions and trajectories. In the process, lived experience and complex flows of time have been brought more centrally into the picture. Thinking through these temporal concepts and processes, and their power to effect change, is a foundational part of the design and development of a QL study. In order to support this process, five timescapes or flows of time have been outlined here, along with some pointers for how they may feed into empirical enquiry.

Overall, Chapters 2 and 3 have illustrated the fundamental importance of engaging with time in the design and development of a QL study. Taking time seriously is vital. But how time is understood, its nature and parameters, is no less so. Our vision will be impoverished if it is fixed solely on the clock and the calendar. QL research has the capacity to bring lived experience and complex flows of time into a common frame of reference and, thereby, to provide a bridge between sociological theories of time and more empirically based life course and longitudinal studies. Adam (1990) observes that seeing things through the lens of time 'quite simply changes everything'. This is no less so when we see things *qualitatively* through the lens of fluid time; indeed, this produces a richness of understanding that can transform our vision of the social world.

Further Reading

There is an extensive literature on the varied themes of this chapter. For life course research, Laub and Sampson's (2003) masterly study of criminal careers over the life course is essential reading. On life course research more generally, Holstein and Gubrium (2000) and the articles in Worth and Hardill (2015) are particularly recommended for their engagement with fluid time. On turning points, transitions and trajectories, Hackstaff et al. (2012) provide an excellent overview, as does Carlsson (2012) from the perspective of criminology. The Timescapes framework is rooted in a vast literature. Particularly interesting insights are provided by Freeman (2010) on the past; Adam and Groves (2007) and Hardgrove et al. (2015) on the future; Brockmeier (2000) on the fluid intersection of past, present and future; Shaw (2001) on the pace of existence in varied spatial contexts; and Hodgetts et al. (2011) on the discontinuities of time for homeless people. Finally, Patrick (2017) is a fine example of research that explores how lived experiences mesh with dynamic policy processes.

Adam, B. and Groves, C. (2007) *Future Matters: Action, Knowledge, Ethics*. Boston: Brill.

Brockmeier, J. (2000) 'Autobiographical time', *Narrative Inquiry*, 10 (1): 51–73.

Carlsson, C. (2012) 'Using turning points to understand processes of change in offending', *British Journal of Criminology*, 52 (1): 1–16.

Freeman, M. (2010) *Hindsight: The Promise and Peril of Looking Backward*. Oxford: OUP.

Hackstaff, K., Kupferberg, F. and Negroni, C. (eds) (2012) *Biography and Turning Points in Europe and America*. Bristol: Policy Press.

Hardgrove, A., Rootham, E. and McDowell, L. (2015) 'Possible selves in a precarious labour market: Youth, imagined futures and transitions to work in the UK', *Geoforum*, 60: 163–71.

Hodgetts, D., Chamberlain, K. and Groot, S. (2011) 'Reflections on the visual in community research and action', in P. Reavey (ed.) *Visual Methods in Psychology: Using and Interpreting Images in Qualitative Research*. London: Routledge, pp. 299–313.

Holstein, J. and Gubrium, J. (2000) *Constructing the Life Course*, 2nd edition. New York: General Hall.

Laub, J. and Sampson, R. (2003) *Shared Beginnings, Divergent Lives: Delinquent Boys to Age 70*. Cambridge, MA: Harvard University Press.

Patrick, R. (2017) *For Whose Benefit? The Everyday Realities of Welfare Reform*. Bristol: Policy Press.

Shaw, J. (2001) 'Winning territory: Changing place to change pace', in J. May and N. Thrift (eds) *Timespace: Geographies of Temporality*. New York: Routledge, pp. 120–32.

Worth, N. and Hardill, I. (eds) (2015) *Researching the Life Course: Critical Perspectives from the Social Sciences.* Bristol: Policy Press.

PART 2

CRAFTING QUALITATIVE LONGITUDINAL RESEARCH

Building on the conceptual foundations for QL research set out in Part 1 of this book, our discussion now turns to research design and practice. The broader contours of qualitative enquiry are detailed elsewhere (see, in particular, Ritchie and Lewis 2003; Lofland et al. 2006; Maxwell 2012, 2013; and Ritchie et al. 2014, who usefully engage with time and processes). Our focus here is on the temporal logic of QL research and how this shapes the research process. This logic, which is threaded through the whole research process, brings **cases**, **themes** and **processes** into a common conceptual framework. Every dimension of the research process is temporally fashioned and informed, from the construction of research questions and the longitudinal frame for a study, to issues of sampling, ethics, data generation and analysis.

Chapter 4 (Design and Sampling in Qualitative Longitudinal Research) introduces the logic of working through cases, themes and processes, and explores how this framework can be used empirically to devise a set of research questions, build the longitudinal frame for a study and determine a sampling strategy. Chapter 5 (Longitudinal Ethics: Walking Alongside) considers the journeys that researchers take with their participants: how they are recruited into a study, their involvement sustained, and the ethical terrain within which these processes occur. Chapter 6 (Generating Qualitative Longitudinal Data) considers the strategies and tools used to explore temporal processes with study participants, and to generate rich QL data. It is here, through the use of ethnographic, narrative and participatory methods, that the researcher generates thick descriptions about unfolding lives.

The title of this section of the book points to an important feature of QL research: as a mode of enquiry in the interpretive tradition, it is as much a craft, involving creativity, skill, dexterity and imaginative artistry, as it is a rigorous social-scientific enterprise (Wright Mills 1959; Pettigrew 1995; Elder and Giele 2009). As a distinctive process, designed to reach a specific goal, QL research fits the classic Greek definition of a method of enquiry. Yet fluid enquiry, with its creativity, flexibility and sensibilities, cannot be reduced to a unified or rigid set of methods with fixed and mechanically applied rules (Kvale 2007: 48–9). Indeed, there is endless scope for variations in design and innovation in the research process. An extensive array of research designs and strategies for engaging with time are showcased in these chapters.

The craft of QL research involves choosing the right design features and tools of investigation, and honing them over time to maximise their descriptive and explanatory power. As shown in Chapter 1, QL researchers are not wedded to one unitary approach; they are able to draw from a repertoire of approaches to produce a unique, tailor-made study (Saldaña 2002). Moreover, the longitudinal frame of a QL study offers scope to blend, develop and refine varied research strategies and tools as a study progresses; design itself is an emerging process (Saldaña 2003). It is important to note, however, that the creativity and flexibility of QL research does not detract from the rigour needed to produce a high quality study. On the contrary, ensuring that a study is in tune with, and able to reflect, dynamic, real-world processes is an inherent part of its methodological rigour: 'It is in the precarious balance between the controlled and the uncontrolled, the cognitive and the affective, the designed and the unexpected that [QL enquiry] finds its distinctive vitality and analytic power' (Barley 1995: 2).

4

DESIGN AND SAMPLING IN QUALITATIVE LONGITUDINAL RESEARCH

Key Points

- **Cases, themes, processes**: QL research is inherently dynamic – the research process is like a journey that unfolds in varied and sometimes unpredictable ways. All social research is driven by a search for connections between social experiences and practices (case data); key ideas (themes, insights); and the nature of social reality (for QL research, fluid, processual reality). QL enquiry is driven by a case-theme-process logic that shapes and anchors the whole research process.
- **Creativity/precision, flexibility/continuity**: The craft of QL research entails finding a balance between creativity and precision, and between flexibility and continuity in research design and practice. The creativity of the process does not detract from its methodological rigour; it is a vital aspect of rigour, ensuring that a study is in tune with and able to reflect dynamic, real-world processes. Clear guiding questions and a conceptual road map can help to structure and navigate the research process.
- **Prospective–retrospective – time frames/tempos**: QL research is prospective but incorporates vital retrospective insights. Time frames (the duration of a study) and tempos (the number and spacing of visits to the field) are flexible. Studies may be conducted intensively, over the short term, or extensively over decades. Clear baseline and closure points can help to frame a study; tempos commonly mirror the process under study.

(Continued)

- **Sampling** and **re-sampling**: QL sampling is purposive, seeking to build insights across a range of complementary cases, rather than measuring differences across strictly comparable cases. Key themes are investigated not only by sampling across cases, but also by sampling through time: time is a unit of sampling and analysis. There is scope to purposively re-sample over the waves of fieldwork, for example to 'grow' or 'condense' cases, or to work intensively with emblematic cases. Sample sizes vary, ranging from a case-led to a cross-case comparative approach. The size and granularity of a QL sample is determined as much by the number of waves of fieldwork as the number of cases; sampling strategies tend to be fluid rather than rigidly stratified. Tempos and samples sizes need to be considered together as integrated aspects of design.

- **Longitudinal panels and cohorts**: Panels are groups of participants, with shared characteristics, who are followed over time. Cohorts are groups of participants who share a particular experience or transition at roughly the same historical time. Drawing different cohorts into a sample, including generational cohorts or intergenerational family chains, can give insights into how unfolding biographies mesh with wider socio-historical processes. These are important mechanisms for working across the micro–macro plane.

Introduction: The Research Process as a Journey

Imagine you're describing a road trip you took across Arizona, a trip where your journey was determined by careful planning ('After spending two days at the Grand Canyon, I was going to drive to Flagstaff'); unexpected opportunities ('But I discovered there was to be a pow wow in Chinle, so I drove there instead'); uncontrollable forces ('The heavy snow fall closed the highway and delayed me'); detours ('I took a state road instead of the highway because of construction, and drove to Jerome'); and revised plans ('When I saw the Red Mountains of Sedona, I just had to drive off the Interstate for a closer look'). Such is the researcher's journey through a longitudinal qualitative study. (Saldaña 2003: 15)

This chapter explores how the key dimensions of time and process introduced in our opening chapters feed into QL design and sampling decisions. All qualitative research is dynamic (Ritchie and Lewis 2003). But, as Saldaña illustrates in our opening quotation, for QL research this dynamism is the central force that drives enquiry. This is evident in many dimensions of the research process. First, key elements of research practice (sampling, recruitment, ethical practice, data generation and analysis) are not discrete, one-off tasks, but recur in iterative cycles that are tied to each wave of fieldwork. A spiral of activities unfolds through the time frame of a study and recurs through repeated visits to the field (this analytical spiral is visualised in Chapter 9, Figure 9.1). The engagement with time at the heart of QL enquiry is mirrored in the research process itself: both can be conceived as journeys through time (Saldaña 2003; McLeod and Thomson 2009).

Second, changing perceptions of research settings and participants, new methodological and theoretical insights, and developments in the researchers' personal and collective circumstances are all likely to influence the research journey. It is for this reason that QL researchers need to be reflexive about their shifting interpretations and practices, and document these as the research progresses (Ottenberg 1990; Filer with Pollard 1998; McLeod, 2003). Third, working through time means that the vantage point from which researchers and participants look back and forth in time is continually shifting (Krings et al. 2013): 'As time passes and more data are collected, we are always standing in a new place from where we can capture a new "perspective"' (McLeod and Thomson 2009: 68). Future time at the start of the study may well have become past time by the conclusion, requiring a continual switching of the temporal gaze. Through these shifting processes, QL researchers become 'time travellers' (McLeod and Thomson 2009).

The Analytical Logic of QL Enquiry

The fluid nature of QL research is reflected in the **case-theme-process logic** that is woven through, and provides an anchor for a research study. As will be shown in Part 3 of this book, analysis is not simply about how we interrogate data. It is a strategy for enquiry that is threaded through and shapes the whole research process.

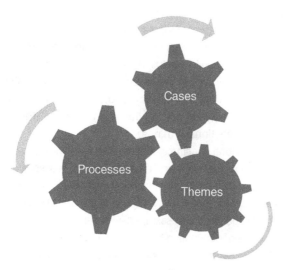

Figure 4.1   Cases-themes-processes: the logic of QL enquiry

In any kind of social research, design is driven by a key methodological question: what kinds of connections are possible between social experiences/practices (situated case data); key ideas (theories, themes, insights); and the nature of social reality (in this case, fluid processual reality)? (Blaikie 2007: 13). The ways in which these dimensions of knowledge and insight are defined and connected produces distinctive designs. For QL enquiry, it is the connections between cases, themes and processes that provide the overriding logic of enquiry (see Figure 4.1).

Box 4.1 Cases, Themes, Processes

- **Cases**: As units of study and analysis, cases are strategically formulated by researchers to address the research questions that drive a study. Depending on how they are defined, they give insights into the situated experiences and practices of individuals and/or varied kinds of collective (families, communities, networks, organisations), located in varied social settings and contexts of time and place. Since they embody concrete, real-life experiences and knowledge, cases constitute the empirical evidence base for a study: they enable researchers to investigate the social world in interpretive fashion, 'from the inside' and to generate thick descriptions of real lives. A detailed exploration of an individual case (a case study) can yield far-reaching insights of value for social enquiry (Flyvbjerg 2007), and provide the basis for complementary, comparative readings across cases (see Chapter 10). A QL case enables a detailed biographical/processual understanding of unfolding lives. How cases are sampled is considered below.
- **Themes** are the conceptual and substantive lenses through which empirical case data are generated and analysed. For QL research, temporality is a theme, as well as the framework through which data are generated. Key themes are likely to be temporally inflected (see Chapter 10). They comprise a rich amalgam of substantive topics (e.g. housing or health trajectories) and an array of theoretical ideas and insights (ranging from sustainability to transformation, evolution to revolution, past to future). Thematic investigation and analysis (see Chapter 10) builds greater breadth into a study and provides a bridge to wider, pre-existing bodies of theory and knowledge. Theories are 'simply ways of piecing the world together' (Plummer 2001: 159), of finding connections in things.
- **Processes** are temporal constructs that reflect a fluid understanding of social reality. They comprise a rich tapestry of events, actions, reactions and interactions that are linked together in a meaningful way through time. With their inherent temporality, they convey a sense of flux and change: of becoming, development, emergence, progression, evolution, and so on. As such, they are an important means of illuminating how lives unfold. They may be thought of as unfolding pathways, but where the course of the path, its nature, momentum and meaning are just as important as the destination reached. In a QL study, cases

---

will be carefully chosen to shed light on temporal processes. Not all processes necessarily have causal dimensions. But the search for causal links and patterns in case data is central to processual enquiry (see the more detailed discussions in Chapter 2, Box 2.4, and Chapter 11).

As Box 4.1 shows, cases, themes and processes are interlocking axes of enquiry that, taken together, form an integrated conceptual framework for a QL study. All three must be held in mind and attended to in the design and conduct of a project, and in the production of insights and interpretations. The analytical connection between cases, themes and processes is an important topic that we will return to at key moments in this book, and explore in some detail in Chapters 10 and 11.

Temporal Design: Key Features

One of the most commonly reported hallmarks of QL enquiry, reflected in our opening quotation, is its openness to creative refinement. The cyclical and cumulative nature of the research process increases the scope for reviewing and refining research questions, samples, fieldwork methods, lines of enquiry (themes), ethical strategies and analytical insights as a study progresses (Saldaña 2003; Yates 2003; Koro-Ljungberg and Bussing 2013; Millar 2021 in press). This gives the flexibility needed to respond to situations of flux and change and 'allows the unexpected to reconfigure the research' as it progresses (Grandia 2015: 312). As Scudder and Colson (2002: 206) observe, 'unexpected events bedevil the planning of long-term research. ... [A] rigid research design becomes a handicap over time'.

At the same time, the flexibility and open-ended nature of this methodology creates some challenges. Working through time adds to the intellectual demands of the process and has resource implications for the timetabling and execution of a study. Moreover, it can engender a sense of adventurous pioneering and uncertainty in equal measure. As our opening quotation illustrates, it can take on the mammoth proportions and meanderings of Odysseus's journey to Ithaca. In Homer's epic tale, and in C. P. Cavafy's Greek poem, *Ithaca*, we are urged to take a long and slow journey, complete with detours, to take time to look carefully and savour each experience along the way, for it is the journey, not the destination, which is the source of our understanding and enrichment. This same sentiment is reflected in recent calls for 'slow' ethnography (Grandia 2015), and it provides a fitting rationale for sustained QL enquiry.

The danger in working with this degree of flexibility and contingency is that researchers may begin to lose track of what their research is about or where it is going (Yates and McLeod 1996: 91; Saldaña 2003: 31). It is all too easy for the original focus to unravel when dealing with nebulous temporal processes that flow into each other, for this creates the temptation to discern flux and change everywhere. As Pettigrew observes:

[W]hen does a change process begin and end, especially where the unit of analysis is the continuous process in context? ... When does the fieldworker start and stop collecting data? Does one stop peeling the layers from the onion only when the vapours inhibit all further sight? There are, of course, no absolute and simple answers to such questions. (Pettigrew 1995: 98)

Maintaining some clarity concerning what processes people are being tracked through (alongside who is being tracked, and how and why) will help to overcome this difficulty. In other words, it helps to be clear at the planning stage about research aims, questions and strategies, and to review, take stock and re-focus at critical junctures in the research process (Saldaña 2003).

Research Questions and Conceptual Mapping

Developing a clear set of research questions at the outset can greatly help to navigate the research journey (examples of research questions are given in Table 4.1, while a variety of processual questions that feed into analysis are set out in Box 11.1). It is here that the analytical logic of QL enquiry, the attendance to case depth, thematic breadth and processual reach, first come into play. The research questions need to be qualitatively pertinent, for example asking *how*, *why* and *where* (Ritchie and Lewis 2003). But they need to be framed in dynamic ways that integrate cases and themes with processual explorations. Questions might be posed, for example, about how dynamic processes unfold; the nature, causes and consequences of change through the life course or across the micro–macro plane; and/or the influence of earlier events on later experiences and circumstances. Other temporal planes outlined in Chapter 3 (e.g. time–space, the tempo of unfolding processes, or ruptures in life experiences) may also be interwoven here as appropriate. Once drafted, the guiding research questions are not fixed; they are likely to be refined and polished iteratively as data are generated and the analysis unfolds. But they are an important starting point in establishing the parameters for a study.

Since it is easy to get lost in the intricacies of a QL study, it is also useful to devise a **conceptual road map**, a chart that sets out the guiding research questions and sub-questions, sources of data, sampling strategies and field methods, and a provisional list of themes that can feed into topic guides and broad-brush thematic analysis (for an example, see Table 4.1). As a study progresses, this map can be an invaluable aid in moving back and forth between theoretical premises and research practice. The map itself can be updated over the course of the study, as new insights develop and research practice is honed. It is not unusual for researchers to modify their research questions over time, as new themes and questions emerge that had not been anticipated at the outset. This is part of the necessary iteration that occurs between theoretical drivers and evolving research practice.

Research questions	Sub-questions	Sources of data: Samples and field methods	Fieldwork themes
Lived experiences: How and why do young people become parents at a young age? How do they manage this transition and its aftermath? How does housing provision impact on young parents? What factors shape their housing pathways, and how are these negotiated and experienced? How is 'home' understood? What forms of supported housing are available for disadvantaged young parents? How do they experience this support over time?	How do the past experiences and life histories of young parents shape their current lives, future aspirations and life chances? How do young parents' housing journeys evolve over time? What are their aspirations for housing and what opportunities and constraints impact on these aspirations over time? How do the housing trajectories of young parents intersect with their family/relational/education/employment and welfare trajectories?	Pre-existing empirical evidence: literature review Analysis of related legacy data: *Following Young Fathers* study – young father interviews New empirical evidence: a qualitative longitudinal enquiry carried out with primarily disadvantaged young parents: life journey interviewing (2 waves); life mapping participatory tools Participant observation at local housing support service	Life histories and journeys: Family background and relationships Childhood experiences Housing and home Education and employment Welfare provision/support Parental pathways/transitions/ Practices/opportunities/constraints Time: past, present, future Space and place: constructions of home, community, security, risk Identities and values (e.g. related to gender, class, parenthood, socio-economic and academic background, support and dependency)
Policy and practice processes: How are supported housing services delivered to young parents and how have such services evolved over time? To what extent are lived experiences of housing provision among young parents in tune with professional practices and expectations and with wider policy processes? How do these intersecting processes evolve over time and what are the implications for the development/sustainability of effective housing policies for young parents?	What kinds of supported housing services are available? What are the issues for professionals in their effective delivery, and in meeting the needs of young parents? How do broader policies (welfare reform, benefit changes, sanctions and conditionality) impact on housing provision and general support for young parents? How are these policies shifting over time? How do practitioners interpret policy directives at local level for young parents? How effective are current policy and professional practice? How might services improve to better support young parents?	Literature review: Review/analysis of policy documents and local practitioner delivery documents Analysis of related legacy data: practitioner interviews from the *Following Young Fathers* study New empirical data: in-depth, one-off interviews with selected local housing practitioners and service commissioners Participant observation at local housing support service	The housing and wider support needs of young parents: how are young parents supported over time? History of housing services, current provision and future plans Specialist and generic provision, referrals to other agencies How do practitioners interpret and implement housing and welfare policies? Opportunities and constraints that impact on service delivery, including housing eligibility, welfare reforms, changes in housing policy over time Hopes and fears for the future Examples of good practice What could be done differently? What resources would be needed?

Source: Developed by Neale and Ladlow for the ESRC funded *Housing Young Parents* doctoral study (University of Leeds).

Building Time into QL Study Design

Crafting a QL study involves working empirically with two of the three foundational planes of time that were introduced in Chapter 1 (Box 1.1). The first involves a balance between looking forward, prospectively, and looking back, retrospectively through time. The second involves crafting the time frames and tempos of a study through intensive/extensive horizons of time. The theoretical possibilities opened up by these planes were explored in Chapter 3; here we focus on how they feed into research design and sampling. As will be shown below, the process involves a series of balancing acts across these two planes.

Prospectively looking forward/retrospectively looking back

Dynamic data can be generated in two broad ways: prospectively (looking forward) or retrospectively (looking back). A prospective approach is the core design associated with longitudinal research, and the prime way to build cumulative knowledge about dynamic processes (Howell and Talle 2012). The same people are followed in real-time, capturing changes and continuities as they occur, and anticipating them in the future. This gives the research a forward momentum. Since revisits are anticipated, each new wave of fieldwork is shaped in relation to the previous waves, with the aim of building a dynamic, cumulative picture. Ideally, prospective real-time studies are planned from the outset, but, as shown in Chapter 1, it is not uncommon for QL studies to be conceived opportunistically, by building on an earlier synchronic (snapshot) study. Since all studies reflect the biographical and/or historical times in which they are located, the original study becomes an important baseline upon which to build cumulative insights.

A **retrospective** approach, in contrast, is essentially historical in nature. It explores dynamic processes through hindsight, a gaze backward in time from the vantage point of the present day (see Chapter 1). Studies that rely solely on retrospective methods require no more than a single visit to the field. This makes them cost-effective and relatively easy to conduct. However, they are temporal rather than longitudinal. For quantitative researchers, this makes them unreliable. Since people's memories are said to be faulty, they often collapse or 'telescope' events and facts (either fast forward or backward) in time, so that a clear and accurate chronology cannot be generated (Scott and Alwin 1998; Ruspini 2002). However, from a qualitative perspective, perceptions of the past are not fixed, and the search for some objective truth beyond the shifting interpretations and practices of the participants will always be elusive. For QL researchers, the drawbacks of a purely retrospective orientation relate rather more to the direction of the temporal gaze: on its own, looking back from one vantage point in time limits the ability to discern the drivers, momentum and impact of changes as they occur (Leonard-Barton 1995).

Nevertheless, a retrospective orientation is vital. It extends the historical reach of a study, enables a re-construction of historical and biographical processes, and can discern fluid, subjective understandings of causality. Prospective and retrospective orientations, then, are not either/or modes of enquiry; they are complementary (Scott and Alwin 1998). In the most effective QL designs, retrospective elements are built into a prospective study in the way research questions are framed, and in the way empirical data are generated and analysed. This enables the temporal gaze to oscillate between past, present and future, and for complex, non-linear processes to be traced backward and forward in time.

Time frames and tempos through intensive–extensive time

There is nothing prescriptive about the overall duration of a QL study, or the number and frequency of visits to the field. Indeed, there are as many time frames and tempos as there are QL studies. But it is possible to identify a spectrum of approaches ranging from intensive to extensive designs. At one extreme, people may be traced intensively through particular processes via frequent or continuous visits to the field. At its most intensive, QL research takes the form of ethnographic immersion. This affords a greater depth of engagement, yielding insights into the rhythms, tenor and synchronicities of daily lives, and the minutiae of change. In these contexts, rather than repeated waves of data generation, which imply periodicity, the process is more akin to a stream or flow of data and insights, which are gathered in 'drops or ripples' (Saldaña 2003: 33). This brings to the fore the 'journey along the way' (Neale and Flowerdew 2003). Instead of making bald comparisons between two snapshots in time, a more intensive approach generates a cyclical, reflexive and processual understanding, 'a description *through* time' (Howell and Talle 2012: 12, 17). This is the prime rationale for working intensively through time, and for utilising ethnographic methods in a QL study.

Intensive styles of research are likely to be conducted over relatively modest lengths of time (several months to several years), leading Saldaña to describe them as 'shortitudinal' (2003: 35). As well as being suited to the short-term funding streams that are currently available, they are ideal for tracking individuals through a transitional process (e.g. getting married, retiring from work, a treatment programme) or a time-bound event (e.g. a period of training, a travel experience or a retreat). Intensive designs can also support the process of staying in touch with mobile or marginalised participants, and enable the production of findings for policy in the short to medium term (Coffield et al. 1980; Molloy et al. 2002; Corden and

Nice 2007). In health, welfare and social care settings, a relatively intensive approach is commonly used to explore the introduction of new policy interventions and their short- to medium-term impact on service users. Examples are provided in Box 4.2.

Box 4.2 — Researching Policy Interventions Using Intensive Designs

- Harocopos and Dennis (2003) tracked a sample of drug users intensively over 18 months to investigate the impact of a health intervention programme. The baseline for the research was the admission of the participants to a treatment and rehabilitation centre, where intensive ethnographic methods were used over several weeks to get to know and recruit the participants into the study. Thereafter, participants were revisited at a less intensive and slowly diminishing tempo (five waves of interviews, conducted at one month, four months, eight months, 13 months and 18 months beyond their discharge from the unit).
- Ferguson et al. (2019) spent 18 months in the field, working intensively with two teams of social workers to discern how they conduct their child protection work. Ethnographic and **shadowing** methods were used to observe social work encounters with a caseload of 30 children and their families, entailing around 20 observations for each case. The researchers also observed organisational practices and cultures, and staff supervision in the teams, and carried out three waves of interviews with the families. Working in this intensive way enabled the researchers to get as close as possible to practitioners and managers as their working practices unfolded. This provided deep insights into the development of their practice; how relationships with families are established; the extent to which these relationships are sustained over time; and how organisational cultures impact on social work practice (reported in Ferguson et al. 2020).

At the other end of the spectrum, people may be traced more extensively through regular, occasional or 'punctuated' revisits to the field (Burawoy 2003). These visits may be spaced out over many years or even decades. As indicated in Chapter 1, such extensive tempos are commonly found in large-scale longitudinal studies, longitudinal ethnographies, and in socio-historical re-studies. The longitudinal frame here is akin to a series of synchronic snapshots, or movie 'stills' gathered at discrete historical moments, while time becomes a linear 'stretch' between two or more points in time (Neale and Flowerdew 2003; Talle 2012). This is one of the ways in which QL researchers can engage with the micro–macro plane; the greater the historical distance between visits, the greater the likelihood of capturing discernible transformations in the social fabric, and of uncovering how longer-term trajectories unfold.

In an extensive design, the distinct temporal boundary between field visits frees the researcher to look anew, with fresh eyes (Talle 2012). However, the time distance between visits diminishes the scope to discern the intricacies of dynamic processes and the ebbs, flows and detours that are continually occurring between the movie 'stills' (Neale and Flowerdew 2003). It also increases the challenge of maintaining a panel of participants; it may be necessary to retrace participants before they can be invited back into a study (see Chapter 5).

Complementary Designs

The different longitudinal frameworks outlined above have long been recognised by anthropologists. For example, Firth (1959) distinguishes between *continuous diachronic* approaches and *dual synchronic* approaches; Foster et al. (1979: 9–10), between *continuous studies* and *re-studies*; and Howell and Talle (2012) between *multi-temporal* studies and *re-studies*. Similar distinctions are made by QL researchers (see Holland et al. 2006; and Warin 2011, who characterises her 14-year study of school children as intermittent ethnography). Yet, as Foster et al. (1979: 9) and Royce and Kemper (2002: xvi) make clear, these are not bald distinctions; there is consideration variation in the overall time frame for a project, the number of field visits, and the intervals between them. Moreover, the intensive and extensive designs outlined above are complementary. They form a spectrum of approaches that may be combined or which merge into each other at different points in the research process. An intensive design, for example, may well evolve over time into a more extensive study or re-study, thereby capturing different flows of time. This is commonly the case for longitudinal ethnographies (Foster 1979; Royce 2002; Gordon and Lahelma 2003; Talle 2012). It is also increasingly evident in interview-based studies, as some of the examples in Box 4.3 show.

Box 4.3 Combining Intensive and Extensive Designs

- Jay MacLeod's (1987, 2009) *Ain't no Makin' It* is widely celebrated for making sociology come alive. It is a study of two groups of disadvantaged American boys, of different ethnic backgrounds, who were growing up in a public housing project in Massachusetts. Conducted in three phases running over 25 years, the research began as an intensive ethnographic and interview-based study of the 15 boys, conducted over four waves of fieldwork in the early to mid-1980s. MacLeod hung out with the boys in their neighbourhoods, explored variations in how they engaged/ disengaged from educational opportunities, and how, over time, they

(Continued)

oscillated between mainstream and subcultural values and practices. He was able to discern what these varied patterns meant for the boys' occupational and family aspirations for the future (MacLeod 1987). MacLeod revisited the young men eight years later (in the early 1990s), exploring how they were faring in a precarious labour market, and in a crime-ridden underground economy, which resulted in a second edition of his book. He returned for a final visit in 2006–7, some 25 years after his initial fieldwork. He was able to trace the biographies of 13 of his participants into middle age, documenting the socio-economic and family events, opportunities and constraints that had shaped their lives over the decades, and exploring how far their original aspirations for a better and 'straighter' future had been realised. For this final phase of the study, MacLeod uses a powerful, **autobiographical** style of reporting, telling the men's tales in their own words, before appending a final sociological reading to their accounts. While the initial phase of MacLeod's study was intensive and prospective, the longer-term follow-up was extensive and retrospective, looking back through life history interviews to explore the many factors that had led the young men to their current circumstances (for similar designs, see Weis's (2004) 15-year follow-up of teenagers from a high school in the USA, and Williamson's (2004) 25-year follow-up of the Milltown Boys in Wales).

Similar strategies have been adopted in a variety of studies:

- A study of parents who were initially tracked intensively through the births of their children, and then followed up 18 years later for a retrospective study, as their children reached legal adulthood (Miller 2005, 2017);
- A 17-year follow-up of a mixed methods study of adolescent mothers in later life (Furstenberg et al. 1987);
- A long-term mixed methods study of delinquent 'boys' who were revisited at the age of 70 (Laub and Sampson 2003; see Box 3.2);
- A study of lone mothers and their children, who initially took part in three waves of interviews and were followed up a decade later (Ridge and Millar 2011; Millar and Ridge 2017; Millar 2021 in press). Going back over the long term yielded new insights into unfolding trajectories, and enabled the researchers to uncover the significant impact of income insecurity on the longer-term fortunes of the mothers and their children:

By the time of the final round … it was continuity rather than change that was the most striking. The women had mainly stayed in work … But many were still on wages at, or not much above the minimum wage. This had major implications for their futures … and their capacity to help and support their children into adulthood … There is often limited capacity to effect a significant and lasting improvement in income and material circumstances over longer periods of time … For the children, the impact of financial insecurity could cast long shadows. (Millar 2021 in press: 3, 5)

Overall, securing funding for extensive research is likely to be a challenge for QL researchers. Most commonly, an extensive time frame evolves in piecemeal fashion through several phases of funding. The *Inventing Adulthoods* study, for example, secured almost continuous piecemeal funding that transformed an original synchronic study into a prospective QL study. This ran over 12 years and involved seven waves of fieldwork and the development of extensive case histories (Thomson and Holland 2003; Henderson et al. 2007, 2012; Thomson 2009). Other notable examples of ongoing, piecemeal funding are Pollard and Filers' *Identity and Learning Programme* (Pollard with Filer 1996; Pollard and Filer 1999), and the *Following Young Fathers/Following Young Fathers Further* research, which began in 2010 and, through four phases of funding, looks set to run until 2027 (Neale et al. 2015; Tarrant and Neale 2017; Tarrant 2020).

Core funding for QL studies over the longer term is extremely rare, and usually secured only where they are nested within large-scale projects (for example, the *Young Lives Project*, core funded from 2001–17 by the Department for International Development (DfiD) as part of a large-scale, international study of childhood poverty (Morrow and Crivello 2015)). Despite these funding constraints, a far-sighted researcher will plan for a potential longer-term revisit to the field and ensure that, as far as possible, contacts with participants are maintained and data generated, documented and preserved in ways that facilitate this process.

Crafting Time Frames and Tempos

As shown in Chapter 1, the **time frame** for a QL study (the overall time span of enquiry) and its **tempo** (the number, spacing and continuity of visits to the field) are intertwined processes. Together, they constitute the longitudinal frame for a study. Researchers who are new to QL research commonly ask how many waves of data are needed to qualify as a QL study, and over what time periods (Saldaña 2003: 33). These are prime questions that form the basis for sampling through time. At a minimum, data need to be generated at two points in time to create the basis for making temporal connections and comparisons. However, there are no rigid prescriptions or easy answers to these questions. As shown above, these uncertainties reflect one of the challenges of QL research: it is always in danger of becoming unbounded, with never-ending possibilities for stretching backward and forward through time.

Time frames and tempos are usually shaped in relation to the research questions, the nature of the process under study, the characteristics of the sample, the practicalities of funding and the availability of resources. Two broad strategies, that give a temporal logic to the research process, are worth highlighting here. The first is the need for clear **baseline and closure points** to frame a study. The second is the need for flexible time frames and tempos that can mirror the process under investigation.

These are an important means of anchoring a QL project, helping to delineate the overall structure and duration of a study, and, crucially, to contain it.

Baseline and closure points

The baseline for a QL study, or for a particular cohort of participants, is a temporal marker of some kind, a key historical or biographical moment. Ideally, QL researchers aim to be there at the beginning of things, for example the moment in which people set up a new initiative such as a re-wilding programme or local community group, become clients of a new service, start a new phase of life, or face a significant change in the external landscape. These markers may be defined biographically, in relation to the changing circumstances of individuals; or historically, in relation to changing external events, or both. These become the conceptual anchors for a study, around which a design can be built. A baseline may not coincide exactly with the start of fieldwork, but a retrospective account can help to capture the event or moment. An example is given in Box 4.4.

Box 4.4 Baseline and Closure Points:
The Lived Experience of Welfare Reform

- Patrick (2017) chose a change in UK welfare legislation, introduced by the Coalition government, as the baseline for her doctoral research on the lived experience of welfare reform. She was able to trace the effects of the reforms on the lives of her participants through the four years of the Coalition's term of office (a process helped by her maternity leave, which enabled her to extend the longitudinal reach of the research; Dwyer and Patrick 2020). Working across the micro–macro plane, she was able to discern the micro-dynamic effects of an increasingly punitive welfare-to-work regime, and to consider, in macro-dynamic context, what these changes meant for the socio-economic status of welfare recipients and the re-shaping of citizenship in the UK.

Baseline and closure points need to be defined conceptually as well as chronologically (Lewis 2007: 552). For those studying discrete transitional processes in individual biographies, such as an entry into parenthood, or the process of retirement, finding such temporal markers may be relatively straightforward. But it can be a challenge where the focus is on a macro evolutionary process that unfolds slowly over the longer term. At what point in such a lengthy process should the researcher begin or end, and what rationale can be used to justify these moments?

These are not easy questions to address. One way forward is to sample comparatively across different cohorts: temporal sub-samples who are at varied points in an evolutionary journey (see Boxes 4.9 and 4.11 for examples; and see below for a discussion of cohorts). Different temporal baselines and/or closure points can then be chosen for each cohort.

While baselines and closure points should, as far as possible, be driven by the temporal logic of a study, in practice both may have to be determined on pragmatic, resource-related grounds, tied to the period of funding (Eisenhardt 1995). Whatever conceptual closure point is arrived at in an unfolding process (the end of a particular transition, for example), a study also needs to be rounded off methodologically and ethically. For example, a final interview is likely to incorporate a retrospective summing up of people's changing lives over the study period, their changing perceptions of the journey that they have been on, and their reflections on the research and the part they have played in it. As will be shown in Chapter 5, closure of a project also needs to be handled and marked in ethically sensitive ways for the participants, while leaving the door open for a potential follow-up in future.

Mirroring the dynamic process: flexible tempos

Working with a temporal logic of enquiry, QL researchers tend to fashion their studies in ways that 'fit' the dynamic process under investigation. For example, studies that track the clients of a service may tie the waves of fieldwork to the frequency and duration of contact between client and service provider. This was the case for Farrell et al. (2006) in their evaluation of New Labour's *Job Retention and Rehabilitation Pilot Scheme*. The study involved six months of fieldwork (six interviews, conducted at monthly intervals) with a panel of 36 people who had taken part in the scheme. The tempo for the research mirrored the tempo of the pilot scheme (cf. also Corden and Nice 2007). As a further example, transition studies are typically built around a 'before and after' model, with waves of fieldwork strategically chosen to capture the overall tenor of the process or to coincide with key landmarks. For example, studies of the transition to parenthood commonly involve three waves of fieldwork conducted over 12–18 months: the early stages of the pregnancy, around the time of the birth, and some months after the birth (Miller 2005, 2015).

The **mirroring process** outlined above suggests the need for a flexible tempo that can be adjusted as a study unfolds. Indeed, whatever tempo is initially chosen, it may evolve in ways that are sensitive to the flux of people's unfolding lives, and responsive to changing conditions. This is one of the ways in which QL research differs from large-scale quantitative longitudinal studies, where participants are more likely to be followed at regular, predetermined intervals, spaced over years (Ruspini 2002: 4). Flexibility of follow-up can enable participants to engage in a study when they are able, or for researchers to respond to critical moments in people's lives as they occur. Calman et al. (2013), for example, report that a flexible tempo would have enabled them to follow their sample of terminally ill cancer patients on a case-by-case basis, mirroring how the disease progressed for each individual. Instead, their 'blanket' schedule meant that several participants declined rapidly and died before the researchers were able to revisit them.

A flexible tempo, tailored to the needs of individual participants, may allow researchers to return to the field opportunistically, not only to capture important historical or biographical moments as they occur (the effects of a recession or pandemic lockdown, for example; see Chapter 6), but also to help sustain relationships or, more pragmatically, to respond to changing circumstances in the research team (Pollard 2007). In the *Following Young Fathers* study, for example, the researcher conducting interviews went on maternity leave, necessitating a re-scheduling of the interviews and the loss of a planned wave of fieldwork (Neale et al. 2015).

The notion that time frames and tempos should be flexible in order to mirror the process under study is a helpful design strategy, but it needs to be tempered by resource and project management considerations. Too much flexibility may unravel a carefully specified study and confound and unsettle existing work schedules and commitments. Building in the capacity for one-off additional visits to the field at pivotal moments in time may be more feasible than building in a blanket extra wave across the whole sample. The latter strategy could be expensive and time-consuming, and add to the complexity and magnitude of data generation and analysis. It is all too easy to be over-ambitious and to underestimate the time needed between waves of fieldwork for rest, reflection, data management, cumulative analysis, and preparations for a return to the field. Even so, building in provision for some flexibility in the field can help to maximise the degree of fit between the tempo of the research and the tempo of the lives and processes under study.

Sampling Strategies

As an integral component of research design, qualitative sampling involves identifying an appropriate range of cases or units of study as the basis for empirical investigation (Ritchie et al. 2014). Choices need to be made about who and/or what to sample, how many cases or units of study to include, what kind of variations to build in, and when and where to sample them. These are interlocking decisions that constitute a **sampling strategy**. Cases may be drawn from a wider population of people, social events, settings, and so on. But given the focus on tracing lives, the main sampling units in a QL study are likely to be individuals or small collectives, alongside the events, settings, time frames and tempos through which their lives are unfolding. As will have become apparent from the discussion of design decisions above, in QL research, time is an important unit of study and a foundational part of any sampling strategy.

However the units of study are defined, the aim is to sample those that have significant explanatory power, that is, those that will give rich insights into the study themes and allow the researcher to read across, compare and synthesise experiences and processes. In qualitative enquiry, **purposive sampling** logic is commonly used to craft an appropriate range of cases. This has a theoretical logic that obviates the need for large or representative samples. The emphasis is on understanding experiences and circumstances across a range of complementary cases, rather than measuring similarities and differences across strictly comparable cases (Pawson 2006). The objective may be to sample for particular, extreme or (supposedly) typical cases, or to work across a spectrum of circumstances and experiences, located within varied settings of time and place. Quotas for each sampling criterion (numbers in each age group, for example) may be drawn up, using a matrix that guides the selection process (Ritchie et al. 2014; although see below for the limitations of **stratified sampling**). This is sometimes preceded by screening questionnaires or the use of national-level statistical data to identify an appropriate range (Ritchie et al. 2014).

Sampling through Time: The Logic of Cases, Themes and Processes

The basics of qualitative sampling outlined above provide the foundation for **sampling through time**. However, adding time into the mix has a transformative effect on how we understand cases and units of study. A QL case is inherently dynamic and process driven. The units of study are likely to be identified not only through the varied characteristics of particular individuals or groups, but through their capacity to reflect the temporal themes of the study. It is not so much the individuals or collectives themselves that are being sampled, but the dynamic events, interactions and processes that they are experiencing, the journeys that they are undergoing (Gobo 2008). Here, processes become important units of study and analysis. The logic of working with cases, themes and processes is an important means of determining a sampling strategy.

For example, time and process impact on the number of cases in a sample, when and how often to sample, what variations to build in, and how comparisons between cases are to be understood. In short, key themes are investigated not only by sampling across cases, but also by sampling through time. **Temporal sampling** is driven by a purposive logic: the aim is not to sample strictly comparable time units that unfold through fixed time intervals, but to thread time into the picture in a way that mirrors complex, fluid, real-world processes. In this way, temporal sampling in a QL study seeks to reflect and uncover the fluidity of lives as they unfold. An example of a QL sampling strategy is given in Box 4.5.

> **Box 4.5**   Sampling in the *Identity and Learning Programme*
>
> • In a 12-year longitudinal ethnography of children's school careers, the units of study were the children, parents and teachers attached to a particular school (cases); the varied micro-settings of the children's lives: classroom, playground and home (case settings); set against a backdrop of shifting educational policies and practices (themes); and the seven school calendar years through which the children were being tracked (processes). This became the conceptual framework for gathering, organising and analysing data about the children's unfolding lives. Time itself became a unit of study, seen in relation to the biographies of the children and the varied micro-cultures and broader education structures that were shaping and re-shaping their school careers. Tracing the lives of these children through these varied settings revealed subtle changes in their fledgling educational trajectories over the years of their primary education (Pollard with Filer 1996; Filer with Pollard 1998; Pollard and Filer 1999; Filer and Pollard 2000; Pollard 2007). (For further details of this study, see Box 4.8.)

Sampling QL Cases: Breadth and Depth

Advice on QL sample sizes tends to be rather vague (Winiarska 2017). This is inevitable, given that the size and breadth of a QL sample will vary from one project to the next. However, a spectrum of approaches is evident, ranging from a **case-led approach** to a broader **cross-case comparative approach** (these same strategies also underpin modes of analysis; see Chapter 10).

A case-led or case study approach identifies a relatively small number of cases, or perhaps one distinctive case that can offer an in-depth, holistic understanding of social process. This produces a case-rich dataset. Sampling across a modest number of individuals, family or community groups or organisations, for example, offers greater scope for a detailed exploration and comparison of how lives unfold (Pettigrew 1995; Yates 2003; Macmillan et al. 2011).

> **Box 4.6**   Case-led Sampling – Intensive Interview and Ethnographic Designs
>
> • Longitudinal Interpretative Phenomenological Analysis (LIPA) involves research with small numbers of cases, enabling an in-depth exploration of lived experiences through time (Farr and Nizza 2019). Interviews are lengthy and detailed. For example, in a study of four participants recovering from kidney transplants, conducted over three waves of fieldwork, the interviews lasted from 45 minutes to 3 hours (Spiers et al. 2016; for further details of LIPA and this study, see Box 10.5).

- A study by Shaw et al. (2016) explored the experiences of four older people as they adjusted to life in a purpose-built, assisted living community. In-depth, exploratory interviews were carried out with the residents within five months of their arrival, and a further 12 and 18 months beyond this. This small dataset (12 in-depth interviews) yielded rich insights into the unfolding biographies of the participants as they adjusted to new patterns of living, and as they reflected on what they had lost and gained from the transition. The negotiation of new relationships was an important theme, along with their developing sense of space and place, and their feelings of opportunity and confinement (one participant described herself as a 'caged bird' in her past life as a carer, but likened her new life to 'being on holiday' and living 'on a cruise ship', with a different but equally palpable sense of confinement). The different trajectories followed by the four participants were highlighted and set against their varied life experiences.
- In their longitudinal ethnographic case study, Coffield and colleagues (1980) sampled four families who were drawn from different social housing estates in an industrial town in the English Midlands (see Box 1.3 for details). The families were experiencing multiple deprivations in their lives. The researchers included as many family members as possible in each of the case study families (children and partners as well as parents). Using a combination of participant observation and life history interviews, the researchers adopted an intensive design of continuous and flexible engagement with the families. Over a period of 18 to 24 months, contact with the families was 'day by day, week by week'. The researchers visited one mother 80 times over the course of the study (Coffield et al. 1980: 72), sometimes for a fleeting visit, and on other occasions for a whole day. A final revisit to each family was arranged some 18 months after the end of the intensive ethnography. The intensive temporal engagement was facilitated by the small number of case study families in the sample.

It is worth noting here that a relatively small number of cases does not necessarily mean a small or simple study, as our examples in Box 4.6 illustrate. The overall size of a QL dataset is determined not just by the number of cases in the sample, but also by the number of waves of field enquiry (Langley et al. 2013). A smaller sample size increases the scope for qualitative richness and depth of understanding.

Alternatively, a cross-case comparative approach identifies a wider range of cases that can bring greater breadth to a study, and may offer scope for discerning variations in experiences across different settings and domains of experience, as well as through time. Multiple samples may be drawn into a study to build such connections (Burawoy 2009; Bartlett and Vavrus 2017; see also Walkerdine et al. 2001 in Box 4.10).

A larger baseline sample can also provide a safety net to mitigate the effects of sample attrition (Harocopos and Dennis 2003; see Chapter 5). Examples of cross-case comparative sampling are given in Box 4.7. These range from modestly sized QL studies to qualitative panel studies, the 'intimate epics' introduced in Chapter 1.

Box 4.7   Cross-case Comparative Sampling

- In the *12 to 18 Project*, Yates and McLeod sampled between six and eight students in each of four Australian high schools, giving a total of 26 students in the overall sample. This strategy enabled them to include students from varied backgrounds in the same schools, and from similar backgrounds across varied schools (Yates and McLeod 1996; McLeod 2003; Yates 2003). The eight years of high school provided the temporal sampling strategy for the study, within which the students were followed up twice a year by the researchers, giving a total of 16 interviews with each young person during their high school careers. This enabled a processual understanding of the young people's changing identities and life experiences through a critical period of growing up. The study yielded a large and complex dataset (350 in-depth interviews), offering scope for a variety of comparative analytical frames within and across the sub-samples, across the different school settings, and through the stream of time. (For a similar study that follows young people in and beyond high school, see Gordon and Lahelma 2003.)
- Qualitative panel studies (QPS or QPR) are prime examples of 'scaled up' studies that work with relatively large and diverse samples, and with large research teams to manage the workload. Burton et al. (2009), for example, traced the lives of 256 low-income mothers in their six-year longitudinal ethnography, a study linked to (rather than nested within) a large-scale longitudinal survey of 2,402 families across three US cities. The ethnographers met with each family once or twice a month for 12–18 months, and then every six months for a further two years. The capacity to combine breadth with depth in this study was made possible by the large team, comprising over 200 field researchers, data analysts and senior research scientists, who were linked to the larger-scale study (for details of the ethnographic methods used in this study, see Box 6.1; for a similarly large-scale, mixed methods design in the context of global poverty research, see Morrow and Crivello 2015).
- More recently, the five-year *Welfare Conditionality* study recruited 480 cases, representing nine varied sub-samples of welfare recipients (including homeless people and migrants), who were drawn from a range of localities across England and Scotland (Dwyer and Patrick 2020). Each sub-sample was followed through three waves of interviews, carried out on a yearly basis by different teams of researchers from six UK universities. The sample also included welfare providers, whose perspectives were sought in one-off interviews. In this study, the large stratified sample was a condition of funding, which created some challenges for the researchers. Completing each wave of fieldwork before the next was due to begin was a challenge with such a large number of participants, and meant that

the team lacked the time to conduct an interim analysis between waves. A new team member was hired to support the thematic coding of the dataset. While this helped with the overall time constraints, it also created some distance between the researchers and their data (Dwyer and Patrick 2020). The team worked hard to ensure that, the breadth of the study did not curtail the depth of researcher engagement and insight.

Overall, the much larger sample sizes illustrated in Box 4.7 are unusual in the canon of QL studies. Whatever the balance between a case-led and cross-case comparative approach, there is a clear trade-off between depth and breadth of investigation. Qualitative researchers, in general, try to keep sample sizes to manageable proportions (averaging around 50 cases), to ensure that the necessary depth of explanation is not compromised (Ritchie et al. 2014). For QL research, this becomes even more of an imperative. A proliferation of varied cases and settings and an accumulation of temporal data, often in quick succession through the cyclical waves of a study, can quickly become unmanageable. Researchers may find themselves grappling with, or sinking under, the mammoth task of generating, re-generating, analysing and re-analysing an increasingly large and unwieldy dataset. Even the average sample sizes used in qualitative research (50 cases) is likely to become much less manageable when a sample is to be followed intensively over several waves of fieldwork, and where the drive is to build cumulative insights as a study progresses. The challenges may be all the greater for lone researchers or small teams with limited resources.

Whatever the attractions of 'scaling up' QL enquiry, depth of explanation and insight is a crucial feature of QL research and should not be compromised. In this context, the trade-off between the depth and breadth of a sample also means a trade-off between the size of a sample and the frequency and intensity with which people are followed up. As noted above, the size of a QL dataset is determined as much by the number of waves of fieldwork as the number of cases followed. In other words, the tempo of a study is a vital consideration in developing a sampling strategy. Since decisions about the nature and size of a QL sample will impact on the tempo of a study, and vice versa, these need to be considered together, as integrated dimensions of QL design.

In sum, the broad aim is to develop a sampling strategy that enables connections and comparisons through time (not simply cross-sectional comparisons at one point in time). For this reasons QL researchers are more likely to recruit a relatively small number of cases, which will yield case-rich, processual data and enable a more detailed engagement with the temporal themes under study. One of the ways in which sample sizes can be contained is to take a broad-brush approach to building sample diversity. Rather than aiming for a stratified sample, based on a range of characteristics that have to be balanced across the cases, QL researchers may opt for a more fluid sampling strategy. This identifies one or two key characteristics (gender and ethnicity, for example, or temporally inflected characteristics, such as age or generation), which will give some shape to the cases, yet will also, through serendipity, reflect a fluid mix of circumstances and characteristics. This more open approach to sampling not only reduces the need for a large-scale, stratified sample, but also allows the researcher to discover all kinds of unanticipated connections between different constellations of circumstances, which a more rigid sampling frame might fail to discern.

Re-sampling through Time

In all forms of qualitative research, sampling is a dynamic process. The criteria for inclusion may change or be refined as fieldwork progresses (Ritchie and Lewis 2003). This is most evident, perhaps, in grounded theorising, where researchers continue to refine their sampling strategy and recruit new cases until they have 'saturated' a particular theoretical category (Charmaz 2014). The logic of enquiry in grounded theorising, however, differs from that of temporal sampling and resampling (and also produces differences in data analysis; see Chapter 9). Sampling in grounded theorising involves an ongoing search for *new* cases that can shed fresh light on emerging theories. Analytical closure, the end point of this process, occurs when categories or themes are 'saturated', that is, when new cases no longer spark new theoretical insights (Charmaz 2014: 213). Yet time, process, continuity and change cannot be 'saturated' in this way: 'you can't build grounded theory while the ground is moving' (Weick, in Huber and Van de Ven 1995: 336). Since temporal understandings are under continual construction and refinement, this creates fresh insights for each case with each return visit to the field.

In QL research, the dynamics of sampling are particularly pronounced. Units of study such as couples, households, organisations or settings may well shrink or grow, or otherwise change shape or composition as a study progresses. Whatever the original criteria used for recruitment, life circumstances, personal and environmental characteristics are never static. This affords the opportunity to trace these transformations as the research unfolds. But there is also increased scope to purposively re-sample cases and processes over successive waves of fieldwork. Sampling itself becomes part of the research journey, requiring researchers to decide how to draw a baseline sample, how and when to follow up the baseline, and whether to recruit new sub-samples at a later date. In what follows, we explore three broad strategies for sampling and re-sampling through time. The first involves condensing or boosting a sample through the longitudinal frame of a study; the second involves working with different cohorts of participants, who have different temporal experiences of a particular process; and the third involves working 'horizontally' with generational cohorts, or 'vertically' with **family chains**. These are creative ways of engaging with historical time and extending the temporal reach of a study.

Condensing or Boosting a Sample

The baseline cases in a study do not necessarily need to be followed through the whole time frame of a study, or at the same times. A study grappling with time constraints, for example, may opt to follow up particular members of a panel after a gap of a year, while the remainder are revisited after two years. This generates two waves of data for the panel, but the tempo varies across different sub-samples (Hastwell and Moss 2019; personal communication). It is also common for a relatively large sample of cases to be recruited at the baseline, from which a more focused longitudinal panel is constructed for the follow-up waves. Among these panel members, certain **emblematic cases** (illuminative, distinctive or archetypal cases) (Weis 2004; Gobo 2008) may then be singled out for more intensive investigation, enabling a more holistic case study treatment.

This is part of a broader ethnographic strategy known as a **funnel approach**, or **progressive focusing** (Agar 1980: 13; Pollard 2007). The emblematic cases are likely to offer greater insights into the themes of the study, for example exemplifying those in stasis or undergoing particular transitions or with diverging trajectories that can be compared; or with distinctive characteristics that provide a focused lens on key issues (Weis 2004; Gobo 2008; Millar 2021 in press). Either way, emblematic cases are likely to be data-rich, compelling or striking in some way: they are the ones that shine (Flyvbjerg 2007). The full baseline of cases may still be followed up at some point, perhaps at the end of the study, but with less intensity and/or frequency, or more indirectly (e.g. via telephone, video or internet contact, rather than in person). A re-sampling strategy such as this enables researchers to build different degrees of granularity into their data and evidence. It is one of the ways in which the balance between breadth and depth in a QL investigation can be maintained, ensuring breadth at the baseline, but depth at follow-up. It can also save on limited budgets, and may be particularly suitable for lone researchers or small teams with limited time and resources.

Alternatively, researchers may choose to boost a baseline sample of cases at follow-up, as the examples in Box 4.8 illustrate. It is worth noting that 'growing' a sample may involve expanding the scope of a case over time, for example where a focus on an individual is broadened to include the constellation of family, community or professional relationships in which the individual is embedded.

Box 4.8   Sample Boosting through Time

- In the *Identity and Learning Programme*, a 12-year longitudinal ethnography of children's school careers (also showcased in Box 4.5 above), the researchers had initially planned to sample children from two contrasting primary schools. When the anticipated funding did not materialise, an opportunity arose to work with a committed head teacher in one particular school. In a prime example of opportunistic sampling, the researchers adopted an ethnographic, case study approach and recruited ten children (the oldest in their year group) from a pool of 22 children in the school reception class. The children were followed on a yearly basis over the seven years of their primary education. A variety of data sources (school records, teacher and parent insights, participant observation in class, in the playground and at home) were drawn upon to create a holistic understanding. Some years later, the researchers were able to boost the sample when they were given access to a further ten children, drawn from the same year cohort, who were attending a contrasting primary school. Most of the 20 children were followed into the years of their high school education, a process that involved expanding the settings for the research from two primary schools to nine high schools (Filer and Pollard 2000; Pollard 2007).
- Similarly, in the *Following Young Fathers* study, the original sample comprised a group of 12 low-income young fathers who were tracked intensively over three waves of interviews. This was also an 'opportunistic' sample, recruited and sustained through the support of a committed practice partner. For the second phase of funding, which followed on seamlessly from the first, the sample was boosted to 31 young men, including those from middle-income families, those without specialist professional support, and a targeted group of young offender fathers. This gave greater insights into the varied circumstances, trajectories and support needs of the young men and how these impacted on their fatherhood journeys (Neale and Ladlow 2015; Neale et al. 2015; Ladlow and Neale 2016; Neale and Davies 2016). Further sample boosting across different UK practice settings, and a cross-national comparative element across different welfare regimes, have subsequently been built into a newly funded phase of the study (Tarrant 2020). Boosting the sample in these ways has enabled an incremental development of this study from its modest beginnings.

Longitudinal Panels and Cohorts

The participants in a prospective longitudinal study are commonly described as a panel. This terminology has its origins in quantitative longitudinal research, where it is associated with representative samples and a relatively long time frame. But it is also commonly employed in QL research, not only for large-scale qualitative panel studies, but also for small-scale studies conducted over intensive periods of time (see, for example, Saldaña 2003; Farrell et al. 2006; Krings et al. 2013). In these contexts, a panel implies an established group of participants with shared characteristics and the capacity for a sustained engagement with the research process.

Using purposive sampling logic, a QL panel may be constructed in varied ways to enable connections and comparisons through time. A common strategy is to build in one or more **cohorts**. These are individuals or groups whose fortunes are shaped by a shared experience, a common passage through the life course or a particular historical process, over *roughly the same period of time*. They are defined as 'aggregates of individuals who experience the same life event within the same time interval' (Ryder, cited in Ruspini 2002: 9, and Nilson 2014). In other words, cohorts are temporally defined samples, or sub-samples, that are anchored by shared experiences in time. This gives a great deal of flexibility in the way that cohorts are constituted. They may share a common age or generation, a common life course experience (e.g. migration, becoming a parent, or retirement), or a con-temporaneous passage through an external landscape (e.g. living through a war or a pandemic).

Perhaps the most well-known cohorts are the birth cohorts – samples born in the same year who may be followed from birth or through a particular segment of the life course (Ruspini 2002). The times into which people are born are among the most powerful influences that shape lives: 'To be young is to be young at a particular time and place: each age cohort is unique' (Colson 1984: 4). Sampling across one or more cohorts is a productive means of engaging with the micro–macro plane of time. Since cohorts are held together by shared experiences that occur contemporane-ously, they become lynchpins for discerning the links between biographical and wider historical processes of change, as our examples in Box 4.9 show. It is also important to note that a cohort is by no means homogeneous: sampling across one particular cohort enables researchers to draw into a study varied sub-samples, with different characteristics and living in varied circumstances.

Sampling across Cohorts

Sampling across different cohorts is a common strategy in longitudinal research, particularly in large-scale, extensive studies that seek to tease out how historical events are synchronised with life course processes (Giele and Elder 1998). Elder (1974; Elder and Pellerin 1998), for example, sampled two age cohorts of children who lived through the Great Depression, and who had radically different experi-ences of the impact of this event on their lives (see Box 3.5, where this research is showcased). By sampling across these two age cohorts, Elder was able to produce new insights about the timing of historical events in people's lives and how biographical and historical events intersect.

Sampling across cohorts is also used in the more intensive designs of QL research, where it can shed light on how experiences vary at different historical moments. Researchers can draw together the experiences of those who began their journeys through a particular process at a different time, and/or who represent different stages in a particular journey. The strategy has been most commonly employed in evaluation studies that seek to assess the delivery and effectiveness of health or social care programmes. But it also has value where a study is exploring an evolutionary (as opposed to transitionary) process that lacks a clear baseline or timescale for development. Both kinds of study are showcased in Box 4.9.

Box 4.9 Sampling across Cohorts

- **Welfare policy interventions**: Researchers who are engaged in evaluating welfare interventions commonly sample across different cohorts. These different cohorts enter a policy programme and are recruited into a study sequentially, or at staggered (overlapping) times; in this way, different baseline and closure points are established for each cohort. For example, an evaluation of New Labour's *Pathway to Work Pilot Scheme* (Corden and Nice 2007) sampled three cohorts of service users (35 cases in each cohort; a total of 105 cases) who were recruited into the pilot at staggered times, and then followed as they engaged in the scheme. The overall time frame for the study was 21 months. Each cohort was interviewed on three occasions, giving a total of nine waves of fieldwork across the cohorts. Similarly, in the *Job Retention and Rehabilitation Pilot Scheme* (Farrell et al. 2006, described earlier), three cohorts of service users (each comprising 12 cases) were interviewed over three separate (rather than overlapping) phases of the study. Each cohort member was interviewed six times at monthly intervals, giving a total of 18 waves of fieldwork over an 18-month period. These studies aimed to discern changes in individual lives (the panel elements), but to also tease out changes in programme delivery and how these impacted on the clients of the service (the cohort elements). The intensive design and sampling strategies yielded a steady stream of data and findings that were fed directly back into the development of the pilot schemes. This iteration between the research process and the unfolding policy process created valuable impacts as these studies progressed, although the researchers also observe that such sampling strategies can be complex to manage, and involve particularly demanding schedules of fieldwork. Overall, these forms of cross-cohort sampling are well suited to applied or evaluation research, where there may be a greater need for a cross-case comparative approach, or where policy funders require quick results and feedback over the short to medium term (Corden and Nice 2007).

- **Co-evolution: The Human–Carnivore Co-existence Study**: Our second example of sampling across cohorts is a doctoral study of a gradual, long-term evolutionary process that lacks a clear baseline, closure point or time frame for development. It focuses on the co-existence and future sustainability of communities of humans and wild carnivores (bears and wolf packs that, after decades of absence, are returning and naturally spreading through rural regions of Europe). The study is exploring the far-reaching socio-cultural transformations at play in this process, and how they intersect with ecological transformations in the natural world. Over a year of fieldwork, the researcher is concurrently following the progress of three community cohorts that are at different stages in this co-evolutionary journey: the first community is anticipating the arrival of the carnivores; a second has experienced their recent arrival; and a third has a long and settled experience of this form of co-existence between the natural and social worlds (Pettersson 2019). This sampling strategy will enable the researcher to shed light on this evolutionary process by piecing together insights across these three historical cohorts, set in different communities, and drawing documentary, historical and policy-related evidence into the picture.

The cross-cohort studies outlined in Box 4.9 use a mixture of longitudinal panel designs (following the same individuals or communities, in these cases intensively over many months) and recurrent cross-sectional designs (following different cohorts of people at the same time, or at staggered or different times). Combining these two forms of longitudinal enquiry is a valuable means of exploring changes in individual or collective experiences (the enduring 'panel' elements), in relation to changes in wider policy or environmental processes (the different 'cohort' elements).

Generational Cohorts and Family Chains

The final group of sampling strategies considered here are bound up with family and generational ties. Sampling within or across generational cohorts, or across intergenerational chains of family members are powerful ways of exploring the interface between generational and historical processes of change. **Generational cohorts** encompass a range of age cohorts. They are broader convoys of individuals who are born and grow up within the same historical period. They are held together 'horizontally' through a shared cultural inheritance and contemporaneous experience of historical circumstances and transformations. When Mannheim (1952 [1927]) first identified generational cohorts, he stressed that they are not defined solely by age;

indeed, on this criterion alone, generations would have no clear definition, given the seamless continuum of daily births and deaths.

Generations are not discrete entities; the temporal boundaries of a generational cohort are fluid and ill defined, and, unless those at the margins are 'sucked into the vortex of social change' (Mannheim 1952 [1927]: 303), they may be inert, or passively orient themselves to those who are born either before or after them (Pilcher 1994; Edmunds and Turner 2002; McLeod and Thomson 2009: 111). It is also worth noting that, as times change, people continually re-evaluate and re-interpret the meaning of their generational identities and experiences (Brannen 2014). Generational belonging, then, is fluid and reflexively constructed (Newman 2014; Wray and Ali 2014).

Despite this fluidity, much like age cohorts, the core members of a generational cohort will share a common sense of destiny that is forged through their shared passage through historical times: macro political and environmental processes, national events, technological advances, the rise of new cultural practices, shifting values, and so on. Such processes may gradually coalesce to create a discernible shift in the social fabric, and the forging of a distinct generational identity (the 'war' generation, the post-war baby boomers, the millennial generation, and so on). Like all cohorts, generational cohorts are far from homogeneous in their life circumstances and experiences. They are likely to comprise varied sub-units that are defined along the axes of gender, class, ethnicity or community, and these too may develop distinctive identities that emerge in contrast or opposition to others (e.g. the 'mods' and 'rockers' of the 20th century post-war era in the UK). An example of a fluid sampling strategy that draws together members of a generational cohort is given in Box 4.10.

Box 4.10 Sampling Generational Cohorts

- In *Growing Up Girl*, Walkerdine et al. (2001) followed the lives of a varied sample of young women from their early childhood through to the cusp of maturity. The researchers used a fluid sampling strategy, drawing together cases that were being tracked prospectively; a second group, designed to boost the sample, who were interviewed retrospectively; and a third group who were sampled (and the data re-purposed) from an earlier legacy study that enabled an extended view backward in time. The composite sample formed a classic generational cohort in the sense proposed by Mannheim. Of mixed class, ethnic and educational backgrounds, the young women were born within a decade of each other. They were forging their adult identities in a specific cultural milieu and at a time of structural inequalities and historical and social transformations leading up to the millennium. For a similar generational sampling strategy, see Henderson et al. (2007).

Sampling across generational cohorts

Drawing different generational cohorts into a study can serve two purposes. It affords access to the dynamics of intergenerational relationships and, depending on the number of generations included, and how they are spaced, it can open a window onto broader processes of historical change. It is one of the key ways of building historical reach into a sample. Bertaux and Delcroix (2000) suggest that a minimum of three generations is needed to achieve the necessary temporal reach. Two examples of cross-generational sampling are given in Box 4.11. The first example is drawn from a retrospective life history study, but is included here to show the potential for creating historical reach in a time-limited study.

Box 4.11   Sampling across Generational Cohorts

- In their life history study of disability across the life course, Shah and Priestley (2011) sampled three generational cohorts of disabled people – those born in the 1940s, those in the 1960s and those in the 1980s. Through a series of 50 life history interviews, they were able to compare the experiences of each cohort as they grew up under very different regimes of health, educational and social care provision. This was a single-visit study that did not follow people through time. But the researchers were able to build a retrospective understanding of historical developments through this approach, and to chart changing experiences of disability that spanned half a century of change.
- Relatively few QL researchers have sampled across generational cohorts, but a re-study conducted by Hermanowicz (1998, 2009) provides an example of how this might be achieved. In his study of the evolving careers of university academics, he sampled three cohorts that were at different stages of their careers (early career, mid-career and late career), basing his criteria on the year in which they received their doctorate (see commentaries in Hermanowicz 2013, 2016). The 55 academics were drawn from different kinds of higher education institution in the USA. Subsequently, he turned what had been a synchronic (snapshot) study into an extensive longitudinal re-study, involving two waves of interviews separated by a decade. At follow-up, his sample of academics had moved into different stages of their career (mid-career, late career and retirement). At each wave, Hermanowicz was able to explore generational and historical differences across the three cohorts. But the re-study design enabled an exploration of the biographical transformations that had occurred for each participant as they moved from one generational position to another. Over a decade of change, this yielded insights into the institutional and social factors that had shaped their varied career trajectories.

Sampling across family chains

Our final sampling strategy is closely related to cross-generational sampling. It involves sampling intergenerational chains of family members who are held together 'vertically' by their genealogical ties. This gives access to the interconnecting lives, influences, legacies and internal dynamics of those who are linked through the bonds of kinship. Their trajectories are interlocking, with the fortunes of each generation (changes in relationships, employment, housing, health, and so on) impacting on the lives of both older and younger generations in the chain (Elder 1985: 39; Bertaux and Thompson 1993).

Working across a number of intergenerational family chains can reveal the many ways in which intergenerational relationships of care or neglect, closeness or distance, are formed and transformed in varied socio-cultural and historical contexts. It is important to note, in this context, that since individuals simultaneously inhabit a place in their 'vertical' family chain, and in their 'horizontal' generational cohort, these two generational systems are perpetually interacting with and influencing each other. They are pivotal points at which biography and history intersect. These dual influences and how they are synchronised are part and parcel of the terrain within which transformations occur in the social fabric of societies (Hareven 1996; Bengston et al. 2002).

In developing this sampling strategy, an 'anchor' generation is usually identified from whom the family chains can be built. It is worth noting that the individual generational groups who make up a family chain (the grandparent generation, for example) do not form generational *cohorts* in the sense described above. These sub-samples will not necessarily experience the same life events at the same historical time, for each family chain will have a unique historical range, depending on the ages of the generations, the spacing of their births, and how many generations are sampled. Nevertheless, family chains can offer valuable insights into the flow of family lives and influences across the generations, and, depending on the historical reach of the chain, may also illuminate broader patterns of social change (Bertaux and Delcroix 2000: 71).

Much like sampling across generational cohorts, sampling across family chains has been utilised, in the main, by researchers using retrospective life history methods (e.g. Bertaux and Delcroix 2000; Nielsen 2003; Brannen et al. 2004; Brannen 2006). But there is ample scope to utilise this sampling strategy within prospective QL designs. Varied examples of this sampling strategy are given in Box 4.12.

Box 4.12   Sampling across Family Chains

- In a retrospective study of changing patterns of care and reciprocity within four-generation families (Brannen et al. 2004; Brannen 2006), the researchers sampled 12 intergenerational family chains, each comprising between five and eight family members (a total of 71 family members). Grandparents were the 'pivotal' kin keepers, who provided links to both older and younger generations. This gave significant historical reach to the study, from the 1930s depression, to the post-war reconstruction and growth of the welfare state, to the neo-liberal economic policies of the 1980s (Thatcherism). In this study, the family chains were recruited and their experiences explored concurrently.

- Family chains have been used in prospective QL studies in varied ways. In the first two examples below, the different links in the chain were recruited sequentially and followed over different periods of time through successive phases of funding. In the third example, the extensive design of continuous engagement over three decades enabled the researcher to work with a continually shifting configuration of family generations.

- A QL socio-legal study of the transition to post-divorce family life was conducted over an eight-year period. In the first phase of the study, two waves of interviews were conducted with a cohort of 60 parents. In the second phase, two waves of interviews were conducted with a sample of children drawn from these families (Smart and Neale 1999; Smart et al. 2001; Flowerdew and Neale 2003; Neale and Flowerdew 2007). Historical reach is limited in a two-generation design, but the researchers explored changing parent–child relationships in the wake of a major disruption in their biographies, and investigated the impact of a landmark legislative change (The 1989 Children Act) that was set to transform the culture of post-divorce family life.

- In a study of transitions to motherhood (Thomson et al. 2011; also Thomson 2011), baseline interviews were conducted with a cohort of 62 first-time mothers (aged 15–48). At follow-up, the researchers funnelled in on 12 of these mothers, who became the anchors for recruiting 12 intergenerational chains of family members into the study. In a further phase of the study, the researchers reconfigured the sample again, funnelling in on six of these 12 chains, for a further two-wave study. The links in the family chains were too limited to permit wider historical analysis, but the prospective intergenerational design study yielded rich insights into changing configurations of family relationships.

- Heath (1983, 2012), a social historian and linguistic anthropologist, carried out a continuous longitudinal ethnography of three generations of working-class American families, conducted over three decades, from the 1970s to the 2000s. The aim was to discern the evolving nature of language use and the varied influences that shaped different linguistic and learning cultures. The baseline study was a decade-long ethnography of 300 families from black and white communities in the mill towns of the Piedmont Carolinas (Heath 1983). As the mills closed, Heath traced

(Continued)

selected families as they migrated to a variety of city locations. Young children became part of the study as they arrived and the family generations were reconfigured. Heath visited as many families as she could on a yearly basis, but for her later work (2012) she focused on six emblematic families with family chains running over three generations (around 50 participants). In a participatory approach to data generation, the family members regularly recorded their talk and play, kept activity logs and generally created an archive of their everyday lives at home, which Heath combined with yearly joint recording and analysis sessions. In this way, she generated naturalistic, participatory data on the evolving linguistic, educational and relational cultures of the families, which she placed against a backdrop of far-reaching socio-historical, technological and environmental changes in US society.

Closing Reflections

The varied examples of temporal design and sampling showcased in this chapter demonstrate the flexibility and creativity of QL research, and illustrate the transformative effect that time has on how such studies are crafted. Working with the temporal logic of QL research, the discussion has highlighted the need to draw cases, themes and processes into a common analytical framework, and to find a balance between prospective and retrospective lenses, and between intensive and extensive time frames and tempos. The need for clear baseline and closure points that can help to anchor and contain a study has been highlighted here, along with the value of a flexible tempo that mirrors the process under investigation. These flexible design features are part of the rigour needed to mirror and capture real-world processes.

Sampling through time is similarly underpinned by the logic of working across cases, themes and processes, and finding different ways to balance the breadth and depth of investigation. Time and the nature of processes are important aspects of sampling, determining when cases are drawn, how long they are followed and how often they are visited. The discussion has explored the basics of purposive sampling and what this means for the size, breadth and depth of cases in a QL study. The parameters of temporal sampling have been considered, including the process of purposively re-sampling over time to either 'grow' or 'condense' a study, and the adoption of a fluid sampling strategy that avoids the need for an overly rigid stratified sample.

Finally, the nature and utility of longitudinal panels and cohorts have been considered, and the potential to sample across generational cohorts or family chains has been explored. The facility to sample and re-sample though biographical, generational and historical time creates a wealth of flexible designs, enabling different sub-samples and cohorts to be followed over varied horizons of time. The importance of attending to these basic design and sampling issues, and thinking through their temporal dimensions, are highlighted here, for they are the crucial springboards for an engagement in real-world processes, and for generating dynamic real-time data and insights.

Further Reading

QL studies routinely document their design and sampling strategies. Across a scattered literature, particularly detailed and insightful accounts can be found in Coffield et al. (1980); Pollard with Filer (1996: Chapter 10); Calman et al. (2013); and Farrall et al. (2014: Chapter 3). For small-scale, case study designs, see the review in Farr and Nizza (2019); and for large-scale studies, Burton et al. (2009) provides an excellent example. For extensive research running over decades, Jay MacLeod (2009) and Heath (2012) are highly recommended. Shah and Priestley (2011) and Thomson et al. (2011) provide valuable insights on sampling across generational cohorts and family chains.

Burton, L., Purvin, D. and Garrett-Peters, R. (2009) 'Longitudinal ethnography: Uncovering domestic abuse in low income women's lives', in G. Elder and J. Giele (eds) *The Craft of Life Course Research*. New York: Guilford Press, pp. 70–92.

Calman, L., Brunton, L. and Molassiotis, A. (2013) 'Developing longitudinal qualitative designs: Lessons learned and recommendations for health services research', *BMC Medical Research Methodology*, 13 (14): 1–10.

Coffield, F., Robinson, P. and Sarsby, J. (1980) *A Cycle of Deprivation? A Case Study of Four Families*. London: Heinemann.

Farr, J. and Nizza, I. (2019) 'Longitudinal interpretative phenomenological analysis (LIPA): A review of studies and methodological considerations', *Qualitative Research in Psychology*, 16 (2): 199–217.

Farrall, S., Hunter, B., Sharpe, G. and Calverley, A. (2014) *Criminal Careers in Transition*. Oxford: OUP.

Heath, S. B. (2012) *Words at Work and Play: Three Decades in Family and Community Life*. Cambridge: CUP.

MacLeod, J. (2009) *Ain't no Making It: Aspirations and Attainment in a Low Income Neighbourhood*, 3rd edition. Boulder, CO: Westview Press.

Pollard, A. with Filer, A. (1996) *The Social World of Children's Learning: Case Studies of Pupils from Four to Seven*. London: Cassell.

Shah, S. and Priestley, M. (2011) *Disability and Social Change: Private Lives and Public Policy*. Bristol: Policy Press.

Thomson, R., Kehily, M., Hadfield, L. and Sharpe, S. (2011) *Making Modern Mothers*. Bristol: Policy Press.

5

LONGITUDINAL ETHICS: WALKING ALONGSIDE

Key Points

- **Walking alongside**: QL researchers are not simply required to maintain samples, but to 'walk alongside' participants and to sustain relationships with them over substantial periods of time. This creates a distinctive form of longitudinal ethics. The ethical and methodological challenges that arise from this dynamic process are explored in this chapter.
- **Recruiting and maintaining a panel of participants**: Methodologically, there are challenges in recruiting and sustaining a panel of participants over time, and in retracing 'lost' panel members after a lapse of years. Attrition of panel members is less likely where they are aware of the longer-term commitment required and can make an informed choice about participating. Efforts to build a sense of panel membership, such as setting up a Facebook page for the project, along with open communications and regular ethnographic engagement in the field, can greatly help. So too can effective partnerships with practice 'gatekeepers', especially when working with marginalised groups. It is also worth keeping a list of key contacts for participants (e.g. details of family members or key workers), who can help to facilitate contact.
- **Re-tracing participants** after a project has lapsed is a time-consuming process that relies on researchers keeping good contact records for their participants. Researchers have had some notable successes in tracing participants from earlier studies, even after a lapse of some decades. However, the persistence needed for this task may lead researchers to think

(Continued)

of themselves as amateur sleuths. In order to respect people's privacy, no more than two requests are usually made for a follow-up visit.

- **Sustaining relationships**: Attrition rates in QL research tend to be low because of the relational nature of the process. The task of maintaining a sample is recast here as a process of sustaining relationships. This is the key to maintaining a panel of participants.
- **The ethics of walking alongside**: Sustaining longer-term relationships with participants makes us sensitive to ethical issues in ways that are impossible to grasp in single-visit studies. Researchers need to work both proactively, establishing broad ethical protocols to guide a study, and reactively, dealing with unanticipated dilemmas as they arise.
- **Ethical balancing acts**: Ethical literacy in a QL study can be thought of as a series of balancing acts. A balance is needed between the methodological drive to maintain a sample, and the ethical drive to revisit consent over the course of the study; consent is not a one-off task but an ongoing process. A balance is also needed between the drive to establish rapport with participants, and the need to respect their privacy; and between reciprocity, the need to 'give something back' to participants, and the need to keep within the bounds of a professional research relationship. Finally, a balance is needed between confidentiality and the equally compelling drive towards authenticity, empowerment, and shared authority with participants. Strategies for bringing ethical closure to a study and for resolving ethical dilemmas as they arise are also set out here.
- **A moral compass**: Ethical literacy in a QL project is a moral compass that helps to set a project on its course and navigate it on its way.

Introduction

Long-term field research, of whatever type it may be … has made us sensitive to ethical issues and responsibilities in ways impossible to grasp from single-visit ethnography. (Royce and Kemper 2002: xv–xvi)

It's a chance to face my own failures of understanding, and, at the same time learning, getting deeper in, and seeing things are always changing and therefore that I am living, as they are, through the stream of time. (Colson, cited in Royce and Kemper 2002: xv)

The real-time nature of QL research has been likened to the process of **walking alongside** a panel of participants (Neale and Flowerdew 2003). The imagery of walking alongside has particular resonance in the context of longitudinal ethnography, where researchers accompany participants in the everyday settings of their lives (see, for example, Corsaro and Molinari 2000; Royce and Kemper 2002; Burton et al. 2009;

Ferguson et al. 2019). Varied forms of experiential walking interviews are also increasingly used within interview-based studies (Thomson 2012; Bates and Rhys-Taylor 2017; O'Neill and Roberts 2020). This is walking alongside in a more literal sense (see Box 4.2 and Box 6.11 for examples). However, the notion of metaphorically walking alongside as 'fellow travellers' (Gordon and Lahelma 2003) is beautifully captured in the opening quotation from Elizabeth Colson, and it has resonance for QL research more generally. It is a useful metaphor for capturing the dynamic tempo of a QL study, its responsive and relational nature, and the central concern with generating deep insights into how lives unfold (Neale and Flowerdew 2003; Kvale 2007, detailed in Chapter 6). In reflecting the sensibilities at the heart of QL research, 'walking alongside' also provides a welcome alternative to the notion of tracking people, which has instrumental (and possibly predatory) connotations.

This chapter focuses on the intricate process of walking alongside a panel of participants. This is as much an ethical as a methodological process. While local and national ethical protocols will vary in detail, the cardinal principles of research ethics are designed to ensure that participants are fully and transparently informed and participate freely in a study, that their confidentiality is protected, and that their dignity, autonomy and privacy are respected at all times (ESRC 2015). It is often held that QL research amplifies existing ethical considerations rather than raising new ones (Farrall 2006: 11; McLeod and Thomson 2009: 76). Yet, as our opening quotations show, researching lives through time makes us sensitive to ethical issues and responsibilities in ways that are impossible to grasp through single-visit studies (Royce and Kemper 2002: xvi). As Scott and White (2005) observe, many of the complex ethical issues that arise in the day-to-day conduct of a QL study are rooted in the sustained relationships between researcher and participant. This highlights the need to tease out the distinctive nature of longitudinal ethics as an integral part of the research process.

We start by considering methodological strategies for recruiting a panel of participants into a QL study, and maintaining their involvement. The challenge of retracing participants whose whereabouts are unknown after a lapse of time is then explored. As the discussion develops, the ethical terrain within which these processes are embedded begins to emerge, culminating in a detailed consideration of the ethics of sustaining relationships in a QL study, and finding respectful ways to represent participants in study outputs. Taking up the themes introduced in our opening quotations, the discussion illustrates the ways in which ethical thinking and practice are transformed through the longitudinal frame of a QL study.

Recruiting and Maintaining Samples over Time

In common with all forms of longitudinal enquiry, QL research relies on being able to recruit and maintain a panel of participants over time. The aim is to minimise **sample attrition** – the process whereby panel members drop out of a study. A refusal to participate or a failure to engage may occur for a variety of reasons, most of which are beyond the control of the researcher. Panel members may lose touch if their circumstances change, for example, through relocation, changing jobs, names or telephone numbers, breaking ties with family or social networks, or when they become ill or die (Farrall et al. 2016). In some cases, drop-out occurs where participants are undergoing particular difficulties in their lives (Harocopos and Dennis 2003). But it may also occur when people are doing better and opt to move on in their lives and leave the past behind them (Farrall et al. 2016).

In large-scale, longitudinal studies, there are varied views on what constitutes an acceptable attrition rate (ranging from 5 per cent to 30 per cent; Desmond et al. 1995). This has to be balanced against the duration of time over which a study runs. A 75 per cent retention rate over a 22-year period is regarded as a significant achievement (Elliott et al. 2008). In small-scale, relatively short-term QL studies, however, the loss of even a few panel members might represent a substantial proportion of the sample and materially alter the balance of experiences under investigation (Farrall et al. 2016). This may skew the sample towards either positive or negative experiences, creating a bias that can impact on the robustness of the evidence (Desmond et al. 1995; Harocopos and Dennis 2003). One way to compensate for this is to over-sample at the baseline, although this needs to be done with care to avoid overstretching project resources (Calman et al. 2013).

The need for **sample maintenance** creates methodological challenges for all longitudinal researchers, albeit at different scales of enquiry (Birmingham 2018). For QL researchers, particular issues may arise where researchers are working with marginalised groups, or where the aim is to retrace a 'lost' sample after a lapse of some years (Dempster-McClain and Moen 1998; Laub and Sampson 2003; O'Connor and Goodwin 2012; Miller 2015; Farrall et al. 2016). A further complication arises where the units of study are families or organisations, for this requires the sustaining of collective commitment, consent and confidentiality over time (Taylor 2015; for an illustration, see Box 5.6). Strategies used by researchers to overcome such challenges are outlined below.

Recruitment

Strategies for keeping in touch with participants need to be built into initial recruitment plans. Preparations for entering the field involve negotiating access to research settings and developing relationships with 'gatekeepers', as well as with potential participants. Recruitment traditionally occurs through leaflets and letters that describe the research (for an example, see Box 5.1).

Box 5.1 Recruiting in the *Following Young Fathers Further* study (Tarrant)

FYFF
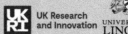

Project Information Sheet

Strand One: Lincoln

UK Research and Innovation

UNIVERSITY OF LINCOLN

Project ID:
Study Title: Following Young Fathers Further   Researcher: Linzi Ladlow

Invitation

We would like you to help us with our research study. Please read this information carefully and feel free to talk to others about the study if you wish. Ask us if there is anything that is not clear or if you want to know more. Take time to decide if you want to take part. It is up to you if you want to do this. If you don't then that's fine, there aren't any consequences.

Why are we doing this research?

We want to try and find out what it is like to be a young dad. We will ask questions about your everyday life and about issues such as housing, family and your future plans.

Why have I been asked to take part?

You have been chosen because we are interested in your views and experiences as a young father.

Do I have to take part?

No. It is entirely up to you. If you do decide to take part:

- You will be asked to sign a consent form,
- You will be given this information sheet to keep.

You are free to stop taking part at any time during the research without giving a reason. If you decide to stop, there will be no consequences.

What will happen if I take part?

- You will be asked to take part in up to 3 interviews over the course of 2 years,
- Each interview will last about 1 hour,
- They can take place in your home or another place that you feel comfortable,
- They will be scheduled at a time and date that suits you,
- In exchange for your time and effort, we will give you a £10 voucher per interview to say thank you.

What will I be asked to do?

The interviews are an opportunity for you to talk about your experiences as a young dad.

Your views will be treated with respect and confidentiality.

The interview will be confidential unless you reveal that you or someone you know is at serious risk of harm. Linzi will talk about it with you so that we can work out together how best to handle it.

You do not have to answer any questions that you don't want to.

(Continued)

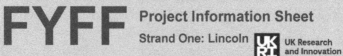

FYFF Project Information Sheet
Strand One: Lincoln

UK Research and Innovation

UNIVERSITY OF LINCOLN

Following Young Fathers Further, Young person info sheet, Strand 1 Lincoln

What happens after the interview?

The interview will be audio-recorded and typed out.

All information that is collected about you during the research will be kept strictly confidential.

Your information will be made anonymous and you will be given a pseudonym (fake name). Only the researchers will know your real name and personal information.

Any publications that are written based on the study will not reveal any of your personal details and your identity will be protected.

Once the study is complete all information will be kept for 12 months by the research team and then archived in the Timescapes Archive (see archiving information sheet).

What if I don't want to do the research anymore?

Just tell the researcher, Linzi, at any time or let John May know and he will speak to her.

What if there is a problem?

Tell us if there is a problem and we will try and sort it out straight away. You can either contact Linzi, or if you remain unhappy after this and want to make a formal complaint you can email ethics@lincoln.ac.uk.

What will happen to the results of the research study?

The results will be shared through things like the publication of a book or the researchers speaking at conferences. We may also share your stories with support workers or on social media. If we do this, we will make sure that you can't be identified. These will be made available to you if you wish to see them.

Who is organising and funding the research?

The research is being organised by the University of Lincoln and is funded by UK Research and Innovation who are a separate organisation.

Who has checked the study?

Before any research goes ahead it has to be checked by a Research Ethics Committee. This is a group of people who make sure that the research is OK to do. This study has been looked at by the University of Lincoln Research Ethics Committee.

Contact for further information

Researcher name: Linzi Ladlow
Telephone: 01522 886 448
Email: LLadlow@lincoln.ac.uk

Study Director: Dr Anna Tarrant
Telephone: 01522 886 170
Email: ATarrant@lincoln.ac.uk

Thank you for taking the time to read this – please ask any questions if you need to.

Figure 5.1 Recruiting in the *Following Young Fathers Further* study

Source: Tarrant 2020

The recruitment process may be initiated via organisations or key workers who can broker the research with participants, or through more direct approaches (in person, by phone or via the web). As shown in Chapter 4, QL researchers may begin a study with a period of ethnographic engagement and/or set up focus groups as a precursor to in-depth interviews. These can be effective ice-breakers, which introduce participants and researchers to each other, and enable participants to learn more about a study before being recruited into a panel.

However, recruitment into a longer-term study is not always straightforward. Recruiting family groups or organisations, for example, may take some time to negotiate with all those involved (Taylor 2015). Whatever the recruitment route, it is best to clarify the proposed time frame for the research, the longer-term commitment required, and the likelihood that researchers will re-contact participants again in the future. Attrition is less likely where participants are aware of the longer-term nature of the study and can make an informed choice (Desmond et al. 1995).

Providing material rewards, particularly for low-income groups, can act as incentives to draw people into a study, at least in the early stages. Gift vouchers or payments in kind may be regarded as a means to professionalise the relationship between researcher and participant (Harocopos and Dennis 2003). In recent studies, QL researchers have offered participants a £20 gift voucher for their time (£50 for a detailed life history interview or for keeping a daily diary), and have provided other forms of in-kind support as appropriate, for example meals, transport costs or taxis to travel to or from an interview (Bytheway 2012; Neale et al. 2015). Such provision needs to be factored into project budgets at the planning stage.

Strategies for maintaining contact

A range of techniques may be employed to keep in touch with a new sample. Posting out letters, project bulletins or other forms of feedback, along with a greeting card, is a common tactic. This provides the foundation for following up informally with a text, phone call and/or house visit. Increasingly, researchers use web-based communications for the same purpose (e.g. text messaging, email and social networking sites such as Facebook, WhatsApp and Instagram). With their speed, ease and relatively low cost, these can be an invaluable means of working flexibly in the field, sustaining links with participants and containing the costs of QL enquiry. Bringing people together in person or virtually (e.g. via a Facebook page, or a members' area of a project website) can foster and help to sustain a sense of group identity and belonging to a study, which can support the maintenance of a panel over time. The use of participatory data-generation tools such as diaries can also provide a rationale for keeping in touch between waves of fieldwork.

Strategies for keeping in touch need to be tailored to the needs and characteristics of the sample. The standard techniques outlined above may not work where panel members are undergoing difficult transitions, or do not have stable homes or regular access to internet or mobile phone technology. In these circumstances, it is worth seeking permission to keep in contact via a participant's social network: family members, friends, key workers, and so on. At the point of recruitment, a contact sheet can be devised to record participants' personal details (including full name and date of birth) and preferred means of contact, along with contact details for selected family members or friends (McNaughton 2008). This can be used to check and update contact details at each research encounter (see Chapter 7 for the safe storage of personal data that conforms to GDPR standards).

When working with transient populations, researchers often leave their contact details with participants, along with details of the next interview, and invite them to get in touch when it suits them (Harocopos and Dennis 2003; Williamson et al. 2014). Setting up a drop-in centre, or tapping into an existing resource that can be accessed by panel members when they wish, is also worth considering. This might offer varied kinds of support or therapies alongside other incentives to keep people's interest or draw them back into a study (Conover et al. 1997). There are few limits on researcher inventiveness. Hagan and McCarthy (1997), for example, sought permission at the outset of their study to take photographs of the homeless men in their sample, and later used the photos to locate the men in their transient communities.

Building ethnographic elements into fieldwork can also be very effective in developing rapport, maintaining communications and sustaining otherwise tentative relationships (Coffield et al. 1980; Hemmerman 2010). This might include informal visits to the home of a participant or family member. Or it may involve attending events or visiting local settings where participants or members of their social networks may be found. In these circumstances, there is a need to be flexible and 'field ready', in particular to be willing to conduct an interview at short notice or on the spot, rather than making a formal arrangement for a later date that may not materialise (Williamson et al. 2014). Being flexible about preferred modes of interview (telephone, internet, face to face, walking interviews) and about data-generation tools and techniques may also help (Warin 2011; Weller 2012). Such strategies may be particularly useful in maintaining contact with transient or marginalised groups, or those with limited access to mobile phone or internet technology (Dempster-McClain and Moen 1998; Calman et al. 2013; Williamson et al. 2014).

Researcher Continuity

Continuity of field researchers is an important means of building rapport and sustaining relationships with panel members over time, as well as preserving the skills and experience needed to build cumulative insights through time (Daniluk 2001; Saldaña 2003: 27; Thomson and Holland 2003; Shirani 2010). The value of such continuity is shown in Box 5.2.

Box 5.2 Continuity of Field Researchers

- In the Timescapes *Men as Fathers* study, participants were asked to reflect on the issue of researcher continuity. Those who had built a continuous and positive relationship with a researcher valued the shared knowledge and understanding that they had forged; there was no need for the participant to start again in explaining the story of their lives. As these participants explain, this continuity creates an important backdrop for building shared understandings through time (Shirani 2010: 53):

  Yeah, it helps, you've got the story. (Barry, *Men as Fathers*, Interview 3)

  It's nice to have that continuity ... its nice as well you can see how I am, and you kind of know from my background, especially with my parents ... that I do cry a lot ... and I think you'd got your head round that really. It's nice 'cause I feel comfortable telling you about my parents, as opposed to somebody else coming along, I'd have to go through all that again. (Joe, *Men as Fathers*, Interview 3)

Over extensive periods of time, continuity of researcher is less likely to be possible. This is not necessarily a drawback for the research team and there may even be some benefits: new researchers may bring fresh perspectives to a project and help to revitalise it (Saldaña 2003: 28; Thomson and Holland 2003; Holland et al. 2006). Handled well, any adverse effects for participants can be mitigated (Shirani 2010). Developing mechanisms for an effective overlap and handover in the field (for example, through carefully planned introductions) will undoubtedly help (Saldaña 2003: 27–8).

Particular care may be needed where incoming researchers do not match the gender or age of their predecessors; participants may be unsettled by such changes (Shirani 2010). To give one example, in the Timescapes *Young Lives and Times* study a participant in her mid-teens was lost to the project when her parents objected to the appointment of a new male researcher, who was perceived as a potential threat to their daughter (on gender matching, see Morrow 2013: 30). In this case, the problem was exacerbated by changes in the research team that led to a break in communication with participants over some months, and the lack of a planned handover in the field.

Working with gatekeepers and practitioners

Building and sustaining relationships with gatekeeper organisations or practice partners can also be a vital means of maintaining a QL sample over time (Pollard with Filer 1996). However, a longer-term commitment from practitioners cannot necessarily be relied on (Saldaña 2003), particularly given the job mobility of professional work-ers and insecure, short-term funding in the public and voluntary sectors. A slow and painstaking process of nurturing working relationships with practitioners over months or years may be undone overnight. This then requires the researcher to switch settings, or start afresh with incoming staff who may have little interest in the research and no knowledge of the participants (Pollard with Filer 1996; Saldaña 2003: 26; Ward and Henderson 2003). The examples in Box 5.3 illustrate some of the pros and cons of working with practitioner gatekeepers.

Box 5.3 Working with Practitioners

- Ward and Henderson (2003) aimed to revisit 30 care leavers after a lapse of six months. However, the social workers who had helped with initial recruitment were too busy to help with re-locating 'lost' members of the sample, and in some cases were hostile to the suggestion. Where they did help, there were administrative delays in releasing new contact details, which held up the fieldwork. It is not clear if the researchers had been able to negotiate longer-term support from these professionals at the outset of their study, a factor that may have made a difference.
- Where sustained professional support can be garnered, it can be of huge benefit. In the *Following Young Fathers* study, a specialist support worker became a practice partner in the project. He played a crucial role in helping to recruit a relatively nomadic and marginalised group of young men into the study, liaised between the researchers and the participants as the research unfolded, and supported the young men in participating (including, on occasion, finding them on the street and bringing them to interview) (Neale et al. 2015). He maintained his role in a subsequent impact initiative, which has translated the findings of the study into professional practice; and his engagement has provided vital continuity and support for an evolving team of researchers (Tarrant 2016).

    In this case, the specialist remit of the practitioner, and his commitment to sustained support for the young men in his care, gave him the time and resources to make these contributions. Clarifying the longer-term nature of the research at the outset and negotiating his role as a practice partner in the project also helped. Attrition rates for panel members recruited through this particular route were very low compared to the rates for a subsequent sample of young men, recruited through a range of different agencies, whose professional support was relatively fleeting and impersonal (Neale et al. 2015; collaborative working in this study is also detailed in Box 5.13 and in Box 12.2).

- As a final example, Ferguson et al. (2019), in a study of social work practice, shadowed two teams of social workers intensively over 18 months to explore their long-term work with clients, and the organisational aspects of their work. The researchers adopted sustained observational rather than participant observational methods for their longitudinal ethnography, and were able to build sensitive, supportive and trusting relationships with the teams and their clients, which were generally valued by all.

Re-tracing Participants over Extensive Time Frames

Where there has been a significant lapse in time since a panel was last convened, or where the aim is to locate a sample from a legacy study carried out by earlier generations of researchers, panel members will need to be re-traced before they can be invited back into a study (Dempster-McClain and Moen 1998; O'Connor and Goodwin 2012; Miller 2015; Farrall et al. 2016). The practical strategies outlined above all come into play here, starting with writing to the last known address, or to named contacts, and following up with telephone calls and visits to field sites, where using personal contacts or simply 'asking around' can be very effective (Dempster-McClain and Moen 1998).

But where these strategies fail, researchers can resort to a range of tracing techniques, based primarily on internet technology and social media (Miller 2015; Farrall et al. 2016). Telephone directories and registers of voters are likely to be available online (in the UK via www.192.com for the electoral roll). Google and Facebook searches can be conducted using people's names, occupations, leisure pursuits or interests; or searches can be made of company registers or the websites of particular organisations or community groups (Miller 2015; Farrall et al. 2016). Revisiting past interview transcripts can be helpful in identifying possible leads.

Where such strategies fail, it is worth checking birth, marriage, death and obituary records (Farrall et al. 2016). Other potential sources are institutional or administrative records, held, for example, by health, welfare, employment or educational agencies, churches or community groups, or the criminal justice system. Researchers report tracing over half of their original samples using these varied routes (Dempster-McClain and Moen 1998; Miller 2015; Farrall et al. 2016). An example of the challenges of retracing a 'lost' sample from a legacy study is given in Box 5.4.

When to give up?

The palette of techniques used to trace a 'lost' QL sample over time, along with the extra time, resources and stamina needed for this task, may seem daunting. Farrall

---

Box 5.4   Tracing Participants in a QL Re-study

- In tracing participants from a project that had been conducted 40 years earlier, O'Connor and Goodwin (2010) had some success with personal contacts in the local community, and the now defunct *Friends Reunited* website. They also advertised their re-study in local print and news media to encourage people to come forward, although this indirect approach was less effective than the standard methods outlined above. Despite the lapse of 40 years, the researchers managed to trace 157 people from a sub-sample of 500 participants, resulting in 97 interviews. In this case, however, only ten of those interviewed were women, despite the efforts of the researchers to trace name changes through marriage registers. Tracing tools, then, can introduce further biases in a sample, but they are clearly effective in enabling researchers to extend the historical and biographical reach of an earlier study.

---

et al. (2016), for example, spent well over two years tracing and re-contacting a sample of 199 probationers before exhausting all possible leads. The process yielded a 50 per cent success rate. A pursuit such as this requires not only earmarked budgets but also skilled, flexible and dedicated researchers who are well versed in longitudinal enquiry (Calman et al. 2013; Williamson et al. 2014; Farrall et al. 2016). Indeed, the process of maintaining or resurrecting a QL sample can require the patience, ingenuity and tenacity associated with private detection.

It can also involve an assertiveness that sometimes borders on aggression (Scott and White 2005). Some research teams offer a 'finder's fee' to practitioners and friends as an incentive to help, or resort to tracing agencies such as Equifax (Dempster-McClain and Moen 1998; Molloy et al. 2002), although, as Molloy and colleagues point out, such methods may breach confidentiality. It has even been known for contract researchers to be offered bonuses if they successfully retrace a sample (Bootsmiller et al. 1998). Perhaps not surprisingly, researchers who find themselves engaged in these ways often describe themselves as amateur sleuths (Dempster-McClain and Moen 1998; Warin 2010: 24; Miller 2015; Sharpe 2017). Regardless of how this practice is managed, it conjures up images of the dubious practice of 'stalking', or coercion, implying that the researcher has turned predator. Understandably, researchers report feeling ambivalent about this, and, for the same reason, may eschew the very notion of 'tracking' participants, with its connotations of a power imbalance between the 'tracker' and the 'prey' (Williamson et al. 2014; Miller 2015).

The language of 'revisiting' or 'walking alongside' is less contentious here. But these ethical concerns reinforce the principle that there have to be limits on how far researchers will pursue people, and the zeal with which they do so. In other words, the methodological drive to maintain or revitalise a sample has to be tempered with the ethical drive to respect people's privacy (an issue elaborated on further below). For this reason, QL researchers commonly adhere to a standard rule of thumb: no more than two approaches are usually made to request a follow-up interview. At the second approach, the researcher clarifies that no further contact will be attempted, but invites participants to get in touch if they would like to re-join a study at a later date (Farrall et al. 2016).

Sustaining Relationships

Whatever the ambivalences around sample maintenance and tracing processes, and the significant commitment of time and resources that they take, it is re-assuring to know that most QL researchers report relatively low rates of attrition, even when working with marginalised groups such as drug users (Desmond et al. 1995). Sample maintenance is generally less of a problem in QL enquiry than in large-scale longitudinal research. This can be explained by the intrinsic nature of the research encounter. It is a sustained interpersonal process that seeks to understand the inner logic of people's lives and which respects their world views. This means attending to the finer details of the research encounter, for example giving participants a choice over interview settings and who is present; cultivating an empathetic, respectful and supportive mode of interaction; and, as shown above, striving for continuity in the fieldworker wherever possible (or an effective overlap and handover where not).

Overall, in QL research the task of maintaining samples is transformed into one of **sustaining relationships** (Neale 2013). Upholding the principles of compassion and respect for research participants may require researchers to recognise them as people first and participants second (Williamson et al. 2014: 82). In applying the ethics of care and respect in their study, Williamson and colleagues maintained an interest in the lives of the homeless women whom they encountered, and provided ongoing forms of emotional support for them (for example, meeting and chatting in a coffee bar) that stretched beyond the time when the women dropped out of the research (for the delicate ethics of this, see below). In the event, the researchers were able to retain over 60 per cent of their sample over the course of a two-year study.

Feedback from participants in QL studies reinforces the fundamental value of sustaining relationships as the key to maintaining a sample. Financial gain is much less often reported as an effective incentive. Farrall et al. (2016) found that when, in desperation, they offered people an increased financial bonus to re-enter their study, this was markedly ineffective. Similarly, the homeless women interviewed by Williamson et al. (2014) reported that their initial financial motivation for taking part quickly gave way to more altruistic feelings, and the sense that they were privileged to be part of the panel (a sentiment that is often expressed among long-term research participants; see, for example, Shirani 2010). A frequently reported motive for a continued engagement is the wish 'to give something back', and to help others in similar circumstances.

Perhaps most significantly, the women interviewed by Williamson et al. (2014) reported an intrinsic satisfaction in being able to reflect on their evolving lives in conversation with the researchers. Indeed, the commitment that participants develop as QL panel members, alongside the sense of privilege and belonging that this can engender, can create challenges in bringing closure to the process (an issue considered below). In sum, whatever strategies are adopted to maintain a QL panel, the relational dimensions of the process are likely to play a crucial role.

The Ethics of Walking Alongside

As the discussion above shows, ethical considerations are woven into the process of walking alongside a panel of participants (Neale 2013). The sustained, interactive nature of the research process opens up new dilemmas, and brings to the fore the transformative potential of well-established ethical principles. For participants, this applies to issues of consent as a process and the changing dynamics of research relationships. It also entails treading a careful path between reciprocity and professional boundary maintenance, and finding new ways to balance confidentiality, privacy, authenticity, protection and empowerment as these evolve through time. Issues of consent, confidentiality and privacy all involve an ethical balancing act that becomes more pronounced as a study progresses (Etherington 2007). There is, of course, no magic formula for how this balancing operates, no prescriptive approach that works for all; finding a balance depends on the field settings, how events unfold, the characteristics of the participants, and the temporal frame for a study.

Researching through time also opens up new ways to think about the relationship between **proactive and reactive ethical strategies** (Neale 2013). Proactive strategies are procedural or advisory, constituted through ethical frameworks and principles laid down by funding bodies and ethics committees, and through bodies of shared knowledge that encourage good practice. Reactive strategies are situated or emergent ethical practices that are context-specific and based on a sensitive appraisal of local circumstances and situated knowledge (Edwards and Mauthner 2002: 27; Guillemin and Gillam 2004; Warin 2011). This approach typically calls for reflexivity and negotiation in resolving ethical questions rather than relying on the application of general rules.

Proactive and reactive strategies are broadly complementary, of course, and both are needed. Yet situated ethics have particular resonance for longitudinal enquiry, given the greater likelihood that unanticipated events, changing circumstances and fresh dilemmas will emerge as a study unfolds. Researchers are likely to find themselves navigating through a changing ethical landscape. The needs and claims of individual panel members or different sub-samples will evolve over time and require flexible responses. Over time, too, a wider constituency of individuals and organisations (from researchers, institutions and data re-users, to family members and practitioners) may become implicated in the process. This requires new thinking about their varied needs and claims, albeit these may not be of equal weight in ethical decision making.

The prime 'stakeholders' in the research process, and the main focus of attention here, are the research participants themselves. In what follows, consideration is given to issues of informed consent, confidentiality, reciprocity, professional boundaries, privacy, authenticity, shared authority, the extent of participation and the ethical closure of a project. The discussion reveals the complex ways in which these varied processes are intertwined in ethical decision making. But, before turning to these themes, it is worth noting that researchers themselves are also key 'stakeholders' in a project, operating within and across research teams (Mauthner 2012). Some of the issues that arise for researchers are outlined in Box 5.5 (see also Chapter 8, where the sharing of legacy data is informed by an ethic of mutual respect between researchers).

Box 5.5 The Ethics of Team Research

- It is generally recognised that the contribution of researchers in a QL study, their professional standing, labour and commitment to a project over time should be all acknowledged, fostered, protected and rewarded. Relationships within QL research teams merit careful attention as part of a proactive strategy for the conduct of a study, for these may operate over considerable periods of time, with implications for the career trajectories and academic livelihoods of contract and junior researchers. Building in guidelines for publishing opportunities and team authorship, for example, and making provision for promotions at the costings stage of a project, can help to support and sustain an effective team. Arriving at agreements for full access to a dataset as a shared resource is also vitally important (Saldaña 2003). There is undoubted merit in facilitating the continuity of skilled and experienced researchers, including those who are engaged in field enquiry and performing the vital and sometimes emotionally challenging task of building and maintaining a panel of participants. QL researchers generally recognise the need to foster a collegial ethic of care, respect and support across team members (Foster 2002: 272; Saldaña 2003: 27–8; Williamson et al. 2014), and for 'senior' researchers (in terms of age as well as experience) to be prepared to 'pass the mantle' to more 'junior' team members over time (Foster 2002; Kemper and Royce 2002).

Process Consent

Informed consent in a QL study is an ongoing process rather than a one-off event (Saldaña 2003: 24; Thomson and Holland 2003). Whether consent is sought in writing or is recorded verbally at the outset, this needs to be revisited over the course of a study, ideally at times when trust has developed. This may be done at each research encounter or through exploratory and flexible conversations that are held with participants at key intervals (what Birch and Miller (2002) refer to as 'ethical talk' or 'moral conversations'). This enables participants to reflect on their consent status with increased understanding of the research and their part in it as a study progresses. Continuity of field researchers can help to facilitate this process.

Process consent undoubtedly creates some challenges. First, consent may be differently 'informed' when the future direction of a project may be flexible and subject to change. As will be shown in Chapter 7, QL researchers tend to address this issue by adopting **enduring models of consent**, which allow for the possibility that research data may be used in new and unknown research contexts. Second, a continual revisiting of consent status may become a burden for participants, suggesting the need for sensitivity in both when and how the issue of consent is subsequently raised. McLeod and Thomson (2009: 74) observe, too, that while participants may agree to each interview, they are unlikely to have a sense of the cumulative power of the data they are providing, and what it may reveal about them over time. On the other hand, time can be a great resource in consent processes. This means that when participants opt out of a wave of fieldwork, they have the option to opt back in at a later date. This flexibility in the field seems to take the pressure off participants when the timing of fieldwork may not mesh well with changing circumstances in their lives (Miller and Bell 2002).

As shown earlier, there is an evident tension between the methodological drive to maintain a sample and the ethical drive to ensure that people can make an informed choice about their ongoing involvement. It is important that the relationship between researcher and participant does not become exploitative over time, as trust and familiarity grow, and that any subtle coercion to continue is avoided (Holland et al. 2006: 28). But care is also needed where the reverse scenario arises: if researchers decide to 'drop' selected participants over time (as part of the 'funnel' approach to re-sampling, outlined in Chapter 4), they run the risk of excluding those who may wish to continue. Taking this step on protective or paternalistic grounds is a last resort that requires fine judgement on the part of the researcher. Ward and Henderson (2003), for example, considered screening out selected young drug users from their study, on the grounds that they might not be ready for an open discussion or that the process might lead them back to their drug habit. Yet the impact on vulnerable participants of a longer-term engagement in a study cannot be known in advance; it is just as likely to have a positive influence on participants' lives (Birch and Miller 2002; Miller and Bell 2002; Harocopos and Dennis 2003).

Additional concerns about whether individuals are consenting freely or being coerced into or out of participation may arise where 'gatekeepers' such as family members or practitioners are involved in recruitment, or where a study is seeking to work with family or organisational groups (Miller and Bell 2002; Warin 2010: 54–5; 2011). Concerns also arise in relation to 'thank you' gifts for participants, and whether these are seen as recompense and reward, or, more dubiously, as incentives or payments that may have a coercive effect (Morrow 2009). As shown above, such gifts can be very helpful in drawing people into a study, and they can also be seen as important elements in the reciprocal offer (see below). Through repeated interviews, participants may well come to anticipate such a reward, which brings a contractual element to the process. Nevertheless, given the longer-term commitment entailed in QL research, and the time required for in-depth interviews, it is equally important to avoid economic exploitation. Some reward or recompense is fully justified in these circumstances, particularly for low-income participants. Being transparent at the outset about the giving of such rewards and their purpose can help to avoid the potential for coercion.

Deciding *how* consent is to be informed also requires consideration. Overall, it is good practice to be transparent from the outset about the objectives of a project, including the longer-term commitment needed from panel members; the steps taken to protect confidentiality; the anticipated outcomes or impact; and plans for archiving and re-using data (see Figure 5.1 and Chapters 7 and 8). This includes the possibility that participants may be contacted after a lapse of time by existing or new research teams seeking to conduct a QL re-study. Finally, in some research settings it may be necessary to allay concerns about ulterior motives, and provide ongoing clarification and re-assurances about the purposes of a study. In particular (and regardless of the principle of reciprocity, discussed below), it may be necessary to clarify how social research differs in its aims and conduct from 'intervention' or 'support', and its limited capacity to effect any desired changes for individuals and the communities to which they belong (best framed as 'hoped for' rather than 'anticipated' outcomes; Morrow 2013; Wiles 2013).

Confidentiality

It is a cardinal principle of social research that researchers should not divulge any identifiable information about participants to third parties (Moore 2012; Wiles 2013; see also Chapter 7). In a UK and European context, this **confidentiality** principle is embodied in the EU General Data Protection Regulation (GDPR) and the UK Data Protection Act 2018, and it is likely to form a core component of international ethics protocols. The commitment to confidentiality is usually built into the process of securing informed consent, thereby setting the standard for how a project will unfold (see Figure 5.1). Reassurances of confidentiality at this stage can perform a vital function in enabling participants to speak freely, without fear that their 'warts and all' accounts, views and experiences will be divulged to others outside the research domain. This in turn can enhance the meaning and authenticity of participants' accounts. As will be shown below, however, this principle needs to be balanced against the need for authenticity and shared authority with participants.

Maintaining confidentiality can be a challenge when the risk of disclosure is magnified over time. The cumulative generation of rich, biographical data creates a unique, holistic 'fingerprint' for a participant, which is increasingly revealing of identities, localities and life circumstances (Hughes 2011). We return to this issue below. But it is worth noting here that even the simple process of re-contacting participants for a revisit needs to be handled with care (Laub and Sampson 2003; Miller 2015). Letters, Facebook or telephone messages may inadvertently reveal to third parties details of past or recent lives that participants may not have disclosed themselves, or may no longer wish to 'own' or be reminded of. In these circumstances, it is best to allude to the research rather than discuss its nature (Harocopos and Dennis 2003; Scott and White 2005).

Issues of confidentiality are also magnified in studies involving groups such as families, organisations and small-scale communities. This is particularly the case where group interviews are held, or participants otherwise know each other. There is an increased danger that, over time, information will leak across participants in the study, or find its way into the public realm (Reiss 2005; Harden et al. 2010; MacLean and Harden 2012; Hall 2014). Issues of **internal confidentiality** are endemic to all group-based studies (Macmillan et al. 2011; Taylor 2015). But, for QL research, they also arise where a group identity is forged across a panel of participants, for example through shared web spaces or via focus groups or other events which bring the panel members together. These are common strategies to keep samples engaged (see above), but they require the panel to commit to internal confidentiality. A useful strategy is to issue ethical guidelines to discourage disclosures about fellow participants, which panel members can pledge to uphold (Patrick 2012). Researchers also need to commit to this principle, to ensure that information gleaned from a panel member is not passed on to other panel members or to family members or practitioners (Scott and White 2005; Bytheway and Bornat 2012a).

The example in Box 5.6, drawn from a perceptive account of the *Real Times* study (Taylor 2015), illustrates the complex ways in which issues of informed consent, confidentiality and group relationships can become entwined as a study progresses.

Box 5.6 Internal Confidentiality in Group-based Studies

- The *Real Times* study tracked a sample of 15 voluntary sector organisations through five waves of interviews, conducted over a four-year period (2010–13). The cases in the study ranged from high-profile organisations to small community-based projects, and included a range of stakeholders within each organisation. A robust confidentiality framework guided the consent process for the study. This was vitally important, particularly for the least powerful interviewees, who would have risked their reputations and possibly their jobs if their views had been divulged. Attending to internal confidentiality was also crucial because the design of the project meant that the identities of participant organisations could not be kept confidential from each other. The research team aimed to foster strong, trusting relationships to ensure that case study data would not be shared across potentially competing organisations or leaked into the public domain. Even so, confidentiality was compromised from the outset. Some organisations, on the basis that they had nothing to hide and did not wish to imply there was some 'cover up', wished to use the research to publicise and promote their work, and did so by setting up links on their project website to the study website.

- The study generated rich, sensitive information about the organisations, some of which revealed instances of malpractice, power imbalances and struggles, staff misconduct, autocratic management and local political positioning. The team had been able to capture this detail precisely because of the reassurances of confidentiality that had been given at the outset. Over time, they also charted some substantial organisational upheavals through times of austerity, including restructuring, rebranding, redundancies and coups. As the study progressed, organisational leaders, who had initially sought to publicise their involvement in the research, were subsequently keen to have their identities obscured.
- The ethical framework agreed with participants early in the process, and the early placing of data in the public domain, served to shape subsequent practices and decision making. There was little scope to negotiate fresh ethical approaches down the line. In the end, however, some of these difficulties were resolved through the simple passage of time. By the close of the study, many of the organisations had changed significantly from their original configuration, with new personnel and branding, and altered trajectories. The data, even over a short space of time, had become historical: both less sensitive and less recognisable through these transformations (Taylor 2015). (For discussion on the management and representation of data in this study, see Box 7.1)

Reciprocal Relationships and Professional Boundaries

As shown above, maintaining a panel of participants over time is an important methodological issue for QL researchers. Ethically, however, the concern becomes

147

one of sustaining and nurturing relationships of trust and respect (Pollard 2007). The process of walking alongside people, the sense of accompanying them on their life journey, may touch the lives of both participants and researchers. Longitudinal ethnographers, for example, describe this process as a deep immersion, whereby they are 'engaging ... with part of who they are' (O'Reilly 2012: 521; see also Royce 2002; 2005; and Burton et al. 2009). Researching in real-time, through a sustained engagement in the field, requires a particular kind of ethical sensitivity that acknowledges the growing personal bonds between researcher and participant, forged through their continuing interactions (Warin 2011).

In some fields of enquiry (policy-related research, for example), the role of the researcher may change over time, from observer, to active collaborator, to advocate, with implications for researcher 'intervention' or 'interference' in interpersonal dynamics or in local systems of power and influence (Royce and Kemper 2002; Saldaña 2003: 29; Scott and White 2005). This creates a new and potent terrain for the ethical conduct of a study. Care is needed in managing these shifting relationships over the course of a study and tailoring ethical practices accordingly (Thomson 2007; Mauthner and Parry 2013). The task involves building trust, mutual respect and reciprocity in ways that do not lead to over-dependence or involvement, intrusion or neglect, to the detriment of either researcher or participant (Pollard with Filer 1996; Birch and Miller 2002; Molloy and Woodfield with Bacon 2002; Scott and White 2005; Morrow 2009).

Sustaining relationships in these ways involves a balance between two ethical principles. The first is **reciprocity**, the notion of an ongoing 'gift' relationship, which is central to qualitative enquiry (Gordon and Lahelma 2003). The second involves **professional boundary maintenance** over time, along with a clear focus on the professional nature of the researcher role (Scott and White 2005; Hemmerman, 2010; Hammersley and Traianou 2012). Projects working with different field methods and with differently constituted samples are likely to balance these principles in varied ways; as indicated above, there is no prescriptive approach that works in all research contexts.

Giving and receiving support

The question of how much and what kind of support may be legitimately and appropriately provided – and received – as part of an ongoing, reciprocal relationship needs to be worked out in relation to local circumstances, contexts and cultures, as well as the overall time frame for a study (Morrow 2013). An example drawn from an extensive longitudinal ethnography is given in Box 5.7.

Box 5.7   Reciprocity over Extended Time Frames

- In his longitudinal ethnography of a Mexican community running over half a century, Foster (2002) was aware that much of his academic reputation, including the royalties from his books, had been built on the sustained research contributions of the local people. While his research benefited the villagers in non-material ways, making them feel listened to, special and valued, he explains that sustained material benefits, given indirectly rather than through direct payments, had also become an essential part of the reciprocal offer:

  > I contribute substantially to such things as public lighting and school funds and my name routinely is found on the list of contributors to any village function. … Each year I leave with the village priest a substantial sum of money to be distributed at his discretion among the village needy. Altogether my continuing contributions have far exceeded any monetary profit to me from publications. … I believe no one is worse off for our presence, and I know that some are better off. A few, without our monetary intervention in medical crises, would almost certainly have died. (Foster 2002: 273)

  The Mexican families with whom Foster stayed in the village were regularly made welcome as guests to Foster's home in the USA. However, local competition for scarce resources also engendered competition for his favours. Some jealousies were directed at these 'favoured' families, which may have affected their close-knit village ties (Foster 2002: 273–4). Foster's account reveals how, over many years, a professional researcher role may evolve gradually and naturally into one of enduring friendship. As shown in Chapter 1, these are common experiences among longitudinal ethnographers, where a strong sense of identity and belonging to a community and its people can develop over the years (Royce 2002). (See also Chapter 1, where the design of Foster's longitudinal ethnography is outlined.)

Maintaining a professional boundary

Whatever the local context, the longer the time frame for a QL study, the greater the likelihood that participants will need or request some form of support, or seek to reciprocate themselves. This suggests the need for researchers to think through the nature of their interpersonal relationships with participants, and to consider how ties of friendship or intimacy (that may involve mutual disclosures and mutual forms of support) sit within a professional research relationship (for a fascinating and provocative account of how the lines between research and intimacy may become blurred, see Wolcott 2002 and the commentary by Strobel 2005).

Attending to these issues can be helped where proactive strategies have been developed to clarify the nature of researcher–participant relationships. Protocols can be developed for how researchers might respond to any need that may arise for participant protection or support (for example, by referring participants to support agencies where needed), yet without risking over-involvement or interference (Scott and White 2005). Boxes 5.8 and 5.9 illustrate some of the issues that may arise in balancing reciprocity with the maintenance of professional boundaries.

Box 5.8 Balancing Reciprocity and Professional Relationships

- In the *Following Young Fathers* study, the researchers were asked by a key worker to provide a character reference for a participant who was facing a custodial sentence. This raised a number of dilemmas for the team: what did the researchers know, but also not know about the young man beyond the confines of the research relationship? What did they owe to the young man and his key worker? Could they breach confidentiality? And could they vouch for the young man's moral conduct in the community, and in a legal context? Keeping within the bounds of the research relationship, the team lacked the knowledge to provide a character reference. However, they provided a general reference for the young man that outlined the valuable and sustained contribution that he had made to the research (Neale et al. 2015).

- On another occasion, the *Following Young Fathers* team offered some educational advice to a young participant whose interviews revealed a persistent and unfulfilled aspiration to go to university. The methodological drawbacks of influencing the life path of the young man were outweighed by the ethics of 'giving something back'.

- Similarly, in *The Lived Experience of Welfare Reform*, Patrick (2013) gave some rudimentary welfare advice to her participants. This was seen as a central part of the reciprocal offer: it would have felt unethical to refrain from providing advice that would materially benefit the participants, although, in the process, she was influencing their welfare journeys.

- On another occasion in this study, an impoverished participant presented Patrick with a gift for her new baby. With no time to consider a response, Patrick graciously accepted the gift: to decline would have been disrespectful and may have damaged the relationship. At a subsequent wave of interviews, however, she clarified with panel members her limited capacity to provide support or to maintain contact beyond the end of her project. She also clarified the limits of her ability to influence welfare policy as an outcome of the project – something that had initially motivated some of the participants to take part in the study (Patrick 2013).

As these examples show, the balancing act between reciprocity and professional boundary maintenance requires some finesse. Finding a balance may become a challenge in particular field settings, Examples are provided in Box 5.9.

Box 5.9 Emotional Involvement and Boundary Maintenance

- The Timescapes *Intergenerational Exchange* study involved repeated interviews with grandparents on a low-income housing estate. In such settings, trust can be fragile and volatile, subject to change at short notice. There is a need to be continuously flexible and 'field ready' to gain access, while sample maintenance becomes a continuous process of frequent, informal visits that run the risk of intrusion. Responding to need in such settings may lead to over-familiarity and over-involvement in the provision of support. Upon arriving for an interview, it was not uncommon for the researcher to help with the washing up or go to the corner shop to buy milk. The usual boundaries of relationship maintenance were severely challenged in this study. Hemmerman was also affected by the precarious lives of her participants and the traumatic events that they shared with her, leading to emotional risks for the researcher.
- Similar experiences were reported by Calman et al. (2013) in their study of terminally ill cancer patients, many of whom died during the research. Walking alongside participants in such circumstances can be very stressful: 'to follow a life will be likely to involve encounters with sickness as well as health, privation as well as prosperity, and sorrow as well as happiness' (Crow, in Neale 2019: ix–x).

The accounts showcased in Box 5.9 suggest the need for ongoing support for researchers who are walking alongside those leading precarious lives, for example through a buddy system (Williamson et al. 2014: 86). More broadly, these accounts raise questions about the nature and extent of researcher involvement in the daily lives of participants (Hemmerman 2010), and they suggest the need to think through the boundaries of emotional engagement and direct support before entering the field. Whatever strategies and solutions are adopted, steering a path through over-dependence, intrusion, neglect and emotional entanglement will be eased where the boundaries of reciprocity and professional research relationships are considered at the outset of a study.

Privacy

The **privacy** principle is closely allied to the need for confidentiality. It requires researchers to consider whether they are intruding into the lives of participants, and to what extent panel members are being asked to disclose sensitive information about their lives that they may find uncomfortable. In both interview and ethnographic settings, the usual protocols of qualitative research enable participants to say as much or as little as they choose. Even so, privacy can quickly unravel over successive waves of a QL study, where building relationships of trust invites greater intimacy (Coffield et al. 1980: 11; Thomson and Holland 2003; Weller 2012; Hall 2014). For example, in their intensive case study research with low-income families, Coffield and colleagues highlight the drawbacks of building friendships with participants: 'Our problem was ... they forgot we were doing research ... They were too open, too honest, too intimate for us to believe that they were consciously providing material for our project rather than discussing problems as friends' (1980: viii).

A related problem may arise on the occasions where researchers witness tense interactions between family members or among staff in organisations, or otherwise become aware of problems or challenges in the lives of their participants that may not have been disclosed directly (Hall 2014; Sharpe 2017). What comes to the surface through a QL study is not just the 'life as told' but also the 'life as lived', and how and why it is unfolding in particular ways. This requires some congruence between how a life is narrated to the researcher, and how it is unfolding. It is an inherently deeper, more reflexive and open process, which requires a greater level of commitment, integrity and willingness to disclose on the part of the participant. While some participants may welcome this and find it enriching, others may avoid it or find themselves unable to engage in this way, particularly at a difficult time in their life, or when they are not (yet) ready to share sensitive issues with a researcher (McLeod 2003: 206).

In finding a balance between privacy and disclosure, time can be an important resource, enabling the researcher to gauge the tenor of the moment and to be flexible about when to touch on sensitive issues. Such issues can then be opened up in retrospect, once the dust has settled and relations of trust have developed further (Macmillan et al. 2011). In the *Following Young Fathers* study, for example, issues relating to illiteracy, anger management, domestic violence, drug use and criminal activities were disclosed over substantial periods of time, often when participants felt they could reflect on them retrospectively, as experiences that they were putting behind them (Neale et al. 2015; see also Burton et al. 2009).

Representing Data: Confidentiality, Authenticity and Shared Authority

Finding ways to represent people's lives in the production and display of research data is an ethical issue in all social research (and a theme detailed further in Chapters 7 and 11). The representational process comes into play in varied contexts:

in the production of field notes and case histories or studies; academic presentations; publications targeted at different audiences; and the preparation and display of data in varied formats: on websites, in archives, in public exhibitions and in media reporting. All researchers feel responsible for participants, but inevitably these feelings strengthen in long-standing relationships, particularly where they run on and are 'live' during the process of analysis and dissemination. The pressure can create mixed effects – a great commitment to handling people's accounts with the utmost care, combined with a great sense of responsibility to get their voices heard so that their stories count.

Safeguarding confidentiality is usually addressed through the task of anonymising data in ways that obscure and protect participant identities (detailed in Chapter 7, Step 5). Yet, whatever the axiomatic nature of confidentiality and privacy as ethical principles, these need to be balanced against the equally compelling drive towards **authenticity** and **empowerment**: that is, towards preserving the integrity of participants' accounts and enabling a more open identification and acknowledgement of their contributions. Regardless of the potential liberation that comes from speaking in confidence, participants may wish to give candid accounts in their own right, and to be acknowledged for doing so (Corden and Sainsbury 2007; Grinyer 2009). This was the case, for example, for a participant in the *Family Fragments* study (Smart and Neale 1999) who opted to be represented in her own right. When she was given a copy of the resulting book, she greatly valued seeing her name in print.

Increasingly, the imperative to anonymise data and obscure identities sits uneasily with the view that the process may strip a dataset of its integrity, diminish its intellectual meaning and scientific value, and do a disservice to participants who are airbrushed out of the historical record (Moore 2012). One way of addressing the latter concern is to ensure that a full, unabridged dataset, complete with participant contact details, is securely preserved in a 'dark' domain of the archive for eventual historical use (see Chapter 7, Step 6).

Treading a delicate path between confidentiality, authenticity and empowerment is a challenging process, one that is complicated further where relationships between researcher and participants are built on trust and enduring commitments that are forged through time. The process raises questions about the status of research data: who 'owns' the data, which 'voices' count, and, in a context where researcher and participant interpretations may shift over time, which versions of events carry authenticity? We return to these broader issues in Chapters 7 and 8. But it is worth noting here that there are no easy answers to these questions and that tensions may exist between opting for the authenticity of gritty realism (showing it like it is) and altering or 'massaging' data in ways that sanitise it and give it a more positive gloss for the benefit or protection of participants (Alldred 1998; Royce and Kemper 2002; Wiles et al. 2008).

One solution to these quagmires, aimed at reducing the disjunctions that may occur between researcher representations of a life and participant perceptions, is to consult with participants about how they wish to be represented in research outputs (Koro-Ljungberg and Bussing 2013; Wiles 2013). There is undoubted merit in preserving some degree of 'fit' between the accounts given by participants and the accounts produced by researchers – part of what oral historians call the principle of **shared authority** (Bornat 2012). Imagining the participants as part of the audience for a published work, and reading it 'through their eyes', may help to ensure that research evidence is presented sensitively and with regard to participants' feelings (Ellis 1995). Working with this principle also enhances the integrity and veracity of a study (see Chapter 12). Examples of what may go wrong are provided in Box 5.10.

Box 5.10   Shared Authority?

- In his longitudinal study of science teaching in a high school, Reiss (2005) gives a candid account of what might happen when participants are not adequately consulted about how they wish to be represented in a study, and how the findings should be conveyed to them. Reiss underestimated how the identities of the teachers might unravel over the course of the study, and how easily the identities that he had assigned could be decoded by other staff in the school. This was of great concern to the teachers, who were also upset at what they saw as an overly critical stance in the way that Reiss reported his findings. He notes that a more respectful, consultative and collaborative approach at the close of fieldwork, perhaps through a preliminary feedback or dissemination event prior to the publication of findings, could have averted these problems.

- Similar experiences are not uncommon among longitudinal researchers (see the accounts in Ellis 1995; Scheper-Hughes 2000; Wolcott 2002; and Hermanowicz 2016). In their ethnographic studies of close-knit rural communities, Ellis (1995) and Scheper-Hughes (2000) give striking accounts of the consequences of not consulting adequately with participants or remaining in tune with local sensibilities. In both cases, the villagers had shared their lives and disclosed sensitive information on the basis of trust and growing friendship with the researchers over extended periods of time. But the villagers subsequently felt used and betrayed by the researchers. When Scheper-Hughes returned to the USA and published her findings, they were feted by her fellow academics but condemned by Irish commentators and local community members. As Scheper-Hughes acknowledges, there was little sense of any shared authority in the way that the study had been conducted or the findings written up. Instead, it was marked by a lack of transparency about the aims and focus of the study, and the times when people were or were not under scrutiny. Moreover, the findings gave a negative portrayal of the villagers, their interpersonal and intimate relationships and their local culture. The researcher had failed to write sensitively about the positive aspects of life in this community and had not consulted participants over identities that were easily decoded by the villagers. When Scheper-Hughes revisited the community after an absence of 25 years, she was shunned by the villagers and eventually expelled by them.

The Extent of Participant Engagement

The extended time frames for QL research open up the potential for participants to play a role in a project that goes beyond their conventional 'informant' role. For example, panel members may be invited to generate data themselves, to read and verify interview transcripts or case materials, and to offer reflections on their past accounts from the standpoint of the present day. In line with the double hermeneutic, they may also be invited to attend feedback forums or research summits, or otherwise act as consultants in the representation or interpretation of data about their lives, and to contribute to dissemination and impact activities.

In some cases, selected participants may opt to become ambassadors for the project and its findings, as part of which their identification in the research process may become explicit, requiring their confidentiality to be waived or re-negotiated. Overall, playing a more active role in a project can have a transformative effect on the confidentiality and privacy afforded to participants. In these ways, QL research shares some affinities with participatory and action modes of research, which are founded on the principles of empowerment, shared authority and the co-production of knowledge (Wiles 2012; Bradbury-Huang 2015; see Chapter 12 for a discussion of these principles in longitudinal impact research).

These extended forms of **participant engagement** would seem to be commendable. As shown earlier, too little consultation runs the risk of breaching trust between participants and researchers, with potentially damaging consequences for all. But, on the other hand, too much consultation may also be problematic. The extended forms of participation outlined above raise questions about how far they should be taken, for which groups of participants and in what specific contexts; there may be costs involved and unintended consequences, as the examples in Boxes 5.11 and 5.12 illustrate.

Box 5.11 Participant-generated Data: Empowering or Exposing?

- In the final stages of the *Growing Up Girl* study, Walkerdine et al. (2001) invited participants to use video diaries to generate data about their everyday lives. The rationale was that this would be less invasive and

(Continued)

more empowering for the young women, enabling them to 'show' their lives rather than necessarily speak about them. However, some of the disadvantaged young women were uncomfortable with this exercise and, on playing back the material they had recorded, chose to delete much or all of the content before handing the tapes back to the researchers. How the young women were represented in the videos generated a sense of shame about their accents and surroundings, and a wish not to appear 'common' to their academic audience (Walkerdine et al. 2001; Pini and Walkerdine 2011; personal communication).

Involving participants in the production of written, audio, video or photographic diaries (detailed in Chapter 6) can be rewarding and interesting. But these processes may also be too revealing, crystallising aspects of a life that participants may not wish to share or would rather disown (Pini and Walkerdine 2011). Researchers who commission such activities remain the prime audience for their production, and, in the process, their scrutiny extends beyond the interview into the realms of a participant's daily life (Pini and Walkerdine 2011). In the end, the idea that such participatory approaches are necessarily empowering may be too idealistic.

Similar considerations arise in the context of recursive interviewing (see Chapter 6), where participants may be invited to revisit their earlier interview transcripts and participatory data such as life maps or visual records. Participants are likely to react in varied ways to such invitations, in some cases finding value in the process and, in others, avoiding the process or finding it disconcerting (McLeod 2003; and see the examples in Box 5.12). An engagement in such exercises can carry emotional risks for participants, for they involve a level of introspection and disclosure that people may find uncomfortable (Miller 2000: 104). Here, too, participants may find themselves confronted with seemingly 'fixed' versions of their past lives that they may not wish to identify with or have moved on from. In the ongoing flow of a life, past events and circumstances are continually open to interpretation as people selectively remember, change plans, modify aspirations, acquire new identities and overwrite their life stories (cf. Miller 2000; Thomson 2012). Being confronted with an earlier version of oneself may mean re-living old hurts or traumas, or it may reveal unfavourable comparisons between how a participant envisaged their lives unfolding and what has actually transpired.

Box 5.12   Revisiting Research Data: Empowering or Exposing?

- In the *Inventing Adulthoods* study, participants were invited to look at and respond to transcripts and video data that had been generated in or between earlier interviews, along with analytical case histories that the researchers had subsequently generated. This opened up the possibility that conflicting interpretations and views on how they were portrayed might emerge. Not all the young people took up this offer and some did not respond. Among those who did, some engaged happily in this activity, while others expressed disquiet at the way they were represented or regretted their disclosures, feeling they were made to look stupid or otherwise exposed (although this was clearly not the intention of the researchers; McLeod and Thomson 2009: 75–6). One participant queried the need for the consultation and expressed regret at her involvement. She felt she would be more wary of talking to the researchers in future: 'cos I never know what you're going to think about me now' (2009: 75–6).

- In a similar vein, Warin (2010: 53–4; 2011; personal communication) recounts how one of the teenage participants in her intermittent ethnography of children's changing identities decided to drop out after he was shown earlier video footage of himself as a pre-schooler. He emphasised his maturity at the follow-up interview, and explained that he felt the study was 'too babyish'. Given the small sample size (ten young people), this was an unfortunate loss to the study.

As the examples in Box 5.11 and 5.12 show, presenting people with data from a past interview, or otherwise reminding them of what they previously said, needs careful handling, for it may intrude on the internal process of 'reworking' the past. The past is an intensely private realm. While QL researchers need to build cumulative understandings by bringing past and future accounts together, this does not obviate the need to respect the privacy of people's past lives, and to accept whatever version of their past, present and future lives they are currently choosing to convey.

Overall, it is possible that relatively few participants may wish to engage in these additional participatory activities. Such extended roles may create additional burdens for them, taking them reluctantly into a process of reflexive interpretation of their lives – a quasi-researcher role – that they may find discomforting (Birch and Miller 2002; McLeod and Thomson 2009). Great care is needed to discern where participants stand on these issues. It has to be acknowledged that seeking to make the research process more democratic by sharing the analytical authority that researchers hold may be an ethical sleight of hand, even somewhat delusional (Back 2007).

Balanced against such sensibilities, however, are the very real benefits for some participants in becoming ambassadors for a study, particularly when fieldwork is completed and they are able to move beyond their 'informant' role. An illustration is provided in Box 5.13.

Box 5.13 Ambassadorial Roles

- In the *Following Young Fathers* study, selected young men took part in a national practitioner conference towards the end of the study, where they contributed to workshops and formed a question-and-answer panel at the close of the day. This was a powerful way to give the young men an audience, as well as a voice. Their contributions were greatly valued by delegates and were a matter of pride for the young men themselves. Using their own voices was immensely powerful and, arguably, carried more weight than the researchers' attempts to speak for them (Neale et al. 2015; Tarrant and Neale 2017). Their capacity and desire to engage with practitioners was a significant finding of the study, yet, in this context, the finding was not simply documented; it was also actively demonstrated to a practice audience.
- Similarly, as part of a collaborative writing project for this study, one participant produced a compelling autobiographical account of his journey into teenage fatherhood (Johnson 2015; for an extract, see Narrative Methods in Chapter 6).
- In a subsequent 'impact' phase of funding for this study (Tarrant and Neale 2017), selected panel members went on to develop mentoring, advocacy and training roles under the aegis of a newly formed *Young Dads Collective* for the North of England.
- In *The Lived Experience of Welfare Reform* (Land and Patrick 2014), several participants contributed to the production of an animated film about the circumstances of low-income welfare claimants, their struggles to find work, and the effects of recent government reforms on their lives. The animation itself protected their identities, but for the launching of the film at varied public venues in the UK, including a high-impact showing at the House of Commons, several of the participants opted to attend in person, to engage in press coverage and to place their stories and their involvement in the study in the public realm (www.doleanimators. wordpress.com/about).

These extended forms of engagement clearly have the potential to empower and enrich the lives of selected panel members, and may be seen as another way for researchers to 'give something back' to participants for their significant contributions. They are also powerful means of creating societal impact from a study (for longitudinal impact studies, see Box 12.2). Yet these forms of participation are not likely to suit all participants. Careful negotiation is needed to determine who to involve and what the nature of the involvement might be. Overall, such engagement is best seen as an optional extra rather than an unmitigated good.

Ethical Closure

The time and effort needed to sustain ethical relationships over time are clearly substantial. At the same time, they create extra challenges for bringing the research to a satisfactory conclusion (Reiss 2005; Hall 2014). Ensuring the **ethical closure** of a project, or the current phase where there may be a follow-up, is vital where participants have had a long-term commitment to a study. Some participants may have a professional investment in the findings. But beyond this, they may have developed relationships and a research identity that they have come to value. Being a fellow traveller is likely to affect researchers too. As shown earlier, walking alongside creates a deeper emotional connection with participants, often at critical moments in their lives, which researchers cannot simply discard. The stories that are entrusted to us are important stores of knowledge and sources of meaning and enrichment that become part of who we are. As any QL researcher in later life will testify, this imprinting is not a temporary state. The people and their stories stay with us, as an enduring part of our emotional core.

In a sensitive reflection on this issue, Hall (2014) acknowledges that where supportive relationships have been sustained, 'letting go' of a longitudinal ethnography and saying goodbye can be emotionally difficult for both researcher and participant, engendering mixed feelings of relief, guilt, regret and anxiety. A clear and well-planned **exit strategy** is therefore needed that goes beyond a formal letter or certificate of participation (Morrow 2009; Neale 2013). For Hall (2014), this involved a gradual process of 'weaning' herself from her participants, and weaning them from her, through a staged disengagement. Strategies included extending the gap between visits; moving gradually to indirect (phone and mail) communications; planning a final goodbye visit, complete with the giving of 'thank you' gifts; and keeping the door ajar for participants if they would like to be in touch in the future.

Further possibilities include a sociable event or a public gathering such as a citizen's forum or research summit, or an exhibition or other form of dissemination event that participants can attend and/or contribute to prior to the final publication of findings (Koro-Ljungberg and Bussing 2013; Neale et al. 2015). Or it may involve creative forms of output, produced in collaboration with selected panel members, and distributed to all as a fitting memento of their contribution. Examples include an anthology of participants' reflections (Neale and Wade 2000; Neale and Flowerdew 2004), or a collaborative film (Land and Patrick 2014; see Box 5.13). Such events and outputs take foresight, time, effort and funding; a proactive strategy can help to build these resources into a study at the design stage.

Resolving Ethical Dilemmas

Varied strategies, both proactive and reactive, can be used to manage ethical literacy in a QL project. An ethical protocol for the conduct of a study, designed at the outset, can be used to think through and anticipate the kinds of issues that might arise, and the various balancing acts that may be needed to resolve them. Researcher training and regular debriefing sessions are useful mechanisms to facilitate ethical mindfulness and reflexivity (Scott and White 2005). The use of reflexive journals that researchers can share with team members may be a useful means to open up and address a range of researcher concerns or worries, both in and beyond the field (Barry et al. 1999; Malacrida 2007). Placing ethical issues as a standing item on the agenda of research team meetings may also help.

Given the extended time frames for QL research, there is an increased likelihood that ethical dilemmas will arise in unforeseen ways as a project unfolds. As we have seen, these dilemmas may take many forms, and relate to changes in the research environment or unanticipated changes in the circumstances of the researchers or participants. It is helpful, therefore, to have strategies in place to re-actively address and respond to such dilemmas as and when they arise. Several models have been formulated (reported in Wiles 2013). A 'belt and braces' model (based on Israel and Hay 2006) is set out in Box 5.14.

Box 5.14 Strategies for Resolving Ethical Dilemmas

- Clearly identify the problem and the stakeholders involved.
- Assess the context for decision making, including the longer-term implications and consequences of alternative courses of action for all.
- Consider this situated knowledge against a backdrop of current ethical principles and guidelines, both internal and external to the project.
- Consult with researchers within the team and with wider research networks or advisory bodies beyond the team.
- Implement a course of action, and reflect on the issue and the outcome, and what may be learned from it.
- Document these processes for sharing with others and to promote good ethical practice.

The last stage in this process is recommended in a context where the minutiae of ethical decision making is often absent from accounts of research methods (Scott and White 2005; Warin 2010: 4).

Our final example in this chapter (Box 5.15) illustrates the strategies that may be used to resolve unanticipated ethical dilemmas and the ethical reflexivity employed by researchers in putting these strategies into practice (Wiles 2013). It also reveals how issues relating to ongoing consent (in this case, for archiving), family involvement, confidentiality and the ethical representation of lives, may merge as a study progresses.

Box 5.15   Resolving an Ethical Dilemma
(*Siblings and Friends* study)

- In 2009, Edwards and Weller (2013) consulted with their advisory group and the Timescapes team on an ethical issue that had arisen in the *Siblings and Friends* study. Following the unexpected death of a teenage participant, who had given verbal consent for archiving his research materials, the team considered whether further consent was needed from the family, and whether any data could be made available to family members in a way that would not violate confidentiality or cause harm. A strategy was worked out in the context of knowledge about the young man, and on the basis of an ethic of care for his family. The researcher visited the young man's mother and consulted with her about what she would like from the project. As a result of this consultation, the mother was presented with selected recordings from her son's interview material, carefully chosen to reflect positive aspects of his life, such as his hobbies and work ambitions, rather than any potentially sensitive information. She was also able to record her memories of her son, which now form part of the material in the Timescapes Archive. The process of consultation with colleagues was documented on the Timescapes website (Edwards and Weller 2011). The online discussions reveal the range of moral principles prioritised by different researchers, their implications for determining varied courses of action, and how these considerations mesh with the situated knowledge held by the team.

Closing Reflections

This chapter has focused on a central practice within QL research: that of 'walking alongside' a panel of participants to discern how their lives unfold. The discussion has explored how participants are recruited into a study and how their involvement is best maintained. It reveals the longer-term commitment required, not only of the central participants, but also of the researchers who engage with them, and of the practitioner and family 'gatekeepers' who facilitate the research. Strategies for retracing people if they become 'lost' to a study have been detailed, along with the need to temper the zeal of private detection with respect for people's privacy.

The chapter illustrates how QL researchers are not simply maintaining samples: they become fellow travellers engaged in the crucial task of building and sustaining relationships of trust and mutual respect. More than any other research strategy, this is the key to maintaining a sample. How this process is managed is the cornerstone of ethical practice in a QL study. We have seen that ethical literacy in a QL study involves a series of balancing acts: between maintaining a sample and respecting and revisiting consent as an ongoing process; between establishing rapport with participants and respecting their privacy; between developing reciprocal relationships and maintaining the bounds of a professional research relationship; and, finally, between protecting confidentiality and addressing the equally compelling drive towards authenticity, empowerment and shared authority with participants. This is **longitudinal ethics**, in which ethical principles and practice are transformed through the longitudinal frame of a QL study.

A concern with research ethics is seen in some quarters as 'ethics creep', a gradual move towards highly regulated systems, or, alternatively, a growing preoccupation that runs the danger of overriding or overwhelming the substantive focus of a study. However, it is simply not possible to take ethical mindfulness or reflexivity out of the equation or to sideline the issues raised (Wiles 2012). For QL research, ethical literacy is an inherent part of the temporal landscape, a moral compass that helps to set a project on its course and navigate it on its way. It relies on a mixture of proactive and reactive ethical strategies, drawing on pre-existing ethical protocols and shared knowledge, and creatively re-working them to address unanticipated ethical dilemmas as they arise. The domain of applied ethics is about making difficult choices in situations where no unambiguous options exist (Bishop 2009). Longitudinal ethics opens up new dilemmas for researchers, as well as magnifying existing dilemmas. But time also operates as a resource in the resolution of ethical issues, and it may uncover and offer new insights into the moral terrain of participants' lives.

Further Reading

Within a growing literature on maintaining samples in QL research, insightful accounts are provided by Harocopos and Dennis (2003) and Williamson et al. (2014). The challenges of re-tracing 'lost' samples from earlier phases of a study are engagingly documented by O'Connor and Goodwin (2010, 2012), Farrall et al. (2016) and Miller (2015).

Most researchers weave brief discussions of ethical considerations into their reporting, but detailed accounts are limited. Valuable overviews of the issues are provided by Saldaña (2003: 22–9) and McLeod and Thomson (2009: 74–6). See also Miller and Bell (2002) and Birch and Miller (2002) on issues of consent and participation in family research; Scott and White (2005) on the ethics of working with drug users; Warin (2011) for a perceptive account of researcher reflexivity in a small-scale educational study; Hall (2014) for letting go and bringing closure to a study; and Morrow (2013) for the ethics of large-scale comparative research with children and families. Finally, for the ethical quagmires that can arise in the making and breaking of research relationships, see the fascinating accounts provided by Ellis (1995), Scheper-Hughes (2000), Reiss (2005) and Wolcott (2002). The *Ethics Knowledge Bank*, created by Timescapes researchers (www.timescapes.leeds. ac.uk/ethicsknowlegebank), is a useful resource for sharing good practice, with scope for further expansion. Case studies of ethical dilemmas and their resolution across a broader range of social-scientific research can be found on the ESRC/UKRI website.

Birch, M. and Miller, T. (2002) 'Encouraging participation: Ethics and responsibilities' in M. Mauthner, M. Birch, J. Jessop and T. Miller (eds) *Ethics in Qualitative Research*. London: Sage, pp. 91–106.

Ellis, C. (1995) 'Emotional and ethical quagmires in returning to the field', *Journal of Contemporary Ethnography*, 24 (1): 68–98.

Farrall, S., Hunter, B., Sharpe, G. and Calverley, A. (2016) 'What "works" when re-tracing sample members in a qualitative longitudinal study?', *International Journal of Social Research Methodology*, 19 (3): 287–300.

Hall, S. (2014) 'Ethics of ethnography with families: A geographical perspective', *Environment and Planning A*, 46: 2175–94.

Harocopos, A. and Dennis, D. (2003) 'Maintaining contact with drug users over an 18 month period', *International Journal of Social Research Methodology*, 6 (3): 261–5.

McLeod, J. and Thomson, R. (2009) *Researching Social Change*. London: Sage.

Miller, T. (2015) 'Going back: Stalking, talking and research responsibilities in qualitative longitudinal research', *International Journal of Social Research Methodology*, 18 (3): 293–305.

Miller, T. and Bell, L. (2002) 'Consenting to what? Issues of access, gate-keeping and informed consent', in M. Mauthner, M. Birch, J. Jessop and T. Miller (eds) *Ethics in Qualitative Research*. London: Sage, pp. 53–69.

Morrow, V. (2013) 'Practical ethics in social research with children and families in *Young Lives*: A longitudinal study of childhood poverty in Ethiopia, Andhra Pradesh (India), Peru and Vietnam', *Methodological Innovations Online*, 8 (2): 21–35.

O'Connor, H. and Goodwin, J. (2010) 'Utilising data from a lost sociological project: Experiences, insights, promises', *Qualitative Research*, 10 (3): 283–98.

O'Connor, H. and Goodwin, J. (2012) 'Revisiting Norbert Elias's sociology of community: Learning from the Leicester re-studies', *The Sociological Review*, 60: 476–97.

Reiss, M. (2005) 'Managing endings in a longitudinal study: Respect for persons', *Research in Science Education*, 35: 123–35.

Saldaña, J. (2003) *Longitudinal Qualitative Research: Analyzing Change Through Time*. Walnut Creek, CA: AltaMira Press.

Scheper-Hughes, N. (2000) 'Ire in Ireland', *Ethnography*, 1 (1): 117–40.

Scott, C. and White, W. (2005) 'Ethical issues in the conduct of longitudinal studies of addiction treatment', *Journal of Substance Abuse Treatment*, 28: 591–610.

Warin, J. (2011) 'Ethical mindfulness and reflexivity: Managing a research relationship with children and young people in a fourteen-year qualitative longitudinal research (QLR) study', *Qualitative Inquiry*, 17 (10): 805–14.

Williamson, E., Abrahams, H., Morgan, K. and Cameron, A. (2014) 'Tracking homeless women in qualitative longitudinal research', *European Journal of Homelessness*, 8 (2): 69–91.

Wolcott, H. (2002) *Sneaky Kid and its Aftermath: Ethics and Intimacy in Fieldwork*. Walnut Creek, CA: AltaMira Press.

6

GENERATING QUALITATIVE
LONGITUDINAL DATA

┌─ **Key Points** ───

- **Data-generation strategies**: This chapter explores varied ways of
  generating data about temporal processes. Strategically, this involves a
  balance between flexibility and continuity. Flexible lines of enquiry allow
  researchers to follow lives where they lead and to respond to changes in the
  social fabric as they arise. Continuity questions, which can be revisited at
  each wave of fieldwork, provide a through-line in the data: a synchronic link
  across cases and themes at each point in time, and a diachronic link *within*
  cases and themes through time. This is founded on the case, thematic and
  processual logic of QL enquiry.
- **Complementary methods**: Three complementary modes of field enquiry are
  outlined here: longitudinal ethnography, life journey interviewing and
  multi-media participatory tools and techniques. Ethnography involves being
  there, walking alongside as lives unfold. Life journey and recursive
  interviewing draws out people's reflections on their unfolding lives and
  gains insight into the life as told, experienced and observed. Ethnography
  and interviewing are commonly combined. Participatory methods enable
  people to document their unfolding lives in their own way.
- **Life journey interviewing**: This is a narrative style of interviewing that draws
  out people's reflections on how processes unfold, and the causes and
  consequences of change. A 'cartographic' strategy involves exploring the
  surface features of a landscape before digging down to explore its

(Continued)

underlying features. Life journey interviewing explores the journey through the landscape: the source of the journey, the route taken, how far people have come along the path, any detours along the way, where they are now and where they are heading. The journey is revisited and recursively updated at each wave, as people revisit and reinterpret past and future.

- **Participatory tools and techniques** include narrative, visual and experiential methods. Narratives may capture past and future times, and/or may be constructed prospectively using diary methods. Diaries are powerful tools that provide valuable continuity between waves of fieldwork. Visual representations include life history charts, creative drawings (life maps), and photography and film (photo elicitation and photo diaries). Life maps are perhaps the most commonly used. They are intuitive tools that reflect the fluidity of unfolding lives, and have the capacity to capture emotional as well as event-based journeys. Photo diaries, in which we see the world, as well as hear about it, have great potential to convey temporal processes in rich and evocative ways.

- **Data-generation tool kit**: Researchers often combine one or more of these field tools and techniques to good effect. For example, life history interviews and diary methods capture different horizons of time. Ethnographies and interviews capture the life as lived and observed as well as told, while participatory tools enhance the capacity to gain an intimate familiarity with a life. Field tools and techniques need to be piloted and chosen with care to ensure that researchers (and participants) are not overloaded with a plethora of activities that complicate field enquiry and analysis.

Introduction

Life stories … capture the continuous, lived flow of historically situated, phenomenal experiences, with all the ambiguity, variability, malleability and even uniqueness that such experience implies. Whether this be the experience of being a nomadic hunter and gatherer, or a North American prostitute … a worker down a mine, … being worried to death in a nursing home, … a teacher, or facing disability … whatever may be of interest to the analyst, a key perspective is the participant's account of this experience. It may not be adequate on its own. But if a study fails to get this 'intimate familiarity' with a life, then such research runs the risk of simply getting it wrong: of speculating, abstracting and theorizing at too great a remove. (Plummer 2001: 37)

In this chapter, we turn to a central task in QL enquiry: generating rich dynamic data about unfolding lives. This task is structured through the successive waves of field-work, where it is intertwined with the process of managing and analysing a QL dataset (detailed in Part 3 of this book). In QL field enquiry, thick descriptive data is generated cumulatively, in real-time, by walking alongside our participants (see Chapter 5). This enhances the capacity to gain an intimate familiarity with a life, which, as Plummer notes in our opening quotation, is vital for fluid, interpretive enquiry. No less than in other phases of a QL study, **data generation** can be seen as an intellectual craft. There are endless possibilities for creativity here (Saldaña 2003; Weller 2012), alongside the ever-present need for careful design and precision.

The chapter begins with a consideration of the strategies used to balance continuity and flexibility through the successive waves of field enquiry. Extending an earlier review (Neale 2017a), the discussion goes on to explore three broad approaches to field enquiry: longitudinal ethnography; life journey and recursive interviewing; and **participatory methods** that utilise multi-media tools and techniques. A fourth **documentary** approach, which utilises and repurposes socio-historical legacy data, is explored in Chapter 8.

Cases, Themes, Processes: Balancing Continuity and Flexibility

We start by considering a basic strategy for generating data through time. Building cumulative data through the longitudinal frame of a study requires a balance between **continuity** and **flexibility** in the field (Ritchie and Lewis 2003: 141). Continuity is needed to ensure that an emerging dataset has some integrity and internal coherence to aid analysis and synthesis (Pollard 2007). A common strategy is to devise a set of core continuity questions for use in the field, which explore key processes, themes and any changes and/or continuities for the participant at each research encounter (e.g. 'then and now' or 'where next' questions; Saldaña 2003; Smith 2003). Building core themes into the conceptual road map that guides the research process can help to ensure thematic continuity across waves (see Chapter 4, Table 4.1). A baseline questionnaire or checklist is also useful for capturing structured demographic and circumstantial information about a case, which can be updated as a study progresses.

These continuity questions can then be revisited at each research encounter, providing the anchors for building an integrated dataset that enables temporal connections and comparisons to be discerned. To paraphrase Saldaña (2003), this attention to continuity creates a **through-line** in the data, a thread that provides a synchronic link *across* cases and themes at any one point in time, and a diachronic link *within* cases and themes through time (Barley 1995; Smith 2003). In this way, the conceptual logic of QL enquiry, the three-dimensional attention to cases, themes and processes, is built into field enquiry.

At the same time, the longitudinal frame allows for flexibility in how data are generated, and what lines of enquiry to pursue. Developing a diachronic understanding of each case requires a cumulative approach, a capacity to build layers of insight from one research encounter to the next to create a unique case narrative. This means tailoring questions to each case, and following the diachronic threads of an unfolding process. What were participants doing at the last wave, and the wave before that? Where are they heading now? Are they pursuing new paths? What led to a change? This same flexibility is needed for the thematic development of the study, and for responding to changes in the social fabric and in the research landscape. As shown in Chapter 4, sampling strategies may involve expanding or condensing a sample (**sample boosting** as new dimensions of the research emerge, or funnelling in on particularly significant or emblematic cases over time). This same logic comes into play in field enquiry. Over time, the researcher may 'funnel in' or progressively focus on **emblematic themes** of particular pertinence to the study or to a particular case, or, alternatively, may boost the scope of enquiry as new themes emerge (Smith 2003; Pollard 2007). The facility to ask new questions and introduce new themes, building on earlier waves of data or responding to changes in the external landscape, is a crucial feature of QL enquiry (Scudder and Colson 2002; Saldaña 2003; Smith 2003; Koro-Ljungberg and Bussing 2013; Grandia 2015). It enhances the capacity of QL research to engage with fluid temporal processes, to follow lives where they lead.

An example of thematic development, drawn from a classic longitudinal ethnography and reflecting far-reaching shifts in the social fabric over several decades, can be found in Chapter 1, Box 1.6. But a changing focus is not only a product of long-term field enquiry; biographical and historical changes can occur in the short term. For example, in 2008, researchers across the Timescapes study (2007–12) responded to the economic downturn as it began to emerge in the UK. They returned to the field armed with a new suite of questions about the recession and its impact on family fortunes (Edwards and Irwin 2010). Similarly, the Covid-19 pandemic, which, in a short space of time, has brought profound changes to the health and well-being of a global population, has created a seismic shift in the social landscape, which is already beginning to impact on the substantive focus of QL studies. Taken together, continuity and flexibility are important strategies in generating QL data. Finding the right balance between these strategies is part of the rigour of QL field enquiry.

Longitudinal Ethnography

As shown in Chapter 1, the longitudinal ethnographies carried out by social anthropologists represent the earliest developments in QL enquiry. An ethnographic approach involves one or more continuous periods of immersion in a particular field setting, working with a particular group of participants. Ethnographers aim to insert themselves, to varying degrees, into the daily lives of the people under study and for sustained periods of time. By participating, observing, listening, asking questions and gathering data from multiple sources, researchers gain insights into the varied conditions under which people live, and begin to see the world through their eyes (Royce 2002; for a recent guide see Hammersley and Atkinson 2019).

The process involves documenting in detail what people do and say in the flow of everyday activities, using recording technology and/or note taking (see Box 8.1, where an early anthropologist is advised to capture the chaos of everyday life, to observe and write down everything). This approach is rooted in the social practice of 'being there' over time, and it functions as an ongoing, joint accomplishment (Royce 2002; 2005; Burton et al. 2009: 73–5). In other words, it is bound up with the process of 'walking alongside' people as fellow travellers (see Chapter 5), shadowing and observing them in their daily activities, sustaining relationships and sharing life experiences, including those of a sensitive nature that may be disclosed gradually over time.

Ethnographic interviewing is an integral part of this methodology, ranging from spontaneous, 'on the hoof' conversations in day-to-day settings, to more focused, pre-arranged conversations in confidential spaces. Combining participant observation and ethnographic interviewing within a processual frame gives longitudinal ethnography a particular strength: it can yield insights into how lives are being *lived* as well as narrated, and how both lived and narrated lives change over time. It has a particular facility, then, for discerning the flux of everyday existence.

As an inherently temporal process, ethnography is a core method used by anthropologists, increasingly used by social scientists across the academy, and commonly employed in QL research (see, for example, Coffield et al. 1980; Pollard with Filer 1996; Corsaro and Molinari 2000; Burton et al. 2009; O'Reilly 2012; Ferguson et al. 2019). Longitudinal ethnography can capture something of the tempo and temporal ordering of day-to-day lives (Zerubavel 1979), the immediacy of the historical moment, and the intricacies and fluid nature of change in the making (Kemper and Royce 2002). With its facility for thick description, illuminating 'lived' lives and fleshing out a holistic picture through varied data sources, longitudinal ethnography is usually associated with small-scale enquiry and a case study approach. But it can also be used when working comparatively with larger samples, as illustrated in Box 6.1.

Box 6.1   Longitudinal Ethnography

- Burton et al. (2009) followed the lives of 256 low-income mothers, located across three cities, to discern the effects of a major change in welfare provision in the USA (see Box 4.7 for the sampling strategy used in this study). Fieldwork took place over a 4–5-year period, from 1999 to 2003, and involved both interviews and participant observation. The interviews

(Continued)

focused on specific topics relating to family lives and relationships, family economics, support networks and neighbourhood environments, but were conducted flexibly to enable new topics to emerge and to gain an understanding of what was important for the women. The ethnographers, who were ethnically matched with the participants, engaged in extensive participant observation, for example attending family functions and outings, accompanying the mothers to health and welfare appointments and to day-care and workplaces, noting both context and interactions in these varied settings. They were also present during extended conversations between the mothers and their families and friends. They met each family once or twice a month over a 12–18-month period, followed by a more extensive tempo of visits every six months. This yielded a rich dataset comprising tape-recorded interview transcripts and detailed field notes for the participant observations. The process of 'being there' and walking alongside revealed the extent of physical and sexual abuse suffered by these women, a major theme that the researchers had not set out to explore but which emerged over the course of the study.

Qualitative Interviewing

This is the most widely used method for generating data in the social sciences. Qualitative interviewing typically takes the form of carefully planned, pre-arranged, in-depth discussions with individuals or small groups, although the encounters may be arranged spontaneously in the field. Interviews range from individual conversations to group-based encounters, such as focus groups, and from face-to-face to indirect discussions. Where mobile phone or web-based technologies are used, interviews may be conducted in real-time or a-synchronically, with a time lapse in the conversation (Weller 2017; Winiarska 2017). A topic guide covering relevant themes and questions is commonly used to guide the process, while the resulting narratives are typically captured via audio-recordings that are transcribed to aid recall and analysis. Being free of note taking also facilitates the development of meaningful conversations with participants.

The longitudinal frame of a QL study gives ample scope to explore processes as they unfold, and build a biographical understanding of lives. Ethnographic techniques can usefully be incorporated into an interview-based study. As shown in Chapter 4 (Box 4.2), an interview study may start with a period of ethnographic immersion to get to know participants and the settings of their lives, before recruiting them for a series of in-depth interviews. Beyond this, walking interviews, or shadowing activities, such as 'day in the life' tracking, are increasingly common (Thomson 2012; Bates and Rhys-Taylor 2017; Ferguson et al. 2019; O'Neill and

Roberts 2020). Researchers may also make informal visits to participants' homes or to field settings (the local pub or community centre, for example), help out in social or health care agencies, attend events or outings arranged by participants or practitioners, or organise events for a panel of participants. This yields complementary forms of data and gives access to lives as they are lived and experienced, as well as lives that are told and retold through time. It is clear that ethnography and interviewing are complementary modes of generating data, which, to varying degrees, may be intertwined in a QL study.

In-depth interviews are described in a variety of ways: as conversational, responsive, dialogical, open-ended, narrative, and so on. But, as the opening quotation for this chapter shows, the overall aim is the same: to gain insights into participants' subjective experiences, feelings and world views, and to build up a picture of how they construct, narrate and make meaning of their lives. While there is no such thing as a totally unstructured interview, qualitative interviewing needs to be sufficiently open to enable participants to reflect on the meaning and significance of their own experiences, and to convey these in their own terms, as accomplished and reflexive individuals. This yields thick descriptive data (see Box 2.1 where the notion of thick description is introduced). It is a process that relies on the quality of the interaction between interviewer and interviewee: on good listening skills, the use of everyday language, and on empathy and encouragement on the part of the interviewer.

Interviewing in QL Research

In QL research, **interviews** are conducted through time to give a cumulative picture of continuities and changes as they occur. In-depth interviews can be used to explore one or more of the planes of time outlined in Chapter 3:

- the flows of past/present/future; continuities/ruptures/transformations in life experience;
- the pace of change, and how people create, manage or adjust to change;
- the tenor and oscillations of unfolding processes, and the interlocking horizons of turning points, transitions and longer-term trajectories;
- the interplay between micro (biographical) and macro (historical) processes;
- the spatial dimensions of time (and/or the temporal dimensions of space).

The simple task of exploring where people were born and have lived, who or what has influenced the direction of their lives, and what relational and socio-economic opportunities and constraints they have faced, will yield insights that span the micro–macro plane (Miller 2000: 74; Plummer 2001: 39–40). Just as time provides a design framework for field enquiry, in an interview setting it also shapes the nature of the interaction and the resulting data. Time, in both its fixed and fluid dimensions, comes into its own here as a rich theme or topic of enquiry.

The idea of narration, that people have a story to tell about what happened, who did what and when, and how things have come about, is central to QL interviewing and analysis (Langley 1999; Plummer 2001; Dawson 2003, 2013). The process of narrating, or telling an unfolding tale, is a frequent and spontaneous occurrence in everyday social interactions. As shown in Chapter 1, by their very nature, narratives have a temporal quality. Tales are rarely narrated in strict chronological order, and may not have a clear sense of a beginning, middle and ending (Brockmeier 2000). Nevertheless, as accounts of biographical or collective events and processes, they are likely to convey a sense of 'plot': of linked events that unfold in a meaningful way, and with an inferred causality, with consequences that arise from people's decisions and actions (Polkinghorne 1995; Elliott 2005; Paavilainen-Mäntymäki and Aarikka-Stenroos 2013). Building on this capacity, narrative styles of interviewing are designed not only to draw out the events of an unfolding life, but also to evoke reflections, interpretations and insights about the meaning of life experiences and how and why events have unfolded in particular ways.

While in-depth interviews are not conversations in the sense of an informal, reciprocal exchange of news and reflections between two or more people, they are nonetheless conversational (in its original Latin, meaning *wandering* or *turning about together*) (Kvale 2007: 19; Ritchie et al. 2014). Kvale (2007) usefully distinguishes between the *miner* interviewer, who digs out nuggets of pre-existing data, and the *traveller* interviewer, who, 'wanders through the landscape, … walks along with the local inhabitants, … enters into conversation with the people he or she encounters, … asks questions and encourages them to tell their own stories of their lived world' (2007: 19). This is a fitting description of the QL researcher, a fellow traveller who walks alongside a panel of participants (see Chapter 5).

In an interview setting, the QL researcher works with the participant to jointly construct and reconstruct meanings and knowledge as the interaction unfolds, enabling participants to find a narrative voice that explores and engages with dynamic meanings, rather than simply stating facts (Elliott 2005; Guenette and Marshall 2009). The resulting accounts are actively produced or *generated*; they are not simply 'out there' in a realist sense, to be 'harvested', 'mined' or 'collected' from participants as if they are passive stores of knowledge. Hareven (1982) eloquently makes this point in her account of oral history interviewing:

> The interviewer is like a medium, conjuring memories through his or her own presence, interests and questions. … [offering] a glimpse not only into the sequence of events in people's lives but how, in their search for a pattern, the different pieces of their lives are re-assembled and dis-assembled as in a kaleidoscope, losing meaning, changing meaning, disappearing, and reappearing in different configurations at different points in time. (Hareven 1982: 373–5)

Hareven observes that this constructionist, narrative understanding of interviewing is part of its value. Rather than detracting from the integrity and meaning of people's accounts, this approach yields explicit interpretations and valuable insights into what matters to people at different moments, and why (Hareven 1982: 374; Elliott 2005; Kvale 2007; Ritchie et al. 2014: 180; Hammersley and Atkinson 2019). This process of jointly constructing meaning and knowledge enhances the overall integrity and veracity of a QL study (see Chapter 12).

A life history or processual interview may be conducted in a variety of ways (Clausen 1998; Miller 2000; Thompson 2000; Wengraf 2000; Plummer 2001; Elliott 2005; Merrill and West 2009; Paavilainen-Mäntymäki and Aarikka-Stenroos 2013). In a relatively unstructured approach, participants are invited to narrate their life story, or segments of it, in their own way, at their own pace, and guided very loosely by the researcher – for instance, 'How would you describe your childhood/ family life/time in …? How did you first come to be involved with …? What was it like for you when you were growing up/starting out/going through …?' (Plummer 2001: 140–2; see also the analytical questions posed in Chapter 10 for working with case data). The aim is to elicit a spontaneous and relatively unmediated narrative. The biographic-interpretive method, for example, begins in this minimalist fashion, with one key question posed to set a life story in train (Miller 2000; Wengraf 2000).

However, not all participants will feel able to respond to such a minimalist prompt, and the lack of guidance and interaction may serve to close down communications and empathy rather than enhance it (Clausen 1998; Thompson 2000; Chase 2005; Elliott 2005; Merrill and West 2009; Brannen 2013). In some cases, a prolonged, empathic interaction may be needed to draw out a narrative, or creative tools may be needed to enable its articulation (Clausen 1998; Guenette and Marshall 2009; see the participatory tools below). In any case, spontaneous narratives may well present a gloss on how a life unfolds, or, at least, a highly edited, partial version (Clausen 1998: 192). For this reason, researchers usually follow these unstructured phases of an interview with probing questions that dig deeper to draw out key themes, or fill in missing elements that are pertinent to the research ('tell me more about…' questions). This is the strategy used in the biographic-interpretive method of data generation (Wengraf 2000; Brannen et al. 2004).

As an alternative to this unmediated strategy, a gentle 'easing in' to an interview can be achieved by adopting a more interactive and guided approach from the outset. A checklist of topics and themes may be devised to guide the interaction, with the option to share these with participants at the start of the discussion or beforehand (Merrill and West 2009). A **cartographic strategy** (a spatial metaphor that nicely complements the others used in QL enquiry) begins with an exploratory, surface mapping of a particular landscape of enquiry (Ritchie et al. 2014: 190–1). More focused questions then follow to explore the terrain in greater detail, before digging down to excavate underlying themes, meanings and reflections (here, 'cartography' shades into 'archaeology'). In this way, the interview moves from concrete life events and experiences to more reflective and abstract insights and interpretations. From the outset, this approach is grounded transparently in the themes of a study, which provide the focus for discussion. Yet, conducted in an open and exploratory way, this approach still gives participants space to construct their own narratives in their own words and to introduce new themes where these are important. And it is likely to achieve the same depth of insight into what matters to people: how salient a particular process or experience is in shaping the course of their lives and its relative significance in relation to other influences and concerns.

Life Journey Interviewing

In QL research, a cartographic strategy can be used dynamically to map and construct a life journey, building insights into particular transitions and trajectories, exploring how participants have arrived at the present day and how they envisage the future. Going beyond a simple mapping of a landscape, this approach explores the movement of people *through* a landscape, giving attention to both surface details and the depths and drivers of the journey. The starting point for enquiry may be a general mapping of present-day circumstances located within the passage of time (identifying where people are on their temporal map, the nature of the current terrain, an outline of the path they are currently following, how far along the path they have travelled, and whether there have been any detours or 'blind alleys' on the way).

This is followed by a retrospective exploration of the 'back story': how participants have arrived at the present moment, and the nature and meaning of the journey as it has unfolded (high and low points, for example). Varied threads of experience may be explored in capturing past time: the pace, tempo, spatial dimensions or synchronicities of the journey; whether it was straightforward (linear) or more fluid: circuitous, meandering or filled with zigzags or peaks and troughs; to what extent it was planned, anticipated or is living up to expectations. A retrospective lens may also be used to explore the opportunities and constraints (across the micro–macro plane) that have shaped the journey so far, and any trigger points or pivotal moments that have provided the driving force for new directions or for reverting back to earlier paths. Such data is vital in the task of process tracing, a core element in data analysis (see Chapter 11). Finally, the interview may move on to explore how participants see their future paths, how they envisage 'getting there' (their plans, aspirations, hopes and fears, again shaped by external opportunities and constraints) and what this means for the longer-term trajectories of their lives.

In **life journey interviewing**, the mapping of a participant's life is inherently dynamic, seeking to locate where people are on their subjectively defined life map, and exploring the nature, meaning and inner logic of the journey as it unfolds. Plummer (2001: 196) suggests that an effective life story or processual narrative needs to address the following questions:

- What was done (act, practice, process)?
- Where and when was it done (scene, setting, beginnings)?
- Who did it (agent)?
- How was it done (agency)?
- Why was it done (purpose)?

To these questions, we might add the following:

- What triggered and propelled the process (multiple influences, impetus)?
- What meaning did it hold for those involved (lived experience)?
- Was it a straightforward path, or were there detours along the way (contours)?
- What (if any) were the effects or consequences at different points in time (impact)?

At each return visit to the field, the journey can be updated. But this is not simply a matter of elaborating the tale by adding another instalment. Instead, the overall narrative is reworked and refined as people look back and forward in time and re-envisage their past and future from a new standpoint (see recursive interviewing below).

In Box 6.2, an extract is provided from the first of four detailed life journey interviews conducted over a period of three years with a young father called Jason. These form part of the *Following Young Fathers* dataset (available through the Timescapes Archive at www.timescapes-archive.leeds.ac.uk). As this first interview progresses, details of the young man's earlier life gradually emerge: periods in care following the death of his mother from a drug overdose; the absence of his father; anger management problems that led to a spell in prison; life on a 'crack-head' estate; disengagement from school and entrenched unemployment; and a volatile relationship with his co-parent. In varied ways, these facets of Jason's life were shaping and colouring his experiences, practices and identity as a father. Even in the early stages of this first interview, temporal data about the past and future are beginning to emerge, and, from the outset, Jason reflects on changes in his perceptions over time. Over the course of the study, these layered experiences, including further spells in custody and the arrival of a second child, were gently and skilfully drawn out by the interviewer (Carmen Lau-Clayton).

Box 6.2 A Journey into Young Fatherhood – Interview Extract

Jason (aged 22), Wave 1 interview, 9 February 2011

Carmen: Well thank you again Jason for coming today. So can you just tell me a little bit about yourself then? Like how old you are, where you live and this sort of thing?

Jason: ... I'm twenty two and I don't really do much except go to the gym and look for work every day. And when I'm not doing that I'm just looking after [son] ... And try to get him things. ... But there's not much you can do, 'cause he's only [eight] weeks old so... ...basically you can only feed, feed him and change his nappies. ... But I've just like, I've opened a savings account and just started putting money away for him because ... he's got hundreds of clothes.

Carmen: So [son] is your only child then? He's your first child then?

Jason: Yeah.

Carmen: So what's it like being a father to a very new baby then?

Jason: Well if I'm honest, before he was born I was a bit negative. I didn't want to be a dad 'cause for starters I'm unemployed. So I can't give him the best possible life. But obviously I can do something about that. But it's quite crazy. Once he were born and I seen him – like I didn't even want to go to watch him being born 'cause I were nervous and scared. ... And I thought because I didn't like his mother that I wouldn't like him. 'Cause me and his mum fell out. ... But once he were born, it's crazy. You just, nothing else matters. ... Everything you do is for him. ... It's impossible to describe, I think. It's just overwhelming. You are responsible for something that's ... that can't be independent and needs help. I don't know. Just, you have to be there for him don't you. You have to sacrifice things to make their life better. But I suppose, obviously I, well, I've got a crap dad so obviously I want to be total opposite and be a good example to him. ... Like I used to, and it's bad, I used to smoke weed. Not too often but since he's been born I just stopped it straight away. ... I realised that's losing money or things I could do for him or, and setting a bad example. So I just stopped.

(Extract from Jason, Wave 1 Interview, 9 Feb. 2011, Following Young Fathers Dataset, Timescapes Archive)

In developing a life journey approach to interviewing, it is worth remembering that lives are rarely narrated in chronological order, while causal processes may unfold in a fluid rather than linear manner (Brockmeier 2000). Even where narratives imply chronology, they are likely to be presented in a fragmented and disorganised way

(Polkinghorne 1995). For this reason, the construction of a chronological case history or case study is usually undertaken in the aftermath of the interview, as part of the analytical process (see Chapter 10). Moreover, the extent to which people envisage their lives as a journey to be planned and executed varies from person to person. As shown in Chapter 3, people may live, either through choice or necessity, in an extended present, without a strong sense of agency over past decisions or future directions. But a life journey approach can help to shed light on these varied orientations, affording insights into the different ways in which people live in the stream of time.

Recursive Interviewing

In QL research, a life journey can be updated and elaborated through the longitudinal frame of a study, enabling insights into how a life is unfolding, and how experiences accrue through time. But this process can also be taken a stage further. As shown in Chapter 3, the unfolding lives of individuals or collectives are not fixed at any one moment, but are constructed, reconstructed and updated through the recursive spiral of time (McLeod 2003; Grbich 2007; Jost 2012). Through successive waves of fieldwork, QL research can illuminate the fluid processes through which people over-write their biographies and reinterpret past events and future aspirations. In other words, recursive interviewing gives insights into changing perceptions as well as changing events. Recursion can be thought of as a form of iteration (feedback), but instead of working across two entities to explore their connections, this is iteration between two versions of the same entity, produced at different moments in time.

Recursive interviewing involves looking both backward and forward in time, revisiting, re-visioning and updating a life journey at each successive interview. Participants are invited to review the past, update previous understandings, and re-imagine the future through the lens of the ever-shifting present (McLeod 2003: 204–5). This makes it possible to compare accounts of intentions and expectations with how events and circumstances actually unfold (Walker and Leisering 1998). Going back to an earlier interview armed with new knowledge of an unfolding life, 'brings out meanings that may have been hidden for a variety of reasons' (Bornat 2013). In the process, researcher interpretations and understandings are continually refined and transformed (Neale and Flowerdew 2007; Millar 2021 in press; see also the examples in Box 3.4 and recursive case analysis in Chapter 10). This iterative approach to past, present and future offers a more nuanced and fluid way of exploring life course dynamics. Time as the framework for conducting a study begins to merge here with time as a rich theme of enquiry.

The value of recursive interviewing is that it takes into account and seeks to capture the flux of lives – recognising that the construction of a life is inherently provisional, and that people are in a perpetual state of 'becoming' (Bergson 1910 [1889]; Worth 2009; see also Boxes 2.2 and 2.3, where fluid understandings of time are introduced). As Plummer (2001: 40) notes, contingencies, volatilities and inconsistencies are an inevitable feature of all unfolding biographies: our lives 'are flooded with moments of indecision, turning points, confusions, contradictions, and ironies', which are likely to be reflected in the way lives are both narrated and lived.

This fluidity is clearly recognised by participants themselves (see Box 3.4). Most notably, it is a feature of the famous autobiographical account produced for Thomas and Znaniecki (1958 [1918–21]) by Wladek, one of their key informants. Similarly, Jason, the young participant from the *Following Young Fathers* study (see Box 6.2), reflects here on his experience of creating and updating a life map and self-portrait over four waves of interviews spanning a period of three years:

> I bet you find I ... put loads of different answers. It just depends on how you are feeling at the time. ... To be honest, every time I've done one, I've come back to it and I've not even known what I've put, because your feelings and opinions change don't they? (Jason, aged 24, Wave 4 interview, 19 Feb. 2014, *Following Young Fathers* dataset, Timescapes Archive)

Researchers seeking a surface, 'factual' account of a life journey may be unable to detect the rich flux of life course processes, or may gloss over or flatten them out (Plummer 2001). Yet uncovering these intricacies and changes in perception is vital if the inner logic and momentum of a life is to be understood. Recursive interviewing, then, uncovers the constant state of flux in which lives unfold and, working with this dynamic, seeks to uncover how the narrative of a life – the life as told, interpreted and understood – is continually re-adjusted to the life as lived and experienced.

Working recursively through time

Strategies for weaving back and forth through time will depend on the focus of a study, the characteristics and circumstances of the participants, and at what point important themes, gaps or anomalies arise in a narrative that need greater attention. Researchers will need to decide how far backward and forward they wish to explore, and at which particular moments. It may be useful to start off with relatively small time horizons (the time since last interview, the last year or a projection over the next year), before moving on to longer horizons that stretch into the more distant past or future. The time frame of a study itself can provide a temporal horizon. At the outset, participants can be invited to reflect on where they envisage they will be by the end of the study, and, at the exit interview, on how far they have come over the study period (Saldaña 2003). A longer-term horizon offers more scope to explore personal, interpersonal or institutional influences across the micro–macro plane, and is a valuable means of contextualising the specific journey under study and discerning how it fits within the longer-term trajectory of a life.

In using recursive interview techniques, researchers need to consider how far and in what ways they will prompt participants about their past and future lives (drawing on knowledge gleaned in previous interviews), and to what extent this might influence or unsettle people's perceptions. For example, participants may be asked simply to recount where they were previously in relation to the present day, or whether their views of past or future have changed at all. It is not uncommon, at this point, for participants to seek clarification on where they were or what they were doing at last interview and to be given a gentle prompt ('you were waiting to hear about ...', ' ... had just started/finished ...', 'you were hoping to go on to...'). This can yield powerful reflections on how the course of a life has changed, and what this means for a participant's changing perceptions.

But, taking the recursive process a step further, researchers may also share with participants some extracts from their earlier interview transcripts, or their analytical case files, as a way of prompting people to explore just how and why they may have moved on or shifted perspective. This approach is illustrated in Box 6.3.

Box 6.3   The Recursive Workbook Interview (Thomson)

- In the Timescapes *Dynamics of Modern Motherhood* study (a follow-up to the *Making of Modern Motherhood* study), the researchers developed a recursive workbook interview, which they shared with participants as a means of rounding off their study (Thomson 2012). Each workbook brought together fragments of data, images and quotations taken from the corpus of interviews for a particular case, and the emergent analytic narratives that the researchers had constructed from these data. Inviting participants to reflect on these fragments and reconstructions generated new discussion and insights about temporal processes in the lives of the participants. It highlighted where their present-day accounts converged or diverged from past accounts, opening up contradictions and incoherencies in their narratives and revealing something of the resilience and/or fragility of their narrated identities.

Here **recursion** is taken to a new level. In line with Giddens's double hermeneutic, it involves a conscious iteration between changing participant perceptions and evolving researcher interpretations. This can be an arresting means of drawing out transformations in people's values, aspirations or identities, and their subjective interpretations of the past and future. However, the process has ethical implications. Responses to this exercise are likely to vary from enjoyment to indifference, and from hilarity to disquiet (McLeod and Thomson 2009; Thomson 2012; and see Box 5.12 for the ethics of taking a crystallised version of a past life back to people). As Thomson (2012) acknowledges, creating a feedback loop between participant narratives and research data and interpretations is a powerful intervention. It needs to be carefully considered and utilised only where it is mediated by robust and trusting relationships and ethical sensitivity.

Multi-Media Participatory Tools and Techniques

Multi-media **participatory methods** for generating dynamic data are commonly used in combination with the field techniques described above. Varied forms of data may be sourced or produced by the researcher, or elicited from or produced directly by participants. The tools and techniques used in these participatory processes fall broadly into three categories:

- **Narrative methods**, through written/audio accounts, e.g. autobiographies or diaries;
- **Visual methods**, through drawings, graphs, maps, photographs or videos;
- **Experiential methods**, through arts-based tools, e.g. music, song, dance and drama.

Our main focus is on narrative and visual methods. But it is woth noting here that experiential arts-based methods (music, dance, drama, visual arts) can render unfolding lives in creative ways, offering powerful forms of embodied knowledge that engage the senses and evoke identities and memories (see, for example, Saldaña 2005; DeNora 2013; Dassa 2018 (featured in Box 6.12), and other rich writings from the fields of ethno-musicology and ethno-drama). In QL research, such tools can be used as part of, or as a precursor to, an interview, or in between waves of fieldwork, and they can be used recursively to capture changing perceptions of events and processes.

Narrative Methods

Varied forms of written or audio narratives may be elicited from participants that are relatively unmediated by the researcher. These complement the oral narratives generated in an interview. Such techniques for fleshing out a life journey have a long history in socio-historical research. Three forms of narrative account are explored here:

- **Past accounts** (autobiographies) that reflect retrospectively on past events;
- **Future accounts** that anticipate an imaginary future;
- **Diary accounts**, constructed in serial form, that chart processes incrementally.

The production of these narratives can create challenges, as the discussion below shows, but they can also provide compelling evidence to enrich a dataset.

Narratives of past and future

Following in the long-established tradition of the Chicago School (Thomas and Znaniecki 1958 [1918–21]; Shaw 1966 [1930]), participants in a QL study may be asked to produce written or audio accounts of their past lives or their journeys through a particular process. In Shaw's (1966 [1930]) classic life history of a young Jack Roller (a thief and mugger), the researcher constructed a chronological case history of the young man, drawn from a succession of in-depth interviews. These case history files were then fed back to the young man, who used them to produce an autobiographical account of his life (Shaw 1966 [1930]: 21–3; Appendix 2). This tradition of soliciting autobiographical writings, either in the form of memoires of past times, of accounts of particular transitions or contemporary patterns of living, has continued through the decades, not least in the work of the *Mass Observation Archive* (see Chapter 8). Such retrospective accounts are vitally important in processual analysis, and in discerning subjective understandings of causal processes.

An autobiographical account of a journey into young fatherhood (Johnson 2015) provides an example. This solicited account, produced with minimal guidance from the researchers, was published in an edited collection designed to explore the issue of young fatherhood from varied perspectives, including the voices of young fathers themselves (Neale and Davies 2015). This is how the narrative begins:

> In late September 2007, merely a few weeks into the final year of high school, I was frantically pacing the upstairs landing of my girlfriend's parents' house. Coming out of the bathroom we caught each other's gaze as she nodded. We were expecting a baby. We both sat down, myself in complete shock. ... Our immediate concern was: What will our parents say? ... What were we going to do? Were we going to keep the baby? If so what would our lives be like? ... What would people say? What would happen next? (Johnson 2015: 319)

Narratives of the future

Autobiographical accounts may also focus on **imaginary futures**. As we have seen above, accounts of future aspirations, plans, hopes and fears are integral to life journey interviewing, and an important means of discerning the seeds of change (see Box 3.4). But future aspirations may also be drawn out using written, audio or visual (life mapping) tools. Written accounts can be produced between waves of field-work or drafted at the time of an interview, usually over a 20- or 30-minute period. These techniques were first used by Veness (1962) in a study of the aspirations of school leavers. More recently, they have been used in several longitudinal studies or re-studies, most notably in 1969 for the *National Child Development* study (1958 cohort; Elliott and Morrow 2007; Elliott 2010b); in 1978 and 2010 for the *Isle of Sheppey* study and re-study (Pahl 1978; Crow and Lyon 2011; Lyon and Crow 2012); and in 2007 for the Timescapes study (Winterton and Irwin 2011). Further details are provided in Box 6.4.

Box 6.4   Narrating Imaginary Futures

- Veness (1962) asked school leavers to imagine they were looking back at their lives from the vantage point of old age, and to write a life story that would span the intervening years. The aim was to explore the fledgling identities, aspirations and expectations of the young people, then aged 14 and 15. In all, 1,300 essays were generated. This technique was combined with 'best moment' essays, questionnaires and short, structured interviews with the young people. Contextualising the essays by interweaving them with these different sources of data greatly enriched the findings. The young people's understandings of unfolding work and family trajectories were examined against a backdrop of post-war optimism and economic growth. A sub-sample of the young people was followed up two years later to find out what occupations they had eventually taken up (Veness 1962: 219). This model was adapted by Pahl in the late 1970s for the *Isle of Sheppey* study (Pahl 1978), and the exercise was repeated 30 years later for Crow and Lyon's re-study (Crow and Lyon 2011; Lyon and Crow 2012, 2020).
- Time spans for constructing the future are likely to vary; the greater the time span, the greater the creativity required in its construction. Writers may be invited to look back from an imaginary older life, as in the Veness (1962) study, or to project forward a number of years from the present day. The teenagers in the *NCDS 1958* cohort, for example, were invited to imagine that they were 25 years old, and to write about the lives they envisaged leading at that age. This same approach was adopted in two Timescapes projects – the *Siblings and Friends* study and the *Young Lives and Times* study. Some of the resulting narratives were short note-form accounts produced during an interview, but the majority were more extensive scripts that were produced independently, between interviews. These were then mailed to the researcher, or brought to the next interview, where they formed the basis for further discussion. Across the two projects, 42 accounts were produced (Winterton and Irwin 2011). Following in the tradition of Veness (1962), the Timescapes researchers were able to locate the essays within the context of interview data about the young people's backgrounds and evolving lives (Winterton and Irwin 2011). Two examples drawn from these accounts are given in Box 6.5.

Box 6.5 Imaginary Futures (*Young Lives and Times* study, Timescapes Archive)

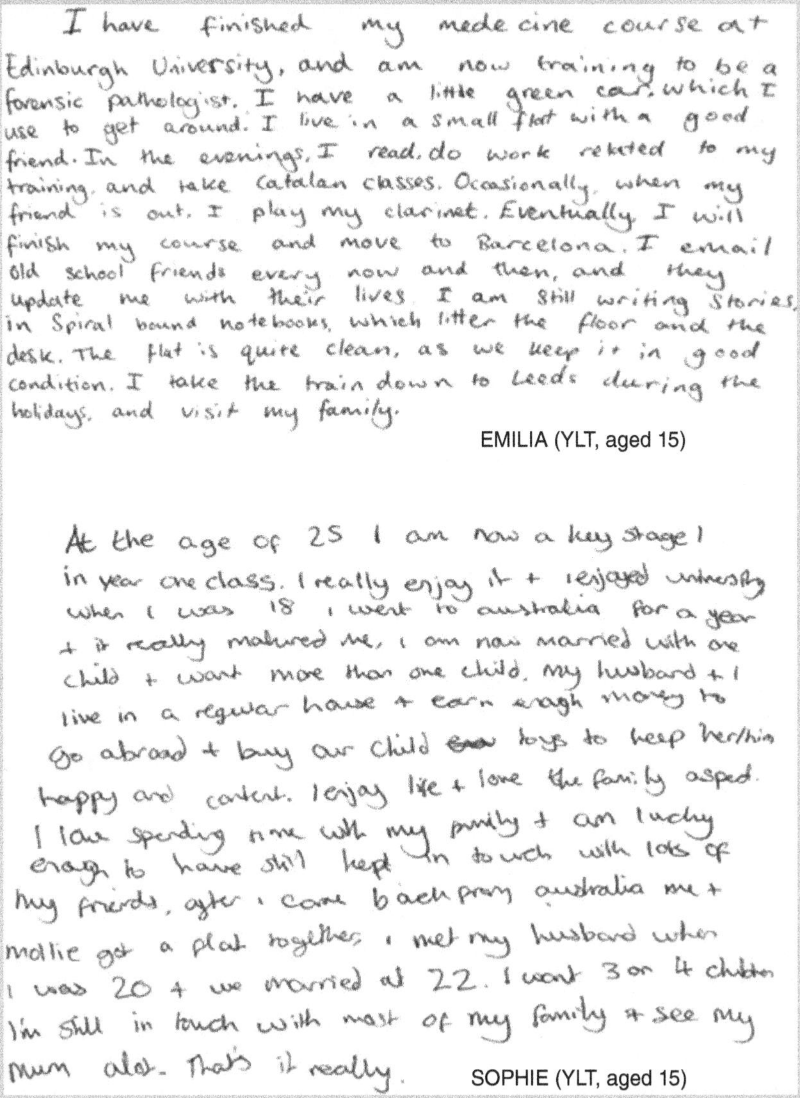

I have finished my medecine course at Edinburgh University, and am now training to be a forensic pathologist. I have a little green car, which I use to get around. I live in a small flat with a good friend. In the evenings, I read, do work related to my training, and take Catalan classes. Occasionally, when my friend is out, I play my clarinet. Eventually I will finish my course and move to Barcelona. I email old school friends every now and then, and they update me with their lives. I am still writing stories in spiral bound notebooks, which litter the floor and the desk. The flat is quite clean, as we keep it in good condition. I take the train down to Leeds during the holidays, and visit my family.

EMILIA (YLT, aged 15)

At the age of 25 I am now a key stage 1 in year one class. I really enjoy it + enjoyed university when I was 18, I went to australia for a year + it really matured me, I am now married with one child + want more than one child. My husband + I live in a regular house + earn enough money to go abroad + buy our child toys to keep her/him happy and content. I enjoy life + love the family aspect. I love spending time with my family + am lucky enough to have still kept in touch with lots of my friends, after I came back from australia me + mollie got a flat together, I met my husband when I was 20 + we married at 22. I want 3 or 4 children. I'm still in touch with most of my family + see my mum alot. That's it really.

SOPHIE (YLT, aged 15)

Figure 6.1 Imaginary futures – *Young Lives and Times* study, Timescapes Archive

The value of future narratives

Narrative accounts of the future serve a dual purpose. They are reflections of the times in which they are produced, illuminating how aspirations are shaped by prevailing structural opportunities and constraints (Sanders and Munford 2008). They have been used to explore the construction of young people's identities, their projections for family, home, leisure and working lives, and the influence of structural factors (class, gender, family background) on these processes (Hallden 1994, 1999; O'Connor 2006; Sanders and Munford 2008; Patterson et al. 2009; McDonald et al. 2011; Winterton and Irwin 2011). The original Isle of Sheppey essays, for example, were gathered at a time of recession in the late 1970s. They reflected an increasingly unpredictable world, one diverging from prescribed pathways, with divorce, unemployment, bereavement and step-family life all emerging as common life course themes (Crow and Lyon 2011). For the re-study, this exercise was repeated with a new generation of young people. This enabled the researchers to explore how imagined futures were being re-scripted against a backdrop of three decades of socio-economic change in this community (Lyon and Crow 2012).

At the same time, these accounts have biographical as well as historical value. They can illuminate dynamic life course processes, how past and future are interwoven, and how aspirations and priorities for the future shift from different vantage points in the life course (O'Connor 2006; Sanders and Munford 2008; Patterson et al. 2009; Crow and Lyon 2011). Interesting insights have also been reported on the turning points and driving forces through which future paths are chosen, forged, sustained or abandoned (O'Connor 2006; Crow and Lyon 2011). The extent to which young people plan out their future lives, or live with truncated time horizons in an extended present, has also been explored (O'Connor 2006).

Revisiting imagined futures recursively, at subsequent interviews, can shed valuable light on how far expectations of the future mesh with what actually happens. As shown in Chapter 3, imagined futures are not predictive of future paths. Yet their very construction can give shape to a range of possible selves and the pathways that may lead to their realisation (Worth 2009; Lyon and Crow 2012; Hardgrove et al. 2015). These accounts may, therefore, offer valuable insights into the seeds of change.

For all their worth, using future accounts as data-generation tools can also create challenges for researchers. The manner in which these writings are produced has a bearing on their meaning and their utility. In the main, they have been used in snapshot, synchronic studies rather than in prospective longitudinal enquiry (the *National Child Development* study (1958 cohort), the Timescapes study and, to an extent, Veness (1962) are exceptions). Related to this, in most existing studies, future accounts have been solicited in school settings and mediated through teachers (not without considerable challenges in some cases, e.g. Patterson et al. 2009; Lyon and Crow 2012). While this can work effectively and yield large pools of data across classrooms of students, it also raises questions about the impact of the setting on the presentation and content of the data (Veness 1962; O'Connor 2006; Elliott and Morrow 2007). Veness (1962: 16) stresses the importance of clarifying the research context in which the essays are being produced, and the need to assure young people that their accounts are confidential and will not be read (let alone marked) by their teachers.

Where school settings have been used, there has been a tendency to hive off the essays and analyse them as stand-alone data, rather than integrating them into an interview setting where they can be used to draw out further reflections (see, for example, Pahl 1978). This reduces the ability to build a contextual understanding of the essay writers and the circumstances of their lives. Similarly, in the *NCDS 1958 Cohort* study, the intention to compare the imagined futures of the essayists with the actualities of their lives as the study progressed, did not materialise (see Elliott and Morrow 2007 for a detailed account). Fortunately, in both these studies the essays were archived, allowing for their subsequent analysis in the context of the broad study findings (Elliott and Morrow 2007; Elliott 2010b; Crow and Lyon 2011; Lyon and Crow 2012, 2020).

A further drawback, common to all writing tasks in a digital age, is that essay writing is increasingly seen as an outmoded form of communication (Lyon and Crow 2012). It has been used most effectively with young people of school age who are familiar with such tasks (Veness 1962); but there is evidence to suggest it may be much less effective with adults (Henwood and Shirani 2012). The way this task is presented to essay writers also requires care, for it can influence how far the accounts reflect thoughtful and relatively realistic expectations, or shade into flights of fancy (for the latter, see Hallden 1994, 1999). The very wording of the instructions can make a difference (Winterton and Irwin 2011).

Writing about the future is inherently creative and imaginative, as essay writers themselves point out (Crow and Lyon 2011: 23). Some researchers stress the importance of encouraging spontaneity and giving participants licence to write in their own style about matters of their own choosing (McDonald et al. 2011). Even so, most researchers, from Veness (1962) onwards, guide participants to write realistically about the future, using their personal experience to imagine how they see their own life unfolding. This generally works well, with researchers acknowledging the powerful and compelling insights that such writings can reveal (Pahl 1978; Crow and Lyon 2011).

Diary accounts

Soliciting or commissioning diaries has a long history in socio-historical research, and remains a popular research tool (Plummer 2001; Bytheway 2011; Bartlett and Milligan 2015). Participants are asked to record their experiences and reflections on events and processes as they unfold, in real-time, either in hand-writing or through internet technology. This technique has been in evidence since the 1930s, most notably in the early work of the Mass Observation Archive (Bartlett and Milligan 2015; see Box 6.8). In their very construction, diaries are temporal records, capturing the immediacy and intimacy of life as it is lived. Unlike autobiographical accounts, diaries work prospectively. They are constructed in the present moment and oriented to the immediate past and future, documenting an unfolding life in an incremental and episodic way (Watson 2013: 107). Whether hand-written or digitally produced, interior thoughts and feelings, alongside events and circumstances of significance to the diarist, are recorded in the stream of time, as they occur, providing a flow of personal reflections on an ever-changing present (Plummer 2001: 48; Fincher 2013).

Given their inherent temporality, narrative diaries constitute a powerful form of longitudinal data. They derive their value from their intimacy, their seriality and their close proximity to the events they describe (Watson 2013). Since they are structured through time, they provide a lynchpin between past and future, following up on previous events, anticipating what is to follow, and illuminating the intricacies of transitions and trajectories, changes and continuities. Capturing the processual nature of experience in this way can provide valuable continuity between waves of QL interviews, and give access to the minutiae of change that could not be gleaned in any other way (Bytheway 2012).

The construction of diaries

Diaries can be produced in a wide variety of ways. At one extreme, they can be used to elicit intermittent 'snapshot' or 'soundbite' data about lives, with limited narrative elaboration. These tell the 'bare bones' of a story which researchers can then flesh out in an interview. Tick-box charts, which are commonly associated with structured time-use studies, fall into this category (Gershuny 2000). For quantitative researchers, these can be used to produce measurable data that is amenable to statistical analysis. This entails logging specific events, for example relating to food, health, financial or time budgets, that give a sequential understanding of a process (for example, eating patterns, disease management, household budgets or the duration of daily tasks).

Daily entries for these data logs may be divided into discrete periods of the day, sometimes by the hour, requiring frequent production. But these diaries may also be used flexibly to record the incidence and timing of acute events as they occur, a process known as **experience sampling**. Examples of multi-media diaries, and **snapshot diaries** that can be used to build a picture of the sequence and tempo of events, are given in Box 6.6.

Box 6.6 Multi-Media and 'Snapshot' Diaries

- **Multi-media diaries**: A range of media may be combined as part of a diary project. For example, creative, pictorial diary formats have been used with young people and those with limited writing skills (Wiseman et al. 2005). In the *Inventing Adulthoods* study, the researchers used *scrapbook diaries* with teenage participants. Writing tools were provided alongside disposable cameras for creating visual records, and glue to attach memorabilia (photos, postcards, event flyers, magazine cuttings, email exchanges, and so on) to the diary. The researchers also distributed sticky labels with thematic prompts (relating to relationships, love, sex, career, and so on) (Thomson and Holland 2005).

- **Web-based diaries**: In recent years, narrative diaries have increasingly been produced using web-based or smartphone technology (blogs, Facebook, WhatsApp, and so on, which are based on 'snapshot' forms of communication); or via audio or video recordings which allow for more expansive reflections (Monrouxe 2009; Fincher 2013; Robards and Lincoln 2017). Snapshot diaries have significant potential and can be tailored for a variety of research purposes, as the example below shows.
- **Experience sampling using snapshot diaries**: Snapshot diaries can be used to capture and explore critical incidents as they occur. In their mixed methods longitudinal study, for example, Koro-Ljungberg and Bussing (2013) used experience sampling to capture the tempo of attention-deficit hyperactivity syndrome among young people. Over a three-month period, whenever an episode of this condition occurred, the participants, along with family members and teachers, sent text messages and internet alerts to the researcher, with a brief description of events. The ease, immediacy and brevity of this approach yielded insights into the nature of these experiences, and their ebb and flow over relatively intense periods of time.

In their more conventional narrative form, diaries are free-flowing written accounts (Bytheway 2012) that give insights into life experiences as they occur. They are produced in a discursive, reflective and interpretive way and may be highly personal or 'confessional' in content. Along with audio or video formats, which also allow for expansive personal reflections, this is the most common form of diary used in QL research. Narrative diaries can be commissioned or solicited over a specified period of time, usually mirroring the process under investigation, or tied to the longitudinal frame of a study. The aim is to capture the ebb and flow of daily lives, and/or key moments in a transition, alongside reflections on their meaning for the participant. For written diaries, participants are given booklets to complete, with dates allocated to each page and clear guidelines on themes of interest to the researcher. Examples are given in Box 6.7.

Box 6.7   Narrative Diaries

- The Timescapes *Oldest Generation* study commissioned a series of diaries from a close relative or carer of the 12 older people in the study. They were designed to run over an 18-month period, with each diary spanning

(Continued)

a one-month period. Participants were asked to complete their entries on a daily basis, and to return the diaries to the researchers at the end of each month. Each diary booklet was dated for the month at hand, and included 60 A5-size pages, allowing for the daily entries to run over to a second page. Participants received a £50 shopping voucher for each diary that was returned to the research team. Several of the diarists fell behind schedule and stopped returning their booklets within the first year (in some cases, the team elicited some limited data by email instead). In two further cases, the older person died, creating a rupture in the diary-writing process. But, overall, the researchers received 162 monthly diaries from the families, of which 116 were handwritten. Full records for the whole 18-month period were secured for seven of the 12 families. These document in great detail the daily lives of the older person and the flow of their family relationships and support needs during the study. In the two cases where the older person died during the course of the research, the diaries contained unique records of their last months of life. The diaries were subsequently deposited in the Timescapes Archive as a valuable component of *The Oldest Generation* dataset (Bytheway 2011, 2012).

- In an organisational study of five managerial entrepreneurs, who were seeking to expand their business into international markets, the researchers set up a nine-month diary project to capture these processes as they occurred. The diary method was the prime means of generating data in this study, although the researchers conducted an initial interview to set up the project, and met with participants several times during the process to encourage them and keep them on track. Diarists were instructed to write freely about business developments, strategies, events, interactions and critical moments as and when they occurred (rather than at set or regular times). In this way, the method was tailored to the fluid, irregular and unpredictable nature of a strategic and evolving process. Diarists were also asked to record their marketing successes and failures, and their reflections and feelings about their experiences. They tended to adopt a rather formal and lengthy style of reporting at the outset, which quickly gave way to a more open, reflexive, informal and briefer narrative style as the project advanced. Notebooks or audio flash drives, provided by the researchers, were used to construct the diaries, which were copied for the use of the research team at the end of fieldwork. The exercise was a positive one for the entrepreneurs, who found that the process of writing about what they were doing helped to focus their efforts, structure their thoughts and hone their strategies for the future. However, the lack of contextual interview data to accompany the diaries, and the shortened time span for what is essentially a long-term evolving process, was a drawback for the researchers (Paavilainen-Mäntymäki and Aarikka-Stenroos 2013).

The value of diary accounts

Diaries present some challenges as data-generation tools. They vary in quality and length, and entries may be incomplete, edited or sanitised (Bytheway 2011, 2012; Watson 2013). Individual entries may be undated, out of sequence, heavily amended or unfinished, creating gaps in the record (Bytheway 2011; Paavilainen-Mäntymäki and Aarikka-Stenroos 2013). They may range from short factual snippets of data, to long reflective narratives, and the content may be highly selective or serendipitous. The entries may be recorded in retrospect, sometimes with a long gap between the event or experience and the diary record. While the temporal distance between events and their recording is much reduced using this tool, it is not eliminated; the problem of recall can still persist in what is, in any case, a highly personalised, interpretive monologue (Bytheway 2012; Watson 2013). Researchers note that participants commonly veer toward reporting positive experiences, and they may quickly lose faith that their mundane existence or the minutiae of their daily activities has any value for the researcher (Bytheway 2012).

Privacy is a key issue: the intimate way in which diaries are produced invites personal or 'confessional' accounts, but diarists may then decide they have revealed too much and opt not to share their writings or recordings, or place restrictions on their use (Pini and Walkerdine 2011). Whether diaries are seen as research documents, that participants will automatically share, or as personal documents that remain their property, or both, is a matter to clarify at the outset. The scrapbook diaries generated for the *Inventing Adulthoods* study, for example, were designated as personal documents that participants would retain. As a result, not all the data could be accessed by the research team, despite some careful negotiations (Thomson and Holland 2005).

Perhaps the biggest drawback is participant fatigue; keeping a narrative diary, particularly on a daily basis, requires time, commitment and motivation that may not be sustainable in the long run. Even a week of regular writing can lead to fatigue (Bartlett and Milligan 2015). However, diarists also comment on the intrinsic value of this creative form of self-expression, including its cathartic power (Thomson and Holland 2005; Paavilainen-Mäntymäki and Aarikka-Stenroos 2013; Bartlett and Milligan 2015). The frequency of entries and the time span for keeping a diary are therefore important considerations for the researcher. Whatever frequency and time span are established, participants may well deviate from them.

Given the challenges noted above, continuous daily entries, particularly of a reflexive kind, are not usually requested for more than a few weeks, although they can be sustained with regular support, encouragement and incentives from the research team, who are the main audience for their production (Monrouxe 2009; Bartlett and Milligan 2015). A chronicle may, for example, be organised around one entry per week or month, in order to enhance its sustainability over a 12–18-month period (Monrouxe 2009; Fincher 2013). But, as some of the examples in Box 6.6 and

Box 6.7 show, there is also value in organising entries flexibly, enabling the diarist to record significant events or encounters as and when they occur, to reflect the ebb and flow of lived experience (Thomson and Holland 2005; Monrouxe 2009; Paavilainen-Mäntymäki and Aarikka-Stenroos 2013).

In Box 6.8, short extracts are drawn from the compelling 20th-century diaries of Nella Last, which were generated for the Mass Observation Archive and span nearly three decades of change (1939–66). They were edited for publication in three volumes many years after Nella's death, and they illustrate the value of diaries as a QL data generation tool.

Box 6.8 Extracts from the Diaries of Nella Last
(housewife, 49, Mass Observation Archive)

- As a newly recruited diarist and recorder for the Mass Observation Archive, Nella began writing in 1939, and continued on an almost daily basis until 1966, two years before her death. She posted the diaries to the Mass Observation team once a week. Nella writes prolifically about her everyday life as a housewife and mother in Barrow-in-Furness (Cumbria, UK), and reflects on her experiences in the Women's Voluntary Service during the war and her return to domestic life in the aftermath. The entries seamlessly flow from world events, to community affairs, to family relationships and the minutiae of everyday life. Nella was a clandestine writer, who did not share her writings with family or friends. Most of her diaries were not read until the 1980s, many years after her death. Her wartime diaries have since formed the basis for a BBC television dramatisation. The extracts below are from Nella's post-war diaries (Malcolmson and Malcolmson 2008):

  15 August 1945: I wonder what work there will be for me? … I've learned my little gifts of cooking and managing. … I've learned to keep people together by a laugh. … I've learned the beauty and worth of sustained service with and for others [through the Women's Voluntary Service]. I'll never go back into a cage of household duties alone, much as my home means and will always mean to me. …

  21 August 1945: I wonder how long before it looks like peace in Japan – and is it really peace, or will it all break out again, or linger like a festering corroding sore for many years? … Little things grow dearer and dearer to me. … The little wood fire that I made for my husband to have his supper by … gleaming bits of brass I'd found time to polish tonight, even my bread and ginger bread seemed real in a world of shadows and doubts. …

  22 August: The dusk fell quickly tonight. … It's grand to think that this winter will have no blackout – that bright lights will be in the streets. …

How remote the last six years are becoming. It's odd to realise how Cliff [her son] has lost such a slice from his life. He has all his limbs. I think of the poor ones who came back handicapped so badly....

29 August: I used to think how happy people would be when the war was over but ... I see few signs of a brave new world. ... People are beginning to fear that they will be paid off. Women are not settling down very well after being at work. After the last slump, a lot of people at Vickers [Barrow's Ship Yard] got a nasty shake up when they were sacked. ...

7 September 1946: Of all gifts I crave, that of 'expression' would be my dearest wish. I have met such interesting people and always heard unbelievable stories about people's lives. If I could put all in written language and sequence, I could write books, I'm sure. Maybe I'll get my wish in some future reincarnation!

Visual Methods: Graphs and Drawings

Alongside written and audio tools, participatory data can be generated using visual representations such as graphs and drawings (discussed here), and photographs and video (sound and picture) recordings (discussed below). Pictorial tools come in a variety of forms, including relational maps and family drawings that can be revisited and updated recursively as a study unfolds (Smart et al. 2001; Akesson 2015; Falola 2015). Two powerful tools for visualising temporal processes are documented here. The first, life history charts, are structured graphic tools designed to elicit details of past lives. The second, life maps, are creative drawing tools with scope to elicit subjective accounts of past, present and future. The relative merits of these tools are explored below.

Life history charts

Life history charts, also known as life history or event history calendars, reviews or life grids, have been in use since the 1960s. These structured graphic tools capture a retrospective view of the life course in an easily accessible and standardised visual record. They were first developed for large-scale longitudinal surveys to improve recall of past events and enhance data reliability, particularly for older participants (Giele 1998; Scott and Alwin 1998; Elliott 2005). More recently, they have been adapted and evaluated for use in a range of qualitative health and social care studies, primarily in single-visit studies (Parry et al. 1999; Bell 2005; Harris and Parisi 2007; Wilson et al. 2007; Feldman and Howie 2009; Richardson et al. 2009; Del Bianco 2015). The example in Figure 6.2 is described below and in Box 6.9.

External Event	Age	Year	A. Personal/Other Life Events	B. Education	C. Lifestyle Smoking	Drinking
		1949	born			
Korean War	1	1950				
	2	1951				
	3	1952				
	4	1953				
	5	1954				
	6	1955				
	7	1956		started		
	8	1957				
	9	1958				
Vietnam War began	10	1959				
	11	1960				
	12	1961				
Cuban Missle Crisis	13	1962				
J.F.K. shot	14	1963			1 pack/2 weeks	
	15	1964		stopped		
	16	1965				
	17	1966	moved out of parents' house		1 pack/2.5 days	
	18	1967	1st car			26 oz rye/ few wks shared with friends
	19	1968	1st wife's child born			
Man on moon/ Woodstock Festival	20	1969			1 pack/day	
	21	1970	met wife & moved in together			
	22	1971			2 pack/day	
Henderson scores goal	23	1972				
	24	1973	1st marriage			
	25	1974	1st biological son born			
End of Vietnam War/ Fall of Saigon	26	1975				
	27	1976				
	28	1977				
	29	1978				
	30	1979	2nd biological son born			
Terry Fox Run/John Lennon shot	31	1980				
Regan & Pope John Paul II shot	32	1981				
	33	1982	wife had brain tumour removed & became vegetative; hospitalized permanently; car accident			drinking alone: 24 beer, 40oz rum & 26 oz rum/day
	34	1983	house fire			
	35	1984	farmhouse repaired			
	36	1985	mom passed away			
Challenger & Chernobyl accidents	37	1986				
	38	1987	first child left home			
	39	1988	started relationship with current partner (has 2 kids)			1 beer/wk
Fall of Berlin Wall	40	1989	divorced			
	41	1990				
1st Gulf War	42	1991	father passed away			

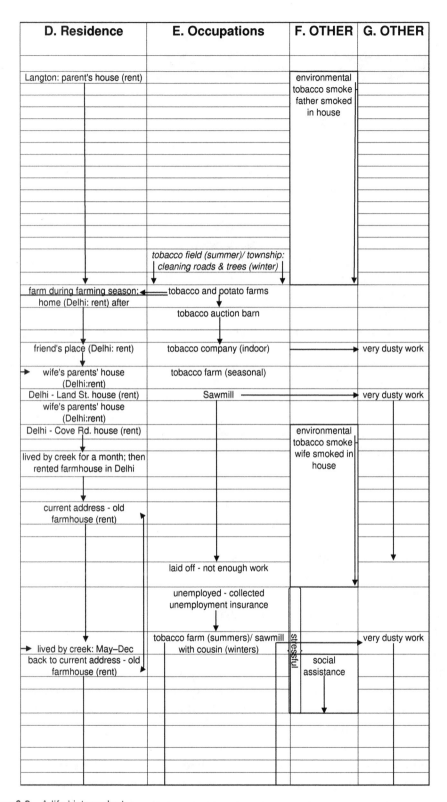

Figure 6.2 A life history chart

Source: Del Bianco 2015, originally published in Worth and Hardill (2015) (eds) *Researching the Life Course*, p. 84, and reproduced with the permission of Policy Press, an imprint of Bristol University Press, UK.

Box 6.9 Constructing a Life History Chart

- Participants are invited to work with the researcher to fill in a pre-prepared chart or grid that chronicles varied facets of a past life over a specified period of time. These charts can be constructed in varied ways, but generally involve plotting time periods along one axis, and key themes along another. Time periods are specified in advance and fashioned to fit the process under investigation (e.g. every year, every five years, or every decade from birth to the present day for a full life history, or covering a discrete period of historical time for a specific process of change). Varied life trajectories (relating to family, employment, housing, and so on) and domains of experience that are pertinent to the study (e.g. unfolding occupational identities, or health or criminal careers) are plotted along the other axis, along with key events or transitions. Time intervals, life trajectories and domains of experience can all be tailored to the needs of the project. This creates a chronology of a past life that graphically maps how varied life events, domains and pathways are connected through time.
- Del Bianco (2015), for example, used life grids with older cancer patients to draw out the connections between their health biographies, drinking patterns and life events such as divorce or loss of a home (illustrated in Figure 6.2). In common with other researchers, Del Bianco added external reference points (a series of world events) to the chart as a way to link biographical and historical processes, and to aid recall of past events.

The value of life history charts

In the main, the use of life history charts in qualitative research has been confined to synchronic, single-visit interview studies that have sought a retrospective understanding of life course events. Evaluations of these tools for in-depth qualitative enquiry reveal a mixed picture. Their ability to capture the fluid, experiential tempo of a life journey is somewhat limited. The focus tends to be on recording events as concrete, factual occurrences, rather than exploring their meaning as life course processes. The precision involved in recalling a past life chronologically does not map easily onto how people narrate their life stories, and the mental effort of pinpointing exactly when an event occurred, and its spacing and sequencing, may be fruitless or frustrating for people.

The use of external historical events as memory aids (for example, the shooting of John Lennon, or the fall of the Berlin Wall; see Figure 6.2) may well misfire. These historical moments may not necessarily be meaningful to participants, even where they have been chosen with a particular generation or socio-cultural group in mind (Richardson et al. 2009). The charts are also complex in their construction and their completion has been found to be daunting for some groups of participants. They can take up a considerable amount of time. Del Bianco (2015; see Figure 6.2), for example, allowed up to four hours for an interview using this tool. Their use may, therefore, dominate rather than facilitate an interview (Richardson et al. 2009). For these reasons, the tools are more likely to be constructed by the researcher on behalf of the participant, so diminishing their participatory value. They are, in effect, analytical tools (with some affinities to the analytical framework grids outlined in Chapter 10), and their use in interviews may reflect the researcher's agenda rather more than the participant's.

Despite these drawbacks, researchers report their effectiveness in chronicling a life, discerning connections between different transitions and trajectories, aiding memory and drawing out narratives of past events. Like all participatory methods, they can provide a welcome diversion from the intensity of speaking about a life, and they may open up sensitive issues in ways that give participants a measure of choice and control over such disclosures (Parry et al. 1999; Wilson et al. 2007).

Where these tools have been adapted for qualitative use and applied flexibly, the drawbacks noted above have been less problematic. For example, in some studies, charts are constructed using a range of colours to give a sense of the flow of life processes, or to convey the different meanings of life experiences (see Wilson et al. 2007; and the life-tapestry approach used by Feldman and Howie 2009). The recognition that these charts may not aid recall so much as aid a meaningful reconstruction of a past life is another helpful development (Richardson et al. 2009). Where these tools are embedded within an interview, with scope for reflection on their construction, it is possible to turn an instrumental recall of past events into a more reflexive understanding.

Life maps

These creative drawing tools are one of the most commonly used participatory tools in QL research. Also known as time maps or timelines (although they are by no means linear in construction), they are designed to visualise dimensions of an unfolding life, or a particular process, in an expressive and intuitive way. Participants are invited to draw a simple map of their life journey (or a segment of the journey) and to highlight key milestones, trigger points, events and transitions along the way. The drawings vary in their construction. In hybrid versions, researchers sometimes set up a simple graph, or suggest a straight line as the basic structure, thereby implying a linear and sequential vision of a life journey (see, for example, Sheridan et al. 2011; Söderström 2019). But participants are more usually given leeway to create their maps in their own way. Even where they are presented with a line, they may well deviate from it or elaborate with roots and branches (Worth 2011).

Participants may choose to draw mind maps, horizontal or vertical lines, parallel lines representing different and overlapping trajectories, or zigzag, criss-crossing, circular, spiral or flowing paths that denote varied ups and downs, historical loops, cul-de-sacs or wandering journeys (Zerubavel 2003). Iantaffi (2011) uses the imagery of a meandering river to introduce this mapping exercise to her participants. The drawings may range over a whole life or varied segments of it, even down to a single day, and they can be used to explore the future as well as the past (Thomson and Holland 2002; Gordon et al. 2005; Worth 2011; Hanna and Lau-Clayton 2012; Falola 2015). They can be used to draw out a particular aspect of a life journey, or to explore the intersection of varied pathways and trajectories (e.g. those relating to work and family life).

Researching emotionally sensitive journeys and embodied experiences can be facilitated through the use of such techniques (Gergen and Gergen 1987). Sheridan et al. (2011), for example, used this tool to explore participants' experience of weight loss and gain in the context of broader relational events and experiences. Figure 6.3 gives an example of a life map produced for a study of the employment journeys of women who had experienced abusive relationships (Guenette and Marshall 2009). The participant provided a running commentary on the map as she drew it, enabling her to represent events that were difficult for her to speak of, and to recall and elaborate on

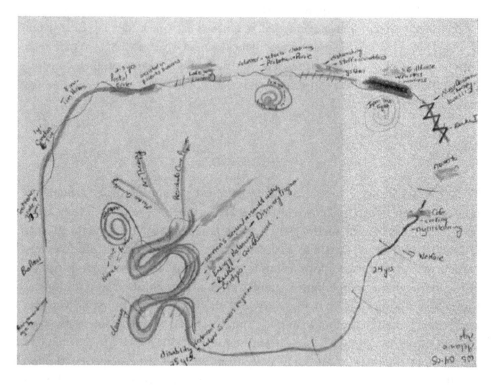

Figure 6.3　Mapping an emotional journey

Source: Guenette and Marshall 2009

varied experiences that occurred at different times during her journey. The map was constructed using coloured pens (the coloured version in the original article is striking). Times of relative calm and anger are denoted by shades of pink and red, while a time of abuse is shown as a jagged black line. Varied whorls of colour denote the exploration of new paths, such as leaving home and starting a new job, while a rainbow in her recent upward journey reflects a time of healing, stability and security in her working life.

As a further example, a creative approach to life mapping was adopted by Nizza et al. (2018) for their longitudinal study of a pain management programme. In this study, the researchers gave heavyweight paper and coloured pens to their participants, and asked them to draw their evolving experiences of chronic pain. By eliciting a sequence of drawings at different points in time, the researchers gained a prospective understanding of pain perceptions at each point in time, and were able to construct a retrospective understanding of pain experiences through time. This gave insights into the complex and emotional journeys that their participants had undergone through their treatment. Figure 6.4 shows the powerful visual images that were evoked in successive interviews by a participant, to convey her transition from feeling submerged and dominated by pain, to gradually taking back control and finding ways to live her life to the full again.

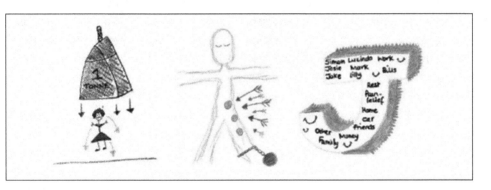

Figure 6.4 Visualising pain experiences through life mapping

Source: Nizza et al. 2018

The value of life maps

While life maps serve a similar purpose to the life history charts outlined earlier, there are notable differences. Life maps are able to overcome some of the limitations of the more structured charts. For example, where the charts are framed around fixed notions of chronological time, life maps are personalised, creative tools that reflect the fluidity of temporal processes and the inner logic of participants' lives. They can vividly convey the peaks, troughs and flowing contours of life journeys. In short, they are ideal as process-mapping tools (see Chapter 11). Since they allow for an understanding of emotional as well as event-based journeys, they do not require accurate recall of the sequencing and chronology of events. They can also allow participants to express in their own way what is unsayable or difficult to articulate through a narrative (Worth 2011).

The simple construction of life maps enables them to be integrated with ease into a biographical interview, where they can enrich and deepen a verbal account (Worth 2011). The ease with which they can be revisited at subsequent interviews, means that they can be recursively updated or modified to reflect changing perceptions through the passage of time. Overall, life maps are good tools to think with, simplifying complex ideas, opening up sensitive life experiences, encouraging self-reflection, and giving tangible, visual shape to an emerging process in ways that would not be possible through a verbal exchange alone.

Visual Methods: Photographic and Video Tools

Photographic and video images provide some of the richest and most tangible data for discerning changes through time (Saldaña 2003: 25). Being able to see the world, alongside hearing about it, offers a powerful form of experiential knowledge. Whether still or moving, photographic images capture and crystallise lives located in time and place, offering, in minute but precise detail, a glimpse of landscapes, people and material cultures (Collier and Collier 1986 [1967]). In capturing fleeting moments in time, photographs are said to make time stand still. At the same time, when a camera produces a series of images that are in sequence, this creates a chronology of events.

As windows onto past times and places, photographic images evoke a strong sense of the passage of time, both biographically (as people gaze at younger versions of themselves and those around them) and historically (encapsulated in changing landscapes, homes, modes of transport, customs, styles of dress, activities, and so on). Photos are taken for posterity; they create a sense of the past within the present, and, as enduring images, they anticipate the future. The meaning and significance of a visual image is tied intimately to this sense of time passing. With each re-viewing, an image is subject to interpretation and re-interpretation by the viewer. As such, snapshots and moving pictures are repositories for creating and recreating memories and meanings (Frith 2011; Reavey 2011).

The use of photography and film as illustrative, documentary data has a long history among ethnographers, going back to the beginning of the 20th century (see, for example, Royce 2002, and for a fascinating overview, Plummer 2001: 59–74). The scope for capturing people and places visually has often been combined with fine artistry (see the wonderfully evocative photographs in Collier and Collier 1986 [1967]). The use of video cameras, which add movement and sound to a visual image, creates particularly rich and value-laden documentary records, generating a sense of 'being there', of seeing the world through the eyes of the participants (Collier and Collier 1986 [1967]). Moving images have traditionally been generated by specialist documentary and ethnographic film makers, but they are beginning to find their place in the standard tool kit of socio-historical researchers (Plummer 2001; see, for example, Royce 2002; Warin 2010; Pini and Walkerdine 2011).

Photographic images, whether still or moving, are increasingly sourced in collaboration with participants or produced directly by them. Exactly how photographic images are generated and used depends on the nature of a study: these are creative tools and techniques that can be adapted in many ways. Our focus below is on the use of still images, although much of the discussion can be applied to moving images. Two main strategies for working with photographic images are discussed here: the first is the use of retrospective images through photo sourcing and elicitation; the second involves generating visual images through photo diaries.

Photo sourcing and elicitation: using retrospective images

Photographic images can be sourced and re-purposed by researchers to create a suite or collage of photos for use in a life journey interview (Collier and Collier 1986 [1967]). In the Timescapes *Men as Fathers* study, for example, Henwood et al. (2011) sourced and assembled a photo-collage of images of fathers as a way to draw out participants' reflections on the role of men in family life. They also sourced and created a sequence of images from Victorian to contemporary times to elicit reflections on the changing nature of fatherhood and family life (see Figure 6.5). In a second phase of the study, the researchers revisited these two suites of photos with their participants. They used the images recursively to explore how responses and interpretations might have changed for their sample of men at different points in their biographies (Henwood et al. 2011).

Figure 6.5   Historical and contemporary images of fatherhood

Source: Henwood et al. 2011. Reproduced with permission from the copyright holders

Photo elicitation is a process in which participants assemble retrospective images of their lives, drawing on their personal picture collections (e.g. family albums or still or moving images shared on Facebook, Instagram or other networking sites). The images are then shared with researchers as part of a life journey interview. Such images can give tangible shape to a narrative, and evoke strong recollections and emotional responses that link past biographies to present-day circumstances (Reavey 2011). An example of how retrospective photographs can be both sourced by researchers, and elicited from participants, is provided in Box 6.10.

Box 6.10   Sourcing and Eliciting Retrospective Photos in a QL Re-study

- In the *Leicester Young Workers* re-study (detailed in Box 1.8), O'Connor and Goodwin (2012: 488–91) uncovered a series of photographs of their field sites, taken by the original researchers in the 1960s. This prompted them to locate the same sites and take contemporary photos that reflected changes in the landscape over four decades. These historical and contemporary images were used in their life history interviews with those participants who had been retraced from the earlier study (see Box 5.4). The aim was to unlock 'memories untapped for decades', helping to explain the 'why' and the 'how' of continuity and change.
- In addition, the researchers elicited photos from their participants. They were asked to bring to their interviews any photos of themselves taken around or since the time of the first study. This produced a rich collection of images, including photographs of their first days at work, in the workplace, or in their work uniforms, which were strongly evocative of biographical and social change over the intervening forty years. These images helped participants to recall details and emotions that may have otherwise remained buried or long forgotten.

Photo diaries: generating images through time

The creation of new photographic images specifically for a research project can be led by researchers and/or participants, or be carried out as a collaborative venture between the two. Collier and Collier (1986 [1967]), for example, took photographs of their participants at work, and used these as the basis for discussions about their favourite images, and their hopes and aspirations for the future. The researchers observe that it is through such active collaborations that the most meaningful and illuminating images can be produced (Collier and Collier (1986 [1967]: 73).

Photo-voice is a process in which participants create photographic data themselves to support the research process. In QL enquiry, such images can be produced dynamically, through the time frame of a study, to create a photographic diary of an unfolding process. Participants are provided with a digital or disposable camera or video recorder, and asked to create a record of aspects of their daily lives, or a particular process that they are going through. The images can then form the basis for discussion in a follow-up interview (Pini and Walkerdine 2011; Bytheway and Bornat 2012b). Illustrations of this approach are given in Box 6.11.

Box 6.11   Photo Diaries – Generating Images through Time

- In a psychological study of health biographies, Frith (2011) invited a panel of women to take part in an intensive photographic and interview study. The images were used to document the women's experience of undergoing chemotherapy for breast cancer, with associated hair loss and change in body image. Following initial interviews, 15 women agreed to create a **photo diary** or record of their journey through this treatment over a period of several months. They were given the freedom to decide what images to create, how many, and at what times; on average, the records consisted of 17 photographs for each case, that captured images of the women themselves and/or the settings in which they were treated. The women recorded significant moments and turning points in the treatment (for example, the point at which their hair began to grow back). In a final interview, held after the treatment, the women shared their photo diaries with the researchers and reflected on their meaning. Gaps in the visual record were just as significant as the photographs that were taken. The women spoke of shocking and distressing experiences that they had decided not to record, for they wished to erase them from their memory. During the interviews, the women used their chosen images to re-work the past, constructing their own narratives and memories of an emotionally difficult process. Plummer (2001: 66) observes that photos do not simply call up the past or provide routes into memory: they are creations that can be used to craft a particular story. This intensive study of a health transition enabled a detailed exploration of biographical disruption and repair, and of how these discontinuities in time were experienced and managed by the women (Frith 2011).
- Similarly powerful visual diaries were constructed by participants in a longitudinal study of the transition of homeless people to a housing re-settlement programme, and (in the majority of cases) their journeys back onto the streets again (Hodgetts et al. 2011). In one case, a photographic diary consisted of four sets of 27 photographs. The first set was produced collaboratively with the researcher during a walking interview, enabling the

(Continued)

participant to explain the significance of each image as it was produced, and to show the street scenes and hidden places where he and other homeless people spent their days. The full set of images, recorded over 12 months, enabled a vivid understanding of the entrenched 'homeless' identities displayed by the participants, their attachment to the street communities where they felt they belonged, and the reasons why a well-meaning resettlement programme was liable to fail.

The value of photographic images

Like all data-generation tools, photographic images have their strengths and weaknesses. As shown above, the meaning of a photograph is not straightforward; it requires interpretation and re-interpretation from the producer of the image and its viewers over time. Images have limited value as 'stand-alone' data for they require accompanying narratives to draw out their significance (Collier and Collier 1986 [1967]); Hodgetts et al. 2011). Linked to this characteristic, photographic images are essentially samples or snapshots, rather than holistic records: they offer no more than a partial vision of people, places and events, and they can therefore be misleading.

The kind of photographs that are appropriate to record varies from one context to the next. Images of conflict, violence, pain, suffering, and so on are the very stuff of investigative journalism but, as shown in Box 6.11, they rarely find a place in personal or domestic collections. Much like narrative diaries, personal photos capture what people wish to preserve; they have a celebratory quality that may not represent the reality of people's lives. While they may be produced spontaneously, they are just as likely to be carefully staged and edited to show the best side of life. Photos that challenge conventional values and collective ideals are generally avoided, since revealing life's difficulties or darker side can 'unfix the gaze' in provocative ways (Plummer 2001: 66). This raises a question mark over how far photographic images can be taken at face value, and suggests the need for accompanying narratives that can shed light on their meaning.

There are further drawbacks. Producing a photo diary can involve participants in a considerable amount of effort and care in gaining access to particular settings (Hodgetts et al. 2011), and in putting into practice the etiquette of seeking permission and avoiding taking images that may reveal people's identities. Deciding which aspects of their lives to record and what to edit out can also engender anxiety (Frith 2011). Where photographic or video diaries are commissioned by researchers, the camera or recorder can become a voyeuristic device, an instrument of surveillance that may engender discomfort for participants and serve to objectify them. Certainly, the task of creating a visual diary of difficult or emotionally charged circumstances may be stressful for participants, confronting them with aspects of their lives that they would sooner not own or would wish to put behind them (Frith 2011; Pini and Walkerdine 2011; the ethics of this are discussed in Chapter 5, see Box 5.11).

At the same time, the use of photographic images by participants can bring many advantages, not least their value in documenting events and processes that the researcher would not otherwise be able to access. Cameras require little skill and experience to use (for the focus is not on the technical aspects of a photo but on the content of the image). Like all visual and creative participatory tools, they allow participants to show as well as tell, thereby playing a valuable role for those who may struggle to produce a verbal narrative. Finally, they increase the participatory nature of a research study, although, as all users of photo voice acknowledge, the extent to which this method can be said to be empowering for participants is far from clear cut. The power of still and moving images to capture temporal processes, however, is beyond doubt. They can engage the senses in ways that powerfully convey the immediacy and emotional tenor of life experiences.

Constructing a Data-generation Tool Kit

The approaches, tools and techniques used to generate QL data form a rich palette of complementary methods that can be combined in creative ways. There is scope to introduce new tools or refine techniques over time, while some researchers offer a menu of creative tools to engage the interest of participants (Saldaña 2003; Weller 2012). Weaving some elements of ethnography into an interview-based study (or vice versa) enhances the capacity to discern lives as they are lived and experienced, as well as how they are narrated. Similarly, researchers commonly supplement interview methods with life maps and/or written, audio or visual diaries. These participatory tools can enrich temporal insights, help sustain participant involvement and interest, and, crucially, increase the capacity to gain an intimate familiarity with a life (Gordon et al. 2005; Monrouxe 2009; Worth 2011; Bytheway 2012; Neale et al. 2015). Such participatory tools are rarely used on their own; they are accessories to a life story, which can be used as a springboard for further discussion and reflection (Plummer 2001). In combination, these varied data sources can give access to different temporalities, interweaving past and future and working across varied horizons and tempos of time (see the *Oldest Generation* study, Box 6.12, for an example).

Yet a caveat arises at this point. If the rigour of QL enquiry is to be maintained, data-generation techniques and tools need to be carefully chosen and piloted, taking into account the design and sampling decisions that shape a study. This should help to ensure that participants (and researchers) are not overloaded by a plethora of different activities that complicate field enquiry and present extra challenges for analysis, particularly when working with large samples or across varied settings.

Similarly, where new field tools are introduced in subsequent waves, this can result in a loss of continuity and reduce the capacity for bringing complementary data together through time. To avoid these pitfalls, most QL researchers aim for a streamlined suite of tools and techniques. Illustrations of the varied ways in which researchers combine field tools and techniques in different research contexts are given in Box 6.12.

Box 6.12 Constructing a Bespoke Tool Kit

- Bornat and Bytheway (2010, 2012) combined life history interviews with narrative diaries and photo-voice techniques in their study of *The Oldest Generation*. The combination of retrospective life histories and prospective diaries enabled the researchers to capture both extensive and intensive horizons of time: the long sweep of lives lived over decades of change, alongside the contingencies of everyday existence for those in later life (Bornat and Bytheway 2012).
- Along with most organisational researchers, Dawson (2003) uses a mixture of in-depth interviewing, observation and documentary and archive materials for his studies of organisational processes. Some iteration between these forms of evidence – the life as lived and observed, and as told – is seen as highly valuable in any study of collective processes, not least because what people say they are doing does not necessarily map on to how things are done (Dawson 2003; see also Pettigrew 1985, showcased in Box 1.3).
- Worth (2011) combined biographical interviews with audio-diaries and life maps in her study with visually impaired youngsters. The life maps were successfully adapted for her participants with the use of tactile materials.
- Dassa (2018) adopted musical autobiography as a field tool in research and reminiscence work with older people, some of whom had dementia and a reduced capacity to narrate or visualise their lives. As noted earlier, experiential art forms such as music offer powerfully evocative ways to conjure a life story.
- The *Following Young Fathers* team combined in-depth life journey interviews with visual drawing tools such as life maps and self-portraits. Future essays and diaries were not considered appropriate for working with a nomadic and marginalised group of young men, some of whom had limited literacy skills (Neale et al. 2015).
- The *Welfare Conditionality* qualitative panel study involved working with a sample of 480 participants, drawn from varied sub-groups across a range of UK settings. In order to keep this study to manageable proportions, three waves of biographical interviews were chosen as the sole method for generating data (Dwyer and Patrick 2020).

Closing Reflections

In this chapter, we have explored the process of generating QL data and outlined the varied field tools and techniques that may be drawn upon to create a rich QL data-set. Particular attention has been given to interviewing and a range of multi-media tools and techniques, including narrative and visual participatory tools. As in other dimensions of QL research, the process of generating data unfolds through the successive waves of field enquiry. This requires a mixture of continuity and flexibility, creativity and precision. Attention also needs to be paid to the three-dimensional logic of QL enquiry, ensuring that an integration of case, thematic and processual understandings is built into field enquiry.

There is ample scope, too, to combine elements from different field traditions, and to draw on new tools and techniques as a study progresses. This capacity to refine data-generation methods as a study progresses is part and parcel of the flexibility afforded by QL research, and a potentially important means of enhancing the integrity and veracity of a study (Saldaña 2003; see Chapter 12 for further discussion on this theme). At the same time, there is the ever-present danger that a field enquiry will unravel. Whatever tools and techniques are utilised, clear rationales are needed for their use, and they need to be piloted, chosen and combined with care. This caveat aside, the tools outlined here demonstrate the many creative ways in which researchers can gain an intimate familiarity with the unfolding lives of their participants.

Further Reading

There is an extensive literature on the themes of this chapter. For insightful accounts on the practice of longitudinal ethnography, see Corsaro and Molinari (2000), Kemper and Royce (2002), Burton et al. (2009), and Howell and Talle (2012). For an array of biographical and narrative forms of interviewing, Plummer's *Documents of Life (*2001) is highly recommended. Other useful works on eliciting biographical data include Clausen (1998), Miller (2000), Merrill and West (2009) and *The Oral History Reader* (Perks and Thomson 2016). The literature on recursive interviewing is sparse, but Rachel Thomson (2012) provides a welcome introduction.

A growing number of commentaries can be found on the use of participatory, multi-media tools for generating real-time life journey data. The following are particularly recommended: on diary methods, Monrouxe (2009), Bytheway (2012), Fincher (2013), and Bartlett and Milligan (2015); on accounts of the future, Veness (1962), Elliott (2010), Winterton and Irwin (2011) and Lyon and Crow (2020); on working with retrospective life history charts, Wilson et al. (2007) and Feldman and Howie (2009); on life mapping, Guenette and Marshall (2009) and Worth (2011); and on visual methodologies, the collection of essays in Reavey (2011).

Bartlett, R. and Milligan, C. (2015) *What is Diary Method*? London: Bloomsbury.

Burton, L., Purvin, D. and Garrett-Peters, R. (2009) 'Longitudinal ethnography: Uncovering domestic abuse in low income women's lives', in G. Elder and J. Giele (eds) *The Craft of Life Course Research*. New York: Guilford Press. pp. 70–92.

Bytheway, W. (2012) *The Use of Diaries in Qualitative Longitudinal Research*. Timescapes Methods Guides Series No. 7, www.timescapes.leeds.ac.uk.

Clausen, J. (1998) 'Life reviews and life stories', in J. Giele and G. Elder (eds) *Methods of Life Course Research: Qualitative and Quantitative Approaches*. London: Sage. pp. 189–212.

Corsaro, W. and Molinari, L. (2000) 'Entering and observing in children's worlds: A reflection on a longitudinal ethnography of early education in Italy', in P. Christensen and A. James (eds) *Research with Children: Perspectives and Practices*. London: Falmer. pp. 179–200.

Elliott, J. (2010) 'Imagining gendered futures: Children's essays from the *"National Child Development Study"* in 1969', *Sociology*, 44 (6): 1073–90.

Feldman, S. and Howie, L. (2009) 'Looking back, looking forward: Reflections on using a life history review tool with older people', *Journal of Applied Gerontology*, 28 (5): 621–37.

Fincher, S. (2013) 'The diarist's audience', in L. Stanley (ed.) *Documents of Life Revisited*. London: Routledge. pp. 77–91.

Guenette, F. and Marshall, A. (2009) 'Time line drawings: Enhancing participant voice in narrative interviews on sensitive topics', *International Journal of Qualitative Methods*, 8(1): 86–92.

Howell, S. and Talle, A. (eds) (2012) *Returns to the Field: Multi-temporal Research and Contemporary Anthropology*. Bloomington, IN: Indiana University Press.

Kemper, R. and Royce, A. (eds) (2002) *Chronicling Cultures: Long Term Field Research in Anthropology*. Walnut Creek, CA: AltaMira Press.

Lyon, D. and Crow, G. (2020) 'Doing qualitative secondary analysis: Revisiting young people's imagined futures in Ray Pahl's Sheppey studies', in K. Hughes and A. Tarrant (eds) *Qualitative Secondary Analysis*. London: Sage. pp. 155–71.

Merrill, B. and West, L. (2009) *Using Biographical Methods in Social Research*. London: Sage.

Miller, R. (2000) *Researching Life Stories and Family Histories*. London: Sage.

Monrouxe, L. (2009) 'Solicited audio diaries in longitudinal narrative research: A view from inside', *Qualitative Research*, 9 (1): 81–103.

Perks, R. and Thomson, A (eds) (2016) *The Oral History Reader*, 3rd edition. London: Routledge.

Plummer, K. (2001) *Documents of Life 2: An Invitation to a Critical Humanism*. London: Sage.

Reavey, P. (ed.) (2011) *Visual Methods in Psychology*. London: Routledge.

Thomson, R. (2012) *Qualitative Longitudinal Methods as a Route into the Psycho-Social*. Timescapes Methods Guides Series Guide No. 13, www.timescapes.ac.uk.

Veness, T. (1962) *School Leavers: Their Aspirations and Expectations*. London: Methuen.

Wilson, S., Cunningham-Burley, S., Bancroft, A. and Backett-Milburn, K. (2007) 'Young people, biographical narratives and the life grid: Young people's accounts of parental substance abuse.' *Qualitative Research*, 7 (1): 135–51.

Winterton, M. and Irwin, S. (2011) 'Youngsters' expectations and context: Secondary analysis and interpretations of imagined futures', in M. Winterton, G. Crow and B. Morgan-Brett (eds) *Young Lives and Imagined Futures: Insights from Archived Data*. Timescapes Working Paper No. 6, www.timescapes.leeds.ac.uk

Worth, N. (2011) 'Evaluating life maps as a versatile method for life course geographies', *Area*, 43 (4): 405–12.

PART 3

JOURNEYS WITH DATA

The many ways of crafting a QL study and generating rich processual data have been considered in Part 2 of this book. Here we turn to an equally important set of issues: how QL datasets are organised and managed and how they are analysed. Their value as legacy data, with the potential for longer-term use and re-use, is also explored here, along with the potential to draw on wider forms of legacy data to enrich QL studies. The title of this section of the book reflects what will, by now, be a familiar refrain: fashioning a QL dataset and making sense of what it can tell us is an ongoing, creative process, rather than a one-off enterprise. Since human lives are continually under construction, the constitution of a growing QL dataset is transformed with each return visit to the field; every time new data are added into the mix, the temporal composition and meaning of the evidence base is recast. This is part of what makes QL data so fascinating, but it takes care to decide how to manage a resource that is continually evolving, and how to formulate insights about processes that are inherently provisional.

Chapter 7 (Managing Qualitative Longitudinal Data: Ethics and Practicalities) explores how an emerging dataset can be managed to support the analytical process, and to facilitate longer-term use. In all qualitative research, generating, managing and analysing data are intertwined phases of a study. But this is particularly pronounced in a QL context, where data management and analysis take place as recurring cycles, tied to each visit to the field. The practical, ethical and legal dimensions of managing QL data are outlined here, with particular consideration given to the timing of these processes over an extended data life cycle.

Chapter 8 (Working with Legacy Data: Ethics and Practicalities) goes on to explore the value of QL datasets, and other forms of legacy data, as retrospective sources of evidence that can shed light on socio-historical processes. QL researchers are both users and producers of legacy data; the nature of these processes and their value are explored here. Legacy data can complement the prospective data generated through the waves of a QL study, and form a valuable baseline for building a new study or re-study, with considerable temporal reach. Different forms of legacy data can also be aggregated to build a broader, more comparative picture of lives and times. The theoretical and ethical issues surrounding the use of legacy datasets are touched on here, and their implications for QL enquiry considered. The central role played by archives in facilitating data sharing and re-use are also outlined here, with a particular focus on the curation and stewardship of QL data.

In considering qualitative longitudinal analysis (QLA), we return to the key conceptual themes that are threaded through this book: the logic of working across and integrating case, thematic and processual insights; and turning synchronic (snapshot) readings of data into diachronic (through-time, processual) readings. This basic logic is set out in Chapter 9 (Qualitative Longitudinal Analysis: Basic Strategies) along with the abductive mode of discovery that underpins interpretive enquiry. Having set the scene in Chapter 9, Chapter 10 considers case and thematic analysis, while Chapter 11 explores processual analysis, the intricacies of tracing processes back and forward in time to discern their multiple causal threads. A range of analytical tools and strategies are outlined here to help translate the conceptual picture into research practice.

Dawson (2003: 99) reflects that working with and analysing processual data 'is an absorbing and often lonely task, which can be difficult to share with others'. It is also challenging, given the sheer scale of these data and their rich complexity. The aim of these analytical chapters is to equip researchers with the strategies to clarify what they are trying to achieve in working with their data, and the practical tools and techniques needed to get there. In this way, hopefully, the data journey may become a little less lonely for the researcher, and a lot more manageable.

7

MANAGING QUALITATIVE LONGITUDINAL DATA: ETHICS AND PRACTICALITIES

┌─ Key Points ───

- **The importance of good data management**: While sample sizes may be small, QL methodology generates large, unwieldy, complex and continually evolving datasets that need to be managed as a project develops. The process is cumulative and recurring. In order to avoid 'death by data asphyxiation', data-management tasks need to be factored in from the outset, and revisited systematically as a study progresses. Research funders in the UK, the USA and across Europe are gradually implementing data-management and sharing policies in order to maximise the openness of data, and transparency and accountability in research design and practice.
- **A dual purpose**: For QL researchers, good data management serves two purposes: it cumulatively builds a QL dataset for ongoing analysis, and it facilitates the longer-term use and safe preservation of the data for the original researchers and for sharing with others.
- **The timing of key tasks**: The ethical representation of data, and preparations and consent for archiving, are not simple administrative tasks that can be 'tacked on' to the end of a project. They are critical issues that need to be addressed from the outset.
- **QL data are inherently personal**: They embody sensitive field materials (biographical interviews, ethnographic and participatory data) and personal

(Continued)

contact details that need to be retained in order to follow participants over time. Ethical safeguards for their use and re-use are therefore essential. Under recent legislation (the General Data Protection Regulation or GDPR), extra safeguards are needed to manage personal data.

- **Managing QL data – six steps**: The guidance here covers data management planning; consent processes; producing, labelling and transcribing data files; systems and structures for organising data; the ethical representation of data – anonymising and safeguarding confidentiality; and archiving a dataset. The guidance is not intended to be overly prescriptive; protocols vary across disciplines, and, for a QL study, are likely to evolve over time. Examples of good practice can be adapted to the needs of individual projects.

Introduction

Anyone who has carried out longitudinal field research … will know that the central problem is dealing with complexity. … There is no release from the overwhelming weight of information, from the task of structuring and clarifying, from the requirements of … conceptualisation. The result is death by data asphyxiation – the slow and inexorable sinking into the swimming pool that started so cool, clear and inviting and now has become a clinging mass of maple syrup. (Pettigrew 1995: 111)

Now all this talk of filing may sound very boring – a long way from the humanistic concerns this book champions! But the fact is that filing – as C. Wright Mills once observed – is indeed an 'intellectual production.' … [A] good filing system harbours your intellectual life. (Plummer 2001: 152)

As our opening quotations describe so graphically, and as each generation of researchers discovers anew, the challenges of managing and working with QL datasets are acute. These datasets are likely to include data transcripts, audio and/or video files, and participatory data (e.g. life maps, diaries, drawings, photographs), along with field notes and case and thematic files (Foster et al. 1979; Huber and Van de Ven 1995; Saldaña 2003; McLeod and Thomson 2009). While QL studies may be 'small' in terms of sample size, the resulting datasets are extensive, unwieldy, complex and continually open to change and growth.

Van de Ven and Huber (1995: xiii) wryly observe that, 'over time, data mount astronomically and overload the information processing capacity of even a trained mind'. For example, a study of the changing citizenship experiences of 65 young people, gathered over three waves of fieldwork, yielded over 4,000 pages of interview transcripts (Smith 2003), while Ferguson et al. (2019) estimate that each of the larger case files produced for their ethnographic study amounts to around 200,000 words.

For large-scale qualitative panel studies (e.g. the *Welfare Conditionality* study, which generated over 1,000 interviews), the size of a dataset will be all the greater. Keeping track of data in waves, cases, themes and formats is all the more challenging when working with data of such scale and complexity. While the danger of data deluge or asphyxiation should not discourage researchers, it is a timely reminder that good data management is vital. It relies, as Plummer notes above, on the disciplined intellectual task of 'filing' along with associated data activities. For QL research, the diligence and precision of data management are the necessary groundings upon which the analysis and longer-term use of data can be built. They are a vital counter-part to the flexibility and creativity of the research process.

This chapter begins by considering the ethical, legal and practical dimensions of producing a well-organised, sustainable QL dataset for future use, along with the critical issue of timing for these processes. The chapter concludes by setting out six steps to good **data management** for QL researchers. The discussion is based on recent guidance and good practice in the UK. The work of the Timescapes Archive, hosted at the University of Leeds in the UK, provides an illustration of how research data can be preserved and shared for the future.

The Timescapes Archive is showcased here because it is a specialist repository for QL research data, and an international resource with scope for further growth and development. It is also a relatively new resource that embodies recent principles of good practice. A wider range of archives, including international resources in the USA and Europe, are outlined in Chapter 8. But it is worth noting here that research funders in the UK, the USA and across Europe are gradually implementing data-management and sharing policies in order to maximise openness of data, and transparency and accountability in research design and practice (Corti et al. 2020). The guidance provided in this chapter, then, reflects broader, international efforts to promote and implement good data management, including the management of qualitative and QL research data resources.

Working with Qualitative Longitudinal Data

For QL researchers, good data management serves a dual purpose. First, it facilitates the analysis and re-analysis of a growing dataset as a study unfolds. Second, it ena-bles the **archiving** of a dataset for longer-term sharing and re-use, for the benefit of both the research team and future generations of researchers (Bishop and Neale 2012; Neale 2013). In this context, the need to build in sufficient time and resources for managing project data at the planning stage is paramount. The process is best attended to in a systematic and co-ordinated way, as an integral part of an evolving study, rather than as an administrative task that is simply 'tacked on' at the end. Indeed, while data management has an important practical dimension, it also has important ethical, epistemological and legal dimensions. In other words, it is an interpretive process that requires careful planning and appraisal (McLeod and Thomson 2009: 133; Neale 2013).

The importance of managing QL research data ethically is sharpened by the fact that these data are inherently personal. As shown in Chapter 5 (Box 5.10), the accumulation of biographical data through the waves of fieldwork creates a unique fingerprint for each participant that is increasingly revealing of their identity. Moreover, personal contact details, that directly identify participants, are vital parts of a QL dataset; they are needed to maintain contact with participants over the course of a study, and for longer-term follow-up that may run over decades (see O'Connor and Goodwin 2010, 2012, and further examples in Chapter 1). The highly personal nature of QL data places particular responsibilities on researchers to adopt robust ethical protocols for their safe preservation. Following the European Union General Data Protection Regulation (GDPR), this imperative has been integrated into UK law in the Data Protection Act 2018. As Corti et al. (2020: 160) note, the inappropriate sharing of data, exposed in the recent Facebook and Cambridge Analytica scandal, reinforces the need for robust safeguards for the protection of personal research data. It is reassuring to know that the ethical and legal sharing of such data is perfectly possible where such safeguards are in place (Corti et al. 2020: 160; for a more detailed discussion of data leaks, see Hughes and Tarrant 2020a).

For QL researchers, future planning is a key priority. This requires researchers to work out in advance how data can best be managed through the cyclical waves of a study, while also maintaining some flexibility to respond to changes in the research and data landscapes. Three key areas where future planning is vital are highlighted here: preparing data for archiving, gaining consent for archiving, and ethically representing data.

Preparing data for archiving

Our first consideration for future planning concerns the preparation of data for archiving, and the timing of this process. Over the past two decades, the preservation of research data through archiving has come to be viewed as a fundamental part of good data management. From a European perspective, at least, it is no longer seen as an optional extra (Bishop and Kuula-Luumi 2017; Neale 2017b). This is underpinned by the idea that, since research datasets are produced with public funds, they should be regarded as an academic resource, rather than something that is 'owned' by the originating team for their exclusive use. In the UK, for example, archiving is mandated for research funded by the major research councils, and recommended by other major funders (e.g. the Joseph Rowntree Foundation), who are increasingly prepared to support the costs of this process. While there are no longer any requirements for research council-funded projects to archive with the UK Data Service, researchers are required to preserve their data for re-use within their own institutional repositories or a suitable specialist archive. In an international context, this same ethos of preserving data for archiving and sharing is also growing, but at different rates and in widely different contexts of infrastructure and funding (see Chapter 8 for a brief exploration of international archiving resources, and reviews of these resources). For QL research, it is worth exploring the options for archiving in local or national repositories. But researchers may also choose to deposit their data in the Timescapes Archive, which has been developed as an international resource (www.timescapes-archive.leeds.ac.uk). Although datasets cannot be translated through the archive, they can be deposited (and analysed) in any language.

The timing for archiving is a delicate ethical issue and is best left to the discretion of the researchers. Given the open-ended nature of QL research, there is often no clear point at which a study can be said to be completed. Moreover, researchers worry that their contribution will be 'scooped' by others if they 'let go' of their data too soon. Whatever the commitment to archiving and sharing data in principle, the push to archive for the common good may be compromised by the pull to retain data for the good of the research team.

These fears can be easily allayed once researchers become aware of the many different ways in which data may be revisited, and the multiple insights that may be produced (Maureen Haaker, personal communication; and see Chapter 8). Dean et al. (2018) provide a convincing demonstration of this: when six researchers, working in different disciplinary/methodological traditions, were asked to analyse the transcripts from a series of radio broadcasts, they produced six varied and equally plausible interpretations. An interpretive framework for analysis, with its abductive underpinnings, allows for – indeed, welcomes – such diversity.

But, given these sensitivities about the 'ownership' of data and findings, there are generally no time constraints laid down by funders or archivists for the deposit of data. Archiving may occur at the end of a funded project, or later if researchers are intending to continue their studies or extend their analysis. For QL researchers, who are engaged in longer-term analysis, flexible time frames for 'letting go' of data are essential. At the same time, however, there are solid professional and practical reasons to archive sooner rather than later.

First, archiving creates a published dataset as an important output from a study that can be cited alongside the publication of findings. For UK researchers, datasets can be included in the Research Excellence Framework (REF), which assesses the quality of research across the academy. Publishing a dataset through an archive increases the visibility of a study, establishes the quality and transparency of its evidence, and promotes it in ways that significantly increase its impact (Corti et al. 2020; see also Chapter 12, where quality issues are explored. For an example of a REF submission for archived datasets, see www.timescapes-archive.leeds.ac.uk/wp-content/uploads/sites/47/2020/07/The-Timescapes-Archive-Report.pdf.

Archiving also transforms a dataset into legacy data, with value for future generations of researchers (see Chapter 8). Where a dataset is revisited for research or teaching purposes, this is evidence of its quality and utility for the academy, giving added value to the funders' investment and enhancing the reputation of the researchers. Moreover, the anticipation of sharing and future use can provide the impetus to produce high quality, verifiable data files. This investment in the data is beneficial in raising standards.

There are also important practical and ethical reasons for depositing a dataset as near as possible to the conclusion of a study, rather than leaving this task for later. While data can be archived retrospectively, few researchers have the time and resources to manage this beyond the end of a project. Once staff resources and budgets are depleted, researchers may move on to new projects, change office or institution, upgrade their computing facilities or equipment, or otherwise lose track of their project and the tacit knowledge that goes with it. The momentum to archive and to preserve and publish a dataset may be lost or severely compromised, unless it is built in at the culmination of the data-management process. This would be a problem not only for the original researchers, who may wish to resurrect a project in the future, but would also mean the loss of an important historical resource for posterity (for examples see Box 1.8 and Box 3.2; see also the issue of data neglect in Box 8.2).

Finally, QL datasets are more secure in a professionally curated, password-protected, access-controlled archive, than in a filing cabinet, or on a computer in a researcher's office, where they are more likely to get lost, destroyed, corrupted or inadvertently disclosed. The conditions under which data can be used (issues of copyright and licensing) are much less clear when data are held outside the archive. Archiving, then, is not so much about 'giving away' a dataset, as transferring the responsibility for its longer-term preservation and stewardship to a data repository, where the data still remain available to the original researchers. For all these reasons, there are strong incentives to archive sooner rather than later, to plan for archiving at the outset of a project, and to prepare for it as an ongoing process.

Gaining consent for archiving

Forward planning is equally important when it comes to seeking consent for archiving. For QL enquiry, gaining consent of any kind can be time-consuming and difficult, particularly if contact with participants has been interrupted or lost (see Chapter 5). For this reason, it is now regarded as standard practice to seek consent for archiving alongside the general consent process prior to fieldwork (Corti et al. 2020). For QL research, such consent can be revisited at key moments in the research process.

At this point, it is worth clarifying exactly what participants are being asked to consent to in relation to the future use of their data. Can consent for archiving be properly informed when future uses of a dataset (lines of enquiry, interpretations, contexts for re-use) are unknown and cannot be anticipated? In the context of an evolving QL study, where the themes under investigation may radically shift over the course of a study, the notion of informed consent is problematic in any case. It can't be specified with any certainty for the work of the original researchers, let alone for the work of others, who may subsequently use a dataset for a different purpose (detailed in Chapter 8).

One way forward is to reframe the consent process in terms of enduring consent. This generic or 'blanket' model of consent clarifies that data may be used in new research contexts, in relation to unanticipated themes, over unspecified timescales, and without the need to re-contact participants in future. **Procedural consent**, i.e. consent for the way that data are to be stored, managed, accessed and generally protected, can be specified in advance and built into this model of enduring consent. Enduring consent is commonly used in medical research, and has obvious utility for longitudinal enquiry and for the future use of archival data (Neale and Bishop 2012b; Neale 2013; ESRC 2016; Hughes and Tarrant 2020b).

It is also worth noting here that, for QL studies at least, the vast majority of participants readily agree to the archiving of their data (Neale 2013). They wish to have their accounts on record as part of social history; indeed, such an agenda may be the driving force for a project (Berriman and Thomson forthcoming). It is important to clarify with participants that, unlike popular archives, research archives are not publicly available resources. Access can be carefully controlled and restricted to those working in officially recognised research institutions, who will pledge to uphold high ethical standards. In these circumstances, participants see little distinction between sharing their accounts with one bona-fide research team or several such teams through the medium of the archive (Kuula 2010–11; Weller 2012; Neale and Bishop 2012a). Kuula's research on participant perceptions of archiving revealed that, 'participants perceive open access to research data for other researchers as self-evident' (Kuula 2010–11: 15). This was certainly our experience within Timescapes, where over 95% of participants consented to archiving. Even where data are virtually impossible to anonymise, or are highly sensitive, consent is not usually withheld. Classic examples include data on the foot-and-mouth outbreak in selected areas of Cumbria, and Seymour's research on end-of-life care (www.ukdataservice.ac.uk/use-data/guides/dataset/foot-and-mouth.aspx; www. ukdataservice.ac.uk/deposit-data/stories/seymour.aspx). Re-thinking the ethics of consent for re-use in these ways may help researchers to move away from an unnecessarily protective stance in relation to their participants.

Ethically representing data

Our final consideration for future planning concerns the ethical representation of QL data. As shown in Chapter 5, there are good reasons for considering at the outset of a study how QL data will be represented, for example in public forums and displays, published findings and archived datasets. This is a vital stage in fashioning a dataset that addresses a fundamental issue: how to balance ethical concerns to respect confidentiality with the epistemological drive to produce an authentic, fully contextualised dataset that reflects real lives (Neale 2013). **Anonymising** (altering or substituting names of people, places, organisations, employment or other identifying features) is the most commonly used strategy, although it is a far from perfect tool. There is a growing appreciation that identities cannot be fully protected (Corti et al. 2020). Nor is anonymising the only route to protecting confidentiality: depositing data in a controlled-access archive also safeguards data and may enable different levels of access for different purposes (Neale and Bishop 2012a; Neale 2013; Corti et al. 2020).

As shown above, data confidentiality is a particular issue in QL research, given the personal nature of the data. In the *Welfare Conditionality* study, for example, an early decision to carry out a light-touch alteration of data was reviewed during the last year of the project, when the politically sensitive nature of the data had become apparent. A decision was taken at this point to fully anonymise the full dataset (1,082 interview transcripts), for deposit in the Timescapes Archive. For this study, each interview had taken, on average, 50 minutes to conduct, and transcribers had been asked to flag up any identifying material in the interview texts. This helped to speed up the anonymising process. The team allowed up to an hour per transcript for the anonymisation process (i.e. 1,000 hours, or approximately 29 weeks of work). Two part-time, trained workers were employed to carry out this task intensively over a six-month period (Fleur Hughes, personal communication; Dwyer and Patrick 2020).

Adopting a clear, systematic and proactive approach to the task of representing data can help to avoid the problems of inconsistency and lack of integrity that may arise if data are altered on a piecemeal basis. A salutary lesson on this issue is provided in the *Real Times* study (Taylor 2015; see Box 7.1; see also Box 5.6).

Box 7.1   Ethically Representing QL Data

The *Real Times* project (Taylor 2015) tracked a sample of 15 voluntary-sector organisations through five waves of fieldwork, over a four-year period (2010–13). Issues of confidentiality for the organisations and the multiple stakeholders who were interviewed were a challenge in this research (see Box 5.6). The study (which had signed up for deposit in the Timescapes Archive) generated rich, sensitive data about the organisations, some of which revealed instances of malpractice, power imbalances and struggles, staff misconduct and autocratic management.

The team had captured this sensitive detail precisely because of the reassurances of confidentiality that had been given at the outset. The researchers used pseudonyms in all public reporting and altered data to obscure locations and other identifying features. However, for the case studies, the rich accumulation of data meant that confidentiality could not always be assured. Moreover, the lack of a strategy for both when and how data would be anonymised created some unanticipated difficulties. The team took an individualised, piecemeal approach to altering data, tied to each separate piece of reporting. Since different researchers produced multiple outputs to diverse audiences over a number of years, this made it difficult to maintain consistency in the way that data were altered, and organisations represented.

By the time the data came to be prepared for archiving, towards the end of the project, its integrity was therefore compromised, with no appreciable or systematic connection between the varied forms of reporting and the evidence in the dataset. A blanket removal of names was all that could be achieved with the limited time and resources available at this late stage. As the author wryly notes (Taylor 2015: 289), future users might well enjoy the contradictions between the data found in the archive, and that presented in publications. Taylor's account highlights the need for careful planning when considering how data are to be represented over the lifetime of a project, and what resources are needed for this task.

The three issues highlighted above reinforce the fact that long-term research requires foresight and future imagination. If QL data are to accrue in historical value, they need to have a long life. This necessitates a willingness to plan for how a QL dataset will be managed and preserved both during and beyond the lifetime of a study.

Managing QL Data: Six Steps

Six key elements of data management for QL research are set out below. This guidance is also available on the Timescapes Archive website, where it includes sample templates such as file management structures, transcription guidelines and anonymisation guidelines (Bishop and Neale 2012; Neale with Hughes 2020; www. timescapes-archive.leeds.ac.uk). Our discussion here draws on the detailed, comprehensive guidance provided for social scientists by the UK Data Service (Corti et al. 2020) and accompanying resources and templates on the UKDS website (ukdataservice.ac.uk/manage-data.aspx). These resources give invaluable advice on a range of legal, ethical and technical issues, including anonymising and confidentiality, file formats and the secure storage and transfer of data files. Since this is a fast-moving field, with new technologies, practices and tools continually coming on stream, websites are likely to offer the most up-to-date advice. For advice and resources beyond the UK, researchers are advised to check local policies and protocols.

The guidance provided here is tailored to the particular challenges faced by QL researchers in working with longitudinal data. But this advice is not set in stone. Good practice will evolve in a QL study and will, in any case, vary according to the nature of the project, its disciplinary roots and any protocols laid down by funders, institutions and archives. Since every dataset is unique, the recommendations set out below are not intended to be overly prescriptive, but to highlight the broad dimensions of the process and the decisions that researchers need to make, along with examples of good practice that can be adapted for individual projects.

The varied tasks involved in good data management follow the **data life cycle** (Bishop and Neale 2012; Corti 2020). While they are presented here as a series of steps, in practice these tasks do not unfold in neat chronological order; they occur in parallel and are interwoven with the processes of generating and analysing data. For QL research, the data life cycle can be imagined as a spiral, a continuously spreading, cumulatively increasing process, rather than a cycle of activity that is relatively stable and repetitive (see Figure 7.1).

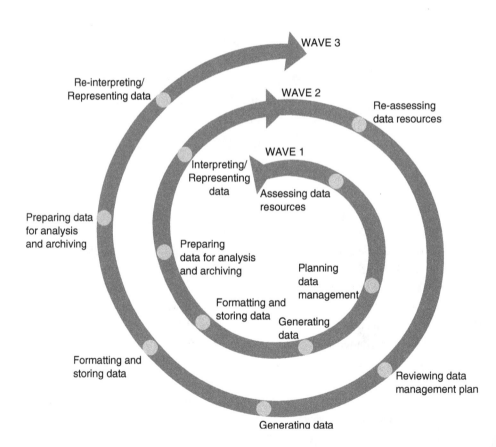

Figure 7.1 The qualitative longitudinal **data spiral**

Source: Adapted from Bishop and Neale 2012

Step 1: Data management planning

The planning process helps researchers to develop a strategy for managing a dataset over the lifetime of a project, and being clear about its end destination.

Step 1: Data Management Planning

- At the design stage, produce a **data-management plan** (a sample plan is available in Neale with Hughes 2020). While this is usually a requirement laid down by funders (with templates provided), it is also good practice for all researchers. The UK Data Service data management checklist is a valuable planning tool: www.ukdataservice.ac.uk/manage-data/plan/checklist.aspx Corti et al. 2020: 49–50. The plan can be reviewed at regular intervals and refined where needed. It should include:
  - **A data planning chart** that sets out the forms of data to be generated, from what sources and over which waves and timescales. This will help to gauge the extent and complexity of the dataset.
  - **An assessment of pre-existing data resources**. Is there a need for new data? How will a new dataset fit with extant data resources, and what is the scope for bringing datasets together to broaden and historicise the evidence base?
  - **An appraisal of data management resources**. Identify who will carry out data management tasks, and set a timetable and budget for this ongoing work. The UK Data Service planning and costing tools are likely to be very helpful here (www.ukdataservice.ac.uk/manage-data/plan/planning.aspx). For a cyclical and cumulative QL project, time needs to be factored in at various points in the project schedule; it is easy to underestimate the resources needed. If working as part of a team, build data management and co-ordination tasks into the remit of a skilled researcher or research manager who understands the data needs of a project. Make this a standing item on the agenda of project team meetings.

- **Identify and liaise with potential data repositories**, who will advise on good practice for the management of a dataset, and on the steps needed for depositing data.
- In order to keep track of a burgeoning dataset, **set up a data log, a record-keeping system** that can document the dataset as it grows. The log should record all forms of data, including contextual data such as interview schedules and consent forms, and descriptive analytical files such as field notes and pen portraits. The log should indicate when,

(Continued)

where and from whom files were generated, and who produced them, and should distinguish between abridged (anonymised) and unabridged (raw) files. For detailed guidance on documenting data, see www.ukdataservice. ac.uk/manage-data/document. Such metadata (data about data) is vitally important for both the originating team and for future users of a dataset.

o The Timescapes Archive (a specialist repository for QL data) provides a spreadsheet as a data log, which is also used to ingest data into the archive (Neale with Hughes 2020; available from the Timescapes Archive website: www.timescapes-archive.leeds.ac.uk).

Step 2: Informed consent for archiving

As indicated above, consent for data archiving now routinely takes place at the start of a project, alongside consent for participation (Corti et al. 2020). As Chapter 5 shows, consent in a QL study is a process rather than a one-off event. Participants can review and change their consent at different points in a study, and before data are finally deposited in a repository.

Step 2: Informed Consent for Archiving

- Before entering the field, **devise a leaflet and consent form for archiving in an approved data repository** (for examples, see Figure 7.2; also www.ukdataservice.ac.uk/consentfordatasharing, and Corti et al. 2020). Consent should be audio or video recorded if written consent is difficult for participants.
- **Assess the requirement for confidentiality**. In line with the ethics of consent outlined in Chapter 5, it is important to ascertain if participants wish for their personal information to be obscured in publications or archives, or whether they wish to be represented in their own right. Both options can be built into the consent form. For disciplines such as anthropology and oral history, which share important affinities with QL enquiry, it is customary to seek and secure consent for an open sharing of personal information (Corti et al. 2020: 196).
- **The wording of consent should be as user-friendly, open and flexible as possible**, in order to comply with data protection legislation, and to meet the requirements of enduring and procedural consent. This is particularly important in QL research because studies are continually

evolving, future data uses are unknown, and some finessing of data protocols and practice may well be needed down the line. The consent leaflet should clarify:

o How confidentiality will be addressed, assuming this is required (i.e. through archive access controls and anonymising data), bearing in mind that complete confidentiality cannot be guaranteed and should not be promised;

o How/where research data will be stored and preserved for the longer term. As for all longitudinal enquiry, it is important to seek consent to store personal contact details, and to clarify the extra safeguards that will be used for these data (encryption, embargo, and storage in a dark archive);

o That data may be shared for future research or teaching purposes;

o That participants have the right to seek to access their data in future, and/or to alter or erase their data from a study and/or archive;

o Details of a contact person that the participant may contact with queries about their data. This may be the researcher as data producer/depositor; the institution as data controller (with legal responsibilities for data use); and/or the archive as data curator/steward.

- A related task at this point is to consider copyright issues. Copyright is an intellectual property right that applies to research data (in written or recorded form) in the same way that it applies to literary or artistic works. Unlike other forms of intellectual property rights (patents, for example), copyright does not need to be registered, but accrues automatically once data are created. This gives the copyright holder control over the use of a dataset, including rights to copy, adapt or loan out the data, the right to communicate the data to the public, and the right to license and distribute it. It is therefore a powerful means to prevent unauthorised copying or publishing of a dataset.

For data produced in interviews that are recorded and transcribed, the researcher holds the copyright in the transcripts and recordings, while participants hold copyright in their recorded words (Corti et al. 2020: 223). This creates a somewhat grey area in terms of protecting data. Archives generally recommend transferring copyright to the research team, so they can control how a dataset is used. However, Haaker (forthcoming) suggests the value of seeking joint copyright for researcher and participant. This still enables researchers to quote freely from a dataset, and to transfer it to an archive with a licence arrangement. But, in the spirit of participatory research and shared authority, participants can also use and control the use of their data, and publish their diaries and memoirs in their own right.

FYFF

Following Young Fathers Further (or FYFF for short!) is a four-year research study based at the University of Lincoln. It is funded by the UKRI Future Leaders Fellowship scheme. We would like to learn more about the lives of young fathers and how we might better support young men in their parenting journeys. To do this, we are gathering information via interviews and other activities through the course of the study.

Archiving Information Sheet

1. Archiving
We would like to store all the interviews and information we generate with you in an archive. This is the space where your data will 'live'. It means that other people will be able to look at them in future and will help them to understand what young fatherhood is like today.

2. What is an archive?
An archive is a bit like a library where the books are all digital only. We would like to store your interviews in an archive based at the University of Leeds, called the Timescapes Archive. It will hold copies of all of the information from you and others who take part in the research. This includes recordings (like sound files) as well as written versions of interviews (usually called transcripts).

Everything will be stored in a digital form in the archive, not as paper in a building.

The archive allows people like researchers and historians to look at the material that we have gathered in our research project now and into the future.

Because we are learning so much and hearing so many interesting things we want to store the interviews and study information to give other researchers a chance to look at them too.

Your information will become an important part of history. What you tell us now will also help researchers to understand young fatherhood in the future too!

UK Research and Innovation

UNIVERSITY OF LINCOLN

timescapes
An ESRC Qualitative Longitudinal Study

Director of FYFF:
Dr Anna Tarrant atarrant@lincoln.ac.uk

Timescapes Archive:
https://timescapes-archive.leeds.ac.uk/

Timescapes Director:
Dr Kahryn Hughes k.a.hughes@leeds.ac.uk

3. Protecting your identity
The archive that your interviews are being stored in will have restricted access. Your interviews, recordings, and personal data will not be available to just anyone. We will make sure that the people who look at your material promise to do so in a responsible manner and protect your identity.

We will make sure that any details that could identify you or anyone you talk about in the interviews will be changed before the material goes in the archive.

Your recordings and personal details, such as address, telephone number and email, will be stored in the archive with extra protections. They will not be made available to anyone during your lifetime. If you want us to take them out of the archive you can do so at any time by contacting the research team or the Timescapes Archive Director. Contact details for the Archive Director are on the Archive website and are listed below.

4. Agreement to archive
To make sure that you agree that we can archive any data we produce with you, we would like you to sign a consent form. The FYFF team will also sign the form, and give you a copy to keep.

The agreement covers ALL interviews and activities that we do with you as part of the FYFF project.

The form also asks you to agree to share 'copyright', or ownership, of the interviews with our research team.

We ask for shared copyright with you because this means that both you and the FYFF team have control over the data. You can still make use of, or withdraw, any data produced should you wish to. However, shared copyright means that the FYFF team can continue to use your data for research purposes.

Because we take our responsibilities very seriously and do not wish your right to privacy to be affected by helping us with our research, we will make sure that nobody else can look at your interview material unless they have our approval and tell us why they want to see it.

FYFF Archiving Consent Form

RESEARCH PARTICIPANT:

• I have read and understood the information leaflet that outlines how my interviews and other data will be archived, and I have had the opportunity to ask questions about it.

• I agree that the material can be included in an archive.

• I understand that my personal details will be stored with protected status in the archive but that I am able to withdraw those details in future by contacting the archive.

• I agree to share copyright, or ownership, of my interviews and activity sheets with Anna Tarrant (Director of 'FYFF' project).

• I accept that including my research data in the archive will mean that, in the future, other researchers may also use my words in their reports, books and magazine articles.

NAME:..

SIGNATURE:..

DATE:..

RESEARCHER:

o I have discussed with the 'FYFF' research participant how their interviews and other data will be archived, and given them the opportunity to ask questions about it.

o The 'FYFF' research team will make sure that recordings, personal contact, and identifying details are archived with extra protections, and know their responsibility to ensure that participants benefit from taking part in the research.

NAME:..

SIGNATURE:..

DATE:..

Figure 7.2 Sample archiving consent leaflet and form

Source: *Following Young Fathers Further* study, UKRI, Tarrant (2020)

Step 3: Producing, labelling and transcribing data files

This is the initial phase in the production of a polished, well-documented dataset. Audio and video recordings produced in the field need to be of high technical quality, for both immediate and longer-term use. High quality recordings will not only aid the transcription process; they are of great value for researchers who wish to get a feel for the conduct of an interview, its interactive dimensions, the oral dimensions of people's speech and identities, and the tenor of their account. Researchers who work only with transcripts (an increasingly common practice, since this is an easier and faster option) are likely to miss these nuanced and revealing dimensions of field enquiry, for these are commonly ironed out or obscured in the process of committing an interview to a two-dimensional page (Alldred and Gillies 2012; Bornat 2020). The technical quality of a recording therefore goes hand in hand with and enhances the intellectual quality of the content.

The long-term accessibility of data depends on the quality and durability of the storage medium, the availability of data-reading equipment for that medium, clear labelling of the files, and high quality transcriptions that produce a written version of an audio file (Corti et al. 2020). All the tasks outlined here can help to generate high quality, well-documented data that are 'future proofed' as far as possible.

Step 3: Producing, Labelling and Transcribing Data Files

- Review methods and equipment for **producing audio/video recordings and photographs of high technical quality**. This may entail seeking expert advice on sound or video recordings, or photographic techniques; reviewing recording equipment; and building in fieldworker training. It is good practice to quality-check recordings as they are produced.
- Consider the quality and future proofing of your chosen **storage media** (optical, magnetic or solid state media, or non-digital paper-based media) and how to create conditions that can optimise their longevity. For a review of these different media and their different vulnerabilities, see www.ukdataservice.ac.uk/manage-data/store/storage.aspx, and Corti et al. 2020: Chapter 6. It is good practice to preserve data files in more than one medium (for example, on a hard drive and a CD), and to copy or migrate data to new media every 2–5 years. Different institutions are likely to have their own policies for the safe storage of data, which researchers will need to follow. Since the storage of paper archives is becoming increasingly difficult for institutions and repositories, aim to create a fully digitised version of a dataset, including digitising handwritten, paper-based files such as drawings and letters.
- Consider what **digital file formats** you will use for your files and apply these consistently. They may be based on widely used proprietary software,

such as MS Office, which is likely to have a long shelf life. But open, non-proprietary software (e.g. PDF/A, TIFF, XML) are less likely to become obsolete and should be considered for longer-term storage. File formats suitable for long-term preservation are listed at: www.ukdataservice.ac.uk/manage-data/format/recommended-formats.

- **A file-naming system** should clearly identify and distinguish between files, and between different versions of files, including abridged and unabridged versions of a dataset. A working copy of a dataset should also be clearly distinguished from backup versions. Careful labelling will ensure that different versions do not proliferate and cause instability in a dataset:

  o In the *Following Young Fathers* study, a **unique digital identifier** was created for each data file (e.g. FYFAdamW2Interview06.doc; FYFAdamW1selfportrait03.tif). These file names start with the initials of the project, followed by the case identifier (the name/pseudonym for the case); the wave of fieldwork in which the file was generated; the type of data (interview, life map, diary, field notes, and so on); a unique number assigned to each file in a particular case, followed by the digital format in which the file is saved (doc = word document; tif = tagged image format). It is worth checking protocols with your data repository; in this instance, the file names are suitable for ingesting in the Timescapes Archive.

- *Create a system for systematically labelling and identifying data files* (recordings, transcripts and other field data) and flagging up their content. For recordings, label the media themselves as well as the packaging (by allowing space to record an audio or video introduction at the start of a recording). For transcripts and other documents, this can be done by creating a one-page template for a front sheet which can be filled in and attached to each file as it is produced (see Neale with Hughes 2020 for an example). The sheet should specify the project name, names of interviewer and interviewee (the case), date and location of interview, wave of fieldwork (temporal data) and file type (e.g. life map, interview transcript, diary). Assigning key words to the front sheet gives a useful indication of its thematic content, ensuring that files can be accessed by theme, as well as by case and wave.

- **Consider how to transcribe audio data files and who will undertake this**. Styles of transcription are likely to vary across disciplines and country contexts. Producing transcripts engages the researcher in a close and systematic reading of the data. Achieving such familiarity with a dataset is an important phase in its analysis. If you are using a transcription service, this same familiarity can be achieved by quality checking the transcripts

(Continued)

against the recordings. The amount of time needed will vary, but some studies allow up to an hour of researcher time to check a transcript (this is considerably less time-consuming than the 2–3 hours needed to transcribe a one-hour interview; Dawson 2003).

- Develop **transcription guidelines and a template**, setting out the rules to be followed in translating audio files into text files. Aim for a rigorous, orthographic reading that preserves as much as possible of the original speech and the nuances of the interaction. Like all data management tasks, transcribing is not neutral. It is an interpretive act that may iron out and lose some of the richness and meaning of the original speech (Alldred and Gillies 2012). Transcription templates need to dovetail with anonymisation protocols and, if required, give guidance on light-touch anonymising. They also need to be compatible with qualitative data analysis (QDA) software, if this is being used. For templates, examples and transcriber instructions, see www.ukdataservice.ac.uk/manage-data/format/transcription.aspx; and www.ukdataservice.ac.uk/media/622355/UKDA-example-transcription-instructions.pdf; also Corti et al. 2020 and Neale with Hughes 2020.
- Produce a **template for a transcriber confidentiality agreement**, including protocols for the safe deletion of all files held by the transcriber once their work is completed (see the example in Neale with Hughes 2020).
- Alongside a system for **quality checking transcripts** as they are produced, develop **protocols for the safe transfer of data files** to transcribers and archivists. File encryption (scrambling data to make it unreadable, except to those who have a key to decode it) is advisable for data on the move, although care is needed to ensure that the key is secure and that data are not lost through this process. Recorders with file encryption facilities are worth considering. A review of encryption practices and software, including *Pretty Good Privacy* (PGP), can be found in Corti et al. (2020: 144–8). Since encryption conforms to the standards laid down by the GDPR for the safe handling of personal data, it is also recommended for the safe storage of personal contact details, both prior to and after archiving.

Step 4: Organising data: filing systems and structures

The aim here is to create an online storage system that enables the easy identification and retrieval of files in a dataset. It is worth considering if data storage and documentation may be facilitated via a QDA software package, if one is being used. In future, it may be possible to transfer file directly from selected QDA packages to a data repository (Corti et al. 2020).

Step 4: Organising Data: Filing Systems and Structures

- **Review where you will locate your digital data, and how you will organise the files**. While there are different options (portable devices, cloud storage, local desktop computers, networked drives, reviewed in Corti et al. 2020: 137–8), a networked drive is likely to be the most robust and secure for personal forms of data. Aim to organise your data files on **a password-protected digital drive** (on a secure server that has daily backups), with access restricted to the researchers. Consider how much storage space you will need for your dataset. If sharing data across teams, set up a system for the safe sharing of files (e.g. *Sharepoint Workspace* software or similar).

- For QL researchers, **the file structure should reflect the temporal logic of working across cases, themes and processes**, thereby supporting multi-dimensional analysis (see Chapters 10 and 11). One strategy is to arrange files alphabetically by case name/pseudonym (or numeral identifier). This brings together all files relating to a particular case, which are then nested by wave of fieldwork and finally by data type. This is a good foundation for building holistic analyses of unfolding biographies, and generating case histories (for an example of this file structure, see Neale with Hughes 2020). The alternative, recommended by Saldaña (2003), is to organise files chronologically by wave of data generation, within which files are nested by case and then by file type. Whichever structure is adopted, it should allow for the cross-referencing of files by case and wave. It should also complement the organisation of files in a QDA package (if one is being used), or in framework grids (see Chapter 10), which label and organise data by theme.

- The file structure should include **contextual and analytical files** as integral components of a dataset. Separate areas can be allocated for files that run across cases and/or waves (e.g. interview schedules, leaflets about the study, sample consent leaflets and forms; and cross-case analytical files such as thematic charts and framework grids – these are described in Chapter 10).

- **Abridged and unabridged versions of the dataset** should be kept in separate folders. The unabridged version will include all 'raw' data files; any identifying or confidential data, such as the personal details of participants, organisations and practitioners and their contact sheets; and any written communications received from participants, their consent forms and the anonymisation code book that links real to assigned identities (see Step 5). This unabridged version should be encrypted to give the additional security needed for personal information.

- It is worth checking local protocols for the safe storage of unabridged files while a project is underway. Some institutions may recommend that these are not held digitally but only in paper format, although paper storage for the longer-term preservation of datasets is becoming increasingly untenable for institutions and archives.

Step 5: Ethically representing QL data: anonymising and safeguarding confidentiality

As shown above and in Chapter 5, the ethical representation of data in public displays, publications and in archives needs to be considered in the early stages of a project, and outlined in participant consent leaflets. Protocols for representing data and safeguarding confidentiality will vary across institutions and country settings; researchers will need to ascertain the protocols and practices used in their chosen repository. Some details relating to the Timescapes Archive are set out below and in Step 6, as an example of how things might be organised, and to highlight the issues that researchers might look out for when negotiating the archiving of their data.

Step 5: Representing QL Data and Safeguarding Confidentiality

- Review varied ways to **safeguard data confidentiality**. Anonymising is usually strongly recommended or mandated by funding bodies, ethics committees, and archives. In the UK, these follow the strictures laid down by the EU GDPR and the Data Protection Act 2018. Yet anonymising is not the only means of protecting identities. Archiving a dataset also provides some protection. Archives control and regulate access to data via a user licence agreement. This places a contractual obligation on new analysts to use data only for research purposes, and to protect identities and preserve confidentiality.

- The Timescapes Archive offers different levels of access (public, registered, restricted) for different categories of data (Neale and Bishop 2012a and b; also Corti et al. 2020: 206–9). This granularity can be very helpful for researchers seeking to fine-tune access to their datasets. Placing personal contact details and other data that have not been anonymised on restricted access adds a further level of security to these data. Researchers can specify that highly sensitive data can only be accessed with the permission of the original researchers, or, in their absence, by an archive access committee that is authorised to make such decisions. There are issues of resourcing and scalability here. In days of stretched budgets, archives are increasingly seeking to automate their procedures. Nevertheless, for personal and unabridged data, a streamlined facility for discretionary permissions, such as that provided by the Timescapes Archive, should be possible.

- **Anonymising** remains a useful tool for protecting identities, although, as noted above, it is not possible to fully anonymise rich, narrative data (for a useful web resource, see www.ukanon.net). Anonymising is a skilled and time-consuming task. It involves substituting the names of people, organisations or localities, or otherwise aggregating or generalising information (e.g. on a participant's employment or family composition) that may identify them, or make them distinctive within a sample (see www.ukdataservice.ac.uk/manage-data/legal-ethical/anonymisation).

- Decide who will undertake this task, and when and how far data will be altered (taking into account the ethical balancing act, outlined in Chapter 5, that seeks to preserve data authentically and with due acknowledgment to the data source). Anonymising is best seen as an ongoing process that follows on from transcribing. In this way, an abridged version of a dataset is gradually created that is ready for public outputs. Audio transcribers may carry out a 'light touch' anonymisation (i.e. changing names and localities), leaving further finessing, or a more thorough 'belt and braces' alteration of data, to the research team. It is worth consulting with your chosen repository and reaching agreement on how a dataset will be altered.
- Multi-media files present particular challenges for anonymising. Audio-visual data such as recordings, photos or videos are very costly, difficult, or may be impossible to anonymise, and are best preserved as part of the unabridged version of the dataset.
- Establish **anonymising guidelines**, and a securely held **code book** that links real to assigned identities and ensures consistency of approach across a dataset (see examples in Corti et al. 2020: 123–4; Neale with Hughes 2020). Using pseudonyms, or replacing text with different or more generalised descriptions, is preferable to simply removing or blanking out data. In this way, the intellectual coherence and integrity of the narrative are less compromised. Words that have been replaced need to be flagged up in the text, ideally in the most unobtrusive way possible, for example, by marking changed text with square [ ] or chevron < > shaped brackets that are unlikely to appear elsewhere in the text.
- Proprietary online tools and services for anonymising text are available, and can automate some of the more straightforward changes. These include the UK Data Service's *text anonymisation helper tool* (http://ukdata service.ac.uk/manage-data/legal-ethical/anonymisation/qualitative.aspx). This identifies capitalised words and numerals in the text, which may help to locate proper nouns, or people's ages or dates of birth. Great care is needed in using general search-and-replace tools, such as those in Microsoft Office Word, since they may unintentionally corrupt a text. Sophisticated tools for technically assisted anonymisation are currently under development (see, for example, the Washington-based *National Institute for Health*-funded project, *Sharing Qualitative Research Data*, led by James Dubois, which aims to produce a new tool kit for ethical data sharing).
- Anonymising creates **two versions of a digital dataset**. As shown in Step 4, a complete, unabridged dataset, including personal contact details, should be digitised, encrypted and stored separately from the abridged (anonymised) version, in its own password-protected folder. Both are integral elements of a dataset that will have value at different historical times.

Step 6: Archiving a dataset

Once the elements of good data management outlined above are addressed, it is a relatively quick and easy task to deposit data in an archive. As shown above, the timing of archiving can be a sensitive matter and is best left to the discretion of the researcher. But there are sound reasons to archive as near as possible to the conclusion of a study, even if this involves placing the whole dataset on embargo for a specified period of time.

Step 6: Archiving a Dataset

- Archives vary in their procedures for depositing a dataset and facilitating their access by others; researchers will need to check the protocols used by their chosen repository. The protocols used by the Timescapes Archive are set out below as an example of what the process might entail. Researchers complete a spreadsheet that logs the cases and files that make up the dataset as they are created (see Neale with Hughes 2020). They also submit a depositors' licence, create a short landing page for the project (see Figure 7.3), and transfer the digital dataset to the repository. Once received, the archive team will assign a unique identifier to a dataset (a digital object identifier, or DOI), which new researchers will use to cite the dataset in their publications. This same identifier is then logged at the UK Data Service, which will then create a catalogue record for the dataset to aid its discovery by a wider pool of researchers (for further details of the Timescapes Archive, see Chapter 8). It is worth checking in advance what procedures are in place for archiving with your chosen repository.
- Any embargoes on the use of research data in the short and longer term need to be agreed with your archive. It is worth seeking to store the full, unabridged, encrypted version of the dataset under long-term embargo in a 'dark' area of the archive, until such time that it can be released as historically valuable data (this may be beyond the lifetime of the participant, when GDPR strictures on the protection of personal data cease to apply). This strategy was adopted by several Timescapes projects; researchers in the *Oldest Generation* study, for example, used the 'dark' archive function of the Timescapes Archive for their collection of unabridged photographs, which are embargoed until 2040 (Bytheway and Bornat 2012b).
- The final stage in the archiving process is the production of a **study guide** for long-term use. This should be archived alongside the abridged dataset. If resources allow, aim for a 'gold standard' guide (e.g. Neale et al. 2015). This will give a detailed account of the study methodology and its development over time, along with details of the participants and how the dataset has been produced. The production of such metadata (data about data) is of

vital importance for legacy data researchers (see Chapter 8). But it is also an essential part of the transparency needed to enhance the veracity of a study (see Chapter 12). The guide is an important way to promote a study and provide the context for its production, ensuring, as far as possible, that data can be independently and appropriately understood; can be interpreted by re-analysts; and have integrity as the evidence base for a study. This documentation can also form the basis for methods discussions in published outputs. A checklist of contents (adapted from Bishop and Neale 2012) includes:

o A description of the project, including title, research aims and questions, theoretical framing, overall design, funders, and details of the research team, institutions, and start and finish dates;

o A description of and rationale for the methods used to generate data, including any ethical or practical issues that have arisen; fieldwork experiences; sampling strategy; any changes in study design or conduct over time; and any protocols used in the management and production of the dataset. Any limitations or challenges that arose in the conduct of the study (e.g. relating to sampling or sample attrition, ethical issues or limitations in data generation or analysis) can be included here, enabling a wider audience to gauge the quality of the study;

o A description of the dataset: numbers and types of data files; numbers of participants, cases and waves; the timing of fieldwork; characteristics of the sample; and themes covered in the interviews;

o Field documents: details of interview schedules, field notes, research diaries, analytical files and thematic key words assigned to the data;

o A list of outputs and publications from the project and links to the project website.

Closing Reflections

This chapter has explored the intricate process of managing a QL dataset and the dual purpose that this process serves: facilitating the ongoing use and analysis of the data by the originating team, and creating legacy data that can be preserved and shared with others. Six areas of good practice in data management have been described here. While these have been presented as a series of steps, in practice they overlap and intersect as a project develops. The timing of these processes is a crucial consideration. A key message is that data management is not a simple administrative task that is tacked on to the end of fieldwork. It is an interpretive process, with ethical and epistemological implications that need to be carefully considered at the outset and addressed as an integral part of a project.

Figure 7.3 Sample project landing page for the Timescapes Archive

It will be abundantly clear by now that managing QL data for prolonged use over time is not a quick and easy task. It requires considerable foresight and planning. But, for a growing dataset that researchers may wish to return to over many years, good data management is essential. A high quality, well-organised, ethically attuned, fully documented and safely preserved dataset provides the foundation for temporal analysis, and for extending a study into the future. It is also an important output from a study that will enhance its credibility and accrue historical value for future generations of researchers.

Further Reading

The guidance provided in this chapter has been reproduced from the Timescapes Archive website (Neale with Hughes 2020; www.timescapes-archive.leeds.ac.uk). The web resource provides a range of templates that researchers may find useful, alongside guidance on archiving with the Timescapes Archive. Beyond this, general state-of-the-art guidance on data management for social scientists is provided in Corti et al. 2020, and on the website of the UK Data Service (www.ukdataservice.ac.uk). In an international context, it is worth checking the web guidance on data management and archiving provided by major funding bodies, professional associations, institutions and archives. A list of international archiving resources of value for qualitative secondary analysts, produced by Kahryn Hughes and Anna Tarrant, is available on the Timescapes Archive website (www.timescapes-archive.leeds.ac.uk/wp-content/uploads/sites/47/2020/04/Resources-for-QSA.pdf). More general overviews of research data provision and services, produced by information scientists and librarians, are available, although they tend to date quickly and the coverage is necessarily selective. For researchers interested in historical developments in research data management services in Europe, Australia and the USA over the past decade, good starting points are Treloar et al. (2012), Whyte (2012) and Matusiak and Sposito (2017); and for the development of European resources for qualitative and qualitative longitudinal research data, see Neale and Bishop (2010–11).

Corti, L., Ven den Eynden, V., Bishop, L. and Woollard, M. (2020) *Managing and Sharing Research Data: A Guide to Good Practice*, 2nd edition. London: Sage.

Matusiak, K. and Sposito, F. (2017) 'Types of research data management services: An international perspective', in *80th Annual Meeting of the Association of Information Science and Technology* (Washington): 754–6.

Neale, B. and Bishop, L. (eds) (2010–11) 'Qualitative and qualitative longitudinal data resources in Europe', *IASSIST Quarterly*, 34 (3–4): Fall/Winter 2010; Spring/Summer 2011.

Neale, B. with Hughes, K. (2020) *Data Management Planning: A Practical Guide for Qualitative Longitudinal Researchers.* University of Leeds Institutional Repository, www.timescapes-archive.leeds.ac.uk.

Treloar, A., Choudhury, G. S and Michener, W. (2012) 'Contrasting national data strategies: Australia and the US', in G. Pryor (ed.) *Managing Research Data*. London: Facet, pp. 173–204.

Whyte, A. (2012) 'Emerging infrastructure and services for research data management and curation in the UK and Europe', in G. Pryor (ed.) *Managing Research Data*. London: Facet, pp. 205–34.

8

WORKING WITH LEGACY DATA: ETHICS AND PRACTICALITIES

- **Legacy data (pre-existing data)**: Using legacy data is a growing practice within socio-historical research. As the name implies, legacy data offer a retrospective understanding of lives and times. They include 'found' forms of documentary and digital data that were not originally produced for research purposes, including processual data such as diaries, blogs and letter collections; and qualitative and QL datasets held in social science and humanities archives. Describing the re-use of existing data as legacy data research highlights the historical nature of this enterprise. Legacy data have value beyond the purposes for which they were originally produced, and, as rich documents of lives and times, they have an inherent temporality which enhances their value for socio-historical research.
- **Legacy data research and QL enquiry**: QL researchers are both users and producers of legacy data. Such data form part of a palette of retrospective, socio-historical resources that can be used to generate new temporal insights, and to complement the prospective data generated through QL field enquiries. There is huge scope for QL datasets, with their inherent seriality, to be used by a wider pool of socio-historical and processual researchers.
- **Working with legacy data**: Beyond a basic, retrospective analysis of these data, they may be used as the baseline to build a new study or re-study with historical reach. Or researchers may produce integrative reviews and

(Continued)

analyses which aggregate legacy data from varied sources. This builds a broader comparative picture that allows for qualitative generalisations.

- **Analytical strategies and challenges**: The aim is to bring disparate data into alignment in order to address new research questions. This typically involves a three-pronged process of searching for, sampling and sculpting new configurations of data. While this is a painstaking process that requires diligence, it is also a voyage of discovery that is founded on intuitive, abductive knowledge-building (see Chapter 9).

- **Ethical and epistemological issues**: The issues that arise in working with legacy data have been extensively debated. It is increasingly recognised that the meaning of legacy data is continually open to interpretation through time. An ethic of mutual respect between data producers and new users can be fostered through data sharing and collaborative initiatives.

Introduction

'The whole of anything is never told,' observed Henry James ... And the richness and value of qualitative studies is not exhausted or fully captured in one reading or telling, or in one time. (McLeod and Thomson 2009: 125)

Over the past two decades, the practice of working retrospectively with **legacy (pre-existing) data** has gradually found a place in the repertoire of socio-historical research methods (Bornat 2013). This chapter explores the nature and value of such data, along with the varied ways in which they can be used, and the ethical and epistemological issues associated with their use. How such data can be accessed and analysed, framed here as a three-pronged strategy of searching for, sampling and sculpting data, is also outlined briefly, including the development of archival resources to facilitate access and re-use. These developments are detailed more fully elsewhere (Hughes and Tarrant 2020a).

It is important to establish at the outset that legacy data, as documents of lives and times, are potentially important resources for QL researchers (Neale 2017b; 2020). As the name implies, legacy data offer a retrospective understanding of lives which complements the prospective real-time focus of QL enquiry. Their retrospective value grows as they age. They form part of a palette of socio-historical resources that QL researchers can use to generate new processual insights, to increase the historical reach of their studies, and to create a broader comparative picture of lives and times. QL researchers, then, are both users and producers of legacy data: the meaning and value of both processes is explored in this chapter.

Among the varied ways in which QL researchers might work with these rich bodies of data, three broad approaches are identified here. First, researchers may conduct retrospective studies of legacy data, including 'found' data that were not originally generated for research purposes. Serial forms of data that tell an unfolding tale (ranging from classic collections of letters and diaries, to digital blogs and QL datasets) offer particularly rich forms of dynamic insight. Second, researchers may use a legacy dataset as a baseline to build a re-study, thereby creating a longitudinal picture of lives and times with greater historical reach. Third, through **integrative reviews and analyses**, they may aggregate legacy data from varied sources to create a broader comparative picture, and to enhance the scope for qualitative generalisations. Overall, the discussion reveals the huge potential to build productive links between QL enquiry and legacy data research.

Legacy Data: Documents of Lives and Times

Among the varied sources of data that underpin qualitative research, documentary and archival sources have been relatively neglected. These data sources form part of a larger corpus of legacy materials that Plummer (2001) engagingly describes as 'documents of life':

> The world is crammed full of human personal documents. People keep diaries, send letters, make quilts, take photos, dash off memos, compose auto/biographies, construct websites, scrawl graffiti, publish their memoirs, write letters, compose CVs, leave suicide notes, film video diaries, inscribe memorials on tombstones, shoot films, paint pictures, make tapes and try to record their personal dreams. All of these expressions of personal life are hurled out into the world by the millions, and can be of interest to anyone who cares to seek them out. (Plummer 2001: 17)

Documents of life also include wills and the detailed holdings of public records offices; reports, memos, confidential and often revealing data held in national and institutional archives; and the rich content of newsprint (e.g. magazines) and media (TV/radio/online) broadcasts. Such data may provide rich, retrospective insights in their own right. But they may also be used to complement the prospective real-time data generated through QL field methods (see Chapter 6). Thomson et al. (2011), for example, drew on newsprint, magazines and internet sites to capture the 'zeitgeist' of motherhood in contemporary times, and to contextualise the empirical data generated in their QL study of first-time motherhood.

Seeking out such rich sources of documentary and archival data, including letters, reports, diaries and autobiographical records, is common among socio-historical researchers, including QL researchers. It has been described as a 'jackdaw' or 'bricolage' approach to research: an open and exploratory process of data discovery that is characteristic of social historians and historically oriented sociologists (Thompson 1981, 2000; Yardley 2008; Neale 2017b, 2019).

There has also been a recent explosion in the use of 'big' digital data, a term that encompasses the vast, dynamic flows of longitudinal and relational data that are continuously created and updated, in real-time, through varied online transactions and exchanges. These include electronic mail, text messaging systems and social networking/micro-blogging websites (Twitter, Facebook, YouTube, and so on) (Kitchin 2014; Tinati et al. 2014; Halford and Savage 2017). Like all longitudinal resources, these digital forms of data offer the possibility of shifting 'from data scarce to data rich studies of societies; from static snapshots to dynamic unfoldings; [and] from course aggregations to high resolutions' (Kitchin 2014: 7). Studies of large-scale digital data are under rapid development, using non-standard computational facilities and software for data storage and analysis (Tinati et al. 2014). But digital forms of legacy data are also beginning to be used by QL researchers working in the interpretivist tradition (see Box 8.3 for an example). In sum, we are witnessing the emergence of a vast, international data landscape that has significant research potential (Hughes and Tarrant 2020a).

Social Science and Humanities Datasets

As Plummer (2001) makes clear, the rich qualitative data held in social science and humanities datasets are also important documents of lives, which can be used for new or evolving research purposes. Qualitative datasets are the most obvious sources of case-rich qualitative data. But useful pockets of such data can also be found in quantitative and mixed method datasets (Savage 2005b; Hughes and Tarrant 2020a; see, for example, the qualitative elements of the large-scale *Born in Bradford* longitudinal study). They may also appear as peripheral traces of data (paradata) that appear in the margins of research datasets, for example in personal notebooks, research diaries and field notes, letters, ephemera such as newspaper cuttings, and in margin notes (Edwards et al. 2017; Goodwin and O'Connor 2020). These can reveal a great deal about the research process and the researchers themselves (see Box 8.1 for an example).

The archiving of legacy datasets and their re-use are not new practices. Booth's (1902–3) extensive survey of working-class lives in London, for example, included vivid case histories of the inmates of Bromley and Stepney workhouses, which were preserved in a series of notebooks in the LSE Library in London (www.booth.lse. ac.uk). There is also a long tradition among socio-historical researchers (longitudinal ethnographers, re-study scholars and oral historians, for example) of preserving their field notes in university repositories, and/or bequeathing them to new generations of ethnographers (Sanjek 1990; Corti and Thompson 2004). An example is given in Box 8.1.

> **Box 8.1** The Early Creation and Sharing of Ethnographic Field Notes
>
> Ethnographic field notes, along with accompanying diaries, correspondence, sketch maps, photos and recordings, represent the core elements of a traditional anthropological dataset. As running logs, written at the end of each day, traditional field notes reflect the immersion of ethnographers in their field settings: their cumulative understandings; their intuition and hunches about what is needed to interpret a culture; and their empathy for those under observation. For much of the 20th century, such notes were intensely personal and revealing documents that were not produced for sharing during the lifetime of the authors. However, they were often preserved in university libraries and/or inherited by the next generation of researchers (Sanjek 1990).
>
> To give one example, in the early 1930s, Camilla Wedgewood, a Cambridge scholar, conducted an ethnographic study among the Manam Islanders in Papua New Guinea. In an experience that will be familiar to contemporary re-analysts, she records her frustration at working with the idiosyncratic and fragmentary field materials left by her predecessor, and the many weeks she spent trying to decipher and re-craft these traces of data for her own use, and for the benefit of her successors. The process left her 'feeling like Alice in Wonderland' (cited in Lutkehaus 1990: 309).
>
> Mindful of the potential value of her own legacy data, Wedgewood, in turn, produced meticulous field notes, recorded in 34 neatly bound notebooks, which she lodged in the library of the University of Sydney. In the late 1970s, some years after Wedgewood's death, these were accessed by Nancy Lutkehaus, her successor in the field. The dataset includes Wedgewood's correspondence with her famous mentor, Malinowski (the 'father' of ethnographic field enquiry), who advises her not to use a soft-leaded pencil when writing up her notes, or be parsimonious with paper, or to rely on memory, but to create 'a chaotic account in which everything is written down as it is observed or told' (cited in Lutkehaus 1990: 304–5). This is perennial advice, which continues to shape the practice of ethnographic fieldwork (Royce 2002). Lutkehaus (1990), in turn, records the value of Wedgewood's dataset for her own research, initially for what it reveals about the life and character of a female ethnographer whose shoes she was about to step into, and subsequently, as a source of insight into the lives of the Manum Islanders in earlier times, and as a means of introducing herself to the Islanders and establishing her credentials as Wedgewood's successor.

Such early examples of the creation, preservation and re-use of legacy data are confined to particular socio-historical disciplines, and tend to occur in small and scattered pockets of scholarship. It was not until the last decade of the 20th century that a more widespread culture of open data access and sharing began to emerge.

This was fuelled by the growing commitment of researchers who wished to preserve and share their field materials, and a new body of literature that was beginning to explore and refine methods for their use (edited collections include Corti et al. 2005; Corti and Bishop 2006; Crow and Edwards 2012; Irwin and Bornat 2013; Hughes and Tarrant 2020a).

Funding initiatives to support and encourage research with legacy datasets have also played a major part in this expansion. As shown in Chapter 7, these include directives by the UK research councils to archive research data as a condition of funding, either within institutional repositories or other kinds of data facility. Archiving is also increasingly recommended and funded by other major funders, such as the UK Joseph Rowntree Foundation, and the EU ERC Horizon 2020 programme.

Qualitative Data Archives

A further critical factor in the development of legacy data research has been the growth in infrastructure to help preserve these resources and facilitate access to them (Bishop and Kuula-Luumi 2017). This includes archives and institutional, specialist and national data repositories. An early venture in the UK, led by Paul Thompson, was the establishment in 1987 of the *National Life Story Collection* within the National Sound Archive at the British Library. In 1991, Thompson carried out a pilot study on qualitative data resources for the UK Economic and Social Research Council. He found that 90% of datasets were either lost or at risk of being lost. Among these were the classic materials gathered for Stacey's (1960; Stacey et al. 1975) community-based study and re-study of the town of Banbury; and a unique longitudinal study of child-rearing, consisting of over 3,000 interviews, that had been generated over a 30-year period by John and Elizabeth Newson (Corti and Thompson 2004). The loss of these datasets is hardly surprising, given that, until recently, the prevailing policy of funders and ethics committees was to destroy such datasets within five years of their creation. Thompson found that the remaining 10% of qualitative datasets had been preserved by their creators, but in many cases without the safeguards and facilities that archives could typically provide (physical, long-term security and shared access, and data discovery through cataloguing) (Corti and Thompson 2004; see Box 8.2 for an example).

These early developments led, in 1994, to the establishment of *Qualidata* at the University of Essex. This was the UK's first dedicated archiving project and clearing house for qualitative research data. By 2001, *Qualidata* had become established as a specialist unit with the UK Data Archive. The priority was a rescue operation for datasets at risk. By 2002, *Qualidata* had archived some 140 datasets (including Goldthorpe's *Affluent Worker* study; see Box 8.3), and catalogued a further 150 that were already located in other archives across the UK (Corti and Thompson 2004).

Building a comprehensive data infrastructure takes time. Data discovery (the process of searching for and finding legacy data that can shed light on new lines of enquiry) remains a challenge for researchers. A *Registry of Research Data Repositories* (www.re3data.org), set up in 2012, is a useful starting point, while a recent inventory of qualitative data repositories, compiled by Hughes and Tarrant, can be found on the Timescapes Archive website (www.timescapes-archive.leeds.ac.uk/wp-content/uploads/sites/47/2020/04//Resources-for-QSA.pdf). A more ambitious project is to create an online *Research Data Discovery Service*, designed to identify and catalogue datasets and their content, and signpost researchers to them, although this has been under development for some years (Bishop 2016; JISC 2018). Currently, there is no centralised data portal for the discovery of legacy datasets, while documentation about archival resources and their holdings is often incomplete.

Perhaps even more worrying, legacy data continue to disappear as rapidly as new data are generated (Hughes and Tarrant 2020a). Currently, many qualitative datasets remain in the stewardship of the original researchers, where they run the risk of being lost to posterity (or fortuitously rediscovered; for examples, see Box 1.8 and Box 3.2). An example of the problems that can arise when legacy data have not been preserved safely is given in Box 8.2.

Box 8.2   Data Neglect

The process of building a re-study from an earlier study can be severely hampered where legacy data have been lost or destroyed, or have not been gathered systematically, adequately documented or archived for future use (Foster et al. 1979: 334–5). This leaves the next generation of researchers with the task of piecing together what they can from fragmented data, published findings, personal archives, and consultations or collaborations with the original researchers. This was the experience of Charles et al. (2008) in their re-study of family and kinship in Swansea (Rosser and Harris 1965). At the conclusion of the original study, the rich dataset had been deposited as a paper resource in the University of Swansea library. But more than three decades later, the data could no longer be found.

The inclusion of one of the original researchers, Chris Harris, in the re-study team helped to compensate for this loss and enabled the researchers to build on and refine the original methodology (Charles et al. 2008; Charles 2012). But the lost opportunity to use the original dataset as the baseline for the re-study was a major blow. These events alert us to the pitfalls of **data neglect**, and the value of building contextual understandings of a study and its methodology through careful and well-preserved documentation.

Despite the fits and starts in developments outlined above, rich sources of legacy data can now be found in a network of generic and specialist archives and data repositories that are scattered across the UK and internationally. In the UK, these

include the *Kirklees Sound Archive* in West Yorkshire, which houses oral history interviews on the wool textile industry (Bornat 2013); the *National Social Policy and Social
Change Archive* (Essex); the *Feminist Archive* (London and Leeds); and the *LSE Archive*
(London) (Hughes and Tarrant 2020a). The principal collections in the UK are held
at the *UK Data Archive* (including the classic *Qualidata* collection); the *British Library
Sound Archive*; the *Northern Ireland Qualitative Archive* (NIQA), including the ARK
resource; and the *Mass Observation Archive*. International resources include the *Irish
Qualitative Data Archive* (Maynooth); the *Qualitative Data Repository* (Syracuse, NY);
the *Henry A. Murray Research Center Archive* (Harvard); the *Finnish Social Science Data
Archive* and the *Swiss Foundation for Research in Social Science* (for a more extensive
review, see Hughes and Tarrant 2020a).

The potential to revisit QL datasets has been greatly enhanced in recent years
through the work of the long-running *Mass Observation Archive* (MOA) and related
biographical life-writing resources. These include the French *APA Archive* (Lejeune
2011); the *Irish Qualitative Data Archive*, with its rich holdings of longitudinal
and life history data (Geraghty and Gray 2017; Gray and Geraghty 2020); and
the more recently established Timescapes Archive, a specialist resource of qualitative
longitudinal data.

The data held in the *Mass Observation Archive* (MOA) is based on a unique national
life-writing project, originally founded in 1937, that captures aspects of everyday life
in Britain. In response to regular directives from the MO project, a panel of some 500
observers across the UK produce narratives of their experiences, thoughts and opinions that are then deposited in the archive. The MOA recorders are currently writing
about their experiences of living through a pandemic. In many cases, the diaries and
accounts of everyday life that make up the collection run across decades of change
(Salter 2017). The numerous studies of these data include reconstructions of single
biographies from a historical collection of hand-written diaries (e.g. Salter 2017; and
the diaries of Nella Last, edited by Broad and Fleming 1981, and Malcolmson and
Malcolmson 2008; see extracts in Box 6.8). The MOA resource also allows for explorations of the changing social fabric of a particular decade; the documenting of
major events or periods in history (the Second World War, for example); and studies
of a variety of changing social and historical practices across cases, themes and time
(see, for example, Shaw 2001; and Savage 2007). Data in this resource is gradually
being digitised, to help data discovery and access.

The Timescapes Archive, a digital resource held within the institutional repository
at the University of Leeds, has been under continual development since its launch
in 2010 (Neale and Bishop 2012a; www.timescapes-archive.leeds.ac.uk). This archive
specialises in the curation of QL datasets, which are gradually being added to the
resource (for an example, see Chapter 7, Figure 7.3). The core collection comprises a
suite of thematically linked datasets, generated through a national-level study of the
dynamics of family and interpersonal lives across the generations (see the Timescapes
study at www.timescapes.leeds.ac.uk). Given its relatively recent development, the

archive has been able to set new standards for the curation of QL datasets. The legacy data held in this resource will grow in historical value as the archive matures. But researchers have already begun to explore new ways to engage with and interrogate these extensive datasets. Pioneering legacy data studies, based on collaborative efforts to share data, were conducted during the lifetime of the Timescapes study (Irwin and Winterton 2012; Irwin et al. 2012; Winterton and Irwin 2012; Irwin and Winterton 2014; Irwin 2020; also Sheldon 2009; Baker 2010). And they have been developed further since (Wilson 2014; Tarrant 2016; Davidson et al. 2019; Tarrant and Hughes 2019, 2020; Edwards et al. 2020; bigqlr.ncrm.ac.uk).

It is worth noting here that specialist archives such as the MOA and Timescapes are not merely passive stores of knowledge; they are crucial lynchpins in the development of a processual understanding of lives and times. They actively curate and organise their collections of QL data in ways that are thematically and temporally linked, and they facilitate the use of their holdings for both research and teaching purposes in ways that shape and advance the field of socio-historical research.

Working with Legacy Data

Legacy datasets may be used for a variety of purposes, in different ways, over varied timescales, by the original researchers or by new generations of researchers. While there is no one shared or settled definition of this process, it is commonly referred to as **qualitative secondary analysis** or QSA (Hughes and Tarrant 2020a). This creates a logical, sequential distinction between 'first' and 'second' stage analysis. However, it is also understood as the analysis of legacy data by 'secondary' researchers, as opposed to the 'primary' researchers who produced them (Kelder 2005; Moore 2007; Largan and Morris 2019). However, this notion of a divide between primary and secondary researchers has some notable drawbacks (a theme explored further below).

Conceptualising the re-use of existing data as legacy data research provides an alternative way of framing this process. It focuses attention on the historical nature of these data, rather than who actually uses them; their key defining feature is that they are inherently temporal. They are *documents of lives and times* that offer a retrospective understanding of temporal processes (Neale 2017b, 2020b; Bornat 2020b; Gray and Geraghty 2020). As Duncan (2012: 313) usefully observes, such research offers a kind of comparative enquiry that compares over time instead of space. As legacy data 'age' through the passage of time, they are placed in new historical, generational and biographical contexts, with the potential to shed new light on the past in relation to the present, and on processes of continuity and change (Irwin 2013: 286; see also Bond 1990; Bishop 2007; Goodwin and O'Connor 2015). Even relatively new legacy data, captured in a contemporary landscape, have this potential, for all data implicitly reflect the times in which they are produced (McLeod and Thomson 2009).

Given their historical nature, another defining feature of legacy data is that they are generally used for purposes beyond that for which they were originally produced (Bornat 2003; Bishop 2009, 2016). In-depth interview data may, for example, be used as teaching resources (Bishop 2012; Haaker 2020), or can be analysed not simply for their content, but also to shed light on their construction as narratives, and what they can reveal about the values of the narrators and/or the producers of the dataset (Prior 2016; see Box 8.5 for examples). As Bornat (2013) observes, asking new questions of data and developing new lines of enquiry are part and parcel of qualitative enquiry. This is precisely what Bornat (2003, 2005) did when she visited a rich dataset, originally produced by Margot Jefferys in the early 1990s, which explored the development of geriatric medicine. Bornat discovered that important historical issues relating to race and ethnicity were implicitly embedded in the interview narratives. These themes became the focus for her re-analysis of these data, and for the development of a new study (Bornat et al. 2012).

The key point here is that working with legacy data is a viable and increasingly used form of socio-historical research, with scope to shed new light on temporal processes. Understanding legacy data as documents of lives and times gives scope for researchers to historicise their insights and explanations, and to work towards an exciting fusion of sociology and history (Wright Mills 1959; Bornat and Bytheway 2012; Duncan 2012; O'Connor and Goodwin 2012; Bornat 2013, 2020).

Three broad ways of working with legacy data are outlined here:

- **Working with retrospective data**: the retrospective analysis of legacy data, including 'found' forms of the data that were not produced for research purposes;
- **Building new studies and re-studies**: using legacy data as the springboard for a new study, or the baseline for a re-study, with significant temporal reach;
- **Working across datasets**: aggregating varied forms of legacy data through integrative reviews and analyses, to produce a broad, comparative picture of lives and times, and to enhance the scope for qualitative generalisations.

Working retrospectively with legacy data

A retrospective analysis of legacy data offers a simple and relatively straightforward form of qualitative enquiry. New themes can be explored in the data, and new insights on past times can be discerned through the lens of present-day knowledge and scholarship. Through these processes, legacy data are re-constructed and reinterpreted from a different historical, theoretical and/or methodological standpoint. A range of studies is outlined in Box 8.3, including those that draw on 'found' forms of data, which were not originally produced for research purposes (Goodwin and O'Connor 2020).

Box 8.3   The Retrospective Analysis of Legacy Data

- Letters, with their inherent seriality, have long provided a rich source of insight into unfolding lives. Stanley's (2013) socio-historical study of the history of race and apartheid in South Africa was based on a retrospective analysis of three collections of letters, written by white South Africans and spanning a 200-year period (1770s to 1970s).

- In their classic study of Polish migration, Thomas and Znaniecki (1958 [1918–21]) analysed news reports and the letters of Polish migrants to the USA. This was an opportunistic source, for a collection of such letters was thrown out of a Chicago window and landed at Znaniecki's feet (Plummer 2001). In this case, the legacy data were used alongside new life history data generated directly from a sample of participants.

- 'Found' forms of legacy data can also take the form of digital data, produced on the internet through social media sites. Alongside the large-scale studies referred to earlier (Tinati et al. 2014), QL researchers are beginning to make use of these data. Robards and Lincoln (2017), for example, set up a participatory study with young people in their 20s to explore the longitudinal narratives that they had created over the previous five years on Facebook, a social networking site. Becoming 'friends' on Facebook enabled the researchers to scroll back through these processual data, which they then co-analysed with their participants. The data revealed how the young people had articulated their stories of 'growing up' and the turning and trigger points in their life stories. The researchers also gained insight into how disclosure practices (what people say and share on social media) change over time. The same scroll-back method could be used with a variety of digital media, as social networking sites develop and diversify over time.

- For his study of social class in Britain, Savage (2005a, 2005b) analysed a rich, historical dataset (a series of detailed notebooks, held in the UK Data Archive) that had been produced in the early 1960s by Goldthorpe and Lockwood for their *Affluent Worker* study. In line with orthodox research practice in the post-war years, the original team generated both qualitative and quantitative data, but prioritised their quantifiable survey data and left their case study evidence on the cutting room floor. Some 40 years later, Savage accessed and read these neglected data in a different way, 'against the grain', making sense of the complexities and nuances of the workers' past accounts through the lens of present-day scholarship. This produced new insights into perceptions and practices of social class in post-war Britain that challenged and refined the interpretations of the earlier researchers (Savage 2005a, 2005b). Savage was also able to

(Continued)

> shed light on the original research process and its theoretical and methodological underpinnings.
> - As well as generating fresh theoretical and historical insights from his analysis, Savage rectified the under-utilisation of a valuable data resource. As each generation of researchers observes, qualitative research generates substantial volumes of data that are rarely fully analysed as part of an original study (Foster et al. 1979; Pettigrew 1995; McLeod and Thomson 2009; and see Box 8.5). This increases the scope to revisit a dataset with a very different purpose in mind.

Building new studies and re-studies

The basic approach to using legacy data outlined in Box 8.3 can be refined and elaborated upon in a variety of ways. Such data can also be used as the springboard for developing new lines of enquiry, including building a re-study with considerable temporal reach (see examples in Box 8.2 and in Boxes 1.7 and 1.8). The process may involve modifying themes and identifying new topics of enquiry, refining methodology (for example, modifying samples and settings) and generating new data to address substantive or conceptual gaps or questions arising from the original research. In these ways, the original study becomes a vital baseline for a newly constituted enquiry (Bornat et al. 2012).

There are many imaginative ways of working with and building on legacy datasets. To give one example, data from a range of studies on young people's imagined futures have been used to shed light on the historical embeddedness of such accounts (see the discussion in Chapter 3, and examples in Boxes 6.4 and 6.5). Where researchers have generated fresh 'futures' data as part of a new study or re-study, they have commonly mirrored the techniques and wording used by their predecessors. This creates comparable data for temporal analysis (see, for example, Crow and Lyon 2011; Winterton and Irwin 2011; Lyon and Crow 2012, 2020; Irwin 2020).

As shown in Chapter 1, the gap between an original study and a re-study is usually a decade or more, giving historical reach to the process. But legacy datasets may also be revisited fast on the heels of their original production, where they can be used as the springboard for developing new lines of enquiry (Bishop 2007; see Box 8.5 for an example). In a contextual mapping exercise, for example, Tarrant (2016; Tarrant and Hughes 2019) worked with data from two QL studies held in the Timescapes Archive: *Intergenerational Exchange* and *Following Young Fathers*. This became the baseline for the development of a new study on fatherhood and practices of care in low-income families and communities.

Working across datasets: building comparative evidence

Finally, there is huge scope for researchers to work across two or more datasets, produced in different settings, with different samples, at different scales of enquiry, and/or through different horizons of time. For example, data from the *Affluent Worker* study (see Box 8.3) was repurposed not only by Savage, but also by the social historian David Kynaston (2005) for his social history of post-war Britain. In a series of publications, Kynaston created a rich mosaic of political, socio-economic and cultural insights drawn from a wide range of sources, including personal accounts held in the *Mass Observation Archive* and social science datasets held in the *UK Data Archive.*

Building a wider pool of data across time and space extends the temporal reach of an enquiry and provides a more elaborate comparative lens for discerning processes of social change (Irwin 2020). It is an approach reflected, for example, in the work of processual sociologists such as Elias (1997 [1977], Abrams (1982) and Tilly (2008), who use a range of archival sources to explore broad socio-historical processes, ranging from class formation and political or religious movements, to imperial expansion and the rise of industrialised societies. Through a growing corpus of studies, researchers are illustrating the creative ways in which data from varied sources, across different scales of the social fabric, and/or across different horizons of time and place, can be brought together to extend and enrich analysis (see, for example, Thompson 2004; Irwin and Winterton 2012, 2014; Gray et al. 2016; Tarrant 2016; Tarrant and Hughes 2019; Edwards et al. 2020; Gray and Geraghty 2020).

To date, much of this research has involved working with relatively small amounts of qualitative data drawn from a small number of datasets. But, through integrative reviews and analyses, researchers have also begun to explore larger corpuses of diverse qualitative material that can be reassembled and re-purposed for new or evolving lines of enquiry. Two developments are worth noting here. First, QL researchers have begun to adapt computational forms of analysis (key word searching, data mining and pattern recognition) that were originally developed for big data analytics (Tinati et al. 2014). This approach has been pioneered by Davidson et al. (2019) and Edwards et al. (2020), who have worked across a large corpus of legacy material on family dynamics drawn from the Timescapes Archive. Second, researchers have begun to develop collective techniques of integrative analysis to build a broader qualitative evidence base (Middlemiss et al. 2019; Wright and Patrick 2019). These developments are showcased in Box 8.4.

The first two examples in Box 8.4 illustrate how a broader evidence base can be built through a combination of qualitative and quantitative legacy data (see also Chapter 1, where the value of such an approach is explored). The last two examples illustrate how the same ends can be achieved when researchers work with and aggregate a critical mass of qualitative data. In the first example, researchers are external visitors to the datasets. In the remaining examples, the researchers are internal users, working collaboratively to link their own data with wider sources of evidence.

Box 8.4 Working across Datasets: Building a Broader Evidence Base

- A mixed longitudinal approach was used by Lindsey et al. (2015) in their study of volunteering. They drew on in-depth data from the *Mass Observation Archive*, which they combined with longitudinal data from the large-scale *British Household Panel Survey* and recurrent cross-sectional data from the annual *British Social Attitudes Survey*. They were able to develop a broad picture of changing cultures of social participation in the UK, which they fleshed out with detailed case study evidence.
- Working collaboratively across their different disciplinary bases, Elder and Hareven (1992) drew on large-scale longitudinal data from the *Berkeley Guidance* study and the *Oakland and Berkeley Growth* studies, which had followed the lives of 500 Californian children over a period of 60 years. These data, which had been extensively analysed by Elder (1974) for his earlier studies, were combined with in-depth data from Hareven's (1982, 2000) rich oral historical study of two generations of mill worker families in Amoskeag in New Hampshire. Reading across these different scales of data, gathered in different settings over the generations, gave new insights into the variable impact of the Great Depression on American families, and the many factors (including military service) that could lift families out of poverty and enhance their life chances.
- Using a collaborative network approach, Middlemiss and colleagues (2019) worked across and integrated an extensive corpus of qualitative data that explored various aspects of energy poverty and its social dimensions. The eight datasets had been generated by network members between 2003 and 2016, in varied settings across the UK. From this broad corpus, the team sampled 197 interviews that showed particular thematic connections and overlaps. From this new pool of data, they developed and explored new research questions concerning energy poverty in different social environments and circumstances. This integrative analysis led them to funnel in on 12 complementary cases for detailed thematic and narrative interpretation. A cross-project collaborative approach was maintained for the interpretation and publication of findings based on these cases.
- Wright and Patrick (2019) aggregated a corpus of QL data drawn from their respective studies on welfare conditionality in the UK. The in-depth data from Patrick's small-scale study (*The Lived Experience of Welfare*

> *Reform*, 15 cases) complemented and fleshed out the broader, more
> comparative picture generated by Wright and her colleagues for the
> *Welfare Conditionality* study (480 cases). Since these studies were in the
> process of being archived, the researchers shared excerpts from their
> thematically coded data rather than full interview transcripts, and relied
> on their respective immersions in their own data to identify key themes.
> They then drew out cases that exemplified the most commonly reported
> and salient experiences across the two panels of participants. Working
> iteratively, a fresh integrative analysis of these cases then led them back
> to their respective datasets to check the emerging insights against the
> original bodies of evidence.

The examples in Box 8.4 illustrate some of the varied ways in which researchers can draw upon and aggregate complementary forms of legacy data to create a broader vision of social processes. The data are likely to be methodologically pluralist (Halford and Savage 2017), involving one or more of the following combinations: small-scale/large-scale; historical/contemporary; situated/comparative; qualitative/quantitative; scholarly/popular; researcher-generated/'found' data. It is not simply the size and extent of these data that gives them their value. They are carefully and strategically chosen to address ambitious and wide-ranging research questions (Halford and Savage 2017). The process creates 'big' rich data with the potential to combine explanatory depth with comparative breadth and historical reach (Neale 2015).

Methodologically, it is worth noting here the advantages of using thematically and/or temporally linked data sources, such as the family projects in the Timescapes Archive (Irwin and Winterton 2014); or the contemporaneous studies on welfare reform used by Wright and Patrick (2019). This can help to overcome the challenge of bringing disparate data into a new conceptual framework (Tarrant and Hughes 2019; Irwin 2020). Drawing on nested QL datasets holds particular promise here (e.g. the *Growing Up in Ireland* study; Gray and Geraghty 2020), for some alignment of samples and/or key themes will already have occurred as part of the original design. (For an example of a nested QL study, see Box 1.5)

Qualitative Generalisations

More broadly, it is worth reflecting here on the potential for these exploratory, data-led modes of research to create a significant shift in social research methodology (Kitchin 2014; Halford and Savage 2017). They raise new questions about the constitution of knowledge, the process of research, and how we engage with and understand data and evidence (Kitchin 2014: 1). For those working with big data analytics, conventional parsimony and theoretical reductionism give way to a more open, imaginative search for multiple forms of empirical evidence, which, through integrative reviews and analysis, can be skilfully woven into a composite picture (Neale 2021). Causality can be established here in new ways: through the elaboration and synthesis of multiple empirical examples, drawn from a carefully chosen range of contexts (Halford and Savage 2017). Insights about patterns and processes of social change are given added credence through the extent, variety and weight of the evidence base and the abductive reasoning though which comparisions and connections are drawn out. Halford and Savage (2017) envisage this process as a 'symphonic' approach to social enquiry, where diverse data are brought into new harmonies through recurring refrains that are endlessly elaborated. In other words, the process creates a rich mosaic of integrated evidence, with each new addition to the picture enhancing our overall understanding (Becker 1966 [1930]: viii; see Box 2.1).

This potential to address broader comparative questions that cannot be addressed through individual datasets alone, offers a powerful incentive for QL and qualitative researchers to pool or aggregate their data to create larger bodies of empirical evidence (Middlemiss et al. 2019; Wright and Patrick 2019; Edwards et al. 2020; Hughes and Tarrant 2020a). This potential will grow rapidly as the ethos of data sharing and re-use becomes more fully established. The aim is to transform the 'little islands of knowledge' derived from small-scale studies into a coherent bigger picture (Glaser and Strauss, cited in Wright and Patrick 2019: 601). Qualitative insights into widespread patterns of social experience and practice, and/or broader structures of knowledge and meaning, are strengthened in these studies, because they remain firmly rooted in careful empirical observations and rich, situated evidence. The process generates a new mosaic of empirical data, drawn from diverse but strategically chosen sources. This creates qualitative forms of generalisation that are based on abductive logic, and perfectly attuned to interpretive enquiry (see Box 2.1 and Box 9.1; also Hallebone 1992; Gobo 2004; Tarrant 2016; Edwards et al. 2020).

Analytical Strategies and Challenges: Searching, Sampling and Sculpting Data

There is a commonly held assumption that working with legacy data is quicker, easier and cheaper than generating data through a field-based empirical study (see, for example, Largan and Morris 2019). Yet the experiences of many legacy data researchers would suggest otherwise (Wilson 2014; Bishop 2016; Tarrant 2016; Hughes and Tarrant 2020a). As shown above, there is the initial challenge of **data discovery**, of searching to find suitable repositories and details of their holdings that may yield suitable datasets. This may be a particular issue for researchers who are starting from scratch and/or operating outside established research networks. Once datasets are located, there is the issue of how to sample data when the researcher may not know in advance which data, or segments of data, might be of use (Bishop 2016). The process involves appraising the quality of legacy data and finding a degree of contextual 'fit' between the data source and a new line of enquiry.

These challenges may be magnified in a variety of ways, for example when working across disparate data sources; when the language and concepts used in the original research have dated or become obsolete; when an initial audit of the data reveals they are too 'thin' or fragmented, or when their quality has been compromised; when there are no links to the data producers; and/or when there is limited accompanying documentation (metadata) that can contextualise the production of a dataset and its contents (Halford and Savage 2017; Irwin 2020; see Chapter 7 for the creation of metadata).

Whatever the circumstances, achieving a degree of contextual 'fit' is likely to require a careful and lengthy process of familiarisation with a dataset, and a diligent sifting through the data (Irwin et al. 2012; Wilson 2014; Irwin 2020). Given the scale of data that may be involved, particularly for a 'deluge' of QL data, researchers tend to sample strategically, using varied filtering techniques to find ways into the data (Irwin 2020). A case-led or depth-to-breadth approach starts with sampling emblematic (illuminative, distinctive or archetypal) cases (Gobo 2004; Weis 2004), potentially in consultation with the original researchers (see below). These emblematic cases provide a starting point for more refined searches of key themes across a dataset as the analysis progresses (Tarrant 2016; Tarrant and Hughes 2019).

A thematically led or breadth-to-depth approach works in reverse (Davidson et al. 2019; Edwards et al. 2020). It begins with systematic thematic searching across the data, using text searching for key words, concepts or themes, or, where the corpus of data is very large, adapting computational methods of data mining, such as Leximancer or a similar software tool. This is followed by an engaged analytic search for selected cases that can provide a more in-depth understanding of the processes under study (Edwards et al. 2020).

Whatever the starting point, the analytical process is likely to involve multiple iterations between cases and themes, and an integration of processual understandings where the data allow. In this, it has some synergies with the abductive, case-theme-process logic of enquiry used in the analysis of QL data (see Chapter 9). The broad aim is to yield new pools of aggregated data. These might be defined in terms of themes, case characteristics (age, gender, generation), temporal location (historical/biographical moment), settings, and/or type of data. This creates a newly configured or 'recast' dataset that is tailored to the new analysis (Laub and Sampson 1998: 218; Bornat 2005; Halford and Savage 2017; Edwards et al. 2020). The process of sculpting data to make them fit for a new purpose may involve re-coding and re-ordering data into new thematic groupings or case histories; harmonising data formats such as file names; and/or re-assigning identities (double anonymising) to provide extra safeguards on confidentiality.

In this new and fast advancing field, new techniques and methodological refinements are continually coming on stream. Whatever methods are used, immersive reading of a whole legacy dataset is not likely to be feasible, particularly for a QL study. Even the more basic process of familiarisation with a dataset requires time and diligence to thoroughly map the resource (Tarrant 2016; Irwin 2020). Searching, sampling and sculpting legacy data, then, is intricate and time-consuming. However, the process becomes more manageable when this detailed, methodical work is placed in a broader, more creative and imaginative framework. Working with legacy data is also a voyage of discovery that relies as much on serendipity, chance discoveries, open explorations and intuitive connections, as it does on diligence and precision (Bornat 2013; Kitchin 2014; Halford and Savage 2017; Middlemiss et al. 2019; Goodwin and O'Connor 2020). In other words, it is founded on an abductive mode of reasoning and knowledge-building that entails iteration between empirical case data and theoretical concepts (detailed in Box 9.1).

Epistemology: The Status and Meaning of Legacy Data

Working with legacy data raises important ethical and epistemological questions about the status and meaning of these data and their value for future use. The issues have been extensively debated elsewhere (see, for example, Mauthner et al. 1998; Kelder 2005; Moore, 2006, 2007; Bishop 2009; Hammersley 2010; Irwin and Winterton 2011, 2012; Mauthner 2012; Irwin 2013; Mauthner and Parry 2013; Hughes and Tarrant 2020a). But some salient points are drawn out here, and in the discussion below on the ethics of mutual respect.

Early debates about the status of legacy data revolved around the extent to which such data are embedded in the contexts of their production, and, therefore, best mediated through the original researchers, with their privileged, experiential knowledge of the field (Mauthner et al. 1998). It was this kind of argument that fuelled debates about the relative worth of 'primary' and 'secondary' forms of analysis. A related concern was that legacy data inevitably give us a partial vision of the social world. As we have seen, there may be a simple 'lack of fit' between the nature and scope of a legacy dataset and the research questions that drive a new study, leaving the new analyst with missing or incomplete data that are not robust enough to contribute new knowledge or evidence (Hammersley 2010; Duncan 2012).

When researchers are working across datasets, and seeking to bring them into analytic conversation and alignment, these challenges are amplified (Irwin 2013,

2020). Careful documentation of an original study and dataset can help to provide contextual understanding (see Chapter 7). But, even with such documentation, legacy data may give us little more than traces of real lives, or 'fragments of past occurrences' (Bond 1990: 287; see the example in Box 8.1). Or, as Steedman observes, 'you find nothing in the archive but stories caught half way through: the middle of things: discontinuities' (Steedman, cited in Tamboukou 2014: 619).

The concerns outlined above raise questions about the viability of transporting legacy data to another research context, and doubts about what (if anything) they may tell us when they are used for a different purpose and/or in a different time. From this point of view, the idea that a researcher can instrumentally revisit a data-set as if it has independent veracity and existence becomes questionable. These concerns reflect a tension between a crude, positivist understanding of data (as resources that are simply 'out there', outside of time), and a narrowly constructionist view that data are not transferable because they are jointly produced and their meaning tied to the context of their production.

The Transformative Potential of Legacy Data

However, these epistemological concerns about the feasibility of working with legacy data have shifted ground over recent years (see, for example, the changing perspectives of Mauthner et al. 1998 and Mauthner and Parry 2013). Researchers now recognise that the problems of contextual understanding and of the fragmented nature of data are not confined to the re-analysis of legacy data. They are foundational issues for all research data, impacting on how data are produced and interpreted in the first place. Whatever the data source, researchers have to appraise the degree of contextual 'fit' and under-standing that can be achieved and maintained (Hammersley 2010; Duncan 2012; Irwin 2013, 2020). Critiquing legacy data research for its lack of contextual fit becomes less valid when these same issues cut across the primary/secondary 'divide'. The status and veracity of research data, then, is not a black and white, either/or issue, but one of recognising the limitations and partial vision of all data sources.

Moreover, while legacy data are by no means simply 'out there', this does not devalue them as sources of knowledge and insight, or mean that they can be under-stood only in the context of their original production (Moore 2006). The process of crafting or recrafting data through time does not empty them of meaning: they are not simply 'made up'. When these data are revisited and re-purposed, they are effec-tively re-generated: re-sampled, re-configured, re-contextualised. Indeed, they are transformed historically simply through the passage of time (Moore 2006; 2007). Visiting legacy data in different social, spatial or temporal contexts does not diminish their 'stand-alone' ontological status or their value for re-analysts, who are seeking to address new or evolving research questions (Moore 2006; 2007; Hammersley 2010;

Bornat 2013). This process of reconstructing data for new purposes is hardly a novel one; it is the very stuff of historical research (Bornat 2008; McLeod and Thomson 2009). Where data have been skilfully generated, are descriptively rich and give voice to participants' own accounts, they can provide vivid and authentic windows onto a variety of social and historical processes.

Layered Meanings

The discussion above points to a crucial feature of research data: they are capable of more than one interpretation, for their meaning and salience emerge in the moment of their use:

> There is no a-priori privileged moment in time in which we can gain a deeper, more profound, truer insight, than in any other moment. ... There is never a single authorised reading ... It is the multiple viewpoints, taken together which are the most illuminating. (Brockmeier and Reissman, cited in Andrews 2008: 89–90)

As McLeod and Thomson (2009) observe in our opening quotation for this chapter, the value of qualitative data is not exhausted or fully captured in one reading or telling, or in one time. It is the combination of different readings, in different contexts, that offers additional layers of meaning and insight. Historical distance is by no means a disadvantage; it provides a new and broader temporal horizon from which to view lives and times (Moore 2006; Duncan 2012; for a re-study example, see Box 1.8). As shown in Chapter 1, Lassiter (2012) carried out a re-study of the Lynds' famous 'Middletown' community studies, which were designed to shed light on processes of socio-economic change in the early decades of the 20th century. Lassiter's re-study shifted the focus to the ethnic composition of the city, revealing the partial insights of the original researchers. It is a prime illustration of how contextual issues relating to time, place and cultural embeddedness can shape very different understandings of the same community. From a temporal perspective, there is not one Middletown, but, potentially, many.

Indeed, understanding data through the lens of time reveals that they have no definitive or fixed meanings; legacy data do not stand still (Moore 2006). Nor do the social contexts in which they can be understood: their contextual anchors are also perpetually transforming (Moore 2006; 2007). The presence or close involvement of a researcher at the point data are generated does not confer on them a privileged understanding of these data (Hammersley 2010; Irwin and Winterton 2012). Interpretations produced in earlier times represent one layer of historical and theoretical insight rather than a definitive picture. This is well recognised by researchers who revisit their own data over time (Thompson 2000; Åkerström et al. 2004), either alone or in the company of others (see Box 8.4). Examples of such internal revisiting are provided in Box 8.5.

Box 8.5 Internal Revisiting

- The practice of researchers returning to the data that they have previously generated, using fresh modes of analysis and interpretation, has a long history. This process is intrinsic to QL research of course, and is standard practice among a broad constituency of socio-historical researchers (Åkerström et al. 2004). Ottenberg (1990) and Andrews (2008), for example, reflect on the process of finding new ways to make sense of the data they have gathered over decades of professional, personal and historical change. For example, in his longitudinal ethnography of the Afikpo community in southeast Nigeria, Ottenberg observes:

  As anthropological theory has changed, so has the way I look at my ... written notes. ... I am constantly re-interpreting Afikpo, ever looking at my field notes in different ways ... through more than 30 years of using these notes. (Ottenberg 1990: 146)

- In a similar vein, Åkerström and Jacobsson (Åkerström et al. 2004) recount how they went back to their earlier studies, re-cycled their data and interpreted them through new theoretical lenses. Jacobsson re-analysed her extensive dataset on the lives of hearing impaired people in Sweden and published a new book from her study just three years after the original publication. The original study was policy driven and used thematic analysis to explore the treatment and education of deaf people. But Jacobsson also found a recurring pattern of talk in her data about the cultures of deaf people that did not fit her analytical framework, and which had been beyond the scope of her original study. These implicit themes became the focus for her re-study. Using conversational analysis, she was able to draw out issues concerning the culture and politics of deafness, in particular the rights of deaf people to maintain their own distinctive identity and sign-language culture, rather than accept cochlear implants that would assimilate them into an unknown world of hearing and speech. The space of three years between these two studies gave Jacobsson little scope to historicise her evidence, but even through this distance of time, she was able to return to her original study with a fresh perspective and new analytical tools.

- Åkerström's original study of criminal lifestyles, based on accounts from inmates of women's prisons, was published in 1985. She describes how her use of cross-case thematic analysis involved fragmenting interview transcripts into descriptive categories. This disintegrated and redistributed

(Continued)

the narratives of her participants, a process that favoured certain lines of enquiry and obstructed others (see Chapter 10 for a detailed discussion of this issue). Like many qualitative researchers, she found that she could not do justice to all of her rich data, some of which did not 'fit' her original analytical framework. The case of 'Annie', in particular, represented an unresolved analytical challenge, a narrative that was at odds with the themes of victimhood and gendered oppression that dominated the women's accounts. Twenty years later, in 2001, Åkerström constructed and published a narrative analysis of this emblematic case, taking her inspiration from similar case study research in her field (Shaw 1966 [1930]). She was able to effect a broad shift from thematic to processual, case-based analysis, and switch her focus from the thematic content of the interview to how Annie spoke about her evolving life. This brought to the fore her values and world view, and her identity as an independent and successful woman in a criminal world, an account that runs counter to dominant cultural narratives about gender and crime.

- The recycling of their respective data led these researchers to the view that there is not just one story that can be told from research data; that interpretations are always incomplete; that recycling a study redefines its material; and that an ongoing exploration of a dataset adds vitality and insight to the original interpretations.

The reflections provided in Box 8.5 alert us to the transformative power of data and the value of multiple readings through time. This is nowhere more evident than in the process of generating and analysing a QL dataset. For QL researchers, returning to and re-interpreting data through time is an integral part of the research process, a continual and cumulative task of building new insights (Bond 1990). The production of new data as a QL study progresses inevitably reconfigures and re-contextualises the dataset as a whole, creating new assemblages of data and opening up new understandings from a different temporal standpoint. Moreover, by their very nature, longitudinal datasets tend to outlive their original research questions (for an arresting example from a longitudinal ethnography, see Box 1.6). This requires researchers to ask new questions of old data, to maximise the degree of 'fit' between them, to conjure new interpretive frameworks and, thereby, to 'breathe new life' into the data (Bond 1990; Elder and Taylor 2009).

In the context of this inherently interpretive and shifting process of meaning making, it is hardly surprising that socio-historical researchers are mindful of the need for modesty in the way they present their findings. As shown in Chapter 2, the aim is to arrive at plausible interpretations of the social world, produced in particular contexts of time and place, which are acknowledged to be provisional and in the making (Cilliers 1998; Åkerström et al. 2004; Elliott 2005).

'Primary/Secondary' Research: Reworking the Boundaries

The discussion above, and the examples in Box 8.5, suggest the need for a fresh appraisal of the interface between 'primary' and 'secondary' research, which will take us beyond the unhelpful notion of a 'divide' between them (Bishop 2007; Moore 2007; McLeod and Thomson 2009). As we have seen above, working with legacy data may involve stepping into the shoes of an earlier self (see Box 8.5), or someone else entirely (see Box 8.3), or it may involve both of these processes simultaneously (see Box 8.4) (Bornat 2006). But, whatever the case, this seems to make relatively little difference to the transformative nature of legacy data, or to the potential for interpretations to shift through time. From a temporal perspective, the boundaries between *primary* and *secondary* analysis begin to break down (Bornat 2005; Moore 2007; McLeod and Thomson 2009; Neale 2013).

This is, perhaps, most evident in the context of QL research, where processual data are continually revisited and the line between primary and secondary analysis is inevitably blurred. But, whatever labels are used to convey the use of legacy data, there is a need to avoid making the divide between primary and secondary researchers its key defining feature, and to scotch the implicit and dubious assumption that, somehow, 'primary' analysis is the privileged lens for analysis, while 'secondary' is merely 'second best' or 'second rate' (Irwin and Winterton 2012; Hughes and Tarrant 2020a).

The Ethics of Data Sharing and Re-use

One obvious way of re-working the boundaries around 'primary' and 'secondary' research is to foster a more collegial culture of data sharing and revisiting, based on trust and mutual respect between researchers (Neale and Bishop 2012b; Mauthner and Parry 2013; Neale 2013; Hughes and Tarrant 2020b). The **ethics of data sharing and re-use** is an important area of debate that is briefly reviewed here. As shown in Chapter 5, how QL researchers relate to their participants is a prime area of ethical concern, which is no less important when working with legacy data. The issues here revolve around informed consent for archiving where the future uses of data are unknown (see Chapter 7); and around the perceived risks of breaching confidentiality, and of exploiting or misrepresenting data about participants' lives. There is an assumption that new analysts are less attuned to the principles of confidentiality and protection for participants than their predecessors, because they are operating at one stage removed from them. But the counter argument holds that it is the very act of engaging with participants' accounts that engenders such sensibilities. If this is so, then new analysts are no more likely to breach ethical protocols than their predecessors (Weller 2017; Hughes and Tarrant 2020a).

Working with legacy data also gives rise to new ethical concerns surrounding the relationships between the original researchers (the data producers) and their successors. For the original researchers, the concerns centre on the potential disregard for their labour and skills as data producers and authors of archived datasets, the dangers of being 'scooped' by others, and risks to their professional standing and reputations in opening up 'their' data to scrutiny (Mauthner et al. 1998; Hadfield 2010). These fears, particularly those relating to reputational harm, are not wholly unjustified (see Box 1.7 for an example). This can make researchers reluctant to archive and share a dataset (although see the counter arguments in Chapter 7). For QL researchers, this reluctance also stems from their commitment to the longer-term nurturing and stewardship of a 'live' study and dataset, where there may be little sense of closure for a project.

One way to overcome these ethical difficulties across the primary/secondary divide is to adopt an **ethic of mutual respect** between the original researchers (the data producers), and new users. This principle is a long-standing one. Re-study scholars such as Lewis (1951) and, more recently, Lassiter (2012) (see above and Box 1.7) were very much aware of the need to avoid **reputational damage** to their predecessors when they uncovered and reported significant gaps and inconsistencies in the earlier studies. They took care to convey their respect for their predecessors, stressed the significant contributions that they had made to scholarship, and acknowledged the common intellectual endeavour that they shared (Lassiter 2012: 435). Lewis dedicated his book to Redfield, his predecessor, noting that, 'the objective and value of re-studies is not to prove one man right and another wrong' (Lewis 1951: 112). In his review of Lewis's re-study, Foster (1952) observes that one of the key factors that made a difference to the findings was 'the fact that each new author has been able to build on the accumulated experience of all his predecessors. Excellent as it is, [the new study] in no way detracts from Redfield's initial study' (1952: 240).

An ethic of mutual respect also comes into its own where standards of researcher behaviour and attitudes that are acceptable in one time or place become unacceptable in another. For example, a re-analysis of the vivid and unguarded field notes produced by Dennis Marsden for his 1960's *Mothers Alone* study revealed attitudes to gender and race that do not meet contemporary ethical standards (Gillies and Edwards 2012; also Evans and Thane 2006, who corresponded with Marsden about these issues before his death in 2009). As part of a broader ethos of openness and the value of critical debate in academic scholarship, such revelations need to be aired (Bornat et al. 2012; Bishop 2016). But they need to be managed with sensitivity to the historical context and cultural specificity of research practices. It greatly helps, too, if they can be placed alongside the achievements of the original researcher (in this case, Marsden was a respected champion of in-depth modes of qualitative interviewing in the field of sociology).

The rationale that is increasingly adopted is to be, '*"better with/because of"* – [rather] than *better than* – those who came before us' (Bracke and Puig de la Bellacasa, cited in Bornat et al. 2012: 10.6). As Bishop observes:

> [R]iver water flowing through a canyon exposes new layers of sedimentation. It would make no sense to criticise earlier geologists for not seeing the previously unexposed layers; the passage of time and water are necessary to be able to tell the more complex, layered story. (Bishop 2016: 400–1)

The principle of mutual respect between the original researchers and their successors has become increasingly important as the sharing of legacy data has grown. However, it is worth observing that the literature in this area tends to focus on the ethic of care that new data users owe to their predecessors. As shown above, new analysts are enjoined to temper their criticisms of what they may perceive as outdated findings, or outmoded attitudes and practices, and to be aware of the different cultural and intellectual environments in which classic legacy datasets were produced (Johnson et al. 2010; Gillies and Edwards 2012). They are also urged to value the legacy data bequeathed to them, and to acknowledge the emotional challenges that data producers face in 'letting go' of these resources (Mauthner and Parry 2013).

But the ethical responsibilities of new analysts should not detract from their own equally valid ethical claims. They have their own integrity, which is founded on intellectual rigour. They need well-produced and fully contextualised datasets to work with (see Chapter 7), and they need the freedom to ask their own questions of these data and produce their own interpretations – all the more so once we acknowledge the inherently provisional nature of interpretations and findings. It is helpful to see the work of new analysts as an enhancement of an original study, rather than a challenge or threat to it. This provides a strong incentive for the original researchers to support and facilitate the work of their successors, so that the ethic of respect runs in both directions (Neale 2013).

Collaborative Ventures

Where timings permit, collaborative ventures between researchers who produce and use legacy data can be of immense value. These may range from fluid consultations and mutual support (Lyon and Crow 2020), to integrated teamwork and joint authorship (Charles et al. 2008; Tarrant and Hughes 2019, 2020; and see the examples in Box 8.4). Three broad collaborative strategies for **data sharing** that have been used by QL researchers are outlined here:

- **intermittent sharing** of data and insights through meetings and workshops;

- **affiliated sharing**: facilitating the use of QL datasets during the lifetime of a study;
- **partnership sharing**: new projects that integrate data to arrive at new insights.

First, an intermittent sharing of data and insights through meetings, workshops and advisory boards is a useful means of building collaborations across teams of data producers and users (for a review of developments and varied practices, see Tarrant and Hughes 2020). Such events can enhance the scope for a critical investigation of a topic (Neale and Bishop 2012a; Bornat 2013; Bishop 2016; Tarrant and Hughes 2020). Events held as part of the Timescapes study, for example, enabled different teams of QL researchers to interrogate their data afresh through different theoretical and substantive lenses, and then return to the field armed with new insights and questions to explore (Bornat et al. 2008; Irwin et al. 2012; Tarrant and Hughes 2020).

Second, building affiliations with new researchers and facilitating their use of a QL dataset during the lifetime of a study is a productive way forward, given that the respective endeavours of the original researchers and their successors are more likely to overlap through these extended time frames. Such collaborations have a venerable history among longitudinal ethnographers, where they are seen as being integral to the success and longer-term sustainability of a study (Foster et al. 1979; Cliggett 2002; Kemper and Royce 2002). Visiting analysts will have their own valuable research agendas, but they can also perform an important role as project affiliates, increasing the utilisation of a growing dataset, extending the scope for theoretical exploration, and providing useful feedback on data documentation and organisation. At the same time, while data producers do not have prior ownership of a dataset, or a monopoly on interpretation, they have a great deal of contextual knowledge that can be of value to a new analyst. Certainly, affiliates can learn much from the core team, and may come to realise gaps in their own earlier research (Wilson 2014: 4.11).

Such collaborations were a feature of three projects in the Timescapes study (*Siblings and Friends, Young Lives and Times* and *The Oldest Generation*: Sheldon 2009; Baker 2010; Winterton and Irwin 2011). More recently, Tarrant (2016; Tarrant and Hughes 2019) carried out an analysis of data from two Timescapes projects (*Intergenerational Exchange* and *Following Young Fathers*) to support her empirical research on fatherhood and practices of care. She became a valued colleague and affiliate of both studies, established a productive working partnership with Hughes, developed joint research and writing projects across both studies; and has subsequently taken forward the *Following Young Fathers* study with a new phase of funding (Tarrant and Neale 2017; Tarrant 2020). She also convened data-sharing workshops across the two teams of researchers that were mutually productive and enjoyable. These workshops were not ends in themselves but valuable springboards to the development of new lines of enquiry (Tarrant 2016; Tarrant and Hughes 2020).

Facilitating the use of QL legacy data in these ways is a productive process, turning the potential overlap between the original research and new research endeavours into a virtue that is beneficial to all (Neale 2013).

Third, there is enormous scope for collaborative networks or teams of researchers to pool and integrate their qualitative data, and to conduct collective analyses that address cutting-edge research questions. As shown above (Box 8.4), this is an important means of building broader, comparative insights; in short, developing qualitative generalisations about social practices and processes that remain grounded in lived experiences.

The collaborative ventures outlined above represent exciting and imaginative departures from more conventional modes of legacy data research. In each case, primary researchers are drawn more directly into the process. There are important substantive and theoretical rationales for these developments. But they may also bring ethical benefits. Pooling data in the ways described above places researchers simultaneously in the role of 'primary' and 'secondary' analysts, part of a collective enterprise of data sharing and re-use that occurs beyond the medium of the archive – data sharing in its literal sense (Neale 2013). There is little sense in these practices of a wholesale 'letting go' of data, or of new researchers 'running away' with data in a way that could be construed as detrimental to the data producers. These are collective processes, based on trust and respect between different teams of researchers, which usefully work across and collapse the 'primary/secondary' boundary (Neale 2013).

Closing Reflections

This chapter has explored the value of legacy data as important documents of lives and times, with scope to shed light on processes of social and historical change. Revisiting legacy data in a new research context, for a new or evolving purpose and/or through new horizons of time, has great potential, regardless of whether this is carried out internally (by the original researchers), externally (by others) or through a mixture of the two. The different forms that legacy data may take, and different ways of working with them, have been outlined here. These include retrospective analyses of data, including serial forms of data such as diaries; the development of new studies or re-studies with enhanced temporal reach; or building a broader evidence base by working strategically across multiple sources of data, produced at different scales and/or in different socio-historical contexts.

This is an open and emerging field, with new methodologies continually under development. The valuable role played by archives in facilitating the use of legacy datasets has been flagged up here, with a particular focus on those that curate QL datasets. But we have also explored collaborative modes of data sharing that are unmediated by the archive, but which rely on the capacity to pool data across research teams and networks. The challenges of working with legacy datasets have also been touched on in this chapter, not least the intricate and time-consuming process of searching for, sampling and sculpting data, appraising their quality and bringing them into fresh alignments and connections that can shed light on new research questions. This recycling process (Åkerström et al. 2004; Bornat 2005) relies on abduction, that is, on a mixture of serendipity, creative intuition, precision and systematic working.

Finally, this chapter has attempted to show the synergies between legacy data research and QL enquiry, not least the common endeavour of revisiting data to discern new meanings and insights through the lens of time. As both users and producers of legacy data, there are many ways in which QL researchers may draw on legacy data to enrich their studies, and/or facilitate the use of their own legacy data by others. The elongated time frame for a QL study enhances this potential. Fostering an ethic of mutual respect and collective working between teams of legacy data producers and users has been explored here, highlighting the imaginative ways in which this can be done, and the significant theoretical, substantive and ethical advantages that may accrue. In sum, the huge potential to build productive links between QL and legacy data research has been highlighted here.

A decade ago, debates about the re-use of legacy datasets were in danger of becoming polarised (Moore 2006; 2007). However, the preoccupations of researchers have begun to move on. The concern with whether or not legacy data *should* be used has given way to a more productive concern with *how* they should be used, not least how best to work with their shifting and partial nature, their sheer size and their layered meanings through time (Neale 2017b, Neale 2020b). Overall, the 'jackdaw' approach to discovering and re-purposing legacy data is the very stuff of historical sociology and of social history more generally (Thompson 2000; Kynaston 2005; McLeod and Thomson 2009; Bornat 2020), and it has huge and largely untapped potential as a means of enriching and extending the scope of QL enquiry.

Further Reading

For state-of-the-art coverage of legacy data research, the collection of articles in Hughes and Tarrant (2020) is highly recommended, including Edwards et al. (2020) on the potential for big data analytics using QL data. For illustrations of the kind of insights that this mode of research can produce, see Bornat et al. (2012), Savage (2005a/b) and Irwin and Winterton (2014). For the potential to revisit varied forms of serial or processual data (ranging from letters to Facebook pages), see Stanley (2013, 2015) and Robards and Lincoln (2017). For illustrations of how (and why) researchers revisit their own datasets over time, either alone or in the company of others, see Åkerström et al. (2004) and Andrews (2008). For more recent examples that seek to pool QL data and build integrative forms of analyses and evidence across datasets, Middlemiss et al. (2019) and Wright and Patrick (2019) are recommended. For an engaging discussion of the significance of this development for social research, along with advances in big data analytics, see Halford and Savage (2017). For the extensive epistemological debates that have helped to shape this field, Moore (2007), Andrews (2008), Bishop (2009), Irwin and Winterton (2011) and Hammersley (2010) are good starting points. For broader discussion of the use of historical and documentary data sources beyond those generated for research purposes, see Plummer (2001) and Gidley (2018).

Åkerström, M., Jacobsson, K. and Wästerfors, D. (2004) 'Re-analysis of previously collected material', in C. Seale, G. Gobo, J. Gubrium and D. Silverman (eds) *Qualitative Research Practice* (concise edition). London: Sage, pp. 314–27.

Andrews, M. (2008) 'Never the last word: Revisiting data', in M. Andrews, C. Squire and M. Tamboukou (eds), *Doing Narrative Research*. London: Sage, pp. 86–101.

Bishop, L. (2009) 'Ethical sharing and re-use of qualitative data', *Australian Journal of Social Issues*, 44 (3): 255–72.

Bornat, J., Raghuram, P. and Henry, L. (2012) 'Revisiting the archives: A case from the history of geriatric medicine', *Sociological Research Online*, 17 (2): 11.

Edwards, R., Weller, S., Jamieson, L. and Davidson, E. (2020) 'Search strategies: Analytical searching across multiple datasets and within combined sources', in K. Hughes and A. Tarrant (eds) *Qualitative Secondary Analysis*. London: Sage, pp. 79–99.

Gidley, B. (2018) 'Doing historical and documentary research', in C. Seale (ed.) *Researching Society and Culture*. London: Sage, pp. 285–304.

Halford, S. and Savage, M. (2017) 'Speaking sociologically with big data: Symphonic social science and the future for big data research', *Sociology*, 51 (6): 1132–48.

Hammersley, M. (2010) 'Can we use qualitative data via secondary analysis? Notes on some terminological and substantive issues', *Sociological Research Online*, 15 (1): 47–53.

Hughes, K. and Tarrant, A. (eds) (2020) *Qualitative Secondary Analysis*. London: Sage.

Irwin, S. and Winterton, M. (2011) *Timescapes Data and Secondary Analysis: Working Across the Projects*. Timescapes Working Paper No. 5, www.timescapes.leeds. ac.uk/knowlegebank/publicationsandoutputs.

Irwin, S. and Winterton, M. (2014) 'Gender and work–family conflict: A secondary analysis of Timescapes data', in J. Holland and R. Edwards (eds) *Understanding Families over Time: Research and Policy*. London: Palgrave Macmillan, pp. 142–60.

Middlemiss, L., Ambrosio-Albalá, P., Emmel, N., Gillard, R., Gilbertson, J., et al. (2019) 'Energy poverty and social relations: A capabilities approach', *Energy Research and Social Science*, 55: 227–35.

Moore, N. (2007) '(Re)using qualitative data', *Sociological Research Online*, 12 (3): 1.

Plummer, K. (2001) *Documents of Life 2: An Invitation to a Critical Humanism*. London: Sage.

Robards, B. and Lincoln, S. (2017) 'Uncovering longitudinal life narratives: Scrolling back on Facebook', *Qualitative Research*, 17 (6): 715–30.

Savage, M. (2005a) 'Revisiting classic qualitative studies', *FQS: Forum Qualitative Social Research*, 6 (1): Art. 31.

Savage, M. (2005b) 'Working class identities in the 1960s: Revisiting the *Affluent Worker Study*', *Sociology*, 39 (5): 929–48.

Stanley, L. (2013) 'Whites writing: Letters and documents of life in a QLR project', in L. Stanley (ed.) *Documents of Life Revisited: Narrative and Biographical Methodology for a 21st Century Critical Humanism*. London, Routledge, pp. 59–73.

Stanley, L. (2015) 'Operationalising a QLR project on social change and whiteness in South Africa, 1770s–1970s', *International Journal of Social Research Methodology*, 18 (3): 251–65.

Wright, S. and Patrick, R. (2019) 'Welfare conditionality in lived experience: Aggregating qualitative longitudinal research', *Social Policy and Society*, 18 (4): 597–613.

9

QUALITATIVE LONGITUDINAL ANALYSIS: BASIC STRATEGIES

Key Points

- **The flexibility of QLA**: Qualitative longitudinal analysis (QLA) is the most complex and least well-documented aspect of the research process. As a flexible mode of analysis, it has no cast-iron rules or procedures, and no fixed sequence or tempo. It encompasses a range of analytical strategies, tools and techniques that may be adapted for the needs of individual projects. Strategies may also evolve over time.
- **The analytical process**: Analysis is more than a discrete phase of a project. It is a process that unfolds throughout a QL project, where it is interspersed with the tasks of generating and managing a growing dataset. The interpretation of QL data is best seen as part of a broader analytical strategy – the logic of working with cases, themes and processes – that runs like a unifying thread through the whole research process.
- **Basic analytical strategies/the logic of abduction**: QLA can be conceived as a conceptual journey that leads from summative to descriptive to interpretive accounts. It is an iterative process that requires the researcher to move back and forth between the data and wider pools of pre-existing theories and insights. The process is rooted in the logic of abduction: a creative and exploratory mode of discovery and knowledge building that transcends induction and deduction.
- **The logic of QLA**: QLA has a distinctive three-dimensional logic, based on a combination of case, thematic and processual readings of a dataset (detailed

(Continued)

in Chapters 10 and 11). These are interlocking facets of analysis (visualised in Figure 9.2) that give depth, breadth and temporal reach to a study. Each reading of a dataset involves an interrogation of case, thematic and processual insights, but from different starting points that open new windows onto the data.

- **The momentum of QLA (working through time)**: The objective of QLA is to piece together a diachronic (through-time) picture from successive waves of synchronic (snapshot) data. The real-time momentum of the research process provides the structure within which this occurs. Broad strategies for weaving analysis through the waves of fieldwork are outlined here; researchers devise their own steps to suit their study design. The varied facets of QLA (case-thematic-processual, synchronic to diachronic) develop iteratively, and quickly merge as the analysis progresses. The effective integration of these readings produces a rich tapestry of temporal insights.

- **Maintaining a processual focus?** Maintaining an analytical focus on time and process can be a challenge. It requires a balance between case and thematic readings of a dataset. Standard forms of thematic analysis (IPA, framework, grounded theory) can be useful springboards for the development of QLA, but need to be adapted for working with temporal processes.

Introduction

Approaches [to QLA] … are as varied as the traditions, disciplines, methodologies and schools within which qualitative research takes place. (Lewis 2007: 551)

There is now much greater visibility about how qualitative data are 'managed' but rather less about the intellectual processes involved in 'generating' findings from the evidence. … [Until recently] analysis was a relatively neglected subject … an almost esoteric process, shrouded in intellectual mystery. … [or] it appeared largely haphazard, with discovery falling from the evidence as if somehow by chance. (Ritchie et al. 2014: 199)

Getting the story can be fun, but making sense of it takes much longer and requires a lot of work. … In many ways this is the truly creative part of the work – it entails brooding and reflecting upon mounds of data for long periods of time until it 'makes sense' and 'feels right' and key ideas and themes flow from it. It is also the hardest process to describe. (Plummer 2001: 152)

Qualitative longitudinal analysis (QLA) is the most complex dimension of the research process, and the least well documented. This is where researchers seek to discover processual connections and patterns, and substantive and conceptual meanings in a dataset, which emerge through careful readings and reconfigurations of the data.

For QL enquiry, these insights are temporally driven. As shown in Chapter 1, the broad aim is to explore how continuities and changes are created, negotiated, lived and experienced, and how temporal processes emerge, develop, grow or dissipate through time.

As our opening quotations show, building qualitative interpretations of the social world has often been characterised as an obscure and enigmatic task, one that 'conjures up images of an unwieldy process characterised by lone researchers wallowing in paperwork' (Henn et al. 2009: 243). While researchers need a clear logic and rationale for their approach, there are no cast-iron rules or procedures for QLA. As Chapter 10 will show, a range of tools and techniques exist for reconfiguring data, which can be tailored to the needs of individual projects. Strategies, then, are varied and may be applied flexibly. They may also evolve within a project, particularly where funding has been built up in piecemeal fashion. Similarly, multiple strategies may be employed in tandem for different cohorts and sub-samples (Calman et al. 2013). Part of the challenge of QLA involves selecting the right combination of tools and techniques for the substantive nature of an enquiry and its theoretical drivers.

It is also worth establishing at the outset that, like any form of qualitative analysis, QLA is more than a discrete stage of a project that follows the completion of fieldwork. It is a process that unfolds throughout a project. This is especially evident for QL enquiry, where analysis is interspersed with the recurring tasks of generating and managing data. The process of interpreting QL data is best seen as part of a broader analytical strategy that runs like a unifying thread through the whole research process.

In this chapter, we introduce the basic analytical strategies that provide the foundation for QLA. The discussion begins with the broad strategies that are common to interpretivist forms of enquiry: first, the conceptual journey from summative to descriptive to interpretive accounts; and, second, the logic of abductive reasoning, which involves iteration between new empirical evidence and wider bodies of theoretical and substantive knowledge. These strategies provide an important grounding for the development of QLA.

We go on to consider the distinctive logic of QLA: the interlocking facets of case, thematic and processual analysis, which have to be held in mind and brought into alignment at key moments in the research process. These facets of QLA enable researchers to combine depth, breadth and temporal reach in their interpretations. This logic has been introduced in earlier chapters (see Box 4.1), but a recap is provided here as a precursor to the more detailed discussions in Chapters 10 and 11. Finally, we explore the distinctive momentum of QLA: how the analytical process is structured through the waves of a QL study, transforming synchronic (snapshot) readings of a dataset into diachronic (through-time) readings. Our discussion concludes with a consideration of a key conceptual issue for QL researchers: how to maintain a processual focus that flows through the research process, from design and sampling decisions, through to the presentation of research findings. This theme is central to our detailed exploration of QLA in Chapters 10 and 11.

Basic Strategies: Summarising, Describing, Interpreting

Like all forms of qualitative analysis, QLA can be conceived as a conceptual journey that leads from summative to descriptive to interpretive accounts. In the process, the researcher moves from finely grained substantive insights, to broader theoretical understandings of social processes (Saldaña 2003; Bygstad and Munkvold 2011). This is an iterative process that requires the researcher to move back and forth between different levels of abstraction, and to make a conceptual leap from description to explanation. The process has been characterised as 'a loop-like pattern of multiple rounds of revisiting the data as additional questions emerge, new connections are unearthed, and more complex formulations develop, along with a deepening understanding of the material. ... [It is] fundamentally an iterative set of processes' (Berkowitz, cited in Srivastava and Hopwood 2009: 77). This neatly reflects the way in which QLA unfolds.

As noted above, a range of analytical tools and techniques can be used to summarise, describe and re-configure QL data (detailed in Chapters 10 and 11). However, this does not represent the whole picture (Saldaña 2003: 63–4, 158). No tools of the trade can make the final conceptual leap from description to interpretation. This relies on the interpretive skills of the researcher, supported by the analytical logic of abduction (set out below). As part of the abductive method, QL researchers commonly report the value of regular analytical discussions (data sharing/analysis workshops, research away-days and other collaborative and dissemination activities) that are designed to share theories and data, debate emerging insights and sharpen thinking (Thomson and Holland 2003; Timmermans and Tavory 2012; Tarrant and Hughes 2020; see examples in Chapter 8). The whole process requires 'a mix of creativity and systematic searching, a blend of inspiration and diligent detection' (Ritchie and Lewis 2003: 199; also Gruber 1981).

Conceptual Scaffolding: The Analytical Spiral of QLA

The basic strategy of summarising, describing and interpreting, outlined above, has been usefully visualised by a number of researchers as a conceptual scaffolding or a ladder of analytical abstraction (Wright Mills 1959: 43; Miles and Huberman 1994; Wengraf 2000: 142–3; Ritchie and Lewis 2003: 212–17; Bygstad and Munkvold 2011). The researcher moves iteratively up and down the scaffolding, drawing on empirical case data at the lower levels, managing and becoming familiar with the data, and going further up the scaffolding to re-configure data into summative and descriptive readings. At the higher levels of the scaffolding, these readings are brought into conversation with broader bodies of theoretical and substantive knowledge (including those that will have informed the enquiry in the first place). The researcher then moves back down the scaffolding to check emerging insights and gauge their credibility and veracity against the corpus of data as a whole.

It is through the process of 'shuttling up and down the scaffolding' (Scheff, cited in Wengraf 2000: 142) that new insights engage with pre-existing theories, yet remain empirically grounded. In this iteration between first-hand knowledge and wider pools of evidence, some initial concepts will be abandoned, others reworked, and new and often unanticipated insights will emerge. The analytical process reaches fruition when the researcher narrates and visualises new insights (and/or refines or confirms existing insights) for a wider audience.

For our purposes here, this scaffolding has been visualised as a spiral of activities that unfolds through the time frame of a QL study (see Figure 9.1).

Figure 9.1 The analytical spiral of QLA

Moving away from the ladder metaphor, which implies a linear, sequential process (Bygstad and Munkvold 2011), the spiral reflects the non-linear, recursive (loop-like) and perpetually emerging nature of QLA. The solid circles in the diagram represent the core analytical tasks, while the outline circles represent the broader, analytically informed stages of the research process. For the core tasks (the solid circles), the researcher shuttles back and forth, changing direction, visiting and revisiting data, building cases and reviewing processual and thematic patterns and connections against a backdrop of evolving theoretical knowledge.

For QLA, this process recurs through cycles or waves of fieldwork that are perpetually advancing and cumulative (see the related data management spiral in Chapter 7, Figure 7.1). Revisiting the field creates a unique opportunity to empirically explore and refine earlier interpretations, to iron out anomalies or puzzles, and to generate a growing pool of temporal data upon which new layers of insight can be built.

Abductive Reasoning

The analytical strategies sketched above and represented in Figure 9.1 are underpinned by **abductive logic** and reasoning. It is this logic which facilitates the conceptual leap from description to interpretation. Abduction was first identified as an analytical method in the late 19th century (Peirce (1934 [1878]). However, it is only in recent decades that it has begun to find a place within interpretive methodologies, particularly among process-oriented researchers (see, for example, Van de Ven 2007; Kitchin 2014; Halford and Savage 2017; Middlemiss et al. 2019). The value of abduction has been recognised, in particular, by ethnographers (e.g. Agar 2006) and critical realists (Blaikie 2007; Blaikie and Priest 2017). It has also found its way into grounded theory, despite the traditional adherence to inductive reasoning (Bajc 2012; Timmermans and Tavory 2012; Charmaz 2014). The core features of abductive reasoning are set out in Box 9.1.

Box 9.1   Abductive Reasoning

- Abduction is an iterative logic of reasoning and discovery. Its roots lie in the interpretivist tradition, for it is grounded in lay perceptions, language and meanings. But abduction explores these facets of life through broader sets of ideas and theories to arrive at new insights. It is a process that zigzags back and forth between theoretical knowledge (ideas, themes, concepts) and rich, situated data (empirical evidence) (Bajc 2012). Previously unrelated ideas are brought together and critically interrogated to discern novel patterns, connections, loops and relationships both within the existing data, through time, and across wider pools of evidence and theory (Agar 2006; Paavola 2014). These varied modes of discovery are gradually refined, delineated and contained as new insights begin to take shape (Agar 2006; Paavola 2014). Iteration emerges here not simply as an instrumental, repetitive task, a mechanical form of feedback, but as a reflexive process of continuous meaning making through which a mosaic of themes, insights and understandings are gradually distilled (Grbich 2007; Srivastava and Hopwood 2009).

- Given its iterative nature, abduction encompasses and supersedes the purely 'bottom up' logic of induction and the 'top down' logic of deduction, both of which are linear and uni-directional. The creativity and openness of abduction enables new insights to be discerned in ways that pure induction fails to do (Gruber 1981; Agar 2006; Blaikie 2007; Timmermans and Tavory 2012; Paavola 2014). It acknowledges, too, the impossibility of starting inductively from 'pure' data, when data are never neutral in their generation, but always theoretically informed (Kitchin 2014). As Burawoy puts it, 'We don't start with data, we start with theory. Without theory we are blind, we cannot see the world' (Burawoy 2009: 13). Moreover, like all creative processes, abduction is theoretically eclectic. It exhibits a fine historical sense that varied ideas and interpretations can be drawn together and aggregated to create broader qualitative insights and generalisations (see Chapter 7).

- As a method of discovery, abduction moves into new realms of imaginative thinking (in its original Latin, to 'lead away'). Peirce's (1934 [1878]) first rule for abductive thinking was the need for researchers 'to wonder', while more recent commentators have identified creative imagination, metaphor, intuition and guesswork as its core attributes (Blaikie 2007: 83). In this, Pierce's abduction and Bergson's intuition (see Chapter 2) are strongly connected (Morris 2005). As a celebrated mathematician once observed, 'Logic ... remains barren unless it is fertilised by intuition' (Poincaré, cited in Gruber 1981: 51). The approach relies on and encourages creative means of knowledge building, including encapsulating and conveying complex ideas and processes through narratives and visual-mapping techniques (see Chapter 11). This intuitive and fluid process of discovery underpins the creativity at the heart of QL enquiry.

- **Retroductive logic** (from the Latin to 'run again' or 'run back') is a crucial facet of abductive logic (and one of the terms originally used by Pierce to describe his analytical method). While abduction is often perceived to have a forward, exploratory momentum, retroduction traces backwards to understand the processes through which events and experiences unfold. This mode of reasoning is recursive as well as iterative: it involves reasoning backwards in time, moving from what is known to the unknown, to make inferences about the underlying driving forces for change (Gruber 1981; Agar 2006; Blaikie and Priest 2017). This involves a great deal

(Continued)

of guesswork, intuition and creative imagination. Retroduction, then, is the reasoning by which retrospective understandings are woven into a processual account. It is a recursive loop of discovery that is in perfect harmony with temporal enquiry.

- In moving back and forth between empirical insights and theoretical precepts, and (for QLA) between depth, breadth and temporal reach, abduction operates in a fluid (non-linear), cyclical and spiralling fashion (Blaikie 2007: 57). Like the spiral envisaged for QLA (Figure 9.1), abduction never returns to the same starting point. It is a cumulative process of discovery which builds new layers of understanding. As an inherently open form of logic, it is not definitive, but subject to continual refinement (Kitchin 2014). It is, therefore, a perfect conceptual fit for the interpretive, dynamic, layered and cumulative nature of QL research.
- The sequence and tempo of abductive reasoning is not fixed; abduction does not have a clear beginning, or unfold through orderly steps and phases. Instead, it evolves dynamically, through the continual interplay of ideas and empirical evidence (Paavola 2014). An early hunch or 'eureka' moment may be followed by a slow and painstaking process of assembling, checking, comparing, re-organising and aggregating disparate theories and pools of empirical data. Or a gradual and meticulous process of evidence building may reach a tipping point or pivotal moment, a point of synthesis from which a new vision of the world suddenly begins to crystallise (Gruber 1981).

The abductive mode of knowledge building set out in Box 9.1 provides the foundation for QLA. It is through the waves of field enquiry that researchers begin to work abductively, embracing serendipity and intuition as they jointly construct meaning and knowledge with participants (Bajc 2012; see Chapter 6). Everyday accounts and lived experiences are full of surprising and unsettling findings, unanticipated effects, small asides, half-expressed thoughts and emotions, puzzles, anomalies, paradoxes and contradictions. These are not inconsistencies that need to be ironed out; rather, they have enormous creative and explanatory value. Such data give rise to fresh conjectures, doubts, guesswork, hunches and flashes of insight that open up an imaginative space for taking analysis in new directions (Agar 2006; Locke et al. 2008; Paavola 2014). In the process, hitherto taken-for-granted notions can be experienced and understood in new, unfamiliar or arresting ways (Timmermans and Tavory 2012). It is here that the ethnographic aim of rendering the strange familiar, and the familiar strange (a phrase drawn from Novalis, an 18th century poet), come into play.

In its retroductive dimensions, abduction supports the task of tracing backwards and forwards through time, discerning and mapping processes, and weaving retrospective and prospective understandings into a fluid, dynamic picture. In spiral fashion, each return to past and future is informed differently, mirroring the way that complex temporal processes unfold in lived experience, and with each iteration building new layers of temporal insight.

As shown in Chapter 2, this creative logic of discovery is increasingly recognised as an essential foundation for understanding a fluid social world. It also gives added weight to the idea of QL enquiry as an intellectual craft, founded on creativity and imaginative exploration. With wry humour, Agar (2006) points out the major differences between this mode of knowledge building and what he calls:

> old fashioned social science. The old guard wants an interview guide. The iterative abductors do a couple of interviews, then obsess about them, then change the interview guide, then do a couple more, and on and on it goes. It makes those who worship standardization break out in a rash. (Agar 2006: 76)

Agar is referring here to the analytical elements of field enquiry. But the cumulative and fluid process that he describes applies equally to the broader analytical logic that shapes the whole research process. It is worth noting that abductive reasoning has provided the impetus for all kinds of major leaps in dynamic knowledge and insight, including the theories of evolution and relativity produced by Darwin and Einstein (Gruber 1981). The overall process is beautifully described by Gruber (1981):

> [The researcher] goes over and over the same ground, many times. [S/he] focuses now on this particular aspect, now on that, now on the problem as a whole. [S/he] looks at it from varying points of view ... diagrams it, verbalises it, ... constructs visual images ... [studies] the relationships among different experiences of the same thing: the same idea worked through by different means and in different modalities; the same idea felt and then thought, and then felt again – but in a new way, for now the feeling contains the new thought. ... Deep understanding of a domain of knowledge requires knowing it in various ways. This multiplicity of perspectives grows slowly through hard work and sets the stage for the *re*-cognition we experience as a new insight. (Gruber 1981: 58)

These same reflections are echoed by Plummer (2001) in our opening quotation. With its multiple iterations and capacity to build layers of interpretation, abduction perfectly captures the analytical process at work in QLA. Moreover, because it is open, inclusive, involves feedback and remains empirically grounded, it plays a major role in enhancing the integrity and credibility of a project's findings (see Chapter 12).

The Case-Thematic-Processual Logic of QLA

QLA is based on an articulation of case, thematic and processual readings of a dataset. These analytical strategies were first introduced and their importance explained in Chapter 4 (see Box 4.1). But a short recap is provided here, as a precursor to a detailed exploration in Chapters 10 and 11. Case, thematic and processual analyses are not discrete, stand-alone modes of investigation (although they are separated out here and in the following chapters for heuristic purposes). Since QL data encompass a rich amalgam of case, thematic and processual elements, they are best seen as interlocking facets of analysis, axes of comparison and synthesis (Barley 1995) that, taken together, create an integrated strategy for QLA (for a visual representation, see Figure 9.2). Each reading of the dataset involves an interrogation of its case, thematic and processual elements, but from a different starting point that opens a different window onto the data.

The interlocking nature of these facets of analysis helps to maintain a focus on the broad processual aims of QLA, and creates a more rounded understanding of the data that combines case depth, thematic breadth and temporal reach. This gives QLA its distinctive, three-dimensional logic. As we have seen in earlier chapters, this logic is woven through the whole research process, helping to shape the questions that drive a study, the construction of a sample, and the generation and management of data. It provides the unifying thread and anchor for the conduct of a QL study.

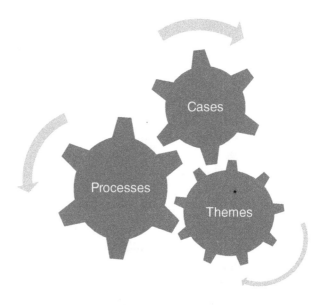

Figure 9.2   The three-dimensional logic of QLA

The Momentum of QLA: Building Insights through Time

The dynamic, processual aspects of QLA are of paramount importance. The longitudinal frame of a QL study provides the real-time structure within which processual insights begin to emerge. Through the successive waves of fieldwork, synchronic (snapshot) readings, reflecting a 'frozen' moment in time (Barley 1995), gradually coalesce into diachronic (processual, through-time) readings, that look both forwards and backwards in time (Van de Ven and Huber 1995; Neale and Flowerdew 2003; Smith 2003; Lewis 2007). The objective of QLA is to piece together a diachronic picture from the cumulative waves of data generation. As shown in Chapter 8, as a study develops, the production of new data inevitably reconfigures the dataset as a whole, creating new assemblages of data and opening up new insights from a different temporal perspective. This transformation of synchronic data into diachronic insights is a core facet of temporal analysis (Barley 1995; Thomson and Holland 2003; Vogl et al. 2017).

In keeping with abductive logic, there is no one right way to structure QLA through the successive waves of a study. This is a flexible mode of analysis with no fixed procedures, sequences or tempos. Researchers tend to work out a number of steps to suit their own design and sampling decisions (see, for example, Lewis 2007; Vogl et al. 2017). However, they are likely to start with a careful reading of the data, and the setting up of a bespoke suite of analytical files (see Chapter 10), which can be used as the basis for building diachronic insights. And they are likely to conclude with an integrated (case study, cross-case and through-time) analysis of the whole dataset following the completion of fieldwork. In practice, the varied facets of QLA (case-thematic-processual, synchronic to diachronic) develop iteratively and quickly merge as the analysis progresses. The critical factor in developing an analytical strategy is not the starting point or order in which these readings occur: it is the capacity for multiple iterations between them. This theme is developed further in Chapters 10 and 11, where we turn to the practice of QLA.

It is also worth teasing out here exactly what researchers are doing when they build layers of understanding through the time frame of a study: the primary aim is to build a dynamic understanding of case data. A recurrent cross-sectional analysis of thematic data after each wave of fieldwork is not likely to be feasible, given time and resource constraints (Calman et al. 2013). Nor is this beneficial, given that the overriding task is to compare and synthesise data through time (see Box 10.5 for the limitations of such a strategy). What is essential, however, is an interim, through-time analysis of case data after each return from the field. This builds a dynamic understanding of each case as the study progresses, and enables researchers to familiarise themselves with their evolving case data in preparation for a return to the field (Smith 2003; Vogl et al. 2017). More broadly, the relative balance of case and thematic analysis in what is essentially a processual form of enquiry is an important issue for QL enquiry. This is considered further below and explored in some detail in Chapter 10.

Finally, it is worth recalling that QLA produces a dynamic, open-ended, kaleidoscopic vision of temporal processes that perpetually evolves as a study progresses (Foster et al. 1979; Stanley, cited in Thomson and Holland 2003; see Chapter 2). In contrast to the aims of grounded theory (see Chapter 4), working with temporal processes means that there is no clear point at which 'saturation' is reached, and no clear-cut or definitive findings. Analytical closure in QLA is an artefact of the research process, although this does not make the emerging insights any less valuable (we return to this theme in Chapter 12).

Maintaining a Processual Focus?

Our review of the analytical strategies underpinning QLA would not be complete without a consideration of a key issue that gets to the heart of the enterprise: how do we ensure that a processual focus, the analytical core of QLA, is maintained in order to shed light on the dynamics of lives? This is also a question about the balance between case and thematic forms of analysis, and their relative capacity to support processual insights. These are important issues to address in a context where, despite some valuable accounts of QLA, analysis is a neglected and fragmented topic of discussion and development. In the rapidly expanding field of QL scholarship, there is currently no integrated body of shared analytical knowledge that researchers can draw upon to inform and develop their own practice (Van de Ven and Poole 1995; Grossoehme and Lipstein 2016; SmithBattle et al. 2018).

This is reflected, for example, in the tendency for researchers to explain their analytical practice with reference to a 'neat label' (Rapley 2016), an off-the-shelf analytical package, rather than documenting how they have worked with temporal processes (SmithBattle et al. 2018). Thematically based packages (e.g. IPA, thematic analysis (TA) and grounded theory) are the most commonly cited. In themselves, these are viable approaches that can be adapted for temporal analysis (see Chapter 10). Yet, where these packages are adopted uncritically, and as the sole or dominant mode of analysis in a QL study, the core aims of QLA may be compromised. This is particularly evident where researchers adopt a highly structured, categorising mode of thematic analysis (see Chapter 10). In their review of QL studies in the field of nursing, SmithBattle et al. (2018) make this observation:

> Where researchers provided little description of procedures for managing and analysing data, we had little confidence that they had effectively mined longitudinal data to capture changes over time: this may be why relatively few studies presented findings with a temporal perspective. (SmithBattle et al. 2018: 5–6)

A similar observation is made in a review of organisational QL studies. The authors note that a processual orientation may be 'killed off' by the researcher in a variety of ways, not least where 'data are reduced to classes, categories or types and where the continuity and causality of the process is left to one side' (Paavilainen-Mäntymäki and Welch 2013: 241). Farr and Nizza, in their review of longitudinal IPA (LIPA) studies, echo this problem: 'it is notable that some articles in the corpus struggled to convey a sense of progression over time' (Farr and Nizza 2019: 8). Where the nature of QLA is poorly specified, there is a greater likelihood that time and process have slipped beyond the grasp of the researcher as the crucial elements of analysis, and the driving force for interpretation.

Further drawbacks may also be evident:

> Researchers … are bewildered by which approach to take – should they try a constructionist approach, IPA, or grounded theory? When they investigate a particular tradition in more detail they may well discover that there are many different versions of that tradition, as well as considerable overlap between them at a practical level. … Many authors counsel against 'epistemological determinism' [and] … unthinking alignment with any one tradition. … Researchers should not be forced into a theoretical or methodological straightjacket. (Ritchie et al. 2014: 19)

An 'unthinking alignment' with orthodox thematic traditions of analysis can be highly problematic for QLA, at least where this is at the expense of a processual, case-led approach. More broadly, QL and 'mixed' longitudinal researchers sometimes resort to using variables, mathematical models or other forms of quantification or measurement to explain their QL data, despite the lack of fit with a fluid, processual methodology (see examples in Saldaña 2003: 40, including his own earlier research; and for mixed longitudinal designs, Van de Ven and Poole 1995 and Van de Ven 2007).

Maxwell (2012) sheds some useful light on this issue. He distinguishes between two broad analytical strategies: categorising and connecting. Thematic analysis is underpinned by **categorising strategies**, which split and fracture data into categories or variables (a task usually referred to as coding):

> Re-ordering the data in terms of particular categories … fragments the actual causal processes embedded in these data … [and] can create analytic blinders, preventing the analyst from seeing alternative relationships in the data. (Maxwell 2012: 44, 113)

Connecting strategies, on the other hand, such as those found in processual analysis and narrative case analysis, are 'particularly important for deriving causal insights in the data' (Maxwell 2012: 44, 109). These methods, which are crucial for the generation of QL data, allow for an exploration of concrete, contiguous, processual connections and links in the data that retain their temporal and contextual sensitivity. Indeed, a narrative analysis of cases is the prime means of piecing together a picture of the flux of lives, and conveying how temporal processes unfold (see, for example, Mishler 1986; and Chapters 6 and 10 for how case data are generated and analysed).

As Maxwell recognises, these categorising (thematic) and connecting (case-led, processual) modes of analysis are complementary; both have value in QL enquiry, and the iterative logic of abduction provides the mechanism for working across them. Currently, however, the recourse to an off-the-shelf analytical package more often leads researchers to a wholesale adoption of structured, categorising modes of thematic analysis, which are not well suited to the aims of QLA. At the same time, narrative case analysis, with its connecting logic and capacity to uncover processual insights, is less well documented or understood (Maxwell 2012). It is all too often relegated to a residual or supplementary approach, and its processual power is overlooked.

In order to overcome these limitations, the aim in Chapters 10 and 11 is to bring temporal processes to the forefront of investigation, to redress the balance between case and thematic analysis, and to explore how thematic modes of analysis can be mobilised to support a processual understanding of lives. The strategies, tools and techniques used by QL researchers to work analytically with time are teased out in these chapters. They form the prototype for a QLA tool kit, which researchers can draw upon to suit their own analytical needs.

Closing Reflections

This chapter has introduced the basic analytical strategies that underpin QLA. The conceptual development from summative to descriptive to interpretive reading of the data clarifies what researchers are aiming to achieve. The abductive, iterative method by which researchers move back and forth between their new evidence, and wider bodies of theory and knowledge, provides an insight into how they might get there.

For QLA, the core analytical focus is on time, processes, continuities and changes. Since time is a slippery concept, maintaining this focus can be a challenge. The strategies underpinning QL research are often poorly specified, while not all studies that purport to be both qualitative and longitudinal capitalise on the temporal dimensions of the research, or follow these through into analysis and interpretation. Achieving an appropriate balance between case and thematic analysis should help to overcome this issue. Indeed, QLA has its own logic of enquiry, which is built around the iteration between case, thematic and processual readings and reconfigurations of a dataset. QLA also has a distinctive momentum: the transformation from synchronic to diachronic insights that emerges through successive waves of a QL study. Engaging in these multiple readings and reconfigurations of a dataset is a challenge that involves a continual switching of the analytical gaze (Thomson and Holland 2003; Holland et al. 2006). But, by combining depth and breadth with temporal reach, QLA produces incomparably rich insights about unfolding lives.

Further Reading

Accounts of the analytical strategies underpinning QLA are limited, but valuable insights can be found in Barley (1995), Thomson and Holland (2003), Smith (2003), Vogl et al. (2017) and the collection of essays in Corden and Millar (2007). Two recent reviews of selected QL literature, SmithBattle et al. (2018), for nursing research, and Farr and Nizza (2019), for IPA, provide useful insights into analytical strategies, and highlight the drawbacks of paying limited attention to processual understandings. Maxwell (2012) provides a helpful discussion of connecting and categorising logic as modes of analysis, and their value for understanding causal processes. For the conceptual scaffolding that underpins QLA and qualitative enquiry more generally, Ritchie and Lewis (2003) is particularly useful, while, for an engaging account of the power and potential of abductive reasoning and knowledge building, Gruber (1981) is highly recommended.

Barley, S. (1995) 'Images of imaging: Notes on doing longitudinal fieldwork', in G. Huber and A. Van de Ven (eds) *Longitudinal Field Research Methods*. London: Sage, pp. 1–37.

Corden, A. and Millar, J. (eds) (2007) 'Qualitative longitudinal research for social policy', in *Social Policy and Society*, 6 (4).

Farr, J. and Nizza, I. (2019) 'Longitudinal interpretative phenomenological analysis (LIPA): A review of studies and methodological considerations', *Qualitative Research in Psychology*, 16 (2): 199–217.

Gruber, H. (1981) 'On the relationship between "aha experiences" and the construction of ideas', *History of Science*, 19 (1): 41–59.

Maxwell, J. (2012) *A Realist Approach for Qualitative Research*. London: Sage.

Ritchie, J. and Lewis, J. (eds) (2003) *Qualitative Research Practice*. London: Sage.

Smith, N. (2003) 'Cross-sectional profiling and longitudinal analysis: Research notes on analysis in the LQ study "Negotiating transitions in Citizenship"', *International Journal of Social Research Methodology*, 6 (3): 273–7.

SmithBattle, L., Lorenz, R., Reangsing, C., Palmer, J. and Pitroff, G. (2018) 'A methodological review of qualitative longitudinal research in nursing', *Nursing Inquiry*, 25 (4): 1.

Thomson, R. and Holland, J. (2003) 'Hindsight, foresight and insight: The challenges of longitudinal qualitative research', *International Journal of Social Research Methodology*, 6 (3): 233–44.

Vogl, S., Zartler, U., Schmidt, E. and Rieder, I. (2017) 'Developing an analytical framework for multiple perspective, qualitative longitudinal interviews', *International Journal of Social Research Methodology*, 21 (2): 177–90.

10

CASES AND THEMES IN QUALITATIVE LONGITUDINAL ANALYSIS

Key points

- **Qualitative longitudinal analysis (QLA)** is designed to build a dynamic tapestry of insights into unfolding processes. The varied interlocking components of QLA – case, thematic and processual – are explored, starting with case and thematic analysis in this chapter, and moving on to process analysis and synthesis in Chapter 11. A prototype for a QLA tool kit is developed across these chapters. Some combination of case, thematic and processual tools and techniques is essential. However, not all of these tools and techniques will be needed for any one project. Researchers need to review, select, adapt, combine and pilot their chosen tools with care, to ensure they support the processual aims of a study.
- **Case analysis** is a connecting mode of analysis that involves a chronological reconstruction and synthesis of case materials. It enables a diachronic, through-time reading of unfolding trajectories. Recursive case analysis enables non-linear understandings of lives to be woven into a case history. Tools to support this form of analysis include summative pen portraits, descriptive case histories, analytical case studies and case-based framework grids. Once a suite of case histories is in place, unfolding trajectories and intersecting pathways can be brought together to build a cross-case diachronic analysis of the data, and to develop **typologies** of different trajectories.

(Continued)

- **Thematic analysis** is a categorising mode of analysis, based on a broad, cross-case, thematic reading and re-organisation of the data. It builds greater breadth into the analysis through an exploration of conceptual and substantive patterns and connections in the data. Two approaches are outlined and contrasted. Recurrent cross-sectional analysis needs to be modified to ensure that data are not fragmented in ways that compromise a processual, case-led vision. Temporal thematic analysis, on the other hand, supports the task of embedding time and processes into the analytical picture. Unfolding trajectories and varied horizons of time become important themes of a study. Tools to support temporal thematic analysis are outlined here, including summative thematic charts and descriptive framework grids.

Introduction

The full, multi-faceted, in depth, textured enquiry of the longitudinal case study should be the mainstay of processual research. (Dawson 2003: 143)

On reading the [ethnographic] ... notes, I initially found it hard to escape those categories I had ... established. ... They exercised a ... powerful physical constraint. ... I am now much less inclined to fragment the notes into relatively small segments. Instead I am just as interested in reading episodes and passages at greater length, with a correspondingly different attitude towards the act ... of analysis. Rather than constructing my account like a patchwork quilt, I feel more like working with the whole cloth. (Atkinson 1992: 458–60)

Building on the basic strategies for QLA set out in Chapter 9, we now turn to the practice of QLA. We start in this chapter with case and thematic analysis, and go on to processual analysis and synthesis in Chapter 11. As Chapter 9 makes clear, these are interlocking dimensions of analysis that combine depth, breadth and temporal reach. Both case and thematic readings of a dataset are essential for QLA, but our discussion aims to tease out how these can be balanced and harnessed to support a processual understanding of lives. A range of analytical tools and techniques are introduced here, which researchers can draw upon and adapt for their own needs. These include the kinds of processual questions that may be posed to focus the analysis and draw out insights.

The discussion begins with the practicalities of longitudinal case analysis, which, for QLA, is inherently processual. This is a crucial element of the analysis which, as our opening quotations make clear, enables us to move beyond a 'patchwork quilt' of themes to discern the 'whole cloth' and (in the dynamic context of QLA) its many processual threads. A QL case is a narrative construction that is organised chrono-logically; it creates a diachronic (biographical, historical), through-time reading of the data. Once a suite of case materials is in place, this forms the basis for building a cross-case, diachronic picture of the data. In this way, breadth can be added to the depth and temporal reach of case analysis. Taking up the issues raised in Chapter 9, we then go on to consider some of the challenges raised by thematic analysis, and explore how time can be more effectively embedded into the themes of a study.

The case and thematic tools outlined in this chapter are cumulative: once they are set up at the baseline, new data can be added at each wave to build a diachronic picture. They also perform a vital practical function. The size and complexity of a QL dataset make it necessary to condense or summarise data into manageable pro-portions, before synthesising them into new configurations. As shown in Chapter 9, this is the first stage in the analytical journey of QLA. The condensing process ena-bles the researcher to 'see' the dataset as a whole, and to read across case, thematic and processual data in new ways. At the same time, the researcher needs to ensure that these condensed readings retain the integrity and meaning of the original data (Flyvbjerg 2007; Gale et al. 2013).

Longitudinal Case Analysis

Longitudinal case analysis is an in-depth, case-led reading and re-sculpting of QL data. Whether a case is an individual, family, organisation or community under-going a particular process, it can be seen as a discrete entity and analysed dynamically in its own right. Sometimes referred to as narrative analysis, or trajectory analysis (Langley 1999; Tsoukas and Hatch 2001; Pearce 2015; Grossoehme and Lipstein 2016), case analysis creates a diachronic, through-time reading of the data. It also enables wider processes of social change to be anchored in and understood through the changing lives of the research participants. As the discussion below will show, constructing a case history is a major act of creation, a central part of the intellectual craft of QL research.

Case analysis involves bringing together data relating to a particular case (indi-vidual or collective lives or segments of these lives), to create a new chronological reading of these data. Participant accounts are usually discursive; they are rarely narrated chronologically (Mishler 1995). But, by carefully selecting and re-scripting/ re-sculpting the data for each case, the researcher creates a narrative that links events and interactions together through time, and tells a plausible, comprehensible, authentic and often compelling tale, complete with causal threads and connections. In working with case data, QL researchers are drawing on a long tradition of case-led research carried out by biographical, narrative and life history researchers (Eisenhardt 1995; Mishler 1995; Polkinghorne 1995; Pettigrew 1997; Bertaux and Delcroix 2000;

Brockmeier 2000; Miller 2000; Plummer 2001; Tsoukas and Hatch 2001; Dawson 2003; Thomson and Holland 2003; Thomson 2007; Henderson et al. 2012; Riessman 2016). Some common themes in this literature are drawn out here.

Crafting a Case History

As a starting point in building a case history, researchers can identify and assemble extracts from a participant's account that get to the heart of an unfolding tale. The extracts exemplify key themes and pathways, and can be drawn from different waves of data to build a dynamic picture. A brief example of this is provided in Box 10.1.

Box 10.1 Crafting a Case History

These interview extracts were skilfully generated by Carmen Lau-Clayton for the *Following Young Fathers* study. Drawn from the case of a young father called Dominic, they convey an outline of his parenthood trajectory, in particular his evolving relationship with his former partner, the mother of his child. This became one of the emblematic themes of this study:

- I just thought, if this is going to come about, this is something that I am going to take on, and I am going to be responsible because I don't understand how, when a child comes along, you can't have that love for him. As much as you don't expect it, it just hits you. ... I want to be the person who [my son] can turn to. And who, obviously, who is always gonna be there for him. ... I found out, ultimately, that I wasn't going to be happy in that relationship [with the mother], but it became quite hard to maintain a separate parent relationship. ... she's tried to make life as hard as possible for me with our son. [Aged 17, Wave 1, contact blocked; court case pending]
- We're civil now. We can have conversations. I think she's grown up and we've become more of a team. I think she sees me more as a form of support as opposed to someone against her. [Aged 21, Wave 4, stable and regular contact]
- I think we're working in the right direction. ... It's a working relationship ... things aren't perfect or ideal but it's working to a degree. ... There's a lot of negative influences in her family. I've got to sort of accept that. ... I have a routine, she doesn't. ... She's acutely aware that she's the decision maker, but ... she depends on me to sort out serious, adult stuff [e.g. school matters]. ... I need to play the game ... compromise and just that sort of way of communicating. ... I'm probably the dominant character within, well for all three of us together. [Aged 22, Wave 5, engaged role as a father]

Source: *Following Young Fathers* dataset, Timescapes Archive

---

These extracts tell the bare bones of this story, but they are embedded in many hundreds of pages of interview transcripts (gathered over a five-year period through five waves of fieldwork). The interviews tell a rich, complex, compelling and sometimes anguished tale of the trials and tribulations faced by this young father in securing and building a relationship with his son, which is mediated through the mother. The narrative begins at a point where Dominic has started court proceedings to regain contact with his son, and concludes at a time when he is engaged in the ongoing work of maintaining his position as a loving father, who plays an indispensable role in his son's life. The extracts provide the grounding upon which to construct an analysis of the parenting trajectory of this young man: how he secured access to his son; how he continues to negotiate his engagement in his child's life; and how his co-parental relationship has evolved over the five years of the study (Neale and Patrick 2016).

Case histories are written as third-person accounts by the researcher, but quotations from the participant are usually inserted to bring the document to life (see Box 10.3 for an example). It is a process of synthesising and re-sculpting data, in contrast to the fracturing of data that may occur with thematic analysis (Polkinghorne 1995; Maxwell 2012). In the process, rich, nuanced threads of individual circumstances and experiences are collated, including multiple tellings and elaborations of an unfolding tale.

Abbott (2001) usefully teases out three elements of a narrative analysis: its order (the flow of events from past to future); its connections (how the elements of a process are meaningfully linked together); and its convergence (how the varied elements converge to achieve change or equilibrium) (this schema is developed further in Chapter 11). In similar vein, Plummer (2001: 196) suggests that an effective narrative needs the following to flesh out a comprehensible and compelling story:

- a sense of ordering – usually linear – of events, to give a recognised form to a story;
- a sense of a person behind a biography – a stability of identity that we can grasp;
- a sense of voice and perspective belonging to the narrator (who tells the story);
- a sense of causality ('plot'): if this, then that; a flavour of how/why things come about.

There are varied ways of finding the person behind an unfolding narrative, including using their own words and creating a narrative that is rich in biographical detail and insight. In their initial reading of case data, researchers may look for evocative language use (metaphor, imagery) and clues to participants' identities, life worlds and experiences, as well as what matters to them as individuals (Shaw et al. 2016; for an example, see Box 4.6). It may be possible to identify particular biographical metaphors, motifs or 'through lines' in the data, which reflect an underlying characteristic of a participant, or a recurrent pattern in the lives of the sample, or the journeys that they are undertaking (Plumber 2001: 195; Saldaña 2002; Henderson et al. 2012). These might be patterns of stability, routine, victimhood, chaos or indecision; living in the moment or in the fast lane; a drive to 'make good'; or strategies for survival or adaptation. Such motifs may well change for individuals or collectives over the course of a QL study, as participants reshape their practices and identity.

To give one example of how a recurring motif may be discerned, in a QL study of participants' journeys into the advanced stages of severe pulmonary disease, Pinnock et al. (2011) found a recurring 'chaos' narrative in the participants' accounts, with no clear starting point, or markers for the stages of the illness or its progression. Meeting the needs of these patients required highly flexible, tailored and responsive modes of care from palliative care nurses, which the researchers found were at odds with the structured, time-bound and overly rigid treatment plans laid down in medical protocols.

Recursive Case Analysis

The issues of linearity and causality (plot) that Abbott (2001) and Plummer (2001) raise above are critical issues for QLA. While, as these authors suggest, a case history is best structured through chronological time, it is important to weave fluid, recursive understandings into the tale. In this way, people's non-linear, circuitous pathways become integral parts of the story. Using retroductive logic, **recursive case analysis** involves tracing backward to see how far earlier aspirations have been fulfilled or redirected, and to gain insights into changing perceptions of events, circumstances and imagined futures. Participants commonly revisit and revise their own accounts and understandings of past events, and of their future hopes, plans or fears (see examples in Box 3.4). But such reflections are all the more likely where a recursive interviewing strategy has been employed (see Chapter 6). Participants may also make new disclosures about their past that change how their account of their lives can be read. The pen portrait in Box 10.2 gives an illustration of this. For this participant, issues of illiteracy and domestic violence were disclosed by the participant at the fourth and fifth waves, some years after the start of the study. Such disclosures are often made in the later stages of fieldwork, and often in retrospect, when events are less 'raw' and a relationship of trust with the researcher has grown (see Chapter 5).

Where participants make such disclosures, or otherwise revise their accounts of past and future, the researcher needs to go back, to retroductively revisit and reinterpret earlier accounts through a new interpretive lens, which may create a shift in the whole analysis (Saldaña 2003: 55; Millar and Ridge 2017; Millar 2021 in press;

for an example, see Box 3.4). This recursive revisiting and revising of researcher interpretations can be built into a case history or case study (see Box 10.2), but the process creates challenges as well as opportunities for the researcher. The constant iterations between then and now, past and future, which are generated and updated at each point in time, certainly complicate the building of interpretations. It may come to feel like an analytical burden that de-stabilises the search for meaning, and introduces too many uncertainties into the process. However, recursive analysis should be seen as illuminating rather than undermining. It allows new layers of insight to be built as a study progresses. It adds immeasurably to our understanding of fluid processes and gives new insights into the shifting relationship between past, present and future. Recursive analysis, then, creates not so much an unfolding tale, but the threads of varied unfolding, overlapping, diverting and cross-cutting tales, which together create a rich and dynamic tapestry.

In sum, an effective case history can capture multiple temporal connections that interweave 'know-how, tacit knowledge, nuance, sequence, multiple causation, means-end relations and consequences into a memorable plot' (Weick and Roberts, cited in Tsoukas and Hatch 2001: 1006). Indeed, Tsoukas and Hatch (2001) suggest that a narrative construction is the only way to convey such complexity: 'narrative time is like a turbulent current, characterised by an overall vector, the plot, itself composed of areas of local turbulence, eddies where time is reversed, rapids where it speeds ahead, and pools where it effectively stops' (Argyros, cited in Tsoukas and Hatch 2001: 1007). The sense of plot embodied in a case narrative gives a concrete, localised non-linear rendition of causality, illustrating its occurrence in the particularities of a case, set in distinctive circumstances and settings of change (Tsoukas and Hatch 2001: 998; for an example, see Box 11.3).

A Balancing Act: Condensing an Authentic Account

As a final point, it is worth stressing that the construction of a case history involves a balancing act between condensing data and retaining the richness and particularities of a case narrative. A case history needs to be authentic: to remain faithful to the lived experiences of participants, and to preserve the complexities, contradictions, ambiguities, tensions and paradoxes that are integral to people's narratives (Flyvbjerg 2007: 401). This ensures the integrity and veracity of case data (see Chapter 12).

At the same time, case histories need to fulfil the task of condensing data to make them more manageable (Smith 2003; Thomson 2010b). Lengthy files that duplicate rather than complement the original data will have reduced analytical power, while the time and resources needed for their construction may prove prohibitive. Ward et al. (2019) liken this to a quantitative 'cleaning' of a dataset that removes background noise and creates temporal order and meaning in the data. This is not just a practical matter; it is an interpretive matter of distilling the essence and essential truth, or verisimilitude, of a tale (Becker 1966 [1930]; Abbott 2001). There are also ethical considerations to be taken into account here. As shown in Chapter 5, the building of rich analytical files creates a unique fingerprint for a participant that is increasingly revealing of identities. Getting the right balance, then, is also an ethical issue of balancing confidentiality with authenticity in the way that analytical case files are constructed.

Case Analysis Tool Kit

Tools to support case analysis (both summative and descriptive), and cross-case diachronic analysis, are outlined in Box 10.2, while the construction of pen portraits and case histories is illustrated in Boxes 10.3 and 10.4.

Box 10.2   Case Analysis Tool Kit

- **Summative mapping tools**: **Pen portraits** are short (one or two page) case files that capture a potted biography or processual development for each case. Scripted by the researcher, the portraits are usually constructed chronologically, with clear headings for fieldwork waves. Past and future can be woven into the script for each wave. The portraits serve to condense and highlight key themes, circumstances and developments in the life of an individual or collective. Since it is surprisingly easy to lose track of the cases in a sample, these condensing tools fulfil a vital mapping role. They can also be used as appendices in reports and published writings to give an overview of the sample (see Box 10.3 for an example).

- **Descriptive tools**: **Case histories** are descriptive tools (also called case profiles or portraits) that create more extensive chronological reconstructions of a participant's account (for an illustration, see Box 10.4). Drawn from varied sources (interview transcripts, field notes, participatory data) and allowing for thick description, they sketch a narrative of change and continuity over time, and present a holistic picture of how varied trajectories unfold and intersect for the participant (Geertz 1973; Langley 1999; Smith 2003; Thomson and Holland 2003; Thomson 2007). Like summative case tools, case histories are commonly organised by wave, but sub-headings can be added to the script that reflect key substantive/processual themes (e.g. educational pathways, family trajectories, medical or legal interventions, or organisational or environmental developments). This interweaving of case data with processual themes creates 'through lines' in the narrative that can be pulled out for detailed investigation (Saldaña 2003; Thomson 2007). As descriptive tools, case histories are closely aligned with and retain the integrity of the original data. For example, key quotations from transcripts may be inserted, and page references to transcripts are commonly added to cross-reference the case history with the participant's own account. The process of constructing a case history relies on a detailed reading of case material and a narrative reconstruction (re-ordering, condensing) of this material. While constructed in chronological fashion, the accounts stretch further into the past and future, incorporating the 'back' story and future hopes and plans. They also weave recursive understandings into the picture, allowing for changing perceptions and non-linear aspects of a journey to be represented. Whether these histories are constructed for all cases depends on the size of the sample. For a large sample, researchers may select a sub-set of emblematic cases, drawn from the much shorter pen portraits, which can be given this more detailed treatment.

- **Interpretive tools (case studies)**: A case history may be elaborated into a **case study** by incorporating researchers' reflections, speculations and emerging insights into the script (Pettigrew 1997; Bertaux and Delcroix 2000; Thomson 2007, 2010b, 2011; Henderson et al. 2012; Brandon et al. 2017). Again, these may be constructed for selected cases, or across all the cases in a sample. Insights can be woven directly into the script, or appear in margin notes, appendices or in different-coloured fonts. In this way, these tools feed into the development of higher-level interpretations, and provide a valuable record of researchers' evolving interpretations (Thomson and Holland 2003).

- **Summative/descriptive tools (case grids or framework grids)**: Biographical or processual data may also be woven into a framework grid or matrix (for a description and illustration, see Box 10.8 and Figure 10.1). The process involves constructing a grid or series of grids for each case in a study, into which summary data on key themes can be added and mapped against temporal developments. The grids create a condensed visualisation that shows how processes and key themes are interwoven for each case, and how varied trajectories (e.g. housing, family and educational pathways) may intersect to create a unique journey for a participant.

Individual Case Analysis: Asking Pertinent Questions

When embarking on an analysis of cases, it can be helpful to devise one or more questions to guide the process, drawing abductively on the research questions/ conceptual map devised at the start of the study (see Chapter 4), and on insights emerging directly from the data (Saldaña 2003). A generic question might be, 'how does a particular trajectory unfold through time in this particular case?' Examples of analyses that address this question can be found in Box 10.1, and in Chapter 6, Figure 6.4, where participants' changing perceptions and management of pain are traced over the course of a study (Nizza et al. 2018). A further generic question might be, 'how do the varied trajectories of a life (e.g. family, education, work, housing), or the interwoven threads of a process (e.g. personal, interpersonal, institutional), unfold in this particular case, and how do they intersect to create a unique journey'? The case framework grid in Figure 10.1 is designed to address this question (see also Box 11.2).

As shown in Chapter 6, in constructing a processual narrative for a case, a range of specific analytical questions can also be posed that provide a focus for the researcher, and help to shape the content of a case history (these are developed from Plummer 2001: 196; for a more detailed treatment of processual questions, see Chapter 11):

- What happened (events, practices, process)?
- Where and when did it happen/over what space of time (setting, time frames)?
- Who was involved (agents)?
- How was it done/how did things evolve (agency)?
- Why was it done (purpose, accident, motives, aspirations)?
- What triggered and propelled the process (multiple influences, impetus)?
- What meaning did it hold for those involved (lived experience)?
- Did these meanings and perceptions shift over time (recursive understandings)?
- Was the path straightforward, or were there detours along the way (pathway)?
- What (if any) were the effects or impact at different points in time (effects)?

By way of illustration, the generic question posed above about intersecting trajectories can be used to interrogate the pen portrait of a young father called Andrew, which is set out in Box 10.3. The portrait gives a basic insight into some of the striking circumstances that are converging to create a downward spiral in Andrew's life at the point of his fifth interview. These include a relatively nomadic existence marked by housing that is, in turns, insecure, transitory or overcrowded; a high level of family poverty; family drug use; criminal activity, social worker involvement and custodial experiences; poor educational engagement and under-achievement; unemployment and conditional welfare support; learning difficulties/illiteracy, mental health issues and domestic violence (all of which Andrew is reluctant to disclose); and the overriding importance that he attaches to his new and fragile family.

The pen portrait alerts us to a rich tapestry of interrelated circumstances that can be pulled out for more detailed analysis through time. The *Following Young Fathers* researchers had not included domestic violence, mental health issues or literacy in the broad-brush themes that were originally assembled for this study, but these emerged from the later waves of data as key issues that warranted a revised understanding of this case, along with further investigation across the whole sample.

Box 10.3 A Pen Portrait of a Young Father – Andrew

Wave 1/2 (merged, Feb./Mar. 2011): Andrew is 16 years old. He has an 8-month-old daughter called Sylvie with his partner; the pregnancy was unplanned and abortion not considered or condoned: 'I wouldn't change Sylvie for the world, but maybe I wish I would have waited until I had a job ... but things happen don't they?' He plays an active role in his child's life: he also explains that he came to the area recently, and has just moved into a local authority hostel where his daughter cannot visit; he is not the primary carer of his child. He describes a close but disjointed and chaotic family. His father is in a relationship with the mother of Andrew's partner; they have just had a child too. He dislikes his father's drug addiction. Becoming a parent has changed Andrew: 'I had to go [to school] on us own. So I didn't go. And that's how come I ended up ... acting an idiot... And look where I've ended now'. He has a criminal record that he regrets. He loves his new family and feels closer to his parents now he is 'more grown up'.

Andrew has learning support needs (disclosed originally through his key worker). He is currently studying at a Community College for his Maths and English GCSEs. He would like to study plastering or plumbing and has thought about the Army. Andrew has a social worker. He explains that this is because of his father's and maternal grandmother's drug use, rather than issues relating to the young couple.

Wave 3 (Jan. 2012): Andrew is 17 and has moved out of the hostel. The council found him a flat but he has since moved in with his partner and child. He is very happy: partner and child are at the centre of his life, relationships are good and the family are settled. Andrew has enrolled on an armed forces training course. He hopes to provide for his partner and child in future.

Wave 4 (Oct. 2013): Andrew is now 18. His father has been sent to prison for a year. Andrew separated from his partner over 'family issues' at the end of 2012 but they were reunited in the spring of 2013 and plan to set up home together again. At the time, Andrew said his feelings towards his partner were mixed: he both loved and hated her. After the split, a court hearing ruled that they could share the care of their child. The court sessions are ongoing. Andrew explains that these are a routine check on the couple's progress. He also discloses that they were placed on a parenting course in relation to domestic violence, which, Andrew explains, is 'both ways'. Last year, Andrew completed level 1 of his armed forces training course, but could not progress to the next level. He is looking for work. He is on welfare benefits and struggling financially.

(Continued)

Wave 5 (Feb. 2014): Andrew, now 19, 'gave up his flat' and now lives with his mother in overcrowded conditions. He thinks it will take a year to be re-housed by the council, since he damaged his old flat in a domestic violence incident. Andrew discloses that there has been domestic violence throughout his relationship, but the parenting course was a help.

Andrew remains unemployed: he has searched everywhere for jobs, tramped the streets, but has had no response. He is on Job Seekers Allowance (JSA), but was sanctioned for not attending a meeting. He discloses that he struggles with reading and writing, and had not read the JSA letter: 'I can't read any communications'. He has had no payments for three weeks, has no money, cannot borrow money from family or afford bus fares to search for work. His partner is supportive but he will not borrow from her. He describes himself as 'going backwards'. He is facing homelessness and is depressed ('sometimes I feel like crying').

Source: *Following Young Fathers* study, Timescapes Archive

Cross-case Diachronic Analysis

Once a suite of case histories is in place across the sample, it becomes easier to identify striking emblematic cases that can be pulled out for more detailed analysis, and/or used to convey empirical insights. It also becomes possible to identify connections, similarities and differences across the cases in the sample, discerning the different pathways that individuals or groups may be following, and how life course trajectories may be converging or diverging. Working across cases enables the development of typologies of different trajectories and pathways – for example, the different 'quit' journeys undertaken by smokers seeking to give up their habit (Ritchie et al. 2014: 390) or the different pathways into politics followed by military veterans (Söderström 2019). Building a further layer of analysis, one that is both diachronic and cross-case, adds breadth to the depth and temporal reach of individual case analysis (see the examples in Box 10.5 and Box 10.7). The important differences between this mode of case-led analysis and recurrent, cross-sectional thematic analysis are clarified below (see Box 10.6).

A useful starting point in building a **cross-case diachronic analysis** is to ask a basic question: 'How do the emerging trajectories of this case compare with the trajectories of other cases?' As an example, it is worth comparing and contrasting the data provided in the pen portrait for Andrew (Box 10.3) with the case history extracts provided for Ben, another participant in the *Following Young Fathers* study. These are set out in Box 10.4.

Box 10.4 A Case History of a Young Father – Ben

Wave 1 (short extract)

Ben is 20 years old. He lives near the university where he is studying but is originally from the town of Southgate. He comes from a supportive, middle-income family. His daughter, Tilly, is 18 months old (born in the summer of 2011). She lives with Ben's co-parent and ex-partner, Jenny, in Northgate, five miles away. He sees his daughter most weekends. Jenny is one year older than Ben and, for the last 9 months, has lived on her own, having moved out of her mother's house. Ben's parents and grandparents, who were initially shocked and upset to hear about the pregnancy, have supported him emotionally and financially through his journey into parenthood.

Education: Ben is a third-year university student. He is enjoying his course:

> Yeah loving it! It's difficult but it's good. The first year is, it's…it's kind of making sure that the course is right for you. … And then the year abroad was … comparatively very easy. And then suddenly you come back to, you know, lecture style classes and stuff. And it's, it's very overwhelming actually, yeah.

He had originally applied to study medicine but failed to get an offer: 'eventually I hope to be able to go back and do medicine but for now, not so much' [laughs].

The pregnancy: Ben found out about the pregnancy two months into his degree:

> It was really difficult actually. She was my girlfriend at the time and I'd, it was, I was having a really hard time kind of adjusting to University life even though I wasn't that far from home. It just, it felt like being really far away and I couldn't, I didn't really get on with my flatmates. And it was a really difficult situation. So I spent a lot of time with her. And then I ended up, I found out that she was pregnant and it just kind of … it's really hard to explain it. I just kind of freaked out a bit. It went … I just kind of … retracted into myself a bit and try – and kind of cut off, cut myself off from the world for a few, a couple of weeks, just while I tried to deal with it. It was really quite difficult.

Planning for parenthood: The pregnancy was unplanned. Ben had not thought about having children at that time, or only as part of a vague plan for the future:

> Not at all, no. Well, only in the sense that, you know, the vague kind of plans of, you know, graduate from Uni, get a job, get married, have kids. Kind of,

(Continued)

it's not, it wasn't anything serious. It was just kind of the general standard life plan, kind of thing.

Career trajectory and parenthood: Ben just missed the birth of his daughter but spent as much time with her as possible before going abroad for a year with his degree course. He feels it is important to continue to invest in his education and career prospects. Although this meant he missed much of the first year of his daughter's life, he reasons that investing in a career is beneficial for his daughter in the long run:

I'm really pleased I went, actually, yeah. Rather than dropping out of Uni and in a sub-standard job. ... I find it quite a difficult situation because on the one hand I don't have the money to provide ... but it's worth a short period of struggling through it for potentially quite a comfortable existence after Uni. And ultimately it would be better for Tilly. ... I can still be a good dad and also do what I want.

Source: *Following Young Fathers* study, Timescapes Archive

The data presented in Boxes 10.3 and 10.4 give only a brief outline of the lives of the participants, but they are enough to highlight a profound contrast in the lived experiences of these two young men: their different family backgrounds, educational and career paths, and their different orientations to parenthood (Andrew keen to be an engaged father; Ben able to invest in a more conventional breadwinner role). These young men share a common experience of entering parenthood in an unplanned way during their teenage years, when they are not ready for this step; nevertheless, both take their fatherhood commitments seriously. However, beyond this, their lives are running along very different tracks. Bringing these cases together highlights the significant impact of family background, material resources, and educational and career trajectories on the identities and practices of young fatherhood, and they warn us of the dangers of stereotyping young fathers (see Neale and Davies 2016 for an analysis of how the parenting trajectories of young fathers intersect with their educational and employment trajectories).

Cross-case comparisons of this sort can be built up in a variety of ways. Researchers may start with a particular theme, or a particular trajectory, to see how it is articulated across the cases (see Box 10.5 for an example). Alternatively, as in the example above, cases can be grouped into pairs, enabling a detailed search for similarities and differences between them. The cross-case analysis can then be extended by bundling cases into groups of three or four. This builds layers of analysis that give insights into the subtle differences and similarities between cases. A further technique is to start with a particular type of case data (life maps or field notes) to draw out insights that are unique to these data sources, before aggregating these insights into a composite picture (Eisenhardt 1995).

It is worth noting here how the articulation between cases, themes and processes emerges in this kind of cross-case analysis. An unfolding trajectory (housing or parenthood journeys, for example) becomes a key theme of a study, which can be drawn out for each case in the study, and then compared across the cases. This ensures an intertwining of case depth, thematic breadth and temporal reach. This is reflected, too, in the LIPA study showcased in Box 10.5, where a cross-case diachronic analysis offers an effective means of integrating case, thematic and processual insights.

Box 10.5   Cross-case Diachronic Analysis

- Longitudinal interpretative phenomenological analysis (LIPA) involves in-depth research with small numbers of cases. The aim is to explore the nuances of unfolding trajectories and to discern vivid insights into processual experiences (Farr and Nizza 2019). Like all QLA strategies, the approach used in LIPA is non-prescriptive: there is no single, structured method but a set of common analytical strategies, including the abductive logic of discovery, that can be applied flexibly by the researcher (Smith et al. 2009; Shaw et al. 2016; Thomson et al. 2017; see Box 4.6 for further details of this methodology, and details of Shaw et al. 2016).
- Spiers et al. (2016) explore the experience of four patients who had undergone a kidney transplant, tracing their medical and health recovery journeys through three waves of interviews (conducted a few weeks before and after the surgery, and a further nine months into the recovery period). A case study approach was made possible by the small sample size. An elegant strategy that combines case and thematic readings of the data was built up through a number of stages:
  - **Familiarisation with the data**: an initial, broad-brush reading of the transcripts for each case. This revealed three broad trajectories (processual themes), representing varied dimensions of the participants' changing experiences and circumstances: strategies for surviving ill health; transformations in identity; and changing perceptions of relationships between kidney recipients and donors.
  - **Teasing out data relating to these different trajectories**: Data relating to these different trajectories were organised into discrete clusters, which were then used as the basis for separate analyses and reporting. In the article cited here (Spiers et al. 2016), the researchers focus on a relational trajectory: the evolving relationships between kidney recipients and their donors.

(Continued)

- o **Case analysis (synchronic to diachronic)**: Individual cases were explored at each point in time, and then through time, building a diachronic understanding of this particular trajectory for each individual case.
- o **Cross-case analysis**: A comparison of this trajectory was then made across the four cases in the sample.

In writing up their findings, the researchers reported on how this trajectory unfolded for each separate case, before reflecting on where they converged and/or diverged across the cases. This maximised the depth of the study, enabling a detailed insight into the life worlds of the participants (Farr and Nizza 2019).

This way of organising and reporting findings was effective for a small-scale study comprising four cases. It would also be feasible where researchers are focusing on a small number of emblematic cases that are drawn from a larger study. However, where the aim is to work across and integrate insights across a larger sample, a more streamlined mode of interpretation and presentation is needed (see Box 10.7 for examples). This highlights the need to tailor case analysis and presentation to design and sampling decisions.

Thematic Analysis

This is a broad, cross-case, thematic reading of a QL dataset. The overall aim is to discern the theoretical, conceptual and substantive connections and patterns of meaning in the data, which can be distilled into key themes. These can then be explored across the whole sample. Thematic analysis is an essential component of QLA. It builds greater breadth into a study, enables a focus on theoretical and substantive ideas, and provides a bridge to broader, pre-existing bodies of knowledge and evidence. It is an important complement to case analysis (Thomson and Holland 2003; Maxwell 2012), enabling unfolding biographies and situated processes to be explored in relation to wider patterns of social and historical change. It also allows for iteration between case and thematic readings of the data, between depth and breadth of insight. In qualitative research in general, thematic analysis involves the following:

- a careful reading of and immersion in the data (familiarisation);
- identifying and labelling (coding, categorising, indexing) segments of data that reflect key conceptual and descriptive themes/sub-themes. A suite of themes with shorthand labels may be derived directly (inductively) from the data. But researchers may start with a broad-brush list of themes and sub-themes, derived abductively from the research questions/conceptual road map. The list of themes can be expanded and refined as each new data source is explored (Ritchie and Lewis 2003; Parkinson et al. 2016; Rapley 2016);

- labelling and re-ordering data is commonly achieved through the cut-and-paste facility in Microsoft Word, or a QDA package (e.g. MaxQDA, NVivo or Dedoose). But this task may also be carried out intuitively, by marking up text manually with coloured pens or highlighters, and/or scribbling margin notes (Rapley 2016);
- the labelled segments of data are collated into new thematic clusters. These can then be explored in a more focused way to shed light on an emerging theme or sub-theme, against a backdrop of wider bodies of theoretical/substantive knowledge. Selected clusters or bundles of data may also be imported into a grid to aid visualisation (see framework grid analysis in Boxes 10.7 and 10.8).

The broad parameters of thematic analysis outlined here form the basis for a number of established analytical methods used in qualitative enquiry (including grounded theory, IPA, thematic analysis (TA) and framework). The latter two are generic, flexible modes of analysis that are not tied to any one theoretical or epistemological position (Ritchie and Spencer 1994; Braun and Clarke 2006; Parkinson et al. 2016; Rapley 2016).

These different methods have their own analytical strategies and language (see the review in Rapley 2016). A structured approach, for example, involves a highly specified, line-by-line coding of data. This produces a proliferation of coded segments of data, often running to well over 100 codes (Parkinson et al. 2016), which then need to be systematically compared, re-grouped and re-aggregated to produce new insights. In contrast, a more flexible, broad-brush approach involves an intuitive reading and conceptual identification of themes at the level of the transcript or case, rather than line by line (see the examples in Box 10.5 and Box 10.7). This more holistic, case-led approach to thematic analysis has particular value for QL enquiry, as our quotation from Atkinson shows at the start of this chapter. It brings greater flexibility and contextual sensitivity to the task of discerning themes and sub-themes in the data, and nicely complements the task of building a diachronic picture of unfolding cases.

Building time into thematic analysis

As shown in Chapter 9, building time into the general modes of thematic analysis outlined above can be a challenge. Across the canon of qualitative research studies, thematic analysis is typically carried out at one point in time, that is, as a synchronic, cross-sectional (or cross-cutting) technique. This prioritises breadth over depth of vision, and segments data into many categories or codes (Maxwell 2012). Unlike 'connecting' case analysis, which brings temporal data together to build a diachronic picture, the tendency here is to think laterally (rather than longitudinally), to prioritise synchronic, cross-case readings at the expense of through-time readings.

This tendency may be compounded where analysis is driven by a highly struc-tured, finely grained method of data coding, of the sort used in grounded theory. This fragments the data, creating a proliferation of data segments that are cast adrift from the case and processual contexts of their production. It is a procedure that 'risks losing the broad pattern of the forest for the descriptive detail of the trees' (Langley 1999: 700). Exactly how researchers incorporate time into this mode of analysis is rarely spelled out in any detail. As shown in Chapter 9, for SmithBattle et al. (2018: 5) this raises suspicions that, in many cases, researchers are simply col-lapsing their temporal data and failing to capitalise on the longitudinal designs of their studies.

To illustrate some of the challenges that may arise in working thematically through time, two broad approaches to thematic analysis are outlined below. The first has been described as **recurrent cross-sectional analysis** (Grossoehme and Lipstein 2016). It involves a series of synchronic readings of the data, produced after each wave of fieldwork. A diachronic reading may be sandwiched into this process, or 'tacked on' at the end (see Box 10.6). But, either way, cross-case and through-time readings tend to be separated out. The second is **temporal thematic analysis**. This is a more integrated, case-led approach, in which themes are harnessed to the case and processual contexts of the analy-sis. Unlike recurrent cross-sectional analysis, this approach enables time and processes to be centrally embedded within the emerging themes of a study (see Box 10.7 for examples).

Box 10.6   Recurrent Cross-sectional Thematic Analysis

As shown in Chapter 1, recurrent cross-sectional designs create a particular kind of longitudinal 'movie'. Panel designs, which follow the same individuals through time, can provide processual insights into unfolding lives. However, this is not pos-sible with recurrent cross-sectional designs. The focus, instead, is on creating time series data that give a snapshot vision of change at each point in time. This cer-tainly produces temporal insights, but only into broad patterns and processes of change at an aggregate or population level.

This same limitation occurs when this approach is used for the analysis of QL data. Imposing a variable-based analytical template on in-depth case data inevitably produces a limited vision of temporal processes. This approach seems to have been employed, in the main, by health and medical researchers, where it is often seen as an adjunct to grounded theorising (Snelgrove 2014; Grossoehme and Lipstein 2016). The following examples illustrate this approach, and highlight its limitations for QL analysis (see also Box 8.5 where a categorising thematic approach is replaced with a connecting case-based approach):

- In their recurrent cross-sectional analysis, Grossoehme and Lipstein (2016) combine two main strategies:

  o a synchronic, cross-sectional analysis of the dataset, carried out after each visit to the field. This creates a recurrent cross-sectional vision of the data;

  o a final, diachronic (through-time) analysis of data across the cases, carried out at the close of fieldwork. The researchers used some of the processual questions posed by Saldaña (2002, 2003) to guide this stage of the analysis (see Box 11.1).

  For the two-wave studies conducted by these researchers, a full synchronic analysis after each wave of data was just about feasible. But it would, in all likelihood, be beyond the scope of a multi-wave study, and would, in any case, leave little room to build in complementary case and cross-case diachronic analysis, or to trace and map processes.

- Descriptions of this mode of analysis and its challenges for processual understandings are rare, but a detailed and perceptive account is provided by Fadyl et al. (2017; Fadyl 2019). Using the principles of grounded theory, these researchers carried out four waves of interviews with a sample of 52 patients who had suffered a traumatic brain injury. The analysis, which aimed to discern how patients had adjusted after their injuries, was conducted in three cumulative stages, with each stage informing the next:

  o a synchronic, cross-sectional analysis after each of the first three waves of fieldwork. Systematic, line-by-line analysis yielded a proliferation of finely grained segments of coded data. Most of the codes provided a snapshot picture at each point in time, although some processual themes were included in the list of codes;

  o a diachronic, through-time analysis of data, carried out at the end of the third wave. The researchers worked here with case materials that were placed in chronological order. The focus was on what (if anything) had changed for the participants;

  o the final stage of the analysis was a combination of cross-sectional and through-time analysis, working with a combined suite of thematic codes.

  For this study, the researchers faced the challenge of managing and keeping track of a large suite of finely grained fragments of coded data. The codes were continually shifting (with old codes modified or discarded, and new codes emerging) as the substantial volume of data expanded across the waves of fieldwork. Since the codes discerned at one wave no longer matched those emerging at subsequent waves, the cumulative dataset had to be re-coded at each wave. This was a painstaking and time-consuming process. The researchers devised an elaborate set of techniques to get to grips with

(Continued)

an evolving picture that seemed to move perpetually beyond their grasp. Strategies included a conceptual mapping exercise; an expert committee for regular consultations on the analysis; the development of a bespoke thematic database to keep track of the codes; and the use of data visualisation software to document the coding structures for each stage.

These strategies and techniques for identifying and managing the coded segments of data seem to have dominated the study and created a significant analytical burden for the researchers; they reflect a mismatch between the temporal objectives of this study (to create a dynamic picture of changing lives) and the categorising analytical strategies that had been employed. Fadyl and colleagues (2017) observe that, while their recurrent, cross-sectional analysis gave broad insights about patient recovery and adaptation at different points in time, it revealed little about the process of change itself. They had created a picture of broad trends at the expense of rich, processual, biographical insights. After the first three waves of fieldwork, the researchers decided to overcome this limitation by building in narrative case portraits that could trace the unfolding trajectories of individual patients:

> This approach felt more appropriate than broad, cross-sectional analysis for examining individual [change]. (Fadyl et al. 2017: 5)

Temporal thematic analysis

The highly structured form of recurrent cross-sectional analysis outlined in Box 10.6 has some evident drawbacks for temporal analysis, but this does not diminish the value of discerning key themes in an emerging dataset, and of following how these emerge, evolve or change within and across the cases in a study. Here is a cogent reminder of the value of cross-case thematic analysis:

> At first I resisted coding. The process seemed mechanical and reductive to me. I didn't want to violate the organic unity of my interviews, many of which had deeply moved me. To fracture these conversations into discrete [segments] seemed like taking a pair of scissors and cutting up family photographs. However, as I started coding ... I found connections between the interviews that I hadn't previously suspected. Not only did my informants share similar experiences, they sometimes used the same language to discuss those experiences. ... a mass of incoherent intractable material did, indeed, have pattern and shape. (Huang, cited in Maxwell 2012: 117)

Nevertheless, the problems identified above (Box 10.6) in using categorising forms of analysis for temporal enquiry need to be addressed. A number of complementary techniques are outlined below that can help to bridge the gap between longitudinal case analysis and thematic analysis, and embed time more centrally into a thematic picture:

- **Harnessing themes to cases**: The use of broad-brush emblematic themes: A closer integration of case and thematic readings eases the task of piecing together a diachronic picture. As the examples in Box 10.5 and Box 10.7 show, thinking in terms of cross-case diachronic analysis, rather than cross-sectional analysis, is a great help here. Working with a relatively small number of broad-brush, emblematic themes ensures that themes retain their contextual sensitivity, are not cast adrift from case data, and the data are not fragmented in ways that can confound the development of diachronic insights. Emblematic themes will emerge from the conceptual road map (Chapter 4, Table 4.1) and from a careful reading of case data.
- **Harnessing themes to processes**: We return here to an idea that is threaded through various chapters of this book: that time is more than the framework within which a study unfolds; it is a rich theme or topic of enquiry in its own right. When looking for themes in the data, we are looking for dynamic insights: for trajectories, transitions, changes, continuities, repetitions and flows of time. In other words, we are looking for processes and how they unfold. Emblematic themes are likely to have dynamic, recurring or cumulative significance. For example, a concern with health or education can be framed in terms of health or educational trajectories, biographies, journeys or developments. Turning nouns into verbs (organisation – organising, migration – migrating, and so on) performs a similar function.

    In these ways, themes acquire a processual quality: they embody the idea of through-time events, activities and experiences (see the examples in Boxes 10.1 and 10.5 where key trajectories are identified as emblematic themes). Building a processual understanding begins at the baseline wave, when a careful reading of the data will uncover emerging themes and sub-themes of a temporal nature. These will include retrospective and prospective accounts that place current lives in the context of past developments and future plans.
- **Developing temporal sub-themes and concepts**: it is possible to identify varied interlocking pathways, or threads of a trajectory, or temporal through-lines in the data that can be pulled out for separate analysis (see Box 10.5 for examples). Pertinent flows of time (detailed in Chapter 3) might form important conceptual themes or sub-themes. Generic conceptual labels, for example, might include change/continuity in events, experiences or perceptions; historical/generational/biographical time; past/present/future time; starting points/mid-points/end points; high/low points; trigger points/

tipping points/turning points; the tempo, momentum and speed of change, and so on. These conceptual sub-themes provide a more finely grained means of exploring different temporal dynamics within the data.

- **Asking processual questions**: As suggested above for case analysis, it helps to develop one or more key processual questions that provide a focus for thematic investigation. Once themes and sub-themes are framed in this dynamic way, it becomes possible to interrogate data in ways that complement and can be integrated with case analysis. Generic questions might include: What factors have led to this process? How have broad transitions or trajectories, and their intersecting threads, unfolded within this case and across cases? What temporal mechanisms are involved and how have they shaped these processes in varied ways across the sample? (See also the case-led questions outlined above, and the suite of processual questions in Box 11.1.)

- **Adopting grid (framework) analysis**: it is worth considering the use of grid or matrix analysis (e.g. framework) alongside, or as an alternative to detailed thematic coding using QDA software (described in Box 10.8 and illustrated in Figure 10.1; see Ritchie and Lewis 2003; Saldaña 2003; Lewis 2007; Parkinson et al. 2016). Grid analysis is of particular value for medium to large-scale studies. It enables a condensed, three-dimensional visualisation of themes in relation to cases and time periods, thereby conveying breadth in relation to depth and temporal reach. Grid analysis requires the use of relatively broad-brush themes that emerge from the case data; it is impossible to incorporate numerous fragments of coded data into a summative/descriptive grid (Parkinson et al. 2016).

Using the techniques outlined above can help to build a diachronic picture into the themes of a study. Here, processes are not separated from themes; instead they become the key themes of a study, which are discerned through rich, detailed longitudinal case data. Box 10.7 gives examples of two studies that have used a temporal approach to thematic analysis, enabling a closer integration of case, processual and thematic insights. A range of thematic tools for QLA are outlined in Box 10.8.

Box 10.7 Temporal Thematic Analysis – Integrating Cases and Themes

- **The BOOST Health Trial** (Ward et al. 2019) used a combination of case histories, of around 4–5,000 words, and framework grids for their three-wave study of 60 participants undergoing a physiotherapy health trial. Case histories were constructed for 10 emblematic cases. These were purposively chosen for their rich data and to reflect key sample characteristics. The histories were then used to draw out key categories (sub-themes) across the emblematic cases. Six sub-themes were identified at the baseline wave. By the time the emblematic data had been analysed across all waves, these themes had been refined and expanded to a total of 27 sub-themes. The researchers then constructed framework grids for each case in the study, with the 27 sub-themes forming rows along the vertical axis, and the three time periods forming columns along the horizontal axis. Summary data, with selected quotations, were imported into the cells of the grid. This enabled a visualisation, interpretation and comparison of the longitudinal trajectories for each case. (See Box 10.8 and Figure 10.1 for a description and illustration of framework grids.)

- **The *Following Young Fathers* study**: This well-resourced project (Neale et al. 2015) used a comprehensive range of techniques to interrogate a rich QL dataset (up to five waves of interview data with 31 young fathers, conducted over five years). Complementary ways of interrogating the data were developed in parallel, enabling ongoing iteration between case depth, thematic breadth and temporal reach:

  o **Diachronic (through-time) analysis** of individual case data, using summative pen portraits and descriptive case histories (see the examples in Box 10.3 and Box 10.4). These case files enabled a finely grained analysis of unfolding processes for each case. A careful reading of the case data at each new wave produced new processual themes, including evolving relationships with grandparents and custodial journeys (reported in Neale and Lau-Clayton 2014; Neale and Ladlow 2015; Ladlow and Neale 2016).

  o **Cross-case diachronic analysis**: Broad-brush thematic analysis of the dataset using a QDA package (NVivo). The researchers worked with up to 20 pre-defined themes and sub-themes (drawn from the research questions), with a focus on those that were framed in processual ways or embodied varied flows of time (for example, evolving parent–child relationships, education, employment, and housing trajectories, and past, present and future time). This was a case-led approach to thematic analysis, working with broad segments of case data that retained their case and processual sensitivity.

  o **Summative thematic charts and descriptive framework grids** were set up for each of the emblematic themes at the baseline, and new charts and grids were added as new themes were identified. Summary data were imported into the charts and grids as the study progressed (see extracts in Table 10.1 and Figure 10.1). These enabled a visual articulation of cross-case and through-time readings of the data for each key theme.

  o **Varied trajectories** were singled out for diachronic analysis, enabling a focused exploration of how they were unfolding within each case, and across the cases in the study (e.g. Neale and Davies 2016 on the employment trajectories of young fathers; Neale and Patrick 2016 on

(Continued)

evolving relationships between young fathers and their co-parents). The researchers also explored how varied trajectories intersect to create distinctive journeys for each case.

Overall, this was an iterative, abductive strategy, a matter of 'feeling one's way' with the data to gradually build up layers of insight. The researchers were able to work across and integrate key processual themes across all 31 cases in the sample, while maintaining a through-time focus (for similar approaches founded on a cross-case diachronic analysis of trajectories, see McDonough et al. 2011; Shaw et al. 2016; and Lloyd et al. 2017).

Box 10.8   Temporal Thematic Analysis Tool Kit

- **Summative mapping tools (thematic charts)**: These tools are 'ready reckoners' that give a graphic display of dynamic circumstances across the cases in the sample over the study time frame. They perform a vital condensing and mapping function, enabling researchers to quickly grasp the core themes of the study across cases and through key time frames. They can be used to identity dynamic patterns in the data that need more detailed investigation (Saldaña 2003). In the *Following Young Fathers* study, for example, a series of thematic charts was produced that enabled the researchers to see, at a glance, how many of the young men had sustained contact with their children, whether they were still in a relationship with their co-parent by the end of the study (see the example in Table 10.1), and the nature, stability or volatility of their education, employment and housing trajectories (Neale et al. 2015; see Saldaña 2003: 54–5, who uses analytical flip charts for this purpose). These charts can be constructed using framework or other QDA software, Microsoft Office software, or manually.
- **Descriptive tools (framework grids)**: These structured tools are particularly suited to temporal analyses, for they enable a condensed, three-dimensional visualisation of themes in relation to cases and time periods (Ritchie and Lewis 2003; Corden and Nice 2007; Lewis 2007; Parkinson et al. 2016). Developed initially by NATCEN, they have since been incorporated into NVivo QDA software, but can also be constructed manually on sheets of A3 paper, or using Microsoft Word or Excel software (Swallow et al. 2003).[1] Framework software was originally designed to map cases against themes

---

[1]Parkinson et al. (2016) report that NVivo framework software is not stable enough to facilitate shared analysis across a research team, necessitating the construction or reconstruction of the grids in other formats. It is worth checking if this issue has been resolved.

(Ritchie and Lewis 2003), but by producing a series of grids, it becomes possible to map key themes against cases and time periods (Lewis 2007).

- The grids can be configured in varied ways to suit the focus and design of a study (for variations, see Molloy et al. 2002; Lewis 2007; Neale et al. 2015; Grossoehme and Lipstein 2016; Brandon et al. 2017; Ward et al. 2019). In the *Following Young Fathers* study, a separate grid was constructed for each key theme in the study. Figure 10.1 gives an extract from a grid that was constructed for the housing journeys of young fathers. The grid lists cases in rows along the vertical axis, and time periods in columns along the horizontal axis. Each cell is filled in with brief summaries of housing data. A 'pre-interview' cell at the beginning of the horizontal axis enables past housing events/circumstances to be documented. A summative cell at the end of the horizontal axis can also be added to provide a summary of housing journeys for each case. Adding key quotations and page references to transcripts enhances the value of these data.

  Once the grids are constructed, the data can be read in varied ways. A vertical' reading gives a cross-case picture of varied housing circumstances for the whole sample at each point in time. A 'horizontal' reading gives a through-time picture of housing journeys for each case in the sample, with a summary for the case in the final cell. A combined, 'integrative' reading gives a vision of varied housing journeys across cases and through time. This facility for multiple visualisations of the data can support the development of higher level interpretations:

- **Case grids:** As noted above, separate grids can also be constructed for each case in a sample, with themes mapped against time periods. In a creative adaptation of framework, researchers in the *Job Retention and Rehabilitation* study (Lewis 2007) established a set of four grids for each case, with each grid representing an emblematic theme of the study. In this instance, time periods (waves of interviews) were charted in rows along the vertical axis, and varied sub-themes were charted in columns along the horizontal axis. The researchers added a further column of cells to the horizontal axis, which summarised the case data at each particular point in time. At the close of fieldwork, a fifth grid was constructed for each case, representing a through-time whole-case summary of the data. Other forms of case grid are illustrated in Figure 10.1, and described in Box 10.7 and in Grossoehme and Lipstein (2016).

- **QDA software**: Qualitative data analysis software tools, such as MaxQDA, NVivo and Dedoose, can aid the process of labelling, sifting and regrouping data into new thematic clusters or bundles. But such software needs to be used with care. Working with a modest number of emblematic themes and sub-themes, and with broad segments of case data rather than line by line, will ensure that the coding process does not create a fragmented thematic picture that is cast adrift from its case and processual contexts and yields limited through-time understandings.

Table 10.1 Summative thematic chart (*Following Young Fathers* study). Relationship with co-parent over the study period (P = partnered; S = separated)

Cases	Start of fieldwork	End of fieldwork
Adam	P	P
Andrew	P	P
Bekele	S	S
Ben	S	S
Cade	P	P
Callum	S	S
Darren	P	P
Dominic	S	S
Iman	S	S
Jackson	P	P
Jakie	P	P
James	S	S
Jason	S	S
Jax	P	P
Jed	P	S
Jimmy	P	S
Jock	P	S
Joe	S	P
Karl	S	S
Kevin	S	S
Manuel	P	P
Marcel	P	P
Martin	P	P
Orlando	S	S
Richard	P	S
Senwe	P	S
Simon	S	S
Tarrell	S	S
Tommy	P	S
Trevor	S	S
Zane	P	P
TOTAL	17 partnered 14 separated	12 partnered 19 separated

Framework Grids: Housing

Participant	Pre-interview	Wave 1	Wave 2	Wave 3
Jimmy	Living with his mum and brother	Lived with partner at her mum's house for a while, now returned to live at his mum's house	Jimmy, his partner and their child are now living between his mum's house and his partner's mum's house	Now lives with a friend from college after a fall out with his mum
Tarrell	Living with his mum (father is deceased)	Still living with mum	Unable to contact participant	Now living with partner and two of his four children at partner's house
Jason	Living alone in local authority flat, after moving out of foster care	Still living alone	In prison	Unable to contact participant

Framework Grids: Jimmy Case Data

Theme	Pre-interview	Wave 1	Wave 2	Wave 3
Housing	Living with his mum and brother	Lived with partner at her mum's house for a while, now returned to live at his mum's house	Jimmy, his partner and their child are now living between his mum's house and his partner's mum's house	Now lives with a friend from college after a fall out with his mum
School employment	In school when became an expectant dad	Had left school and without a job	Temporary job but was sacked. Looking at training schemes	Joined a college course
Relationship with co-parent	In relationship with mother at age of 15	Volatile but still in relationship during pregnancy	Relationships positive: living with partner and child across households	Relationship with partner highly volatile

Figure 10.1 Grid analysis (framework) *(Following Young Fathers* study)

Closing Reflections

This chapter has explored case and thematic analysis as central and complementary components of QLA. We have seen that case analysis enables a diachronic, through-time and recursive understanding of people's unfolding transitions or trajectories. Once a suite of pen portraits or case histories is in place, it becomes possible to read across these analytical files to build a cross-case, diachronic picture. Case analysis is inherently processual, but, as will be shown in Chapter 11, it can be supported and sharpened through a concerted focus on process tracing, using a series of processual questions to aid the task.

Thematic analysis builds greater breadth into an emerging picture, by exploring theoretical and substantive patterns and connections across the cases in a dataset. It provides a crucial bridge to pre-existing bodies of theory and knowledge. But the discussion here has alerted us to a potential pitfall in adopting a recurrent, cross-sectional mode of thematic analysis. An over-emphasis on categorising forms of coding and recoding data can create multiple fragments of thematic data that are cast adrift from their case and processual contexts, and can only be understood as snapshots in time. This can confound the task of creating a through-time picture. However, a temporal, case-led mode of thematic analysis, which ties themes, cases and processes more closely together, and maintains a focus on cross-case (as opposed to cross-sectional) analysis, can help to overcome this problem. This highlights the need to work not just with emblematic cases, but also with broad-brush emblematic themes that reflect varied journeys through time. More generally, where standard analytical packages such as grounded theory are being used, these need to be tailored to address the temporal aims and demands of QLA.

In exploring the practicalities of case and thematic analysis in this chapter, two broad challenges have been identified. First, there is the challenge of working ana-lytically with large volumes of QL data and keeping the process to manageable proportions. The tools and techniques assembled here are designed to condense data, enabling researchers to 'see' the dataset as a whole, and to read across data in new ways, while, at the same time, ensuring that the reconstructed data retain their integrity and remain faithful to their case origins. Case analysis (the production of case histories and case studies) and framework grid analysis, for example, are useful combinations (see e.g. Pollard 2007; Neale et al. 2015; Ward et al. 2019). But it is important to note that not all of the tools and techniques outlined here will be needed; researchers will need to review, select, adapt, combine and pilot their cho-sen tools with care, ensuring that they support the processual aims of the analysis rather than becoming a burden. There is also undoubted merit in drawing out emblematic cases and themes for focused attention in order to illuminate how processes unfold.

Second, there is the challenge of not only teasing out the case, thematic and processual components of QLA, but also of reconnecting and synthesising them to create coherent and compelling interpretations. Whatever tools and techniques are adopted, some combination of case, thematic and processual readings of a dataset is essential. Processual understandings are the driving force for QLA and need to be threaded through the whole process. In Chapter 11, the processual dimensions of QLA are given focused attention, along with the means to create a final synthesis of QLA through the use of narratives and process mapping tools. This is where the analytical journey, begun in Chapter 9 and progressed in this chapter, reaches fruition.

Further Reading

QL researchers have produced some valuable accounts of the analytical strategies adopted for their own studies. For longitudinal and narrative case analysis, Mishler (1995), Polkinghorne (1995), Plummer (2001), Thomson and Holland (2003), Thomson (2007), and Henderson et al. (2012) are particularly recommended. Spiers et al. (2016) give an excellent account of cross-case diachronic analysis as a means to integrate case, thematic and processual data. For temporal thematic analysis, the literature is sparse. Grossoehme and Lipstein (2016) and Fadyl et al. (2017) provide insights into recurrent cross-sectional analysis, including some salutary lessons on its challenges and limitations. For framework grid analysis, the discussion provided by Lewis (2007) is a valuable starting point.

Fadyl, J., Channon, A., Theadom, A. and McPherson, K. (2017) 'Optimising qualitative longitudinal analysis: Insights from a study of traumatic brain injury recovery and adaptation', *Nursing Inquiry*, 24 (2).

Grossoehme, D. and Lipstein, E. (2016) 'Analysing longitudinal qualitative data: The application of trajectory and recurrent cross-sectional approaches', *BMC Research Notes*, 9: 136.

Henderson, S., Holland, J., McGrellis, S., Sharpe, S. and Thomson, R. (2012). 'Storying qualitative longitudinal research: Sequence, voice and motif', *Qualitative Research*, 12 (1): 16–34.

Lewis, J. (2007) 'Analysing qualitative longitudinal research in evaluations', *Social Policy and Society*, 6 (4): 545–56.

Mishler, E. (1995) 'Models of narrative analysis: A typology', *Journal of Narrative and Life History*, 5 (2): 87–123.

Plummer, K. (2001) *Documents of Life 2: An Invitation to a Critical Humanism*. London: Sage.

Polkinghorne, D. (1995) 'Narrative configuration in qualitative analysis', in J. Hatch and R. Wisniewski (eds) *Life History and Narrative*. London: Falmer. pp. 5–23.

Spiers, J., Smith, J. and Drage, M. (2016) 'A longitudinal interpretative phenomenological analysis of the process of kidney recipients' resolution of complex ambiguities with relationships with their living donors', *Journal of Health Psychology*, 21 (11): 2600–11.

Thomson, R. (2007) 'The qualitative longitudinal case history: Practical, methodological and ethical reflections', *Social Policy and Society*, 6 (4): 571–82.

Thomson, R. and Holland, J. (2003) 'Hindsight, foresight and insight: The challenges of longitudinal qualitative research', *International Journal of Social Research Methodology*, 6 (3): 233–44.

11

PROCESS AND SYNTHESIS IN QUALITATIVE LONGITUDINAL ANALYSIS

┌─ Key Points ─

- **Process analysis**: This vital and intellectually challenging aspect of QLA is currently poorly documented and under-utilised. The temporal dynamics of processes, their purpose, scale, duration, pattern and tempo, are infinitely varied: they may have no clear or uniform purpose or structure, and their effects may be unpredictable. Teasing out the threads of processes is therefore a challenge and may only be possible in retrospect. Given their complexity, processes are most easily grasped in localised contexts, through rich case data.
- **The nature of processes**: Processes are temporal constructs that convey a sense of flux and change. They comprise a rich tapestry of events, actions and interactions that are linked together in a meaningful way through time. As a starting point for analysis, it is helpful to focus on how a process is ordered, how the threads are connected, and how they may converge at key moments in time. It is also helpful to tease out the fixed and fluid elements of processes, their multiplicity and their relational dimensions, which provide insights into the complexities of causality.
- **Temporal flows, patterns and tempos**: The power of processes lies in their temporal constructions and connections. Understanding *how* they unfold is therefore important. Time frames, patterns and tempos are infinitely varied

(Continued)

but some of the most commonly observed temporal flows are set out here. A focus on sequences needs to be balanced with a consideration of non-linear, loop-like patterns (cyclical and spiralling events and actions), while tempos are likely to embody times of volatility and stability, change and continuity.

- **Process tracing**: This involves following processes where they lead, through situated pockets of time, space and the social fabric. It relies on an abundance of rich case data. Processes can be traced recursively forward and backward in time; through intensive and extensive horizons of time; through their fixed (linear, predictable) and fluid (non-linear, unpredictable) dimensions; and through their micro–macro influences. The iteration between these modes of analysis produces new lines of discovery and insights on causal processes.
- **Asking processual questions**: A suite of generic questions is provided to help focus the analysis (Box 11.1). These straddle descriptive 'what' questions and discursive 'how' questions that flesh out the picture. An example of process tracing is provided in Box 11.2.
- **Synthesis**: We return to an overview of QLA and its elements of case, thematic and processual analysis. QLA culminates in a full-scale, integrative (case-led, cross-case, through-time) analysis of data at the close of fieldwork. Insights are finally developed and crystallised through the process of narrating and visually conjuring temporal processes and conveying these to varied audiences. The ethics of representing data and findings is touched on here. Techniques for visually mapping processes are outlined, illustrated and appraised. The discussion highlights the value of intuitive, empirically grounded mapping tools that offer vivid windows onto unfolding processes.

Introduction

Analysis is often the hardest task of all, as the researcher seeks to do justice to the data that may have taken years to collect. This is also the period when researchers may question their sanity in embarking on such a study in the first place. ... Processual analysis ... examine[s] the whole picture over time as a dynamic tapestry, with competing histories, future trajectories and ongoing multiple narratives of change. (Dawson 2003: 86, 114)

Some processes may be linear, directional, cumulative and perhaps irreversible, while others may be non-linear, radical and transformational. Openness to these possibilities is a key intellectual requirement for the process scholar. (Pettigrew 1997: 339)

The process researcher needs to follow the process, back and forth, through time and space. ... We are exploring a maze of links and paths distributed through time and space. ... The whole point is to follow the process wherever it takes you. (De Cock and Sharp 2007: 243)

The processual dimensions of QLA are of critical importance, yet they are currently poorly documented and under-utilised. As we have seen in Chapters 9 and 10, holding temporal processes at the forefront of our thinking can be intellectually challenging, given the slippery and ineffable nature of time. However, as shown in Chapter 10, there are ways to overcome this. Achieving a balance between case depth, thematic breadth and temporal reach, requires a focused attention on the dynamics of things, how events, actions and interactions are linked together and unfold in a rich dynamic tapestry (as Dawson refers to it above). It requires insight into the nature of processes and how they may be pieced together through time.

This chapter explores **process analysis** as a vital dimension of QLA. Techniques of process tracing (and, to a lesser extent, **process mapping**) are outlined here, drawing on ideas developed in narrative inquiry, organisational process research, and in causality and complexity theory (see Chapter 2). The discussion begins with broad-brush ideas about the nature of processes and their temporal dynamics, drawing together the range of rich ideas explored in Chapter 2. These ideas are then distilled to highlight strategies for building processual insights, and then distilled further to produce a generic list of processual questions that can help to focus the analysis.

The final part of this chapter takes us back to a broader consideration of QLA. It examines how we synthesise the varied facets of QL analysis to create a dynamic tapestry of insights into unfolding lives. Some combination of case, thematic and processual interpretations of a dataset are essential for QLA. But there are different ways to achieve this, and to find the right balance between them. The discussion concludes by exploring the culminating act of analysis: how temporal processes are narrated and visually mapped, and how the findings of a study may be conjured and conveyed to a wider audience.

The Nature of Processes

Processes are temporal constructs with a forward momentum. They may be thought of as unfolding pathways, but where the course of the path, its nature, momentum and meaning are just as important as its starting point or the destination reached. Processes comprise a rich tapestry of events, actions, reactions and interactions that are linked together in a meaningful way through time. The social world is an intricate web of these multiple, intersecting elements, operating at different scales of enquiry, from the unfolding of micro biographies to the unfolding of macro socio-historical events. Processes are perpetually flowing, oscillating and interacting through recursive feedback or feedforward loops, which may converge at key moments in time to reaffirm, grow, adapt or otherwise transform the lives of those involved. With their open, intersecting and porous boundaries, processual pathways are intertwined with others, like skeins of thread, or a confluence of streams flowing within a river basin or across a flood plain (Pettigrew 1997).

The causal power and influence of processes lie in their very nature; given their inherent temporality, they convey a sense of flux and change: of becoming, development, emergence, progression, evolution, revolution, transformation, dissipation, decay, and so on (Lofland et al. 2006: 152). They are narratives of becoming. Understanding how events unfold requires a shift in focus from the form that social events take, their structural components, to their processual nature, to their multiple, fluid and relational elements (Neale 2021). The aim of QLA is to capture this dynamic reality in flight (Pettigrew 1997), to follow processes where they lead, discerning their constituent threads, how these threads are connected through time, space and the social fabric, and how they may coalesce to create the momentum for change.

As shown in Chapter 2, the varied threads or elements of a process are closely intertwined and flow into each other in unpredictable ways, making the task of teasing them for analysis rather challenging. There are many permutations of different processual threads in the methodological literature, which are defined and labelled in varied ways (see the different schemas offered by Pettigrew 1987, 1997; Langley 1999; Brockmeier 2000; Tsoukas and Chia 2002; Lofland et al. 2006; Bidart et al. 2013; Bidart 2019; see Box 11.2). Abbott (2001: 190) for example, identifies three dynamic components of unfolding processes (which are slightly reformulated here):

- **their order** – the flow of events and interactions from past to future;
- **their connections/connectors** – how the threads of a process are linked together; the driving forces and trigger points that create the connections;
- **their convergence** – how these threads converge at pivotal moments to achieve change or equilibrium.

In a fluid world, of course, there is nothing straightforward about finding a structured order in things, or discerning how events are connected, or how or indeed whether they converge. While this is a useful way to think about the contours of processes, and how the threads are connected through time, it is also important to explore the nature of the threads and their causal powers. Their multiple, fluid and relational elements are set out below (and also elaborated in Neale 2021).

Processes are Fluid

Some processes may have a clearly defined purpose, a fixed sequence of events or practices, discrete start and end points, and clear milestones along the way.

The more instrumental, time-bound, habitual, routine or prescribed a process, the more likely this will be. Enduring life course transitions, such as becoming a parent, will exhibit many fixed processual features. However, lives do not necessarily unfold in chronological order, in one linear direction, or at a uniform pace. Nor do people experience their lives in these orderly ways. Myriad fluid elements may be identified that are not linear, consistent or planned, but have ill-defined and recursive (loop-like) pathways and effects that extend over varied horizons of time. Even relatively fixed processes are likely to exhibit a multitude of fluid characteristics. These fixed and fluid processual threads, then, are not mutually exclusive: they are present and, to varying degrees, intertwined in most processes. This requires a recursive, retrospective lens, to complement a focus on linear, unidirectional sequences.

How processes are understood depends on how time itself is understood. From a fixed 'events in time' perspective, entities such as events, groups and institutions are assumed to have a fixed and stable nature, and change is something that happens to them through a variety of processual mechanisms. Time is an external, overarching force that brings about the change. In contrast, from a fluid 'time in events' perspective, events and interactions are not fixed or stable but in a continual state of becoming. Everything in nature is in a state of flux, with changes occurring through a maze of interwoven interactions, influences and feedback loops (Langley et al. 2013: 6). Time, then, inheres in processes. The ontological focus shifts from change as something that happens to things, to change as an inherent part of the nature of things. In like vein, causality is not something that happens mechanically as a process unfolds: it is embedded in the *way* processes unfold. These distinctions between fixed and fluid understandings of temporal processes are commonly drawn by QL researchers (see, for example, Tsoukas and Chia 2002; Langley et al. 2013; Jarzabkowski et al. 2017; see Chapter 2 for a detailed discussion).

Processes are Multiple

While not all processes will have overtly causal dimensions, the search for links and connections that provide the momentum for change is central to process analysis. However, as shown in Chapter 2, there may be no single or clear-cut outcome, or discrete link between cause and effect. A process may have no a priori purpose, and no fixed or unitary driving force or trigger point for change. The purpose may be ill-defined, exploratory or experiential. For example, it may be as much about sense making, learning, adapting or experimenting, as about concrete decision making and tangible changes (dealing with events, undergoing a transition of some sort, altering or creating things to produce something new or different) (Langley et al. 2013). Processes may have flexible, opportunistic, arbitrary or accidental starting points, no clear sequence, flow or end point, and they may develop in unpredictable or random ways, or have unanticipated or arbitrary effects or consequences.

The idea of a clear-cut series of events that leads to definitive outcomes, then, may or may not fit the empirical reality. Moreover, future outcomes are inherently unpredictable. Fluid processes are essentially unfinished, requiring us to capture them 'in flight' through small windows in time, and in small corners of the social fabric. 'Outcomes' are better framed here as 'ephemeral way stations in the ongoing flow of activity ... rather than static termination points' (Langley et al. 2013: 10). While processes are by no means necessarily chaotic or random, future effects are characterised by multiple possibilities, particularly where they evolve slowly, imperceptibly and without visibility (for example, the slow-burn, hidden effects of climate and environmental change; Adam 1998).

The historical antecedents and consequences of processes, the traces of past and future that inhere within them, shape how they unfold and reinforce their emergent qualities. Indeed, every event has multiple antecedents that spiral backwards into the past, and multiple consequences that spiral forwards into the future. This creates a vast constellation of causal flows (Abbott 2001: 144, 192). Tracing effects back to a single cause, or through a clear-cut, linear sequence of events, is too simplistic when they are rooted in entangled webs of causality (Nowotny 2005). Since a multitude of interacting processual threads are at work at any one time, operating at varied scales of the social fabric and unfolding through varied tempos and horizons of time, there are no simple or unitary relationships between causes and effects.

The multiplicity of processual threads, and the distributed nature of influences across the social fabric requires a shift in thinking about the relationship between a process and the context in which it occurs. Our tendency to separate these out, to hold one constant while the other moves, becomes less viable: 'context is not something that is held constant and outside the changes being analysed, but is itself continually reconstituted ... [through] chains of activity and events in which actors, environments and organisations are all in constant and mutually interacting flux' (Langley et al. 2013: 5). Contexts, then, have no fixed constitution; they are part of the fluid threads that make up an unfolding process. What constitutes a context shifts through time, requiring a more nuanced, open and exploratory understanding of the driving forces that shape a process and its cumulative effects (Pettigrew 1997; Langley et al. 2013).

Processes are Relational

Processual understandings rely on an abundance of longitudinal case data, and thick descriptions of interacting events, actions, meanings and motives. Lived experiences of processes, which embody human agency and subjectivity, are vital to our understanding. It is important, for example, to discern how and why individuals or collectives actively pursue, overcome, resist or create the conditions for change, or otherwise respond or adapt to shifts in the social fabric. Opportunity, constraint, motive, moral values, circumstance, chance, hope, fear, surprise and ingenuity may all be implicated, along with the varied nature of interpersonal dynamics (conflictual, coercive, competitive, collaborative, supportive, inspirational, and so on) (Dawson 2003).

In this way, process tracing can capture emotional, value-laden journeys, as well as those that are chronological and event-based. In sum, an understanding of the influence of human agency, reflexivity and moral sensibilities on how processes unfold is central to their analysis, giving insights into the shifting meanings that processes hold for those who experience and craft them.

These relational factors are likely to play a part in our understanding of what triggers a process, and what provides the momentum to carry it forward. These are key questions for process analysis. They require an understanding of the driving and restraining forces that connect the threads of a process. These forces may set a process in train and sustain it, or alternatively, may lead to stasis, lock-in, stagnation, dissipation or collapse (Lofland et al. 2006: 154–5; Boulton et al. 2015). Driving or restraining forces may take varied forms, ranging from nudges, push/pull factors, feedback/feedforward loops and random events, to sudden ruptures, discontinuities, accumulations or oscillations in time and space. There are, indeed, a multitude of ways in which the threads of a process are connected. Turning and trigger points are important conceptual tools in understanding how new paths may be opened up, as are the pivotal moments through which events converge or coalesce to create the momentum for change (Lofland et al. 2006: 154–5; Boulton et al. 2015).

Temporal Flows, Patterns and Tempos

As shown in Chapter 2 (Box 2.4), exploring *what* unfolds, in a somewhat descriptive, instrumental fashion, needs to be complemented with a more nuanced focus on *how* things unfold, *how* events and actions interact, and *how* they coalesce to create change or equilibrium through time (Van de Ven and Huber 1995; Pawson and Tilley 1997). This is particularly important given the insight (above) that time, change and causality are embedded within processes. 'How' questions are inherently processual. Arguably, they precede and encapsulate 'what' and 'why' questions, which require relatively clear-cut responses (Plummer 2001; Lofland et al. 2006: 158; Bidart et al. 2013). The advice in our opening quotations to follow processes where they lead comes into its own here.

There are as many time frames, patterns and tempos as there are processes, inviting consideration of their duration (short to long term), and their speed, pace and momentum (fast/slow; continuous/discontinuous; sudden/gradual). At one end of the spectrum, for example, a conversation can be seen as a process that unfolds intensively over a few minutes, inviting analysis of its linguistic and dialogic elements, and the iterative nature of the exchange through which meanings emerge and lives move on (Doehler et al. 2018). At the other end of the spectrum, 'slow burn' processes evolve almost imperceptibly through microscopic nudges or slippages, influences that spread slowly and indirectly through time, space and the social fabric, inviting analysis of broad, intertwined patterns of social and historical change (Elias 1997 [1977]; Tsoukas and Chia 2002; Tilly 2008). Processual analysis, then, may involve anything from the 'close-up' of an intimate movie to the 'long shot' of an epic movie.

A retrospective lens can be used to discern the multitude of temporal patterns and tempos that shape processes. The patterns may be sequential, zigzag, branching, loop-like, cyclical or spiralling. They unfold through varied tempos, which help to shape how the threads of a process are connected and how they converge. Fragmentary pathways that occur randomly or show no clear patterning are also discernible (Brockmeier 2000; Zerubavel 2003; Lofland et al. 2006). Summative data (e.g. pen portraits; see Chapter 10), which afford a broad overview of a case, may be of particular value in bringing these patterns and tempos to light.

Among the varied ways in which processes flow, their patterning and tempos, the following have particular analytical power and are explored in the discussion below:

- linear, unidirectional patterns: horizontal and diagonal sequences;
- linear, multidirectional patterns: zigzags and branches;
- non-linear patterns: cycles and spirals;
- tempos: the temporal rhythms, pace and momentum of a process.

Linear, unidirectional patterns: horizontal and diagonal sequences

Processes are most commonly equated with chronologies, creating an overriding preoccupation with sequences and the discrete events, steps or stages through which an end point is reached (known as sequence analysis; Halinen and Mainela 2013: 194). Sequences are commonly unidirectional, occurring along a historical line from start to finish. The line may be horizontal (stone age, iron age, bronze age; 1960s, 1970s, 1980s; youth, adulthood, old age). Or it may be angled to give a trajectory a particular meaning (Zerubavel 2003). For example, it may reflect an upward trajectory, the march of progress, climbing the ladder, or a rags-to-riches tale. Alternatively, it may reflect a downward trajectory, a more pessimistic or tragic pattern of decline, irreparable loss and nostalgia for bygone, happier times (Zerubavel 2003: see, for example, the pen portrait of a young father in Box 10.3, whose trajectory is described in terms of a downward spiral). Zerubavel (2003) notes that these upward or downward patterns are commonly thought to be predetermined and inevitable, as if they are shaped through some grand historical design. While such ideas may have little grounding in empirical reality, they have salience as explanatory motifs, which can be applied to events in retrospect (see Chapter 10 on the value of motifs in case analysis).

Linear, multidirectional patterns: zigzags and branches

Linear patterns, which convey a sense of serial progression, are not necessarily unidirectional; pathways may run in more than one direction. Zigzag patterns alternate between different pathways, or between upward and downward trajectories, reflecting the peaks and troughs, or high and low points in a process, or otherwise representing a change in the path. They are found, for example, at times of recovery, descent, adjustment or conversion (Zerubavel 2003). Zigzags are striking in that they embody a significant change, an upward or downward turn that is commonly seen as a turning point (Zerubavel 2003). A longer-term, retrospective account can often reveal such zigzag paths (see, for example, the use of this pattern in Laub and Sampson's (2003) study of delinquent boys in later life, detailed in Box 3.2). But these patterns may also be discernible in the shorter term, in lives marked by particularly arresting events, insecurities or volatilities, or where collective lives are synchronised with times of global instability or change (wars, recessions or pandemics). Multidirectional branching patterns may also be discernible, with a mass of paths leading in different directions, some of which peter out, while others become more established and well-trodden (Zerubavel 2003).

Non-linear patterns: cycles and spirals

As we have seen above, searching for linear sequences and patterns, whether they run in one or more directions, is a reasonable starting point for process analysis. Such an approach may have particular resonance where a process has a clearly defined purpose and/or change is being actively crafted or managed. However, a narrow focus on sequences alone would obscure the accumulations, recursions, discontinuities, irregularities, sudden accelerations, stabilisations or de-stabilisations that may also develop through time (Stich and Cippolone 2017). A preoccupation with change at the expense of continuity, for example, may leave little room to consider the oscillations between the two. Similarly, organisational process researchers commonly use the idea of 'bracketing' processes into discrete episodes or phases, which are separated by distinct markers along the way (Langley 1999; Langley et al. 2013; see the visual representation of this in Figure 11.1, linear, fixed time; and an example in Box 11.2). These phases are understood to be descriptive rather than predictive (Langley 1999; Van de Ven 2007). But, nevertheless, they may or may not fit the empirical reality. Moreover, as Abbott (2001: 192) observes, events or occurrences have duration and may overlap in their effects, undermining the idea that things have a clear conceptual order. A focus on sequences, therefore, needs to be set within a broader consideration of the non-linear, loop-like patterns that inhere in events and interactions, and which may unfold in cyclical or spiralling ways.

Cyclical patterns reflect the constant, repetitive and cumulative recursions which characterise unfolding processes. It takes only a small shift to turn a linear construction into a circular, loop-like process that embodies both past and future in the ever-shifting present (Brockmeier 2000). Linear and cyclical patterns are not incompatible (Zerubavel 2003). As shown in Chapter 2, recurring cycles are not closed or static circular loops, but have a forward momentum (much like a wheel that simultaneously turns but travels forwards along a path).

Recurring cycles of events are often tied to the seasons, or the rhythmic momentum of the life course, or the repetitive practices of organisations (e.g. cycles of production, or cycles of family renewal and celebration). Each recurring cycle moves the process on in subtle, incremental ways. Cyclical patterns may also have a fractal quality, whereby never-ending, repeating patterns occur at different scales of time and place: 'small swirls, nested within swirls, nested, in turn, within yet larger swirls', that create a 'recursive symmetry' of temporal flows (Tsoukas and Hatch 2001: 988). The nested horizons of turning points, transitions and trajectories (detailed in Chapter 3) have this never-ending recursive symmetry.

It takes only a small shift to turn cyclical patterns into **spiralling patterns** that encompass ever-widening spheres of influence and activity. These patterns are most commonly discerned as cumulative processes which build through their own momentum, with each new step triggering the next step in a domino effect (Lofland et al. 2006: 154). Spiralling patterns may encompass escalating/accelerating or de-escalating/dissipating flows of interaction and influence through time and space. Or they may be marked by alternating patterns of expansion and contraction, or divergence and convergence (Lofland et al. 2006: 153; Dooley and Van de Ven 2017). As Lofland et al. (2006) note, since these patterns may spread through opposing dialectical paths, or a chain reaction of events and influences, they do not have the degree of stability found in institutional cycles. They may have value in discerning the upward or downward fortunes of individuals (e.g. journeys to incarceration or homelessness), but they are also a common feature of organisational change, and of social movements (e.g. the Black Lives Matter movement), which may reach a tipping point at key moments to challenge oppressive forms of dominance and social control.

As Brockmeier (2000) notes, only small shifts are needed for all kinds of mutual transformations to occur between the different temporal patterns outlined above. They are not mutually exclusive and they may flow into one another. This means that it may not be possible to identify one discrete pattern in a process, particularly where it is unfolding organically across extensive horizons of time. The greater the flow of a process through time and space, the greater the likelihood that random or unpredictable threads or influences will begin to appear.

Tempos: the temporal rhythms and pace of a process

Processes exhibit a range of tempos that give a temporal rhythm or pace to unfolding events and interactions. Tempos reflect times of volatility and stability, change and continuity, and can be strongly implicated in the momentum for change.

But they are endlessly varied and not mutually exclusive. Like the patterns outlined above, they are more easily discerned in retrospect. Across the range, the following are commonly found:

- **slow/fast**: ranging from gradual to sudden; evolutionary to revolutionary;
- **erratic**: a relatively stable process punctuated by defining moments or times of erratic change (also known as punctuated equilibrium);
- **oscillating**: a process marked by alternating times of change and continuity, activity and rest, growth and decline; or where conflicting tempos (e.g. work and family life) are reconciled;
- **incremental**: cumulative actions in which each new event is triggered by the previous one, until equilibrium breaks down or a watershed moment is reached: a tipping point, catalyst or 'final straw' that may result in drastic change (Gladwell 2000; Lofland et al. 2006: 152–4). These incremental tempos are commonly associated with spiralling patterns, where small fluctuations in one time or place can lead to disproportionate effects elsewhere (also known as path dependency);
- **synchronic/a-synchronic**: where the different threads of a process are either synchronised in time, or marked by dissonance (delays or time lags) that may slow things, inhibit the momentum for change or create a rupture in a process;
- **lock-in**: a process marked by inflexibility, inertia or stagnation, where the momentum for change or innovation dissipates or collapses, or is actively suppressed (Gerrits 2008).

The complex intertwining of the different threads outlined above gives each process a unique, kaleidoscopic swirl of movement (Dawson 2003: 86). There is no common, predictable, regular or universal patterning, no fixed driving force, mechanism, trigger point or context, for events and actions are overlapping and interchangeable in their influence and effects. There may be no clearly defined hierarchy or order. How a process unfolds in practice, and what it means for those involved, depends on the complex configuration of its constituent elements, operating in particular contexts of change. As shown in Chapter 10 for case analysis, this creates more than an unfolding tale; it creates the threads of varied unfolding, overlapping, diverting and cross-cutting tales, which together create a rich dynamic tapestry. As Cilliers (1998: 114) observes, we arrive at narrative understandings that are portrayed through a plurality of smaller stories.

Process Tracing

As our opening quotations show, analysing processes means following lives where they lead, through time, space and the social fabric. This is process tracing, which, in Bergson's terms, involves 'following reality in all its windings' (Bergson 1946 [1903]: 190). Some of the rich ideas presented above are distilled here to create a clearer understanding of what process tracing entails, and to suggest the kinds of processual questions that can be posed to focus enquiry. It is worth noting at the outset that process tracing is not confined to interpretive enquiry. Mechanistic, reductive 'cogs and wheels' forms of exposition can be found across the social sciences, including those that create predictive models of contexts, causal mechanisms and outcomes (see Chapter 2, and the review in Hedström and Ylikoski 2010). The focus here, in contrast, is on qualitative process tracing. This is firmly rooted in the analysis of rich case data, and makes overriding use of narrative forms of exposition that can best convey the flux of lives.

Varied temporal dynamics can be harnessed in the task of tracing processes. They offer complementary ways of drawing out the threads of a process, how they are linked together, what the connectors are, and how they converge at pivotal moments to create the momentum for change. Three intersecting strategies are set out below, and visualised in Figure 11.1. They draw on the foundational timescapes (flows of time) that were introduced earlier in this book (see Box 1.1 and Box 3.3):

- fixed–fluid: sequential and recursive process tracing;
- prospective–retrospective: tracing back, tracing forward;
- intensive–extensive: tracing over varied horizons of time.

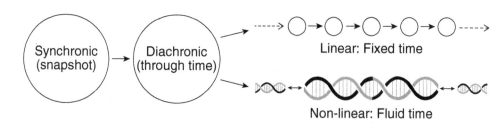

Figure 11.1 Building processual insights

Fixed–fluid: sequential and recursive process tracing

As shown above, fixed (linear, predictable) and fluid (recursive, unpredictable) processual elements are intricately interwoven, and give different insights into how processes are patterned and what they mean. Both are therefore important in the analysis of processes; both are visualised in Figure 11.1, running in parallel to each other as different ways of conceptualising diachronic (through-time) analysis.

A fixed temporal perspective compares data gathered at discrete moments in time and discerns what has changed (or remained constant) from one time point to the next. Glick and colleagues, for example, suggest that, 'examining change is analogous to time lapse photography; change processes can be inferred by researchers who look for differences across a series of snapshots taken at fixed time intervals' (Glick et al. 1995: 138). As visualised in Figure 11.1, this orthodox mode of process analysis is linear, sequential and unidirectional. It is commonly represented as a series of snapshots, or a string of beads on a necklace. It is here that the order of things emerges. The visualisation also conveys the idea that processes can be bracketed into discrete phases or episodes that are punctuated by clear events, turning points or milestones along the way.

A fluid temporal perspective, on the other hand, represents a more nuanced, recursive layer of process analysis. This takes us beyond bald comparison over time (then versus now), to focus on the complex ways in which the multiple threads of a process are linked or connected through time (Saldaña 2002: 3; 2003). These multiple temporal dynamics, with their complex, recursive flows and powerful, intertwined connections and convergences, are visualised in Figure 11.1 as a double helix. These intersecting threads of a process are by no means planned, and their influence can only be fully discerned in retrospect. There is nothing fixed about these threads and connectors: they are subjectively defined, suggesting that, whatever their broader effects, they can be discerned most easily through the particularities of their operation and impact.

A fluid perspective allows recursive understandings to be woven into the processual picture. Moving beyond changing events to consider changing perceptions of events, how past and future are revisited and revised, is vital for recursive analysis. A consideration of these subtle, more subjective and experiential processual understandings brings to the fore their idiosyncratic, oscillating, anomalous, paradoxical, inconsistent, contradictory and unpredictable nature (Saldaña 2003; Dawson 2013). It becomes possible, for example, to gauge perceptions of the optimal timing of events in an unfolding process, along with moral or pragmatic judgements about the speed at which change should occur, or how it can best be managed. And, as shown in Chapter 10 for recursive case analysis, it necessitates a continual revisiting and re-interpretation of earlier data in the light of more recent disclosures, as people rework and reveal more of their past lives.

The process of working across these fixed and fluid representations, and discerning how far they are synchronised, opens up new lines of enquiry. What was supposed to happen? What was anticipated but did not materialise? What occurred spontaneously or through chance? Did any unanticipated events occur and did they take a participant along a different path? Data from recursive interviewing (see Chapter 6) are likely to yield rich insights of this nature. Micro–macro influences are integral to this evolving picture: for example, to what extent are processes prescribed and their timing and order laid down? How far does a process unfold in conformity with social values and expectations about the right thing to do, at the right time and in the right way? How far do broader institutional influences (policy processes and interventions, for example) mesh with lived experiences, individual agency and creativity? Overall, it is worth exploring how far a process is consciously planned and crafted, and/or socially prescribed, with a clear sequence and purpose;

or, conversely, to what extent it is nebulous, ill-defined and unpredictable, with an emerging or unclear purpose, and with effects that may be residual or unanticipated (Jarzabkowski et al. 2017).

Prospective–retrospective: tracing back, tracing forward

The fixed–fluid dimensions of process tracing outlined above are complemented by and elaborated through the task of tracing events backward and forward through time. The researcher looks forward prospectively to build a picture from past to present to future. The analysis is incremental and cumulative: insights from each new wave of data are sharpened and refined in relation to the previous waves (Pettigrew 1997; Royce 2005). This is visualised in the fixed flow of time in Figure 11.1 as a series of connecting arrows that are unidirectional.

It is possible, for example, to trace forward from a recent event or a set of present circumstances, to explore the pathways that people are taking or plan to take from this point in time; and what, if any, continuities or changes are occurring along the way, and what impact they are having as they unfold (Lofland et al. 2006). Where imaginary futures have been constructed (see Chapter 6), these can provide powerful benchmarks for tracing the paths that people subsequently take. This prospective strategy is only possible through the distinctive longitudinal frame of a QL study, in which synchronic (snapshot) readings of QL data gradually coalesce into diachronic (processual, through-time) readings (detailed in Chapter 9 and represented in Figure 11.1).

At the same time, researchers can reconstruct a process retroductively, tracing backward to discern how the threads of a process have intersected and what effects may have occurred at discrete moments leading up to the present day. Tracing backward from a particular event (for example, the arrival of a pandemic, a series of riots, becoming homeless) enables a reconstruction of how past lives have led to present-day realities, and helps to identify the factors that may have shaped a pathway and led to equilibrium or change (Lofland et al. 2006). As shown in Chapter 3, such understandings may only be possible in retrospect, and they rely on an abundance of detailed retrospective data from which an unfolding process can be pieced together.

Once again, these two modes of tracing back and forward through time are complementary. By combining them, the analyst gives equal weight to past, present and future and allows for recursive, loop-like understandings between them. Part of the power of QL enquiry resides in its capacity to merge these temporal dynamics, weaving retrospective and prospective understandings into an integrated whole, and using abductive/retroductive logic to discern the constant interplay of past, present and future (Gray et al. 2013). These combined readings are visualised in Figure 11.1 through the arrows in the double helix, which run in both directions.

Intensive–extensive: tracing over varied horizons of time

As a further elaboration of process tracing, events and processes can unfold over varied horizons of time, from short-term incremental or revolutionary changes to longer-term evolutionary changes. These dynamics are likely to be most vivid over the immediate time frame of a study, where they can be discerned in some detail and as they occur. But they will also extend beyond this, into the more distant past and future. In Figure 11.1, these more extensive time horizons are visualised as distant extensions into the past and future, which run beyond the longitudinal frame of a study. Taking these extended time horizons into account gives greater scope to discern how biographical processes are intertwined with wider historical processes of change. These more extensive temporal insights can be discerned through a careful reading and re-reading of retrospective and 'futures' data. These will have been generated through life journey interviewing and participatory methods, and through sampling across generations to build historical insights (see Chapters 4 and 6). The use of legacy data can also yield valuable insights into longer-term historical processes (see Chapter 8).

Once again, there is scope to combine these analytical strategies: to bring intensive insights about events and actions, gleaned through the time frame of a study, into alignment with more extensive temporal insights to discern their historical links, connections, continuities, discontinuities and synchronicities through time. The oscillations that occur between continuity and change, for example, are likely to become more apparent over extensive time. How longer-term trajectories relate to transitions, and to turning points that occur in the moment, is also likely to become clearer.

Seeing processes through different time horizons produces a different density of understanding (Zerubavel 2003). How are processes elaborated and understood through the immediacy and intensity of the present day? Conversely, how do people telescope events, selecting and filtering them through a more extensive historical lens? When looking into the past (or future), we commonly compress events, focusing on chronological or biographical markers or anchors that we use to locate ourselves in time (e.g. before the war, after the war), while discarding much of the rest (Zerubavel 2003: 90). This process of selectively remembering may occur not just through extensive historical time, but in the way we rework our recent biographies (see examples in Box 3.4 and Box 6.11). Seeing events and processes through a combination of intensive and extensive temporal lenses can shed valuable light on their tempo, and on shifting interpretations of their meaning and significance as they recede into the distant past, or as future events or decisions begin to loom large and are suddenly upon us.

As the discussion above shows, process tracing opens up many new lines of exploration and insight. It enables insights into a range of temporal dynamics, including the constant interplay between past, present and future, between biographical and historical horizons of time; between fixed and fluid dimensions of processes, and between micro and macro scales of change. Tracing processes through one or more of these temporal dynamics creates a rich tapestry of insights about unfolding lives.

Asking Processual Questions

As suggested in Chapter 10, it can be helpful to pose a series of generic questions that provides a focus for process analysis. The suite of questions set out in Box 11.1 provides a starting point for process tracing. They are drawn from the rich ideas on processes explored above, which have been further distilled for our purposes here.

Box 11.1   Asking Processual Questions

Two suites of questions are set out here. The first are descriptive 'what' questions. With a focus on sequences and the construction of chronologies, they offer ways to measure processes: their continuity and development, scale and duration, rate of change and trend, order and tempo; and a bald measure of their overall value or impact (Monge 1995). The second are more discursive 'how' questions, designed to flesh out the descriptive questions and yield insights into the fluidity of processes and their subjective, experiential and recursive dimensions. In varied ways, these questions attempt to tease out how the threads of processes are connected and converge, along with insights into the multiple, fluid and relational dimensions of causality. The analytical questions posed by Saldaña (2002, 2003) have been incorporated into this broad schema.

Descriptive 'What' Questions

What changes through time? What continues or endures?

- What increases or cumulates? What decreases, dissipates, ceases? By how much?
- What emerges or fails to emerge? Over what scale and span of time and space?
- When do changes occur? Through what sequences, stages, episodes, tempos?
- What improves or worsens? Are there upwards or downwards trajectories?

Discursive 'How' Questions

How are processes constituted and experienced (purpose, impact, duration, scale, pattern, tempo)?

- **Lived experience (agency, subjectivity, reflexivity)**: How are processes experienced (made sense of, (re)interpreted, (re)assessed)?

- **Agency**: Is a process planned, sudden, prescribed, imposed, joyous, traumatic?
- **Antecedents**: How do past events, actions, interactions and historical circumstances feed into a process?
- **Order, pattern and tempo**: How do these threads intersect and unfold (linear, sequential, multidirectional, fluid, random, up or down, smooth, volatile, meandering, cyclical, spiralling, unpredictable, running in parallel, interconnecting)?
- **Connections**: How are the threads of a process linked or connected through time? What is the scale of these connections and to what extent are they synchronised?
- **Driving forces (connectors)**: What are the driving forces that connect the processual threads? How is a process initiated, and what carries it along? How does the momentum for change build (trigger points, turning points, epiphanies, goals, plans, micro–macro influences, nudges, incremental steps, tipping points)?
- **Continuities/restraining forces**: How is continuity sustained/equilibrium reached (delays, repairs, deflections, redirections, stability, inertia, stagnation, lock-in)?
- **Convergence**: How/when/how far do events coalesce to create a pivotal moment or tipping point for change?
- **Consequences/effects**: What outcomes are envisaged for a process (hopes and fears)? How far are they realised? What remains unfinished? What consequences arise (predictable, planned, random, unanticipated, cumulative, incremental)? How is the future understood and faced at different moments in the process?

A suite of generic questions, such as those set out in Box 11.1, can help to shed light on how processes unfold for each case in a study, and how trajectories converge or diverge within and across cases. The questions are designed to capture the emotional, value-laden elements of processual pathways, as well as the more descriptive chronological elements.

An example of how a processual analysis may be constructed is given in Box 11.2. The case data are presented in Bidart et al. (2013) and have been drawn out and reconstructed for our purposes here. The data were generated as part of a large-scale, mixed longitudinal study (the *Biographical Bifurcations* study), which explored the career pathways of a mixed cohort of young people from varied European localities. Six waves of interviews were conducted at three-yearly intervals over a 20-year period (1995 to 2015), starting from the participants' last year in high school. The segments of rich case study data presented by the researchers have been reconfigured here, and the analysis extended to illustrate how the threads of a process may be connected, and how they may converge to create the momentum for change.

Box 11.2 Process Tracing – Alban's Work Trajectory

Bidart et al. (2013) draw on rich case study data from the *Biographical Bifurcations* study to suggest a framework for processual analysis. Their focus is on sequences, driving forces and turning points as the key contextual elements of an unfolding process. The overall aim of the study is to move beyond linear understandings of the life course to explore the bifurcations that may occur in young people's career trajectories. The case study extracts presented by these researchers are reconstructed here in a more connected narrative and summative form. The reconstruction illustrates how a processual analysis may be developed, and further draws out the constellation of causal threads that may coalesce to shape the course of a life.

The case study concerns the career path of Alban, a young man from Caen in Normandy in France. We learn that Alban has Portuguese roots. He grew up in an immigrant family with few resources, an alcoholic father, and family transitions marked by a difficult divorce between his parents. Although Alban had aspired during his childhood to be a dentist, his experiences while growing up helped to shape a strong aspiration to find employment upon leaving school, in order to gain some financial security and status as a high earner. He moves to Paris, where the labour market is more buoyant, to take up training in sales and marketing.

Several years later, Alban makes a number of changes in his life that reconfigure his career path and his work and family priorities and values. By 2007 his life is on a completely different track from where it had been in 1995, at the start of the research. The intersecting threads that make up this trajectory, and that precipitate these changes, are set out below:

- **Pivotal moment**: Leaving school, a major life transition, gives Alban the opportunity to move to Paris to take up training in sales and marketing for a national retail company. This seems to be a fresh start, where Alban forges his own life beyond his family.
- **Driving force**: A money-oriented disposition, a desire to accrue status as a high earner, seen as compensation for a lack of resources and financial and emotional stability in his upbringing.
- **A 'slow burn' process**: Gradual disillusionment and weariness with his chosen employment, and with big city life, set in over several years, sharpened by the contrast with his sister, who has a professional career. She is Alban's inspiration, the benchmark by which he gauges his own development.
- **Trigger point**: The death of his father and reconfigured family relationships.
- **Pivotal moment/turning point**: These circumstances coalesce to create an opportunity for Alban to take up a new retail job in Caen, where he can return to a reconfigured family, support his mother and seek to revitalise his career. A lack of commitment to his girlfriend in Paris enables him to prioritise this move; he has little to lose by moving away from the city.

Returning to live with his mother, who is very welcoming and encourages him in his ambitions, makes this change possible and brings him closer to her: 'I want to help her make up some of the lost time'.

- **Meso-macro constraints**: Alban finds that the new job in Caen is no more fulfilling than the one in Paris; opportunities to pursue his career in marketing prove to be limited in this local labour market, despite his years of skill and experience.
- **Trigger point**: A change in an inner biographical disposition: Alban revisits and revives his childhood aspiration to become a dentist. He is now inspired by a desire to do something valuable for others (rather than simply earn money); to prove his worth as the son of an immigrant; and to meet expectations in French society about what counts as a good profession: 'it is the best job in the world. Someone who saves you from pain, he's like a god'. Building on his employment track record, he also has a newfound confidence in his ability to develop his skills and support himself financially.
- **Pivotal moment/turning point**: Alban enrols on a dentistry course at a pivotal point where a range of circumstances and influences converge to make this possible: lack of fulfilment in his current work; the resurrection of a long-held dream to work as a dentist; the offer of a place at a local dentistry school; the funds he has accrued to enable him to finance his studies; low living costs while living with his mother (enabling his survival as a student); and his shifting orientation away from material wealth and towards job satisfaction as the driver for success.

In terms of the overall contour of Alban's work trajectory, Bidart et al. (2013) usefully discern a career sequence bracketed into three phases: a phase of retail development in Paris; a transitional phase of disillusion with his current job, which, combined with the death of his father and lack of meaningful relationships in Paris, presents a rationale for moving back to Caen; and a third phase of reviving and pursuing an aspiration to train as a dentist, in which work becomes a matter of personal and social fulfilment.

Running alongside this sequential framework, Alban's trajectory can also be understood in a fluid, non-linear way, with unforeseen developments and a recursive revisiting and reworking of past aspirations. There are elements of loop-like circularity here, of a journey come full circle: Alban reclaims the past in his return to his childhood locality, his reconfigured family of origin and the resurrection of a childhood dream. There are also elements of a spiralling effect in terms of the development and unravelling of Alban's employment in the retail trade. Work, family, relationship and housing/home trajectories are clearly important, creating multiple, fluid and relational causal threads that impact on Alban's unfolding biography. At pivotal moments, influences across the micro–macro plane (from personal aspirations and dreams, to micro family and relationship connections, ruptures and sensibilities, to macro institutional opportunities, pressures and constraints) converge to create the momentum for change.

As noted above and in Chapters 2 and 3, the task of effectively identifying the interwoven threads of a process, let alone discerning how they are linked to create change or reach equilibrium, is intellectually challenging. That these elements are continually evolving and flowing into each other complicates the picture further (Bidart et al. 2013). Nevertheless, some degree of teasing out these different threads, their connections and the forces that connect them, is part and parcel of process analysis. Multiple iterations are likely to be needed to gain a plausible picture, with each iteration building a new layer of insight. This is the abductive logic of analysis, which is at once slow, careful and painstaking, but also exploratory, creative and intuitive. As shown in Chapter 2, where it is possible to identify the driving forces and trigger points for change, and/or the pivotal moments where the threads of a process coalesce, this can greatly enhance the bigger picture. The aim, overall, is to develop a plausible and comprehensible narrative in which the varied threads of an unfolding tale can be interwoven. It will be apparent by now that qualitative process tracing relies on an abundance of rich, dynamic empirical case data, of the sort generated in real-time through QL field techniques. Our discussion has come full circle, back to the interlocking nature of case, thematic and processual readings of a dataset, which is the hallmark of QLA.

Synthesis

In the concluding part of this chapter, we return to a broad overview of QLA. We consider how the varied elements of case, thematic and process analysis set out here and in Chapter 10 can be brought together to ensure an effective synthesis of empirical, theoretical and processual insights. The work of synthesis will have begun in the early stages of analysis, but will reach fruition following the completion of fieldwork, where researchers are able to engage in a full-scale, integrative (case study, cross-case and through-time) analysis of the whole dataset. Sometime during this process, the conceptual leap from a largely descriptive to an interpretive level of insight is likely to occur (see Chapter 9). This sometimes results in a creative 'aha' or eureka moment, where varied disparate ideas and patterns, painstakingly and intuitively worked and re-worked by the researcher, begin to coalesce into a picture that tells us something new (Gruber 1981; Jarzabkowski et al. 2017).

Analytical files are compared and synthesised to discern similarities and differences within and across cases, across temporal themes, through the time frame of the study and further back and forward in time as appropriate. The analytical gaze oscillates between single and multiple cases, micro and macro historical processes, past and future, and short- and long-term time horizons. It also oscillates between fixed and fluid temporal understandings, and between transitions, trajectories and the fleeting trigger points, drivers and inhibitors of change. Plausible accounts of dynamic processes may have already begun to coalesce from a dataset that is rich in descriptive detail and explanatory insights. But here the process is sharpened through a systematic examination of the whole corpus of data, seen in relation to pre-existing theories and insights. The process culminates in the construction of narratives, typologies and visual representations that help to crystallise emerging insights (Ritchie and Lewis 2003: 244–8).

At this point, two further considerations need to be borne in mind in our over-view of QLA. First, the discussion here and in Chapter 10 suggests a prototype for a QLA tool kit, comprising a suite of case-led, thematic and processual tools and tech-niques (see Boxes 10.2 and 10.8; and 11.1 to 11.3). As suggested in Chapter 10, these tools and techniques will need to be used selectively, ensuring that effort is not duplicated or resources overloaded with the task of re-ordering data into many dif-ferent configurations. However, some combination of case, thematic and processual readings of a dataset is essential for QLA, despite the greater analytical burden that this entails. Moreover, whatever the balance of case and thematic readings, proces-sual tools and techniques are vital, particularly in a context where they are currently poorly specified and too easily overlooked.

Second, the strategies that are chosen to work across cases, themes and processes, and, thereafter, to shape the presentation of findings, need to be tailored to the nature of the project and its intended audiences. Researchers will need to take into account the epistemological groundings of a study, the research questions that drive it, and the design and sampling decisions that shape it, not least the priority accorded to breadth or depth of investigation (see Chapter 4). For example, research-ers working with very small samples, or with emblematic cases drawn from a larger sample, may prioritise the analysis of rich, processual case data, and work more selectively or broadly with key themes (a depth-to-breadth approach). Findings are more likely to be structured around detailed case studies, within which processual and thematic insights are embedded (see, for example, Pollard with Filer 1996; Neale and Flowerdew 2007; Thomson 2009, 2010a; Warin 2010; Compton-Lilly 2017, and the recent work of Longitudinal IPA researchers, reviewed in Box 10.5).

Alternatively, when working across larger samples or with a greater focus on micro–macro understandings, researchers may structure analysis around key tempo-ral themes or trajectories across the sample, and work selectively with rich processual and case materials to flesh out the picture (a breadth-to-depth approach, commonly used with framework). Findings are more likely to be structured around a particular trajectory, or the intersection between related trajectories, within which rich proces-sual and case study evidence is embedded (see, for example, Smith 2003; Henderson et al. 2007; Lewis 2007; Neale and Davies 2016).

These different approaches are not mutually exclusive and may be adopted by the same researchers at different times and for different purposes. This is as much about tailoring evidence to present it in the best possible way, as it is about analytical differences. Both approaches have distinctive value and are equally grounded in a commitment to processual understandings and explanatory depth. Given the flexibility of QLA, there is no one right approach. The critical factor in developing an analytical strategy is not the starting point or the sequence in which the different readings of a dataset occur: it is the capacity for multiple iterations between them (what, in another context, Tarrant and Hughes (2019) call a nuanced depth-to-breadth-to-depth approach). In sum, there are many ways of achieving an effective synthesis of case, thematic and processual insights.

Narrating and Visualising Temporal Processes

We conclude our analytical journey by considering the culminating act of analysis: how temporal processes are narrated and visually conjured and conveyed to the varied audiences for a study. Our starting point is the recognition that writing and reporting findings is an analytical task, the final stage in the analytical journey. Narrating is fundamentally an interpretive act (Tsoukas and Hatch 2001: 997), part of the abductive logic of discovery. It is through the process of narrating and visually representing processes that interpretations are crystallised: 'writing no longer merely captures reality, it helps to construct it' (Plummer 2001: 171). For Wolcott, writing is thinking (cited in Ritchie et al. 2014: 374). This reinforces the value of writing as a daily, ongoing task and a skill that can be honed and refined as a study progresses (Wright Mills 1959). Indeed, for QL research, some form of interim writing, tied to each wave or to a midpoint in a study, can be a valuable mechanism for developing insights, as well as for interim sharing with others and for seeking feedback (Ritchie et al. 2014: 64; and see Chapter 12). Ongoing writing also ensures that researchers do not become so bound up in the research process that they lose track of the end point of a study.

In qualitative enquiry, creative ways of representing an unfolding tale have expanded in recent years, to include 'split page writings, theatre, poetry, photography, music, collage, drawing, sculpture, quilting, stained glass and dance' (Creswell, cited in Ritchie et al. 2014: 369; see also Plummer 2001, who elaborates on this list). This trend is evident across the disciplines. Anthropologists such as Anya Royce, for example, cross the divide between the practical and the poetic in their presentation of findings, preferring this to the more static and 'antiseptic' forms of presentation that characterised earlier scholarship:

> Why ... is so much anthropological writing so antiseptic, so devoid of anything that brings people to life? There they are, pinned like butterflies in a glass case, with the difference, however, that we often cannot tell what color these specimens are; and we are never shown them in flight, never see them soar or die except in generalities. (Read, cited in Royce 2002: 12)

We find ourselves in a more imaginative realm for grasping and conveying the dynamics of lived experiences. Saldaña (2003: 38), for example, uses ethno-drama alongside narrative reporting to convey his findings, while poetic forms of representation and analysis are powerful ways to distil experiences, to convey changing identities and to understand the social world 'from the inside' (Bergson 1946 [1903]; see, for example, Murray et al. 2009; Edwards and Weller 2012; and for poetics as an analytical tradition, see Freeman 2017).

Styles of reporting vary across disciplines and in different institutional and cultural settings, ranging from the somewhat discursive, reflexive styles commonly found in oral and life history research, anthropology and narrative enquiry, to more formal modes of academic presentation found in much social science writing, particularly in the UK. Beyond this, reporting styles are commonly tailored to different audiences. The formal styles of journal articles aimed at academic audiences, for example, differ markedly from the creative findings produced for policy and practice audiences, or developed for, or in collaboration with, participants (see, for example, the animated film produced for Patrick's study of welfare reform: Land and Patrick 2014, showcased in Box 5.13; and the glossy policy briefing papers produced for the Timescapes and *Following Young Fathers* studies: www.timescapes.leeds.ac.uk; www.followingfathers.leeds.ac.uk).

These creative outputs are likely to convey their messages more succinctly, and in visually arresting and accessible ways. But they are also a reminder of how ethical considerations, notably the principle of shared authority, can shape the production of findings and evidence (detailed in Chapter 5; see Boxes 5.10 and 5.13). For example, in two linked QL studies of post-divorce childhoods, an anthology of the young people's reflections and drawings was produced in collaboration with the participants and a children's charity. A sequel was produced following the second phase of funding (Neale and Wade 2000; Neale and Flowerdew 2004). Copies were provided for each young person and the publications were widely used to support the work of court welfare officers. Where the voices of the participants take centre stage, and researchers take on the role of editors and producers, this can increase the participatory and, potentially, the emancipatory potential of a QL project, along with its real-world impact. Such writings are often produced in parallel with academic outputs, but the two can be effectively combined. Jay MacLeod (2009) provides an excellent example in his third and final book from his 25-year QL study. He used a powerful autobiographical style of reporting, telling his participants' tales in their own words, before appending a final sociological reading to their accounts (this study is showcased in Box 4.3).

Whatever the style of reporting, dynamic processes are most commonly conveyed through narrative forms of presentation. These are ideally suited to process tracing. As shown in Chapters 2 and 10, unfolding narratives, with their rich metaphors and motifs, are the ideal means, perhaps the only means, of tracing the complexities, nuances and paradoxes of fluid processes. They can offer compelling accounts of continuity and change, past and future, hindsight and foresight (Van de Ven and Huber 1995; Tsoukas and Hatch 2001; Langley et al. 2013; Plummer 2019).

This is particularly so where researchers draw out and showcase their striking, emblematic cases, 'the cases that shine' (Flyvbjerg 2007). The narratives produced for case histories (see Chapter 10) can form the basis for producing case study evidence in research reports and drawing out typologies of different trajectories. By their very nature, narratives convey a sense of 'plot' that has causal connections and addresses important how and why questions (Langley 1999; Plummer 2001; Bidart et al. 2013; Langley et al. 2013: 9). They also reveal ambiguities rather than tidying them away, enabling us to tell an evolving story that, by its very nature, is in a state of becoming and open to fresh interpretations.

Process Mapping

While narratives are likely to form the bedrock of reported findings, it is increasingly common for QL researchers to enhance their processual narratives with complementary visual maps (drawings, diagrams, flow charts and graphs; Langley 1999). Such maps can be created not only in the field, as part of data generation, but also as analytical tools to aid interpretation. In some forms of processual research (conducted, for example, by critical realists, and in fields such as system dynamics, network analysis and process organisational research), such visualisations are standard analytical tools.

It is worth noting that processual maps do not present an unmediated view of empirical data. Their designs shape and filter what we see and do not see (Halford and Savage 2017). They can be used to focus on particular insights, filter out uninteresting data, select a particular trajectory and convey how its varied threads intersect. Halford and Savage (2017) also suggest that they create a kind of optical consistency that can hold diverse data sources together. A series of maps, for example, can provide the means to aggregate diverse data and enable qualitative generalisations to be made.

Process mapping tools take a variety of forms. Graphs are commonly used for mapping peaks, troughs and directions of travel for a trajectory, and for presenting a visual comparison of trajectories across a sample. In a life history study of the political careers of military veterans, for example, Söderström (2019) used life maps as a participatory method for generating data. These depicted the shape and curve of the men's trajectories of political engagement, including key points of transition, and tracks of stability, change, troughs and peaks. She then used these images to develop a typology of the varied political life paths followed by her participants, which were displayed in a series of graphs.

'Box and arrows' network maps, or flow charts, are equally popular. A series of labelled boxes or circles, representing events or stage posts in a journey, are connected through a network of branching and bifurcating arrows, straight, curved or wavy lines, and feedback loops. These connectors may or may not be labelled, but will nevertheless give a sense of a multiplicity of connections and the direction of travel (Langley 1999; Langley et al. 2013: 8; Feldman 2017). In some designs, boxes are dispensed with in order to give greater prominence to the linked connections and pathways themselves (Feldman 2017; for varied examples, see Huber and Van de Ven 1995; and the collection of articles in Langley et al. 2013).

Process mapping clearly has some value in distilling complex processes and clarifying conceptual insights and relationships. Visualisations are more than just a means of reporting and displaying findings. They may enable an argument to be clearly summarised in a more accessible manner than complex tables or dense narratives. As shown in the context of participatory life maps (Chapter 6), they are good tools to think with, an opportunity to make data intelligible, to interrogate data differently, to see things in a new way, as well as to visualise and discern new things (Halford and Savage 2017). As part of the abductive method explored by Gruber (1981), visualisations are not merely illustrative, for they help to shape the nature of interpretations, and may capture ideas in ways that are not possible to grasp in any other way.

Even so, the construction of processual maps and models can present researchers with challenges. The abstract and rather mechanical nature of some mapping techniques can obscure rather than illuminate, particularly where the maps are not tied closely enough to explanatory narratives, and/or lack descriptive detail and labelling. At the same time, attempts to faithfully capture a many stranded process in one condensed visual image can result in diagrams that are far too busy and complex, and equally opaque. Either way, trying to aggregate or reduce data into one tidy processual map, which is intended to convey something typical or archetypal about a process, may obscure or iron out the very complexities, particularities and idiosyncrasies that a QL study aims to illuminate. A series of maps is likely to be needed to represent a typology of different trajectories, or to illustrate the temporal dynamics of individual pathways. Overall, researchers may struggle 'to creatively but accurately project the dynamics of living processes onto the static two dimensional page' (Langley et al. 2013: 8).

However, there are more qualitative (intuitive, grounded) ways of mapping processes. Process mapping tools will, ideally, have been built into the generation of QL data in the field, most usually in the form of participatory life maps, drawings, or pictorial or photographic diaries that convey subjective, fluid journeys (see Chapter 6, Figures 6.2 and 6.3 for examples). These are ideal ways of conveying fluid processes. A suite of life maps, or images from a photographic diary, for example, may be integrated into a final narrative to vividly illuminate unfolding pathways, both within and across cases. More generally, there is undoubtedly some merit in ensuring that process mapping remains qualitatively driven, empirically grounded, and that it seeks to convey no more than a relatively simple, easily grasped set of ideas that can be explained in an accompanying narrative (see Box 11.3 for an example).

Box 11.3 Process Mapping

Mishler (1995) carried out a narrative analysis of the work histories of craft workers in order to understand how they arrived at their art-and-craft identities. This was a retrospective life history (rather than QL) study, but Mishler used the mode of case analysis outlined in Chapter 10 (Box 10.1) to create a series of chronological narratives and narrative summaries about the life journeys of his participants. The processual map below conveys, in a simple format, the career history of a crafts-man furniture maker. Running from the top to the bottom of the map is a chronology

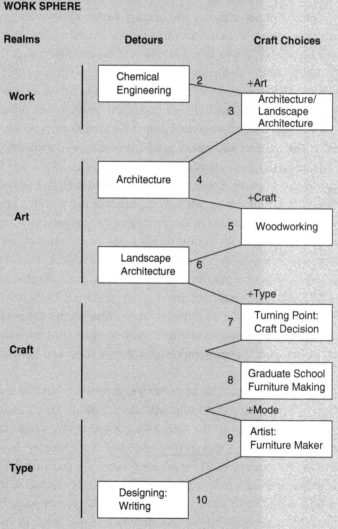

WORK SPHERE

Figure 11.2 An example of process mapping in the work sphere

Source: Reproduced from Mishler 1995: 97

of the nine different jobs held by this craftsman over the course of his career, and a tenth which is a future aspiration. The tempo shows a steady, incremental, cumulative pathway of increasing refinement and specialisation, represented on the map by varied interwoven realms of activity (work, art, craft and craft type), along with a turning point that marks a transition into the realm of specialist craft work. The overall visualisation also shows a fluid, oscillating journey that zigzags between two intertwining pathways: the participant's central craft choices and activities, and the detours (alternative side paths) that also make up his career path. The map nicely supports Mishler's observation that an emerging career and work identity 'is not a linear, continuous, developmental process, but proceeds through a series of shifts that may or may not be progressive' (1995: 96).

Closing Reflections

The practice of qualitative longitudinal analysis has been explored in some detail in this chapter and in Chapter 10. A number of case, thematic and processual tools and techniques have been introduced, which are designed to generate temporal insights. The focus here has been on how case and thematic analysis can be supported and sharpened through a concerted focus on qualitative process tracing and mapping, using a series of processual questions and techniques to aid the task. The discussion here and in Chapter 10 reveals some of the challenges involved in teasing out the varied facets of QLA, and then synthesising them to strike a balance between case depth, thematic breadth and temporal reach.

Achieving this balance is complicated by the fact that temporal reach is not a simple linear construct. It entails an understanding of a complex constellation of processual threads that create and sustain the momentum for change. Getting to grips with process analysis can be helped by focusing on how processes are ordered, how the threads of a process are connected, and how they may converge at key moments in time. Beyond this, it is possible to discern the fluid, multiple and relational dimensions of causal processes, and to uncover the processual patterns and tempos that shape how lives unfold. The oscillations between prospective–retrospective and intensive–extensive temporal horizons can yield many insights, along with an exploration of how the fixed (linear, sequential) and fluid (non-linear, recursive) elements of a process intersect.

QLA culminates in the task of narrating and visualising processes. The pros and cons of process mapping have been considered here, including ways to empirically ground mapping tools and tie them more closely to their accompanying narratives. These tasks are bound up with important representational and ethical considerations, which impact on how findings are conveyed to different audiences.

In a context where there are no rigid procedures or prescriptions for QLA, a prototype for a QLA tool kit has been outlined here, which encompasses the case-thematic-processual logic of QL enquiry (see Boxes 10.2 and 10.8, and, above, Boxes 11.1–11.3). The need to be selective in the use of these tools and techniques has been stressed, ensuring that effort is not duplicated and researchers not overloaded with the task of re-ordering data into many different configurations. The critical factor is not the precise tools and techniques that are adopted, but their capacity to draw case, thematic and processual readings into a common framework. However, the development of processual tools and techniques is a priority, ensuring that these crucial dimensions of QLA are not overlooked.

Overall, QLA is a labour-intensive and intellectually demanding process that requires a continual shift in the analytical gaze (Thomson and Holland 2003). As Dawson (2003) suggests in our opening quotation, researchers may well question their sanity when confronted with these challenges. But, having robust strategies, tools and techniques in place for mapping, condensing, and reading across data can help greatly. Gaining insights into the temporal dynamics of unfolding lives is also exhilarating (Philip 2017). Building case, thematic and processual insights into an integrated picture, and discerning how myriad pathways unfold through and beyond the waves of a QL study, takes the researcher into realms of lived experience that are invariably unexpected and arresting. Whatever the challenges, it is an intensely rewarding process.

Further Reading

Overviews that straddle the varied approaches to QLA outlined in these chapters are relatively rare, but important contributions that engage with time and processes can be found in Saldaña (2002, 2003) and Dawson (2003). For a wealth of ideas on qualitative process tracing, Pettigrew (1997), Lofland et al. (2006), Langley et al. (2013), Bidart et al. (2013) and Bidart (2019) are particularly recommended, while Mishler (1995) and Halford and Savage (2017) are good starting points for process mapping. Finally, for those wishing to delve into the patterns and tempos of a treasure trove of autobiographical and historical processes, Brockmeier (2000) and Zerubavel (2003) make for engaging reading.

Bidart, C. (2019) 'How plans change: Anticipation, interference and unpredictabilities', *Advances in Life Course Research*, 41 (September).

Bidart, C., Longo, M. and Mendez, A. (2013) 'Time and process: An operational framework for processual analysis', *European Sociological Review*, 29 (4): 743–51.

Brockmeier, J. (2000) 'Autobiographical time', *Narrative Inquiry*, 10 (1): 51–73.

Dawson, P. (2003) *Reshaping Change: A Processual Perspective*. London: Routledge.

Halford, S. and Savage, M. (2017) 'Speaking sociologically with big data: Symphonic social science and the future for big data research', *Sociology*, 51 (6): 1132–48.

Langley, A., Smallman, C., Tsoukas, H. and Van de Ven, A. (2013) 'Process studies of change in organisation and management: Unveiling temporality, activity and flow', *Academy of Management Journal*, 56 (1): 1–13. Special issue on process studies.

Lofland, J., Snow, D., Anderson, L. and Lofland, L. (2006) *Analysing Social Settings: A Guide to Qualitative Observations and Analysis*, 4th edition. Belmont, CA: Wadsworth.

Mishler, E. (1995) 'Models of narrative analysis: A typology', *Journal of Narrative and Life History*, 5 (2): 87–123.

Pettigrew, A. (1997) 'What is a processual analysis?', *Scandinavian Journal of Management*, 13 (4): 337–48.

Saldaña, J. (2002) 'Analysing change in longitudinal qualitative data', *Youth Theatre Journal*, 16 (1): 1–17.

Saldaña, J. (2003) *Longitudinal Qualitative Research: Analyzing Change through Time.* Walnut Creek, CA: AltaMira Press.

Zerubavel, E. (2003) *Time Maps: Collective Memory and the Social Shape of the Past.* Chicago: University of Chicago Press.

PART 4
CONCLUSION

12

LOOKING BACK, LOOKING FORWARD: THE VALUE OF QUALITATIVE LONGITUDINAL RESEARCH

- **Strengths and challenges**: This final chapter weighs the strengths and challenges of QL methodology. Working with time is never straightforward; it creates a range of challenges in the research process, from design and sampling, through to data generation and analysis. It requires new thinking about the logistics of sustained research, of longitudinal ethics, the status and management of data, the interface between temporal theory and method; and the challenges of working recursively through the shifting horizons of past, present and future. It requires an abundance of time, resourcefulness, sound organisation, commitment, stamina, good luck and a dogged faith in the value of the journey and its eventual destination. However, the benefits of working with and through time are beyond doubt. The flexibility to follow lives where they lead, to uncover changing practices and perceptions, to address and to respond to new issues as they arise, and to shape methods accordingly, gives QL research unique value as an intellectual craft.
- **Value and integrity**: The value of QL research and the status of its interpretations and findings are crucial yet neglected issues. Precise positivist criteria (validity, reliability, generalisability) have little purchase in

(Continued)

this context; a more flexible, value-laden language is needed to convey the quality of QL enquiry. The integrity of QL methodology resides in the conceptual alignment between case depth, thematic breadth and temporal reach. This requires fidelity to a fluid ontology and epistemology, and to an interpretive framework of understanding, through which fluid processes can best be accessed. QL accounts have verisimilitude (trustworthiness, moral truthfulness), not because they are based on bald facts or definitive evidence, but because they are in tune with, mirror and faithfully portray a world that is in flux, where understandings are inevitably partial, plural and unfinished. A range of strategies for enhancing the quality of QL research are outlined here, including the use of iteration to build a mosaic of insights.

- **Longitudinal impact studies**: QL methodology is commonly employed in policy contexts where individuals or groups are required or encouraged to change their behaviour, or adapt to changing conditions. It has significant potential as a design, navigational and participatory tool that runs alongside and evaluates new initiatives, in collaboration with policy and practice partners, and with participants themselves. This capacity enhances the value of QL enquiry. Examples of such research are showcased in Box 12.2, demonstrating the potential to create real-world impacts as an integral part of a study.
- **Future directions**: Suggestions are made for taking QL research forward and, in keeping with the interdisciplinary focus of this book, for exploring the interface with other research traditions. These straddle methodological, substantive and theoretical developments. A plea is also made for looking back as well as forward, to re-search and re-discover important historical ideas and insights that we may have lost sight of.

Introduction

Methodology [is] work in progress rather than an abstract and ossified set of technical prescriptions. (Dey 2007: 92)

[T]o be convinced of the veracity of an interpretation ... [we need] fidelity to the phenomenon ... the living, loving, suffering, dying human being. ... The most believable interpretation of data about human beings ... follows as closely as possible all the twists and turns of what it means to be human – a meaning which is neither absolute or enduring. (Andrews 2008: 92)

We hold out this hope ... That we do whatever we do with passion and a belief that our scholarship can make a difference, that is, move people to action. (Holstein and Minkler 2007: 26)

This book has explored the contours of qualitative longitudinal research, from its theoretical underpinnings to the intricacies of research design and practice.

The broad aim has been to illustrate how QL research has developed across a range of disciplines and research traditions, in the process exploring the multi-faceted nature of this methodology and the many creative ways in which it may be utilised. In this final chapter, key themes are drawn together to consider the strengths and challenges of QL methodology, its status and value as a source of knowledge and insight, and its rich potential to create impact as an integral part of the research process. Finally, we explore its potential for future growth and development, bearing in mind Dey's observation (above) that qualitative methodology is a work in progress, a craft that may be fashioned anew in a rich variety of ways.

Two particular issues are highlighted in this chapter. The first concerns the quality and veracity of a method of enquiry that has no temporal fixity, where there is no analytical closure and where findings are built on shifting sands. Andrew's insights (above) provide an excellent starting point for this discussion. The second issue concerns what kind of societal impact can be made, and to what extent this methodology might be used to address pressing issues for policy and professional practice when, by its very nature, it takes time to unfold. As our third opening quotation shows, this is part of a value-laden approach to social research, a passionate and compassionate form of scholarship that seeks to make a difference in the world. In addressing these issues, this chapter makes the case for the utility and value of a unique and powerful form of social enquiry.

The Power of QL Research

QL research has many compelling attractions, not least its capacity to discern change 'in the making' (Wright Mills 1959). It can shed light on the human factors that shape lives, the varied ways in which transitions and trajectories unfold, and how and why these pathways converge or diverge across a panel of participants. QL enquiry has significant explanatory power. It can uncover the subjective causes and consequences of dynamic processes: the stability or inertia of continued states, the triggers and mechanisms of change, and the creativity, resilience and/or fragility of individuals and groups in shaping or accommodating to these processes. With its recursive power, QL enquiry captures how individuals overwrite their biographies, continually adjusting the narratives of their lives to their evolving experiences. In the process, the messy, complex, subtly shifting facets of human experience are brought to light (Farrall et al. 2014). QL researchers are able to:

- intensively 'walk alongside' people, in 'real' time, as their lives unfold;
- extensively follow people over decades, to discern longer-term trajectories;
- explore the journey along the way, as well as the destination reached;
- weave back and forth through time to gain a more processual understanding;

- uncover the inner logic of lives, and the dynamics of human agency and subjectivity;
- investigate the driving forces and trigger points for change;
- capture the fluidity, multiplicity and relationality of causal processes;
- discern the place of lived experience within a broader landscape of socio-historical and/or structural transformations;
- build qualitative generalisations through a mosaic of socio-historical evidence;
- mirror real-world processes;
- flexibly trace, navigate and evaluate policy developments and interventions;
- create 'real-world' impacts as an integral part of a study.

We have seen that the longitudinal label can be applied to any form of qualitative enquiry, creating a rich mosaic or patchwork of studies that, together, make up the QL canon. These fields have their own subtle methodological inflections and favoured labels. Yet they share a common purpose and core approach: a commitment to a dynamic, real-time tracing of lives, using a processual logic of enquiry that is grounded in the interpretivist tradition. The qualitative and longitudinal dimensions of QL enquiry are entwined and captured in the notion of 'walking alongside' people, creating an intimate 'movie' of their unfolding lives, and discerning something of the life as lived and experienced, as well as the life as told. Its application across a variety of qualitative research traditions and settings illuminates its versatility: it is an intellectual craft founded on creative skills, innovation, flexibility, sensibility, an open knowledge base and fine judgement on the part of the researcher. This is cutting-edge research that offers creative ways to grasp the dynamics of social processes in a fast-moving world. It transforms our monochrome visions of the social world into vivid shades of colour and contrast (Ridge 2015).

Weighing the Strengths and Challenges

While the longitudinal frame of a QL study is a vital resource that offers many benefits and opportunities, it also brings challenges to the research process (Pollard 2007). Working with time is never straightforward, for it is a slippery and pervasive entity that can evade the precision of interrogation and defy neat, tidy, definitive categorisation and explanation. We have seen that QL researchers face challenges in building time into research design and sampling, and in maintaining a processual focus in the analysis and interpretation of data (see Chapters 4, 9 and 10). Moreover, the vantage point from which researchers and participants look back and forward continually shifts: future time at the start of a study will have become past time by the conclusion (Krings et al. 2013). Working recursively through time and engaging with multiple, shifting horizons of time compounds these complications. This continual switching of the temporal gaze places intellectual demands on researchers.

Added to this, the time frame and tempo of a QL study may not match the momentum of a participant's life, while the temporal window that a QL study affords may be a relatively modest one. Caveats are therefore needed about the limited longitudinal reach of a QL study and how much it can reveal about longer-term trajectories, or more extensive processes of historical change (Corden and Nice 2007).

The cyclical nature of the research process (visualised in Chapter 7, Figure 7.1 and Chapter 9, Figure 9.1) creates more tangible, logistical hurdles. Gaining consent, recruiting samples, generating, organising and analysing data are not one-off tasks but recur repeatedly through the waves of fieldwork. The process is intricate and the workload substantial and relentless. The cumulative nature of QL enquiry, with its forward momentum, complicates the process further. As shown in Chapter 5, maintaining a longitudinal panel is vital, yet longitudinal ethics involves long-term ethical vigilance, and a commitment to sustaining relationships with panel members that may last for years. In addition, there are the pressures of seeking ongoing funding to maintain a study and its core researchers (Pollard 2007). The repeated visits to the field make QL research an expensive option in comparison to single-visit qualitative studies, although, to put this in perspective, the costs of QL designs, even for medium-scale qualitative panel studies, are modest in comparison to the costs of large-scale longitudinal and cohort studies (Pearson 2016).

Added to these challenges, the task of managing a complex QL dataset that accumulates through time can be overwhelming, as each new generation of researchers discovers (Foster et al. 1979; Saldaña 2003). The contemporary issue of 'data deluge' is commonly documented, but for QL researchers the issues are magnified: there is the ever present danger of 'death by data asphyxiation' (Pettigrew 1995: 111). As shown in Chapter 7, a rigorous approach to data management is all the more important in this context.

Furthermore, trying to maintain a robust study that is clearly specified and well-structured, with identifiable goals and guiding research questions, can be a challenge where key elements of the process may lose their clarity or be subject to revisions along the way. A study may unravel and become unfocused if researchers lose sight of their key goals and the drivers for their research. In policy-related studies, for example, funders searching for solutions in rapidly developing policy areas may drive the introduction of new themes and the abandonment of old ones (Corden and Nice 2007). This can create instability in the whole process. At the same time, such flexibility is part of the rigour of a process that seeks to mirror fluid, real-world processes. Overcoming these hurdles requires a strategic balance between flexibility and continuity, and between creativity and precision in how a project is designed and executed. The time and resources necessary to meet the varied challenges outlined above need to be realistically appraised and built proactively into project planning and management. In short, QL researchers need an abundance of time, resourcefulness, sound organisation, commitment, stamina, good luck and a dogged faith in the value of the journey and its eventual destination.

Whatever the hurdles, however, the benefits of working prospectively through time are beyond doubt. QL researchers are driven by an abiding concern for the changing fortunes of their participants, and a deep curiosity about how their lives are unfolding (Colson 1984; Weis 2004; Warin 2010; Compton-Lilly 2017). As shown above, the flexibility to follow lives qualitatively wherever they lead, to discern the tenor of lived experiences, to uncover changing practices, perceptions and fortunes through the stream of time, to address new issues and themes as they arise, and to hone and shape methods of working and responses in line with changing realities, gives QL research unique value as an intellectual craft.

And Then What?

In his reflections about dynamic policy making, Ellwood (1998: 54) observes that 'when you think dynamically you must confront the "and then what?" question'. This broad question lends itself to many interpretations and responses, but it prompts us to consider the destination of a QL study and its impact: in particular, its status and value as a form of evidence and knowledge and its capacity to make a difference in the real world. More broadly, it invites consideration of the potential of QL studies to evolve and grow through new developments and innovative applications. These important areas of methodological debate and development have been touched on in various places in this book, but are given more focused attention below.

The Value and Integrity of Qualitative Longitudinal Research

Perhaps the overriding issue raised by Ellwood's 'and then what?' question concerns the value and integrity of QL enquiry, and the status of its interpretations and findings. These crucial issues need to be addressed in all forms of qualitative research (Flick 2018), but they have yet to be given focused attention by QL researchers (Calman et al. 2013). Part of the issue concerns the lack of analytical closure in a mode of research that has no temporal fixity, where findings are inherently provisional and where not only do participant perceptions and external circumstances change over time, but researchers themselves also change over time, both professionally and personally (Colson 1984; Andrews 2008; Neale 2019). Narrative researchers have long been attuned to these issues: 'We are in the middle of our stories and cannot be sure how they will end; we constantly have to revise the plot as new events are added to our lives' (Polkinghorne, in Hatch and Wisniewski 1995: 130).

While the provisional nature of findings is a trait that is common to all research evidence, it becomes particularly transparent through the prospective, open-ended design of a QL study: 'each time you look, you see something rather different' (Stanley, in Thomson and Holland 2003: 237). This can create challenges in knowing when to bring a study to a close, and uncertainty about the status of research insights and interpretations at any one moment (Thomson and Holland 2003). In some quarters, this feature of QL enquiry is seen as a particular limitation. De Cock and Sharp (2007), for example, ask, 'if we cannot draw boundaries and we cannot generalise, what value can there possibly be in such a form of [longitudinal] process research?' (De Cock and Sharp 2007: 248). This suggests the need to clarify how the quality of a QL study can be understood and demonstrated by QL researchers.

Evaluating Qualitative Research

Before turning to the specific quality issues faced by QL researchers, it is worth reviewing the issues that all qualitative researchers routinely face. Qualitative studies are 'frequently criticised for lacking scientific rigour, with poor justification of the methods adopted, lack of transparency in analytical procedures, and the findings ... merely a collection of personal opinions, subject to researcher bias' (Noble and Smith 2015: 34). Judgements about the integrity of a project, including the coherence of its design and execution and the veracity (verisimilitude, trustworthiness) of its findings, are usually made by considering how the methods have been applied, how interpretations have been reached, and whether they are supported by sufficient evidence. But, as the discussion below will illustrate, these simple formulae mask a host of more complex issues. We draw here on the more detailed accounts provided by Hatch and Wisniewski (1995), Maxwell (2012), Ritchie et al. (2014), Flick (2018) and Seale (2007, 2018).

In the positivist tradition, the quality of a study is commonly measured in terms of three main criteria:

- **Validity**: Its objective 'truth' value and accuracy; gauged largely through the methods used to generate findings and the precision with which the findings reflect the data. If more than one way of interpreting the evidence exists, this is a threat to validity;
- **Reliability**: The consistency of the method: whether observations found at one point in time can be replicated at a different time, necessitating a standardised approach and the removal of any sources of bias;
- **Generalisability**: Whether results obtained in one setting or for one population can be applied to other settings or broader populations (creating the need for a 'representative' sample of cases). Note that this differs from the qualitative forms of generalisation outlined in Chapters 2 and 8.

These criteria are closely tied to the idea of a single, objective, knowable reality. Perhaps not surprisingly, if QL research was judged on these criteria, it would be an abject failure on all counts. There is always more than one way to interpret evidence; no replication of findings is possible from one point in time to another; and findings from one setting or set of circumstances cannot be simply generalised to other settings or contexts. Indeed, in the interpretivist tradition, there are no fixed, stable, universal or ultimate truths to discover or verify. The truth of something undoubtedly exists, but this is understood not in terms of bald facts, but in terms of its verisimilitude: the truth-like, persuasive and compelling nature of people's interpretations, and their moral worth as situated forms of knowledge and insight (Plummer 2001; Saldaña 2003). Verisimilitude is about finding the inherent meaning in events and processes (Tsoukas and Hatch 2001). It resides not in the generality of things, but in the particularities of things. It is found in the distinctive nature and faithful representation of the cases under study, and in fidelity to people's lived experiences, which have their own moral worth and integrity (Blumenfeld-Jones 1995; Plummer 2001; Flyvbjerg 2007). Verisimilitude goes hand in hand with the notion of situated knowledge and interpretation, for it encompasses the idea that there may be multiple realities and truths to discern in different social, spatial and temporal contexts.

Related to these points, the quality of qualitative enquiry cannot be judged purely by the methods that are employed; it is not simply a procedural effect, a matter of following a set of technical prescriptions. Quality inheres in the methodological integrity and coherence of a project, which can be understood in two senses. First, as shown above, it resides in the integrity (veracity, verisimilitude, trustworthiness, honesty) of the researcher's interpretations and insights. This requires fidelity to the real-world, lived experiences of the participants, and to the moral and ethical principles that guide the conduct of a study. As will be shown below (Box 12.1), these relational aspects of integrity can be perceived and enhanced in a variety of ways that inhere in the research process itself. Second, integrity resides in the methodological coherence of a project, the degree of fit between the ontological and epistemological drivers for a study, and its explanatory power (how interpretations are arrived at). As Blaikie (2007: 13) shows, it is how these dimensions of a study are connected that is important, for they shape not only how a study is designed, but also how the findings are produced and what they can tell us.

If the quality of a qualitative study is tied to its methodological and interpretive integrity, this means that there are no generic criteria, no blanket or overarching standards about the precision of methods, or how these link to the findings, that can be applied across the board to judge its worth. The narrowly defined criteria used in positivist research are not likely to be appropriate, let alone useful here, and, for QL research, they may be counter-productive. The pressure to meet a specified list of criteria that may or may not match the broad methodological drivers for a project has been likened to the tail wagging the dog (Flick 2018). Worse still, the positivist enterprise to 'purge research of all ... sources of bias is to purge research of human life. ... It is through these "sources of bias" that "a truth" comes to be assembled' (Plummer 2001: 156–7). This is why qualitative researchers working in different methodological traditions commonly develop their own standards by which to judge the worth of their studies. Doing so is far preferable to having narrow external criteria imposed on them (Flick 2018).

Temporal and Interpretive Integrity in QL Research

The integrity of a QL study is shaped by the distinctive nature of its methodology. As we have seen in Chapter 2 (and elsewhere in this book), QL research is founded on the articulation between three facets of its methodology: its processual ontology (that the world is fluid and unpredictable); its epistemology (if the world is fluid, we need fluid (interpretive, processual) methods to access it); and its explanatory power (that theoretical and substantive insights need to be in tune with these temporal drivers for a study). These research components form the analytical logic of QL enquiry, articulated through the alignment of case depth, thematic breadth and temporal reach. The integrity of a QL study resides, in large part, in how these facets of a study are connected – the coherence with which they are aligned. This requires fidelity to the notion of 'real-time' fluid enquiry, which is both processual and interpretive.

Where these alignments are not maintained, this can undermine the aims of a project and compromise the explanatory power of the findings. This occurs, for example, where QL researchers adopt categorising or variance forms of thematic analysis, when what is needed is fidelity to connective forms of analysis that are driven by a processual logic of enquiry (see the discussion in Chapter 9, and illustrations in Box 10.5). Certainly, positivist notions of validity, reliability and generalisability (as outlined above) are simply not relevant in a processual, interpretive mode of research that takes as axiomatic the notion that the world we are investigating is inherently fluid and diverse, and that our insights will inevitably be multiple and continually shifting through time.

It is worth teasing out the two interrelated dimensions of integrity that reflect the dual nature of QL enquiry:

- **Temporal integrity**: This is fidelity to the real-time flux and dynamism of the world. We have seen that the rigour of QL research depends on its capacity to mirror, reflect and flexibly follow real-world processes, in all their flux; to trace processes forward and backward in time to understand their recursive nature; to attempt the tricky task of teasing out multiple causal connections and convergences; in short, to follow reality in all its windings. This requires a sustained engagement in the field, and the generation of real-time longitudinal knowledge and insights. As part of this, a strategic balance is needed between flexibility and continuity, and between creativity and precision in how a project is designed and executed. **Temporal integrity** ensures that a dynamic, processual logic runs through the whole research process, from the way that questions are framed, to the way data are generated and analysed, and how findings are presented.

- **Interpretive integrity**: This relates to the interpretive, relational nature of QL enquiry. It entails fidelity to the real-world, lived experiences and inner logic of lives, garnered through field enquiry that takes agency, subjectivity and reflexivity seriously, and that adheres to the principles of longitudinal ethics (see Chapter 5). Interpretive integrity accords priority to the generation of situated, case-rich data and thick (interpretive) descriptions. As shown in Chapter 6, our aim is to gain an intimate familiarity with an unfolding life, to 'reveal the experiences of real people, in real situations, struggling with real problems' (Hatch and Wisniewski 1995: 127). Case narratives have their own veracity, a moral heart that emerges through the particularities of an unfolding tale (Flyvbjerg 2007; see Chapter 10). Like temporal integrity, interpretive integrity is threaded through the whole research process, from the way that questions are framed to the way that findings are generated, interpreted, narrated and visualised (see Chapter 11).

The integrity of QL enquiry is also enhanced through its abductive logic. As shown in Chapter 9, abduction relies on two oscillating modes of discovery. The first is intuition, an imaginative and creative mode of exploration and discovery that enables us to discern the essential truth of things. The second is precision, a painstaking and meticulous process of piecing together a mosaic of substantive and conceptual insights. Abduction relies on a continuous **iteration** between existing theories and bodies of evidence, and newly emerging data and insights. Iteration is more than an instrumental, repetitive task, a mechanical form of feedback. It is a reflexive process of continuous meaning making through which a mosaic of themes, insights and understandings are gradually distilled (Grbich 2007; Srivastava and Hopwood 2009).

In QL enquiry, iteration flows through the whole research process. It occurs through the cumulative waves of QL field enquiry, where synchronic understandings are continually transformed into diachronic insights. Iteration can be harnessed in varied ways to spark and ignite new thinking, and to reach new meanings. It inheres in the oscillations between prospective and retrospective understandings: between tracing back and forward in time, and between the linear (sequential) and fluid (recursive) facets of temporal experience. It is also evident in the constant interplay between researcher and participant understandings, between the life as lived and the life as told, and between micro–macro and local–global frames of reference. It emerges too in constructive exchanges and collaborations across the research/

policy interface (see below). These multiple, iterative readings may not be invoked in every study, and they cannot produce definitive evidence. But by building in varied layers of insight, researchers are able to generate persuasive, plausible and compelling accounts of dynamic processes.

Overall, the interrelated dimensions of integrity outlined above, and their abductive underpinnings, create a deeper understanding of the quality and value of QL enquiry. This mode of research has its own internal logic, through which its quality and integrity emerge. The fact that it has no temporal fixity, and that findings are inherently provisional, is rarely construed as a problem by QL researchers (Koro-Ljungberg and Bussing 2013; Farrall et al. 2014: 75). If there is nothing definitive about our findings, this is because there is nothing definitive about a fluid social world:

> [O]ur conclusions are always and only provisional ... forever subject to new
> readings. Far from being problematic, this characteristic of narrative data
> is evidence of its resilience and vitality and of its infinite ability to yield
> more layers of meaning when examined from yet another [historical] lens.
> (Andrews 2008: 98–9)

The transformative nature of temporal data and insights as a study unfolds is part and parcel of its power. By its very nature, QL enquiry confounds the search for theoretical saturation and definitive conclusions. Instead, it alerts us to an ever-changing kaleidoscope of lives 'in the making', perpetually unfolding through a complex and unpredictable web of events and influences.

An interpretive lens recognises the verisimilitude of multiple, partial, provisional and sometimes contradictory tales, which are filtered through shifting horizons of time and space in particular pockets of the social fabric: 'we can no longer chart the life in a simple, linear fashion, in which one logical step leads to the next. ... When the representations are more complex, we, as interpreters, find that ... lives are more open to multiple interpretations, and, therefore, our interpretations become less authoritative' (Bloom, in Hatch and Wisniewski 1995: 123). This requires us to dispense with the idea that only one story holds the truth about changing lives or the causes and consequences of social events and actions, and to work, instead, with multiple layers of truth and shifting interpretations through time.

Indeed, it is only through an interpretive lens, with its narrative power, that we can faithfully capture and represent this fluid reality, and convey the inherently partial and provisional nature of the world that we are investigating. An interpretive lens, then, is not simply an optional extra, a gloss that we can choose to place on the findings of a study. For fluid enquiry, it is the nub of what we have. It is a modest, realistic and authentic way of discerning and conveying the flux of the world, an essential foundation for responsible social enquiry. The location of QL enquiry in the stream of time is not, then, a problem to be somehow circumvented; it is the very reality that we wish to capture and convey. It is through its fidelity to the fluid nature of social reality, and the flux and indeterminacy of human lives, that QL research acquires its quality and integrity.

Strategies for Enhancing the Quality of a Study

While qualitative researchers are likely to eschew abstract lists of validity criteria that may constrain or simply not fit their studies, they commonly adopt one or more broad strategies for gauging and enhancing the integrity of their studies. These strategies are woven into the research process and set out in Box 12.1.

Box 12.1   Strategies for Enhancing the Quality of a Study

- **Design (asking pertinent questions and choosing the right cases):** The quality of a study is greatly enhanced where it addresses important, relevant and timely questions that will fill important gaps in our knowledge: 'The formulation of a problem is often more essential than its solution' (Einstein, cited in Van de Ven 2007: 71). A robust sampling strategy will ensure that these questions can be addressed through strategically chosen cases that can shed light on varied aspects of the topic.
- **Field engagement:** Prolonged, in-depth engagement in the field can help to build detailed, situated knowledge and discern unfolding processes in the making. The iterative process of jointly constructing meaning and knowledge with participants in the field (see Chapter 6) provides the foundation for enhancing the interpretive integrity of a study. A commitment to thick description (that embodies the interpretations of the participants, alongside faithful representations of their practices and actions) is also essential. Flexibility in the field (carefully balanced against continuity of enquiry) enables researchers to refine and enhance the quality of their data-generation methods (Saldaña 2003).
- **Longitudinal ethics:** Ethical literacy and integrity are vital elements of research quality and integrity. Alongside the various ethical balancing acts set out in Chapter 5, there is the vital issue of nurturing shared authority with participants and practice partners. Where appropriate, facilitating new forms of participant engagement (e.g. ambassadorial or partnership roles) can consolidate interpretive integrity (see impact studies below).
- **Iteration:** This abductive strategy brings together and works across a mosaic of insights, generated through different sources of data and evidence, to build an emerging picture. Iteration provides an alternative to **triangulation**. This is conventionally understood as a means of generating insights through more than one method, theory or source of data, which

can then be compared to iron out factual inconsistencies (so-called 'negative' or 'deviant' cases that do not fit a theory) (Ritchie et al. 2014: 42; Flick 2018). But, as a rather blunt tool, triangulation rarely provides a coherent story. It is more likely to yield multiple insights that will have equal veracity. Iteration works with a different logic of discovery: it is connective, multiple and inclusive. Complementary sources of data are drawn together so that each new addition to the theoretical pool changes the overall shape and meaning of the interpretations. Iteration, then, is more nuanced and finely grained than triangulation, for it is deeply embedded in the fabric of the research process. It allows for a greater density and diversity of evidence and meaning making, and a more integrated and cumulative approach to building insights (see above and Chapter 9);

- **Researcher reflexivity and field/data documentation**: This is an open approach to gauging quality, and refining research practices, achieved through the use of research diaries and field notes; through analytical files (case study documents) that chart evolving interpretations; and through high standards of data management and documentation, including the production of a gold standard study guide (see Chapter 7). These allow researchers to document critical reflections on their methods, such as any limitations in design, sampling, data-generation or analysis techniques, or any personal biases that may have influenced the research; evolving interpretations; lessons learnt: and reflections on remaining gaps in knowledge and on methodological and ethical refinements that need to be addressed.
- **External consultation, feedback, audit**: This involves the use of research advisory groups, peer review and other forms of academic and policy-related feedback (e.g. through seminar and conference presentations, or consultations or events with other academics, practice partners or community groups about provisional findings and outputs) (Pettigrew 1995; Bygstad and Munkvold 2011). Saldaña (2003: 43) recommends a mid-stream audit to keep a project on track. Millar (2020 in press: 3) notes: 'As we presented the research, we often had follow up conversations with audience members who spoke to us … about recognising the accounts: "that was me." This sort of authenticity is an important source of validation of researchers' interpretations of qualitative data'. Feedback from participants, commonly called participant verification, can also be sought (not only for validating their own data and evidence, but, in some cases, also for more general interpretations – what Bygstad and Munkvold (2011) call 'talk back'). This can be thought of as a natural extension of the interpretive integrity that is built into field enquiry (see above). It is worth recalling that, in a context where events and perceptions are continually shifting, there may be both methodological and ethical drawbacks in taking a crystallised version of the past back to people for

(Continued)

355

their verification, or otherwise inviting them to take on a broader analytical role (see Chapter 5). In practice, participant verification may turn out to be a selective strategy, with take-up limited to participants with ambassadorial roles, who are attuned to the analytical aims of a study.

- **Presentation of findings**: This involves using narratives, visuals, case study evidence and direct quotations that are persuasive, compelling and accessible to different audiences. These should authentically reflect the particularities and distinctiveness of case material, while also teasing out the similarities and differences across cases. The transparency of findings can be enhanced through the addition of reflexive accounts of the methodology.

- **Publishing a dataset through the archive**: This increases the visibility of a study, establishes the quality of its evidence base, creates legacy data with historical value, and promotes the research in ways that increase its impact. The overall value of a study can be significantly enhanced through a transparent and open approach to data sharing (see Chapters 7 and 8).

Attending to the methodological integrity of a study and engaging in the embedded research strategies set out in Box 12.1, are important parts of the intellectual craft of QL enquiry. The quality of the process is just as important as the quality of the end results. The skills of the craft are honed on the job, through evolving research practices (Seale 2007). But they are also grounded in and remind us of a broader set of guiding principles that help to maintain fidelity to the craft:

> All we have ... is a general sense of the value of careful scholarship, commitment to rigorous argument, attending to the links between claims and evidence, consideration of all viewpoints before taking a stance, asking and answering important rather than trivial research questions. ... The very fragility of these ideals ... is what makes it worth devoting one's life to their support. (Seale 2007: 379–80)

Longitudinal Impact Studies

The second area of development prompted by Ellwood's 'and then what?' question relates to the potential for QL research to create impact, to make a difference in the real world, and how this might be achieved. This idea of 'making a difference', through the passionate form of scholarship identified by Holstein and Minkler (2007) in our opening quotation, is often seen as a fundamental aim of social research. It builds on the ideas developed above about the value and worth of QL enquiry, and illustrates how the power and integrity of this methodology might be actively harnessed and demonstrated, particularly where the research is bound up with the navigation or crafting of a change process.

Qualitative research can create impact in a variety of ways. Beyond capacity building impacts (the scope to build capacity in research skills, or enhance training in
research methodology), two forms of impact are worth highlighting here:

- **conceptual impacts**: which produce new or distinctive forms of knowledge,
  change perceptions, reframe debates and enable people to 'see' things in a
  different way;
- **instrumental impacts**: which have direct influence and create tangible
  changes in practice and policy.

Clearly, these forms of impact are not mutually exclusive and are likely to be intertwined in the research process. 'Making a difference' may be focused on one or more
specific target groups: the academic community; research participants; practitioners
across public, private and voluntary sectors; policy makers; community groups and/
or the general public. The strategies employed are also likely to be varied. It might
be a matter of asking the right kinds of questions, finding the right methods to convey ideas (for example, through the power of narratives rather than 'killer' statistics;
see Chapter 11) and/or the use of creative and visually arresting means of dissemination. It may occur through a 'bottom up' approach that involves working closely
with practitioners, and creating grassroots knowledge that percolates upwards. Or it
may occur through a 'top down' approach that involves working closely with policy
makers or broker organisations to try out new and more effective ways of shaping
and delivering interventions.

It is also likely to entail some form of monitoring, feedback or evaluation to gauge
the impact of a study. Like all unfolding processes, impacts may be diffuse, pervasive
and widespread, emerging through a rich constellation of actions and interactions
that are unpredictable and hard to identify. Gauging research impacts is likely to
require careful documentation of engagement with research users, and methods of
tracking back from a particular policy or practice change, to discern how impact has
emerged (ESRC Research Evaluation Committee 2011; Buchanan 2013). Whatever
the routes, 'making a difference' requires ongoing personal commitments from
researchers and dedicated resources.

As shown in the introduction to this book, QL research is increasingly used as an
exploratory, evaluation or navigational tool in a variety of policy and applied
research settings. Understanding processes of change and continuity is vital where
people are required or encouraged to change or refine their practices, to advance
their skills and knowledge, or where they need to adapt to changing circumstances
or environments (a range of studies are illustrated in Box 1.2; Boxes 4.2 and 4.4;
Box 6.11 and Figure 6.4; and Box 10.5). But, even where this is not part of the
rationale, QL research can create conceptual impacts that provide new ways of seeing and understanding the social world. Since QL research is flexible and grounded
in real-time developments, the longitudinal frame of a QL study gives space to

explore the interface between lived experiences and policy processes, and develop productive collaborations with policy and/or practice partners, and with participants themselves (see examples in Box 4.9 and Boxes 5.3 and 5.13). Policy and/or practice partners are increasingly likely to play an active role in agenda setting, mediating field enquiry, steering future directions, providing various forms of feedback on data and interpretations, and disseminating findings (Corden and Nice 2007; Bygstad and Munkvold 2011; Neale and Morton 2012; Neale et al. 2015).

But, in a more elaborate rendition of the double hermeneutic, these processes can also be taken a stage further. In the 1970s, the research/practice interface was commonly conceived in terms of *knowledge transfer*, seen as a linear, one-way process. This subsequently gave way to the more interactive idea of *knowledge exchange*, a productive exchange of ideas between two parallel domains of practice and expertise, occurring at key moments in the research process (e.g. through advisory groups and dissemination events). More recently, this has been superseded by the notion of **knowledge co-production**, a more integrated approach that fosters practitioner-informed research, and research-based practice (Best and Holmes 2010; Neale and Morton 2012). Van de Ven (2007: 9–10) calls this *engaged scholarship*, a mode of research that is conducted in collaboration with practitioners to advance knowledge as a collective achievement. The appeal of this approach is that it encourages a sense of investment in and local ownership of a project, which enables the take-up of research findings. But more than this, it offers scope for a greater merging of research and professional practice, in which research findings are embedded within and emerge from practice developments (detailed further in Neale 2021).

The longitudinal frame of a QL study is ideally suited to facilitate the co-production of knowledge with policy, practice or community partners (Bygstad and Munkvold 2011). As noted in Chapter 5, longitudinal impact research shares important affinities with **participatory action research**. The core rationale for action research is to bring about productive changes in collective practices, and thereby improve the quality of participants' lives, using the principles of participant engagement, empowerment, shared authority and the co-production of knowledge (Kemmis et al. 2014; Bradbury-Huang 2015; see also www.actionresearch plus.com and the journal *Action Research*). Working on the principle of shared authority supports the process of building crucial relationships of trust and mutual respect with research partners, and helps to avoid the ethical quagmires that, in some cases, have bedevilled the work of longitudinal ethnographers (see Chapter 5 for the ethics and practicalities of sustaining long-term relationships with policy or practice partners).

Two varied examples of **longitudinal impact studies** are provided in Box 12.2. In both cases, there is an ongoing iteration between research and professional practice, through which momentum builds. In the first example, both instrumental and conceptual impacts are designed into the study from the outset. This is an evaluation study that is carefully planned and occurs in a series of well-ordered, anticipated and chronological stages. In the second study, impact is a longer-term goal that occurs in a more fluid, non-linear fashion. Conceptual and instrumental impacts occur here incrementally, on the understanding that changes in perception are the necessary foundations upon which to build concrete changes in practice. Both studies are based on the insight that 'what works' requires a prior understanding of 'how things work' (an essentially processual question), and 'what matters' to people, along with insights into 'what helps', in particular contexts of change (see Chapter 2).

Box 12.2   Longitudinal Impact Studies

Pharmacy Training **study (Kinsey)**

For her doctoral research, Kinsey (2020), a qualified hospital pharmacist, developed, co-ordinated and evaluated a new hospital placement scheme for pre-registration pharmacist trainees, which was conducted by 'walking alongside' a group of trainees and their trainers. In doing so, she was guided by the principles of design-based educational research (McKenney and Reeves 2018). This does not simply investigate educational or training interventions; it designs, implements and evaluates them. Kinsey took on multiple roles as designer, facilitator and evaluator of the new training process. The aim was to give trainees an extended period of time (three months) on a particular hospital ward, enabling them to build teamwork skills and experience, and interact directly with patients. The first phase of the research revealed that these sustained elements were missing from existing rotational training models, where trainees typically move around between specialities, spending a maximum of two weeks in any one setting.

The study was conducted in four phases:

- In the first phase, Kinsey interviewed a range of stakeholders (hospital pharmacists, nurses, doctors, pharmacy educators) about the pros and cons of existing training provision. At this stage, she also consulted with hospital pharmacy departments to identify wards in two hospitals with highly effective, innovative teams, who would make ideal hosts for testing out the new placements. These were easily recruited.
- This fed into the second phase, in which Kinsey worked with nine key stakeholders from these wards to design the new training placements. As part of this developmental work, she produced a workbook that gave guidance to the trainees on their roles and responsibilities, learning objectives, a timeline for activities, and workplace assessment tools. The guide also helped the ward teams (pharmacists, ward sisters and consultants) who were supporting the trainees.

(Continued)

- The third phase involved setting up and evaluating a short (four-week) prototype for the new placement, to test out its feasibility and acceptability in a clinical setting.
- The final phase involved setting up the placements and following three trainees through the process. They were drawn from the national pharmacy training programme, and had volunteered to take up the new placements and participate in the study. The placements were rolled out on the wards over a period of 13 weeks. The impact of the training was evaluated for both trainees and staff. For ethical reasons, it was not possible to carry out ward observations, but Kinsey carried out four waves of interviews with each trainee (at weeks 0, 4, 8 and 14), enabling her to track their development through this new and evolving process. Having worked closely with the ward staff at the development stage, she also carried out final interviews with them at week 14.

The study yielded new insights into the dynamics of team building, on-the-job learning, and the development of person-centred care. Kinsey was able to develop detailed case studies of the new training process undertaken by the three trainees, and to explore similarities and differences in their experiences. Trainees reported that their longitudinal placements had been far more effective and fulfilling than other phases of their rotational training. By week 8, they had begun to settle well into their roles, and by the end of the placement had become such valuable and fully integrated team members that they did not wish to leave 'their' wards. In a similar vein, ward staff reported the success of the placements and the value of the new training and trainees. As a result, they lobbied the pharmacy department to adopt the three-month placements as standard practice. There is clear potential to extend the scope of this study and to roll out and further gauge the value of this new model of on-the-job pharmacy training across hospital settings (for further discussion of this model of longitudinal impact research, see Neale 2021).

Following Young Fathers study (Neale et al. 2015)

The Kinsey study is a well-structured, intensive and localised implementation and evaluation study, with a clear purpose and time frame. It also demonstrates what can be achieved within the confines of a doctoral research project. But it is also possible to build longitudinal impact through an incremental approach, using more extensive and evolving designs. The Following Young Fathers study, which explored how lived experiences mesh with policy processes, provides an example:

- The initial study was conceived in 2010 in collaboration with a regional network of teenage pregnancy co-ordinators, who identified a major gap in professional knowledge and practice in relation to young fathers. This initial consultation, which identified a new and pressing research question, provided the foundations for the eventual impact of the study. It led to the formation of a partnership model of research, working with several committed practitioners with specialist skills in working with young fathers, which was developed and sustained over a six-year period (see also Box 5.3).

- Over the course of the study, the practice partners developed a dual role as partners in the development of the research, and key participants in the production of insights and findings. They were engaged in recruiting the participants and helping to maintain their involvement in the research (Neale et al. 2015). But they also became internal research brokers, jointly presenting findings with the research team at conferences and parliamentary meetings, circulating policy briefing papers, and working with local practitioners to translate the evidence into practitioner goals and strategies. Their input into the development of the briefing papers and their feedback on our analytical skills in representing their practices helped to gauge the quality of the research. When we received comments that we had 'hit the nail on the head' or had managed to encapsulate what they were trying to do, or enabled them to think about their practice in new and productive ways, we knew we were on the right track.

- A broader practitioner strategy group was set up across a range of statutory and voluntary organisations, which met on a regular basis over the course of the study. This created a forum for sharing good practice and advancing ideas about future developments. Entering into the world of the practitioners, learning their language and seeing professional development as it evolved were hugely enriching processes for the research team, and ensured our findings were in tune with cutting-edge grassroots ideas and thinking.

- At the end of the first phase of the study, a policy briefing paper series, aimed at policy and practice communities, was produced and launched at a national practitioner conference (www.followingfathers.leeds.ac.uk). The conference was jointly organised with the partners, who convened varied sessions and supported the young fathers who were contributing to the event (see Box 5.13).

- A collaborative writing project was also undertaken, which brought together a variety of voices about the issues facing young fathers: from researcher, practitioner, policy think tank and political perspectives (the All Party Parliamentary Group on Fatherhood, chaired by David Lammy), and from young fathers themselves (Neale and Davies 2015).

- Embedding this study in a policy and practice landscape paved the way for a practitioner-led, one-year impact initiative, *Supporting Young Dads (SYD)*, which followed on seamlessly from the empirical study. Co-ordinated by the researchers, this initiative enabled the findings of the study to feed directly into new practice developments. Selected

(Continued)

practitioners were funded to pilot and test out new ways of working, particularly in developing tailored forms of specialist support for young offender fathers upon their release from custody. Practice partners also trained selected young fathers as 'experts by experience' under the aegis of a new northern arm of the *Young Dads Collective*. The young men developed advocacy, mentoring and training roles, and tested their skills in training health and social care practitioners in how to engage effectively with young fathers. The initiative was documented through a collaborative writing project (Tarrant and Neale 2017).

- More recently, this long-term partnership working has provided the springboard for a new and extended study that is building an international comparative dimension into this research (*Following Young Fathers Further*, UKRI, Tarrant, 2020–27).

Longitudinal impact in this study has grown incrementally through a collaborative, partnership model of research, which has evolved gradually and gained strength and momentum through cumulative phases of funding. In a related example, Bygstad and Munkvold (2011) give a valuable account of a collaborative, longitudinal process study. They reveal how the active engagement of practitioners in the development and interpretation of findings may necessitate a diplomatic reconciliation of conflicting views (for further insights on the challenges of collaborative models of researching, see Neale 2021).

The studies showcased in Box 12.2 demonstrate the huge potential for QL enquiry to be used as a design and navigational strategy in policy settings, running alongside new initiatives in real-time, and working collaboratively to bring people together at key moments to take stock, review developments and plan new ways forward. In this way, it is possible to create real-world impacts as an integral part of the research process, and to circumvent the oft-cited critique that, in a fast-moving policy world, longitudinal enquiry simply takes too long to be of value.

Future Developments: Exploring the Boundaries

The final consideration prompted by Ellwood's 'and then what?' question concerns the huge potential for future innovation and growth in this field. As Dey (2007) notes in our opening quotation, methodology is a work in progress, not a set of technical prescriptions. In keeping with the interdisciplinary focus of this book, some of the rich ways of pushing the boundaries of this methodology, and forging productive links with related traditions of enquiry are drawn together and outlined in Box 12.3.

Box 12.3 Future Developments – Exploring the Boundaries

Some pointers for interdisciplinary developments in QL research, which straddle methodological, substantive and theoretical advances, are suggested here:

- **Advancing the field**: First, to advance QL research across new fields of substantive enquiry and in new disciplinary and interdisciplinary contexts and research traditions. There is enormous scope to address some of the pressing global issues of the day: in environmental and biodiversity issues that become more urgent by the day; in global public health and well-being; in evolving political processes and shifting international alignments; and in enduring and far-reaching issues surrounding racial, ethnic, religious and other forms of intolerance, oppression and inequality. Second, to facilitate advances in QL methodology through the development of detailed integrative reviews and analyses in particular disciplines and fields of enquiry. These move beyond the scope of edited collections to create a more holistic and methodologically useful knowledge base (e.g. Calman et al. 2013; SmithBattle et al. 2018; Farr and Nizza 2019).
- **Advancing QL design**: To refine and advance existing methods and pioneer new methods, tools and techniques for building a range of temporal dynamics into research design. Possible areas for development include creative modes of sampling; advances in life journey and recursive interviewing and participatory modes of data generation; advances in case, thematic and processual forms of analysis; and refining strategies to enhance the quality of QL enquiry (Chapters 4, 6, 10 and 11).
- **Mixed longitudinal methods**: To advance ways of working across different scales of longitudinal enquiry, through nested and linked designs that bring QL data into alignment with large-scale survey data (see Chapter 1 and Box 8.4).
- **Longitudinal socio-historical studies**: To develop longitudinal ethnographies, longitudinal re-studies and longitudinal biographies in new research settings and across new fields of socio-historical enquiry; and to advance ways of researching the complex connections between individual lives and wider processes of socio-historical change (Chapters 1 and 3).
- **Time, space and international comparative studies**: To advance scholarship on the spatial dimensions of time and the temporal dimensions of space, and to develop the international comparative dimensions of QL enquiry (Chapter 3).
- **Longitudinal ethics**: To build and advance understandings of the practice of walking alongside people, and the application of longitudinal ethics in new and innovative terrains of enquiry; to enhance ethical literacy through the documentation and sharing of ethical dilemmas and their resolution (Chapters 5 and 8).

(Continued)

- **Managing and archiving data**: To grow the culture of managing, archiving and sharing QL data for longer-term use. As part of this, to advance data infrastructure and facilities for data discovery; to enhance strategies for the preservation of legacy datasets; and to further develop the role of archives as mediators of socio-historical knowledge (Chapters 7 and 8).
- **Legacy data**: To advance the use of legacy data as important documents of lives and times that complement other methods of generating QL data and insights. This would involve refining methods for analysing legacy data, and for working across and aggregating data from existing studies, including the application of big data analytics, and the collaborative sharing of datasets. It also means advancing the case for qualitative (data-rich, empirically grounded) forms of generalisation that build a mosaic of evidence from diverse sources (Chapters 2 and 8).
- **Longitudinal impact research**: To build a body of methodological insight and knowledge on QL impact studies, and enhance the potential to use QL research as a design and navigational tool in policy initiatives and interventions. Related to this, to draw productive links between this emerging field and the growing canons of participatory action research and educational design research; and to build research designs that bring lived experiences and policy and practice processes into a common framework of understanding (see above and Box 12.2; see also Chapter 3).
- **Theoretical advances**: To explore and elaborate the varied temporal dynamics that underpin QL enquiry, and increase the scope for working with varied timescapes as rich themes or topics of enquiry. The broader enterprise is to create more robust links between theory and method, including a more practice-based understanding of the power of abductive logic and discovery. There is huge scope to advance processual modes of research and analysis; to forge productive links between QL enquiry and social complexity theory (a fledgling field that lacks a methodological tool kit); and to further develop our understanding of complex causality, and the crucial role played by QL enquiry in illuminating causal processes (Chapters 2, 3 and 11).
- **Imagining the future**: Finally, in keeping with John Law's (2004) suggestion at the start of Chapter 2, and mindful that QL methodology is an unfinished and partial work in progress, to nurture the capacity for creative imagination, to think six impossible things before breakfast, and to forge new pathways for dynamic real-time enquiry that are undreamt of here.

As Box 12.3 shows, the scope to develop new and exciting directions for QL research is extensive, including the growth in experiential, arts-based methodologies, and the transformative potential of digital technologies for research design and practice, and their value as emerging sites of temporal enquiry. The longitudinal frame, in itself, offers abundant scope for methodological innovation, for example in building collaborative research relationships and networks over time, in developing and refining imaginative research tools and techniques for discerning the past and the future, and in bringing creative and participatory forms of output to fruition (see, for example, Johnson 2015; and Land and Patrick 2014).

There is huge potential, also, for theoretical advances. The study of time in all its rich variety remains an open field, with scope for new explorations at the interface of temporal theory and research practice. In this avowedly temporal field, it is also worth considering the enormous scope for historically embedded explorations and rediscoveries. New research is, by its nature, exciting and, in most cases, innovative (see, for example, the QL doctoral studies of Gerrits (2008), Patrick (2017), Pettersson (2019) and Kinsey (2020), showcased above and in Chapters 2 and 4). But working through time brings a heightened sensitivity to the value of past scholarship, and the need to re-search and re-discover past wisdom and insights, alongside whatever is new or currently fashionable. For QL enquiry, this historical sensitivity is part and parcel of robust and careful scholarship. Just as datasets may be lost, it is all too easy to lose sight of ideas and theoretical concepts that have developed over decades of scholarship, and that underpin our present-day understandings (not least where these ideas have, at various times, been suppressed or discredited by powerful academy elites). This was the case for both Bergson and van Gennep, whose ground-breaking ideas about time and processes, and fine sense of what is real and meaningful for people, have provided solid conceptual foundations for this book. Looking forward, then, may benefit from looking back to regain and revitalise lost ideas. We can see the craft of QL research in a new way, as part of the rich, historical development of a field that builds new layers of insight through the decades.

Closing Reflections

Researching qualitatively through time undoubtedly brings challenges. But, in the view of this enthusiastic advocate, these are far outweighed by the benefits. As a responsive mode of research, QL enquiry does more than investigate dynamic processes; it is implicated in the very changes that it seeks to study. This capacity to walk alongside a panel of participants, and to respond with sensibility to the rich flux of human experience, makes for a powerful and rewarding research journey. Engaging with time requires a leap into the unknown, a capacity to see beyond the visible. Qualitative longitudinal researchers may not know exactly where their research will lead, how long it may last or what they may find, but they are likely to uncover some compelling insights along the way. This 'slow' and careful mode of research, which looks again and again to create an intimate portrait of changing lives, has unique power and potential to follow reality in all its windings.

Further Reading

Sources that explore the quality of QL research are scarce, but Saldaña (2003) provides a helpful and concise discussion. Valuable discussions on the quality of narrative and life history research can be found in Hatch and Wisniewski (1995), Plummer (2001) and Andrews (2008). Among more general sources on the quality of qualitative enquiry, Flick (2018) and Seale (2018) are recommended, while a concise discussion that captures the essence of the arguments is usefully provided by Noble and Smith (2015). Sources on longitudinal impact research are also scarce. Kinsey's (2020) pharmacy training study provides an excellent example of what can be achieved, while Bygstad and Monkvold (2011) provide a valuable review of the broader issues involved in sustaining collaborative research through time. These themes are also explored further in Neale (2021). For general sources on creating impact, action research, and design-based educational studies, see Best and Holmes (2010), Buchanan (2013), Kemmis et al. (2014), Bradbury-Huang (2015) and McKenney and Reeves (2018).

Andrews, M. (2008) 'Never the last word: Revisiting data', in M. Andrews, C. Squire and M. Tamboukou (eds) *Doing Narrative Research*. London: Sage, pp. 86–101.

Best, A. and Holmes, A. (2010) 'Systems thinking, knowledge and action: Towards better models and methods', *Evidence and Policy*, 6 (2): 145–59.

Bradbury-Huang, H. (ed.) (2015) *The Sage Handbook of Action Research*. London: Sage.

Buchanan, A. (2013) 'Impact and knowledge mobilisation: What I have learnt as Chair of the Economic and Social Research Council Evaluation Committee', *Contemporary Social Science*, 8 (3): 176–90.

Bygstad, B. and Munkvold, B. (2011) 'Exploring the role of informants in interpretive case study research in IS', *Journal of Information Technology*, 26: 32–45.

Flick, U. (2018) *Managing Quality in Qualitative Research*. London: Sage.

Hatch, J. and Wisniewski, R. (eds) (1995) *Life History and Narrative*. London: Falmer.

Kemmis, S., McTaggart, R. and Nixon, R. (eds) (2014) *The Action Research Planner: Doing Critical Participant Action Research*. London: Springer.

Kinsey, H. (2020) *Integrating a Longitudinal Ward Placement into the Hospital Pharmacist Pre-Registration Year: A Design-based Research Approach Informing Design, Implementation and Evaluation* (unpublished doctoral thesis). Norwich: University of East Anglia.

McKenney, S. and Reeves, T. (2018) *Conducting Educational Design Research*, 2nd edition. London: Routledge.

Neale, B. (2021 in press) 'Fluid enquiry, complex causality, policy processes: New agendas for qualitative longitudinal research' *Social Policy and Society.*

Noble, H. and Smith, J. (2015) 'Issues of validity and reliability in qualitative research', *Evidence Based Nursing*, 18 (2): 34–5.

Plummer, K. (2001) *Documents of Life 2: An Invitation to a Critical Humanism*. London: Sage.

Saldaña, J. (2003) *Longitudinal Qualitative Research: Analyzing Change through Time*. Walnut Creek, CA: AltaMira Press.

Seale, C. (2018) 'Research quality', in C. Seale (ed.) *Researching Society and Culture*, 4th edition. London: Sage, pp. 567–81.

GLOSSARY

Abductive logic An iterative form of reasoning based on two modes of discovery: intuition, an imaginative, creative and interpretive mode of exploration that discerns the essential truth of things; and precision, a painstaking and meticulous process of piecing together a mosaic of substantive and conceptual insights. Abduction relies on iteration between different sources of meaning: between existing theories/evidence and newly emerging data/insights. It embodies both induction (a 'bottom-up' approach that derives theories from observations) and deduction (a 'top-down' approach that starts with theoretical hypotheses and tests them in the field). Abduction also encompasses retroductive logic, which traces backward in time, enabling iteration between prospective and retrospective understandings. *See also*: Iteration; Bricolage; Qualitative generalisation

Agency (human) The capacity to act, to interact, to make choices, to influence the shape of one's life and the lives of others. It is a dynamic concept, embodying ideas of change, continuity, action, motivation and endurance, and it brings notions of subjective causality to the fore. Agency is a core feature of interpretive enquiry and central to processual and causal understanding. *See also*: Subjectivity; Reflexivity; Interpretivist tradition

Analysis *See* Qualitative longitudinal analysis (QLA)

Anonymising The process of altering research data in order to protect the confidentiality of participants, that is, substituting names of people, places, organisations, employment or other identifying features. This creates two versions of a dataset: abridged and unabridged. Anonymising is a less than perfect tool, since it does not guarantee confidentiality, and it runs counter to the need for data authenticity. Anonymising is not the only way to protect confidentiality; identities can also be safeguarded through archiving data. *See also*: Longitudinal ethics; Confidentiality/authenticity; Archiving.

Archiving The process of preserving and safeguarding new research data through deposit in a research archive or data repository. This creates legacy data, which can be safely stored, discovered, shared and re-used. Archives control and regulate access to data, thereby placing safeguards on their use. Archiving is fundamental to good data management. The timing of archiving is a vital consideration; some flexibility is helpful for researchers, but archiving within the lifetime of a project avoids issues of data neglect, and the potential loss of a valuable historical resource. *See also*: Legacy data research; Data sharing; Ethics of data sharing and re-use; Data management

Assemblages (process tracing) Unstable, open, dynamic structures, comprising moving elements that collide, break apart, form new connections and offshoots, or fold into new structures. They can be thought of as dynamic mosaics that change in their composition with each new addition to the conceptual picture (Deleuze 1988 [1966]). *See also*: Abductive logic; Processes; Process analysis; Complexity theories; Complex causality

Attrition *See* Sample attrition/maintenance

Authenticity (of data) *See* Confidentiality/authenticity

Autobiographical accounts Retrospective, first-person accounts of past events and processes, usually in narrative or audio form. Such accounts can be generated through life journey interviewing, but also produced directly by participants as part of a suite of participatory data generation tools. They complement other forms of participatory accounts, including accounts of the future. *See also*: Participatory methods; Data generation; Imaginary futures

Baseline/closure points Important design tools in determining the time frame of a QL study. Clear baseline (starting points) and closure points help to define a study conceptually and contain its temporal reach. The baseline is a temporal marker of some kind, a key historical or biographical moment (e.g. a change in the external landscape, or a life course transition). Different baselines may be chosen for different cohorts. Where a baseline does not coincide with the start of fieldwork, it can be explored retrospectively with participants. Baseline and closure points may have to be determined on pragmatic, resource-related grounds, tied to the period of funding. *See also*: Intensive–extensive (time frames and tempos)

Biographical studies A broad umbrella term for a range of socio-historical studies (biographical, life history, oral history and narrative studies) that are concerned with the unfolding lives of individuals. The focus is on observing and recording people's life experiences. Much of this research has been retrospective, using single visits to the field, although longitudinal biographical studies are beginning to appear. Biographical methods have informed QL methods of data generation and case analysis. *See also*: Socio-historical studies

Bricolage/bricoleurs The skill of using whatever materials are at hand and re-combining them in a patchwork, montage or mosaic of evidence to create new insights (Levi-Strauss 1966). Bricolage works with the logic of abduction and suits perfectly the enterprise of socio-historical and legacy data research. *See also*: Abductive logic; Qualitative generalisations

Cartographic strategy *See* Interviewing

Case analysis A connecting mode of analysis, based on a chronological reconstruction and synthesis of case material. A central part of the qualitative longitudinal analysis (QLA) tool kit. It enables a diachronic, through-time reading of unfolding trajectories. Tools to support this analysis include pen portraits (short documents that summarise case data generated through time); case histories (descriptive files that give a detailed picture of an unfolding case); case studies (elaborated case histories that incorporate researcher insights and feed into reporting findings); and framework grids (constructed for each case). Recursive case analysis enables non-linear, fluid understandings of lives to be woven into a case history.

Reading across a suite of case histories (cross-case diachronic analysis) enables an analysis of trajectories across cases, and the development of typologies. *See also*: Recursive interviewing/analysis; Thematic analysis; Process analysis; Qualitative longitudinal analysis; Categorising/ connecting strategies; Framework grids; Typologies; Cross-case comparative approach

Case histories *See* Case analysis

Case-led approach An approach to sampling that identifies a relatively small number of cases, or perhaps one distinctive case, that can offer an in-depth, holistic understanding of social processes. This produces a case-rich dataset. For QL research, a relatively small number of cases may not mean a small or simple study; it depends on the number of waves of fieldwork and the length and detail of generated evidence. *See also*: Sampling strategies; Sampling through time; Cross-case comparative approach

Cases Cases are units of study that provide the empirical evidence base for a study. They are an integral part of the analytical logic that drives QL enquiry. Encompassing individuals/groups, settings/circumstances, practices/processes, cases are strategically formulated, sampled, investigated and analysed to address the driving research questions. They enable qualitative researchers to investigate the social world in interpretive fashion, 'from the inside', and to generate thick descriptions of real lives. A QL case enables a detailed biographical/processual understanding of lives as they unfold. *See also*: Emblematic cases; Thick description; Case analysis; Cross-case comparative approach; Case-theme-process logic; Themes; Processes

Case studies *See* Case analysis

Case-theme-process logic The analytical logic that is threaded through and shapes the QL research process. Cases, themes and processes are interlocking axes of enquiry that form an integrated conceptual framework for a study, ensuring case depth, thematic breadth and processual reach. The relative weight of these facets of analysis will vary, but some balance between the three is essential. They ensure that QL research builds distinctive connections between social experiences and practices, key ideas, and the fluid nature of social reality. *See also*: Cases; Themes; Processes

Categorising/connecting strategies Strategies for sampling and analysing cases. Cases can be divided into categories as part of a stratified sampling strategy. In thematic analysis, categorising splits, fractures or codes data into categories or 'variables'. This gives limited insights into processual links and causal relationships between categories. Connecting strategies are used by QL researchers to explore the contiguous, processual and temporal connections, similarities and differences between different sources of data. Categorising strategies create and analyse strictly comparable cases and data. Connecting strategies create and analyse complementary cases and data to give a more fluid, intuitive understanding of how cases are connected across a sample and through time. *See also*: Sampling strategies; Sampling through time; Qualitative longitudinal analysis

Causality/causal processes *See* Complex causality

Closure *See* Baseline/closure points; Ethical closure

Cohorts Groups of individuals who share life events and experiences at roughly the same period of time. Anchored by their shared temporal experiences, cohorts are the lynchpins for connecting biographical and wider historical processes of change. Birth cohorts (born in the same year) or generational cohorts (born within 2–3 decades of each other) are well known, but a cohort can be defined in many ways, depending on the shared temporal experience under investigation (e.g. a cohort of first-time mothers, or a cohort entering a new therapy programme). Including different cohorts in a sample, such as generational cohorts or cohorts of service users, can extend the historical reach of a study, and yield insights into how unfolding biographies mesh with wider policy or socio-historical processes. Family chains (where several generations of a family are included in a study) are not strictly cohorts, but they also capture the intersection of biographical and historical processes. *See also*: Sampling through time

Complex causality Causality is our way of making sense of the world: discerning how and why things happen, and identifying the threads of events, interactions or experiences that shape, influence, impact on or transform lives. Researchers are often enjoined to explain these deeply embedded processes. With its real-time design, QL research can uncover an unfolding tale and explore the causes and consequences of change and continuity in human affairs. Complex causality alerts us to the multiplicity, fluidity and relationality of causal processes. It is not singular, linear or neatly ordered, but involves multiple, intersecting, loop-like antecedents and consequences. These can be understood through an interpretive (retrospective/subjective) lens. *See also*: Complexity

theories; Fluid enquiry; Fluid time; Turning points; Transitions; Trajectories

Complexity theories A combination of systems theory and processual thinking. Social complexity theory holds that social systems (connected groups of individuals, operating at different scales of the social fabric) are in a constant state of flux. As relational assemblages, these systems have open and fluid boundaries. The varied entities within a system interact with and influence each other reflexively, through recursive feedback or feedforward loops that may re-shuffle (reaffirm, grow, adapt, condense) or transform the system. Influences that produce change, or lead to recurring states, are multiple and flow in all directions. It is the rich flow and patterning of interactions between system entities which is important (rather than the entities themselves). The focus is on how interactions occur, the direction of influence and paths being followed, and the effects. Simple, linear, cause-and-effect models of change give way to a dynamic, fluid, unpredictable vision of social processes. *See also*: Assemblages; Processes; Process analysis; Complex causality

Conceptual road map A design tool that provides a map to the guiding research questions and sub-questions, sources of data, sampling strategies and field methods, and a provisional list of themes that can feed into topic guides and broad-brush thematic analysis. These maps are an invaluable aid in moving back and forth between theoretical premises and research practice. They can be updated as new insights develop, research practice is honed and new questions arise. This is part of the necessary iteration between theoretical drivers and evolving research practice.

Confidentiality/authenticity This is a core consideration in how data are ethically generated and represented when presenting findings and archiving datasets. It requires a balance between the principle of safeguarding the confidentiality of people's accounts, and the epistemological drive towards producing authentic accounts that reflect and acknowledge real lives. *See also*: Longitudinal ethics; Anonymising; Internal confidentiality; Shared authority

Connecting strategies See Categorising/connecting strategies

Consent (for participation/archiving) The process of seeking informed consent from participants for taking part in a study and for archiving the resulting data. Both forms of consent need to be sought at the outset of a study, although, for QL researchers, process consent requires a careful revisiting of consent at appropriate moments. QL researchers seek a mixture of procedural consent, which specifies how data will be handled to protect participants, and enduring consent, which allows for unspecified future uses of data, and enables researchers to contact participants again in the future. *See also*: Longitudinal ethics

Continuity/flexibility (in field enquiry)
QL research requires a balance between continuity and flexibility, and between precision and creativity in design and data generation. Continuity and precision are important strategies for working through time, ensuring that cumulative data have some integrity and internal coherence to aid analysis and synthesis. Revisiting continuity questions at each research encounter creates through lines in the data that build connections across the waves of fieldwork. Flexibility and creativity, the

capacity to modify research practices and strategies as a study progresses, enables a study to follow lives where they lead, respond to changes as they arise, and mirror the flux of real-world processes. This creativity is a hallmark of QL enquiry, but tempering it with continuity and precision ensures that a study does not lose its focus or direction. A conceptual road map can support this balancing act. *See also*: Data generation; Conceptual road map

Critical realist tradition Realism is based on the drive to understand a real world, comprising real relationships and processes, a world that is seen to exist independently of how we perceive or construct it. Critical realists start from the observation that there can be no objective or certain knowledge of this world. Regardless of its independent existence, the social world can only be known through the interpretations of its members. This means that alternative interpretations have to be accommodated. This stance chimes with interpretivist thinking. Critical realism brings a strong processual focus to social enquiry, and employs abductive logic, but, to date, has paid little attention to time and fluid notions of temporality. *See also*: Interpretivist tradition; Positivist tradition; Paradigms; Abductive logic

Cross-case comparative approach This is an approach to sampling and analysis that seeks to build connections and synergies across a range of cases in a sample. Identifying and working across a range of cases brings greater breadth to a study, and offers scope for discerning variations in experiences across different settings and contexts of change. Multiple cases or sub-samples may be drawn into a study to build such connections. Cross-case analysis supports the process of discerning the different pathways that individuals or groups may be following, and how life course trajectories may be converging or diverging. It facilitates the development of typologies of these different trajectories. A cross-case approach builds greater breadth into an investigation, which can be balanced against the depth of a narrative, case-led approach. *See also*: Cases; Sampling strategies; Sampling through time; Case-led approach; Case analysis; Qualitative longitudinal analysis (QLA); Typologies

Cross-case diachronic analysis *See* Case analysis; Cross-case comparative approach

Cyclical time/patterns Recurring or seasonal events and activities that have a loop-like, repetitive pattern. Cyclical patterns may mirror and elaborate on the rhythms of the natural world (the diurnal cycles of day following night, the turning of the earth, the passing of the seasons); the rhythmic momentum of the life course; or repetitive communal practices in families or organisations. Each recurring cycle moves the process on in subtle, incremental ways. In process analysis, cyclical patterns reflect the enduring repetitive and cumulative nature of events and experiences. Cyclical time creates a bridge between fixed and fluid time. *See also*: Fixed time, Fluid time; Process analysis; Spiral patterns

Data discovery *See* Archiving

Data generation The process of generating data in field enquiry, using varied combinations of longitudinal ethnography, interviewing, participatory methods and legacy (documentary) data research. These approaches are not mutually exclusive and are commonly combined. The idea of *generating* (as opposed to collecting or gathering) data recognises that

knowledge and meaning are jointly produced by participant and researcher. *See also*: Longitudinal ethnography; Interviewing; Participatory methods; Legacy data research; Diary methods; Narrative methods; Visual methods; Continuity/flexibility

Data life cycle/data spiral The data life cycle follows the research process, from planning how to generate data, through to the analysis, preservation and re-use of data. For QL research, the data life cycle can be imagined as a spiral, a continuously spreading, cumulatively increasing process, rather than a cycle of activity that is relatively stable and repetitive. *See also*: Data management; Archiving

Data management The effective and ethical management of research data to support data analysis; and to facilitate the preservation and re-use of data through archiving. Elements of good data management include: planning; seeking consent; the production of high quality, sustainable data files, including transcribing aural interviews into narrative texts; devising systems and structures for organising files; the ethical representation of data; and preparations for archiving. In QL research, these cumulative processes recur through the data spiral. *See also*: Archiving; Data life cycle/data spiral; Longitudinal ethics; Confidentiality/authenticity

Data neglect *See* Archiving

Data sharing The ethos of data sharing drives the practice of preserving and archiving data for longer-term use. It also underpins the practice of pooling data among teams or networks of researchers, who aim to create new forms of knowledge and build qualitative generalisations. Such direct sharing can occur through workshop events, affiliations to research teams, or through collaborative network analyses. *See also*: Ethics of data sharing and re-use; Legacy data research

Deduction *See* Abductive logic

Design (of QL studies) QL studies combine longitudinal designs (following people in real-time), with qualitative methods of sampling, field engagement and analysis. Designs include stand-alone prospective studies; re-studies; and nested QL studies linked to large-scale quantitative longitudinal research. Prospective designs incorporate a retrospective lens, and may engage with time intensively (over the short term) or extensively (over the long term), or both. QL studies are generally small scale in terms of sample size and setting, while qualitative panel studies work with larger samples and greater geographical coverage. *See also*: Qualitative longitudinal research; Movies; Panels/panel designs; Recurrent cross-sectional designs; Re-studies; Mixed longitudinal designs; Prospective–retrospective; Intensive–extensive; Longitudinal impact studies

Diachronic A through-time perspective, concerned with the way in which a process evolves, develops, changes, grows, and so on. In longitudinal research, this refers to the process of generating and/or analysing data through time. *See also* Synchronic; Movies

Diary methods A participatory approach that generates processual data either within an interview or between interviews. Diaries may take various forms, including conventional narrative diaries; 'snapshot' diaries that sample discrete events or experiences (experience sampling); or visual diaries that build an evolving picture

of a process. *See also*: Data generation; Narrative methods; Participatory methods; Visual methods

Documentary methods *See* Legacy data research

Double hermeneutic Refers to two interacting systems of understanding and interpretation: the interpretations of social actors (their world views) and the interpretations of researchers. These two systems of interpretation (lay/expert, participant/researcher) are understood to interact and influence each other (Giddens 1984). *See also*: Interpretivist tradition; Hermeneutics/hermeneutic circle

Emblematic cases Illuminative, distinctive or archetypal cases that may be singled out for more intensive investigation in the field, and/or for analysis. They are 'cases that shine', that is, that are particularly data-rich, compelling or striking. They may reflect distinctive characteristics within a sample, or provide greater insights into key dynamic themes and issues. Working with emblematic cases allows for a more holistic, case study treatment of data. It capitalises on scarce resources when detailed treatment of all cases is beyond the scope of a project. *See also*: Cases; Emblematic themes

Emblematic themes Researchers may choose to work with emblematic themes in the same way that they choose to work with emblematic cases. For QL research, emblematic themes are broad-brush, dynamic themes that effectively link thematic with process analysis. They avoid the pitfalls of fragmenting data into categories that dislocate data from their temporal and case contexts. *See also*: Themes; Emblematic cases

Empowerment *See* Shared authority

Enduring consent *See* Consent

Epic movies *See* Movies

Ethical closure The process of bringing longitudinal field enquiry to an ethical and satisfactory conclusion. This may be a challenge where participants have developed a long-term commitment to a study and value their contribution and the relationships that have been built. Researchers too may need mechanisms to 'let go' of relationships that they have painstakingly built and sustained over time. A range of exit strategies may be employed, including a celebratory event or the production of collaborative outputs. *See also*: Longitudinal ethics

Ethical literacy *See* Longitudinal ethics

Ethics of data sharing and re-use
Revisiting legacy data requires an ethic of mutual respect between the original data producers and re-users. This ensures that reputational damage is avoided when early findings are overturned or outmoded forms of conduct or attitudes are uncovered. It also encourages the original data producers to facilitate the work of their successors and to pass the mantle when appropriate. Working within an interpretive framework that acknowledges the provisional and partial nature of research findings is helpful here. *See also*: Data sharing; Archiving; Longitudinal ethics

Ethics of mutual respect *See* Ethics of data sharing and re-use

Ethnography *See* Longitudinal ethnography

Ethnomethodology The study of how, in practice, people construct and find meaning in their social relationships, and make sense of the social fabric. The focus is on specific, situated meanings and practical reasoning, rather than the production of broader generalisations. The approach has developed from phenomenology. *See also*: Phenomenology; Interpretivist tradition

Events in time *See* Fixed time

Exit strategy *See* Ethical closure

Experience sampling *See* Diary methods

Experiential methods These are arts-based participatory methods for generating data that rely on evoking memories, embodying experiences or creatively conveying or encapsulating ideas. They include the use of music, dance, drama, and a range of visual tools. These may be employed during a field encounter or set up as complementary events. Such creative tools may also be used to convey research findings in arresting and accessible ways. *See also*: Participatory methods; Narrative methods; Visual methods; Data generation

Family chains *See* Cohorts

Fixed time This is linear, absolute, measurable time, the structured realm of the clock and calendar. Also known as 'events in time': a broad 'umbrella' force within which lives are lived and events unfold. A linear view of temporal processes underpins positivist social research, exemplified in the logic of Newtonian physics. Fixed understandings of time complement fluid time. *See also*: Fluid time; Cyclical time/patterns; Spiraling patterns; Movies

Flexibility (in field enquiry) *See* Continuity/flexibility

Fluid Enquiry Processual research that engages with fluid time

Fluid time This is non-linear, multi-dimensional, relative time, the social and experiential realm of lived experiences. Also known as 'time in events': time is not external to our social practices and day-to-day lives; it inheres within them. Time in this formulation is a social construct, our creation. An interpretive lens is needed to discern fluid time. Fluid time complements fixed time. *See also*: Fixed time; Cyclical time/patterns; Spiraling patterns; Movies; Process analysis; Fluid enquiry

Framework grids Structured analytical tools, particularly suited to QL research, that enable a condensed, three-dimensional visualisation of themes in relation to cases and waves of data (time periods). They can be constructed for each case in a study, and/or for each key theme. *See also*: Case analysis; Thematic analysis; Qualitative longitudinal analysis

Funnel approach *See* Sampling through time

Generational cohorts *See* Cohorts

Grid analysis *See* Visual methods; Framework grids

Grounded theory A structured method for generating and analysing qualitative data, based on the systematic production of theory from data. It uses finely grained categorising, coding and constant comparison of data segments to build insights. Theoretical sampling of new cases continues until concepts are 'saturated'. This is conventionally understood as a broadly inductive logic of enquiry, although it is also recognised as abductive. The approach developed from symbolic interactionism. *See also*: Symbolic interactionism; Abductive logic; Categorising/connecting strategies

Hermeneutics/hermeneutic circle Hermeneutics is an interpretive framework of social understanding that seeks meaning in social actions/interactions (Dilthey 2002 [1920]). The hermeneutic circle is an iterative process by which researchers oscillate between the particular and the general, individual and social, interpreting the fragmented parts of a social system from multiple vantage points, to produce new understandings. The idea of the circle recognises that social events and practices are always situated within a larger socio-historical context, and that any interpretation of the social world requires an investigation of how the parts of this system are related to the whole. It is also conceptualised as a holistic or gestalt approach. *See also*: Interpretivist tradition; Micro–macro; Double hermeneutic; Phenomenology

Horizons of time *See* Timescapes

Idiographic Encapsulates the aim of phenomenologists and ethnomethodologists to explore specific experiences and meanings rather than produce broader generalisations about the social world. An idiographic stance reflects a commitment to the uniqueness of individuals and the particularities of their lives. *See also*: Interpretivist tradition; Phenomenology; Ethnomethodology

Imaginary futures Autobiographical accounts of future lives, aspirations, plans, hopes and fears. Such accounts are generated as part of life journey interviewing but can also be produced directly by participants. They may be drawn out using written, audio or visual (life mapping) tools. They reflect how participants locate themselves in the stream of time, and may give important insights into the seeds of change.

See also: Data generation; Autobiographical accounts; Participatory methods

Induction *See* Abductive logic

Integrative reviews and analyses *See* Qualitative generalisations

Intensive–extensive (time frames and tempos) This plane of time is concerned with the time frames or duration of temporal processes, the tempo of events, their spacing and regularity, and whether they occur intensively over the short term or extensively over the long term. Methodologically, a spectrum of QL designs is evident: cases may be traced *intensively* via frequent or continuous visits to the field; or *extensively* through regular, occasional or 'punctuated' revisits over decades. In QL research, these two tempos may be combined as a study evolves. Ideally, the tempo of a study will mirror real-world processes. *See also*: Timescapes; Design; Baseline/closure points

Internal confidentiality The process by which participants pledge to uphold the confidentiality of their co-participants. This is an important component of longitudinal ethics. Internal confidentiality needs to be secured when working with groups who know each other, including those who are brought together as part of a panel in a QL study. *See also*: Confidentiality/authenticity; Longitudinal ethics

Interpretative phenomenological analysis (IPA) *See* Phenomenology

Interpretive integrity The relational, real-world dimensions of quality in a QL study. Interpretive integrity is based on fidelity to the tenets of interpretative enquiry, i.e. on fidelity to lived experiences and the inner logic of lives, garnered through field

enquiry that takes agency, subjectivity and reflexivity seriously, and which embeds these in the analysis and presentation of findings. *See also*: Temporal integrity

Interpretivist tradition This tradition of enquiry holds that the social world is experienced, interpreted, constructed, reconstructed and transformed by its members through their everyday actions and interactions with others. This provides the foundation for QL research. Interpretivist thinking encompasses social constructionist ideas, and draws on both hermeneutics and phenomenology. It accords priority to human agency, subjectivity and lived experience as the means to reach a deep understanding of the social fabric and its dynamic nature. Since this research is situated in time and space, findings are provisional and subject to reinterpretation. *See also*: Phenomenology; Hermeneutics/hermeneutic circle; Agency; Subjectivity; Reflexivity; Lived experience; Critical realist tradition; Positivist tradition; Paradigms

Interviewing One of four broad ways of generating data in a QL study. Interviews are in-depth and qualitative. Life journey interviewing explores the processes that shape people's journeys through time, including the 'back story' and orientations to the future, alongside current experiences and circumstances. A cartographic strategy can be employed to explore the surface features of the journey, before digging down to excavate underlying themes. Recursive techniques are also employed to revisit/reinterpret experiences and orientations to past and future. *See also*: Data generation; Recursive interviewing/analysis; Narrative methods; Imaginary futures; Participatory methods;

Longitudinal ethnography; Legacy data research

Intimate epics *See* Movies

Intimate movies *See* Movies

Iteration The core method of abductive logic. Iteration is not simply an instrumental, repetitive task, a mechanical form of feedback. It is a reflexive, oscillating process of continuous meaning making, which brings together varied sources of evidence and insights, and gradually distils a rich mosaic of concepts, themes and interpretations. *See also*: Abductive logic; Recursion

Knowledge co-production *See* Longitudinal impact studies

Legacy data/legacy data research One of four broad ways of generating data in a QL study. Pre-existing, archival or legacy data are used to enrich and complement QL field enquiry. Legacy data are important documents of lives and times that can increase the temporal reach of a study. QL researchers are both producers and users of legacy data. Working with legacy data entails searching, sampling and sculpting data to maximise the degree of 'fit' with evolving research questions. Researchers who pool their legacy data for integrative analysis can build more extensive bodies of knowledge and evidence. *See also*: Data generation; Archiving; Data sharing; Ethics of data sharing/re-use; Qualitative generalisations; Interviewing; Longitudinal ethnography; Participatory methods

Life course research A concern with how lives flow through time, how biographies are shaped, how causal processes unfold through time, and how these processes intersect with broader shifts and transformations in the social fabric. This is a central organising framework for QL research. It encompasses the study of collective as well as individual biographies, and the nested horizons of turning points, transitions and trajectories. *See also*: Turning points; Transitions; Trajectories; Complex causality

Life history charts/life grids *See* Visual methods

Life journey interviewing *See* Interviewing

Liminality The state of being 'in limbo', betwixt and between two worlds. Liminality was first identified by van Gennep as the central element in his rites of passage: a state that separates life experiences and creates a bridge from the old to the new. *See also*: turning points

Linear time *See* Fixed time

Lived experience A central concept in the interpretivist tradition (Dilthey 2002 [1910]). Defined as a complex mix of experiences, social practices and values, in which imaginative and accomplished humans interact with others to create and recreate their social worlds. Lived experiences are essentially temporal; experiences are necessarily lived through time, for they are part of a dynamic, interconnected system in which meaning is derived from understanding of the past and anticipation of the future. *See also*: Interpretivist tradition; Hermeneutics/hermeneutic circle

Lock-in (process tracing) Inflexibility or stagnation, where the momentum for change dissipates or is actively suppressed. *See also*: Process analysis; Complexity theories

Longitudinal case analysis *See* Case analysis

Longitudinal ethics Refers to the ethical literacy needed in 'walking alongside' a panel of participants, and sustaining ethical relationships over time. Maintaining a panel of participants in a QL study relies on maintaining good quality relationships. Proactive strategies (working with pre-defined ethical protocols) need to be balanced with reactive strategies (responding to unanticipated dilemmas as they arise). Standard ethical considerations (consent, confidentiality, maintaining professional boundaries, privacy – not intruding on personal matters) are transformed when relationships develop through time. New dilemmas also arise (for example, around reciprocity over time and the ethical closure of a project). The principle of shared authority and the ethics of data sharing and re-use are important components of longitudinal ethics. *See also*: Consent; Confidentiality/authenticity; Internal confidentiality; Ethical closure; Shared authority; Ethics of data sharing and re-use

Longitudinal ethnography One of four broad ways of generating data in a QL study. These studies typically involve a continuous or recurrent ethnographic immersion in the field, using participant observation and shadowing techniques. This may be followed by a more extensive engagement that may run over decades. Longitudinal ethnographers use both prospective and retrospective methods. They explore how lives are being lived, as well as narrated, and how both lived and narrated lives change through time. Longitudinal ethnographic methods represent the earliest forms of QL enquiry. *See also*: Data generation; Interviewing; Participatory methods; Legacy data research; Prospective–retrospective; Narrative methods; Socio-historical studies

Longitudinal impact studies QL studies that seek to make a difference by working collaboratively with policy, practice or community partners to design and conduct a study, and/or to navigate and craft a change process. This integrated approach to brokering the research-policy interface is based on the principles of knowledge co-production. Superceding earlier linear models based on knowledge transfer and knowledge exchange, it fosters practice-informed research and research-based practice. These studies have affinities with participatory action research and design-based educational research, which are founded on the principles of empowerment and shared authority. The broad aim is to bring about productive change in collective practices and thereby to improve the quality of lives. The impact from longitudinal impact studies is a joint accomplishment. Since the research is harnessed to practice developments, impact is created as an integral part of the research process.

Longitudinal studies *See* Qualitative longitudinal studies; Quantitative longitudinal studies

Macro *See* Micro–macro

Meso *See* Micro–macro

Micro–macro (scales of time) This plane of time is concerned with how events and experiences unfold at different scales of the social fabric (from micro dynamic understanding of personal lives, through meso understandings of interpersonal, collective and institutional lives, to macro understandings of broader socio-historical processes). A rounded process analysis will need to explore how these different facets of the social fabric intersect; how, for example, lived experiences mesh with and unfold against a backdrop of shifting policy processes. In QL enquiry, socio-historical processes are anchored in and understood through the unfolding lives of individuals and groups. *See also*: Timescapes; Hermeneutics/hermeneutic circle

Mirroring process *See* Intensive–extensive (time frames and tempos)

Mixed longitudinal designs QL studies may be nested within or linked to large-scale quantitative studies, enabling researchers to work across different scales of enquiry, to link research questions and different forms of data, and to combine qualitative depth with quantitative breadth. *See also*: Design; Qualitative longitudinal research; Quantitative longitudinal studies

Movies Longitudinal designs, whether qualitative or quantitative, create 'movies' of unfolding processes. There are several kinds of longitudinal movie. Quantitatively driven epic movies trace broad patterns and trends across larges samples of the population, and create a surface picture of social dynamics. Qualitatively driven intimate movies provide an up-close-and-personal picture of how lives unfold for particular individuals or groups. Intimate epics are hybrid, medium-scale qualitative panel studies that combine breadth of coverage with depth of insight. *See also* Diachronic; Qualitative longitudinal research; Quantitative longitudinal studies; Design

Narrative/narrative methods Narratives are written or spoken accounts of connected events and experiences that tell an unfolding tale. As styles of telling, stories of experience and ways of knowing, they are

the means by which we story our lives and make sense of lived experiences. Narrative methods are central to research in the interpretivist tradition. In QL enquiry, they are used to generate data about dynamic processes, complete with a sense of 'plot' that suggests how and why things unfold. Narrative methods are used to generate QL data; they underpin life journey and recursive forms of interviewing, narrative diaries and other forms of autobiographical account. Narrative methods are important means of analysing/making sense of data, and conveying findings. *See also*: Interviewing; Diary methods; Imaginary futures; Autobiographical accounts; Qualitative longitudinal analysis

Neo-positivist *See* Positivist tradition

Nested QL studies *See* Mixed longitudinal designs

Panels/panel designs A panel study follows the same individuals or collectives (a 'panel' of participants) prospectively, as their lives unfold, to discern change as it occurs. A panel design is synonymous with, and a good short hand for, a prospective longitudinal study. The process is also captured in the notion of 'walking alongside' participants. A panel implies an established group of participants, with shared characteristics and a shared identity, with the capacity for a sustained engagement with the research process. *See also*: Design; Recurrent cross-sectional designs; Walking alongside

Paradigms Integrated sets of conceptual ideas that feed into and acquire a dominant position in social research (interpretivist, positivist and critical realist thinking are prime examples). Paradigms provide a methodological blueprint for researchers to follow, but they have porous boundaries and are continually shifting as new ideas come to prominence. There is no one-to-one correspondence between paradigms and research methods; strict adherence to one paradigm is unnecessary and undesirable. They are described here in more fluid terms as research traditions. *See also*: Interpretivist tradition; Critical realist tradition; Positivist tradition; Pragmatism

Participant engagement *See* Shared Authority

Participant observation *See* Walking alongside; Longitudinal ethnography

Participatory action research *See* Longitudinal impact studies

Participatory methods One of four broad ways of generating data in a QL study. Participatory methods involve the production of data by participants that is relatively unmediated by the researcher. This includes autobiographical accounts and diaries of past, future and evolving lives; visual methods (drawings, graphs, photography, video); and experiential arts-based methods. A participatory ethos may also run more broadly through a project, engaging participants in shaping lines of enquiry and in the way data are analysed, represented and conveyed to a wider audience. *See also*: Data generation; Narrative methods, Diary methods; Visual methods; Experiential methods; Shared authority; Interviewing; Longitudinal ethnography; Legacy data research

Path dependency (process tracing) Conveys the idea that the momentum for change builds through incremental and cumulative events and interactions, that is, that the path being followed helps to shape the destination reached. How this shaping occurs is open to debate. From a fixed, linear, predictive perspective, the past determines the present, which in turn determines the future: it is portrayed as a relentless, inexorable process from which individuals cannot escape. From a fluid perspective, however, the past is a creative as well as constraining force, which may lead people to choose new and exploratory directions, or to modify the pace at which they travel the path. *See also*: Process analysis; Complexity theories; Turning point

Pen portraits *See* Case analysis

Phenomenology A descriptive and experiential framework of social understanding that explores how individuals experience phenomena in the world (Husserl 1964 [1901–10]). The focus is on subjective meanings, human consciousness (judgement, perception, emotion) and lived experience. This has fed into the development of ethnomethodology and interpretative phenomenological analysis, which is used by psychologists to explore how people understand and make sense of the world. *See also*: Ethnomethodology; Hermeneutics/hermeneutic circle; Interpretivist tradition; Idiographic

Photo diaries *see* Visual methods

Photographic elicitation/sourcing *See* Visual methods

Positivist tradition This scientific tradition holds that the social world can be measured statistically and understood objectively (from the outside) through careful observation, and that social laws can be formulated to explain behaviour.

Neo-positivist thinking moves away from the idea of universal laws/ definitive findings. It seeks to generalise through a deductive approach that tests hypotheses through large-scale, statistically representative empirical studies. *See also*: Interpretivist tradition; Critical realist tradition; Abductive logic; Paradigms; Quantitative longitudinal studies

Pragmatism An ethos of social enquiry that holds that theories should be useful, derived from experience and practice, and that rather than adhere to one paradigm, researchers should design a bespoke set of methods that best fits their research questions (Pierce, James, Mead). For many researchers, pragmatism is understood to increase the quality of social research. *See also*: Paradigms

Privacy *See* Longitudinal ethics

Proactive/reactive ethical strategies *See* Longitudinal ethics

Procedural consent *See* Consent

Process analysis A through-time mode of analysis that traces and maps the pathways and trajectories which are under investigation. It is a central component of qualitative longitudinal analysis. It enables an understanding of how processes are ordered (sequence analysis), and how the threads of a process are connected and how they converge to produce change. It also entails attention to the multiple, fluid and relational nature of these processual threads, including an understanding of the **tempo** of events (their volatility, stability, speed, pace) and their patterning (linear, multi-directional, cyclical, spiralling). Overall, it relies on asking processual questions, looking back as well as forward in time, following processes where they lead, and tracing and mapping

how they unfold. *See also*: Processes; Path dependency; Lock-in; Punctuated equilibrium; Cyclical time/patterns; Spiralling patterns; Qualitative longitudinal analysis; Complexity theories; Complex causality; Assemblages; Typologies

Process consent *See* Consent

Processes Temporal constructs that convey a sense of flux and change, and illuminate how lives unfold. They are an integral part of the analytical logic that drives QL enquiry. They comprise a rich tapestry of events, actions and interactions that are linked together in a meaningful way through time. They may be thought of as unfolding pathways, but where the course of the path, and its nature, momentum and meaning, are just as important as the destination reached. In a QL study, cases will be carefully chosen to shed light on temporal processes. The search for dynamic links and causal patterns in case data is central to processual enquiry. *See also*: Process analysis; Cases; Themes; Case-theme-process logic

Process mapping *See* Process analysis; Visual methods

Process tracing *See* Process analysis; Assemblages; Lock-in; Path dependency; Punctuated equilibrium; Cyclical time/ patterns; Spiralling patterns

Processual turn A paradigmatic shift in focus from static structures to dynamic processes. This turn is evident across the social and natural sciences. It has led to new investigations into causality, the development of complexity theories, and has created a bridge between interpretive, neo-positive and critical realist thinking. *See also*: Temporal turn; Paradigms

Professional boundary maintenance *See* Longitudinal ethics

Progressive focusing *See* Sampling through time

Prospective–retrospective (past, present, future) This plane of time is concerned with how people orient themselves to time: prospectively (looking forward to the future) and/or retrospectively (looking back to the past). The purest forms of longitudinal research are *prospective*, with a forward momentum. They follow the same people in real-time, capturing changes and continuities as they occur, anticipating them in the future and yielding insights into change in the making. A *retrospective lens* explores dynamic processes through hindsight, a gaze backwards in time from the vantage point of the present day. This is vitally important in generating and analysing QL data, where it forms the basis for tracing processes through time and for developing recursive understandings. In QL research, the temporal gaze oscillates between the two. *See also*: Process analysis; Recursion; Recursive interviewing/analysis; Timescapes

Punctuated equilibrium (process tracing) Erratic changes following periods of relative stability. *See also*: Process analysis

Purposive sampling *See* Sampling strategies

Qualitative generalisations These are not discerned through statistical prevalence, or by extrapolating from a presumed archetypal or typical case. Instead, using abductive logic, they are pieced together (aggregated) through a mosaic of empirical evidence on social practices, lived experiences and structures of meaning and knowledge. Integrative forms of analyses, alongside integrative reviews, enable the use of legacy data, as well as published

findings, to build new forms of evidence. Insights about patterns and processes of social change are given added credence through the extent, variety and weight of this evidence base, and the strategic way in which data and findings are brought into alignment. *See also*: Bricolage; Abductive logic; Legacy data research

Qualitative longitudinal analysis (QLA) A flexible mode of analysis, with no cast-iron rules, procedures or fixed sequence. It has a distinctive three-dimensional logic, based on a combination of case, thematic and processual readings of a dataset. It also has a distinctive temporal momentum. The objective is to piece together a diachronic (through-time) picture from successive waves of synchronic (snapshot) data. *See also*: Case analysis; Thematic analysis; Process analysis; Case-theme-process logic; Synchronic; Diachronic; Recursive interviewing/analysis; Typologies

Qualitative longitudinal (QL) research These studies follow the same people closely, in real-time, to discern how their lives unfold. They turn a 'snapshot' of social life into a longitudinal 'movie' that can shed light on processes of change and continuity. In their qualitative dimensions, QL studies use in-depth, ethnographic, case study, narrative and participatory methods. This creates an intimate movie of changing lives, akin to 'walking alongside' participants as their lives unfold. This combination of real-time and real-world enquiry gives QL research its rich explanatory power. *See also*: Walking alongside; Design; Panels/panel designs; Movies; Longitudinal impact studies; Quantitative longitudinal studies

Qualitative panel studies *See* Movies; Design

Qualitative secondary analysis *See* Legacy data research

Quality of QL research *See* Interpretive integrity; Temporal integrity

Quantitative longitudinal studies These studies chart broad changes in patterns of social behaviour through the generation of big 'thin' numerical data that can be analysed using event history modelling or other statistical techniques. These studies are able to measure what changes, for whom, the direction and extent of change, and where, when and how often change occurs. This gives a bird's eye view of social trends, a long shot, a broad, surface picture of social dynamics. The result is an epic movie. *See also*: Movies; Qualitative longitudinal research; Positivist tradition; Recurrent cross-sectional designs

Reciprocity *see* Longitudinal ethics

Recurrent cross-sectional designs/ analysis Unlike panel designs, these longitudinal studies recruit different cohorts at each wave of data collection. Each person is interviewed just once. Such studies give a snapshot view of change across the population at each point in time. They generate time series data, which discerns broad patterns of change at an aggregate or population level, but not at the micro level of the individual. Similarly, recurrent cross-sectional analysis gives a synchronic (snapshot) picture of key themes across the data, generated at discrete points in time. *See also*: Design; Panels/panel designs; Thematic analysis; Categorising/ connecting strategies; Synchronic; Diachronic; Positivist tradition; Quantitative longitudinal studies

Recursion *See* Recursion. This play on words, loved by mathematicians, conveys the loop-like, recurring and self-referential nature of recursion (also reflected in Lewis Carroll's *Alice through the Looking Glass*). It is a process in which events, interactions, experiences or processes in the past or future are revisited and re-examined from a new temporal standpoint, to shed fresh light on their meaning and significance. Recursion can be thought of as a form of iteration (feedback), but, instead of working across two entities to explore their connections, this is iteration between different versions of the same entity, produced at different moments in time. Recursion is inherently temporal and retrospective. The longitudinal frame of a QL study has a unique capacity to generate recursive understandings. *See also*: Recursive interviewing/analysis

Recursive case analysis *See* Recursive interviewing/analysis

Recursive interviewing/analysis Recursive techniques are used in interviewing and analysis to draw out recursive understandings. Recursive interviewing involves looking both backward and forward in time, revisiting, re-visioning and updating a life journey at each successive interview. Participants are invited to review the past, update previous understandings and re-imagine the future through the lens of the ever-shifting present. This makes it possible to compare accounts of intentions and expectations with how events and circumstances actually unfold. Recursive case analysis aims to weave fluid, recursive understandings into a case history. It involves tracing backward to see how far earlier aspirations have been fulfilled or redirected, and gaining insight into changing perceptions through time. *See also*: Recursion; Iteration; Reflexivity; Data generation; Interviewing; Case analysis

Reflexivity The process of examining one's thoughts, feelings, beliefs, values and practices to question taken-for-granted assumptions, and to reinforce or modify understandings. In QL research, participant reflexivity is invited through life journey and recursive interviewing, and occurs more generally through the longitudinal process of revisiting participants at different points in time. In the interpretive tradition, reflexivity applies to the understandings of researchers as well as participants. The theoretical drivers for a study, the joint production of insights in interviewing and the interpretive frame that shapes enquiry (the double hermeneutic) mean that researchers cannot take themselves out of the picture. They are deeply implicated in the processes that they seek to describe and explain. Researcher reflexivity enhances the quality of QL studies. *See also*: Subjectivity; Interpretivist tradition; Double hermeneutic; Recursion; Interviewing; Interpretive integrity

Repeated cross-sectional designs *See* Recurrent cross-sectional designs

Reputational damage *See* Ethics of data sharing and re-use

Re-sampling *See* Sampling through time

Re-studies Socio-historical re-studies revisit and update an earlier study, creating the means for a comparison between the two. The orientation is retrospective, and the research usually framed over extensive periods of time (a decade or more). QL re-studies often develop opportunistically. They turn an earlier synchronic 'snapshot' study into a longitudinal study with an extensive temporal reach. Unlike broader socio-historical re-studies, QL re-studies

seek to trace the same individuals (a panel) through extensive time. Wider socio-historical changes are anchored in and understood through the changing lives of individuals or groups. *See also*: Design; Socio-historical studies

Retroductive logic *See* Abductive logic

Retrospective *See* Prospective–retrospective

Sample attrition/maintenance Sample attrition is the process by which panel members drop out of a study because they decline to participate or cannot be contacted. The loss of panel members is a potentially serious drawback. Researchers seek to avoid this by developing varied sample maintenance techniques. For QL researchers, where attrition tends to be low, maintaining a sample depends, in the main, on maintaining good quality relationships between participant and researcher. *See also*: Longitudinal ethics

Sample boosting/condensing *See* Sampling through time

Sampling across cohorts *See* Sampling through time

Sampling strategies These identify an appropriate range of cases or units of study (people, events, settings) as the basis for empirical investigation, that is, deciding who or what to sample, in what settings, how many cases to include and what variations to build in. For QL enquiry, when and how often to engage people are key questions: time, as a unit of study, becomes part of the sampling strategy. Stratified sampling (based on categorising logic) aims to include a numerically balanced number of cases with varied characteristics that are assumed to be representative of a wider population.

Purposive sampling (based on connecting logic and used by qualitative researchers) has a theoretical basis that obviates the need for large or representative samples. It samples experiences/circumstances/processes across a diverse range of complementary cases, rather than measuring similarities/differences across strictly comparable cases. A fluid sampling strategy takes a broad-brush approach to building sample diversity, based on connecting rather than categorising logic. *See also*: Categorising/connecting strategies; Sampling through time; Case-led approach

Sampling through time In QL enquiry, researchers sample through time as well as sampling for particular case characteristics and experiences. Fluid sampling strategies are used to engage with time in creative ways. Time and processes become important units of sampling and analysis. The aim is to thread time into a study in a way that mirrors dynamic processes. QL researchers also re-sample through time. They may boost or 'grow' a sample, or condense it (a funnel approach or progressive focusing). They may also sample across different generational cohorts or family chains to build historical reach into a study. *See also*: Sampling strategies; Cohorts; Categorising/connecting strategies; Intensive–extensive

Sequence analysis *See* Process analysis

Shadowing *See* Walking alongside; Longitudinal ethnography

Shared authority An important dimension of longitudinal ethics, based on consulting with participants, or engaging with them in decisions about how they are involved in a study: what roles they may take on beyond an 'informant' role

(e.g. ambassadorial roles); how they are represented in research outputs; and how findings about their lives are produced and conveyed to a wider audience. The longitudinal frame of a QL study invites such engagement. *See also*: Longitudinal ethics; Longitudinal impact studies

Snapshot diaries *See* Diary methods

Social complexity theory *See* Complexity theories

Social constructionism The insight that knowledge and interpretations are actively constructed by people rather than being passively received by them. *See also*: Interpretivist tradition

Socio-historical re-studies *See* Re-studies

Socio-historical studies A broad umbrella term for varied fields of research that engage qualitatively with time and temporal processes, including the general fields of social history and historical sociology. Longitudinal ethnography, re-studies and biographical (oral, life history, narrative) research are singled out here for their synergies with QL enquiry. These fields of study engage with time in different ways. As a form of socio-historical research, QL research draws on these fields to shape its design features and field techniques. *See also*: Longitudinal ethnography; Re-studies; Biographical studies

Spiralling patterns (process tracing) These are continuously spreading, cumulatively increasing processes that encompass ever-widening spheres of influence and activity. These patterns build through their own momentum, with each new step triggering the next step in a domino effect that grows and then recedes through time. Spiralling patterns may encompass escalating/

de-escalating, expanding/contracting or diverging/converging patterns through time and space. Spiral patterns never return to the same starting point, but move events and experiences on in subtle ways. *See also*: Cyclical time/patterns; Process analysis; Complexity theories

Stratified sampling *See* Sampling strategies

Subjectivity People's thoughts, feelings, beliefs, values, preferences and perceptions – for QL enquiry, the shifting meaning that events, interactions and processes hold for those who experience them. These are foundational dimensions of the interpretivist tradition for social research. *See also*: Reflexivity; Agency; Interpretivist tradition

Sustaining relationships *See* Walking alongside; Sample attrition/maintenance; Longitudinal ethics

Symbolic interactionism A tradition of interpretive enquiry which focuses on the interactions between people and the symbolic meanings and interpretations that people attach to their actions and practices. This has fed into the development of grounded theory. *See also*: Grounded theory; Interpretivist tradition

Synchronic A synchronic (snapshot) approach is concerned with an entity or state (e.g. a social practice, the nature of an organisation, an institution or a language) as it exists at one particular moment in time. In longitudinal research, it refers to the process by which data are generated or analysed at one moment in time. *See also*: Diachronic

Tempo *See* Intensive–extensive; Process analysis

Temporal horizons *See* Timescapes

Temporal integrity The methodological dimension of quality in a QL study. Temporal integrity is based on the coherence or degree of fit between the ontological and epistemological drivers of a QL study (which are grounded in a fluid temporality), and the capacity of its methodology to reflect and capture this fluidity. *See also*: Interpretive integrity

Temporal sampling *See* Sampling through time

Temporal Thematic analysis *See* Thematic analysis

Temporal turn A paradigmatic shift that recognises time and temporality as foundational dimensions of human experience. This broad shift in thinking towards the dynamics of individual and social lives is evident across the academy. *See also*: Processual turn; Paradigms

Thematic analysis A categorising mode of analysis, based on a broad, cross-case thematic reading and re-organisation of data. It is a central part of the qualitative longitudinal analysis (QLA) tool kit. It builds greater breadth into the analysis through an exploration of conceptual and substantive themes, patterns and connections across the data. Tools to support thematic analysis include thematic charts (summative tools that give a graphic display of changing circumstances across the sample for each key theme); framework grids; and qualitative data analysis (QDA) software tools. While recurrent cross-sectional analysis gives a synchronic picture of themes at each point in time, temporal thematic analysis gives a diachronic through-time picture of key processual themes. *See also*: Themes; Framework grids; Typologies; Categorising/connecting strategies; Recurrent cross-sectional designs/

analysis; Case analysis; Process analysis; Qualitative longitudinal analysis

Thematic charts *See* Thematic analysis

Themes The conceptual and substantive lenses through which empirical case data are studied and analysed. They are an integral part of the analytical logic that drives QL enquiry. For QL research, temporality is a theme (as well as the framework through which data are generated). Key themes are likely to be temporally inflected (e.g. a switch in focus from health to health trajectories). Thematic investigation and analysis build greater breadth into a study and provide a bridge to wider, pre-existing bodies of theory and knowledge. *See also*: Emblematic Themes; Thematic analysis; Typologies; Cases; Processes; Case-theme-process logic

Thick description The generation of empirical data that give insights into the inner logic of lives, and the world views of participants. Thick description is not simply **rich data** – a detailed description of practices and circumstances (however valuable that is). It also encompasses how participants find and convey meaning in their daily interactions, and how they interpret the social world (Geertz 1973).

Through-line *See* Continuity/flexibility

Time frame *See* Intensive–extensive

Time in events *See* Fluid time

Timescapes Flows or planes of time. A scape is a vista, a view of the world that changes in kaleidoscopic ways, depending on the position and disposition of the observer. In QL enquiry, varied planes of time can be discerned as the basis for empirical investigation: prospective–retrospective, intensive–extensive, micro–macro, time–space and continuity–

discontinuity. These flows of time overlap and flow into each other; they are not mutually exclusive. Within these planes of time, a multitude of time horizons exist, near and far, stretching into the past and future, which move as the observer moves. *See also*: Prospective–retrospective; intensive–extensive; micro–macro

Time series data/studies *See* Recurrent cross-sectional designs

Tipping point A point of no return that may lead to a radically altered state; also characterised as a watershed moment, catalyst or 'final straw'. *See also*: Turning point

Trajectories The unfolding contours of lives that stretch across the life span; the broader and more extensive paths that people follow. Turning points and transitions are nested within trajectories, and influence how trajectories unfold. *See also*: Turning point; Trigger point; Transitions; Life course research

Transcription *See* Data management

Transitions Changes from one state or circumstance to another. These may unfold over varied periods of time, at different paces and intensities, and they may or may not be planned, prescribed, managed or desired by those involved. These temporal constructs give insights into how lives unfold, both individually and collectively. They are nested within longer-term trajectories and likely to be constituted through a series of turning and trigger points. *See also*: Turning point; Trigger point; Trajectories; Life course research

Triangulation Using more than one method, theory or source of data, and comparing the insights to iron out factual inconsistencies and verify the findings. This strategy is conventionally used to enhance the quality of a study. The alternative approach, advocated here, is iteration, a more finely grained strategy for drawing together and working across a mosaic of evidence and meanings, which is integral to abductive logic. *See also*: Abductive logic; Iteration

Trigger point An event, experience or interaction that acts as the trigger point for change; a change in an inner biographical disposition. Multiple trigger points may create the conditions for change. *See also*: Turning points

Turning points A loose umbrella term to denote a plethora of critical events, pivotal moments, epiphanies and tipping points that may act as the trigger or driver of change. They are the connecting forces that link events, actions and interactions together to create the momentum for change. The varied metaphors used to describe these phenomena reflect subtle differences in their nature and the way they operate. They occur in striking moments in time and their longer-term power and influence are best understood in retrospect, with hindsight. They are nested within transitions and longer-term trajectories. Viewing these phenomena together and discerning their intersections can provide insights into how causal processes unfold. *See also*: Tipping point; Trigger point; Transitions; Trajectories; Life course research; Complex causality; Process analysis; Complexity theories

Typologies Analytical tools that identify and distinguish between varied conceptual or substantive patterns in research data, e.g. relating to case characteristics, human agency, practices or processes. Used, for example, in qualitative longitudinal analysis to discern varied pathways/trajectories across the cases in a sample. *See also*: Qualitative longitudinal analysis; Case analysis

Visual methods These are important components of the methods used in the field to generate dynamic data, and are also used to convey the findings of a study. Spanning drawings, graphs, charts, photography and video recordings, they are often used as participatory tools. Drawings and graphs, such as life maps or life grids/life history charts, can be constructed to map out a life story and draw out an accompanying narrative. Intuitive life maps are the most commonly employed, and can be used recursively to revisit and update an earlier narrative. Photography and video recordings are powerful ways of visualising lives, and of capturing processes beyond the confines of an interview. Photos can be sourced by the researcher, elicited from participants or created especially for a study, including by participants themselves (known as photo voice). Photo diaries (an elaboration of photo voice) tell an unfolding tale of events and are increasingly popular tools. *See also*: Participatory methods; Data generation; Diary methods

Walking alongside A metaphor that conveys the distinctive nature of qualitative longitudinal research. It captures the real-time tempo of QL enquiry, its responsive and relational nature, and the central concern with generating deep and personal insights into the dynamics of lives. It has particular resonance in the context of longitudinal ethics, for it creates a new landscape for ethical practice. Where QL researchers aim to 'be there' ethnographically, walking alongside may occur in a more literal sense, through walking interviews, or through shadowing (accompanying participants and observing what happens), or participant observation (joining in). *See also*: Qualitative longitudinal research; Design; Longitudinal ethnography; Longitudinal ethics

REFERENCES

Abbott, A. (1995a) 'Sequence analysis: New methods for old ideas', *Annual Review of Sociology*, 21: 93–113.

Abbott, A. (1995b) 'A primer on sequence methods', in G. Huber and A. Van de Ven (eds) *Longitudinal Field Research Methods*. London: Sage, pp. 204–27.

Abbott, A. (2001) *Time Matters: On Theory and Method*. Chicago: University of Chicago Press.

Abbott, A. (2016) *Processual Sociology*. Chicago: University of Chicago Press.

Abrams, P. (1982) *Historical Sociology*. Ithaca, NY: Cornell University Press.

Adam, B. (1990) *Time and Social Theory*. Cambridge: Polity Press.

Adam, B. (1995) *Timewatch: The Social Analysis of Time*. Cambridge: Polity Press.

Adam, B. (1998) *Timescapes of Modernity: The Environment and Invisible Hazards*. London: Routledge.

Adam, B. and Groves, C. (2007) *Future Matters: Action, Knowledge, Ethics*. Boston: Brill.

Agar, M. (1980) *The Professional Stranger: An Informal Introduction to Ethnography*. London: Academic Press.

Agar, M. (2006) 'An ethnography by any other name', *Forum: Qualitative Social Research*, 7 (4): Art. 36.

Agren, M. (1998) 'Life at 85 and 92: A qualitative longitudinal study of how the oldest old experience and adjust to the increased uncertainty of existence', *International Journal of Aging and Human Development*, 47 (2): 105–17.

Åkerström, M., Jacobsson, K. and Wästerfors, D. (2004) 'Re-analysis of previously collected material', in C. Seale, G. Gobo, J. Gubrium and D. Silverman (eds) *Qualitative Research Practice* (concise edition). London: Sage, pp. 314–27.

Akesson, B. (2015) 'Using map-making to research the geographies of young children affected by political violence', in N. Worth and I. Hardill (eds) *Researching the Life Course: Critical Perspectives from the Social Sciences*. Bristol: Policy Press, pp. 123–41.

Alexander, K., Entwisle, D. and Olson, L. (2014) *The Long Shadow: Family Background, Disadvantaged Urban Youth, and the Transition to Adulthood*. New York: Russell Sage Foundation.

Alheit, P. (1994) 'Everyday time and life time: On the problems of healing contradictory experiences of time', *Time and Society*, 3 (3): 305–19.

Alldred, P. (1998) 'Ethnography and discourse analysis: Dilemmas in representing the voices of children', in J. Ribben and R. Edwards (eds) *Ethics in Qualitative Research*. London: Sage, pp. 147–70.

Alldred, P. and Gillies, V. (2012) 'Eliciting research accounts: Re/producing modern subjects?', in T. Miller, M. Birch, M. Mauthner and J. Jessop (eds) *Ethics in Qualitative Research*, 2nd edition. London: Sage, pp. 140–56.

Anderson, G. and Scott, J. (2012) 'Towards an intersectional understanding of process causality and social context', *Qualitative Inquiry*, 18 (8): 674–85.

Andrews, M. (2007) *Shaping History: Narratives of Political Change*. Cambridge: Cambridge University Press.

Andrews, M. (2008) 'Never the last word: Revisiting data', in M. Andrews, C. Squire and M. Tamboukou (eds) *Doing Narrative Research*. London: Sage, pp. 86–101.

Andrews, M., Squire, C. and Tamboukou, M. (eds) (2008) *Doing Narrative Research*. London: Sage.

Ansell-Pearson, K. (2018) *Bergson: Thinking Beyond the Human Condition*. London: Bloomsbury Academic.

Apted, M. (1999) *Seven Up!* (ed. B. Singer). London: Heinemann.

Archer, M. (1982) 'Morphogenesis versus structuration: On combining structure and action', *British Journal of Sociology*, 33 (4): 455–83.

Ariès, P. (1962) *Centuries of Childhood: A Social History of Family Life*. New York: Vintage.

Atkinson, P. (1992) 'The ethnography of a medical setting: Reading, writing and rhetoric', *Qualitative Health Research*, 2: 451–74.

Back, L. (2007) *The Art of Listening*. Oxford: Berg.

Bajc, V. (2012) 'Abductive ethnography of practice in highly uncertain conditions', *Annals of the American Academy of Political and Social Science*, 642 (July): 72–85.

Baker, S. (2010) *Reflections on Secondary Analysis of the Siblings and Friends Data*, www.timescapes-archive.leeds.ac.uk/publications-and-outputs.

Baraitser, L. (2013) 'Mush time: Communality and the temporal rhythms of family life', *Families, Relationships and Societies*, 2 (1): 147–53.

Barley, S. (1995) 'Images of imaging: Notes on doing longitudinal fieldwork', in G. Huber and A. Van de Ven (eds) *Longitudinal Field Research Methods*. London: Sage, pp. 1–37.

Barnard, A. (2012) 'Widening the net: Returns to the field and regional understandings', in S. Howell and A. Talle (eds) *Returns to the Field: Multi-temporal Research and Contemporary Anthropology*. Bloomington, IN: Indiana University Press, pp. 230–49.

Barry, C., Britten, N., Barber, N., et al. (1999) 'Using reflexivity to optimise teamwork in qualitative research', *Qualitative Health Research*, 9 (1): 26–44.

Bartlett, L. and Vavrus, F. (2017) 'Comparative case studies: An innovative approach', *Nordic Journal of Comparative and International Education (NJCIE)*, 1 (1).

Bartlett, R. and Milligan, C. (2015) *What is Diary Method?* London: Bloomsbury.

Bastian, M. (2014) 'Time and community: A scoping study', *Time and Society*, 2 (4).

Bates, C. and Rhys-Taylor, A. (eds) (2017) *Walking through Social Research*. London: Routledge.

Becker, H. (1966 [1930]) 'Introduction', in C. Shaw (ed.) *The Jack-Roller: A Delinquent Boy's own Story*. Chicago: University of Chicago Press, pp. v–xviii.

Becker, H. and Geer, B. (1957) 'Participant observation and interviewing: A comparison', *Human Organisation*, 16 (3): 28–32.

Bell, A. (2005) '"Oh yes I remember it well!" Reflections on using the life grid in qualitative interviews with couples', *Qualitative Sociology Review*, 1 (1): 51–67.

Bell, C. and Newby, H. (1971) *Community Studies*. London: Allen & Unwin.

Bengston, V., Biblarz, T. and Roberts, R. (2002) *How Families Still Matter: A Longitudinal Study of Youth in Two Generations*. Cambridge: CUP.

Berger, P. and Luckmann, T. (1971 [1966]) *The Social Construction of Reality: A Treatise in the Sociology of Knowledge*. London: Penguin University Books.

Bergson, H. (1908 [1896]) *Matter and Memory*, 5th edition (trans. N. Paul and W. Palmer). London: Zone Books.

Bergson, H. (1910 [1889]) *Time and Free Will* (trans. F. Pogson). London: Allen & Unwin.

Bergson, H. (1944 [1911]) *Creative Evolution*. New York: Modern Library.

Bergson, H. (1946 [1903]) 'Introduction to metaphysics', in *The Creative Mind*. New York: Citadel Press, pp. 159–200.

Bergson, H. (1946 [1922]) 'Introductions 1 and 11', in *The Creative Mind*. New York: Citadel Press, pp. 11–90. [A collection of essays published between 1903 and 1922.]

Berriman, L. and Thomson, R. (forthcoming) 'Starting with the archive: Principles for prospective collaborative research', *Qualitative Research*.

Bertaux, D. (ed.) (1981) *Biography and Society: The Life History Approach in the Social Sciences*. London: Sage.

Bertaux, D. and Delcroix, C. (2000) 'Case histories of families and social processes', in P. Chamberlayne, J. Bornat and T. Wengraf (eds) *The Turn to Biographical Methods in Social Science*. London: Routledge, pp. 71–89.

Bertaux, D. and Thompson, P. (eds) (1993) *Between Generations: Family Models, Myths and Memories*. Oxford: OUP.

Berthoud, R. (2000) 'Introduction: The dynamics of social change', in R. Berthoud and J. Gershuny (eds), *Seven Years in the Lives of British Families*. Bristol: Policy Press, pp. 1–20.

Berthoud, R. and Gershuny, J. (eds) (2000) *Seven Years in the Lives of British Families: Evidence on the Dynamics of Social Change from the 'British Household Panel Survey'*. Bristol: Policy Press.

Best, A. and Holmes, A. (2010) 'Systems thinking, knowledge and action: Towards better models and methods', *Evidence and Policy*, 6 (2): 145–59.

Bevan, P. (2014) 'Researching social change and continuity: A complexity-informed study of twenty rural community cases in Ethiopia in 1994–2015', in L. Camfield (ed.) *Methodological Challenges and New Approaches to Research in International Development*. Basingstoke: Palgrave Macmillan, pp. 103–40.

Bidart, C. (2019) 'How plans change: Anticipation, interference and unpredictabilities', *Advances in Life Course Research*, 41 (Sept.).

Bidart, C., Longo, M. and Mendez, A. (2013) 'Time and process: An operational framework for processual analysis', *European Sociological Review*, 29 (4): 743–51.

Birch, M. and Miller, T. (2002) 'Encouraging participation: Ethics and responsibilities', in M. Mauthner, M. Birch, J. Jessop and T. Miller (eds) *Ethics in Qualitative Research*. London: Sage, pp. 91–106.

Birmingham, K. (2018) *Pioneering Ethics in a Longitudinal Study: The Early Development of the ALSPAC Ethics and Law Committee*. Bristol: Policy Press.

Bishop, L. (2007) 'A reflexive account of reusing qualitative data: Beyond primary/secondary dualism', *Sociological Research Online*, 12, www.socresonline.org.uk/12/3/2.html.

Bishop, L. (2009) 'Ethical sharing and re-use of qualitative data', *Australian Journal of Social Issues*, 44 (3): 255–72.

Bishop, L. (2012) 'Using archived qualitative data for teaching: Practical and ethical issues', *International Journal of Social Research Methodology*, 15 (4): 341–50.

Bishop, L. (2016) 'Secondary analysis of qualitative data', in D. Silverman (ed.) *Qualitative Research*, 4th edition. London: Sage, pp. 395–411.

Bishop, L. and Kuula-Luumi, A. (2017) 'Revisiting qualitative data reuse: A decade on', *SAGE Open*, Jan.–Mar.: 1–15.

Bishop, L. and Neale, B. (2012) *Data Management for Qualitative Longitudinal Researchers*. Timescapes Methods Guide Series No. 17, www.timescapes-archive.leeds.ac.uk/publications-and-outputs.

Blaikie, A. (1999) *Ageing and Popular Culture*. Cambridge: CUP.

Blaikie, N. (1993) *Approaches to Social Enquiry*. Cambridge: Polity Press.

Blaikie, N. (2007) *Approaches to Social Enquiry*, 2nd edition. Cambridge: Polity Press.

Blaikie, N. and Priest, J. (2017) *Social Research: Paradigms in Action*. Cambridge: Polity Press.

Blows, E., Bird, L., Seymour, J. and Cox, K. (2012) 'Liminality as a framework for understanding the experience of cancer survivorships: A literature review', *Journal of Advanced Nursing*, 68 (10): 2155–64.

Blumenfeld-Jones, D. (1995) 'Fidelity as a criterion for practicing and evaluating narrative inquiry', in J. A. Hatch and R. Wisniewski (eds) *Life History and Narrative*. London: Falmer Press, pp. 25–35.

Bond, G. (1990) 'Fieldnotes: Research in past occurrences', in R. Sanjek (ed.) *Fieldnotes: The Makings of Anthropology*. Ithaca, NY: Cornell University Press, pp. 273–89.

Booth, C. (1902–3) *Life and Labour of the People in London*, 3rd edition. London: Macmillan.

Bootsmiller, B., Ribisi, K., Mowbray, C., Davidson, W., Walton, M. and Herman, S. (1998) 'Methods of ensuring high follow up rates: Lessons from a longitudinal study of dual diagnosis participants', *Substance Use and Misuse*, 33 (13): 2665–85.

Bornat, J. (2003) 'A second take: Revisiting interviews with a different purpose', *Oral History*, 31 (1–2): 47–53.

Bornat, J. (2004) 'Oral history', in C. Seale, G. Gobo, J. Gubrium and D. Silverman (eds) *Qualitative Research Practice*. London: Sage, pp. 34–47.

Bornat, J. (2005) 'Recycling the evidence: Different approaches to the re-analysis of gerontological data', *FQS: Forum: Qualitative Social Research*, 6 (1): Art. 42.

Bornat, J. (2006) *Secondary analysis of one's own and others' data*. Paper presented to the Practice and Ethics in Qualitative Longitudinal Research Seminar, University of Leeds, January.

Bornat, J. (2008) 'Biographical methods', in P. Alasuutari, L. Bickman and J. Brannen (eds) *The Sage Handbook of Social Research Methods*. London: Sage, pp. 344–56.

Bornat, J. (2012) *Oral History and Qualitative Research*. Timescapes Methods Guides No. 12, www.timescapes-archive.leeds.ac.uk/publications-and-outputs.

Bornat, J. (2013) 'Secondary analysis in reflection: Some experiences of re-use from an oral history perspective', *Families, Relationships and Societies*, 2 (2): 309–17.

Bornat, J. (2020) 'Looking back, looking forward: Working with archived oral history interviews', in K. Hughes and A. Tarrant (eds) *Qualitative Secondary Analysis*. London: Sage, pp. 137–53.

Bornat, J. and Bytheway, W. (2008) 'Tracking the lives of the oldest generation', *Generation Review*, 18 (4).

Bornat, J. and Bytheway, W. (2010) 'Perceptions and presentations of living with everyday risk in later life', *British Journal of Social Work*, 40 (4): 1118–34.

Bornat, J. and Bytheway, W. (2012) 'Working with different temporalities: Archived life history interviews and diaries', *International Journal of Social Research Methodology*, 15 (4): 291–9.

Bornat, J., Raghuram, P. and Henry, L. (2012) 'Revisiting the archives: A case from the history of geriatric medicine', *Sociological Research Online*, 17 (2): 11.

Bornat, J., Bytheway, W. and Henwood, K. (2008) *Report of Meeting between the Timescapes 'Men as Fathers' and 'The Oldest Generation' projects*, University of Cardiff, 21st July 2008, https://timescapes-archive.leeds.ac.uk/wp-content/uploads/sites/47/2020/07/report-fathers-oldest-generation-projects-july08.pdf

Boulton, J., Allen, P. and Bowman, C. (2015) *Embracing Complexity: Strategic Perspectives for an Age of Turbulence*. Oxford: OUP.

Bradbury-Huang, H. (2015) *The Sage Handbook of Action Research*. London: Sage.

Brandon, M., Philip, G. and Clifton, J. (2017) *Counting Fathers In: Understanding Men's Experiences of the Child Protection System*. Centre for Research on Children and Families. Norwich: University of East Anglia.

Brannen, J. (2006) 'Cultures of intergenerational transmission in four generation families', *Sociological Review*, 54 (1): 133–55.

Brannen, J. (2013) 'Life story talk: Some reflections on narrative in qualitative interviews', *Sociological Research Online*, 18 (2): 15.

Brannen, J. (2014) 'From the concept of generation to an intergenerational lens on family life', *Families, Relationships and Societies*, 3 (3): 485–9.

Brannen, J. and Nilsen, A. (2002) 'Young people's time perspectives: From youth to adulthood', *Sociology*, 36 (3): 513–37.

Brannen, J., Moss, P. and Mooney, A. (2004) *Working and Caring over the Twentieth Century*. London: Palgrave.

Braun, V. and Clarke, V. (2006) 'Using thematic analysis in psychology', *Qualitative Research in Psychology*, 3 (2): 77–101.

Broad, R. and Fleming, S. (eds) (1981) *Nella Last's War: The Second World War Diaries of Housewife, 49*. Bristol: Falling Wall Press.

Brockmeier, J. (2000) 'Autobiographical time', *Narrative Inquiry*, 10 (1): 51–73.

Bronfenbrenner, U. (1993) 'Ecological models of human development', in T. Husen and T. Postlethwaite (eds) *International Encyclopaedia of Education*, Vol. 3, 2nd edition. Oxford: Pergamon Press, pp. 1640–7.

Bruner, E. (1984) 'The opening up of anthropology', in E. Bruner (ed.) *Text, Play and Story: The Construction and Reconstruction of Self and Society*. Washington, DC: American Ethnological Society, pp. 1–18.

Brunswick, A. (2002) 'Phenomenological perspectives on natural history research: The longitudinal Harlem adolescent cohort study', in E. Phelps, F. Furstenberg and A. Colby (eds) *Looking at Lives: American Longitudinal Studies of the Twentieth Century*. New York: Russell Sage Foundation, pp. 219–44.

Bryant, A. and Charmaz, K. (2007) 'Grounded theory in historical perspective: An epistemological account', in A. Bryant and K. Charmaz (eds) *The Sage Handbook of Grounded Theory*. London: Sage, pp. 31–57.

Bryant, R. (2016) 'On critical times: Return, repetition and the uncanny present', *History and Anthropology*, 27 (1): 19–31.

Byrne, D.,Olsen, W. and Duggan, S. (2009) 'Causality and interpretation in qualitative policy-related research', in D. Byrne and C. Ragin (eds) *The Sage Handbook of Case-Based Methods*. London: Sage, pp. 511–21.

Buchanan, A. (2013) 'Impact and knowledge mobilisation: What I have learnt as chair of the Economic and Social Research Council Evaluation Committee', *Contemporary Social Science*, 8 (3): 176–90.

Burawoy, M. (2003) 'Revisits: An outline of a theory of reflexive ethnography', *American Sociological Review*, 68 (Oct.): 645–79.

Burawoy, M. (2009) *The Extended Case Method*. Berkeley, CA: University of California Press.

Burton, L., Purvin, D. and Garrett-Peters, R. (2009) 'Longitudinal ethnography: Uncovering domestic abuse in low income women's lives', in G. Elder and J. Giele (eds) *The Craft of Life Course Research*. New York: Guilford Press, pp. 70–92.

Bury, M. (1982) 'Chronic illness as biographical disruption', *Sociology of Health and Illness*, 4 (2): 167–82.

Bygstad, B. and Munkvold, B. (2011) 'Exploring the role of informants in interpretive case study research in IS', *Journal of Information Technology*, 26: 32–45.

Bynner, J. (2007) 'Re-thinking the youth phase of the life course: The case for emerging adulthood', *Journal of Youth Studies*, 8 (4): 367–84.

Byrne, D. and Callaghan, G. (2014) *Complexity Theory and the Social Sciences*. London: Routledge.

Bytheway, W. (2011) *Unmasking Age*. Bristol: Policy Press.

Bytheway, W. (2012) *The Use of Diaries in Qualitative Longitudinal Research*. Timescapes Methods Guides Series No. 7, www.timescapes-archive.leeds.ac.uk/publications-and-outputs.

Bytheway, W. and Bornat, J. (2012a) *Ethical Issues in the Oldest Generation Project*, www.timescapes-archive.leeds.ac.uk/publications-and-outputs.

Bytheway, W. and Bornat, J. (2012b) 'The oldest generation as displayed in family photographs', in V. Ylanne (ed.) *Representing Ageing: Images and Identities*. London: Palgrave Macmillan, pp. 169–88.

Calman, L., Brunton, L. and Molassiotis, A. (2013) 'Developing longitudinal qualitative designs: Lessons learned and recommendations for health services research', *BMC Medical Research Methodology*, 13 (14): 1–10.

Camfield, L. (ed.) (2014) *Methodological Challenges and New Approaches to Research in International Development*. London: Palgrave Macmillan.

Carlsson, C. (2012) 'Using turning points to understand processes of change in offending', *British Journal of Criminology*, 52 (1): 1–16.

Cartwright, N. (2007) *Hunting Causes and Using Them: Approaches in Philosophy and Economics*. Cambridge: Cambridge University Press.

Chamberlayne, P., Bornat, J. and Wengraf, T. (eds) (2000) *The Turn to Biographical Methods in Social Science*. London: Routledge.

Chaplin, D. (2002) 'Time for life: Time for being and becoming', in G. Crow and S. Heath (eds) *Social Conceptions of Time: Structure and Process in Work and Everyday Life*. Basingstoke: Palgrave Macmillan, pp. 215–29.

Charles, N. (2012) 'Families, communities and social change: Then and now', *The Sociological Review*, 60: 438–56.

Charles, N. and Crow, G. (2012) 'Introduction: Community studies and social change', *Sociological Review*, 60: 399–404.

Charles, N., Davies, C. and Harris, C. (2008) *Families in Transition*. Bristol: Policy Press.

Charmaz, K. (2014) *Constructing Grounded Theory*, 2nd edition. London: Sage.

Chase, S. (2005) 'Narrative enquiry: Multiple lenses, approaches, voices', in N. Denzin and Y. Lincoln (eds) *Sage Handbook of Qualitative Research*, 3rd edition. London: Sage, pp. 651–78.

Cilliers, P. (1998) *Complexity and Postmodernism: Understanding Complex Systems*. London: Routledge.

Cilliers, P. (2001) 'Boundaries, hierarchies and networks in complex systems', *International Journal of Innovation Management*, 5 (2): 135–47.

Cilliers, P. (2005) 'Complexity, deconstruction and relativism', *Theory, Culture and Society*, 22 (5): 255–67.

Clark, T. (1973) *Prophets and Patrons: The French University and the Emergence of Social Science*. Cambridge, MA: Harvard University Press.

Clausen, J. (1995) 'Gender, contexts and turning points in adult lives', in P. Moen, G. Elder and K. Luscher (eds) *Examining Lives in Context: Perspectives on the Ecology of Human Development*. Washington, DC: APA Press, pp. 365–89.

Clausen, J. (1998) 'Life reviews and life stories', in J. Giele and G. Elder (eds) *Methods of Life Course Research: Qualitative and Quantitative Approaches*. London: Sage, pp. 189–212.

Cliggett, L. (2002) 'Multi-generations and multi-disciplines: Inheriting fifty years of Gwembe Tonga research', in R. Kemper and A. Royce (eds) *Chronicling Cultures: Long Term Field Research in Anthropology*. Walnut Creek, CA: AltaMira Press, pp. 239–51.

Coffield, F., Robinson, P. and Sarsby, J. (1980) *A Cycle of Deprivation? A Case Study of Four Families*. London: Heinemann.

Cohler, B. and Hostetler, A. (2004) 'Linking life course and life story: Social change and the narrative study of lives over time', in J. Mortimer and M. Shanahan (eds) *Handbook of the Life Course*. New York: Springer, pp. 555–76.

Collier, J. and Collier, M. (1986 [1967]) *Visual Anthropology: Photography as a Research Method*. Albuquerque, NM: University of New Mexico Press.

Colson, E. (1984) 'The re-ordering of experience: Anthropological involvement with time', *Journal of Anthropological Research*, 40 (1): 1–13.

Compton-Lilly, C. (2017) *Reading Students' Lives: Literacy Learning across Time*. New York: Routledge.

Conover, S., Berkman, A., Gheith, A., Jahiel, R., Stanley, D., Geller, P., et al. (1997) 'Methods for successful follow-up of elusive urban populations: An ethnographic approach with homeless men', *Bulletin of the New York Academy of Medicine*, 74 (1): 90–108.

Corden, A. and Millar, J. (eds) (2007) 'Qualitative longitudinal research for social policy', in *Social Policy and Society*, 6 (4). Themed Section.

Corden, A. and Nice, K. (2007) 'Qualitative longitudinal analysis for policy: Incapacity benefits recipients taking part in "Pathways to Work"', *Social Policy and Society*, 6 (4): 557–70.

Corden, A. and Sainsbury, R. (2007) 'Exploring "quality": Research participants' perspectives on verbatim quotations', *International Journal of Social Research Methodology*, 9 (2): 97–110.

Corsaro, W. and Molinari, L. (2000) 'Entering and observing in children's worlds: A reflection on a longitudinal ethnography of early education in Italy', in P. Christensen and A. James (eds) *Research with Children: Perspectives and Practices*. London: Falmer, pp. 179–200.

Corti, L. and Bishop, L. (eds) (2006) 'Defining and capturing context: The qualitative archiving and data sharing scheme' *Methodological Innovations Online*, 1 (2).

Corti, L. and Thompson, P. (2004) 'Secondary analysis of archived data', in C. Seale, G. Gobo, J. Gubrium and D. Silverman (eds) *Qualitative Research Practice* (concise edition). London: Sage, pp. 297–313.

Corti, L., Ven den Eynden, V., Bishop, L. and Woollard, M. (2020) *Managing and Sharing Research Data: A Guide to Good Practice*, 2nd edition. London: Sage.

Corti, L., Witzel, A. and Bishop, L. (eds) (2005) 'Editorial introduction: Secondary analysis of qualitative data', *Forum: Qualitative Social Research*, 6 (1).

Crow, G. (2002) 'Community studies: Fifty years of theorization', *Sociological Research Online*, 7 (3).

Crow, G. (2012) 'Community re-studies: Lessons and prospects', *The Sociological Review*, 60: 405–20.

Crow, G. and Edwards, R. (eds) (2012) 'Editorial introduction: Perspectives on working with archived textual and visual material in social research', *International Journal of Social Research Methodology*, 15 (4): 259–62.

Crow, G. and Heath, S. (eds) (2002) *Social Conceptions of Time: Structure and Process in Work and Everyday Life*. Basingstoke: Palgrave Macmillan.

Crow, G. and Lyon, D. (2011) 'Turning points in work and family lives in the imagined futures of young people on the Isle of Sheppey in 1978', in M. Winterton, G. Crow and B. Morgan-Brett (eds) *Young Lives and Imagined Futures: Insights from Archived Data*. Timescapes Working Paper No. 6, www.timescapes-archive.leeds.ac.uk/publications-and-outputs.

Dall, T. and Danneris, S. (2019) 'Reconsidering 'what works' in welfare to work with the vulnerable unemployed: The potential of relational causality as an alternative approach' *Social Policy and Society*, 18 (4): 583–596.

Daniluk, J. (2001) 'Re-constructing their lives: A longitudinal qualitative analysis of the transition to biological childlessness for infertile couples', *Journal of Counseling and Development*, 79 (4): 439–49.

Dassa, A. (2018) 'Musical auto-biography interview (MABI) as promoting self-identity and well-being in the elderly through music and reminiscence', *Nordic Journal of Music Therapy*, 27 (5): 419–30.

Davidson, E., Edwards, R., Jamieson, L. and Weller, S. (2019) 'Big data qualitative style: A breadth and depth method for working with large amounts of secondary qualitative data', *Quality and Quantity*, 53 (1): 363–76.

Dawson, P. (2003) *Reshaping Change: A Processual Perspective*. London: Routledge.

Dawson, P. (2013) 'The use of time in the design, conduct and write-up of longitudinal processual case study research', in M. Hassett and E. Paavilainen-Mäntymäki (eds) *Handbook of Longitudinal Research Methods in Organisation and Business Studies*. Cheltenham: Edward Elgar, pp. 249–68.

Dean, J., Furness, P., Verrier, D., et al. (2018) 'Desert island data: An investigation into researcher positionality', *Qualitative Research*, 18 (3): 273–89.

Dearden, G., Goode, J., Whitfield, G. and Cox, L. (2010) *Credit and Debt in Low-Income Families*. York: Joseph Rowntree Foundation.

De Cock, C. and Sharp, R. (2007) 'Process theory and research: Exploring the dialectical tension', *Scandinavian Journal of Management*, 23: 233–50.

Del Bianco, A. (2015) 'A method for collecting life course data: Assessing the utility of the life grid', in N. Worth and I. Hardill (eds) *Researching the Life Course: Critical Perspectives from the Social Sciences*. Bristol: Policy Press, pp. 81–100.

Deleuze, G. (1988 [1966]) *Bergsonism*. New York: Zone Books.

Dempster-McClain, D. and Moen, P. (1998) 'Finding respondents in a follow-up study', in J. Giele and G. Elder (eds) *Methods of Life Course Research: Qualitative and Quantitative Approaches*. London: Sage, pp. 128–51.

DeNora, T. (2013) 'Music and talk in tandem: The production of micro-narratives in real time', in L. Ole Bonde (ed.) *Musical Life Stories: Narratives on Health Musicking*. Oslo: MNH-Publikasjoner.

Denzin, N. (1977) *Childhood Socialisation*. San Francisco, CA: Jossey-Bass.

Denzin, N. (1989) *Interpretive Biography*. London: Sage.

Derrington, M. (2019) *Qualitative Longitudinal Methods: Researching Implementation and Change*. Washington, DC: Sage.

Desmond, D., Maddux, J., Johnson, T. and Confer, B. (1995) 'Obtaining follow-up interviews for treatment evaluation', *Journal of Substance Abuse Treatment*, 12 (2): 95–102.

Dey, I. (1999) *Grounding Grounded Theory: Guidelines for Qualitative Inquiry*. Bingley: Emerald.

Dey, I. (2007) 'Grounded theory', in C. Seale, G. Giampietro, J. Gubrium and D. Silverman (eds) *Qualitative Research Practice* (concise edition). London: Sage, pp. 80–93.

Dilthey, W. (2002 [1910]) 'The formation of the historical world in the human sciences', in R. Makkreel and F. Rodi (eds) *The Selected Works of William Dilthey*, Vol. 3. Princeton, NJ: Princeton University Press.

Doehler, P., Wagner, J. and Gonzales-Martinez, E. (eds) (2018) *Longitudinal Studies on the Organisation of Social Interaction*. London: Palgrave Macmillan.

Donmoyer, R. (2012) 'Can qualitative researchers answer policymakers' "what works" questions?', *Qualitative Inquiry*, 18 (8): 662–73.

Dooley, K. and Van de Ven, A. (2017) 'Cycles of divergence and convergence: Underlying processes of organisation change and innovation', in A. Langley and H. Tsoukas (eds) *The Sage Handbook of Process Organizational Studies*. London: Sage, pp. 574–90.

Duncan, S. (2012) 'Using elderly data theoretically: Personal life in 1949/50 and individualisation theory', *International Journal of Social Research Methodology*, 15 (4): 311–19.

Du Plessis, C. (2017) 'The method of psychobiography: Presenting a step-wise approach', *Qualitative Research in Psychology*, 14 (2): 216–37.

Dwyer, P. and Patrick, R. (in press) 'Little and large: Methodological reflections from two qualitative longitudinal policy studies on welfare conditionality', *Longitudinal and Life Course Studies*, online.

Economic and Social Research Council (ESRC) Research Evaluation Committee (2011) *Branching Out: New Directions in Impact Evaluation*, www.esrc.ukri.org/research/ research-and-impact-evaluation/developing-impact-evaluation/

Economic and Social Research Council (ESRC) (2015) *Framework for Research Ethics*, https://esrc. ukri.org/files/funding/guidance-for-applicants/esrc-framework-for-research-ethics-2015/.

Edmunds, J. and Turner, B. (2002) *Generations, Culture and Society*. Buckingham: Open University Press.

Edwards, R. and Irwin, S. (eds) (2010) 'Editorial introduction: Lived experience through economic downturn in Britain – Perspectives across time and across the life course', *21st Century Society: Journal of the Academy of Social Sciences*, 5 (2): 119–24.

Edwards, R. and Mauthner, M. (2002) 'Ethics and feminist research: Theory and practice', in M. Mauthner, M. Birch, J. Jessop and T. Miller (eds) *Ethics in Qualitative Research*. London: Sage, pp. 14–31.

Edwards, R. and Weller, S. (2011) *Dealing with the Death of a Participant: Ethical Dilemma Correspondence in a Study of Siblings and Friends*, www.timescapes-archive.leeds.ac.uk/ publications-and-outputs/knowledge-bank.

Edwards, R. and Weller, S. (2012) 'Shifting analytic ontology: Using I-poems in qualitative longitudinal research', *Qualitative Research*, 12 (2): 202–17.

Edwards, R. and Weller, S. (2013) 'The death of a participant: Moral obligation, consent and care in qualitative longitudinal research', in K. te Riele and R. Brooks (eds) *Negotiating Ethical Challenges in Youth Research*. London: Routledge, pp. 125–36.

Edwards, R., Goodwin, J., O'Connor, H. and Phoenix, A. (eds) (2017) *Working with Paradata, Marginalia and Fieldnotes: The Centrality of By-Products of Social Research*. Cheltenham: Edward Elgar.

Edwards, R., Weller, S., Jamieson, L. and Davidson, E. (2020) 'Search strategies: Analytical searching across multiple datasets and within combined sources', in K. Hughes and A. Tarrant (eds) *Qualitative Secondary Analysis*. London: Sage, pp. 79–99.

Eisenhardt, K. (1995) 'Building theories from case study research', in G. Huber and A. Van de Ven (eds) *Longitudinal Field Research Methods*. London: Sage, pp. 65–90.

Elder, G. (1974) *Children of the Great Depression: Social Change in Life Experience*. Chicago: University of Chicago Press.

Elder, G. (1985) 'Perspectives on the life course', in G. Elder (ed.) *Life Course Dynamics: Trajectories and Transitions, 1968–1980*. Ithaca, NY: Cornell University Press, pp. 23–49.

Elder, G. (1994) 'Time, human agency and social change: Reflections on the life course', *Social Psychology Quarterly*, 57 (1): 4–15.

Elder, G. and Giele, J. (eds) (2009) *The Craft of Life Course Research*. New York: Guilford Press.

Elder, G. and Hareven, T. (1992) 'Rising above life's disadvantage: From the Great Depression to global war', in J. Modell, G. Elder and R. Parke (eds) *Children in Time and Place: Developmental and Historical Insights*. New York: Cambridge University Press, pp. 47–72. (Reprinted in T. Hareven (ed.) (2000) *Families, History and Social Change*. Oxford: Westview Press.)

Elder, G. and Pellerin, L. (1998) 'Linking history and human lives', in J. Giele and G. Elder (eds) *Methods of Life Course Research: Qualitative and Quantitative Approaches*. London: Sage, pp. 264–94.

Elder, G. and Taylor, M. (2009) 'Linking research questions to data archives', in G. Elder and J. Giele (eds) *The Craft of Life Course Research*. London: Guilford Press, pp. 93–116.

Elias, N. (1997 [1977]) 'Towards a theory of social processes: A translation', *British Journal of Sociology*, 48 (3): 353–383.

Elias, N. (2007 [1984]) *An Essay on Time*. Dublin: University College Dublin Press.

Elliott, J. (2005) *Using Narrative in Social Research: Qualitative and Quantitative Approaches*. London: Sage.

Elliott, J. (2010a) 'The social participation and identity project', *Ko'hort: CLS Cohort Studies Newsletter*, Summer: 3–4, www.cls.ioe.ac.uk.

Elliott, J. (2010b) 'Imagining gendered futures: Children's essays from the "National Child Development Study" in 1969', *Sociology*, 44 (6): 1073–90.

Elliott, J. and Morrow, V. (2007) *Imagining the Future: Preliminary Analysis of NCDS Essays Written by Children at Age 11*. London: University of London, Institute of Education, Centre for Longitudinal Studies, CLS Working Paper 2007/1, www.cls.ioe.ac.uk.

Elliott, J., Holland, J. and Thomson, R. (2008) 'Longitudinal and panel studies', in P. Alasuutari, L. Bickman and J. Brannen (eds) *The Sage Handbook of Social Research Methods*. London: Sage, pp. 228–48.

Elliott, J., Miles, A., Parsons, S. and Savage, M. (2010) *The Design and Content of the 'Social Participation' Study: A qualitative sub-study conducted as part of the Age 50 (2008) sweep of the National Child Development Study*. London: University of London, Institute of Education, Centre for Longitudinal Studies, CLS Working Paper 2010/3, www.cls.ioe.ac.uk.

Ellis, C. (1995) 'Emotional and ethical quagmires in returning to the field', *Journal of Contemporary Ethnography*, 24 (1): 68–98.

Ellwood, D. (1998) 'Dynamic policy making: An insider's account of reforming US welfare', in L. Leisering and R. Walker (eds) *The Dynamics of Modern Society*. Bristol: Policy Press, pp. 49–59.

Entwisle, D., Alexander, K. and Olson, L. (2002) 'Baltimore beginning school study in perspective', in E. Phelps, F. Furstenberg and A. Colby (eds) *Looking at Lives: American Longitudinal Studies of the Twentieth Century*. New York: Russell Sage Foundation, pp. 167–93.

Etherington, K. (2007) 'Ethical research in reflexive relationships', *Qualitative Inquiry*, 13 (5): 599–616.

Evans, T. and Thane, P. (2006) 'Secondary analysis of Dennis Marsden's *Mothers Alone*', *Methodological Innovations Online*, 1 (2): 78–82.

Fabian, J. (1983) *Time and the Other: How Anthropology Makes its Object*. Columbia, NY: Columbia University Press.

Fadyl, J. (2019) 'Seeing the changes that matter: Qualitative longitudinal research focused on recovery and adaptation', *MethodsNews*, 2019 (1): 3.

Fadyl, J., Channon, A., Theadom, A. and McPherson, K. (2017) 'Optimising qualitative longitudinal analysis: Insights from a study of traumatic brain injury recovery and adaptation', *Nursing Inquiry*, 24 (2).

Falola, B. (2015) 'Life geo-histories: Examining formative experiences and geographies', in N. Worth and I. Hardill (eds) *Researching the Life Course: Critical Perspectives from the Social Sciences*. Bristol: Policy Press, pp. 101–22.

Farr, J. and Nizza, I. (2019) 'Longitudinal interpretative phenomenological analysis (LIPA): A review of studies and methodological considerations', *Qualitative Research in Psychology*, 16 (2): 199–217.

Farrall, S. (2006) *What is Qualitative Longitudinal Research?* LSE Methodology Institute, Papers in Social Research Methods: Qualitative Series No. 11, www.scribd.com/document/303619551/Stephen-Farrall-Qual-Longitudinal-Res,

Farrall, S., Hunter, B., Sharpe, G. and Calverley, A. (2014) *Criminal Careers in Transition*. Oxford: OUP.

Farrall, S., Hunter, B., Sharpe, G. and Calverley, A. (2016) 'What "works" when re-tracing sample members in a qualitative longitudinal study?', *International Journal of Social Research Methodology*, 19 (3): 287–300.

Farrell, C., Nice, K., Lewis, J. and Sainsbury, R. (2006) *Experiences of the 'Job Retention and Rehabilitation Pilot'*. Department for Work and Pensions, Research Report No. 339. Leeds: Corporate Document Service.

Feldman, M. (2017) 'Making process visible: Alternatives to boxes and arrows', in A. Langley and H. Tsoukas (eds) *The Sage Handbook of Process Organizational Studies*. London: Sage, pp. 625–35.

Feldman, S. and Howie, L. (2009) 'Looking back, looking forward: Reflections on using a Life History review tool with older people', *Journal of Applied Gerontology*, 28 (5): 621–37.

Ferguson, H., Leigh, J., Cooner, T., Beddoe, L., Disney, T., et al. (2019) 'From snapshots of practice to a movie: Researching long-term social work and child protection by getting as close as possible to practice and organisational life', *British Journal of Social Work*, online, www.doi.org/10.1093/bjsw/bcz119.

Ferguson, H., Warwick, L., Singh, T., Leigh, J., Beddow, L., Disney, T., et al. (2020) 'The nature and culture of social work with children and families in long-term casework: Findings from a qualitative longitudinal study', *Child and Family Social Work*, 2020: 1–10.

Filer, A. with Pollard, A. (1998) 'Developing the Identity and Learning Programme: Principles and pragmatism in a longitudinal ethnography of pupil careers', in G. Walford (ed.) *Doing Research about Education*. London: Falmer Press, pp. 57–75.

Filer, A. and Pollard, A. (2000) *The Social World of Pupil Assessment: Processes and Contexts of Primary Schooling*. London: Continuum.

Fincher, S. (2013) 'The diarist's audience', in L. Stanley (ed.) *Documents of Life Revisited*. London: Routledge, pp. 77–91.

Firth, R. (1959) *Social Change in Tikopia: Re-study of a Polynesian Community after a Generation*. London: Allen & Unwin.

Flaherty, M. (2011) *The Textures of Time: Agency and Temporal Experience*. Philadelphia, PA: Temple University Press.

Fleetwood, S. (2014) 'Bhaskar and critical realism', in P. Adler, P. du Gay, G. Morgan and M. Reed (eds) *Oxford Handbook of Sociology, Social Theory and Organisation Studies*. Oxford: OUP, pp. 182–219.

Flick, U. (2018) *Managing Quality in Qualitative Research*. London: Sage.

Flowerdew, J. and Neale, B. (2003) 'Trying to stay apace: Children with multiple challenges in their post-divorce family lives', *Childhood*, 10 (2): 147–61.

Flyvbjerg, B. (2007) 'Five misunderstandings about case-study research', in C. Seale, G. Gobo, J. Gubrium and D. Silverman (eds) *Qualitative Research Practice*. London: Sage, pp. 390–404.

Foster, G. (1952) 'Review of Oscar Lewis: Life in a Mexican village – Tepoztlan revisited', *American Anthropologist*, 54: 239–40.

Foster, G. (1979) 'Fieldwork in Tzintzuntzan: The first thirty years', in G. Foster, T. Scudder, E. Colson and R. Kemper (eds) *Long-Term Field Research in Social Anthropology*. New York: Academic Press, pp. 165–84.

Foster, G. (2002) 'A half-century of field research in Tzintzuntzan, Mexico: A personal view', in R. Kemper and A. P. Royce (eds) *Chronicling Cultures: Long-Term Field Research in Anthropology*. Walnut Creek, CA: AltaMira Press, pp. 252–83.

Foster, G., Scudder, T., Colson, E. and Kemper, R. (eds) (1979) *Long-term Field Research in Social Anthropology*. New York: Academic Press.

Frankenberg, R. (1990) 'Village on the border: A text revisited', in *Village on the Border: A Social Study of Religion, Politics and Football in a North Wales Community*. Prospect Heights, IL: Waveland Press, pp. 169–93.

Freeman, M. (2010) *Hindsight: The Promise and Peril of Looking Backward*. Oxford: OUP.

Freeman, M. (2017) *Modes of Thinking for Qualitative Data Analysis*. London: Routledge.

Frith, H. (2011) 'Narrating biographical disruption and repair: Exploring the place of absent images in women's experiences of cancer and chemotherapy', in P. Reavey (ed.) *Visual Methods in Psychology*. London: Routledge, pp. 55–68.

Furstenberg, F., Brooks-Gunn, J. and Morgan, S. (1987) *Adolescent Mothers in Later Life*. Cambridge: CUP.

Gale, N., Heath, G., Cameron, E., Rashid, S. and Redwood, S. (2013) 'Using the framework method for the analysis of qualitative data in multi-disciplinary health research', *BMC Medical Research Methodology*, 13: Art. 117.

Geertz, C. (1973) 'Thick description: Towards an interpretive theory of culture', in C. Geertz, *The Interpretation of Cultures: Selected Essays*. New York: Basic Books, pp. 3–30.

George, L. (2009) 'Conceptualising and measuring trajectories', in G. Elder and J. Giele (eds) *The Craft of Life Course Research*. New York: Guilford Press, pp. 163–86.

Geraghty, R. and Gray, J. (2017) 'Family rhythms: Re-visioning family change in Ireland using qualitative archived data from *Growing Up in Ireland*, and *Life Histories and Social Change*', *Irish Journal of Sociology*, 25 (2): 207–13.

Gergen, K. (1973) 'Social psychology as history', *Journal of Personality and Social Psychology*, 26 (2): 309–20.

Gergen, K. and Gergen, M. (1987) 'The self in temporal perspective', in R. Abeles (ed.) *Life Span Perspectives and Social Psychology*. Hillsdale, NJ: Erlbaum, pp. 121–38.

Gerrits, L. (2008) *The Gentle Art of Co-Evolution* (doctoral thesis). Rotterdam: Erasmus University. www.Researchgate.net/publication/254805429.

Gershuny, J. (1998) 'Thinking dynamically: Sociology and narrative data', in L. Leisering and R. Walker (eds) *The Dynamics of Modern Society*. Bristol: Policy Press, pp. 34–48.

Gershuny, J. (2000) *Changing Times: Work and Leisure in Post-Industrial Society*. Oxford: OUP.

Giddens, A. (1979) *Central Problems in Social Theory: Action, Structure and Contradiction in Social Analysis.* London: Macmillan.

Giddens, A. (1981) *A Contemporary Critique of Historical Materialism*, Vol. 1. London: Macmillan.

Giddens, A. (1984) *The Constitution of Modern Society: Outline of the Theory of Structuration.* Cambridge: Polity Press.

Giddens, A. (1991) *Modernity and Self Identity: Self and Society in the Late Modern Age.* Cambridge: Polity Press.

Gidley, B. (2018) 'Doing historical and documentary research', in C. Seale (ed.) *Researching Society and Culture.* London: Sage, pp. 285–304.

Giele, J. (1998) 'Innovation in the typical life course', in J. Giele and G. Elder (eds) *Methods of Life Course Research: Qualitative and Quantitative Approaches.* Thousand Oaks, CA: Sage, pp. 231–63.

Giele, J. (2009) 'Life stories to understand diversity: Variations by class, race and gender', in G. Elder and J. Giele (eds) *The Craft of Life Course Research.* New York: Guilford Press, pp. 236–57.

Giele, J. and Elder, G. (eds) (1998) *Methods of Life Course Research: Qualitative and Quantitative Approaches.* London: Sage.

Gillies, V. and Edwards, R. (2012) 'Working with archived classic family and community studies: Illuminating past and present conventions around acceptable research practice', *International Journal of Social Research Methodology*, 15 (4): 321–30.

Gladwell, M. (2000) *The Tipping Point: How Little Things Can Make a Big Difference.* London: Abacus.

Glaser, B. and Strauss, A. (1971) *Status Passage.* Chicago, IL: Aldine.

Glick, W., Huber, G., Miller, C., Doty, D. and Sutcliffe, K. (1995) 'Studying changes in organisational design and effectiveness: Retrospective event histories and periodic assessments', in G. Huber and A. Van de Ven (eds) *Longitudinal Field Research Methods.* London: Sage, pp. 126–54.

Gobo, G. (2004) 'Sampling, representativeness and generalisability', in C. Seale, G. Gobo, J. Gubrium and D. Silverman (eds) *Qualitative Research Practice* (concise edition). London: Sage, pp. 405–26.

Gobo, G. (2008) 'Reconceptualising generalisations: Old issues in a new frame', in P. Alasuutari, L. Bickman and J. Brannen (eds) *The Sage Handbook of Social Research Methods.* London: Sage, pp. 193–213.

Gomm, R. and Hammersley, M. (2001) *'Thick Ethnographic Description and Thin Models of Complexity.'* Paper presented at the British Educational Research Association (BERA) conference, University of Leeds, 13–15 September.

Goodwin, J. (ed.) (2012) *Sage Biographical Research* (4-volume set). London: Sage.

Goodwin, J. and O'Connor, H. (2015) 'A restudy of young workers from the 1960s: Researching intersections of work and life course in one locality over 50 years', in N. Worth and I. Hardill, (eds) *Researching the Life Course: Critical Perspectives from the Social Sciences.* Bristol: Policy Press, pp. 63–80.

Goodwin, J. and O'Connor, H. (2020) 'Imagination and the analytical potential of working with non-interview or unusual data', in K. Hughes and A. Tarrant (eds) *Qualitative Secondary Analysis.* London: Sage, pp. 173–94.

Gordon, T. and Lahelma, E. (2003) 'From ethnography to life history: Tracing transitions of school children', *International Journal of Social Research Methodology*, 6 (3): 245–54.

Gordon, T., Holland, J., Lahelma, E. and Thomson, R. (2005) 'Imagining gendered adulthood: Anxiety, ambivalence, avoidance and anticipation', *European Journal of Women's Studies*, 12 (1): 83–103.

Grandia, L. (2015) 'Slow ethnography: A hut with a view', *Critique of Anthropology*, 35 (3): 301–17.

Gray, J. and Geraghty, R. (2020) 'Using quantitative data in qualitative secondary analysis', in K. Hughes and A. Tarrant (eds) *Qualitative Secondary Analysis*. London: Sage, pp. 195–215.

Gray, J., Geraghty, R. and Ralph, D. (2013) 'Young grandchildren and their grandparents: A secondary analysis of continuity and change across four birth cohorts', *Families, Relationships and Societies*, 2 (2): 289–98.

Gray, J., Geraghty, R. and Ralph, D. (2016) *Family Rhythms: The Changing Textures of Family Life in Ireland*. Manchester: MUP.

Grbich, C. (2007) *Qualitative Data Analysis*. London: Sage.

Grenier, A. (2012) *Transitions and the Life Course: Challenging the Constructions of Growing Older*. Bristol: Policy Press.

Grinyer, A. (2009) 'The anonymity of research participants: Assumptions, ethics and practicalities', *Pan*, 12: 49–58.

Grossoehme, D. and Lipstein, E. (2016) 'Analysing longitudinal qualitative data: The application of trajectory and recurrent cross-sectional approaches', *BMC Research Notes*, 9: 136.

Gruber, H. (1981) 'On the relationship between "aha experiences" and the construction of ideas', *History of Science*, 19 (1): 41–59.

Guenette, F. and Marshall, A. (2009) 'Time line drawings: Enhancing participant voice in narrative interviews on sensitive topics', *International Journal of Qualitative Methods*, 8 (1): 86–92.

Guillemin, M. and Gillam, L. (2004) 'Ethics, reflexivity and "ethically important moments" in research', *Qualitative Inquiry*, 10 (2): 261–80.

Gusfield, J. (1967) 'Tradition and modernity: Misplaced polarities in the study of social change', *American Journal of Sociology*, 72 (4): 351–62.

Haaker, M. (2020) 'Qualitative secondary analysis in teaching', in K. Hughes and A. Tarrant (eds) *Qualitative Secondary Analysis*. London: Sage, pp. 119–34.

Haaker, M. (forthcoming) *Conceiving Subjectivity: An Exploration of Pregnant Women's Experiences* (unpublished doctoral thesis). Colchester: University of Essex.

Hackstaff, K., Kupferberg, F. and Negroni, C. (eds) (2012) *Biography and Turning Points in Europe and America*. Bristol: Policy Press.

Hadfield, L. (2010) 'Balancing on the edge of the archive: The researcher's role in collecting and preparing data for deposit', in F. Shirani and S. Weller (eds) *Conducting Qualitative Longitudinal Research: Fieldwork Experiences*. Timescapes Working Papers No. 2, pp. 60–73, www.timescapes-archive.leeds.ac.uk/publications-and-outputs.

Hagan, J. and McCarthy, B. (1997) *Mean Streets*. Cambridge: CUP.

Halbwachs, M. (1992) *On Collective Memory*. Chicago: Chicago University Press.

Halford, S. and Savage, M. (2017) 'Speaking sociologically with big data: Symphonic social science and the future for big data research', *Sociology*, 51 (6): 1132–48.

Halinen, A. and Mainela, T. (2013) 'Challenges of longitudinal field research in process studies on business networks', in M. Hassett and E. Paavilainen-Mäntymäki (eds) *Handbook of Longitudinal Research Methods in Organisation and Business Studies*. Cheltenham: Edward Elgar, pp. 185–203.

Hall, S. (2014) 'Ethics of ethnography with families: A geographical perspective', *Environment and Planning A*, 46: 2175–94.

Hallden, G. (1994) 'Establishing order: Small girls write about family life', *Gender and Education*, 6 (1): 3–18.

Hallden, G. (1999) '"To be or not to be?": Absurd and humoristic descriptions as a strategy to avoid idyllic life stories – boys write about family life', *Gender and Generation*, 11 (4): 469–79.

Hallebone, E. (1992) 'Use of typologies for "measuring" self-identity change: Methodological issues in longitudinal qualitative research', *Quality and Quantity*, 26: 1–17.

Hammersley, M. (2008) 'Causality as conundrum: The case of qualitative inquiry', *Methodological Innovations Online*, 2 (3): 1–15.

Hammersley, M. (2010) 'Can we use qualitative data via secondary analysis? Notes on some terminological and substantive issues', *Sociological Research Online*, 15 (1): 47–53.

Hammersley, M. and Atkinson, P. (2019) *Ethnography: Principles in Practice*, 4th edition. London: Routledge.

Hammersley, M. and Traianou, A. (2012) *Ethics in Qualitative Research: Controversies and Contexts*. London: Sage.

Hanna, E. and Lau-Clayton, C. (2012) *Capturing Past and Future Time in QL Field Enquiry: Timelines and Relational Maps*. Timescapes Methods Guide Series No. 5, www.timescapes-archive.leeds.ac.uk/publications-and-outputs.

Harden, J., Backett-Milburn, K., Hill, M. and MacLean, A. (2010) 'Oh, what a tangled web we weave: Experiences of doing "multiple perspectives" research in families', *International Journal of Social Research Methodology*, 13 (5): 441–52.

Harden, J., Maclean, A., Backett-Milburn, K. and Cunningham-Burley, S. (2012) 'The "family–work project": Children's and parents' experience of working parenthood', *Families, Relationships and Societies*, 1 (2): 207–22.

Hardgrove, A., Rootham, E. and McDowell, L. (2015) 'Possible selves in a precarious labour market: Youth, imagined futures and transitions to work in the UK', *Geoforum*, 60: 163–71.

Hareven, T. (1982) *Family Time and Industrial Time: The Relationship between Family and Work in a New England Industrial Community*. New York: Cambridge University Press.

Hareven, T. (ed.) (1996) *Ageing and Generational Relations: Life Course and Cross-Cultural Perspectives*. New York: Aldine de Gruyter.

Hareven, T. (2000) *Families, History and Social Change: Life Course and Cross-Cultural Perspectives*. Oxford: Westview Press.

Hareven, T. and Masaoka, K. (1988) 'Turning points and transitions: Perceptions of the life course', *Journal of Family History*, 13: 271–89.

Harocopos, A. and Dennis, D. (2003) 'Maintaining contact with drug users over an 18-month period', *International Journal of Social Research Methodology*, 6 (3): 261–5.

Harris, C. (1987) 'The individual and society: A processual view', in A. Bryman, W. Bytheway, P. Allatt and T. Keil (eds) *Rethinking the Life Cycle*. Basingstoke: Macmillan, pp. 17–29.

Harris, D. and Parisi, D. (2007) 'Adapting life history calendars for qualitative research on welfare transitions', *Field Methods*, 19 (1): 40–58.

Hart, N. (1976) *When Marriage Ends: A Study in Status Passage*. London: Tavistock.

Hassett, M. and Paavilainen-Mäntymäki, E. (eds) (2013) *Handbook of Longitudinal Research Methods in Organisation and Business Studies*. Cheltenham: Edward Elgar.

Hastwell, P. and Moss, C. (2019) *Our Lives, Our Journey: Disabled Children and their Families*. London: Scope. Report No. 1, www.scope.org.uk/campaigns/research-policy/our-lives-our-journey.

Hatch, J. and Wisniewski, R. (eds) (1995) *Life History and Narrative*. London: Falmer.

Heath, S. B. (1983) *Ways with Words: Language, Life and Work in Communities and Classrooms*. Cambridge: CUP.

Heath, S. B. (2012) *Words at Work and Play: Three Decades of Family and Community Life*. Cambridge: CUP.

Hedström, P. and Swedberg, R. (1998) 'Social mechanisms: An introductory essay', in P. Hedstrom and R. Swedberg (eds) *Social Mechanisms: An Analytical Approach to Social Theory*. Cambridge: CUP, pp. 1–31.

Hedström, P. and Ylikoski, P. (2010) 'Causal mechanisms in the social sciences', *Annual Review of Sociology*, 36: 49–67.

Heidegger, M. (1980 [1927]) *Being and Time*. Oxford: Blackwell.

Heinz, W. (2003) 'Combining methods in life course research: A mixed blessing?', in W. Heinz and V. Marshall (eds) *Social Dynamics of the Life Course*. New York: De Gruyter, pp. 73–90.

Heinz, W. (2009a) 'Transitions: Biography and agency', in W. Heinz, J. Huinink and A. Weymann (eds) *The Life Course Reader: Individuals and Societies across Time*. Frankfurt: Campus Verlag, pp. 421–9.

Heinz, W. (2009b) 'Status passages as micro-level linkages in life course research', in W. Heinz, J. Huinink and A. Weymann (eds) *The Life Course Reader: Individuals and Societies across Time*. Frankfurt: Campus Verlag, pp. 473–86.

Hemmerman, L. (2010) 'Researching the hard to reach and the hard to keep: Notes from the field on longitudinal sample maintenance', in F. Shirani and S. Weller (eds) *Conducting Qualitative Longitudinal Research: Fieldwork Experiences*. Timescapes Working Paper Series No. 2, pp. 7–19, www.timescapes-archive.leeds.ac.uk/publications-and-outputs.

Henderson, S., Holland, J., McGrellis, S., Sharpe, S. and Thomson, R. (2007) *Inventing Adulthoods: A Biographical Approach to Youth Transitions*. London: Sage.

Henderson, S., Holland, J., McGrellis, S., Sharpe, S. and Thomson, R. (2012) 'Storying qualitative longitudinal research: Sequence, voice and motif', *Qualitative Research*, 12 (1): 16–34.

Henn, M., Weinstein, M. and Foard, N. (2009) *A Critical Introduction to Social Research*, 2nd edition. London: Sage.

Henwood, K. and Shirani, F. (2012) *Extending Temporal Horizons*. Timescapes Methods Guides Series No. 4, www.timescapes-archive.leeds.ac.uk/publications-and-outputs.

Henwood, K., Shirani, F. and Finn, M. (2011) '"So you think you've moved, changed, the representation got more what?" Methodological and analytical reflections on visual (photo-elicitation) methods used in the "Men as Fathers" study', in P. Reavey (ed.) *Visual Methods in Psychology*. London: Routledge, pp. 330–45.

Hermanowicz, J. (1998) *The Stars Are Not Enough: Scientists – Their Passions and Professions*. Chicago, IL: University of Chicago Press.

Hermanowicz, J. (2009) *Lives in Science*. Chicago: University of Chicago Press.

Hermanowicz, J. (2013) 'The longitudinal qualitative interview', *Qualitative Sociology*, 36: 189–208.

Hermanowicz, J. (2016) 'Longitudinal qualitative research', in M. Shanahan, J. Mortimer and M. Johnson (eds) *Handbook of the Life Course* (Volume II). New York: Springer, pp. 491–513.

Hitlin, S. and Elder, G. (2007) 'Time, self and the curiously abstract concept of agency', *Sociological Theory*, 25 (2): 170–91.

Hochner, N. (2018) 'On social rhythms: A renewed assessment of van Gennep's *Rites of Passage*', *Journal of Classical Sociology*, 18 (4): 299–312.

Hockey, J. and James, A. (2003) *Social Identities across the Life Course*. Basingstoke: Palgrave Macmillan.

Hodgetts, D., Chamberlain, K. and Groot, S. (2011) 'Reflections on the visual in community research and action', in P. Reavey (ed.) *Visual Methods in Psychology*. London: Routledge, pp. 299–313.

Holland, J. and Thomson, R. (2009) 'Gaining a perspective on choice and fate: Revisiting critical moments', *European Societies*, 11 (3): 451–69.

Holland, J., Thomson, R. and Henderson, S. (2006) *Qualitative Longitudinal Research: A Discussion Paper*. Working Paper No. 21. London: South Bank University.

Holstein, J. and Gubrium, J. (2000) *Constructing the Life Course*, 2nd edition. New York: General Hall.

Holstein, J. and Gubrium, J. (eds) 2008) *Handbook of Constructionist Research*. New York: Guilford Press.

Holstein, M. and Minkler, M. (2007) 'Critical gerontology: Reflections for the 21st century', in M. Bernard and T. Scharf (eds) *Critical Perspectives on Ageing Societies*. Bristol: Policy Press, pp. 13–26.

Howell, S. (2012) 'Cumulative understandings: Experiences from the study of two Southeast Asian societies', in S. Howell and A. Talle (eds) *Returns to the Field: Multi-Temporal Research and Contemporary Anthropology*. Bloomington, IN: Indiana University Press, pp. 153–79.

Howell, S. and Talle, A. (eds) (2012) *Returns to the Field: Multi-Temporal Research and Contemporary Anthropology*. Bloomington, IN: Indiana University Press.

Huber, G. and Van de Ven, A. (eds) (1995) *Longitudinal Field Research Methods: Studying Processes of Organisational Change*. London: Sage.

Hughes, K. (2011) 'Ethics in qualitative longitudinal research: A special case?' *Presentation for the Timescapes QL Methods Training Programme*, University of Leeds, October.

Hughes, K. and Tarrant, A. (eds) (2020a) *Qualitative Secondary Analysis*. London: Sage.

Hughes, K. and Tarrant, A. (2020b) 'The ethics of qualitative secondary analysis', in K. Hughes and A. Tarrant (eds) *Qualitative Secondary Analysis*. London: Sage, pp. 37–58.

Husserl, E. (1964 [1901–10]) *The Phenomenology of Internal Time Consciousness*. The Hague: Martinus Nijhoff.

Iantaffi, A. (2011) 'Travelling along rivers of experience: Personal construct theory and visual metaphors in research', in P. Reavey (ed.) *Visual Methods in Psychology*. London: Routledge, pp. 271–83.

Irwin, S. (2013) 'Qualitative secondary analysis in practice: Introduction', *Families, Relationships and Societies*, 2 (2): 285–8.

Irwin, S. (2020) 'Qualitative secondary analysis: Working across datasets', in K. Hughes and A. Tarrant (eds) *Qualitative Secondary Analysis*. London: Sage, pp. 19–35.

Irwin, S. and Bornat, J. (eds) (2013) 'Qualitative secondary analysis in practice', *Families, Relationships and Societies*, 2 (2): 285–8.

Irwin, S. and Winterton, M. (2011) *Timescapes Data and Secondary Analysis: Working across the Projects*. Timescapes Working Paper No. 5, www.timescapes-archive.leeds.ac.uk/publications-and-outputs.

Irwin, S. and Winterton, M. (2012) 'Qualitative social analysis and social explanation', *Sociological Research Online*, 17 (2).

Irwin, S. and Winterton, M. (2014) 'Gender and work–family conflict: A secondary analysis of Timescapes data', in J. Holland and R. Edwards (eds) *Understanding Families over Time: Research and Policy*. London: Palgrave Macmillan, pp. 142–58.

Irwin, S., Bornat, J. and Winterton, M. (2012) 'Timescapes secondary analysis: Comparison, context and working across datasets', *Qualitative Research*, 12 (1): 66–80.

Israel, M. and Hay, I. (2006) *Research Ethics for Social Scientists*. London: Sage.

Jahoda, M., Lazarsfeld, P. and Zeisel, H. (1972 [1932]) *Marienthal: The Sociography of an Unemployed Community*. London: Tavistock.

Jarzabkowski, P., Lê, J. and Spee, P. (2017) 'Taking a strong process approach to analysing qualitative process data', in A. Langley and H. Tsoukas (eds) *The Sage Handbook of Process Organizational Studies*. London: Sage, pp. 237–53.

JISC (2018) *UK Research Data Discovery: Making Research Data and Collections in Universities and Data Centres Discoverable*, www.jisc.ac.uk/rd/projects/uk-research-data-discovery.

Johnson, D. (2015) 'Not your stereotypical young father, not your typical teenage life', *Families, Relationships and Societies*, 4 (2): 319–22.

Johnson, J., Rolph, S. and Smith, R. (2010) *Residential Care Transformed: Revisiting 'The Last Refuge'*. London: Palgrave Macmillan.

Jost, G. (2012) 'Biographical structuring through a critical life event: Parental loss during childhood', in K. Hackstaff, F. Kupferberg and C. Negroni (eds) *Biography and Turning Points in Europe and America*. Bristol: Policy Press, pp. 125–42.

Kelder, J. (2005) 'Using someone else's data: Problems, pragmatics and provisions', *FQS: Forum Qualitative Social Research*, 6 (1): Art. 39.

Kelly, A. (2008) 'Living loss: An exploration of the internal space of liminality', *Mortality*, 13 (4): 335–50.

Kelly, J. and McGrath, J. (1988) *On Time and Method*. London: Sage.

Kemmis, S., McTaggart, R. and Nixon, R. (eds) (2014) *The Action Research Planner: Doing Critical Participant Action Research*. London: Springer.

Kemper, R. and Royce, A. (eds) (2002) *Chronicling Cultures: Long Term Field Research in Anthropology*. Walnut Creek, CA: AltaMira Press.

King, H. and Roberts, B. (2015) 'Biographical research, longitudinal study and theorisation', in M. O'Neill, B. Roberts and A. Sparkes (eds) *Advances in Biographical Methods: Creative Applications*. London: Routledge, pp. 106–22.

Kinsey, H. (2020) *Integrating a Longitudinal Ward Placement into the Hospital Pharmacist Pre-Registration Year: A Design-based Research Approach Informing Design, Implementation and Evaluation* (unpublished doctoral thesis). Norwich: University of East Anglia.

Kitchin, R. (2014) 'Big data, new epistemologies and paradigm shifts', *Big Data and Society*, April–June: 1–12.

Knight, D. and Stewart, C. (2016) 'Ethnographies of austerity: Temporality, crisis, and affect in Southern Europe', *History and Anthropology*, 27 (1): 1–18.

Kohli, M. (1981) 'Biography: Account, text, method', in D. Bertaux (ed.) *Biography and Society*. London: Sage, pp. 61–75.

Koro-Ljungberg, M. and Bussing, R. (2013) 'Methodological modifications in a longitudinal qualitative research design', *Field Methods*, 25 (4): 423–40.

Krings, T., Moriarty, E., Wickham, J., Bobek, A. and Salamonska, J. (2013) *New Mobilities in Europe: Polish Migration to Ireland post 2004*. Manchester: Manchester University Press.

Kupferberg, F. (2012) 'Conclusion: Theorising turning points and decoding narratives', in K. Hackstaff, F. Kupferberg and C. Negroni (eds) *Biography and Turning Points in Europe and America*. Bristol: Policy Press, pp. 227–59.

Kuula, A. (2010–11) 'Methodological and ethical dilemmas of archiving qualitative data', *IASSIST Quarterly*, 34 (3–4): 12–17.

Kvale, S. (2007) *Doing Interviews*. London: Sage.

Kynaston, D. (2005) 'The uses of sociology for real-time history', *FQS: Forum Qualitative Social Research*, 6 (1): Art. 45.

Ladlow, L. and Neale, B. (2016) 'Risk, resource, redemption? The parenting and custodial experiences of young offender fathers', *Social Policy and Society*, 15 (1): 113–27.

Land, E. and Patrick, R. (2014) *The Process of Using Participatory Research Methods with Film-Making to Disseminate Research: Challenges and Potential*. SAGE Research Methods Cases. London: Sage. [Report on the development of the Dole Animators Film (2015) *All in this together? Are benefits ever a lifestyle choice?* www.doleanimators.org.uk]

Langley, A. (1999) 'Strategies for theorising from process data', *Academy of Management Review*, 24 (4): 691–710.

Langley, A., Smallman, C., Tsoukas, H. and Van de Ven, A. (2013) 'Editorial introduction: Process studies of change in organisation and management – Unveiling temporality, activity and flow', *Academy of Management Journal*, 56 (1): 1–13.

Langley, A. and Tsoukas, H. (eds) (2017) *The Sage Handbook of Process Organizational Studies*. London: Sage.

Largan, C. and Morris, T. (2019) *Qualitative Secondary Research: A Step-by-Step Guide*. London: Sage.

Lassiter, L. (2012) '"To fill in the missing piece of the Middletown puzzle": Lessons from re-studying Middletown', *The Sociological Review*, 60 (3): 421–37.

Laub, J. and Sampson, R. (1993) 'Turning points in the life course: Why change matters to the study of crime', *Criminology*, 31 (3): 301–25.

Laub, J. and Sampson, R. (1998) 'Integrating quantitative and qualitative data', in J. Giele and G. Elder (eds) *Methods of Life Course Research: Qualitative and Quantitative Approaches*. London: Sage, pp. 213–30.

Laub, J. and Sampson, R. (2003) *Shared Beginnings, Divergent Lives: Delinquent Boys to Age 70*. Cambridge, MA: Harvard University Press.

Law, J. (2004) *After Method: Mess in Social Science Research*. London: Routledge.

Lee, J. (2015) 'Using a life history approach within transnational ethnography: A case study of Korean New Zealander returnees', in N. Worth and I. Hardill (eds) *Researching the Life Course: Critical Perspectives from the Social Sciences*. Bristol: Policy Press, pp. 183–98.

Leisering, L. and Walker, R. (eds) (1998) *The Dynamics of Modern Society: Poverty, Policy and Welfare*. Bristol: Policy Press.

Lejeune, P. (2011) 'The story of a French life-writing archive: "Association pour l'autobiographie et le patrimoine autobiographique"', *FQS: Forum Qualitative Social Research*, 12 (3): Art. 7.

Lemke, J. (2000) 'Across the scales of time: Artifacts, activities and meanings in ecosocial systems', *Mind, Culture, and Activity*, 7 (4): 273–90.

Leonard-Barton, D. (1995) 'A dual methodology for case studies', in G. Huber and A. Van de Ven (eds) *Longitudinal Field Research Methods: Studying Processes of Organisational Change*. London: Sage, pp. 38–64.

Levi-Strauss, C. (1966) *The Savage Mind*. Chicago: Chicago University Press.

Lewis, J. (2007) 'Analysing qualitative longitudinal research in evaluations', *Social Policy and Society*, 6 (4): 545–56.

Lewis, O. (1951) *Life in a Mexican Village: Tepoztlan Restudied*. Urbana, IL: University of Illinois Press.

Lincoln, Y. and Guba, E. (1985) *Naturalistic Inquiry*. Thousand Oaks, CA: Sage.

Lindsey, R., Metcalfe, E. and Edwards, R. (2015) 'Time in mixed methods longitudinal research: Working across written narratives and large scale panel survey data to investigate attitudes to volunteering', in N. Worth and I. Hardill (eds) *Researching the Life Course: Critical Perspectives from the Social Sciences*. Bristol: Policy Press, pp. 43–62.

Lloyd, L., Calnan, M., Cameron, A., Seymour, J., Smith, R. and White, K. (2017) 'Older people's perspectives on dignity: The benefits and challenges of a qualitative longitudinal approach to researching experiences of later life', *International Journal of Social Research Methodology*, 20 (6): 647–58.

Locke, K., Golden-Biddle, K. and Feldman, M. (2008) 'Making doubt generative: Rethinking the role of doubt in the research process', *Organisation Science*, 19 (6): 907–18.

Lofland, J., Snow, D., Anderson, L. and Lofland, L. (2006) *Analysing Social Settings: A Guide to Qualitative Observations and Analysis*, 4th edition. Belmont, CA: Wadsworth.

Lopez-Aguado, P. (2012) 'Working between two worlds: Gang intervention and street liminality', *Ethnography*, 14 (2): 186–206.

Lovgren, M., Hamberg, K. and Tishelman, C. (2010) 'Clock time and embodied time experienced by patients with operable lung cancer', *Cancer Nursing*, 33 (1): 55–63.

Lubbock, J. (1892) *The Beauties of Nature and the Wonders of the World We Live In*. London: Macmillan.

Lutkehaus, N. (1990) 'Refractions of reality: On the use of other people's fieldnotes', in R. Sanjek (ed.) *Fieldnotes: The Makings of Anthropology*. Ithaca, NY: Cornell University Press, pp. 303–23.

Lynd, R. and Lynd, H. (1929) *Middletown: A Study in Contemporary American Culture*. New York: Harcourt Brace.

Lynd, R. and Lynd, H. (1937) *Middletown in Transition: A Study in Cultural Conflicts*. New York: Harcourt Brace.

Lyon, D. (2017) 'Time and place in memory and imagination on the Isle of Sheppey', in G. Crow and J. Ellis (eds) *Revisiting Divisions of Labour: The Impacts and Legacies of a Modern Sociological Classic*. Manchester: Manchester University Press, pp. 149–68.

Lyon, D. and Crow, G. (2012) 'The challenges and opportunities of re-studying community on the Isle of Sheppey: Young people's imagined futures', *The Sociological Review*, 60 (3): 498–517.

Lyon, D. and Crow, G. (2020) 'Doing qualitative secondary analysis: Revisiting young people's imagined futures in Ray Pahl's Sheppey studies', in K. Hughes and A. Tarrant (eds) *Qualitative Secondary Analysis*. London: Sage, pp. 155–71.

MacLean, A. and Harden, J. (2012) *Generating Group Accounts with Parents and Children in Qualitative Longitudinal Research: A Practical and Ethical Guide*. Timescapes Methods Guide Series No. 8, www.timescapes-archive.leeds.ac.uk/ publications-and-outputs.

MacLeod, J. (1987) *Ain't no Making It: Levelled Aspirations in a Low Income Neighbourhood*. London: Tavistock.

MacLeod, J. (2009) *Ain't no Making It: Aspirations and Attainment in a Low Income Neighbourhood*, 3rd edition. Boulder, CO: Westview Press.

Macmillan, R., Arvidson, A., Edwards, S., Soteri-Proctor, A., Taylor, R. and Teasdale, S. (2011) *First Impressions: Introducing the 'Real Times' Third Sector Case Studies*. Third Sector Research Centre Working Paper No. 67. Birmingham: University of Birmingham Third Sector Research Centre.

Makkreel, R. (2003/4) 'The productive force of history and Dilthey's formation of the historical world', *Revue Internationale de Philosophie*, 226: 495–508.

Malacrida, C. (2007) 'Reflexive journaling on emotional research topics: Ethical issues for team researchers', *Qualitative Health Research*, 17 (10): 1329–39.

Malcolmson, P. and Malcolmson, R. (eds) (2008) *Nella Last's Peace: The Post War Diaries of Housewife, 49*. London: Profile Books.

Mannheim, K. (1952 [1924]) 'Historicism', in *Essays on the Sociology of Knowledge: The Collected Works of Karl Mannheim*, Vol. 5 (ed. P. Kecskemeti). London: Routledge, pp. 84–133.

Mannheim, K. (1952 [1927]) 'The problem of generations', in *Essays on the Sociology of Knowledge: The Collected Works of Karl Mannheim*, Vol. 5 (ed. P. Kecskemeti). London: Routledge, pp. 276–322.

Mari, C. and Meglio, O. (2013) 'Temporal issues in process research', in M. Hassett and E. Paavilainen-Mäntymäki (eds) *Handbook of Longitudinal Research Methods in Organisation and Business Studies*. Cheltenham: Edward Elgar, pp. 204–28.

Massey, H. (2015) *The Origin of Time: Heidegger and Bergson*. Albany, NY: State University of New York Press.

Matusiak, K. and Sposito, F. (2017) 'Types of research data management services: An international perspective', *80th Annual Meeting of the Association of Information Science and Technology* (Washington): 754–6.

Mauthner, N. (2012) 'Accounting for our part of the entangled webs we weave: Ethical and moral issues in digital data sharing', in T. Miller, M. Birch, M. Mauthner and J. Jessop (eds) *Ethics in Qualitative Research*, 2nd edition. London: Sage, pp. 157–75.

Mauthner, N. and Parry, O. (2013) 'Open access digital data sharing: Principles, policies and practices', *Social Epistemology*, 27 (1): 47–67.

Mauthner, N., Parry, O. and Backett-Milburn, K. (1998) 'The data are out there, or are they? Implications for archiving and revisiting qualitative data', *Sociology*, 32 (4): 733–45.

Maxwell, J. (2004) 'Using qualitative methods for causal explanations', *Field Methods*, 16 (3): 243–64.

Maxwell, J. (2012) *A Realist Approach for Qualitative Research*. London: Sage.

Maxwell, J. (2013) *Qualitative Research Design: An Interactive Approach*. Thousand Oaks, CA: Sage.

May, J. and Thrift, N. (eds) (2001) *Timespace: Geographies of Temporality*. New York: Routledge.

McAdams, D. (2008) 'Personal narratives and the life story', in O. John, R. Robins and L. Pervin (eds) *Handbook of Personality: Theory and Research*, 3rd edition. New York: Guildford Press, pp. 242–62.

McCoy, L. (2017) 'Longitudinal qualitative research and interpretative phenomenological analysis: Philosophical connections and practical considerations', *Qualitative Research in Psychology*, 14 (4): 442–58.

McDonald, P., Pini, B., Bailey, J. and Price, R. (2011) 'Young people's aspirations for education, work, family and leisure', *Work, Employment and Society*, 25 (1): 68–84.

McDonough, M., Sabiston, C. and Ullrich-French, S. (2011) 'The development of social relationships, social support and post-traumatic growth in a dragon boating team for breast cancer survivors', *Journal of Sport and Exercise Psychology*, 33: 627–48.

McIntosh, I. and Wright, S. (2019) 'Exploring what the notion of "lived experience" offers for social policy analysis', *Journal of Social Policy*, 48 (3): 449–67.

McKenney, S. and Reeves, T. (2018) *Conducting Educational Design Research*, 2nd edition. London: Routledge.

McLeod, J. (2003) 'Why we interview now: Reflexivity and perspective in a longitudinal study', *International Journal of Social Research Methodology*, 6 (3): 201–11.

McLeod, J. and Thomson, R. (2009) *Researching Social Change*. London: Sage.

McNaughton, C. (2008) *Crossing the Continuum: Understanding Routes out of Homelessness, and Examining 'What Works'*. Glasgow: Simon Community Project.

Mead, G. (1959 [1934]) *Mind, Self and Society*. Chicago: University of Chicago Press.

Merrill, B. and West, L. (2009) *Using Biographical Methods in Social Research*. London: Sage.

Middlemiss, L., Ambrosio-Albalá, P., Emmel, N., Gillard, R., Gilbertson, J., et al. (2019) 'Energy poverty and social relations: A capabilities approach', *Energy Research and Social Science*, 55: 227–35.

Midgley, M. (2014) *Are You an Illusion?* London: Routledge.

Miles, M. and Huberman, A. (1994) *Qualitative Data Analysis*, 2nd edition. Thousand Oaks, CA: Sage.

Millar, J. (2007) 'Qualitative longitudinal research for policy', *Social Policy and Society*, 6 (4): 529–94.

Millar, J. (2021 in press) 'Families, work and care over time: Reflections on a qualitative longitudinal study', *Social Policy and Society*. Themed section.

Millar, J. and Ridge, T. (2017) *Work and Relationships over Time in Lone-Mother Families*. York: Joseph Rowntree Foundation.

Miller, R. (2000) *Researching Life Stories and Family Histories*. London: Sage.

Miller, T. (2005) *Making Sense of Motherhood: A Narrative Approach*. Cambridge: CUP.

Miller, T. (2015) 'Going back: Stalking, talking and research responsibilities in qualitative longitudinal research', *International Journal of Social Research Methodology*, 18 (3): 293–305.

Miller, T. (2017) *Making Sense of Parenthood: Caring, Gender and Family Lives*. Cambridge: CUP.

Miller, T. and Bell, L. (2002) 'Consenting to what? Issues of access, gate-keeping and informed consent', in M. Mauthner, M. Birch, J. Jessop and T. Miller (eds) *Ethics in Qualitative Research*. London: Sage, pp. 53–69.

Mishler, E. (1986) *Research Interviewing: Context and Narrative*. Cambridge, MA: Harvard University Press.

Mishler, E. (1995) 'Models of narrative analysis: A typology', *Journal of Narrative and Life History*, 5 (2): 87–123.

Molloy, D. and Woodfield, K. with Bacon, J. (2002) *Longitudinal Qualitative Research Approaches in Evaluation Studies*. Department for Work and Pensions Working Paper No. 7. London: HMSO.

Monge, P. (1995) 'Theoretical and analytical issues in studying organisational processes', in G. Huber and A. Van de Ven (eds) *Longitudinal Field Research Methods*. London: Sage, pp. 267–98.

Monrouxe, L. (2009) 'Solicited audio diaries in longitudinal narrative research: A view from inside', *Qualitative Research*, 9 (1): 81–103.

Moore, N. (2006) 'The contexts of context: Broadening perspectives in the (re)use of qualitative data', *Methodological Innovations Online*, 1 (2): 21–32.

Moore, N. (2007) '(Re) using qualitative data', *Sociological Research Online*, 12 (3): 1.

Moore, N. (2012) 'The politics and ethics of naming: Questioning anonymization in (archival) research', *International Journal of Social Research Methodology*, 15 (4): 331–40.

Morris, D. (2005) 'Bergsonian intuition, Husserlian variation and Peircian abduction: Toward a relation between method, sense and nature', *Southern Journal of Philosophy*, 43: 267–98.

Morrow, V. (2009) *The Ethics of Social Research with Children and Families in 'Young Lives': Practical Experiences*. Young Lives Working Paper Series No. 53. Oxford: University of Oxford, Department of International Development.

Morrow, V. (2013) 'Practical ethics in social research with children and families in "*Young Lives*": A longitudinal study of childhood poverty in Ethiopia, Andhra Pradesh (India), Peru and Vietnam', *Methodological Innovations Online*, 8 (2): 21–35.

Morrow, V. and Crivello, G. (1915) 'What is the value of qualitative longitudinal research with children and young people for international development?', *International Journal of Social Research Methodology*, 18 (3): 267–80.

Murray, S., Kendall, M., Worth, A., Harris, F., Lloyd, A., et al. (2009) 'Use of serial qualitative interviews to understand patients' evolving experiences and needs', *British Medical Journal*, 339: b3702.

Neale, B. (1985) *Getting Married: An Ethnographic and Bibliographic Study* (unpublished doctoral thesis). University of Leeds, School of English, Institute of Dialect and Folk Life Studies.

Neale, B. (2007) *Timescapes: Changing Relationships and Identities through the Life Course – Study Overview*. University of Leeds, www.timescapes-archive.leeds.ac.uk/publications-and-outputs.

Neale, B. (2008) *Linking Questions and Data in Longitudinal Research: Re-thinking Mixed Longitudinal Methods*. Briefing Paper for the ESRC Research Resources Board, www.timescapes-archive.leeds.ac.uk/publications-and-outputs.

Neale, B. (2013) 'Adding time into the mix: Stakeholder ethics in qualitative longitudinal research', *Methodological Innovations Online*, 8 (2): 6–20.

Neale, B. (2015) 'Time and the life course: Perspectives from qualitative longitudinal research', in N. Worth and I. Hardill (eds) *Researching the Life Course: Critical Perspectives from the Social Sciences*. Bristol: Policy Press, pp. 25–41.

Neale, B. (2016) 'Editorial introduction: Young fatherhood – Lived experiences and policy challenges', *Social Policy and Society*, 15 (1): 75–83.

Neale, B. (2017a) *Generating Data in Qualitative Longitudinal Research: A Review of Field Tools and Techniques*. Timescapes Working Paper No. 8, www.timescapes-archive.leeds.ac.uk/publications-and-outputs.

Neale, B. (2017b) 'Research Data as Documents of Life', *Guest post no.* 13, bigqlr.ncrm.ac.uk.

Neale, B. (2019) *What is Qualitative Longitudinal Research?* London: Bloomsbury Academic. (re-published as *Qualitative Longitudinal Research*, 2021).

Neale, B. (2020a) 'Researching eduational processes through time: The value of qualitative longitudinal methods' in M. Ward and S. Delamont (eds) *Handbook of Qualitative Research in Education*. 2nd edition. Cheltenham: Edward Elgar, pp 101–13.

Neale, B. (2020b) 'Documents of lives and times: Revisiting qualitative data through time', in K. Hughes and A. Tarrant (eds) *Qualitative Secondary Analysis*. London: Sage, pp. 61–78.

Neale, B. (2021 in press) 'Fluid enquiry, complex causality, policy processes: Making a difference with Qualitative Longitudinal Research' *Social Policy and Society*.

Neale, B. and Bishop, L. (eds) (2010–11) 'Qualitative and qualitative longitudinal data resources in Europe', *IASSIST Quarterly*, 34 (3–4): Fall/Winter 2010; Spring/Summer 2011.

Neale, B. and Bishop, L. (2012a) 'The Timescapes Archive: A stakeholder approach to archiving qualitative longitudinal data', *Qualitative Research*, 12 (1): 53–65.

Neale, B. and Bishop, L. (2012b) *The Ethics of Archiving and Re-Using Qualitative Longitudinal Data: A Stakeholder Approach*. Timescapes Methods Guide No. 18, www.timescapes-archive.leeds.ac.uk/publications-and-outputs.

Neale, B. and Davies, L. (2015) 'Editorial introduction: Seeing young fathers in a different way', *Families, Relationships and Societies*, 4 (2): 309–14.

Neale, B. and Davies, L. (2016) 'Becoming a young breadwinner? The education, employment and training trajectories of young fathers', *Social Policy and Society*, 15 (1): 85–98.

Neale, B. and Flowerdew, J. (2003) 'Time, textures and childhood: The contours of longitudinal qualitative research', *International Journal of Social Research Methodology*, 6 (3): 189–99.

Neale, B. and Flowerdew, J. (2004) *Parent Problems 2! Looking Back at our Parents' Divorce*. East Molesey, Surrey: Young Voice.

Neale, B. and Flowerdew, J. (2007) 'New structures, new agency: The dynamics of child–parent relationships after divorce', *International Journal of Children's Rights*, 15 (1): 25–42.

Neale, B. with Hughes, K. (2020) *Data Management Planning: A Practical Guide for Qualitative Longitudinal Researchers*. University of Leeds Institutional Repository, www.timescapes-archive.leeds.ac.uk/publications-and-outputs.

Neale, B. and Ladlow, L. (2015) *Young Offender Fathers: Risk, Resource, Redemption?* Following Young Fathers Briefing Paper No. 5, www.followingfathers.leeds.ac.uk.

Neale, B. and Lau-Clayton, C. (2014) 'Young parenthood and cross-generational relationships: The perspectives of young fathers', in J. Holland and R. Edwards (eds) *Understanding Families over Time: Research and Policy*. London: Palgrave Macmillan, pp. 69–87.

Neale, B. and Morton, S. (2012) *Creating Impact through Qualitative Longitudinal Research*. Timescapes Methods Guides Series No. 20, www.timescapes-archive.leeds.ac.uk/publications-and-outputs.

Neale, B. and Patrick, R. (2016) *Engaged Young Fathers? Gender, Parenthood and the Dynamics of Relationships*. Following Young Fathers Working Paper Series No. 1, www.followingfathers.leeds.ac.uk.

Neale, B. and Wade, A. (2000) *Parent Problems: Children's Views on Life when Parents Split Up*. East Molesey, Surrey: Young Voice.

Neale, B., Henwood, K. and Holland, J. (eds) (2012) 'Researching lives through time: The timescapes approach', *Qualitative Research*, 12 (1): 1–15.

Neale, B., Lau-Clayton, C., Davies, L. and Ladlow, L. (2015) *Researching the Lives of Young Fathers: The Following Young Fathers Study and Dataset*. Briefing Paper No. 8, www.followingfathers.leeds.ac.uk.

Negroni, C. (2012) 'Turning points in the life course: A narrative concept in professional bifurcations', in K. Hackstaff, F. Kupferberg and C. Negroni (eds) *Biography and Turning Points in Europe and America*. Bristol: Policy Press, pp. 41–64.

Nelson, E. (2004) 'Wilhem Dilthey: The formation of the historical world in the human sciences – Review', *Journal of the History of Philosophy*, 42 (1): 113–15.

Neumann, I. (2012) 'Introduction to the forum on liminality', *Review of International Studies*, 38: 473–9.

Newman, J. (2014) 'Telling the time: Researching generational politics', *Families, Relationships and Societies*, 3 (3): 465–8.

Nielsen, H. B. (2003) 'Historical, cultural and emotional meanings: Interviews with young girls in three generations', *Nordic Journal of Women's Studies (NORA)*, 11 (1): 14–26.

Nilson, A. (2014) 'Cohort and generation: Concepts in studies of social change from a lifecourse perspective', *Families, Relationships and Societies*, 3 (3): 475–9.

Nizza, I., Smith, J. and Kirkham, J. (2018) '"Putting the illness in a box": A longitudinal interpretive phenomenological analysis of changes in a sufferer's pictorial representation of pain following participation in a pain management programme', *British Journal of Pain*, 12 (3): 163–70.

Noble, H. and Smith, J. (2015) 'Issues of validity and reliability in qualitative research', *Evidence Based Nursing*, 18 (2): 34–5.

Nowotny, H. (1994) *Time: The Modern and Postmodern Experience*. Cambridge: Polity Press.

Nowotny, H. (2005) 'The increase in complexity and its reduction: Emergent interfaces between the natural sciences, humanities and social sciences', *Theory, Culture and Society*, 22 (5): 15–31.

Oakley, A. (1979) *Becoming a Mother*. Oxford: Martin Robertson.

O'Connor, H. and Goodwin, J. (2010) 'Utilising data from a lost sociological project: Experiences, insights, promises', *Qualitative Research*, 10 (3): 283–98.

O'Connor, H. and Goodwin, J. (2012) 'Revisiting Norbert Elias's sociology of community: Learning from the Leicester re-studies', *The Sociological Review*, 60: 476–97.

O'Connor, P. (2006) 'Young people's construction of the self: Late modern elements and gender differences', *Sociology*, 40 (1): 107–24.

O'Neill, M. and Roberts, B. (2020) *Walking Methods: Research on the Move*. London: Routledge.

O'Reilly, K. (2012) 'Ethnographic returning, qualitative longitudinal research and the reflexive analysis of social practice', *The Sociological Review*, 60: 518–36.

Ottenberg, S. (1990) 'Thirty years of field notes: Changing relationships to the text', in R. Sanjek (ed.) *Fieldnotes: The Makings of Anthropology*. Ithaca, NY: Cornell University Press, pp. 139–60.

Paavilainen-Mäntymäki, E. and Aarikka-Stenroos, L. (2013) 'Narratives as longitudinal and process data', in M. Hassett and E. Paavilainen-Mäntymäki (eds) *Handbook of Longitudinal Research Methods in Organisation and Business Studies*. Cheltenham: Edward Elgar, pp. 138–60.

Paavilainen-Mäntymäki, E. and Welch, C. (2013) 'How to escape an unprocessual legacy: A viewpoint from international business research', in M. Hassett and E. Paavilainen-Mäntymäki (eds) *Handbook of Longitudinal Research Methods in Organisation and Business Studies*. Cheltenham: Edward Elgar, pp. 229–48.

Paavola, S. (2006) *On the Origin of Ideas: An Abductive Approach to Discovery*. Philosophical Studies from the University of Helsinki: 15. Helsinki: University of Helsinki, Department of Philosophy.

Paavola, S. (2014) 'From steps and phases to dynamically evolving abduction', in M. Bergman, S. Paavola and J. Queiroz (eds) *Commens Working Papers (Digital Companion to C. S. Peirce)*, No. 5, www.commens.org/papers/paper/paavola-sami-2014-steps-and-phases-dynamically-evolving-abduction.

Pahl, R. (1978) 'Living without a job: How school leavers see the future', *New Society*, November: 259–62.

Parkinson, S., Eatough, V., Holmes, J., Stapley, E. and Midgley, N. (2016) 'Framework analysis: A worked example of a study exploring young people's experiences of depression', *Qualitative Research in Psychology*, 13 (2): 109–29.

Parry, O., Thomson, C. and Fowkes, G. (1999) 'Life course data collection: Qualitative interviewing using the life grid', *Sociological Research Online*, 4 (2).

Patrick, R. (2012) *Recruiting and Sustaining Population Samples over Time*. Timescapes Methods Guide Series No. 3, www.timescapes-archive.leeds.ac.uk/publications-and-outputs.

Patrick, R. (2013) *The 'Gift' Relationship: An Ethical Dilemma in Small Scale Research*, www.timescapes-archive.leeds.ac.uk/publications-and-outputs/knowledge-bank.

Patrick, R. (2017) *For Whose Benefit? The Everyday Realities of Welfare Reform*. Bristol: Policy Press.

Patrick, R., Treanor, M. and Wenham, A. (eds) (2021 in press) 'Qualitative longitudinal research for social policy: Where are we now?', *Social Policy and Society*. Themed Section.

Patterson, L., Forbes, K. and Peace, R. (2009) 'Happy, stable and contented: Accomplished ageing in the imagined futures of young New Zealanders', *Ageing and Society*, 29: 431–54.

Pawson, R. (2006) *Evidence Based Policy: A Realist Perspective*. London: Sage.

Pawson, R. and Tilley, N. (1997) *Realistic Evaluation*. London: Sage.

Pearce, S. (2015) 'Going beneath the surface in a longitudinal qualitative narrative study with young adults with cancer', *BMJ Open*, 5 (4): 1–9.

Pearson, H. (2016) *The Life Project*. London: Allen Lane.

Peirce, C. (1934 [1878]) *Collected Papers Vol. 5* (eds C. Hartshorne and P. Weiss). Cambridge, MA: Harvard University Press.

Pember Reeves, M. (2008 [1913]) *Round About a Pound a Week*. London: Persephone Books.

Perks, R. and Thomson, A. (eds) (2016) *The Oral History Reader*, 3rd edition. London: Routledge.

Pettersson, H. (2019) *The Future of Human–Carnivore Co-existence in Europe: Design for a NERC-funded Doctoral Study*. University of Leeds: School of Earth and Environment, Sustainability Research Institute.

Pettigrew, A. (1979) 'On studying organisational cultures', *Administrative Science Quarterly*, 24 (4): 570–81.

Pettigrew, A. (1985) *The Awakening Giant: Continuity and Change in Imperial Chemical Industries*. Oxford: Blackwell.

Pettigrew, A. (1987) 'Context and action in the transformation of the firm', *Journal of Management Studies*, 24 (6): 649–70.

Pettigrew, A. (1995) 'Longitudinal field research on change: Theory and practice', in G. Huber and A. Van de Ven (eds) *Longitudinal Field Research Methods*. London: Sage, pp. 91–125.

Pettigrew, A. (1997) 'What is a processual analysis?', *Scandinavian Journal of Management*, 13 (4): 337–48.

Phelps, E., Furstenberg, F. and Colby, A. (eds) (2002) *Looking at Lives: American Longitudinal Studies of the Twentieth Century*. New York: Russell Sage Foundation.

Philip, G. (2017) *Working with Qualitative Longitudinal Data*. Guest blog, www.bigqlr. ncrm.ac.uk.

Pilcher, J. (1994) 'Mannheim's sociology of generations: An undervalued legacy', *British Journal of Sociology*, 45 (3): 481–95.

Pini, M. and Walkerdine, V. (2011) 'Girls on film: Video diaries as auto-ethnography', in P. Reavey (ed.) *Visual Methods in Psychology*. London: Routledge, pp. 139–52.

Pinnock, H., Kendall, M., Murray, S., Worth, A., Levack, P., et al. (2011) 'Living and dying with severe chronic obstructive pulmonary disease: Multi-perspective longitudinal qualitative study', *BMJ Online*: 342.

Plummer, K. (2001) *Documents of Life 2: An Invitation to a Critical Humanism*. London: Sage.

Plummer, K. (2019) *Narrative Power*. Cambridge: Polity Press.

Plumridge, L. and Thomson, R. (2003) 'Longitudinal qualitative studies and the reflexive self', *International Journal of Social Research Methodology*, 6 (3): 213–22.

Polkinghorne, D. (1995) 'Narrative configuration in qualitative analysis', in J. Hatch and R. Wisniewski (eds) *Life History and Narrative*. London: Falmer, pp. 5–23.

Pollard, A. (2007) 'The Identity and Learning programme: "Principled pragmatism" in a 12-year longitudinal ethnography', *Ethnography and Education*, 2 (1): 1–19.

Pollard, A. with Filer, A. (1996) *The Social World of Children's Learning: Case Studies of Pupils from Four to Seven*. London: Cassell.

Pollard, A. and Filer, A. (1999) *The Social World of Pupil Career: Strategic Biographies through Primary School*. London: Cassell.

Portelli, A. (2016 [1979]) 'What makes oral history different?', in R. Perks and A. Thomson (eds) *The Oral History Reader*, 3rd edition. London: Routledge, pp. 48–58.

Prigogine, I. (1980) *From Being to Becoming: Time and Complexity in the Physical Sciences*. San Francisco: W. H. Freeman.

Prior, L. (2016) 'Using documents in social research', in D. Silverman (ed.) *Qualitative Research*, 4th edition. London: Sage, pp. 171–85.

Radin, P. (1987 [1933]) *The Method and Theory of Ethnology: An Essay in Criticism*. South Hadley, MA: Bergin & Garvey.

Rapley, T. (2016) 'Some pragmatics of qualitative data analysis', in D. Silverman (ed.) *Qualitative Research*, 4th edition. London: Sage, pp. 331–45.

Reavey, P. (ed.) (2011) *Visual Methods in Psychology*. London: Routledge.

Redfield, R. (1930) *Tepoztlan: A Mexican Village*. Chicago: University of Chicago Press.

Reiss, M. (2005) 'Managing endings in a longitudinal study: Respect for persons', *Research in Science Education*, 35: 123–35.

Reiter, H., Rogge, B. and Schoneck, N. (2011) 'Times of life in times of change: Sociological perspectives on time and the life course', *BIOS*, 24 (2): 171–4.

Richards, A. (1956) *Chisungu: A Girls' Initiation Ceremony among the Bemba of Zambia*. London: Faber and Faber.

Richardson, J., Ong, B. N., Sim, J. and Corbett, M. (2009) 'Begin at the beginning … Using the life grid for exploring illness experience', *Social Research Update*, 57: 1–4.

Richardson, K. and Cilliers, P. (2001) 'What is complexity science? A view from different directions', *Emergence: Complexity and Organisation*, 3 (1): 5–23.

Ricoeur, P. (1984–5) *Time and Narrative*. Chicago: University of Chicago Press.

Ridge, T. (2015) *Understanding the 'family-work' project: Researching low income families over time*, Researching Relationships Across Generations and Through Time Conference, held at the FLAG (Families, Life course and Generations) Research Centre. University of Leeds, 9th June.

Ridge, T. and Millar, J. (2011) *Following Families: Working Lone-mother Families and their Children*. Department for Work and Pensions Research Report No. 536. London: Stationery Office.

Riessman, C. (2008) 'Concluding comments', in M. Andrews, C. Squire and M. Tamboukou (eds) *Doing Narrative Research*. London: Sage, pp. 151–6.

Riessman, C. (2016) 'What's different about narrative inquiry? Cases, categories and contexts', in D. Silverman (ed.) *Qualitative Research*, 4th edition. London: Sage, pp. 363–78.

Riley, M. (1998) 'A life course approach: Autobiographical notes', in J. Giele and G. Elder (eds) *Methods of Life Course Research: Qualitative and Quantitative Approaches*. London: Sage, pp. 28–51.

Ritchie, J. and Lewis., J. (eds) (2003) *Qualitative Research Practice*. London: Sage.

Ritchie, J., Lewis, J., McNaughton Nicholls, C. and Ormston, R. (eds) (2014) *Qualitative Research Practice*, 2nd edition. London: Sage.

Ritchie, J. and Spencer, L. (1994) 'Qualitative data analysis for applied policy research', in A. Bryman and R. Burgess (eds) *Analysing Qualitative Data*. London: Routledge, pp. 173–194.

Robards, B. and Lincoln, S. (2017) 'Uncovering longitudinal life narratives: Scrolling back on Facebook', *Qualitative Research*, 17 (6): 715–30.

Roberts, B. (2002) *Biographical Research*. Buckingham: Open University Press.

Rosa, H. (2013) *Social Acceleration: A New Theory of Modernity*. New York: Columbia University Press.

Rosser, C. and Harris, C. (1965) *The Family and Social Change*. London: Routledge & Kegan Paul.

Rothman, K., Gallacher, J. and Hatch, E. (2013) 'Why representativeness should be avoided', *International Journal of Epidemiology*, 42: 1012–14.

Rowntree, S. (1901) *Poverty: A Study of Town Life*. London: Macmillan and Co.

Royce, A. P. (2002) 'Learning to see, learning to listen: Thirty-five years of fieldwork with the Isthmus Zapotec', in R. Kemper and A. P. Royce (eds) *Chronicling Cultures: Long-Term Field Research in Anthropology*. Walnut Creek, CA: AltaMira Press, pp. 8–33.

Royce, A. P. (2005) *The Long and Short of It: Benefits and Challenges of Long-term Ethnographic Research*. Paper presented at the ESRC seminar series: *Qualitative Longitudinal Research: Principles, Practice, Policy*. University of Leeds, UK, 30 September.

Royce, A. P. and Kemper, R. (2002) 'Long-term field research: Metaphors, paradigms and themes', in R. Kemper and A. P. Royce (eds) *Chronicling Cultures: Long-term Field Research in Anthropology*. Walnut Creek, CA: AltaMira Press, pp. xiii–xxxviii.

Ruspini, E. (2002) *Introduction to Longitudinal Research*. London: Routledge.

Saldaña, J. (1995) 'Is theatre necessary? Final exit interviews with 6th grade participants from the ASU longitudinal study', *Youth Theatre Journal*, 9: 14–30.

Saldaña, J. (2002) 'Analysing change in longitudinal qualitative data', *Youth Theatre Journal*, 16 (1): 1–17.

Saldaña, J. (2003) *Longitudinal Qualitative Research: Analyzing Change through Time*. Walnut Creek, CA: AltaMira Press.

Saldaña, J. (2005) *Ethnodrama: An Anthology of Reality Theatre*. Walnut Creek, CA: AltaMira Press.

Salter, A. (2017) 'Reading time backwards: Archival research and temporal order', in N. Moore, A. Salter, L. Stanley and M. Tamboukou (eds) *The Archive Project: Archival Research in the Social Sciences*. London: Routledge, pp. 99–126.

Sanders, J. and Munford, R. (2008) 'Losing sense to the future? Young women's strategic responses to adulthood transitions', *Journal of Youth Studies*, 11 (3): 331–46.

Sanjek, R. (ed.) (1990) *Fieldnotes: The Makings of Anthropology*. Ithaca, NY: Cornell University Press.

Savage, M. (2005a) 'Revisiting classic qualitative studies', *FQS: Forum Qualitative Social Research*, 6 (1): Art. 31.

Savage, M. (2005b) 'Working class identities in the 1960s: Revisiting the *Affluent Worker* Study', *Sociology*, 39 (5): 929–48.

Savage, M. (2007) 'Changing social class identities in post-war Britain: Perspectives from mass-observation', *Sociological Research Online*, 12 (3): 6.

Savage, M. (2010) *Identities and Social Change in Britain since 1940: The Politics of Method*. Oxford: Oxford University Press.

Sayer, A. (1992) *Method in Social Science: A Realist Approach*, 2nd edition. London: Routledge.

Sayer, A. (2000) *Realism and Social Science*. London: Sage.

Scheper-Hughes, N. (2000) 'Ire in Ireland', *Ethnography*, 1 (1): 117–40.

Scott, C. and White, W. (2005) 'Ethical issues in the conduct of longitudinal studies of addiction treatment', *Journal of Substance Abuse Treatment*, 28: 591–610.

Scott, J. and Alwin, D. (1998) 'Retrospective versus prospective measurement of life histories in longitudinal research', in J. Giele and G. Elder (eds) *Methods of Life Course Research: Qualitative and Quantitative Approaches*. London: Sage, pp. 98–127.

Scudder, T. and Colson, E. (1979) 'Long-term research in Gwembe Valley, Zambia', in G. Foster, T. Scudder, E. Colson and R. Kemper (eds) *Long-term Field Research in Social Anthropology*. New York: Academic Press, pp. 227–54.

Scudder, T. and Colson, E. (2002) 'Long-term research in Gwembe Valley, Zambia', in R. Kemper and A. P. Royce (eds) *Chronicling Cultures: Long-term Field Research in Anthropology*. Walnut Creek, CA: AltaMira Press, pp. 197–238.

Seale, C. (2007) 'Quality in qualitative research', in C. Seale, G. Gobo, J. Gubrium and D. Silverman (eds) *Qualitative Research Practice*. London: Sage, pp. 379–89.

Seale, C. (2018) 'Research quality', in C. Seale (ed.) *Researching Society and Culture*, 4th edition. London: Sage, pp. 567–81.

Shah, S. and Priestley, M. (2011) *Disability and Social Change: Private Lives and Public Policy*. Bristol: Policy Press.

Shanahan, M. and Macmillan, R. (2008) *Biography and the Sociological Imagination: Contexts and Contingencies*. New York: Norton.

Sharland, E., Holland, P., Henderson, M., Zhang, M., Cheung, S., et al. (2017) 'Assembling life history narratives from quantitative longitudinal panel data: What's the story for families using social work?', *International Journal of Social Research Methodology*, 20 (6): 667–79.

Sharpe, G. (2017) 'Sociological stalking? Methods, ethics and power in longitudinal criminal research', *Criminology and Criminal Justice*, 17 (3): 233–247.

Shaw, C. (1966 [1930]) *The Jack Roller: A Delinquent Boy's Own Story*. Chicago: University of Chicago Press.

Shaw, J. (2001) 'Winning territory: Changing place to change pace', in J. May and N. Thrift (eds) *Timespace: Geographies of Temporality*. New York: Routledge, pp. 120–32.

Shaw, R., West, K., Hagger, B. and Holland, C. (2016) 'Living well to the end: A phenomenological analysis of life in extra care housing', *International Journal of Qualitative Studies on Health and Well-Being*, 11 (1): 1–12.

Sheldon, R. (2009) 'Breaking a "strange silence": The potential for reusing existing qualitative data to inform policy', *Public Policy Research*, Jun.-Aug.: 97–102.

Sheridan, J., Chamberlain, K. and Dupuis, A. (2011) 'Timelining: Visualising experience', *Qualitative Research*, 11 (5): 552–69.

Shirani, F. (2010) 'Researcher change and continuity in a qualitative longitudinal study: The impact of personal characteristics', in F. Shirani and S. Weller (eds) *Conducting Qualitative Longitudinal Research: Fieldwork Experiences*. Timescapes Working Paper Series No. 2, pp. 49–59, www.timescapes-archive.leeds.ac.uk/publications-and-outputs.

Shirani, F. and Henwood, K. (2011) 'Taking each day as it comes: Temporal experiences in the context of unexpected life course transitions', *Time and Society*, 20 (1): 49–68.

Smart, C. and Neale, B. (1999) *Family Fragments?* Cambridge: Polity Press.

Smart, C., Neale, B. and Wade, A. (2001) *The Changing Experience of Childhood: Families and Divorce*. Cambridge: Polity Press.

Smith, J., Flowers, P. and Larkin, M. (2009) *Interpretative Phenomenological Analysis: Theory, Method and Research*. London: Sage.

Smith, N. (2003) 'Cross-sectional profiling and longitudinal analysis: Research notes on analysis in the LQ study "Negotiating Transitions in Citizenship"', *International Journal of Social Research Methodology*, 6 (3): 273–7.

SmithBattle, L., Lorenz, R., Reangsing, C., Palmer, J. and Pitroff, G. (2018) 'A methodological review of qualitative longitudinal research in nursing', *Nursing Inquiry*, 25 (4): e12248.

Snelgrove, S. (2014) 'Conducting qualitative longitudinal research using interpretative phenomenological analysis', *Nurse Researcher*, 22: 20–5.

Söderström, J. (2019) 'Life diagrams: A methodological and analytical tool for accessing life histories', *Qualitative Research*, 19 (3): 1–19.

Spiers, J., Smith, J. and Drage, M. (2016) 'A longitudinal interpretative phenomenological analysis of the process of kidney recipients' resolution of complex ambiguities with relationships with their living donors', *Journal of Health Psychology*, 21 (11): 2600–11.

Srivastava, P. and Hopwood, N. (2009) 'A practical iterative framework for qualitative data analysis', *International Journal of Qualitative Methods*, 8 (1): 76–84.

Stacey, M. (1960) *Tradition and Change: A Study of Banbury*. Oxford: OUP.

Stacey, M., Batstone, E., Bell, C. and Murcott, A. (1975) *Power, Persistence and Change*. London: Routledge & Kegan Paul.

Stanley, L. (2013) 'Whites writing: Letters and documents of life in a QLR project', in L. Stanley (ed.) *Documents of Life Revisited: Narrative and Biographical Methodology for a 21st Century Critical Humanism*. London: Routledge, pp. 59–73.

Stanley, L. (2015) 'Operationalising a QLR project on social change and whiteness in South Africa, 1770s–1970s', *International Journal of Social Research Methodology*, 18 (3): 251–65.

Stich, A. and Cippolone, K. (2017) 'In and through the educational "reform churn": The illustrative power of qualitative longitudinal research', *Urban Education*, 6 Feb.: 1–27.

Strauss, A. (1997 [1959]) *Mirrors and Masks: The Search for Identity*. New Brunswick, NJ: Transaction Publishers.

Strauss, A., Schatzman, L., Bucher, R., Ehrlich, D. and Sabshin, M. (1963) 'The hospital and its negotiated order', in E. Friedson (ed.) *The Hospital in Modern Society*. Glencoe, IL: Free Press, pp. 147–68.

Strobel, K. (2005) 'After the aftermath: A reply to Wolff-Michael Roth's review of Harry Wolcott's "Sneaky kid and the aftermath" published in FQS 5 (1)', *FQS Forum: Qualitative Social Research*, 6 (3): Art. 6.

Swallow, V., Newton, J. and Van Lottum, C. (2003) 'How to manage and display qualitative data using Framework and Microsoft Excel', *Journal of Clinical Nursing*, 12: 610–12.

Szakolczai, A. (2014) 'Living permanent liminality: The recent transition experience in Ireland', *Irish Journal of Sociology*, 22 (1): 28–50.

Sztompka, P. (1991) *Society in Action: The Theory of Social Becoming*. Chicago: University of Chicago Press.

Talle, A. (2012) 'Returns to the Maasai: Multi-temporal fieldwork and the production of anthropological knowledge', in S. Howell and A. Talle (eds) *Returns to the Field: Multi-Temporal Research and Contemporary Anthropology*. Bloomington, IN: Indiana University Press, pp. 73–94.

Tamboukou, M. (2014) 'Archival research: Unravelling space/time/matter entanglements and fragments', *Qualitative Research*, 14 (5): 617–33.

Tarrant, A. (2016) 'Getting out of the swamp? Methodological reflections on using qualitative secondary analysis to develop research design', *International Journal of Social Research Methodology*, 20 (6): 599–611.

Tarrant, A. (2020) *FYFF: Following Young Fathers Further*, https://fyff.blogs.lincoln.ac.uk.

Tarrant, A. and Hughes, K. (2019) 'Qualitative secondary analysis: Building longitudinal samples to understand men's generational identities in low-income contexts', *Sociology*, 53 (3): 538–53.

Tarrant, A. and Hughes, K. (2020) 'Collective qualitative secondary analysis and data sharing: Strategies, insights, challenges', in K. Hughes and A. Tarrant (eds) *Qualitative Secondary Analysis*. London: Sage, pp. 101–18.

Tarrant, A. and Neale, B. (eds) (2017) *Learning to Support Young Dads: Responding to Young Fathers in a Different Way*. Policy Briefing: Supporting Young Dads Impact Initiative, www.followingfathers.leeds.ac.uk/impact.

Taylor, R. (2015) 'Beyond anonymity: Temporality and the production of knowledge in a qualitative longitudinal study', *International Journal of Social Research Methodology*, 18 (3): 281–92.

Thomas, W. and Znaniecki, F. (1958 [1918–21]) *The Polish Peasant in Europe and America.* New York: Dover Publications.

Thompson, E.P. (1967) 'Time, work-discipline, and industrial capitalism', *Past and Present,* 36: 52–97.

Thompson, E.P. (1978) *The Poverty of Theory.* London: Merlin.

Thompson, P. (1981) 'Life histories and the analysis of social change', in D. Bertaux (ed.) *Biography and Society: The Life History Approach in the Social Sciences.* London: Sage, pp. 289–306.

Thompson, P. (2000) *The Voice of the Past,* 3rd edition. Oxford: OUP.

Thompson, P. (2004) 'Researching family and social mobility with two eyes: Some experiences of the interaction between qualitative and quantitative data', *International Journal of Social Research Methodology,* 7 (3): 237–57.

Thomson, R. (2007) 'The qualitative longitudinal case history: Practical, methodological and ethical reflections', *Social Policy and Society,* 6 (4): 571–82.

Thomson, R. (2009) *Unfolding Lives: Youth, Gender and Change.* Bristol: Policy Press.

Thomson, R. (ed.) (2010a) *Intensity and Insight: Qualitative Longitudinal Methods as a Route to the Psycho-Social.* Timescapes Working Paper No. 3, www.timescapes-archive.leeds.ac.uk/publications-and-outputs.

Thomson, R. (2010b) 'Creating family case histories: Subjects, selves and family dynamics', in R. Thomson (ed.) *Intensity and Insight: Qualitative Longitudinal Methods as a Route to the Psycho-Social.* Timescapes Working Paper No. 3, pp. 6–18, www.timescapes-archive.leeds.ac.uk/publications-and-outputs.

Thomson, R. (2011) 'Using biographical and longitudinal methods: Researching mothering', in J. Mason and A. Dale (eds) *Understanding Social Research.* London: Sage, pp. 62–74.

Thomson, R. (2012) *Qualitative Longitudinal Methods as a Route into the Psycho-Social.* Timescapes Methods Guides Series No. 13, www.timescapes-archive.leeds.ac.uk/publications-and-outputs.

Thomson, R. and Holland, J. (2002) 'Imagined adulthood: Resources, plans and contradictions', *Gender and Education,* 14 (4): 337–50.

Thomson, R. and Holland, J. (2003) 'Hindsight, foresight and insight: The challenges of longitudinal qualitative research', *International Journal of Social Research Methodology,* 6 (3): 233–44.

Thomson, R. and Holland, J. (2005) '"Thanks for the memory": Memory books as a methodological resource in biographical research', *Qualitative Research,* 5 (2): 201–19.

Thomson, R. and McLeod, J. (2015) 'Editorial introduction: New frontiers in qualitative longitudinal research – An agenda for research', *International Journal of Social Research Methodology,* 18 (3): 243–50.

Thomson, R., Bell, R., Henderson, S., Holland, J., McGrellis, S. and Sharpe, S. (2002) 'Critical moments: Choice, chance and opportunity in young people's narratives of transition to adulthood', *Sociology,* 36: 335–54.

Thomson, R., Plumridge, L. and Holland, J. (eds) (2003) 'Longitudinal qualitative research: A developing methodology', *International Journal of Social Research Methodology,* 6 (3): 185–7.

Thomson, R., Kehily, M., Hadfield, L. and Sharpe, S. (2011) *Making Modern Mothers*. Bristol: Policy Press.

Thomson, R., Martin, J. and Sharples, S. (2017) 'The experience of couples being given an oxygen concentrator to use at home: A longitudinal interpretative phenomenological analysis', *Journal of Health Psychology*, 22 (6): 798–810.

Tilly, C. (2008) *Explaining Social Processes*. London: Paradigm.

Timmermans, S. and Tavory, I. (2012) 'Theory construction in qualitative research: From grounded theory to abductive analysis', *Sociological Theory*, 30 (3): 167–86.

Tinati, R., Halford, S., Carr, L. and Pope, C. (2014) 'Big data: Methodological challenges and approaches for sociological analysis', *Sociology*, 48 (4): 663–81.

Treloar, A., Choudhury, G. S. and Michener, W. (2012) 'Contrasting national data strategies: Australia and the US', in. G. Pryor (ed.) *Managing Research Data*. London: Facet, pp. 173–204.

Tsoukas, H. and Chia, R. (2002) 'On organisational becoming', *Organisation Science*, 13 (5): 567–82.

Tsoukas, H. and Hatch, M. (2001) 'Complex thinking, complex practice: The case for a narrative approach to organisational complexity', *Human Relations*, 54 (8): 979–1013.

Tunstall, R. and Coulter, A. (2006) *Twenty-Five Years on Twenty Estates: Turning the Tide?* Bristol: Policy Press and the Joseph Rowntree Foundation.

Urry, J. (2005) 'Editorial introduction: The complexity turn', *Theory, Culture and Society*, 22 (5): 1–14.

Van de Ven, A. (2007) *Engaged Scholarship: A Guide for Organisational and Social Research*. Oxford: OUP.

Van de Ven, A. and Huber, G. (1995) 'Introduction', in G. Huber and A. Van de Ven (eds) *Longitudinal Field Research Methods: Studying Processes of Organisational Change*. London: Sage, pp. vii–xiv.

Van de Ven, A. and Poole, M. (1995) 'Methods for studying innovation development: The Minnesota Innovation Research Program', in G. Huber and A. Van de Ven (eds) *Longitudinal Field Research Methods: Studying Processes of Organisational Change*. London: Sage, pp. 155–85.

van Gennep, A. (1960 [1909]) *The Rites of Passage*. London: Routledge & Kegan Paul.

Veness, T. (1962) *School Leavers: Their Aspirations and Expectations*. London: Methuen.

Vogl, S., Zartler, U., Schmidt, E. and Rieder, I. (2017) 'Developing an analytical framework for multiple perspective, qualitative longitudinal interviews', *International Journal of Social Research Methodology*, 21 (2): 177–90.

Wajcman, J. (2015) *Pressed for Time*. Chicago: Chicago University Press.

Walker, R. and Leisering, L. (1998) 'New tools: Towards a dynamic science of modern society', in L. Leisering and R. Walker (eds) *The Dynamics of Modern Society*. Bristol: Policy Press, pp. 17–33.

Walkerdine, V., Lucey, H. and Melody, J. (2001) *Growing up Girl: Psycho-social Explorations of Gender and Class*. London: Palgrave Macmillan.

Ward, J. and Henderson, Z. (2003) 'Some practical and ethical issues encountered while conducting tracking research with young people leaving the "care" system', *International Journal of Social Research Methodology*, 6 (3): 255–9.

Ward, L., Lamb, S., Williamson, E., Robinson, R. and Griffiths, F. (2019) *Drowning in data! Designing a novel approach to longitudinal qualitative analysis*, Powerpoint presentation for the Qualitative Health Research Network Bi-annual Conference, London, 20 March [Abstract available in BMJ Open, 9 (supp. 1): 021].

Warin, J. (2010) *Stories of Self: Tracking Children's Identity and Wellbeing through the School Years*. Stoke-on-Trent: Trentham.

Warin, J. (2011) 'Ethical mindfulness and reflexivity: Managing a research relationship with children and young people in a fourteen-year qualitative longitudinal research (QLR) study', *Qualitative Inquiry*, 17 (10): 805–14.

Watson, C. (2013) 'Between diary and memoir: Documenting a life in war time Britain', in L. Stanley (ed.) *Documents of Life Revisited*. London: Routledge, pp. 107–19.

Weis, L. (2004) *Class Re-Union*. New York: Routledge.

Weller, S. (2012) 'Evolving creativity in qualitative longitudinal research with children and teenagers', *International Journal of Social Research Methodology*, 15 (2): 119–33.

Weller, S. (2017) 'Using internet video calls in qualitative (longitudinal) interviews: Some implications for rapport', *International Journal of Social Research Methodology*, 20 (6): 613–25.

Wenger, C. (1999) 'Advantages gained by combining qualitative and quantitative data in a longitudinal study', *Journal of Aging Studies*, 13 (4): 369–76.

Wengraf, T. (2000) 'Uncovering the general from within the particular: From contingencies to typologies in the understanding of cases', in P. Chamberlayne, J. Bornat and T. Wengraf (eds) *The Turn to Biographical Methods in Social Science*. London: Routledge, pp. 140–64.

Westhorp, G. (2018) 'Understanding mechanisms in realist evaluation and research', in N. Emmel, J. Greenhaugh, A. Manzano, et al. (eds) *Doing Realist Research*. London: Sage, pp. 41–57.

Whitehead, A. (1978 [1929]) *Process and Reality: An Essay in Cosmology*. New York: Free Press.

Whyte, A. (2012) 'Emerging infrastructure and services for research data management and curation in the UK and Europe', in G. Pryor (ed.) *Managing Research Data*. London: Facet, pp. 205–34.

Wiles, R. (2012) 'Developing ethical literacy: An unnecessary burden or a benefit to researchers?', *NCRM Methods News*, Winter, 7.

Wiles, R. (2013) *What are Qualitative Research Ethics?* London: Bloomsbury Academic.

Wiles, R., Prosser, J., Bagnoli, A., Clark, A., et al. (2008) *Visual Ethics: Ethical Issues in Visual Research*. National Centre for Research Methods, eprints.ncrm.ac.uk/421.

Williamson, E., Abrahams, H., Morgan, K. and Cameron, A. (2014) 'Tracking homeless women in qualitative longitudinal research', *European Journal of Homelessness*, 8 (2): 69–91.

Williamson, H. (2004) *The Milltown Boys Revisited*. Oxford: Berg.

Wilson, M. (1977) *For Men and Elders: Changes in the Relations of Generations and of Men and Women among the Nyakyusa-Ngonde People, 1875–1971*. London: International African Institute.

Wilson, S. (2014) 'Using secondary analysis to maintain a critically reflexive approach to qualitative research', *Sociological Research Online*, 19 (3).

Wilson, S., Cunningham-Burley, S., Bancroft, A. and Backett-Milburn, K. (2007) 'Young people, biographical narratives and the life grid: Young people's accounts of parental substance abuse', *Qualitative Research*, 7 (1): 135–51.

Wingens, M. and Reiter, H. (2011) 'The life course approach – It's about time!' *BIOS*, 24 (2): 87–203.

Winiarska, A. (2017) *Qualitative Longitudinal Research: Applications, Potentials and Challenges in the Context of Migration Research*. University of Warsaw: Centre for Migration Research, www.migracje.uw.edu.pl.

Winterton, M. and Irwin, S. (2011) 'Youngsters' expectations and context: Secondary analysis and interpretations of imagined futures', in M. Winterton, G. Crow and B. Morgan-Brett (eds) *Young Lives and Imagined Futures: Insights from Archived Data*. Timescapes Working Paper No. 6, www.timescapes-archive.leeds.ac.uk/publications-and-outputs.

Winterton, M. and Irwin, S. (2012) 'Teenage expectations of going to university: The ebb and flow of influences from 14 to 18', *Journal of Youth Studies*, 15 (7): 858–74.

Wiseman, V., Conteh, L. and Matovu, F. (2005) 'Using diaries to collect data in resource-poor settings: Questions of design and implementation', *Health Policy and Planning*, 20 (6): 394–404.

Wolcott, H. (2002) *Sneaky Kid and its Aftermath: Ethics and Intimacy in Fieldwork*. Walnut Creek, CA: AltaMira Press.

Woodman, D. and Wyn, J. (2013) 'Youth policy and generations: Why youth policy needs to "re-think youth"', *Social Policy and Society*, 12 (2): 265–75.

Worth, N. (2009) 'Understanding youth transitions as "becoming": Identity, time and futurity', *Geoforum*, 40: 1050–60.

Worth, N. (2011) 'Evaluating life maps as a versatile method for life course geographies', *Area*, 43 (4): 405–12.

Worth, N. and Hardill, I. (eds) (2015) *Researching the Life Course: Critical Perspectives from the Social Sciences*. Bristol: Policy Press.

Wray, S. and Ali, N. (2014) 'Understanding generation through the lens of ethnic and cultural diversity', *Families, Relationships and Societies*, 3 (3): 469–73.

Wright Mills, C. (1959) *The Sociological Imagination*. Oxford: OUP.

Wright, S. and Patrick, R. (2019) 'Welfare conditionality in lived experience: Aggregating qualitative longitudinal research', *Social Policy and Society*, 18 (4): 597–613.

Yardley, A. (2008) 'Piecing together: A methodological bricolage', *Forum: Qualitative Social Research*, 9 (2): Art. 31.

Yates, L. (2003) 'Interpretive claims and methodological warrant in small-number qualitative longitudinal research', *International Journal of Social Research Methodology*, 6 (3): 223–32.

Yates, L. and McLeod, J. (1996) '"And how would you describe yourself?" Researchers and researched in the first stage of a qualitative longitudinal project', *Australian Journal of Education*, 40 (1): 88–103.

Zerubavel, E. (1979) *Patterns of Time in Hospital Life: A Sociological Perspective*. Chicago: University of Chicago Press.

Zerubavel, E. (1981) *Hidden Rhythms: Schedules and Calendars in Social Life*. Chicago: University of Chicago Press.

Zerubavel, E. (2003) *Time Maps: Collective Memory and the Social Shape of the Past*. Chicago: University of Chicago Press.

INDEX

CPSIA information can be obtained
at www.ICGtesting.com
Printed in the USA
FSHW010410210122
87621FS